The Guru Chronicles

The Making of the First American Satguru

First Edition

Copyright © 2011
Himalayan Academy

 Published by
Himalayan Academy
India • USA

PRINTED IN THE USA BY QUAD GRAPHICS

Library of Congress Catalog Card Number 2011933013

ISBN: 978-1-934145-39-5 (HARDCOVER)
978-1-934145-40-1 (EBOOK)

The Guru Chronicles

**The Making of the
First American Satguru**

By the Swamis of
Kauai's Hindu Monastery

 வ

Dedication

Hindu history is replete with stories of noble, courageous, high souls who are born to uplift and guide mankind, men and women who come "from up down" in response to humanity's needs—the more dire the need, the greater the soul sent to meet it. Satguru Sivaya Subramuniyaswami, affectionately known by his devotees as Gurudeva, was such a soul. He was born in modern times to meet modern challenges—born, he would say, "to protect, preserve and promote the Saiva dharma," to bring the knowledge, worship and realization of God Siva into the 21st century. How he did that is a story you are about to read. But he would be the first to caution that this is not about him. He was only the latest guru in a lineage that had preserved the knowledge of the Self within man since the dawn of history, a lineage that existed before him, thrived during his lifetime and carries on today. ¶Those close to Gurudeva lived the stories in these pages, saw his communion with the inner worlds, experienced his life of revelation and realization. He looked and acted like Siva Himself, tall, powerful, compassionate, urgent. He did things people don't do: created a new language, talked to the light-bodied devas, established America's first South Indian monastery, founded Hinduism's first international magazine, saw and then recreated the future. Little wonder he was chosen by Yogaswami to carry on the Nandinatha Kailasa lineage. Little wonder he was recognized in the East as the West's first authentic satguru. Everything he did was to meet a need, to elevate consciousness, to preserve Hindu dharma for the future—not the nearest future, but the far future of thousands of years, what he loved to call "the future of futures." His temple was built to last a thousand years. His monastery and yoga order were crafted to last even longer. His magazine continues to inspire and transform not merely individuals and institutions but entire nations. His realization of Absolute Reality supersedes it all. Yet he could explain karma to a child. ¶In this tenth year since his Great Departure, we dedicate this book to Gurudeva, an Eastern soul in a Western body, a man who loved all that is modern and used it to protect all that is ancient. We fall at his feet, humbled by the certainty that we have no more captured him and his predecessors here than one can snare the midday sun. Enjoy his story and that of his guru and his guru's guru and so on back in history, and hope in your heart that you will one day meet someone like him. Jai! Satguru Sivaya Subramuniyaswami! Jai!

Contents

Preface

At an auspicious moment during the around-the-world 1972 Indian Odyssey, Satguru Sivaya Subramuniyaswami (Gurudeva) gave diksha in Sri Lanka to several of his devotees. One, a teacher, received the mission to remain with his wife and pre-teen son in the village of Alaveddy near Subramuniya Ashram in order to collect oral and written histories about Yogaswami's lineage of gurus. The timing was critical. Yogaswami's Great Departure had happened in 1964, and the memories of those who were close to him were still fresh. They saw the need to chronicle their guru's life, so they put aside their usual distrust of outsiders and eagerly shared their experiences. It was important to capture their recollections at this time, for it assured a faithful telling of Yogaswami's life and teachings. To wait for decades would invite a sketchy history and stories forgotten.

It was discovered during this one-year sojourn that years earlier Yogaswami had told devotees: "My biographer is coming. He's in a white body, and he's coming here to tell my story." Once when an Englishman arrived in Jaffna, devotees ran to Swami, saying, "This is your biographer." Yogaswami retorted curtly, "No. He is coming later, much later." During the devotee's stay, more than a few of the villagers had dreams indicating that the American schoolteacher living in Alaveddy was the biographer Yogaswami had spoken of. Word swept through the Jaffna peninsula. One by one visitors came to the humble home of Swami's biographer to share their stories of their guru, Sri Lanka's lion of dharma, and of his guru, Chellappaswami, and his guru's guru, Kadaitswami. The teacher sat on a mat listening to hundreds of narratives, carefully penning them by hand. Later he wove them into a 120-page manuscript entitled *Soldiers Within,* which he presented to Gurudeva after returning to America.

This book began with those papers. In fact, *Soldiers Within* was studied within the monastery for decades and shared with only a few close devotees. It remained unpublished until now. In the intervening years, Gurudeva asked his monks to undertake further research. We collected more oral histories and written biographical material, translating as needed from Tamil in consultation with Tamil elders. Finally we assembled the material into this tome. In 1998 Gurudeva sat with his editing team of monks to review, line by line, a preliminary 400-page version, which did not include his own biography.

Pass a sentence around a room of people, and you may be amused by the difference between the first iteration and the last. Similarly, real-life stories told again and again are naturally altered, and ultimately distorted. Yet much of history has been chronicled in this manner. It's not completely reliable, but often it is all we have. This biography of seven mystics contains their actual writings, which is the bedrock of the book, alongside stories by their contemporaries, some of which are probably not perfectly accurate. But they are the stories told. This was a primary and persistent challenge confronting the editors of this book.

For years we compared hundreds of sources, working hard to assure the nearest thing to historical fact. In particular, recorded details are scarce for the book's earliest gurus—Maharishi Nandinatha, Rishi Tirumular and the nameless rishi from the Himalayas. Tirumular's history, for example, is known only in its broadest details, derived primarily from references in the ancient *Periyapuranam* and Tirumular's few cryptic autobiographical references in his *Tirumantiram*.

To fill in the historical lacunae in those sections, we adopted a free-flowing style of embellishment to bring light and detail to lives that would otherwise be hidden in the oblivion of non-history. The stories of those early gurus, as told in this book, are a partially fictionalized recreation of events based on rudimentary historical facts supplemented with a modern historian's understanding of life in that region in those days. The closer our story comes to now, the more founded in fact it becomes.

For the chapters about Gurudeva's life, the situation was completely different; we had a surfeit of resources. The challenge was to identify the five percent of his biographical material that we had room for. To allow him to tell his story in his own words as much as possible, we referenced a his 1970 talk called "Making of a Master," in which he detailed the mystical experiences of his youth. We also transcribed videos of seven classes he gave aboard a ship during the 1999 Alaska Innersearch Travel-Study Program, one on each decade of his life. Details of his early life were found in the monastery archives. We examined certificates of birth and death, old passports, newspaper clippings and other documents, childhood photo albums, letters he wrote from Sri Lanka in the late 1940s, and letters later written to him and his monks relating the events of his visit there from the observers' point of view. Gurudeva's own handwritten notes from those days proved indispensable.

To structure the storyline of his life from the time he began teaching, we consulted an exhaustive monthly chronology kept by his monks over the years, along with the personal testimonies of those who lived and studied with him. Many events of the historic early Innersearches were recovered from participants' diaries. Other facets of Gurudeva's life were drawn from our April/May/June 2002 memorial edition of HINDUISM TODAY. But still there were many gaps in the history—briefly worded bullet points in the chronology and partially disclosed memories of Gurudeva's monks—that represented stories needing to be told. Thus, for five years, beginning in 2007 until the completion of this book, Gurudeva's editing team of monks set most other work aside, writing those stories and weaving them into this first full account of the life of this modern-day rishi.

Gurudeva placed tremendous value on the use of artwork for its ability to convey teachings and tell stories. The extensive paintings in this book were created with that principle in mind, to bring these stories to life, to capture visually the places and events seen only by a few. They are the masterful work of Tiru S. Rajam (1919-2009) of Mylapore, Tamil Nadu. Though his first gift was music, his art was equally remarkable, created in a unique style rooted in the purely South Indian genre. He spoke of it as his worship, and he regarded himself as a kind of aesthetic monk, which made his work with us, the ascetic monks, especially effectual, as these pages reveal. When others went to the temple, he adjourned to his canvas, always to paint something spiritual. In a somewhat dusky second-story studio, Rajam worked at his easel up to fourteen hours a day from 2002 to 2003 to create fifty-six canvases for this book, each with multiple stories. His brush was guided by descriptions, photos and illustrations that we, the sannyasin editors living at Kauai's Hindu Monastery in Hawaii, provided. The creative genius and cultural nuances are all his.

The book you hold in your hands took some thirty-eight years to complete; but it is a first edition, and first editions are seldom perfect. We welcome additional stories, photos, corrections and ideas, which will make for fuller and more flawless future editions. You can send your stories and changes to sadasivanatha@hindu.org. This book is available in PDF and e-book formats at www.himalayanacademy.com.

Introduction

These are the stories of remarkable souls who knew the Unknowable and held Truth in the palm of their hand. They confounded their contemporaries, revealed life's purpose and path, and became inexplicably aware of the future. They worshiped God as Siva, knowing Him as All and in all, as the God—by other names—of every faith and path. Many are the gurus; but these knowers of God—those who have achieved the ultimate goal of yoga, transcending the mind itself—are called satgurus. Their successors still live, their powers transmitted and maturing from one to the next, now flourishing in the 21st century. But their stories have remained largely untold, a kind of universal spiritual secret. Here, for the first time, what moved and motivated them is revealed, to the extent they let it be known. Here, for the first time, what they said and did is shared outside the circle of initiates.

Scholars and scientists in our time have probed the past for the story of man and discovered how astonishingly little they could find. Our species has peopled the Earth for over two million years, but we can account for barely a trace of that history today. How many unknown civilizations have come and gone? We live as if they never did, for they left so little. Piecing together the human events of a mere fifty centuries reveals dozens of cultures that flourished for ages and vanished almost entirely.

Where are the ancient religions of Egypt, Sumeria, Greece or Peru, Italy, Britain or Persia? With precision, historians trace out their histories and their influence on modern times, but this is only scholarship. Buried cities, broken walls, enigmatic shards, excerpts of their laws and scraps of their art are not the living traditions that made each of them great in its time. Apart from clusters of survivors here and there, the continuity of nearly all of Earth's ancient religions and cultures has been broken in recent millennia due to religious wars and, in the larger time frame of geology, by the obscuring power of recurring ice ages.

The remarkable exception is ancient Bharata, modern-day India, the

homeland of Hinduism, the world's oldest living faith. Knowledge of the religion's antiquity is traditional among Hindus and has been more or less proven by modern research. Though the Sanatana Dharma, the "Eternal Path," belongs by its nature to the whole world and has spread in many guises and tongues to distant continents throughout history, only in India did it survive and thrive in unbroken continuity throughout the millennia, flourishing today as a billion-strong, global Hindu faith.

India has always been the cradle of spirituality. During his 1895 lecture tour to India, Mark Twain wrote, "India is the cradle of the human race, the birthplace of human speech, the mother of history, the grandmother of legend, and the great grandmother of tradition. Our most valuable and most instructive materials in the history of man are treasured up in India only!"

What spared Hinduism the oblivion that claimed every other ancient faith? It cannot have been mere good fortune. India is a difficult land in itself, and its history is marked by the repeated absorption of whole races and religions from beyond its borders. In addition, it has had more than its share of foreign invaders, natural disasters and internal wars. Yet, drawing from some secret sustenance, Hinduism flourished with persistent vitality and retained its grip on the soul of India, never failing to inspire, never fading, ever renewed and strengthened from within. We can well ask who is responsible. Who kept the religion alive in the mind of man through all these millennia? Who keeps it vibrant and inwardly strong today? How many were they? Where do they live? How was it done? The answers lie, in part, in the pages of this book. Satguru Sivaya Subramuniyaswami, whose life story ends this biography, explained:

Among a thousand [devout] Hindus, one or a few will abandon the world for a stricter path, living in seclusion by a river, in a cave in the hills or wandering, the sky his roof, God his landlord. Each Hindu looks up to the swami or sadhu, knowing they will one day be where he is now. Among a hundred thousand such *tapasvins* who search for God, one, or ten, will find That which all souls are seeking, so high is the summit, so steep the ascent. Realized saints and sages are rare, but never absent in India. Their absence would leave it a land like any other. Their presence makes it holy.

Every Hindu generation has produced its farmers, lawyers, mothers, kings, beggars, scholars, priests, swamis and God-men. Yet all of these souls together do not carry or sustain the full force of the Sanatana Dharma, for they cannot. They are each engaged in their own desires, their own affairs or their own quest. Their search continues. They do not yet possess the fullest knowledge; they have yet to accrue their soul's full maturity. Even after God Realization, the soul continues to evolve. It does not vanish, nor does the world disappear. An enlightened man can help many forward on the spiritual path, according to his maturity of soul. Whose mission is it to guide whole generations? Who turns from their search to guide hundreds of millions on their way? Only those whose search is utterly ended, only the perfected souls who have become the goal itself.

Such men live; such men have always lived. They are known as siddhas, which means "accomplished ones" or "perfected ones." They are a special class of yogis, each a fully matured soul and heir to the inner force and subtle knowledge of the Sanatana Dharma even as the masses of India are heir to its outer precepts and practice. They hold the power of it and protect its destiny. One with Siva, they speak and behave only in expression of the will of God.

All gurus differ one from another depending on their param-para, or lineage, as well as on their individual nature, awakening and attainments. Basically, the only thing that a guru can give you is yourself to yourself. That is all, and this is done in many ways. The guru would only be limited by his philosophy, which outlines the ultimate attainment, and by his own experience. He cannot take you where he himself has not been. It is the guru's job to inspire, to assist, to guide and sometimes even impel the disciple to move a little farther toward the Self of himself than he has been able to go by himself.

The satguru is needed because the mind is cunning and the ego is a self-perpetuating mechanism. It is unable and unwilling to transcend itself by itself. Therefore, one needs the guidance of another who has gone through the same process, who has faithfully followed the path to its natural end and therefore can gently lead us to God within ourselves. Remember, the satguru will keep you on the path, but you have to walk the path yourself.

It is the disciple's duty to understand the sometimes subtle guidance offered by the guru, to take the suggestions and make the best use of them in fulfilling the sadhanas given. Being with a satguru is an intensification on the path of enlightenment—always challenging, for growth is a challenge to the instinctive mind. If a guru does not provide this intensification, we could consider him to be more a philosophical teacher. Not all gurus are satgurus. Not all gurus have realized God themselves. The idea is to change the patterns of life, not to perpetuate them. That would be the only reason one would want to find a satguru.

Some teachers will teach ethics. Others will teach philosophy, language, worship and scriptures. Some will teach by example, by an inner guidance. Others will teach from books. Some will be silent, while others will lecture and have classes. Some will be orthodox, while others may not. The form of the teaching is not the most essential matter. What matters is that there be a true and fully realized satguru, that there be a true and fully dedicated disciple. Under such conditions, spiritual progress will be swift and certain, though not necessarily easy. Of course, in our tradition the siddhas have always taught of Siva and only Siva. They have taught the Saiva Dharma, which seeks to serve and know Siva in three ways: as Personal Lord and creator of all that exists; as existence, knowledge and bliss—the love that flows through all form—and finally as the timeless, formless, causeless Self of all.

While the millions lead their lives along the length and breadth of India, the yogis and sages who unveil Eternal Truth within their souls sit for years in silence or gather in conclave, high above the world, in fulfillment of their duty and their mission as guardians of the Truth in man. Carrying the knowledge and force of Hinduism through an age of ignorance, the Himalayan seers have revealed and passed on the Sanatana Dharma to every generation, reawakened knowledge of it in the minds of the population during troubled times, rekindled the lamps of faith when devotion wearied, and carried to every corner of India, year after year, the knowledge that Siva is within you, within all things, that Siva is all things. When all is said and done in this world, naught else matters than to have lived in such a way as to come a little closer to the Infinite within.

In Asia this is well understood, hence the deep reverence the devout extend to the gurus who walk among us, guiding and showing the way of dharma that leads to liberation. Gurudeva spoke further of the guru's role in the Hindu tradition:

In a traditional Saivite family, the mother and the father are the first teachers, or gurus, of their children, teaching by example, explanation, giving advice and direction until their children are old enough to be sent to their next guru, in the arts, sciences, medicine and general education. Families that have a satguru will often choose the most promising religious young son to go to his ashrama, to study and learn the religion and become a sannyasin or a family pandit in later years, depending on how his life works out. In this case, the mother and father, the first gurus, turn the entire direction of their son over to the satguru, the second guru, who then becomes mother and father in the eyes of the son, and in the eyes of his parents as well.

A satguru doesn't need a lot of words to transmit the spirit to another person; but the shishyas have to be open and be kept open. The little bit of spirit extends like a slender fiber, a thin thread, from the satguru to the shishya, and it is easily broken. A little bit more of that association adds another strand, and we have two threads, then three, then four. They are gradually woven together through service, and a substantial string develops between the guru and the shishya. More strings are created, and they are finally woven together into a rope strong enough to pull a cart. You've seen in India the huge, thick ropes that pull a temple chariot. That is the ultimate goal of the guru-shishya relationship.

Upon the connection between guru and shishya, the spirit of the parampara travels, the spirit of the sampradaya travels. It causes the words that are said to sink deep. They don't just bounce off the intellect; the message goes deep into the individual. Between the guru and shishya many threads are all woven together, and finally we have a firm rope that cannot be pulled apart or destroyed even by two people pulling against one another. That is sampradaya. That is parampara. That is the magical power of the Nathas.

As we look at this great line of satgurus—coming from Lord Siva Himself through Nandinatha and countless ones before Nandinatha, to Rishi Tirumular and countless rishis after him to the Rishi of Bangalore, to Kadaitswami, Chellappaguru and Yogaswami—we see the same spiritual force flowing. We see an undaunted, rare succession of individuals who considered adversity as a boon from the Gods, wherein all the accumulated karmas to be wiped away come together in one place to be taken care of all at once.

In Sri Lanka and India, men commonly prostrate themselves full face on the ground when they come into the presence of a holy man, no matter when or where they meet him. In this way, they offer their devotion to the Divinity or superconsciousness they sense in him. When they come to worship at his ashram, they bring fruit or flowers or some other offering to show their respect. This tradition of worship is known in Sanskrit as guru bhakti. There are entire scriptures exalting the guru and his importance on the spiritual path, and chants to the guru sung when one enters his presence. By expressing such devotion, people remind themselves powerfully that they are on this Earth not for the pleasure of the senses, not for the acquisition of wealth, not for the storing of knowledge, not for the development of a powerful ego, but for the realization of God within themselves, that ineffable and absolute Truth which the mystics in this book held in the palm of their hand.

Without a satguru, all philosophy, knowledge and mantras are fruitless. Him alone the Gods praise who is the satguru, keeping active what is handed down to him by tradition. Therefore one should seek with all effort to obtain a preceptor of the unbroken tradition, born of Supreme Siva.

KULARNAVA TANTRA 10.1

Chapter One

Seeking a Guru in Ceylon

Having saved his funds by living a frugal, almost ascetic existence, Robert Hansen, 20, boarded a steamer in February of 1947, sailing from San Francisco under the Golden Gate Bridge en route to Sri Lanka (then called Ceylon), heading the five-member American-Asian Cultural Mission. Months before, he had danced on the stage of the San Francisco Ballet Company, reveling in the joys of being their premier danseur. But the lifelong spiritual urge within him would not be subdued by worldly success, and he was determined to leave for the exotic East, there, he hoped, to find a true and authentic guru who would guide him to the Self within.

In sharing that departure with the monks of his yoga order 25 years later, he described it as a dark, dreary day and noted the Dutch merchant marine boat, the MS Mapia, sailed with an English crew. He was free of responsibilities for the first time in years, and it was a freedom he savored. The month-long voyage was aboard a working ship with rough accommodations. Robert's berth was the cheapest available, a tiny, one-man chamber below deck right above the engine room. This was to provide an unexpected encounter with the supranormal, which he shared aboard another ship during a 1999 Alaska travel-study cruise with 45 disciples.

I took the first ship after the war leaving the port for Sri Lanka. It was a freighter. My cabin was right over the engine room, and that was very disturbing. I remember one time I was in deep meditation, really deep meditation, not really hearing anything. Then I came out of that silence and heard this roaring engine—rrrrrrr. I said to myself, "I wish this noise would just stop," and it did. Immediately, the whole ship stopped. We floated for three days, going off course a little bit. They couldn't find out what was wrong. Finally, they found that two screws had come loose in the engine. They fixed the problem and the

. . . .

Robert took to meditating in his tiny cabin, right above the engine room. Coming out of meditation one day, he was jarred by the giant engine's piercing noises. He mentally called for the noise to stop, and the engines halted for days.

engine started up again. It was a lucky thing because we were going through mine fields. It was just after the war. The ship could have been blown up very easily, and only toward the end of the voyage did we know what the cargo was. It was munitions. That would have been a big bang for all of us—something you would want to miss.

In a later recounting, he reflected on how this experience impressed on him the power of the meditative mind, a power that was unleashed spontaneously that day on the ship.

The cultural troupe practiced on the wooden deck of the moving ship and built a small pool in which they could splash around on hot days. They shared meals with the crew, even the captain. The captain took his gallant young passenger to the wheel room one day and told Robert, "See that pen on the table? If I even pick it up, I relinquish my job as captain." Robert would recall this later in life when describing his duties as a guru.

The troupe disembarked in Bombay on March 8, but as their Indian visas designated them as "through passengers," they stayed just a few days before boarding a train for the South of India. From Madras, they

took a ferry across the narrow Palk Strait to Talaimannar on the Western side of Ceylon. Boarding another train, they reached Colombo in mid-March of 1947. On March 23, Robert wrote from his new home on Galle Road:

> Ceylon is much better than our hear-say before arrival; if you hear anything good about this country, double it and you'll have the truth. It truly is the garden spot of the world. The people are alert, strong, wide awake, healthy and desirous of modernizing their country in every way.
>
> Ceylon is nothing like India. The day after my arrival some friends, a Sinhalese man and his wife and driver, took me up to Kandy. You should have been there. We went to the Temple of the Tooth and the old Kandy palace which is in ruins now. Everywhere you look, all over the Island, you see nothing but green trees all year around. People plowing with elephants, and by hand. The men wear sarongs or pants; the ladies wear saris. In Kandy they dress in a different way. A man is walking by with a box balanced on his head—that's the way people carry things here.
>
> There are several boys that take care of the house—every time you pass they come out with a big "Hello, sir." It's about all the English they know. They are so polite they always say yes to everything, whether they understand or not.
>
> We thought it would be very hot, but it's not at all; and rather cool at night, and though this is their hot season, I can still wear a wool sport coat and not sweat too badly. We have to keep everything under lock and key, because we are not living in an age of saints, though Ceylon and India are both very spiritual countries. They respect people a lot who don't eat meat, take coffee or tea or drink or smoke, so I have won many fine friends, and being universally minded, can mix with any type of people, class or faith, which is a big advantage.
>
> On Saturday my friends and I (Mar 29) were going up to Adam's Peak, about 6,000 feet above sea level (it's very cold there) to see the sunrise on Sunday morning. Every full moon people of all beliefs go

*From Bombay, Robert traveled south by train to Tamil Nadu, then took
a ferry across Palk Strait to Colombo, Ceylon, his destination.*

there and shout, "LOVE TO ALL! LOVE TO ALL!" whether they are
Buddhist, Hindu, Mohammedan or Christian, rich or poor.

You see many strange and wonderful things, such as snake charm-
ers, fortune tellers that can tell from old Sanskrit records just how
many in your family and describe them all to a T, and all your past and
future. The records are thousands of years old and take a long time
to read. Elephants walking down the street, bargaining, new tongues,
beautiful sunsets. Tea at 3:30 pm. Driving on the other side of the
street makes it hard for US pedestrians. Love to all—write soon. Bob

Robert's journey to Lanka was choreographed by his early catalysts. In
fact, his first teacher, Grace Burroughs, received him when he reached
Colombo, welcomed him to her dance studio there and saw to his well-
being for the first year of his stay.

Meeting His Mentor's Challenges

In Ceylon, he studied with his fourth catalyst on the path, Dayananda Priyadasi (Darrel Peiris), a Sinhalese Buddhist who, during his first visit to the US in 1934, had established an ashram at the Oakland home of Robert's second catalyst, Mother Christney. Dayananda was a dynamic teacher of meditation and occultism and a great patriot of this island nation.

Ceylon was then in the final stages of 21 years of active struggle for independence from Great Britain, which it gained in 1948. The times were unsettled; and the fiftyish Dayananda, who was both meditative mystic and charismatic politician, took advantage of the situation to train his new protege personally in the art of getting positive things done in the world. Within months of his arrival, Robert helped found two schools for village children, assisted in reviving the dormant Kandyan dance and introduced electric power saws to carpenters, who had never seen such contraptions. These down-to-earth projects were a part of his training.

I was happy and awed to meet my fourth catalyst on the island of Sri Lanka, a Buddhist. He was a strong, active Sinhalese man dedicated to spiritual awakening and bringing this through in a vitally helpful way to all of humanity. He had been high in Ceylonese government and was practical and forceful as a teacher. I studied with him for one year and a half.

In earlier years, Dayananda attained enlightenment in a cave in Thailand by sitting in the morning, eyes fixed upon the sun, following its travel across the sky all day long until it set at night. He practiced under his guru this most difficult sadhana. Then one night while meditating in a cave, the cave turned to brilliant light, and a great being appeared to him, giving him his mission and instructions for his service to the world.

My fourth catalyst taught me how to use the willpower, how to get things done in the material world. He was a real father to me. I needed this at twenty-one years of age. I wanted to meditate, but he wanted me to work to help the village people in reconstructing the rural areas. He assigned me to do different duties, sometimes several at a time, which I had to work out from within myself. One was seeing that a new village bridge was put up that had been washed out in a flood, bringing into another village modern saws and carpentry equipment to replace traditional tools used in building furniture.

I had to take a survey of all the carpenters using handsaws on the west coast of Sri Lanka. I went around with a notebook and listed all

. . . .

His mentor, Dayananda, was a Buddhist mystic, politician and social activist who engaged Robert in a difficult project—introducing the electric circular saw to the village carpenters of Ceylon who were using simple hand saws.

their names and addresses and the types of saws they were using, for my assignment was to see that they all would eventually be provided with electric saws. Getting modern equipment into the Moratuwa area was one of the biggest assignments I had ever had, and I had no idea how to begin, for I had never done anything of this nature in my life. Occasionally my catalyst would ask, "Well, have they gotten their saws yet?" All I could say was, "Well, I'm working on it."

Executing governmental changes was strange to me. My life had been quiet, with no exposure to methods of business. But even worse, I was in a foreign country that had different customs, subtle ways of relating and suggesting. Most of the educated could speak English beautifully. In the villages, however, only the native languages, Sinhalese and Tamil, were spoken and understood. The craftsmen were accustomed to the old ways, their fathers' ways, of making furniture,

and were not easily persuaded that electric saws would improve their work. Some had grown up in remote regions where there was no electricity, no running water. So naturally they resisted such a massive change. They made good, sturdy furniture already. Why complicate life further, they must have thought.

My natural shyness was the biggest barrier though. I had to interview people, do research and convince people of the practicality of electric equipment. Finally, it unfolded to me from the inside how to go about it. I drew up an elaborate proposal, long and wordy, with myriad details, diagrams, names and addresses. I gave it to him. He was pleased and said, "Now what I want you to do is take this fine proposal to the head of the Department of Rural Reconstruction. You

Robert lived as a guest in Buddhist temples and monasteries, conversing with the monks, observing and absorbing their strict lifestyle, ways of life he would later implement in his own monasteries.

Page 9

Chapter 1

give it to him, and I will do the rest. But while you are in his office, sit down with him and tell him how fast work is done in your country by using modern equipment to make furniture."

I was happy. At last I had something definite to do that would bring this project to a successful end. I went into Colombo to the Office of Rural Reconstruction and presented the proposal. The government was convinced, and not many months later the modern electric saw became available and popular in the Moratuwa villages for any carpenter who needed one. Sri Lanka had just that year received its independent dominion status from the Crown, and there was a lot to do to bring the rural areas up to better standards. I did my part in the best way I knew how and was glad to do it.

One assignment like this after another was given to me. This fourth catalyst of mine worked on the philosophy that you do what you're told. If you are given an assignment, do it to perfection. Finish it. And don't come back with excuses. If he sent you on a mission, you wouldn't dare return until you had completed that mission, not to your satisfaction but to his. He might have nothing more to do with you if you failed. I knew that, so I was very, very careful. Inside myself, as I struggled to do tasks that seemed impossible, I could hear him saying, "Don't fail, don't fall short. You create the obstacles. You can overcome anything, do anything, be anything." He challenged me to work problems out from within myself, offering little advice and often assigning a task and then just leaving.

He was quick to point out my mistakes, even though he knew I was sensitive and couldn't stand being scolded. Still, he scolded and criticized harshly. This was good for me, and I am still thankful for his direct and powerful ways. He made me use my own inner intelligence to complete each assignment, and most of them were of a worldly nature. At this time in my life that is exactly what I needed, to strengthen the outer shell, to learn to accomplish duties in the world. It was invaluable in later years.

Dayananda had me meditate in the villages. I would sit in the lotus position for an hour or two while he talked to the village people about meditation, *bhavana*. They were all Buddhists. They appreciated the

Buddha's philosophy but did not meditate. So, together we would go
from village to village encouraging the people to meditate, to put the
enlightened teachings into practice. Finally I was getting my own
meditating done while he was teaching the people and the Buddhist
priests about it.

Prior to my arrival in Sri Lanka, Dayananda had worked with Thailand's Buddhist priests to build a wonderful school of meditation that
served to uplift the Thai people. Because of his efforts, many priests
now meditate in Thailand, as do the lay people of the country.

Every once in a while I remarked, "I want to go into a cave and meditate. I want to realize the Self." He said, "Plenty of time for that. You
can go into a cave and meditate after you have finished the next two
or three assignments. Anyway, the cave is inside of you." So, I continued with the assignments month after month.

From time to time I reminded him, "You know, I came to Sri Lanka
to find my guru." It had been impressed on me by my teacher in California that this would happen in Sri Lanka but that I should have total
realization of the Self first. So, I had come to Sri Lanka to meditate to
realize the Self and to find my guru. Yet, here I was in governmental
agencies and wandering around in the villages. I deeply felt that if I
could get away from doing external things and go into a cave, which is
traditionally the ideal place to meditate, I really could realize the Self.
In fact, I was sure of it. If he would just give me a little time off. But
would he? No.

I confess, I rebelled. Inwardly I criticized this incessant concern
about business and social change. After all, I thought, he is not my
guru, and I am not here to change the world. I'm here to meditate.
Maybe I should just go off to a cave without telling him. The rebellion externalized my awareness. Suddenly it was more difficult to
do the assignments. I was too preoccupied, divided between what I
wanted personally and what my teacher wanted me to do. I struggled
for a while, but then conquered this rebellion within a week and
never allowed it to occur again. The biggest enemy on the path is a
rebellious nature, wanting to do things our own personal way, being
inflexible and unable to give up our own will for a greater purpose.
I settled down to obey him exactly and directly, becoming an even
more positive person. I was a very positive person at that time, and
remain so today.

I visited and lived in many Buddhist temples in Sri Lanka. I was

. . . .

Dayananda campaigned constantly in rural villages. One day he
showed the American visitor his powers, closing his eyes and entering
the mind of a speaker on the stage, who suddenly began talking about
a subject Dayananda and Robert had shared earlier that day.

received by the monks there. I saw how they lived, saw how they
dressed, and that influenced in a very strict way the monastic protocols that we later put into action in our own monastic order.

Dayananda was campaigning incessantly on the road, taking his protege
from village to village. He aspired to be the head of the country, and many
thought he would be, though it never happened. He once took Robert to
a Buddhist home where they lived for three days. The teacher took the
opportunity to stretch the young American's discipline, and demanded
that he meditate through the night, without respite.

Dayananda was a skillful speaker and would often hold forth from a
makeshift stage or under a tree, his American executive secretary standing nearby. One day, in a remote village, they were standing together as
the local chieftain was speaking words of introduction, working the
crowd for Dayananda's speech. Almost playfully, he turned to Robert and
said, "Watch this." Dayananda closed his eyes, his concentration etched
on his brow. Within a minute, the speaker completely changed subjects,
talking of things that Dayananda and Robert had shared earlier. Robert
soon realized that Dayananda had gone within himself and entered the
man's mind, and was in fact speaking through him. It was a demonstration of white magic that he never forgot. Impressive, he would later say,
but not all that useful. Dayananda was full of such magic-making, something Robert would later regard as an obstacle to spiritual unfoldment, not
a demonstration of it.

At one point Dayananda gave his young charge a wind-up clock and
instructed him to follow a Buddhist meditation practice. Robert was to
set his clock to wake him in two hours. When the alarm went off, he was
to sit in lotus posture and meditate for a time as deeply as he could. Then
he would reset the clock, lie down on the floor and sleep, waking in two
hours to meditate again. Throughout the night, day after day, he followed
this discipline, meant to bring the consciousness of meditation into other
states of mind.

While working with Dayananda, Robert remained busy with the travels of the cultural troupe. They traveled north and south, performing at
the nation's formal musical and dance halls, in small towns and on college
stages. They raised funds for the Child Protection Society at Royal College
Hall in Colombo and mesmerized the crowd at Bishops College on July 23,
1947, where the reviewer noted, "Robert Hansen again proved himself a
clever ballet and character dancer." He worked his body hard, and drank

. . . .

*Led by young Robert Hansen, the American-Asian Cultural Mission
toured Ceylon for months, dancing in every important venue, with the
goal of bringing East and West together through dance and music.*

so much hot water to purify himself that the Sinhalese called him Unu Wathura, which means "hot water" in that language.

From the Town Hall in Kalutara to Wales College Hall in Moratuwa to the Young Men's Buddhist Association, they brought their dynamic fusion of East and West song and dance to audiences who had never seen such performances, let alone the Matchless Muchachos and the acrobatic tango during Latin American Night at the Silver Fawn Club.

Dance took great effort, with all that travel, yet Robert managed to squeeze in another of his loves: organizing. Again and again, the newspapers reported on his efforts to bring the people of Ceylon together for good causes. He formed the World Fellowship of Youth on March 20, 1948, and soon established the World Fellowship of Artistes, which grew into the Opera and Ballet Guild of Ceylon, established on July 23.

One of the spiritual disciplines given to the young American was a sleep sadhana.
He was required to rise every two hours throughout the night to meditate.

Robert was about to embark on his greatest challenge, the struggle to realize Parasiva, the Self within all. Every experience in life had led him to this moment, a moment that would transform the young American into an enlightened being who would one day transform and guide Hinduism in the United States and beyond. To understand the experience he would soon have in the deep southern jungles of Ceylon, and the spiritual tradition he had discovered, it is necessary to go back in time, to the Himalayan mountains and the mystical sages who first charted the path Robert now found himself on.

Maharishi Nandinatha

The Himalayan Hindus of two thousand years ago lived a rustic life, close to the land, close to their spiritual roots, close to one another, on whom they depended for sustenance. Hamlets and ashrams were always built near a river, fresh water being central to survival. Their thatched cottages took many shapes, mostly round and rectangular, engineered with four or six posts inside, over which a sheet of woven branches, grasses and leaves was layered. This thick sheet of thatch, rightly constructed, could keep the region's brutal weather out. For further protection from the elements, the simple dwellings were sheltered strategically amid and beneath large trees. The huts were organic, providing warmth in the winter while being cool during the high-altitude, sun-intense summers. The floors, made of cooling earth mixed with cow dung and straw, were antiseptic and served the important task of repelling insects. Each day the dung floor was sprinkled with fresh water and buffed to renew the surface.

Mountainous lands are severely sloped, so the Himalayan agriculturalists terraced the hills, a difficult but necessary task. They grew rice, cereals and garbanzo beans, lentils and root crops. (Roots were kept as famine foods, saved for the hardest of times). Fruits were abundant, and every home was planted with apricots and apples. Families kept bees for the honey and wax, cows for milk, goats for meat (not everyone was vegetarian, though most were) and to serve as beasts of burden, being so adept at rock climbing. They learned to cultivate grasslands for cattle grazing. They crushed their oil from mustard seeds, for eating, cooking and lighting the lamps. Mustard was so crucial to life that the oil was poured on either side of the home's threshold when important visitors arrived.

The mountains were crisscrossed with trails along which life-sustaining commodities traveled, to be traded at distant marketplaces. So narrow were the passageways that a single man or goat was all that could pass. These paths were called *aja-patha*, meaning "goat path" in Sanskrit. Each goat could only carry a few kilograms, so goods were chosen thoughtfully. The two primary routes of the day passed through Joshimath (a Saiva center), Badrinath (a Vaishnava center) and Kedarnath (a Saiva stronghold).

This pastoral life offered many opportunities for gatherings, especially

. . . .

Maharishi Nandinatha is the famed guru of Patanjali, Vyaghrapada and Tirumular, the Himalayan-dwelling siddha yogi and progenitor of the Nandinatha Sampradaya. He was the first known preceptor of this lineage, which imparts the advaitic (monistic) teachings of Saivism.

in the ashrams, and the Himalayan Hindu holy men loved nothing more than to hold philosophical discourse and debates, often under the wide canopy of a ficus tree. Everyone would sit on the ground for these meetings. There were no books. Learning in those days was conveyed orally and committed to memory by the students. The spiritual elders had small mat-seats or wooden tables, called *pitha,* some six inches high, on which they would sit to guide the others and impart instructions to students of different ages. These rishis were often married men, not sannyasins. Some sannyasins also had disciples living with them, while others engaged in their spiritual meditation and other practices in strict seclusion.

Students were of every age, having found their way to the remote teaching/living centers to be schooled in the ancient arts and sciences, to learn Sanskrit and to master a variety of skills for practical living. Every household served as a training center of farming skills and apprenticeship in other arts. Life in the Himalayan uplands was arduous, challenging and particularly conducive to religious and spiritual pursuits. It was regarded as a sacred region, where holy persons conversed with Divinities and lay persons traveled to ascend to paradise. The Joshimath-Badrinath route, famous for its pilgrimage sites, has been celebrated as the "path of ascent to heaven" *(svarga-arohana)* since the age of the epic *Mahabharata.*

A Lineage of Masters
In this Himalayan remote there lived a great yogi known as Maharishi Nandinatha, a rare and illumined soul whose inner eye was opened to the perfection of the universe, a knower of Siva, of the Self God within. He himself derived from a long line of satgurus, whose names and biographies are lost, and thus he is regarded as the first known preceptor of the lineage known today as the Nandinatha Sampradaya, the Agamic tradition that Robert Hansen had discovered in Ceylon.

Nandinatha had for his direct disciples the four sages—Sanaka, Sanantana, Sanatana and Sanatkumara—all bearing the title of Nandi. Besides them were Sivayoga Muni, Patanjali, Vyaghrapada and Tirumular (also known as Sundaranatha). All eight were the spiritual leaders of one of the initial Agamic schools and were known as Nathas. Of them, the first four received Lord Siva's special grace and were commanded by Him to disperse themselves in the four directions, carrying the message of the *Agamas.* Once at their appointed destinations, they practiced intense yoga in the Agamic way—through sun and rain, hail and storm—and in time

• •

Lord Siva beats His drum fourteen times, issuing forth fourteen primal sounds to create the universe. High in the Himalayas, siddha Nandinatha sits with his eight yogic disciples to teach, for the first time in known human history, the revelatory truths of the monistic tradition of Saiva Siddhanta.

ascended to celestial status.

The yogis around Maharishi Nandinatha were well versed in the *Siva Sutras,* whose aphorisms were regarded as the voice of Siva Himself—a puzzling, mathematically sophisticated set of fourteen couplets that seem to be about the Sanskrit alphabet, but on deeper reflection are a key to understanding the composition of the cosmos, showing how this language creates a mystical connection to the Divine from its very roots. The early tantric traditions, from Kashmir Saivism to Saiva Siddhanta, share a love of the *Siva Sutras,* those obscure, arcane, mysterious verses that yogis study even in the 21st century to delve into the mystical apprehension of the universes, gross and subtle.

These fourteen sutras—revealed to Panini, who wrote them down as a kind of yogic science notebook for its time—emanated from the drum held in the raised right hand of Lord Siva Nataraja. This science of sound and words remained a secret to most, for only the illumined could comprehend it, being unspoken knowledge directly from the Supreme Lord and beyond the reach of the ordinary mind.

Sages like Sanaka, Sanatana, Sanatkumara, Patanjali and others were able to hear the transcendental sounds of Siva's drum but were unable to grasp the inner, core meaning of the aphorisms. Legend says they approached Maharishi Nandinatha seeking an explanation. Moved by the sincerity of their search for this rare knowledge, the satguru proceeded to elucidate the essence of the sutras. He offered 27 verses, which are the only written teachings of this primal preceptor that have survived the tides of time, and thus form the

. . . .

Maharishi Nandinatha sits on a tiger skin explaining a scriptural verse to Sundaranatha, as the other disciples confer, examine sacred texts and offer praise to God Siva.

oldest scriptural text from this Saiva Siddhanta lineage. Terse and wise, it is known as the *Nandikeshvara Kashika. Kashika* means "the illuminator."

It is said that Sri Nandikeshvara, as Maharishi Nandinatha is also known, accomplished the feat of explaining the inexplicable due to two things: his profound God Realizations, which gave him a oneness with Siva within, and the completion of a difficult, some would say impossible, austerity, that of reciting the epic chant Sri Rudram ten million times.

Nandinatha's *Kashika* is more a meditation than an explanation, a contemplation on thirty-six constituents of the universe, from the most subtle to the very earth on which we stand—Lord Siva's unfoldment of the cosmos through sound, specific sounds that are embedded forever in the letters of the Sanskrit language. These constituents, or *tattvas*, are at the heart of the cosmology of Saiva Siddhanta, for in them can be found every level of consciousness, every element, every sense and color, every energy, vibration and sound that exists. Saiva Siddhanta speaks of 36 *tattvas* in all. Knowing the *tattvas,* one knows all.

The ancient texts are dense, convoluted and opaque, for in those days the secrets of yoga and inner consciousness were thought too precious to be openly expressed. So they were concealed in a special kind of language, like a cryptogram, assuring that only those who were qualified would have access; others would be confounded. Indeed, reading these texts today is confounding, as this glimpse into the far past, into the heart of the progenitors of yoga, the Himalayan masters, proves. On the following pages is a selection of sutras from Maharishi Nandinatha's 2,200-year-old philosophical text.

Without the insights and commentary of knowers of God and Sanskrit pandits of the highest order, even these aphorisms, composed to elucidate the even more arcane fourteen *Siva Sutras*, may defy understanding. Here is Nandinatha's verse ten, followed by a commentary by Sabharathnam Sivachariar:

The Supreme Lord of all, denoted by the letter *ṛi* (ऋ), being in union with Sivashakti, denoted by the letter *lṛi* (ॡ), whose form is of the nature of pure consciousness, enters maya, activates it slightly, creates the world of movables and immovables and makes them expand. He does all this solely and absolutely, being One.

COMMENTARY: When it is said that the Supreme Lord is absolutely One only, and that being in union with Shakti and by entering into maya He creates the world, it is observed that the concept of the nondual Lord gets affected. A defect occurs in the concept of advaita, as it is seen that, apart from the One Lord, there is the role of Siva-shakti and maya. In this verse and in the succeeding three verses it is explained that there is no such defect in the concept of non-dual Lord. *Ri* (ऋ) denotes the Supreme Lord and *lri* (ॡ) denotes Shakti and maya. As stated in the *Shri Tantra,* the mind-form of Siva is Shakti, denoted by the letter *lri* (ॡ). The last letter, *ka* (क), the root word, means "brings out from the unmanifest." Shakti constitutes the form of the Lord, and maya is a part of His form. A person is not in need of external help in making his bodily movements. So also, the Supreme Lord does not need an external help to make His form move and act. This is expressed by the term *kevala.* Apart from Siva, there does not prevail a separate existence for Shakti and maya.

Two Streams of Teaching

Natha means "lord" or "master," a knower of the Self who has mastered the intricacies of his inner bodies and states of mind. Through the millennia, Nathas have been conveyors of esoteric knowledge and wielders of siddhis, powers of the soul. Natha siddhas delve deep into the mind, invoking Siva's grace, controlling the kundalini shakti. They worship with full heart and mind the Lord of Lords, Siva, and in yogic contemplation experience identity in His Being.

The divine messages of the Eternal Truths and how to succeed on the path to enlightenment are locked within the Natha tradition. All that we know as Saivism today—Agamic temple worship, *homa,* sannyasa, sadhana, *tapas,* yoga, tantra and the theology of monistic theism—has been carried forward by the Himalayan orders of the Natha Sampradaya. *Sampradaya* means a living stream of tradition or theology. The Nathas are considered the source of hatha as well as raja yoga.

This oldest of Saivite sampradayas existing today consists of two major streams: the Nandinatha Sampradaya and the Adinatha Sampradaya. The Adinatha Sampradaya's earliest known exemplars were Maharishi Adinatha, Matsyendranatha and Gorakshanatha (ca 950), expounder and foremost guru of Siddha Siddhanta Saivism and founder of the well-known order of Kanphata yogis.

In the twenty-first century, the Adinatha and Nandinatha Sampradayas are both vibrant and vital. They share a common ground of theology, principles, sadhanas and many scriptures, including the *Vedas, Agamas* and Patanjali's *Yoga Sutras,* though historical, societal and geographical forces over the past 1,000 years have shaped differences between them.

Much of what is written by scholars about the Nathas refers to the northern Gorakshanatha school and lifestyle, rather than the Tirumular school.

The two streams diverge in important ways. The foremost exposition of the Nandinatha Sampradaya is Tirumular's *Tirumantiram* (ca 200 bce), while that of the Adinatha Sampradaya is Gorakshanatha's *Siddha Siddhanta Paddhati* (ca 950 ce). Most texts of the Nandinatha Sampradaya are in the Tamil language, while those of the Adinatha are in Sanskrit. The Nandinatha Sampradaya is most influential in Sri Lanka and the South of India, while the Adinatha Sampradaya is most prominent in the North of India. The philosophy of the Nandinatha Sampradaya is known as Saiva Siddhanta, while that of the Adinatha Sampradaya is known as Siddha Siddhanta. The primary philosophical difference concerns the means of liberation from rebirth: Adinathas hold that liberation is entirely dependent on our own thoughts and actions, while Nandinathas believe it cannot be attained without Siva's grace.

The Nandinatha Sampradaya values highly the necessity of a living preceptor who keeps the channels open to Lord Murugan, the first renunciate and traditional progenitor of the lineage. Tirumular wrote:

> Illuminating it is to perceive the guru's sacred person;
> Illuminating it is to chant the guru's sacred name;
> Illuminating it is to listen to the guru's sacred word;
> Illuminating it is to reflect on the guru's person.   139

The Nandinatha Sampradaya is a siddha yoga tradition (*siddha* means "attainment"), and its gurus have often demonstrated great mystical abilities and wisdom. It is said that these teachers have realized their oneness with the Supreme God Siva and have merged as completely as humanly possible with this Divine source of all. With such realization comes limitless bliss and direct command of every power in the universe. There are many accounts of miraculous powers demonstrated by the masters of this lineage. The aid, even the glance, of such a highly realized siddha can quicken

. . . .

The yogis of yore lived in the forests and jungles, often on the banks of rivers. There they performed spiritual disciplines, restraining the senses and driving consciousness deeper and deeper within. That inner worship was balanced by outer worship, commonly through a fire ceremony called homa, a mystical communion with the Deities and the inner worlds still performed by Hindus around the world.

spiritual practice. It is believed that without the *diksha* (initiation) of
such teachers, the human instincts will always fail to lead to this highest
realization.

The Natha Sampradaya is an initiatory guru-shishya tradition. Membership in the sampradaya is always conferred by initiation from a *diksha* guru, either the lineage-holder or another member of the sampradaya whose ability to initiate has been recognized by his *diksha*-guru.

The Natha initiation is conducted as a formal ceremony in which some portion of the awareness and spiritual energy (shakti) of the guru is transmitted to the shishya (student). The neophyte, now a Natha, is given a new name with which to support his new identity. This transmission, or "touch," of the guru is symbolically fixed by the application of holy ash to several parts of the body. In *The Phantastikos,* Shri Gurudev Mahendranath, a preceptor of the Adinatha Sampradaya, wrote:

> The passage of wisdom and knowledge through the generations
> required the mystic magic phenomenon of initiation, which is valid to
> this day in the initiation transmission from naked guru to naked novice by touch, mark and mantra. In this simple rite, the initiator passes
> something of himself to the one initiated. This initiation is the start of
> the transformation of the new Natha. It must not be overlooked that
> this initiation has been passed on in one unbroken line for thousands
> of years. Once you receive the Natha initiation, it is yours throughout
> life. No one can take it from you, and you yourself can never renounce
> it. This is the most permanent thing in an impermanent life.

Indian alchemy, known as *rasayana*—involving the ritual, spiritual and medicinal uses of mercury, cinnabar and other minerals, crystal preparations and elixirs—is practiced by the Natha siddhas. The primary aim of the Natha siddhas is to achieve liberation, or moksha, during their current lifespan.

According to Gurudev Mahendranath, another aim is to avoid reincarnation: "Our aims in life are to enjoy peace, freedom and happiness in this life, but also to avoid rebirth onto this Earth plane. All this depends not on divine benevolence, but on the way we ourselves think and act." This last statement would not find agreement among proponents of the Nandinatha Sampradaya, however. In Saiva Siddhanta, as expressed by Tirumular himself, it is precisely Siva's grace, and only that, which bestows the ultimate gift of liberation.

Himself will create, Himself will protect,
Himself will annihilate, Himself will obscure,
Himself having done these, He will bestow liberation.
Himself will pervade and be the chief, too.   1809

A Selection of Sutras from Maharishi Nandinatha's Philosophical Text

1. Compassionately willing to elevate the siddhas such as Sanaka and others and to install them in the highest plane of consciousness related to the transcendental sound, Lord Nataraja, the absolute and unparalleled Lord of cosmic dance, sounded the drum (held in His raised right hand) fourteen times at the ending phase of the dance. The transcendental sounds emanating from the drum assumed the form of fourteen aphorisms and came to be known as the collection of *Siva Sutras*. Now I proceed to explain the core meaning of those fourteen sutras.

3. The Supreme Lord, who is eternally free from the association of three qualities, having entered the cosmic flux known as maya, through His Conscious Energy becomes all-pervasive, assumes the form of the worlds and governs them.

4. The letter *a* (अ) is the first and foremost of all the 51 letters; it is self-luminous in nature. Because of its total identity with the Supreme Lord, it shines forth as the Supreme Ishvara Himself. Upon the union of the first letter, *a* (अ), and the final letter, *ha* (ह), the word *aham* gets formed.

9. The letter *a* (अ) is of the nature of cogitability alone, being the unmanifest. The letter *i* (इ) denotes *chitkala*. Because of its pervasive nature, the letter *u* (उ) denotes Vishnu. That which is in the state of cogitability alone, having associated with *chitkala,* assuming a form for the sake of cosmic function, creates the worlds and enters into them by means of pervasive nature (Vishnu) and becomes cogitable as the Great Lord (Maheshvara).

10. The Supreme Lord of all, denoted by the letter *ṛi* (ऋ), being in union with Sivashakti, denoted by the letter *ḷṛi* (ऌ), whose form is of the nature of pure consciousness, enters maya, activates it slightly, creates the world of movables and immovables and makes them expand. He does all this solely and absolutely, being One.

11. Not even a slight difference can be seen between the moon and the moonlight and between a word and its meaning. So also, not even the slightest difference can be seen between the modifications and the One which sustains those modifications.

12. Through His own energy, known as Chit-Shakti, and through His own will, the Supreme Lord makes the entire range of worlds to unfold from the causal source known as maya. The knowers of the scriptures realize that the letter *ṛi* (ऋ), which denotes the Supreme Lord, and the letter *ḷri* (ॡ), which denotes Shakti, are the specific letters belonging to the category of neuter.

13. The letters *e* (ए), *o* (ओ) and *ṅa* (ङ) indicate the unified state of maya and Ishvara. This kind of unification is seen in all the existents. Since He is the witness-consciousness for all the manifested things, it is ascertained that the Supreme Lord is solely One only, having nothing apart from His own existence.

16. What is known as space evolves from *ha* (ह). Air evolves from *ya* (य). Fire evolves from *ra* (र). Water evolves from *va* (व). Thus declares the exalted King of Sivayoga through His *Agamas*.

18. The five subtle elements from which the gross elements arise—namely, sound, touch, form, taste and smell—evolve from the five letters *ña* (ञ), *ma* (म), *ṅa* (ङ), *ṇa* (ण) and *na* (न). Sound, touch, form, taste and smell are respectively the qualities of space, air, fire, water and earth. The presence of these five elements is to be realized in all the existents.

21. It has been declared that for all embodied beings, the five organs of knowledge—namely ear, skin, eye, nose and tongue—evolve from the five letters *ja* (ज), *ba* (ब), *ga* (ग), *ḍa* (ड) and *da* (द) respectively.

25. The Great Ishvara, the Absolute Lord of the universe, having well associated Himself with the three qualities—sattva, rajas and tamas—which evolve prior to the creation of the worlds, constantly plays, presenting Himself in each embodied being. The three qualities—sattva, rajas and tamas—evolve from the three letters *śa* (श), *sha* (ष) and *sa* (स).

27. Lord Siva is beyond all these *tattvas* whose evolution has been told so far. He is the Supreme One. He is the sole witness of all beings and their actions. He assumes a form fit enough to bestow His abounding grace on all beings. "I am the Self of all, and I am one with the supreme letter *ha* (ह)." Having imparted this final message, Lord Nataraja concealed Himself from the vision of the sages. Thus ends the *Nandikeshvara Kashika*.

Tirumular Is Sent on Mission

Having achieved the eight siddhis and perfect enlightenment at the feet of the Natha guru Maharishi Nandinatha in the Himalayas, Rishi Sundaranatha, later to become known as Rishi Tirumular, joined the venerable Natha lineage, and later became one of its most celebrated yogis. Of the centrality of his guru he wrote in *Tirumantiram:*

By Nandi's grace, master I became;
By Nandi's grace, I sought Mular;
What can happen without Nandi's grace?
I remained, seeking to expound Nandi's path.   68

By the grace of Nandi, I sought Mular;
By the grace of Nandi, I became Sadasiva;
By the grace of Nandi, I became united with supreme wisdom;
What I am is by the grace of Nandi.   92

A View of Oneness
Following his initiation, Sundaranatha was sent by his satguru to revive Saiva Siddhanta in the South of Bharat. Taking leave of Nandinatha and his brother monks, Sundaranatha began his life's mission, to bring the true knowledge of the *Agamas* and *Vedas* to the southern parts of India in the Tamil language. It was a long and arduous journey in those days, thousands of kilometers by foot on simple roads and paths. Scripture notes that Rishi Sundaranatha took pains to visit the sacred Saiva centers en route, beginning with Kedarnath in the North, a remote stone shrine in the snowy Himalayan peaks, at the fountainhead of the river Ganga, near the border of Tibet. Now apart from his satguru, he sat at the headwaters of the river Ganga. His life's work lay ahead, his years of learning were complete and his mystical experiences were swirling all about. He would later write of these early realizations, of the four forms of Saivism, the four stages, the four relationships the soul has with God, the four realizations attainable, the four aspects of the descent of grace and the power of true renunciation of the world:

. . . .

The great siddha Nandinatha blesses his disciple, Sundaranatha, instructing him to undertake the arduous journey to the South of India, there to promulgate monistic Saiva Siddhanta in order that mankind may overcome the illusion of separation in the ultimate experience of Parasiva, where God and soul are one.

Purposeful is my learning; body and soul together,
I experienced the Lord in close intimacy;
Nothing to stop Him, He entered my soul;
So immaculate and sublime was my learning.   290

The four—charya and the rest—the four resultant realizations,
The six, like the elaborate Vedanta and Siddhanta,
Are established by Nandi leaving His golden abode,
For the sake of ignorant people to worship.   1449

Ask six historians when Tirumular lived, and you may well get six answers. This biography, based on statements in Tirumular's *Tirumantiram,* makes him a contemporary of Yogi Patanjali, author of the *Yoga Sutras,* who lived around 200 bce. In another analysis, Sundaramurti Nayanar mentions Tirumular in his list of Nayanars. The common view that Sundaramurti Nayanar lived in the period between 840 to 864 ce would mean that Tirumular lived before that period. Then there is a reference by Tirumular himself in the *Tirumantiram* to the Golden Hall of Chidambaram. Since the roof was first thatched in gold for the first time by the Pallava king Simhavarman, who lived in the fifth century ce, many historians conclude that Tirumular must have lived in the later fifth or early sixth century ce. But this ignores the possibility that Tirumular was, in *Tirumantiram,* describing Chidambaram from his mystic vision rather than from the sight of his physical eyes. Still others place him in the 10th century ce, noting that a sage by the name of Kalangi (the not uncommon name of one of Tirumular's disciples) was the guru of Bhogar Rishi, who lived during that period and was connected to Rajaraja Chola. Others point to his linguistic style and suggest he lived as late as the 11th or 12th century. India's history is notoriously debatable, and the period in which these great gurus lived may forever defy certainty.

His travels south, simply chronicled in the *Periyapuranam* by Sekkilar in the twelfth century, are envisioned in the tale below. The lone Sundaranatha traveled next to Pashupatishvara Temple in Kathmandu, Nepal. Gautama, the Buddha, had preceded him 300 or 400 years before, traveling from Nepal to South India and then to Sri Lanka, bringing with him his philosophy. At the Siva temple, Sundaranatha reflected on the Buddha's life and teaching, and his own destiny. In pondering the life of Gautama, he gained courage and prepared to continue his pilgrimage. But there was a difference. Tirumular was immersed, as Buddhism is not, in

. . . .

*Sundaranatha's arduous journey from the Himalayas, entirely on foot,
took years, culminating in Tamil Nadu, a land covered with palmyra
trees, shown here with a toddy-tapper collecting the sweet nectar.*

the overwhelming, ever-consuming, passionate love for Siva. He saw first hand that Divine Love incinerates impurities and purifies the soul.

Use the bone as firewood, chopping the flesh,
Fry it hard in the golden fire;
Unless one's self mellows and melts with tender love,
One cannot attain Siva, the priceless gem.   272

Search! You will find no God like Lord Siva;
None here can compare with Him; He transcends all worlds;
Golden-hued, His matted locks glow like fire;
He is in the lotus of the hearts.   5

Walking out of the lofty valleys of Kathmandu, he proceeded south and east to Kashi, the city of light, Siva's city, today known as Varanasi, where he was to have darshan of Lord Siva at the Vishvanatha Temple. Here he came close to his great Lord and bathed the Sivalingam with his own hands, as is the custom for all devotees in this northern shrine. During his worship, Sundaranatha longed to be with his guru, Maharishi Nandinatha, deep in the Himalayas again, listening to him expound the Vedic-Agamic truths he had learned so well. In an instant, the Sivalingam spoke to him from inside himself, reminding him that his guru was indeed within him, traveling with him, and that this oneness could never be altered.

Bowing out of the temple, walking backwards, at the door he turned to the right and departed, filled with confidence and assurance. For months Sundaranatha continued on his holy trek, walking along the village paths, roadways and trails beside mosaic paddy fields, out of the northern plains of India.

Entering the South of India

His chronicles tell of having darshan of Siva at Vindhya, Sri Parvatan and Kalahasti. He sojourned at the Sri Kalahasti Sivan Koyil, which is connected with the air element and the shadowy "planets," Rahu and Ketu. Here he would have observed the prevalence and popularity of pluralistic Saiva Siddhanta, and felt the immediacy of his mission, to convince the peoples of the South of the Advaitic Saiva Siddhanta truths. He understood Siva as beyond all, yet saw Siva everywhere and in everyone he met.

Sundaranatha proceeded to Tiruvilankadu, from where he set out to Kanchipuram, in what is now Tamil Nadu, the land of the Tamil Dravidian people, one of the oldest Caucasian races on the planet. The first temple

Sundaranatha reached Chidambaram in the deep South of India. He lived in the wilderness, not drawn to the townships and their activities. He bathed in the streams and slept on the ground, and occasionally in the crook of a tree to avoid animals and insects.

to be visited was a Siva sanctuary in Kanchipuram representing the earth element, where the healing powers of Lord Siva are pronounced, profound and famous. In each temple Tirumular's love of God grew stronger, his immersion in Siva more complete. He wrote:

The light that shines in the hearts of devotees,
Holy God, who sports in such hearts;
Extolling His greatness, adoring Him as my Lord,
We shall get closer and obtain His grace.   39

Seek refuge, in distress, in the resonant holy feet of the Lord,
Brighter than the rays of the purest gold;
Praise Him free of pretence and obstinacy;
He will not ignore, but let Himself abide in you.   40

His holy feet I shall place on my crown;
I shall keep them in my heart; His glory I shall sing;
I shall dance, offering flowers variegated;
I shall seek Him, the God of gods; this is all that I know.   50

In his astral body, sage Sundaranatha approached the dead cowherd, psychically entered the corpse and brought it back to life. His first sight upon awakening in the Tamil body was the herd of cows, happy to see their caretaker alive and well again.

• •

From here, Sundaranatha trekked to Chidambaram, where he stayed longer, having the darshan of God Siva's ananda *tandava* dance. Living the contemplative life, going inward and observing great austerities, Tirumular experienced consciousness as a dance within himself. So timeless were the yogic states he entered, he wrote figuratively of spending yugas, hundreds of thousands of years, at Tillai, another name for Chidambaram.

Saiva Agamas, so well spoken, I had received
From their exponent, the gracious Nandi;
Blessed I was with the Lord's dance at Tillai;
Thus I remained during several yugas.   74

One day, walking about as he was wont to do, he entered a dense forest. There Sundaranatha stumbled upon a Sivalingam and immediately fell to the ground in spontaneous surrender. It was a potent Lingam, about fifty centimeters high in its black granite base. Sunda-ranatha's worship was so complete, so one-pointed and so oblivious of himself that in a powerful experience of unity, he felt one with the Lingam. This I-am-God experience further empowered the icon. Today it is worshiped in its own sanctum within the thirty-five-acre Chidambaram Temple compound.

Pati, God, is the gracious Sivalinga in the sanctum.
Pashu, soul, is the powerful bull, standing before it.
Pasha, world, becomes the altar behind the bull.
Thus exists Siva's shrine for the seekers.   2411

The form of the human body is Sivalingam.
The form of the human body is Chidambaram.
The form of the human body is Sadasivam.
The form of the human body the sacred dance.   1726

The story passed down at Chidambaram Temple is that Sage Vyaghra-pada, a brother monk of Sundaranatha, established that original Lingam within an enclosure of thorny, marsh-loving *tillai* shrubs *(Excoecaria agallocha),* which gave protection from intruders, and performed his *sadhana* and worship near a small pond. The pond was later turned into the temple tank, where devotees wash their feet and hands before entering the temple.

Reborn Without Dying

Leaving the sleepy village of Chidambaram, he crossed the Kaveri River and reached Tiruvavaduthurai, a Saiva center which holds the samadhi shrine of this Natha siddha, though present-day managers of the sacred monastery say the disposition of his remains is actually not known. Lord Siva captured him here, and he was reluctant to leave.

Walking one day on the banks of the Kaveri, he came upon a herd of cows bellowing in distress near the dead body of their cowherd. Sundaranatha's compassion proved overwhelming as he felt the anguish of these bereaved creatures. His soul reached out to bring solace to the cows. Being a great adept of siddha yoga, he conceived a strategy to assume the herder's body.

He first looked for a place to hide his physical body and found a hollow log. Crawling into the log, where his body would be safe, he entered a mesmeristic, cataleptic trance, stepped out in his astral body, walked over to the dead cowherd, whose name was Mular, lay down on top of the corpse, entered it and slowly brought it back to life. The first thing he saw upon reanimating Mular's body was one of the cows looking into his face, crying big tears from both eyes, tears of joy. All the cows now gathered round their beloved Mular, licking his face and body with their abrasive tongues and bellowing in bovine joy. After a time, they began to graze as usual, and the sight gladdened Sundaranatha's heart.

As evening fell, the cattle began their daily walk home, leading the new Mular behind them. The cowherd's wife was waiting at the gate. She felt a strangeness in her husband and began to weep. Sundaranatha told her he had no connection with her whatsoever, and instead of entering the home, he went to a monastery that he had passed on the way.

Mular's wife informed the village elders of her husband's strange behavior. They approached the monastery, speaking with her supposed husband, whose deep knowledge and presence of mind baffled them.

. . . .

Legend speaks of Tirumular's years alone in a cave, deep in samadhi. At the end of each year he would write a single verse, scribed with a stylus into a palm leaf, capturing in that verse the sum of one year's meditations. Thus, patiently, he composed the mystical text, Tirumantiram.

Returning to Mular's wife, they told her that far from being in a state of mental instability, as she had described, he appeared to be a Saiva yogi, whose greatness they could not fathom. Mular's wife was troubled, but soon resigned herself to the fact that her husband was somehow no longer the same person. The villagers began to call the cowherd Tirumular, meaning "holy Mular." The mysteries of life and death were not mysteries to Tirumular, who wrote of life's impermanance and people's dismissiveness of this basic fact of life:

> Clandestine love and wedlock thereafter;
> Sated love and memories die with time;
> The body is carried on the bier and copious tears shed;
> Love and body offered to fire, a ritual offering.   150

> The wise that see the dead carried and put away seek
> The precious One that is the unswerving axle of the soul.
> They will follow Him ardently, the seed of their liberation.
> The rest, caught in the world, waste away.   156

> The sun rises in the East and sets in the West;
> People see and learn not.
> A young calf becomes a bull; in a few days it dies;
> People see and learn not.   177

> Childhood, youth and old age—
> Everyone worries about their inevitable transit;
> But with great ardor, I seek and abide in the holy feet of Him
> That penetrates and transcends the many worlds.   181

Tirumular sought out the body he had left near the pasture. Returning to the hollow log, he looked inside and found that his body was not there. He searched for days and days, looking in every hollow log he could find. Finally, in desperation, he sat in *padmasana* upon the log where he had left his North Indian body. Entering deep yoga samadhi, he contacted his guru, Maharishi Nandinatha. They communed, as mystics do, and he learned that Lord Siva Himself, through His great power of dissolution, had dissolved the atomic structure of the North Indian body after he was well settled and adjusted to his Tamilian cowherd's body, with the boon that he could now speak fluent Tamil. He realized that now he could

The footsteps of the hundreds of disciples of the disciples of Tirumular have been lost in the shifting sands of time, and we have neither names nor biographies for the many gurus (pictured above) who lived in the centuries between 200 bce and 1700 ce, when Rishi from the Himalayas appeared in Bangalore.

effectively give out to the Tamil-speaking world the truths of the *Saiva Agamas* and the precious *Vedas,* uniting Siddhanta with Vedanta for all time. He wrote of Siva's giving him this mission:

> Of what use will the subsequent births be
> If the previous one is not marked by austerities?
> A purposeful birth God gave me,
> That I may well render Him in Tamil.   81

3,000 Years of Yoga

Rishi Tirumular returned to Tiruvavaduthurai and there worshiped Siva, sitting locked in *padmasana* under the sacred *arasu,* or *bodhi,* tree to the west of the shrine. These years were deeply yogic, an inner journey that brought many unfoldments of the *nadis,* pranas, lights, mantras and yantras as awareness broke through the chakras following the rise of kundalini to the crown, there to find Siva's grace waiting, there to attain final liberation, moksha. The great yogi wrote of these inner explorations in hundreds of esoteric verses of the *Tirumantiram*.

> Fix the two eyes upon the nose,
> Contain the prana, and regulate it within.
> Seek to abide deep in the peace and freedom from the senses,
> There shall be no fear of birth. This is the fruit. 605

> The triangle-shaped *muladhara* is
> From where the kundalini rises, through the *sushumna*
> To the crescent moon facing the middle of the eyebrow.·
> Myriad shapes spring forth in a beauteous spectacle. 627

> Within you blossom the seven chakras.
> They are the Lord's abode you know not.
> When you know how to be one with Him,
> There you will see Him, sweet as sugar. 768

> Meditate upon that light of kundalini.
> Direct it upwards to the top with the breath.
> The ruddy flame of Siva transcending the cosmic *adharas*
> I sought and found this truth within. 1017

Legend says that once each year he came out of samadhi and gave forth from his meditations a single verse and spoke briefly on its meaning. Since he wrote over 3,000 verses, this would mean he lived over 3,000 years, and was born earlier than two millennia ago. Others postulate that he gave forth one verse a day for 3,000 days, and the poetic legend of 3,000 years arose because so much profundity is condensed into these 3,000 verses. It would take a full year of the deepest meditation to comprehend the full import of each four-line stanza.

Whatever actually happened, Tirumular's sacred text has persisted and flourished for 2,200 years. Even today new translations and editions are being published, and thousands of institutions count it among their philosophical and linguistic treasures. Its final verses speak of the unspeakable Siva, who is omnipresent and all-pervasive.

> The one with the graceful matted locks, the body of golden hue,
> Is non-attached, yet totally united;
> One who has no cessation, no birth; the Lord
> Is distinct from the seven worlds and yet merged in them.   3034

> As the Supreme Being, He transcends the seven worlds;
> He is the Earth surrounded by the seven seas;
> He is grace standing in its true nature;
> He is the vision (of the jivas) and stands merged.   3037

> My virtuous Lord! He is the leader of the universe;
> He is the mahout who controls the world;
> He is the one who manifests as the innumerable souls;
> He is the one revered as the Supreme God.   3039

> He is the resplendent indwelling prana;
> He is the Lord of the spreading rays of the sun in the firmament;
> He is the wind that blows on the Earth;
> He is the wisdom that gleans in the thought.   3040

> He is the light behind the perishable body,
> Water, earth, sky, fire and air;
> His name is Parapara; He is Siva, the destroyer;
> My Lord is limitless, pervasive everywhere.   3045

It would be difficult to overstate the importance of the *Tirumantiram* in Saiva Siddhanta philosophy. It is the earliest full statement of Siddhanta, "the end of ends." It is perhaps the most complete and profound exposition of the subtle theology of Saiva Siddhanta ever written, and it is the most extensive of the texts of the early gurus of the Nandinatha Sampradaya. Within the context of other Saiva scriptures of South India, the *Tirumantiram* is the tenth of the twelve *Tirumurai* or "Holy Books."

The *Tirumurai* are collected works in the Tamil language written mostly during the first millennium ce by various Saivite saints and gathered together in the eleventh and twelfth centuries. They constitute a Saiva canon and hymnal in which may be found all forms of spiritual expression, from the advaitic principles of non-dualism and Self Real-ization to heart-melting devotional praises to God Siva. The *Tirumurai* have come to be regarded as the very life breath of the devotional stream of Saivism. Second in importance only to the *Vedas, Upanishads* and *Agamas,* they are sung daily in temples throughout South India and elsewhere in the world where Saivites worship. In addition to the *Tiru-mantiram,* the *Tirumurai* consist of the *Devaram* hymns of the Samay-acharyas—Saints Appar, Sundarar, Sambandar and Manikkavasagar—the *Periyapuranam* of Saint Sekkilar, and other works.

In his life and writing Rishi Tirumular erased philosophical divisions, bringing much-needed unity to the kingdoms and their peoples. This togetherness created an integrated culture that gave rise to countless Siva temples throughout the South and 1,008 Siva temples in Sri Lanka. The ever-enduring philosophy of monistic Saiva Siddhanta—mystic yoga in union with total surrender—satisfied the masses, brought wealth, politi-cal stability and the flourishing of culture. There was peace in those days. Each Sivalingam was regularly bathed. Each yogi and rishi was treated with a reverence usually reserved for God.

Rishi Tirumular had seven disciples: Malangan, Indiran, Soman, Brah-man, Rudran, Kalangi and Kanchamalaiyan, each of whom established one or more monasteries and propagated the Agamic lore. In the line of Kalangi came the sages Righama, Maligaideva, Nadantar, Bhogadeva (who, some claim, is Bhogar Rishi of Palani) and Paramananda. All this we know from the *Tirumantiram* itself. But that is precious little, and history offers no trace of subsequent transmissions of power and the great *tapas* and sadhana performed by those early generations of gurus between 2,200 bce and 1710 ce. We do know that the Kailasa Parampara survived those hidden years and remains alive today. The gurus spoke of their gurus and their gurus' gurus, bringing us the first clear story in modern times, that of an anonymous siddha whom we know as Rishi from the Himalayas.

HIMALAYAN RANGE

Kedarnath Badrinath

Kathmandu

Kashi

INDIA

Bombay

Sri Kalahasti

Bangalore Madras

Mysore Kanchipuram

Chidambaram

Tiruvavaduthurai

Palani

Madurai Jaffna

Rameswaram

CEYLON

Tiruchendur

Colombo

Rishi from the Himalayas

What little we know of the next satguru in the Kailasa Parampara, a Natha siddha who had some 157 satgurus before him, of which 155 remain nameless, is but an oral legend. In the absence of even a name, he is called Rishi from the Himalayas, and the details of his life are tellingly sparse. There have been mystic intimations of his life and times, little more, into which the following fictive story breathes vivid detail and color, telling of India's hoary tradition of world renunciation, self-inquiry, sitting at the feet of masters, and God Realization.

A Boy Becomes a Sadhu

One day in a village in the North of India, the sun began to crackle on the far horizon. The villagers, soundly sleeping in their thatched huts, barely noticed, concentrating instead on clinging to the last few shreds of sleep. This day may have been like any other, were it not for one village member. Today that youthful villager would not just arise and go about his business. Today he would awaken.

The young man slowly stretched himself in his humble cot and looked about his hut. He had prepared for this day for so long. His abode was bare; nothing of value remained—only the memories, which now seemed so faint. Yet, as he scanned the room, the travails of his life until now exerted pangs of poignancy. His eyes lost focus, revealing a memory of his mother preparing a warm breakfast for his father and him before the day's work. Immersed in the memory, he scented the hot chapatis and fresh ghee. His mother would laugh as his father attempted to steal chapatis from the simple skillet.

He had no family now. He might have slipped away unnoticed, except in turning around he saw nearly the whole village gathered quietly near his hut—cousins, uncles, aunts and friends he had known since his youth. There was an awkward silence. One of their sons was simply leaving to become a sadhu. Duty to his father had kept him in the village for the last year. During that time, all of the village elders knew of his inclinations and tried to steer him toward family life. In these attempts, there was no ill intent. India has known this conflict for eons. On one hand, the sadhus, swamis, yogis, mendicants, rishis and siddhas are accorded

. . . .

It is traditional that a sannyasin's past and personal history remain unknown, as the source of a river should remain a mystery. Aptly, almost nothing is known of the lone wanderer who captured the imagination of the people of Bangalore in the southern hills of India.

great reverence once they are established in their calling. Oddly enough (or perhaps not, given humanity's
attachments), when one chooses to tread this path, he
or she usually meets great resistance and discourage-
ment from family and community. It is a path which is
supremely challenging; but for the select few who try,
and even fewer who realize what is to be realized, its
rewards are beyond words.

Though his mind wavered, his soul stood firm. He
smiled with affectionate detachment, brought his
hands together and softly bowed toward all before
him. Spontaneously, everyone raised their hands in a
blessing gesture. At last, the young man turned and
took his first step. He never looked back and was never
seen again in his village.

On the Road
Once alone and on the road, he strode with a determined power, halting only to rest. For days he walked
along the Himalayan rivers, visiting the occasional village temple and crossing fields to keep off the roads
where he knew people might be. It was a joyous time,
a time of discovery of something new each day. Rising late one morning, the groggy wanderer made his
way down to the river to bathe and honor the Sun.
Cleansed, he performed his morning sadhanas, then
continued on his southbound path. Days passed,
weeks and months.

A band of sadhus, less than a dozen, befriended him,
clothed him in their simple attire and let him join in their peripatetic
caravan, making their way to Palani Hills. The saints of history worshiped
here; it is one of the six foremost temples in South India, called *arupadai-
vidu,* dedicated to the powerful God Murugan (known as Karttikeya in
North India), whose mission it is to hold the path of the realization of Siva
open on the planet. He joined them full-heartedly on this long pilgrimage to see the Lord of Renunciates, his ideal in throwing down the world.

So much happened as he drew closer to his traveling brothers, learning
of their ways, their secrets, their view of life and life's beyond. From them
he learned to use a *neti* pot, to heal himself with herbs from the forest, to
bathe using nothing but sand, to eat from the land, to use pranayama in

The Himalayan sadhu's long trek to the South took him along the great rivers and through roadless forests and countryside. Each day was a joy, as he greeted Lord Siva and performed his daily sadhanas.

. . . .

a hundred ways, to see the perfection of the world that ordinary people miss or dismiss. He found it easy to see God in everyone he met, and his love for God Siva was deepened each day in their presence. They saw in him themselves, but younger, and they appreciated his eagerness, his gentleness, curiosity and quiet profundity. He had an uncanny stillness during their long nighttime meditations, something they silently envied.

They learned much from the novice, for he was well schooled in the ancient philosophies, articulate and capable of holding his own in their nightly debates around the campfire. They found him to be something of a prodigy, and they enjoyed ganging up on him, their combined skills and knowledge being roughly equal to his own. He never noticed the ploy, lost as he was in the spiritual joy of it all. He was living his dream. He was a sadhu among sadhus, and what could be more wonderful than that?

Weeks turned to months as the ragged band made its way, ten to fifteen kilometers a day, depending on conditions, toward their destination, the legendary Palani Hills Temple in Tamil Nadu, some 2,500 kilometers from the sadhu's village. Even today, Palani Hills Temple is one of the most popular in all of India, so much so it is the second richest temple in a nation that boasts hundreds of thousands of temples.

The group picked up its pace as it grew closer and closer to the temple. Pilgrims were converging on the well-used road, walking, many in bare feet to intensify their journey to God, in clusters past ragi, red chili and cotton fields on either side, threading their way through flocks of geese and herds of goats, all using the same road. Many groups of pilgrims dressed alike and sang and chanted in unison. This was not, for them, a solitary journey, but a fellowship and a sharing, a spiritual family united on the same holy trek.

Not all were skilled musicians, but each was inspired and sang fervently in praise of (and in petition to) Dandayuthapani, the Lord they sought—the beautiful youth wearing but a loincloth, his head shaven, carrying the staff of the renunciate, the radiant and eternal bachelor, tutelary Deity of the Tamil land, the second son of Lord Siva. One devotee among the band led an hour-long bhajan of only two words. He bellowed "Haro! Hara!" and all would respond "Haro! Hara!"—some feebly, for their real work was the walking. Passing them, the sadhus joined in the choir, still hearing the incantations when they were half a mile ahead.

The thicker the flow of pilgrims became, the more their strides filled with enthusiasm. Finally, the towers of the temple, set atop a 500-foot-high outcropping, could be seen. Lord Murugan was calling them to His feet, and they were answering His call. The sun was setting as they entered Palani, the town that hugs the bottom of the twin hills. The exhausted mendicants quickly found shelter at one of the many sadhu ashrams. They would climb to the top tomorrow. It was time now to rest and rejoice.

. . . .

Rishi's adventures on the road included many village encounters. In one story, he was accused by a food vendor of purloining a dosai and escaped an angry crowd who came to her aid.

Awash in Inner Light

Our young sadhu arose sharply in the morning, just before the first crack of light, for pilgrims know the importance of taking the climb in the cool morning hours before the sun makes it arduous. It's hard enough when the air is pleasant. He peered at all the pilgrims still sound asleep.

Pulling himself to his feet and donning a fresh *veshti*, he bathed at the open well, bringing up buckets of water to splash over his body, water that was bracingly cool and helped drive the sleep from his mind. He was not the first up, so he was able to follow others through the small township to the gate that stood at the bottom of the hill and betokened the beginning of the ascent he had so longed for. He paused in silent thanks, grateful to be here, to be safe and healthy and able to make this climb. Then he was off, determined, as he had heard was the ideal, to not stop en route, a rigorous approach to a challenging climb. But he was young and would do it.

He walked up the 659 steps, many carved crudely into the rock hill, worn by the bare feet of millions of earlier pilgrims. Finally, the top. Breathless, he stopped and scanned the immensity below. He could see in every direction—a view he had never had, a view of the villages and homes, the fields and roads that circumnavigate Murugan's home, a view of a thousand morning fires with their promise of breakfast, and of thousands of pilgrims just arriving, as he had the night before. He turned, walked thrice around the temple and entered for the first puja of the day.

After worshiping, he found his way to the cave shrine of Bhogar Rishi, the temple founder and disciple of Tirumular's disciple Kalangi. It was Bhogar, the great siddha, alchemist and healer—some say he was Chinese—who first worshiped Lord Murugan here around the year 200 bce and who magically fashioned with his own hands a 43-inch tall icon that still stands in the modern-day temple sanctum. He did not make it of stone or metal, but combined nine poisons, *nava-bhashana*, with various herbs to form a rock-like amalgam which cannot, even today, be precisely replicated, though master craftsmen made repairs to the aged icon in 2006 using approximated formulas.

Bhogar's shrine holds a power that gives credence to the local story that he is still alive and, impossibly old, living in a cave within the mountain. True or not, the young man felt the vibrant energy of the place and found a quiet corner where he sat down.

He was completely empty: no doubts and no expectations. No past, no future. Only the now. Effortlessly, he dove into deep meditation. His breath slowed, then virtually stopped; his awareness turned in upon itself and was soon washed in pure light, pure energy and a stillness that held the cosmos. He was everywhere and everything, infinitely expansive, without limit or body. While he was in that state, Murugan, the great God of the Pleiades, appeared in the form of a resplendent light. The light was so brilliant that he could not hold it as a vision and had to let himself be absorbed by it. He and Lord Murugan were one. He sat there transfixed as the kundalini soared upward, bringing him to a state beyond light.

He remained in that samadhi for some time. Finally, he became aware of the light once again, then beheld another vision in which Lord Murugan revealed to him the complete unfoldment of his life. Everything from past lives to his future life was suddenly known to the young sadhu. Once the revelation faded, he sat like a sponge, absorbing every drop of its energy. Completely satisfied, he got up and, without looking around, walked down the hill and went on his way.

Tremulous, the yogi felt remade, as if he had been given new life. After this rapturous encounter, he moved from one experience to another as in a dance. Life's energies flowed gracefully through him. His timing was perfect. Everything he needed came to him without effort. Food appeared when he was hungry. There would be someone on the way just standing there with food or beckoning him to their home for a meal. Shelter came. There would always be a fellow seeker's hut or a temple *devasthanam* awaiting him at the end of the day. After an evening meal, a mat would be offered for him to stay the night. He never thought, "Is this the way or is that the way?" He simply went here and there, following orders from within. His vision of the Lord and the kundalini experience was so vivid that he did not even need to think about it; it lived within him constantly.

In mystic Bharat people sense when a soul has attained spiritual maturity and renounced the world, and they seek some shared blessings from him for their own journey to moksha. Intuiting that he is on a mission, they part to let him pass, cautious never to re-involve him in the things of the world. They take care of him, offering what he needs without engaging him in idle conversation. They prepare him food and let him eat it alone in respect for his chosen solitude. So it was with this young sadhu. Villagers would offer him a place to sleep and take care to not let their householder life intrude upon him. In such a culture, like a knife cutting through water, the nameless sadhu walked his path alone and unhindered.

The Sadhu Meets His Guru

A year after his first samadhi, having trekked northward from Palani Hills, he arrived at a small temple high in the Himalayan mountains. He sat down to rest. Sensing that he was at the end of his journey, he went into deep contemplation of the beyond of the beyond. The intense vibration he had felt since his vision of God Murugan subsided into Saravanabhava bliss. Now it was as if he had finished everything, as though he were not, and yet as if he were the core of Being itself. He basked in the ocean of peace that engulfed him.

When he opened his eyes, he saw an old man sitting across from him who seemed to be in the same blissful state. The young sadhu stayed with him, sitting and waiting. For three or four days he waited for the man to move or speak. After a few more days, he stopped waiting and wondering. Soon he became absorbed within the Oneness and peace and lost all consciousness of being in a particular place. In that silent communion he received all the teachings he would ever need for moksha in this life. They came to him in an orderly way. For days he sat there absorbing and assimilating the silently eloquent shakti emanating from the old man.

The old man was taken care of by his devotees from neighboring villages and by pilgrims who came to worship at this small temple. They attended equally to the needs of the young man, distantly aware of the guru's protection of the profound experiences his shishya was going through. They were together in those mountainous regions for years. Most days were spent in meditation, not talking, not doing anything, immersed, absorbed in the bliss that is the aftermath of the great non-experience of Absolute Reality.

The young sadhu finally spoke out certain concerns to his silent guru, though not expecting a verbal response. He told of a spiritual need he had cognized during earlier days in the South. The sadhu implored his master's grace, explaining in the wee hours of the morning that things had gone awry there and the Saiva Siddhanta teachings were no longer correctly understood. Someone was needed to reestablish the pure monistic Saiva Siddhanta philosophy, which emphasizes worship and affirms that God and man are one, that jiva, in truth, is Siva.

One day, after a long meditation, the guru, who had barely looked at his disciple for many years, opened his eyes and smiled. They were pure and clear and luminous beyond description. The sadhu saw in them the same resplendence he had seen in the eyes of Lord Murugan at Palani Hills Temple many years before. He understood at that moment his guru's unspoken directive and turned to be on his way. He did not wait one minute, not a second. The next phase of his life had begun.

By the time he stepped again on South Indian soil, the sadhu from the Himalayas was an old man, a white-haired rishi. No one ever knew his name, or if he had one, so people called him Rishi. Only the barest facts have come down about him—that he was a sannyasin from the North and was probably born around 1790. He once told his one known disciple, Kadaitswami, that he had lived in the Himalayas all his life and that his guru sent him to the South on a mission. Once there, he wandered from village to village for nearly ten years, nameless and homeless, unknown and unnoticed.

A Teashop in Bangalore

Around 1850 Rishi began to frequent a small village near Bangalore, returning to beg from the houses often enough to become a familiar sight. He may have been drawn to the Natha mystics who lived in Karnataka state, and felt an affinity with their ways. Like them, he was not your everyday yogi. Always barefoot and empty-handed, he carried no bowl, no staff, no water pot or shawl. He ate once a day, from one house, and only what his two hands could hold. Many had thought of approaching him for blessings or asking him who he was, but Rishi came and went like the wind and did not brook intrusions or the curious. He appeared out of doorways and disappeared just as quickly. He stepped out of the crowd in the marketplace, and before you could catch him he walked around a corner or into a shop and was gone. Where Rishi came from, where he stayed, no one in the village knew. No one had been able to talk to him about such things.

He was described as a man of medium height with a thin, wiry build, intensely active and always in motion. He never strolled or ambled the roads; he marched wherever he was going, strong and straight despite his age. He wore a *kavi* dhoti (the rusty orange hand-spun, hand-woven, cotton garb of the Hindu saint) and two rudraksha malas, nothing more. His beard was silvery grey, his hair still quite dark, matted and piled in a crown above his head. His eyes, though, are what men remembered most about him—like two dark pools they were, large and round, black as coals and full of fire. They say he was an unusually quiet man, with an aura of unbridled power, like a river at its mouth, like the air before a storm. That heat, that current, was overwhelming, making it hard to be near him for long.

A man named Prasad owned a tea shop in the village, located right off the market square. It was a solid building with concrete walls and a timber-hatch roof, and he made a modest living serving tea, sweets and buttermilk there. Business was brisk, as it is in most Indian tea shops. The rishi walked into his place one morning and sat down on a wooden bench against the back wall. Prasad looked up to see an old sadhu leaning back against the cool wall, resting from the heat outside. Even as he watched, Rishi looked once around the room, pulled his legs up under him and closed his eyes in meditation. Prasad wasn't sure what to make of it, so he let the holy man be. In this time and place, holy men were revered, and even the most eccentric among them were held in awe, their movements unrestrained by ordinary society.

When it came time to close the shop for the day, Rishi was still sitting there. He hadn't moved. In fact, he didn't seem to be breathing at all. Prasad came over. "Has he died?" he wondered. No, the body was warm. He sat by Rishi for over an hour, wondering what to do. Finally, he reluctantly locked the shop and went home, leaving Rishi inside.

The following morning, Prasad found Rishi still in samadhi, exactly as he left him. He hadn't stirred at all. Word got around quickly, and villagers crowded in through the day to see—standing around, staring at him and talking it over. Despite the commotion, Rishi never moved. His face was radiant, but unmoving, like a mask.

That night Prasad again locked him inside the tea shop, and again the next morning Rishi was there, entranced, upright and unmoving. This went on for days, then weeks, then month after month. Word spread. People started coming from hundreds of kilometers away to see the silent saint. The tale grew more unbelievable each time it was told. In legends such things happened, in folk stories perhaps. Not in a little village in the hills. Not in modern times. And yet, there he was.

The rishi didn't eat, didn't drink, didn't move, didn't breathe, as far as anyone could tell. He was like a log of wood, like a corpse, but he wasn't dead, they knew. He was absorbed in God, in samadhi, keeping only a tenuous hold on the physical plane.

Eventually Prasad closed his tea operation and cleared out all the rough-hewn tables and benches. He didn't mind. His devotion filled him with the confidence that all his family's needs would always be met, and they were. Once he made the decision to surrender himself to caring for the Rishi and managing the crowds that came every day for darshan, everything always seemed to flow smoothly.

They came from before dawn and stayed until after dark. Some were there for the mystery of it all, and others for the chance to be with

. . . .

Walking the 2,200 kilometers from the Himalayas to Bangalore was not merely arduous, it could be life-threatening. It required enormous stamina, and it called forth a simplicity few could sustain. Here Rishi from the Himalayas makes the journey carrying only a water pot and yoga danda for meditation.

philosophically astute comrades. Others were superstitious, and a few were there just to debunk the whole thing. The evenings were always busy, for there were few in the village who didn't visit Rishi almost daily. Eventually, pilgrims from all corners of India made their way to Bangalore, to be part of history, to see something remarkable.

The crowds grew. It became difficult to keep them from crowding Rishi, as most wanted to touch him, to touch a bit of holiness. Prasad put up a brass railing to keep them back. It worked. Only he and his sons could go beyond it, and at least one of them was on duty whenever the shop was open.

The various offerings people brought were passed over the railing to the "priest" on duty, who spread them out on a low, copper-clad table in

front of the bench where Rishi sat. Also within the railing was a row of brass oil lamps, a dozen of them, large and small, no two alike, donated by pilgrims. These were kept burning night and day. A shallow bronze pot was added later, out in front of the railing, where devotees burned great quantities of camphor. The soot from the fires soon blackened the room, especially after Prasad bricked in all the windows for security. The remaining door he bolstered with great iron hinges and bars, and he kept the key to the shop on his person at all times.

His business gone, Prasad maintained his family by taking what he needed each day from the piles of cooked food, fruits, flowers, incense and money the pilgrims brought as offerings. The rest he distributed back to the devotees as prasadam, as temples do after each puja, so little or nothing was left by nightfall. The rishi attracted an astonishing amount of wealth. No one came or went away empty-handed.

Things eventually settled down to a routine, for there was really very little to do or see. People came to be with Rishi, staying a few hours or a few days, and then going. No pujas were done; no one chanted, sang or talked. The room was always silent, the lamps were always lit, Rishi was always there, and this went on year after year after year.

Seven Years in Meditation
A visit to the tea shop was the experience of a lifetime, and many said once was more than enough. Stepping through the iron doorway was like stepping into another world, from the glaring heat of the Indian sun to the cool interior of a cave. One end of the room was illumined by sunlight streaming in through the open door. Only oil lamps lit the far end and the bench where Rishi sat.

You see Rishi first, like an apparition, a wraith against the wall beyond. If chiselled in stone, he would look the same. Ringed by oil lamps, no shadows approach, so his face reflects the ruddy color of fire. He is thin and old, his ribs show through, and he is covered with a film of *vibhuti,* holy ash, from head to toe. No one applies it, but it is always there, powdering down on the bench and floor, the only thing about him that changes from day to day. Looking at him, the thrill in his limbs is unmistakable; it can be seen. His face is an open expression of indrawn joy, radiant and shining, mingled with the fire glow.

On the table in front are heaps of bananas and mangoes, rice and pomegranates, clay jugs, brass pots, incense and coins all spread in profusion on

. . . .

Like Starbucks today, tea shops were gathering places back in the 1800s, the traveler's place of respite and rejuvenation. Here a shopkeeper prepares hot tea, deftly pouring the boiling brew back and forth between two cups held a meter apart to cool it to the perfect temperature.

a gorgeous cloth of red and green. The whole room is strewn with flow-ers. Everything looks polished and new—the railing, the lamps, the table—everything but the camphor bowl, blackened and bent. It must glow red on a busy day. New straw mats hide the earthen floor, and a few devotees are seated upon them. Prasad stands guard in the shadows, a portly figure in spotless white.

It is perfectly quiet, perfectly still. A ringing silence fills the air and can be heard by those inwardly attuned, a sound as of a thousand vinas play-ing in the distance, a sound divine, the sound, some say, of the workings of the subtle nervous system, or, others claim, the sound of consciousness itself coursing through the mind, the sound that binds guru to disciple through the ages. It is a sound that many visitors have never heard till now, and it fills them with an inexpressible and familiar joy.

The dim room smells of camphor and earth and the perfume of ripe mangoes piled on the table. It feels alive; it looks empty. Sitting on the mats with the other devotees, one suddenly feels the impact of Rishi's presence. The skeptical mind is stunned, and it seeks a rational explana-tion: "He is an old man napping, nothing more. He is asleep or lost in a thought. Surely that's all." But for seven years? Seven years he has been here, they say, rapt in his soul, absorbed in God. Can it be believed? It boggles the imagination. The mind struggles and comes away baffled and yet changed by having been here, having been in Rishi's scintillating presence.

Pilgrims from all over India reached the tea shop in Bangalore, on the 3,000-foot-high Mysore Plateau. Many said they had been called there, having seen Rishi in a dream or vision. Prasad knew a thousand such sto-ries, and delighted in telling them to whomever would listen. The pil-grims came with problems more often than not, and always they were helped; none was denied. Few would claim that Rishi had answered their prayers himself, for no one felt that kind of personality in him. He wasn't there in that sense. And yet, things happened around him that didn't hap-pen elsewhere.

In Rishi's presence the mind was so clear for some pilgrims, so calm, that answers often became self-apparent. Even problems that had gone unsolved for years dissolved in minutes before him. The answers came from within the pilgrim. For others the answers were more elusive, com-ing after they left his presence, even days later. A visitor would pray or merely think over his life while sitting before Rishi and then be on his

· ·

Rishi from the Himalayas became a legend when he sat for seven years in a tea shop without moving. People came from far and near to witness this miracle, so many that a brass railing was installed to keep the crowds from touching him and disturbing his meditation.

way. Whatever the question or problem or need, the answer soon came, clear as a bell—in a scrap of conversation overheard on the street, in a song sung by a child skipping to school, or simply from intuition, from the inner sky. Sitting with Rishi opened the mind to its depths, and everything adjusted itself naturally. It wasn't the answer itself but the way it hit the mind, the impact of it, that showed where it came from—it was straight to the point in a roundabout way, said but unsaid, seen but unseen, like Rishi himself. Always the answer hit the nail on the head, with stunning power, leaving no room for doubt. And that power did not diminish with time, as everyday thoughts do, but grew in certainty and clarity.

Then there were the notes. On rare occasions, a pilgrim would receive a note, a message out of thin air, answering problems he had brought, silently, before Rishi. These notes appeared in the room where he sat, written on a scrap of paper. A rustling sound as it hit the floor was all anyone knew of where the note came from. These messages were never personal, never addressed to anyone, and didn't answer questions specifically. Rather, they spoke in general terms, talking around the subject and usually explaining the way things were done in the old days.

If a mother was worrying about the marriage of her daughter, the note might explain a bit about how marriage was looked at in the *Vedas*, what the ancients looked for in a family, why a man marries, why a woman marries, how to tell if the choice is good, and so on. Though brief, the notes were more than enough to show what was needed and why. Because they spoke to everyday problems, their content was seldom remarkable. Similar statements could be found in any Hindu scripture. Indeed, the notes occasionally quoted scripture, especially the *Upanishads*. But the way they were written, and the medium of the message, had a remarkable effect on the one who received it. The language of the notes was usually Kannada, though Telugu, Tamil, Hindi, Sanskrit—and even German, on one occasion—were also used.

A widowed businessman came from Tuticorin, deep in the South of India, after finishing his career and leaving the estate in his son's hands. Bringing no plans, no problems, no needs, he simply came to see Rishi. A note appeared while he was there, referring to the four stages of life—brahmacharya, *grihastha, vanaprastha* and sannyasa (student, householder, elder advisor and renunciate)—which are the natural patterns of the soul's earthly vitality and karma. The man captured the subtle direction

. . . .

The tea shop eventually became a shrine, as people came to see a spiritual giant of remarkable yogic powers. Those powers were nowhere more evident than in the magical way that prayers were answered in his presence. Sometimes answers fell from above on small pieces of paper.

and entered a life of service in a nearby ashram, visiting Rishi often.

Five years after Rishi had come to the tea shop, four young men, students at the University of Berlin, arrived in the village to see him. They were all in their early twenties, all Sanskrit scholars, three of them quite competent. Like many of their generation, they were enthralled by the *Vedas* and *Upanishads*. They had even founded an ashram in Germany to spread the lofty teachings they so admired.

These four had heard about Rishi from travelers in far away Berlin and decided to come to India to see him for themselves. If the reports were true, he was just the man they were looking for to guide them in practicing and realizing the ideals of the *Upanishads*. Two of them were wealthy enough to pay passage for four out of pocket, and so—their hearts aglow with dreams and plans, pinning their hopes on bringing Rishi back to the fatherland to head up their ashram—they shipped off to India.

Landing in Bombay, they proceeded south to Bangalore and the village where Rishi sat. Because they spoke only Sanskrit, of the Indian dialects, a brahmin man accompanied them as a guide and translator. The people of the village were impressed with their sincerity and a bit surprised by their knowledge of Hinduism. They were hosted and entertained by the best of families, treated like princes and practically adopted by everyone. They would gladly have stayed on forever, if not for their comrades in Berlin and the mission they had come East to fulfill.

Once they met Rishi, their world turned around him alone. They spent two days sitting in the tea shop, coming outside only to hear Prasad's stories. After two weeks, each of them had their own stories to tell, of wonderful experiences, inner and outer. The rishi surpassed their wildest dreams. They were sure they had found their teacher. The future of Hinduism in Germany looked bright. They talked about it excitedly: Could Rishi be aroused? Would he even speak? Could he travel in his present state? Dare we disturb him? Most important, would he agree to go to Berlin? What if he refused? Then what?

A message materialized one day, the kind Prasad always talked about, written in German and obviously meant for them alone. That note convinced them utterly. They were walking on air for days afterward, reciting it to each other like a hymn, like a mantra. The note was in Rishi's usual style, indirect, talking all around the question, yet plain enough:

"All things can be—according to karma and opportunity. A man's karma is threefold: that which awaits a future birth, that which awaits an opportunity and that which is in motion now. Sadhana spares the least of men a thousand future lives."

Such profound thoughts simply had to be heard back home. For most of the next week, the four debated about how Rishi lived without food. They made plans to inquire, ending up at Prasad's home one evening where they broached the subject for the first time, questioning him through their brahmin interpreter.

"Does a man in samadhi ever eat?" they asked. "How long can he go without food?" "Just supposing Rishi had to be moved to a larger building someday—how would you go about it?" Prasad answered them as best he could, smiling all the while. He didn't understand their intentions until they asked him about coming past the railing. Then he said, "No, it might disturb Rishi." They asked again. He said no, he didn't let anyone past the railing. The students tried another tack. One began to describe their ashram in Germany, going on at length about how much the people there needed a genuine teacher, someone like Rishi, for example.

Prasad listened with growing horror until he got wind of a scheme involving crates, carts and steamships, when he jumped to his feet and let loose a speech that brought tears to his eyes. He talked himself hoarse in five minutes, and not a word of it got through. The brahmin man wasn't translating; he was busy himself explaining to his clients the consequences of even thinking of such things, and they were arguing back at him. Prasad went inside and slammed the door.

They didn't see him again until the next morning, when they walked over to the tea shop for their daily meditation. Prasad was there, sitting in the dirt out in front, slumped against the wall, his hair disheveled, his *veshti* trailing, the picture of misery in the extreme. The shop was still locked.

"What's wrong?" they asked. "Prasad, what's the matter?" Prasad told a tale of woe to the brahmin, who nodded his head sadly and rolled his eyes as he listened. Then he turned to the Germans and translated. "My friends, a calamity has come to us all. Not an hour ago, when Prasad opened the shop for the day, what should meet his eyes but an empty room! The rishi has vanished in the night. They have searched the town and no one can find him. He is gone. Ah! What have we done to deserve this? This is bad news, indeed."

Then he sat down beside Prasad and put his head in his hands. The students were skeptical. They wanted to see for themselves. "Why is the door locked if Rishi isn't here?" Prasad didn't hear the question. One of them stepped up and rattled the door. "Where is the key?" he demanded. In the wink of any eye, the veranda was crowded with men, a half dozen stalwarts, and the village headman was crossing the square. "What's all

the noise?" he inquired. "Can I help you?"

The Germans explained Prasad's tricks. The headman was surprised. "Perhaps you have misunderstood," he apologized. "You must permit me to explain. My friend Prasad is an honest man. I have known him many years. All of us here can vouch for him. If he said Rishi is gone, Rishi is gone. I do not think you will ever see him again."

The students understood exactly what was being said, and they withdrew. Too late, they realized their opportunity had gone. They lingered on in the village three days more, to no avail. The rishi was still "gone" and so was their welcome. They ate alone for the first time since coming to India.

Rishi was regarded variously by those who visited the tea stall: yogi, magician, oracle and Deity. No matter how they saw him, visitors approached with trepidation and reverence for the remarkable man who lived apart from ordinary consciousness.

· ·

They had no callers, and no one spoke to them, even on the street, except to inquire about their travel plans. They left on the fourth day for Bombay, and they never came back.

There were other foreign visitors to the little tea shop during the following two years, though no one ever again tried to disturb Rishi. Life went on as it always had, until one day Rishi opened his eyes and looked at everyone present. A few minutes later, he stood up, stepped out of the shop and walked down the road. He had taken great care during those years, through practice of pranayama, to maintain the flow of life through his body. So he was able to get up and move about with the merest instability, more like someone who had sat in one position for too many hours.

Word spread quickly, as it does in small villages. Everyone came running, from the fields, from the shops, from the houses. Everyone was there. The mere fact that he could walk after seven years astounded the villagers. They didn't want to lose their silent saint. His being there had transformed their lives; they wanted him to stay with them. They couldn't imagine life without him, so they acted quickly.

With everyone pooling the best that they had, a two-room cadjan hut was built that afternoon on a low hill overlooking the village, on virgin ground next to a stream. They stocked it and overstocked it with utensils and food, bedding and more. Now, should he want it, Rishi had a hermitage—remote enough for him and close enough for the villagers who had grown to love and revere him so.

No one had seen Rishi, so the following morning men and boys fanned out and searched the countryside for miles around. They found him in the late afternoon, asleep under a tree. The village elders hurried to the spot, bearing gifts. The rishi sat up when they came and made their pranams. He was staring at them in surprise. They placed their offerings at his feet and everyone begged him to stay, talking all at once and by turns. All his needs would be met. His hermitage was ready, they told him, and if it wasn't just right, they would build a bigger one. They assured him they were there to serve and obey him always, their children, too. "You must stay," they pleaded, "Please don't go." He sat impassively and they knew enough to take their leave.

Before daylight the next day, the village headman was awakened from his slumber by little boys shouting at his gate: "Come quick! Come and see!" They pointed to the hill. The rishi was sitting out in front of his hermitage, tending a small fire to keep away the cold that comes many nights at 1,000 meters above sea level, looking out over the village, right where they wanted him! The headman and others gathered up baskets of fruits and flowers and, walking single file, approached as Rishi looked on while adding sticks to the fire. Laying their offerings at his feet, they prostrated, then stood with folded hands, nervous and uncertain after yesterday's encounter, not knowing how to approach this man who had been immobile all those years and now was on the move. The rishi offered no response, and, after some awkward moments, the villagers nodded one to the other and turned back to their homes, saying not a word along the way.

In time, the courageous villagers returned to enjoy his darshan. But he was different. He absolutely refused food prepared for him. Instead, he ate a meager fare that he picked and prepared himself and shared with the crows, content to sit on the bare ground. He seemed almost crazy. He didn't behave the way they had imagined he would.

His eyes were so fiery and intense that people who had once so devotedly worshiped him while he was sitting in samadhi no longer felt the same rapport. In fact, they became afraid of him; such a potent spiritual presence being more than they bargained for. Some even wished the holy man gone from their lives and pondered how to be rid of him. Their fears and confusions were not unknown to Rishi. One afternoon, some of the distraught villagers went to speak with him, but found the thatched shed burnt to the ground. The rishi was gone.

It was a month before the regular stream of pilgrims coming to the village showed some sign of abating. People still came to see Rishi, and the

Rishi's serenity during the silent years in the tea shop gave no indication of his fiery nature, which was experienced later. Villagers wanted him gone, but before they could engineer his departure, he torched his simple thatched hermitage and left the region forever.

• •

villagers found it hard to explain why he had gone away without accusing one another, but there was an unspoken agreement on all sides not to do that. The tea shop was left open at all hours, if only to convince skeptics that Rishi had ever been there at all. No one talked about his leaving, though. In the wise old way of a Hindu village, it was one of those disasters that had never happened, a thing that wasn't talked about or thought about. Life went on. Instead, the pilgrims heard about how sublime Rishi was, how he sat in that one place for seven years, answered prayers in magical ways and never moved once until the day he got up and walked out of the village. No, no one knew where he went. No, they didn't think he would return. At least, it didn't seem likely.

A few months after Rishi's departure, a towering sadhu arrived, a huge man, two meters tall. He stood head and shoulders over everyone. Entering the village, he walked straight to the tea shop as if he'd been there before, and sat down inside to meditate. He didn't come out for several hours. Then he started asking around about Rishi's departure and where he had gone. Prasad told him what he knew.

He had dinner at Prasad's house that evening; and afterwards, rumor had it, the two of them talked in private long into the night. The townspeople thought Prasad probably gave the sadhu some information not usually shared with strangers.

The lanky sadhu stayed for a week, and talked to just about everyone about Rishi, even going out into the fields to chat with farmers. He walked up the hill to Rishi's place, but came right back down, saying there was nothing up there. A good part of his day was spent talking with people in this way, and the rest of it in meditation. He slept several of the nights he was there on the floor of the tea shop itself; otherwise, he could be found at Prasad's house. Whenever he was asked his name, he would only say that he was from Rishikesh. From his accent, though, people guessed that his native tongue was Telugu, though he spoke Kannada, Tamil and English around the village.

The opinion of most villagers was that Rishi had gone north, back to the Himalayas, but no one knew for sure; so the sadhu left the village, still not knowing where in India Rishi was. Later tales spoke of Rishi's presence in Sri Lanka, where the miracles and the magical notes appearing from nowhere and falling to the floor occurred again. In fact, it is said that he was better accepted in Sri Lanka than in India.

"I Will Not Sentence Him to Death"

One day, in High Court in Bangalore, Karnataka, a magistrate presided over a murder case. The verdict was never in doubt, and the jury was unanimous. When the time came to pronounce the mandatory death sentence, the judge stood up to address the court. His tall, imposing stature brought silence to the courtroom. Before he spoke, he removed his shastri's shawl, his robes and ornaments. Looking around the courtroom for the last time, he announced, "God created this man. Who am I to decree his death?" Refusing to deliver the death sentence, he solemnly walked away from the bench and was never seen in that region again.

Years later, he would be found in Northern Ceylon, a swami and spiritual force who deeply changed not only individual lives there, including the future satgurus of the Nandinatha Sampradaya, but the course of that nation's history as well. What happened between these known events is vague, and stories don't all agree. Here an attempt is made to intuit the most likely course of events, based on those oral histories and the cultural patterns of the time.

It is likely that this thirty-something bachelor had little to hold him beyond his work in the courts and that the murder trial provoked deep reflections about life and death, reflections that intensified his naturally spiritual turn of mind. Finally, he made the pivotal decision to seek a satguru and devote the remainder of his life to realization of God and service to his Hindu faith.

Speaking to others about his inclinations toward sannyasa, he came to know of the rishi in the tea shop. He was regaled with stories of this remarkable sage, stories that moved him deeply and led him to seek to meet that awakened being in person. The erstwhile High Court judge became a wandering sadhu, following the Indian roads on foot, in search of the rishi, walking from village to village, here and there, looking on the inside, looking on the outside for the man he increasingly knew beyond any doubt was his guru. This was no intellectual certainty, for they had never met. Rather it was a truth, a subsuperconscious knowing, that welled up from deep within him.

His unusual height and beggar's way of life attracted attention wherever he went. It was no use trying to blend into the background, and he didn't try. On reaching a village, his usual method was to stand in the center

. . . .

Duty demanded that an Indian judge sentence a guilty murderer to death, but he could not bear that karma. Instead, he removed his wig and judicial robes, stood and walked out of the courtroom, never to return, never to practice law again.

of the marketplace as if he were waiting for someone. Seeing him there, people would gradually set aside what they were doing and come over to find out what he wanted. He would talk with them for a few minutes and have them laughing and smiling, until a crowd had gathered. Then he would tell all the little boys who were there about the swami he was looking for and send them to ask their parents and relatives, aunts and uncles, everyone they knew, whether the sannyasin had been to their village.

While they were gone, he would stroll through the marketplace, talking with the buyers and sellers and accepting alms from the shopkeepers. They offered him the best they had. He had a natural affinity for people and a charm that was irresistible. Added to this, he was at ease with people and gifted in his speech. He could communicate readily and fluently and was never at a loss for words. People trusted and befriended him without hesitation, most of them calling him Appar, or "father," without thinking twice. As the children returned from their errands, they brought him news of every swami, sadhu or pilgrim that had been there in the past ten years. Usually, the rishi wasn't among them.

Sometimes, he was. Clues to the rishi's whereabouts came now and again, from out of the air. At one point the sadhu was directed to the tea shop near Bangalore, where he stayed a while in the aftermath darshan that could still be felt there. But no one knew where the rishi had gone, so the search continued from place to place.

One day the sadhu had reached a small town just south of Mysore and was asking his way to the marketplace, when he suddenly stopped in front of a large house in the merchant's quarter. After some time, a young man came out and asked who he was. He explained he was a sadhu, and he was looking for a certain swami, an old sannyasin. Had he seen him? The youth didn't reply, but stared at him, blinking for a moment before he turned and disappeared into the house again.

A minute later, his father came out and respectfully invited the sadhu into his home to share a meal. He explained that he and his youngest son had just returned that day from a long pilgrimage to Palani Hills Temple and the welcoming home was still going on in his house. They ate somewhat absently, as their conversation interested both more than the food.

The merchant had seen, at Palani, the very swami his guest described, an old rishi with dark eyes, matted hair wrapped up in a crown, very thin, but as lively as a boy of six. He didn't know where he might have gone, but he had seen him there one day. He said the rishi's face would stay fresh in his memory as long as he lived. "I am sure he is the one you seek," he said. "You will not meet such a man twice in your lifetime." After the meal, the sadhu thanked his host and set out on the long trek to Palani, 300 kilometers to the southeast in the state of Tamil Nadu.

Meeting the Rishi

They finally met at Palani Hills Temple, the famed hilltop sanctuary where Lord Murugan presides as the loincloth-clad yogi. This had been the sacred site of the rishi's initial vision of Murugan, the experience that took him north to the Himalayas and into a lifetime of sadhana and divine realizations. He had returned to this place of his spiritual beginnings.

Like the two men, their meeting was not ordinary. The sadhu was engaged in worship when the rishi came up from behind and motioned him to follow. It is said they were together for most of a year, wandering through the Tamil lands from temple to temple, shrine to shrine—at Chidambaram for several days, later at Tiruvannamalai, and as far north as Madras and Nellore.

People long remembered seeing them, for they were an unusual sight, the rishi and his disciple. Wherever they went, people looked twice or stopped to stare. The rishi walked with long strides and kept his eyes on the way ahead. If people looked at him, he looked away, showing nothing of himself. His towering disciple, though, walked with a long, lumbering gait, one stride for the rishi's two, his gaze fixed between the clouds and treetops.

They walked side by side, like old friends, staying each night wherever they happened to be at day's end—in a village, at someone's home, a temple or under a tree by the road. A typical day would find them meditating together in the pre-dawn darkness, having sat up most of the night. Before the sun came up, they would bathe at a well or river and stretch a bit, then the rishi would sit down facing the east, his shishya nearby. The rishi talked to his disciple for several hours each morning, then sent him to beg the day's meal. They would sleep through the hot hours, and in the afternoon move on, covering a few kilometers each day at a leisurely pace.

Wherever they stayed, people soon gathered, even in a wild spot, a clearing in the jungle, so they never stayed a third day anyplace. On the second day, more people would appear, coming to see, coming for blessings, coming with food—wanting to catch them, the rishi said. When they weren't staying in a village proper, the sadhu would walk to the nearest hamlet to beg their meal and, as often as not, would return with five or ten of the boys of the village tagging along. They had never seen such a tall man, and they wanted to be with him, so they carried his beggings and umbrella and brought along milk, mangoes and treats from their mothers' kitchens. When the rishi saw such a parade approaching, he would laugh and laugh. His disciple was really helpless to stop it; there was nothing he could do. Even if he bellowed, the children simply followed playfully a little farther behind.

Sacred Instructions

It is said that the rishi and his disciple were last together around 1860 near Siva's classical city of Thanjavur, where they stayed several weeks at a private temple. Our creative narrator peers back through the mists of time to pen the following story, based on the culture of the day.

Leaving the holy town, on the road south from Madras, the capital, they passed a large estate. A well-dressed man came out from the house and hurried forward to meet them. Saluting them in all reverence, he introduced himself as the landlord and enthused that he had seen his visitors in a dream the night before, the two of them sitting in his family shrine, and had been waiting all morning, hoping they might appear. He begged them to accept his hospitality for as long as they pleased. They walked with him up to the house, a palatial mansion, to be met at the door by a host of excited servants.

The landlord washed their feet himself, offering handfuls of flowers he had gathered just in case his dream was prophetic. He took his guests inside and introduced his family. Afterwards, he showed the way to his family's private temple, across a wide courtyard behind the house. It was a pillared hall with a high roof, the outside painted with traditional red and white stripes, the building surrounded by *bilva* and mango trees. Inside the hall was a small stone shrine. "This temple is as old as I am," he exclaimed, with a sweeping gesture of his arm. "My grandfather built it while I was a boy. My father worked very hard on it, too." Within the shade of the portico sat a small stone Nandi, which the landlord bowed to fondly as they passed.

The shrine was flawless and scrupulously clean. Teak-wood doors swung open to reveal a floor of polished granite and walls almost covered over with superb wooden and plaster carvings of sacred import. The Sivalingam in the sanctum was bedecked with garlands of flowers and crowned with jewels. The *pujari* had just left, and the air was full of incense. The wealth of the owner was evident. All the puja articles were of silver and gold—the bell, the trays, even the hanging pot above the Lingam. The atmosphere was quiet and sublime, a world unto itself.

A thin brahmin lad walked in through a side door. He withdrew as

· ·

The young sadhu found his guru, Rishi from the Himalayas, at Palani Temple. The two were inseparable, and always on the road, never staying more than two nights in one place, true mendicants, begging for their meals and living under no man's roof.

soon as he saw them, but the landlord called him back. "This is Ramesh," he informed his two guests. "His father has been the priest here for many years, and Ramesh will take his place one day."

Their host showed them through the rest house he maintained for pilgrims, and offered them anything they wanted from a storeroom full of supplies. Water pots, *veshtis*, shawls, umbrellas, mats, walking sticks, fans, sandals, trays—every conceivable pilgrimage item was there, from needles to blankets, even a small basket overflowing with large rupee coins.

"There is no counting the devotees of the Lord that pass this way in the dry months," he explained. "They go on to Thanjavur and Chidambaram, and often they return through here as well. Our family has always tried to look after them as best we can." He paused for a moment, then quickly added, "Of course, this is not the pilgrimage season. You will be alone here. No one will disturb you."

Outside, he showed them the family well, its wooden bucket hanging above the 12-foot-wide, stone-lined opening in the earth, and again turned to them with folded hands. "It is a very great honor for me to serve you," he said. "You must rest here for a while. Stay as long as you please. This is a duty given me by Siva to do; you cannot refuse." Against his childlike sincerity and imploring looks, they could not, and he was elated. He bowed once more, announced that their first meal would arrive in minutes, and marched off to the house without looking back.

They stayed for a week at this little temple. No one else was there, no one disturbed them. They suspected other guests had been softly sent away. Within the solid stone walls of the shrine, no thought of the outside world, no memory of anything other than Siva could intrude; and in this blissful atmosphere they felt free to undertake the pilgrimage to the heights of consciousness without concern for the events of the day.

They sat through most of the night and day in deep meditation. Each morning they would bathe at the well—its cold, clear waters poured from the bucket onto head and body—and walk around a bit, after which the rishi would talk to his disciple, giving him strong instructions and insights that would carry him through the rest of his life. After the noon meal, they would sleep for several hours and then return to their meditations as the tropical sun waned. They sat for hours together in deep, inner communion, in perfect harmony. The only words between them were the rishi's, and those were intermittent.

He told his disciple that he would go to Yalpanam, the northern peninsula of Sri Lanka, but to wait until he received his inner orders. "It is a

. . . .

On the last day they were together, Rishi initiated his shishya into the great Kailasa Parampara, pouring the light and love of Siva into this new vessel with a simple, but puissant, touch on the knee.

place where the Saivite path is followed more strictly than anywhere else in the world. Recently there has been a falling away there due to Western influence, but it is not destroyed. With hard work, the path can be reestablished. The people are pure; they cherish their traditions; they live the Saivite path; but they do not know the spirit of Siva. His power and presence sleeps within them. Their lives run on in the orthodox ways, but the depths of things are closed to them. They have forgotten that the strict Saiva culture is a vehicle for spiritual unfoldment.

"Go there and revive that spirit. Show them. Tell them. Be a worker of miracles. You will have more siddhis than you even know about. You will work wonders, live long and have many disciples. The people there will try to catch you and hold you, but don't let them. When you have done your work, for their sake, shake them off. There will be many to claim you but few to understand or appreciate what you do for them, and fewer still to ask for what you alone can give. The others will come to you for everything. Give them everything they need. Thus you will leave nothing undone."

The rishi spoke of the being who would eventually inherit his disciple's spiritual mantle. He would be quiet, crystal pure, but he would act as if he were a madman. "Teach others your siddhis," he admonished, "but give the gems of jnana only to this one. By his guise of madness he will preserve the power of the guru lineage during foreign rule, and pass it along to his disciple." Each day the rishi would talk like this, giving his disciple detailed instructions.

The last day they were together, as they sat before a fire before dawn, he smeared *vibhuti* abundantly on his disciple's forehead, as is done in Saiva funeral rites, thus initiating him into the renunciatory life known as sannyasa. Rubbing freshly ground sandalwood paste on the disciple's chest, the satguru spoke out the initiate's monastic name, Muktiyananda, meaning "he who enjoys liberation's bliss."

The rishi reached over and, with focused intent, touched Muktiyananda on the knee, a touch that was never forgotten, and abruptly sent him on his way, out into the world to do his work. Muktiyananda stood up, prostrated to his preceptor and, as instructed, left that minute, and the rishi remained behind in the temple.

The rishi stayed at the private temple for a few days longer. Then he went south, stopping briefly at the Subrahmanya Temple in Tiruchedur, then south to Kanyakumari, a Goddess temple at the southern tip of India. He found a niche on the coast and remained there for untold years, experiencing the ever-evolving encounters with samadhi until he finally left his body.

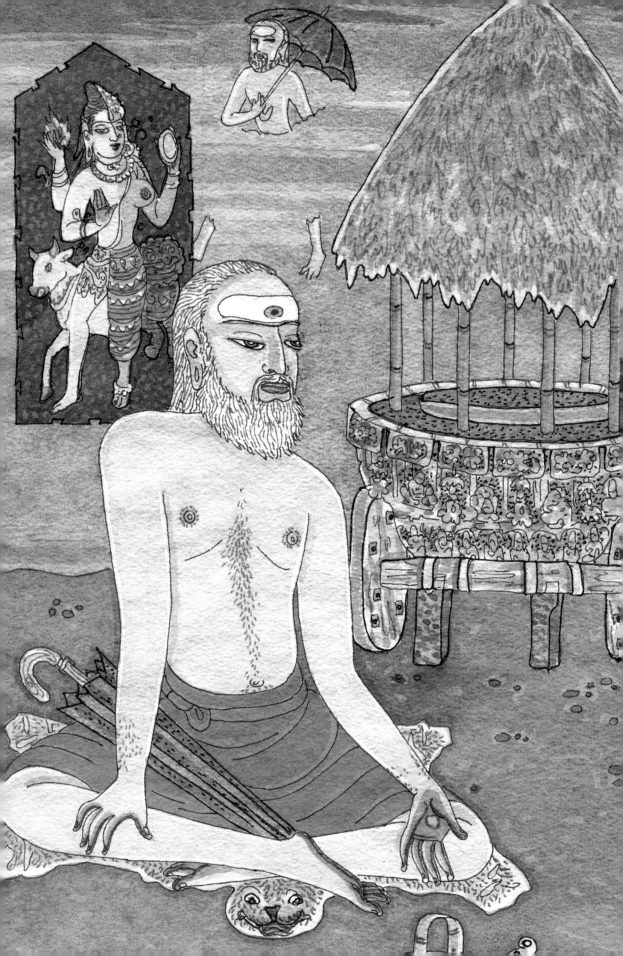

Muktiyananda Sails to Sri Lanka

Jaffna, which had once boasted its own king, was culturally and spiritually under siege. Over the past two centuries it had fallen under the successive dominion of a triumvirate—the Portuguese, the Dutch and the British. These bands of colonizers came to this idyllic island to extend their hegemony: political, business and religious. Many churches were built in and around Jaffna, and Hindu temples were destroyed in the process. The need for a spiritual leader was never greater.

Muktiyananda made his way from South India to Ceylon as he was instructed, though that sounds easier than it actually was. On foot for hundreds of kilometers, he reached India's southern shore sometime in the 1860s. Though a Tamil legend claims he magically flew across the 65-kilometer-wide Palk Strait, biographers tell us he came by more mundane means. In *Eelathu Sitharkkal* (translated as *Siddhars of Eelam),* author Muthaiyar narrates:

> In those days, Oorkavalthurai [Kayts] in northern Ceylon was an important port. Big ships used to come from India to Ceylon. Eluvaitivu is the first place that ships sailing to Sri Lanka from Nagapattinam in India will see. Muktiyananda reached Oorkavalthurai on a ship like this. From Oorkavalthurai he walked all the way to Jaffna. The first place he stayed was Mandaitivu.

Mandaitivu is an island off the Jaffna peninsula that measures 800 meters by 3.2 kilometers. It became a spiritually awakened place due to Swami's presence. Even today, the island is known for its spiritual prowess and Siva temples.

When Swami landed, he met a man named Nanniyar, who let the stranger stay in a hut near his home. It became Swami's abode. The hermitage had a cow-dung floor and plaster walls, with a coconut-wood roof covered with thatched palm fronds. His bed was a small wooden platform, oddly just 1.25 meters long. Even today, there are remnants of his years there, including his bed; and residents of the area still fondly recall their great grandfathers' stories of his presence.

Before Muktiyananda sailed to Ceylon, a Chettiar named Vairamuthu

. . . .

Muktiyananda arrived in northern Sri Lanka in the 1860s. Though he came anonymously to the island, this single soul would one day awaken the Tamils who slumbered under colonial rule, reigniting their faith in God Siva and their ancestral religion, Hinduism.

had seen him at a temple in South India and invited him to come back with him to Sri Lanka. Muktiyananda replied, "You go; I will come." One day Swami showed up at Vairamuthu's home in Jaffna. When the wife said her husband was at the temple, Swami asked for some food and instructed her to set a banana leaf also for her husband. As soon as the wife was finished serving the visitor, her husband walked in and Swami offered, "Sit and eat."

Ultimately, Vairamuthu gave Swami his house and all his wealth and became a sadhu himself, known as Chinnaswami. Swami made the home into an ashram called Kantharmadam Annathaanasataran near Nallur; and with the money created an endowment to feed devotees every day.

Walking the six kilometers to Jaffna from Mandaitivu on the sandy isthmus became Kadaitswami's daily habit, entering the market to give forth his spiritual wisdom. He would return to Mandaitivu in the evening,

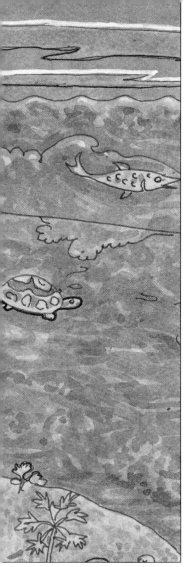

Muktiyananda's boat landed on a small island just off the northwest coast of Sri Lanka. There he moved into a simple hut. Soon he began walking daily to Jaffna on the narrow ithsmus to perform his marketplace mission.

· ·

or stay in Jaffna, making camp on the steps of the Vannarpannai Sivan Temple or staying at the nearby public rest house. In subsequent years, he made use of centers built by his devotees in Ussan, Kantharmadam and Erlalai, where a bed and basic food was provided for pilgrims.

Muktiyananda was a mysterious sadhu for whom there is no written record and no photograph, only a few crude artistic sketches. However, it is known that he had been a High Court judge in the state of Karnataka, and that he had mastered English, Sanskrit, Kannada and Tamil. His close devotees knew that he had taken the robes of a sannyasin due to a deep-seated change of heart.

There is speculation, unsubstantiated, that Muktiyananda was given sannyasa *diksha* by Sri Narasimha Bharati, 32nd Shankaracharya of the Mysore Sringeri Math. In *Siddhars of Eelam,* N. Muthaiya observed:

Between 1817 and 1879 Sri Narasimha Bharati was the 32nd leader of the Mysore Sringeri monastery's Shankaracharya Pitham. He was a great siddhar who created many jnanis, yogis, siddhars and *jivanmuktas.* During his 62-year tenure, 40 years were spent outside [i.e., traveling]. His last 12 years were spent in spiritual service in Tamil Nadu. Together with his primary disciple and fellow siddhar Sri Sachidhanantha Siva, he traveled from village to village to create spiritual awakening among the people. At such an opportunity, the judge became Swami Muktiyananda.

An early biographer, Brama Sri A. Subramaniya Iyer (1857-1912), wrote

that Muktiyananda was born in 1810. Swami told the people of Jaffna precious little about himself. He told them that he had been sent to Jaffna by a rishi who had come down from the Himalayas, a man who ate among the crows. Muktiyananda ate with the crows. When he sat alone on the ground under a tree, crows would gather nearby, watching for scraps from the meal. It is said that he ate and drank almost anything that was given to him.

Kadaitswami swept through the Jaffna markets, carried by lengthy strides and ever aware of his presence among the people. He was a mystery to one and all, an affable sage who somehow always brought joy to shoppers and prosperity to shopkeepers.

· ·

Marketplace Monarch

Muktiyananda spent his days at Jaffna Grand Bazaar, walking about or sitting under a huge, shade-giving banyan tree. The shops on the northern and western streets of this marketplace belonged mainly to the Chettiars, or trading community. Muktiyananda did not say his name, so people took to referring to him as Kadaitswami (*kadai* means "shop" in the Tamil language, so his name simply meant the swami who frequents the marketplace). It is common in Tamil culture to name holy men after places, for they often do not let people know any other name. History also knows him as Adikadainathan, "Lord of the Marketplace."

Kadaitswami would go to a shop and take a piece of bread. While they might object to such filching by an ordinary customer, shopkeepers were always pleased to relinquish a little of their stock to the swami, for they had come to learn that business was bountiful on days he visited. They would even pray that the tall sadhu might come and help himself to something. People observed, and these small signs gave them faith in the swami, faith in his powers to bless and magically influence the world around him. That is one reason Chellappaswami, his future disciple, was not as popular in Jaffna, for he refused to perform such miracles. Muthaiyar shares the following:

Sometimes Swami would dance in the market and on occasion enter a stall and touch the coins. It soon became known that this brought prosperity to the proprietor, and every merchant waited eagerly for him to enter their premises and give his blessing. But not everyone received it.

At times Swami would take a handful of coins and run down the road like a madman, with many kids running after him. Suddenly he might turn around and throw the money in the air, dancing in joy as the children rushed to pick up the coins.

The real-life stories of Kadaitswami are full of miraculous happenings and healings. Chroniclers allege that he turned honey into arrack and arrack into honey. It was claimed that he never used a toilet, or had to. Decades later, his disciple's disciple, Yogaswami, told his disciples that Kadaitswami performed more miracles than were attributed to Krishna. One day, Yogaswami narrated, Kadaitswami came upon a dead and decomposing cat, touched it with his foot and commanded it to get up. The cat came to life and walked away.

Muthaiyar narrates another story:

Thaandel of Valvettithurai, a devotee of Swami, went to see him at Vannarpannai. Hearing that Swami had gone to Mandaitivu, he set out walking there. It was high noon, and the sandy path soon became so hot that his legs and body were burning. Unable to tolerate it, he shouted, "I can't stand the heat, Gurunatha!" At that moment, Swami, who was lying on his bed in Mandaitivu, got up and shouted, "Terrible, terrible, I can't stand the heat!" He told one of his devotees to open an umbrella and shade his feet. The devotee did so without understanding why. After some time, Swami told him to put the umbrella away. Thaandel came in just then, prostrated at Swami's feet, then stood, tearfully grateful for Swami's grace.

Muktiyananda was described as lean and tall, dressed in a dark *veshti*, carrying an umbrella under his arm. They say he was six feet four inches tall, had curly hair, piercing eyes and a long, pointed nose; his body was gangly, but well formed and of charming appearance. K. Ramachandran provided the following description on a radio talk he gave in the mid 20th century on Sri Lanka Broadcasting Corporation.

No photograph of Kadaitswami was ever taken. The pictures of him

· ·

Life and death held no mystery for Kadaitswami. Striding through the villages one day, he came upon a dead cat in the road. As witnesses watched, he nudged the carcass with his foot, as if to wake it up. Moments later the cat, revived, got up and walked away.

that now exist are, in fact, drawings by an artist who was his devotee. These drawings depict him as having broad shoulders, long hands and a radiant smile constantly shining on his face. His long nose, lightly hooked at the tip, lent beauty to his face. There was a spring in his brisk, stately walk and humor in his talk that gave charm to his personality, say those who had seen him.

He often smoked cigars. People would throw themselves down in an effort to have his cigar spittle land on their back as a blessing. K. Ramachandran noted in his radio talk:

> It is said that many are those who had swallowed his saliva and been cured of illnesses. Some gained siddhis. A person from Suddumalai became an expert astrologer. Another became a famous medical practitioner. In trying to explain the greatness of Kadai Swami, sage Yogaswami had said: "Even if Kadai Swami were to hold hands and dance with naked maidens, he would not lose his composure. Indeed, he is many times greater than even Buddha, Christ and the rest of them."

Perhaps because of the radical behavior of Kadaitswami and his devotees, the most orthodox Saivites did not closely mix with him, and he no doubt liked it that way. They were strict vegetarians who did Siva puja daily and followed a conservative path, while Kadaitswami placed no such rules or restrictions on himself.

His heterodoxy reaches a zenith in the tale of his visit to a cremation ground where, to teach a radical lesson to a shishya, he bit into the charred flesh of a corpse. Such tales of outrageous behavior were the proud insignia of the Nathas. Many sadhus in and around Jaffna took Kadaitswami as their preceptor. In their world, such outlandishness was a sign of transcendence of social norms, a certificate of extraordinariness.

In addition to Chellappaswami, Kadaitswami had a number of close brahmachari disciples, including Arulambalaswami, Kulandaivelswami and Sadaivarathaswami. Arulambalaswami met Kadaitswami as a young child of two and followed him from youth. Kadaitswami eventually sent Arulambalaswami to manage the Kantharmadam Annathaanasataran ashram. Kulandaivelswami was a district court secretary who gave up his career to follow Kadaitswami. The samadhi shrines for Arulambalaswami and Kulandaivelswami are at Keerimalai, where a hall was built in

. . . .

Honored as the guru of the land, Kadaitswami was unmoved by the adulation of the many or the animosity of the few. He lived simply, unto himself, accountable to none, aware of all. He would eat alone, among the crows, sharing his food with these creatures who, it is said, always call their clan to join.

their honor near the Naguleshwaram Siva Temple.

Sadaivarathaswami went to Kadaitswami with some other children when he was eight years old. The moment Kadaitswami saw him, he jumped for joy and took him aside, gave him a hug, took off the hat he was wearing and put it on the boy's head, saying, "This is your initiation. One day you will be a fine swami." The hat given by Kadaitswami was later put in a shrine and received daily puja.

Two other men who gave up their worldly life were Sergeant Swami, also known as Chinnathambyswami, who renounced his career with the police force, and Vairamuthu Chettiar, Kadaitswami's first Sri Lankan devotee, who met him in India, eventually renounced the world and became known as Chinnaswami.

Miracle of the Iron Rod

Kadaitswami lived life striding through the countryside and various townships, stopping and staying in patterns discernible to no one. As his reputation grew, everyone wanted blessings from him. With the passing years, he had a sizable contingent of devotees, and anecdotes of his miracles were the devotional coin of the kingdom. We could imagine one such blessing, based on a true report, as follows.

Kadaitswami burst into the entrance of a bustling market one day, with shoppers vigorously negotiating for the slightest amounts of everything from flour to fish. Down the road to his right were fresh fruits and vegetables in lavish variety, each kind stacked in neat geometrical pyramids at open stalls tended by the farmer's family. Bullock carts were still lumbering in from the farther fields, laden with the morning's yield. Every region had its market, a giant version of the modern farmer's market, with the growers engaging directly with the buyers in a frenzied melee. In those days, everyone was a locavore. Villagers had no refrigerators, not even ice, so visiting the market was an almost daily chore for every household, and food was always fresh. The age-old drama played out, with the merchants trying to maximize their take and villagers trying to minimize their expenditure.

A medley of prepared foods were on display in a separate sector. *Pittu*, a mixture of rice flour and shredded coconut steamed in cylindrical bamboo tubes, laid in steaming pots, fresh and ready to eat—the fast food of those days, but much healthier. *Idiyappam* (known as stringhoppers in English), that strangely wonderful spaghetti-pancake-looking treat made of a thick rice flour dough, were being steamed. *Dosai* and *appam*, made from a fermented batter of rice and dal, were being skillfully cooked on wood-heated iron griddles. *Iddli, vadai, biryani, uthappam* and *uppama* were all available.

Each stall purveyed a plethora of curries, along with the obligatory triad of red, green and cream colored chutneys, stone ground from fresh coconut and herbs to complement the main dish. Here, at a glance, one could see and enjoy 8,000 years of culinary evolution which has resulted in the most varied and healthful vegetarian palette on the planet. Saivites were so uniformly vegetarian in those days that the word for *vegetarianism* in Tamil is *saiva*. No wonder they mastered the veggie diet, having no fleshy distractions.

A man named Kandiah was part of a circle of devotees dedicated to Kadaitswami, but the two had never spoken. Suddenly, there the guru stood, an arm's length away, his tall frame towering above the crowd. Looking down at Kandiah, Kadaitswami spoke in a deep, resonant voice, "I am coming to your home for lunch tomorrow, and I am bringing many guests!" It was not a request or a negotiation.

Looking up at the improbably tall swami, Kandiah folded his hands together and paused for a moment in the hopes of saying something inviting, yet profound, grateful and reverent. All he could muster was a lame smile and a barely audible "Yes, Swami." Swami turned around and left without a word. The rumor spread like wildfire. Kandiah had been chosen by Swami. Down the line of stalls, people greeted the news with joy, curiosity and downright envy.

As he wandered home, Kandiah's mind wandered to food. He had not eaten a full meal in five days. His family had simply sustained themselves on a little dal, the milk of the family cow and a compassionate neighbor's occasional offerings. They owned the famous CSK Coconut Oil Mill, which was started by Kandiah's grandfather, but the business had floundered. They lost their land and had to sell off the family jewelry, all except his wife's *tali* (wedding pendant). Kandiah was too proud to ask anyone for help. How then would he serve the swami?

Reaching home, he was struck by the oddly placed reminders of his old life: the tile floors, a luxury compared to the cow dung floors of neighboring huts, a finely carved chair with a silk cushion, a silver-plated chest with engraved artistry. He lost himself for a moment, remembering how, when times were better, they lived and had servants in a home five times this size.

Kandiah announced to his wife, Ponnamma, "Kadaitswami is coming tomorrow for lunch!" Her immediate reaction was enthusiastic, for a spiritual master was about to step foot in her home. But as fast as the smile came to her face, it left when she pondered how to receive him. Turning to her husband, she queried as diplomatically as possible, "How would you like to receive the swami?"

Her husband said nothing, but handed her a small pile of rupees. Looking at him with love and admiration, the good wife joyfully glanced at the handful of notes without counting it and confidently announced, "I will go to the market and be back with the food for tomorrow." An experienced market-goer, she knew the money in her hand was woefully inadequate.

Ponnamma headed for the door, pausing a moment to clutch her *tali,* the gold pendant worn on a golden chain around the neck of all Hindu wives. Wives never remove this sacred symbol of marriage, and most faithfully worship it each morning. To lose it is considered unthinkably inauspicious. Nevertheless, setting out to the market, Ponnamma stopped surreptitiously at the goldsmith's shop to pawn the *tali* for the need of the hour.

The next day arrived almost immediately, or so it seemed since there was so much to do. The couple conscripted their two sons to help, and everyone was scrambling. By a quarter to noon, the last of the dishes was ready, kept fresh in the kitchen to be served hot only after the swami had seated himself on the woven palm mat that served as the dining room. Their scurrying was interrupted by a thundering thump on the door, "Kandiah, I have come!" And with him a grand following of guests, numbering, according to one biographer, in the hundreds!

Ponnamma grabbed the camphor, Kandiah the lamp and the two boys held the tray as their parents placed the camphor on the lamp and lit it. Kandiah opened the door. Hands held in *anjali mudra,* he offered a reverent "Vanakkam, Swamiji." But as they tried to offer the camphor flame in the traditional salute to holy men and women, Kadaitswami marched past and into the house. Obviously in good cheer, he gave Kandiah a hearty thwack on the back, "It's a fine day, young fellow!" Swami sat on the mat prepared for him, indicating not so subtly that there had been enough niceties and he was ready to eat.

Taking an unadorned clay basin in one hand and a jug in the other, Ponnamma poured water over Swami's right hand as he turned it over and flexed his fingers in the cleaning gesture that begins all Tamil meals. Kandiah went to the kitchen where, one by one, his wife handed him the items to be served onto the banana leaf in an exacting order. Only men would serve a swami in those days, and the family would eat only after

. . . .

When a once-wealthy family sacrificed to feed Kadaitswami in their home one day, he was moved by their hardship which did not diminish their hospitality. He called for an iron bar, turning it by his touch into gold. The family eventually sold the bar and prospered from that day onward.

their guests had finished.

Ponnamma had purchased an abundant supply of every savory staple and treat for the large group. But Kadaitswami was a big and active man, with a matching appetite. As is customary in a Tamil home to this day, the host kept offering his guests more of each item as it disappeared, giving the sense that there was a never-ending supply. "It was a fine meal, Amma!" Kadaitswami finally announced, folding in half the banana leaf that had been his plate, thus indicating that he was finished. Relieved, Ponnamma relaxed. She literally had nothing more to serve.

The next day, Swami visited again, alone this time, and asked Ponnamma to bring a piece of iron. Searching the family compound, she found a rusted piece of iron half-hidden in the soil and brought it to Swami. He took the rod in his hands and began to slowly chant, "Aum Namasivaya, Aum Namasivaya...." then placed it back in her hands, instructing her to clean off the rust, wrap the rod in cloth and store it away. Abruptly, Swami then stood up and left. It was an odd departure, but Kadaitswami was nothing if not eccentric. A bit overwhelmed by it all, the family basked in the aftermath of Swami's presence, so pure, so noble and mysterious.

Four days later, when Ponnamma opened the cupboard, curiosity beguiled her to look at the rod. To her astonishment, it had turned to gold! Her husband had it tested by a goldsmith, and indeed, it was solid gold. Tears of joy in their eyes, Kandiah and Ponnamma later thanked Swami for his grace. Eventually they sold the gold rod, and their family business prospered once again.

Saving a Fisherman

One stormy evening, Kadaitswami arrived shortly before dark at the house of a man who owned a fishing boat. The fisherman was not at home, and the swami acted strangely, so his wife was reluctant to let Kadaitswami through their compound gate. So adamantly did he insist that she relented.

Entering the front yard, he went to a tree and sat down. About two hours later, the wife, who was still waiting up for her husband's return, noticed that Kadaitswami was holding a stout pole and sitting on the ground digging in the dirt beside him as if he were trying to push himself along with this makeshift oar, all the while repeating "Ellello," a word fishermen chant when working together to pull their nets. Yes, she

. . . .

When a massive storm capsized the fishing boat of a devotee one dark night, Kadaitswami sensed the danger from afar. He rushed to the man's house and sat in the rain-soaked yard, thrashing about as if rowing, much to the consternation of the man's wife who watched from inside in fear. Later, she learned, her husband's life had been mysteriously saved at that same time.

thought, it looks as if he is pretending to row a boat, sitting in the mud in the dark. She went out in the torrential rain and pleaded with Kadaitswami to stop, afraid of the weird goings-on in her garden as much as what her husband would say when he came home to find the yard dug up. But Kadaitswami would not desist; in fact, amid the intensity of the storm and his work he seemed not even to hear her.

Three hours passed as the lanky sage performed this strange and strenuous drama. Unable to chase him away, she kept watch from the safety of her home. Finally, the swami stopped, rose to his feet and disappeared into the moonless night.

The husband did not return until dawn, something that had never happened before. Many local fishermen's wives had lost their husbands to the turbulent sea. The wife was waiting anxiously at the gate when her beloved approached, deeply relieved to see him but afraid of the scolding he might give her when he saw the yard. Mustering her courage, she shared the tale of the swami's visit and the wild rowing episode. Hearing this, her husband prostrated at the spot where Kadaitswami had been sitting. Only then, dishevelled and exhausted, did he go to the open well to bathe.

She brewed fresh coffee as he recounted that a severe storm had ravaged the sea just before dusk, capsizing his small boat. Struggling in the churning waters, he grew fatigued and felt death near, but wrestled with all his might to turn the boat aright. It was not working, and he grew weaker with every effort. Suddenly, one of the oars whacked him on the head, knocking him unconscious. When he came to, he found himself clinging to a plank, the boat right side up nearby in a becalmed sea.

He told his astonished wife of a vision he had just when death seemed certain, a vision of Kadaitswami rowing the boat toward him, rescuing him from the sea. He had been saved, he said, by the grace of the guru. Both marveled at the miraculous interconnectedness of their experiences. They knew they had been touched by something rare and beyond their understanding. For the rest of their lives, they spoke of Kadaitswami's supernatural efforts to save a drowning fisherman.

Confounding Conduct

One day in the marketplace in Jaffna, Kadaitswami was begging at the stalls when he observed two elderly women stealing from the shops. They would take their concealed produce to the far quarter of the market, put it down on a piece of burlap, and quickly sell it below market price. No one was willing to apprehend the pair. They were surly nags, but they probably needed the money. Deciding their exploits should be stopped, Kadaitswami went after them one afternoon and provided each one a sound beating, one they would not soon forget. A policeman came by as he was knocking their heads together. Horrified to see an able-bodied man assaulting two feeble ladies, he arrested Kadaitswami and threw him into jail.

In the middle of the night there was a loud commotion in the jail. Kadaitswami was pulling on the bars from inside and shouting at the top of his voice, "Don't fear! I'm here to set you free." He shouted that way for a long time until the jailer came to quiet him forcibly. Arriving at the cell, the jailer found the prisoner had vanished. He searched the yard, to no avail. The jailer awakened his superior to notify him of what was happening. When they reached the cell, the two found Kadaitswami asleep inside. The superintendent went back to bed, thinking his jailer was crazy or had had a bad dream.

Within minutes the raucous scofflaw's taunting began again, "Don't worry! I will set you free!" Running again to the cell, they found it empty. A few minutes later, they saw the swami sleeping under a tree in the compound. Rushing to catch him, they were mystified by another disappearance. Again they heard him yelling from the cell. Shaking the bars, he called out, "Oh, I'm working on it. Soon you will be free!" Realizing they could do nothing to contain the man, they let him go. One of the guards was a sergeant named Chinnathamby. In later years, he renounced the world and became known as Sergeant Swami.

One day Kadaitswami went into a shop to beg a few cents. The cashier ignored him for some time, then decided to have some fun with this old beggar, "I have a diamond ring here. If you can tell me what hand it is in, I'll give you what you ask for." The merchant put the ring in his hand and, placing his hands behind his back, switched it back and forth, then challenged Kadaitswami to guess. The swami declared that the ring was in neither hand. The merchant roared with laughter, thinking that he had really found a fool. Bringing both hands forward to reveal the ring, he was dismayed to find the swami was right. The ring was gone! Kadaitswami turned and walked out of the shop, followed by the distraught merchant. After some distance, Kadaitswami halted and spat the ring out of his mouth. The fellow was flabbergasted. Kadaitswami smiled and deadpanned, "Now you are caught."

At one time a group of boys followed Kadaitswami day and night, knowing that he sometimes drank arrack (the potent liquor made from palm tree juice, also known as toddy) and hoping to entertain themselves at his expense. But it was Kadaitswami who had fun with them. With the boisterous band not far behind, he visited several toddy shops, down-ing the potent drink. Continuing the game, Kadaitswami entered a shop where a metal worker had a pot of wax boiling on an open fire. He picked up the cauldron, drank some of the wax, then turned to offer it to the boys. But hot wax was not the intoxicating brew they had hoped would be his offering. Frightened by this bizarre spectacle, they fled down the lane, never to bother the swami again.

Many thought Kadaitswami mad. He often danced in the streets and threw money into the air. One Dipavali day, in October, people were enjoying the festivities, buying new clothes for the year on this annual holy day. A merchant took his richest scarf from the shelf and gave it to Kadaitswami—who swiftly placed it on the shoulders of an approaching beggar and gave him a few coins. When asked later about this unusual gesture, he explained, "That man was the King of Nepal in a previous life." Like the siddhas of yore, his vision was not limited to this time and this place. But seeing a deeper reality came with a price, the price of being misunderstood by ordinary folks.

Several times, the police arrested him. As they took him away by the arms, Swami would lower his head and go along courteously. Two con-stables once took him before a judge, claiming he was mad and should be committed. It was customary for officers to wait outside while defen-dants stood before the judge. The magistrate asked Swami some questions, to which he responded in lucid English. The two got along well, in part, no doubt, because Swami had once been a judge himself. Both enjoyed the conversation. The judge summoned the police and scolded, "Release this gentleman immediately. There is nothing wrong with him. He is per-fectly normal."

Combatting Christianity

In those days, the British Christian missionaries controlled most of the education in Jaffna. They had the best schools, based in the English lan-guage; and if Hindus wanted their children to attend these schools and get the most promising education, the children had to give up wearing their traditional clothing, their holy ash and *pottu*, submit to attending Chris-tian religious classes and even attend daily mass. This insidious attempt to convert the children to Christianity was effective. Often unbeknownst to their parents, the children slowly adopted the Christian teachings. As

• •

Like most Asian masters, Kadaitswami taught more indirectly than intellectually. When a band of truant boys took to following and needling him, he did not send them away. Instead, when they were watching one day, he grabbed a flask of molten wax in a jeweler's shop and drank from it. This so frightened the boys, they never bothered him again.

Kadaitswami, famed for his ever-present umbrella, was a judicial officer turned mendicant, an Indian who guided the spiritual life of Sri Lanka, a linguist who preached in the commoners' marketplace and led a renaissance of Saivism among the Tamil people of Jaffna.

intended by the Christians, this strategy disrupt-
ed the Hindu unity of the family.

Since they had to have a Western education
to get a decent job with the British government,
many were sent to the missionary schools, and
among those many converted to Christianity, to
their family's dismay. These innocent children
would attend morning prayers in school, then
share in pujas in their homes, where their family life remained true to Saivite tradition. The
compromise ruined their spiritual lives, which
was exactly the missionaries' purpose. Children
found themselves on two different paths at once,
one at home with mother and another in the
classroom with the nuns. What Saivite rituals
they performed were done without understanding, and what Christian services they took part
in were performed hollowly as part of the daily
school regimen.

Kadaitswami served as a counterweight to this
dogmatic onslaught. He was more articulate than
any previous holy man in Sri Lanka, having been
a lawyer and judge. He frequented Vannarpannai
Siva Temple, about two kilometers from the marketplace, and there sang songs to Parvati. After
worship, he gave rousing spiritual discourses.
During his years in Jaffna, Kadaitswami spoke so
often in front of the Siva temple that a thatched
pavilion was built for him there. He stood on a
platform in the pavilion and lectured to hundreds of men and women who came to worship
or were on their way to nearby markets. An eloquent orator, he spoke with missionary verve.
Though Swami's native tongue was Telugu, he
also spoke proficient Tamil (though in a dialect
that was difficult for Sri Lankans to follow), along
with Kannada, Malayalam and English.

His *upadeshas* about the greatness of Saivism inspired renewed devotion in the people, who were accustomed to hearing sermons only from
the Christian fathers seeking to convert them. Not for a long time had

someone stood so boldly in public and said what was in their heart of hearts. Kadaitswami became the voice of their heritage, the protector of Saiva dharma, as he boldly reminded them of the beauties and potencies of their born faith. Over the years, tens of thousands heard him speak from the Vannarpannai platform, and large numbers of those were reinspired to hold fast to their ancient ways of Saivite Hindu life.

There was, during those years, a learned scholar in Jaffna, twelve years Kadaitswami's younger, by the name of Arumuga Navalar, the father of Sri Lankan Tamil prose. Before him, all Tamil was written in verse form. At one point in his life, Navalar translated the Bible, which he regarded as inferior to the Hindu scriptures, into Tamil to show his people the teachings it actually contains.

These two firebrands were deeply dedicated to preserving Saivite culture in Sri Lanka, having clearly cognized the threats their people faced. They worked together to open several Hindu schools to offset the prevailing Christian education that so direly threatened the faith and futures of Tamil children. The first of these, known simply as Hindu High School, was begun at Vannarpannai in Jaffna, by the side of the Siva temple where Kadaitswami preached to crowds. This later became the Jaffna Hindu College, the foremost educational institution of the North.

Magical Moments at Mandaitivu

One day at his place in Mandaitivu, Kadaitswami was preparing lunch with two disciples, Niranjananandaswami and Chinmayanandaswami. This was observed by Nanniyar's wife. Suddenly, Kadaitswami shouted, "A karmi is coming! Quick, we must go." Placing all the pots in a wooden box used for storing leftover foods, they ran away. Before long, a disgruntled man arrived and told the woman he was looking for Swami. She said he had just left. The man waited and waited all day, but Swami never returned. He waited for three days and Nanniyar's wife fed him. As soon as the man left, Swami reappeared with his two brother monks and said, "Now we can eat." They went to the storage box. The woman was thinking, "Ugh, they are going to eat spoiled, three-day-old food!" As they opened the box, steam was rising from each pot as if it had just been cooked, and— to the wife's astonishment—the three enjoyed a fresh, hot lunch.

On one visit to the island, Swami called Nanniyar's family together and performed a *homa* in the backyard, as if doing an *antyeshti* (funeral

· ·

Chellappaswami's initiation came in the marketplace where his guru reigned. Kadaitswami had seen something in the eccentric young man that eluded others, the promise of a truly spiritual life and awakening, and he empowered his shishya by placing a large rupee coin in his hand, touching his back with the umbrella and sending him away.

ceremony). They assumed Swami was performing his own last rites, as a sign that he might soon leave his body. After the *homa*, he told them not to go to the temple for 31 days. "Now this," they thought, "is strange, because Swami is still alive." In a few days the family received news that their son had died in India during a pilgrimage to Chidambaram. Swami's magical rites all came clear.

Kadaitswami's magic had a style, a kind of mystical DNA. How often he would know the events in people's lives, events happening beyond the ken of the immediate players, events that affected friends and family, events separated by space, but often not by time. And he, the knower, the intermediary of the two seemingly unconnected events, would provoke some change that defied reason.

Chellappa Meets Kadaitswami

One day a young sadhu came to the pavilion. His eyes revealed a profound depth, and Kadaitswami recognized something special in him. After they spent an unknown time together, Kadaitswami met his disciple in the marketplace. Fetching a rupee from a woman peanut vendor, he wrapped it in a betel leaf and gave it to the young shishya. In those days rupees were large coins. The bundle covered half the palm of the sadhu who would later become known as Chellappaswami. Kadaitswami then struck him on the back with his umbrella and sent him away.

Future devotees spoke of the coin-giving as Kadaitswami's unconventional Natha way of initiating his shishya into sannyasa, the state of world renunciation. Decades later, Chellappaswami's disciple, Yogaswami, recounted this great spiritual experience as it was told to him:

> Lo, with a silver rupee coin did Kadai Swami infuse his grace on Chellappar! The world looked upon him as a madman. From his empyrean height, he stood aloof, far from the madding crowds' ignoble strife.

The two met often during the next four years and went on long walks together. Chellappaswami said little or nothing of the time he spent with Kadaitswami, and history has almost no memory of it. S. Ampikaipaakan offers the following anecdote.

> To Kadaitswami, all devotees were the same regardless of differences in race or creed, high or low, rich or poor. He treated one and all with equal affection and remedied their physical and mental ills and their poverty, too. Knowing this, the devotees began to flock around him

in larger numbers. There were many humble requests even from the poor to visit their homes. At such times they offered him their usual nonvegetarian meals, including liquor. Above likes and dislikes, he accepted what was offered.

When this became known, there was anger and resentment amongst orthodox Hindu Saivites. Chellappaswami, the guru of Siva Yogaswami, could not bear to hear from devotees that Kadaitswami, whom he honored, takes liquor. It was something altogether unbelievable. Wishing to test him, he went to Grand Bazaar in search of Kadaitswami with a bottle of liquor carefully concealed under his shawl.

As Chellappar went and sat beside him, Kadaitswami cried, "Oh ho, so you too have begun to treat me with liquor! All right, take the bottle that you have concealed under your shawl and open it. Let me share this with you and all these devotees here!" Chellappaswami, trembling, took out the bottle, but upon opening it found that the bottle was empty. The dismayed disciple asked forgiveness and returned back to Nallur *teradi*.

On another occasion, Kadaitswami presented a bottle of arrack to Chellappaswami, saying it was time for his disciple to have his first drink. After all, did he consider himself better than his guru? Chellappaswami, unable to refuse anything his guru offered, took the bottle and tipped it up to his mouth. What had the smell of arrack to his nose tasted like honey on his tongue.

What to imagine of the years they shared—a powerful siddha from South India and his inwardly inclined shishya from Jaffna exploring the depths of consciousness, the profundities of Saivism, that were so dear to them both? But imagine is all we can do.

The Grand Departure
During the last few years of his life, Kadaitswami ceased going back to Mandaitivu and remained in the Jaffna area. He took a liking to a small, privately owned temple to Lord Nataraja in Neeraviady, a few kilometers from the marketplace. A hut was built for him in the compound behind the temple, where he stayed with Kulandaivelswami. This became his domain, a place of solitude and communion. He declared to his followers, "This is Chidambaram," referring to the renowned temple of Lord Nataraja, the Cosmic Dancer, in South India, which is mystically thought of as the center of the universe.

It was at this spot, on October 13, 1891, Shatabhishak *nakshatra*, that Kadaitswami made his Great Departure from this Earth plane. Kulandai-velswami was with him in those final moments. He had instructed his shishyas to inter his body in a crypt, as is often done with illumined souls. Kulandaivelswami oversaw the samadhi ceremony and entombment at the site of his hut. Soon afterwards, a large stone was placed on the spot, and pujas to it were regularly conducted by devotees. A year later, in 1892, in keeping with Swami's orders, a sizable temple was built enshrining a Sivalingam from Benares, India, which took the place of the large stone.

Nearly a century later, when the samadhi temple had fallen into dis-repair, a group of boys who played cricket nearby began having dreams about a tall, slim man who told them they should restore the structure. When the parents heard about the dreams, they realized it was Kadait-swami the boys had seen and told them not to play there anymore. The boys rallied together, involved the Chettiar community and in the early 1980s began renovating the temple.

In 1983, during Satguru Sivaya Subramuniyaswami's (the disciple of the disciple of Kadaitswami's foremost disciple, Chellappaswami) last visit to Jaffna, the Kadaitswami Temple temple committee, mostly youth, invited him to set the first stone for a new tower above the sanctum. He climbed a rickety, bamboo ladder to the top, set the stone and a small puja was per-formed. The renovations continued and the final consecration ceremony was held in 1985.

. . . .

When Kadaitswami departed from his body in the hut near the Nataraja temple, devotees interred the body in a crypt and built a Sivalingam temple at the sacred site. To this day, pujas are held in that temple.

Chellappaswami, the Siddha of Nallur

Toward the middle of the 19th century, a farmer named Vallipuram of Vaddukkoddai married Ponnamma of Nallur. They built their home near Nallur Temple and cultivated the fields. The couple had two girls and two boys, one of whom was named Chellappa. From his youth, Chellappa devoted himself one-pointedly to the pursuit of the divine within himself. He was so introverted that his parents thought him addled. Eccentric as he was, Chellappa was a pure person, strict with himself and others. By all accounts he was born a yogi—people had predicted sannyasa for him even as a youngster. He would never ask for things, even food or clothing. If he wasn't given what he needed, he went without. He had no friends. In fact, he went to any length to hide from people, spending every free minute alone. He was close to no one. His family never knew what he was thinking, nor could they coax him out of his shell. He only withdrew all the more for their efforts.

As a young man, he had to be taken to school or he wouldn't go. Once there, he would sit through the day hearing and speaking nothing. It was sheer torment for everyone. His classmates mocked him, and his teachers punished him constantly for his "daydreaming." But nothing they did brought his mind down to earth. At home, he habitually sat quietly apart from others, lost in his thoughts or meditating, much to his parents' dismay. They felt he was too serious and told him he should laugh and play like other children. He attended a Tamil primary school called Saiva Prakasa Vidyasalai at Kantharmadam, a mile from Nallur Temple.

By the time he was sixteen, Chellappa's peculiar distance from people was so pronounced that he routinely went for days without speaking to anyone at all. His parents feared something was seriously wrong with him, and from time to time took him to various doctors, astrologers and other learned men, seeking a sensible diagnosis. No one could help them understand their boy. His health was sound, though he was unusually thin, but no one knew his aloof mind. Nonetheless, he attended Jaffna Central College, a secondary school, where the medium of instruction was English.

Later Chellappa took to wandering away into the countryside, to a far-off temple or village, where his family would inevitably find him, after a

. . . .

Chellappaswami was a difficult man to be near, fiery and outspoken, bold and taunting, preferring his own company and often mumbling nonsense. With his tattered veshti *and unforgiving manner, it is little wonder only a few strong disciples drew close.*

desperate search, meditating under a tree or aimlessly walking the roads. He patiently bore with their pleading and punishments but before long wandered off again. They learned finally to let him go. He would turn up, hungry and tired, after a week or two. It moved his mother to tears, and she prayed for him all her life.

A Penchant for Solitude

After leaving school, Chellappa worked as a night watchman guarding a building adjacent to a cremation ground, spending the whole night outside in the weather, making an occasional circuit of the property. He was in his late teens at the time. His parents had resigned themselves to his austere predilections, yet he managed to appall them even further. It seems that after perfunctorily checking the building he was hired to watch, he would enter the cremation yard and sit through the night meditating, often near a still-smoking pyre. It is said he later worked at a small government office, but his penchant for solitude overcame his need for a salary.

K.C. Kularatnam gave details of this period in *Yalpana Nallur Terati Cellappa Cuvamikal* (translated by Dr. Vimala Krishnapillai as *Chellappa Swami of Nallur):*

Chellappa discontinued his studies after some years and commenced his employment as an *arachi* [public relations officer] at the Jaffna Kachcheri [District Secretariat]. Being a very efficient worker he received the admiration and the confidence of the authorities and was many a time entrusted to be in charge of the treasury. Though Chellappa enjoyed the high prestige of a privileged post, he was not enamored by it. He was ever dwelling on the inner kindling of his being. Irresistibly drawn towards jnanam, spirituality, there appeared changes in his habits, dress and movements. This intrigued many. Outwardly he carried on with his normal work without giving any room for others to talk about it. Inwardly, during the night when others were all fast asleep, he was engaged in mystic communion with Lord Murugan of Nallur and began to prate, "Father! Father!"

When this flood of jnanam surged and overflowed outwardly, he appeared like a madman, like one possessed by the spirits, like an innocent child. He would speak to himself, repeat "Om, Om," shaking his head, raise his right hand high, wave and shout loudly. He

* * *

Chellappaswami frequently found refuge in Nallur Temple's chariot house, a 12-meter-tall thatched tower in which Lord Murugan's parade images and elaborate carts were stored. It was a dark chamber, well suited to the sage's urge to be alone, to meditate for hours without distraction.

would not let anyone get close to him. He chased them away as they approached him. He neglected his job and finally left the Kachcheri. He then sat all day in the corner of his hut.

Kadaitswami visited Chellappaswami often, watching over his shishya's meditations. The two were often seen marching together through the villages that dot the Jaffna peninsula, going nowhere in particular.

· ·

Seeing him withdraw more and more into states they interpreted as aberrant, his relatives arranged special pujas for him in which the priests tried to exorcise the spirits they assumed had possessed him. To no avail. Chellappa was unmoved by all the fuss and unfazed by not being understood. On occasion he even took advantage of being thought mad. It could be his ticket to do just as he pleased, to wander or be a hermit as and when he was moved to. He would mix with the sadhus of Sri Lanka, listen to their stories and watch quietly as they debated philosophical intricacies. These were the things that engaged his mind.

Understandably, the question of Chellappa's marrying never came up, and when he met his satguru, Kadaitswami, he was perfectly free to follow him. Released, if reluctantly, by his family and society at large, he lived as a sannyasin from his early twenties. His already intense inner life was so heightened by the spiritual transformation his guru wrought within him that his relatives hardly knew him, nor did he know them from strangers. Everything about him changed and changed again.

In a very short time, Kadaitswami carried him to the heights of God Realization, but Chellappa was a long time adjusting to the aftermath of this profound nonexperience. He spent long hours in deep meditation near the portico adjacent to the Nallur Temple *teradi,* a large shed in which Lord Murugan's ornate festival chariot is stored, forty-five meters from the temple entrance. It was in those days a thatched chamber, about twelve meters tall and six meters on a side, housing the wooden parade chariot, with its two-meter-high wheels, and other parade paraphernalia which were brought out only during major festivals. In front stood a three-sided open pavilion bordered by a wrought iron fence.

We read of the eminent history and grandeur of Nallur, Jaffna and Sri Lanka in *Chellappa Swami of Nallur:*

Our country, Lanka, land of Siva, glows like gold in the Indian Ocean. The Tamil word *eelam* means "gold." Saint Tirumular in his *Tirumantiram* has said that this Ellankai [Lanka, "island"] is an abode of Siva. There were many Iswaran temples dedicated to Lord Siva in this land and many siddhas lived and roamed this land. The traditions of the Siddha Parampara are deep rooted here. The greatness of these saints, who immersed their minds at the feet of Lord Siva, is beyond comprehension.

Samadhi temples of these great siddhas abound in the Jaffna peninsula and throughout the Northern Province. Many jnanis and siddhas, from Kadaitswami to Yogaswami, have left their sacred footprints in and around Jaffna. Guru puja *mandapams*, the halls constructed near such temples, were not only centers of charity but also the seats of cultural and religious activities.

Nallur [literally "good place"] is an ancient city in Jaffna. It was the capital city of Emperor Ariya Chakravarthi, whose sovereignty (1215–1240) was widespread. In fact, Rameswaram in Tamil Nadu was under his administration, and he earned the title Sethukavalar, the protector of Sethu [the isthmus between Tamil Nadu and Jaffna]. It was in Nallur that pure, refined Tamil and Saivaneri [the Saiva path] flourished. Situated very close to the king's ancient palace was the Nallur Kandaswami [Sanskrit: Skandaswami] Temple of Lord Murugan. Around this temple, in the four directions, were built the sentinel temples for protection; Veyilukanda Pillaiyar Kovil in the East, Kailasanatha Sivan Kovil in the West, Veerakali Amman Kovil in the North and Sattanatha Kovil in the South. The royal flag and the royal seal carried, in the insignia, the symbol of the Nandi, which was continued by successive kings.

Though the Portuguese destroyed the Nallur Kandaswami Kovil and even uprooted the foundation, there was a Saiva revival during the Dutch rule, around 1734. During this period, there lived several bards and poets who composed great religious hymns. Thus, Nallur was once again flooded with religious wisdom, jnanam. Srimat Ragunatha Mappana Mudaliyar, who was holding a high position in the Jaffna Kachcheri, appealed to the Dutch and got their permission to set up a Vel Kottam, where the *vel*, the insignia of Lord Murugan, could be installed for worship.

Nallur Temple was a center of life for Chellappaswami. An ancient Murugan temple, with a shakti *vel* enshrined within its innermost sanctum, it is even today the most prominent Hindu temple of the Jaffna peninsula, some say because of the presence of the lineage.

Kadaitswami visited Chellappaswami there often, and together they went on long walks and meditated at out-of-the-way places. One afternoon, on a particularly scorching day, while Chellappaswami was sitting in the shade in the Nallur compound, he suddenly put up his umbrella and held it there as if he were in the sun. Ten minutes later Kadaitswami arrived, and Chellappaswami put the umbrella down. Witnesses surmised that Chellappaswami had felt his guru coming and put up his umbrella to mystically shelter him from the hot sun as he walked.

In the Guise of a Madman
In the weeks following Kadaitswami's departure from the Earth plane, Chellappaswami lost all outward coherence, behaving like a madman, wild and unpredictable. He sat in the Nallur *teradi* portico for days and nights, motionless, hardly breathing, showing no hunger or thirst. He was an awesome figure, living in another world. Yet physically he was awkward, with protruding teeth and thin, hay-colored hair. People brought offerings of camphor, fruit and flowers, and sat blissfully at his feet. He spent so much time there that people referred to him as Nallur Siddhar, or Teradi Siddhar.

He sat, meditated and ate in the shade of the *bilva* tree near the entry. At some point he took up use of a hut with clay walls and thatched roof across the road from the *teradi* in a corner of his sister Chellachi's property. For some time she brought meals for him, but he would shout, "Go! Take it away! You have brought me poisoned food." He cooked his own meals at the hut, and slept there or on the concrete steps of the *teradi* on a thin straw mat, living a simple life that would have great impact on others—that would, in fact, change the future of Saivism in Sri Lanka.

When he wasn't in samadhi, his demeanor was fierce. He threw things at anyone who approached for blessings, running and shouting after people who merely looked at him twice. People kept their distance, not comprehending this amazing being, yet sure, somehow, that he was special. Chellappaswami's successor, Siva Yogaswami, wrote of the enigmatic sage:

> In derogatory language would he, my father, look at those
> who linger in the streets, and rebuke them menacingly.
> They note his insanity, Sinnathangam dear. His gait ever so
> stately, he rambles from place to place. All those who sight
> him feel inclined to mock and jeer at him, my dear.

These were the days of British Christian domination, when a Hindu sage or swami had to disguise himself to continue his inner work, when sannyasins wore white, not orange, lest they be persecuted or thrown in jail. Indeed, Chellappaswami was not mad, but was likely instructed by his guru to behave this way to avoid harassment. Chellappaswami was a jnani who cloaked his greatness in *unmatha avastha,* the guise of a madman. Indeed, to the locals he was known as "*visar* (mad) Chellappaswami." To protect him, at one point his family had him put in chains, giving even more credence that his behavior was for real.

Chellappaswami would stagger in a rapture through the streets of Jaffna, talking aloud to himself in cryptic phrases, complex and confounding, addressing everyone and no one at the same time, perhaps to discourage unworthy devotees and perhaps to throw off suspicion from the British-controlled government that he might be a spiritual leader and therefore a threat to them and their evangelical efforts. It was a time in Jaffna when well over half of the traditional Saivite families had come under the influence, temporarily as it turned out, of the conversion-hungry Catholic, Anglican and other Protestant faiths.

Years later, Yogaswami was under similar pressures and was also considered a madman by local people. But discerning villagers knew that these were the ones who were truly sane; these were the knowers of the Unknown spoken of in the *Vedas.* These men were sadhus in their last lives, and thus were naturally inclined to sit absorbed for hours or even days in meditation, fathoming the depths of consciousness. That the community as a whole did not comprehend this was of little concern to them. *Chellappa Swami of Nallur* offers this insight:

> Though Chellappa Swami had openly declared, "Chellappa will not
> reveal himself," devotees in large numbers came to him, affirming

· ·

*In telling of their travels together, Yogaswami shared his amazement
at how Chellappaswami would walk, eyes on the clouds, and yet he
never stepped on the anthills that strew the land, while he, Yogaswami,
managed to step into their fire even when he was watching for them.*

"Chellappa is our father, a good father who showers mercy on us, the golden father of Nallur." Even people from far off places came to him with deep faith—to mention a few: Tiru Gnanasambanthar, Ramalingam, Thuraiyappah and Ponnaiah of Columbuthurai, Arumugam, Elayathambi, Thamotharampillai of Kantharmadam and Murugesu of Kambantharai.

Swami was very kind to them. When some of his pupils said they wanted to follow the ascetic path, he remarked, "That life and you are poles apart. You had better get married." When some said that their relatives were compelling them to get married and sought his permission, the swami would say, "Why should you ask me to get married? Go, go at once." If anyone spoke about marriage, he would chide in a humiliating tone, bluntly saying, "Did you hear? The government agent wants me to marry his daughter. He wants me to marry. Shall I?"

Chellappaswami told Yogaswami that to make it known you are a guru, a realized one, is even madder than appearing insane. Ordinary people would give you no peace. They would chase you night and day to extract blessings, almost by force, without doing anything to deserve that grace. They would come for material blessings, to have their future revealed, or just to stand near in hopes of something miraculous.

Mrs. Inthumathy (Amma) Navaratnarajah shares this image of Chellappaswami and thoughtful insights into his guise of lunacy in her manuscript *Yogaswami, Life and Teachings.*

The great personage Chellappar sat on the chariot house step every day. Yet no divinity was visible on the dark-complexioned sadhu who sat with a vacant look on his face. Coarseness was the only visible sign. Even during festival times when the crowd was so dense that a ray of light would not pass through, he would sit on the step, his face shining, laughing to himself. Sometimes he would lie on the step, looking at decriers. Sometimes he would berate with belittling words those who were wandering about aimlessly. They would in turn abuse him, call him a lunatic and go away. He would not bother about this abuse and would continue to harangue them, taunting them to oppose him.

Sometimes he would stand in Lord Skanda's presence, before the sanctum, wearing rags, and scold in foul language those coming and going. At times he would wander to Tirunelveli, Columbuthurai and other places. People seeing him wander around would ridicule him as insane. He would stand begging before houses, accepting whatever was given. On some days he cooked rice and a curry. He did not sleep much. After midnight, using his hands as a pillow, he could be seen sleeping on the ground.

His versatility with his hands in weaving palmyra and coconut leaves into various objects of art was the only factor that showed that he was not mad. But is this one factor alone enough for the crazy world to realize his sanity?

Chellappaswami lived exhibiting the qualities of a madman and a great sage immersed in spiritual meditation. Those who were deluded by him considered him a madman. Those thirsting for spiritual knowledge saw him in his true colors—a man of deep knowledge. Siva Yogaswami saw him as the royal sage, who in the form of a guru redeemed and saved him. "At the *teradi*, I saw him, the crescent jewel of grace. He made me his own and showed me the way of bliss."

With these baffling disguises Chellappa wandered alone, hiding his real nature; so that no one realized his true self. Even scholars who were well-versed in Vedanta and Siddhanta, even those who had a long-standing friendship with him could not realize his true inner nature. Chellappa acted well the role of a lunatic he had taken on himself. Yogaswami once noted, "For forty years he acted the role he took without anyone suspecting, and went away."

Chellappaswami spoke cryptically, in a language that had to be deciphered. Yogaswami himself recorded some of his gems:

"Intrinsic evil there is not," and "Absolute is Truth which none can ever comprehend"—so saying, he would remain mute. "It is what it is, and there is none who can know fully, as it is concealed in dissimulation"—so uttered the lofty Chellappan, clad in ragged clothes, and haunting Kandan's frontal courtyard. At those who frequent that resort, he will hurl abuse, my fond one.

"That is so from endless beginning," he would say and wander hither and thither. "It's all illusive phenomena," he muttered, "Who knows?" and "It was all settled long ago" and went about the outer courtyards of Nallur Temple and sat in the dirt, saying that all that dirt would frighten away the people who came to fall at his feet. I don't think anyone ever got from him an answer to a question. I merely stood and waited behind him for the occasional gem that fell out of all the mad talk.

Among the Sri Lankan Hindus, there are countless marvelous stories about the powers of a realized person, stories that would bring curiosity seekers if a guru proclaimed himself. Chellappaswami said that devotees who are ready, those few souls who understand the true nature of a satguru, will go through any barrier to be with him. Such a seeker will recognize and pursue the satguru in any disguise he wears. Were the satguru a homeless mendicant, a village pariah, the seeker would grow strong withstanding the disapproval the community might express in seeing him follow someone considered socially unworthy.

The devotee seeking realization will not let anything stop him. Even if the guru chases him away, he will not be dissuaded from his path. He accepts as a blessing anything the guru does. He will change his form, his opinions, his intellect, his very nature, to bring himself into harmony with the guru. There are endless stories of people being sent away by a guru, only to come back in disguise. If that didn't work, they would go away and undertake life-transforming *tapas* until they changed their nature and were able to return in good stead.

Chellappaswami's nephew, his sister's son, lived in her house. The young man was hot-tempered and, even though he acknowledged Chellappaswami was a sage, often lost his temper with the swami because Chellappaswami used such harsh and filthy language toward him, his mother and other members of the family, sometimes offending their friends and visitors.

One day Chellappaswami was standing by the open water well in the family compound, scolding his sister in a loud, angry voice. Running out of the house to defend his mother, the youth began screaming at Chellappaswami to stop. Chellappaswami yelled back at him, mocking his words. Suddenly the boy jumped across the two-meter-wide well to get at the swami, both fists flying as he landed on the other side. Chellappaswami touched him lightly on the chest and immediately all his anger was stilled. It vanished entirely. The boy just stood there, dumbfounded, blinking in shock, not knowing where he was.

The family learned through the years to respect Chellappaswami's advice. Once they and a few close friends planned a pilgrimage to Kataragama, the most famous of Sri Lanka's Skanda temples, located in the tiger-infested jungles deep in the southern hills. They saved their money and talked about the journey for months ahead of time. Chellappaswami knew they were going. When the day finally came to depart, though, he said, "Why go searching? God is here." They unpacked immediately, all

· ·

Chellappaswami kept a tight rein on his desires and appetites. His meals were taken in solitude most of the time, prepared on a simple wood fire in the shade of the Nallur temple bilva *tree.*

but one of the party, who set out by himself. As it turned out, he never reached Kataragama. He fell desperately ill with malaria along the way and returned to Jaffna only after six months in the hospital and thousands of rupees in doctor's fees.

Works of Wonder

Most of the time Chellappaswami could be found in the shade of his thorny *bilva* tree, the famed *Aegle marmelos,* sacred to Lord Siva, since its leaves form a *trishula.* Protected from the tropical sun under its massive canopy, he talked to himself, meditated, ate his meals, sat and made fans and containers of various shapes from palmyra and coconut palm leaves. He often worked all day in the hot sun weaving the leaves into fans. Mastering the art requires patience and skill, and none was better at it than he. Each fan was of a unique design, no two alike. He gave the fans away to devotees and bystanders. It was a form of communion and blessing, imbued as they were with the implied meaning of protecting, cooling and relief from suffering. He also wove cadjan from coconut fronds, a thatch used for roofs, walls and fences.

The mysterious siddha wielded great influence. One of the honored sons of Sri Lankan culture was Sir Ponnambalam Ramanathan, who founded the Ramanathan College for young ladies at Maruthanamadam at the edge of Jaffna town during Chellappaswami's time. On the day of its grand opening, Swami was among the first to arrive. He walked in through the open doors and presented Ramanathan with one of his best fans, and said, "There is no intrinsic evil; finished long ago; everything is true; we know nothing."

The community attributes the school's success to Chellappaswami's blessing that day. The whole staff considered it extraordinary that this holy man had come to their school at this particularly auspicious moment on this most important day.

Ramanathan did much for Saivism, including rebuilding the Sivan Koyil at Kochikadde, Colombo, with his own funds, decreeing that it be carved entirely from granite. The original temple had been built by his father, Mudaliyar Ponnambalam, in 1856. The reconstruction was completed in 1910.

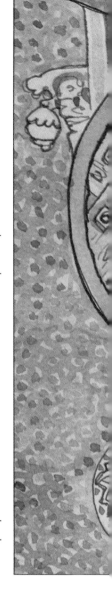

Chellappaswami would spend hours cutting and weaving the rigid fronds of the palmyra tree to make traditional fans, which people used to fend off the sweltering heat. Those who received his fans regarded themselves immensely blessed.

Chellappaswami expected to be left alone. Even his own devotees approached only on invitation, visiting less on their initiative than his. If they needed anything from him, they would already have received it. He knew their minds. Devotees often sought his help at crucial times in their life. Here is an example from *Chellappa Swami of Nallur:*

A child of Ramalingam of Columbuthurai was seriously ill. The parents were eager to take the child to Swami, but his mother-in-law

warned them, "We do not know to what caste that madman belongs. Do not take the child to him." Brushing off this old woman's words, Ramalingam and his wife took the child to Swami. When he saw them, Swami ordered, "Kanakamma, bring the child here!" Giving instructions to take the child to a native physician for a particular medicine, he declared, "Your mother is speaking of caste. I swear by the Sun and the Moon that we are no other than Vellala caste from Vaddukkottai." When Swami touched the child, the temperature went down, and upon receiving the prescribed medicine, the child was fully cured.

If strangers drew near, stopping out of curiosity to see what he was doing,

Chellappaswami's extraordinary self-discipline can be seen in the control of his appetite. If, during the preparation of any food, his mouth began to water in anticipation, he would shatter the clay cooking pot and forego that meal. This happen so often, Yogaswami described him as "one surrounded by broken pots."

• •

he would scold, throw things and chase them away. He would throw anything—dirt, mud, rocks, cow dung, garbage—just so they would let him be.

In every scolding, Chellappaswami corrected devotees' misdeeds and touched the sorest and most sour area of their inner mind. They trusted him to know just where they were imperfect, just where they needed to change for spiritual progress.

They hated these upbraidings, not only because they revealed those things most wanting to be hidden, but also because they were delivered with a spiritual force so penetrating that it felt like a deep psychic surgery. Yet, again and again they went back for more, receiving those incisive corrections as divine blessings. They invariably improved in the days and months after his fiery grace descended on them in all its terrible fury. Just being in his presence, receiving a modicum of that infinite shaktipata, transformed them, made them different, somehow better.

Thus, he spoke like a spiritual king to those with an inner ear. Those few, the lawyers, the judges, all who were of a subtle mind, loved and feared Chellappaswami. He would curse them, beat them verbally and even physically. He was their inner guide, the guru that inspired them to fully live a spiritual life, and spiritual life was universally understood in Northern Sri Lanka to be the most exalted of human inquiries.

Chellappaswami continued the parampara's mighty mission of slowly but surely, step-by-step, awakening Saivism within the hearts and souls of Tamils everywhere on this lush, garden island. Were it not for him, there is no way of knowing whether Saivism would have survived into the 21st century.

Then again, on rare occasions he paid no attention at all when people he had never seen before brought him flowers or prostrated in his presence. He sat impassively while they made their pranams. It was hard for them to discern if he knew they were there at all. No one ever knew what to expect from this perplexing spiritual giant. Yet all got exactly what they needed.

This was Chellappaswami's way—always the sage, never the saint. Many times he treated Yogaswami as if he had never seen him before, chasing him away and calling instead to some common passersby off the street, people who weren't much interested in spiritual things. He would coax them sweetly to come near, then lecture, then berate in the vilest language imaginable, telling them what scum they were—living like animals, with no thought of God or their own souls, filling their bellies like pigs by day and sleeping like dogs at night, wallowing in endless desires, rushing down the royal road to hell, and so forth. He might go through every individual in the group, naming their secret vices, ticking off their private sins, abusing them right there in public. If they tried to leave, he followed them until he was through. He was unrelenting in giving forth his blessing, revealing the truth, no matter how great the humiliation.

His greatest siddhi was to change the life force within people, hence change their lives. These psychic powers, which he received from Kadaitswami, Chellappaswami passed on to Yogaswami. The righteous anger of our sages is to this day called "white anger" by the Tamil people, the opposite of the hurtful black anger of the *vitala* chakra, below the *muladhara* chakra.

Whenever in life the issue of the guru's fierce scoldings arose, Yogaswami challenged, "Is not a big fire necessary to burn rubbish?" In his later years, Yogaswami was himself a gifted scolder, and many people were afraid to come near him. But he said that anyone who thought he was harsh should have stood for a single second before his guru's scolding.

Yogaswami explained that most people try to get you to love them by giving you something you like so you will pay more attention to them; you transfer some of your attachment from the thing you like to the person who gave it to you. He told disciples, "Chellappaguru, through subtle guile, pulled me to his side by taking everything away. He did not allow me to put on any show, nor to do any service, nor to know the future, nor to have any siddhis, nor to associate with other saints or sadhus. He did not even allow me to wonder."

About fifty bulls were attached to the project to do the hauling and heavy work. Mr. Brown insisted they receive the best of care and did not permit them to be abused. After the day's work, their drivers led them to the river to wash and feed them, and every day Mr. Brown walked down to see that they did it right. It was a lesson Yoganathan never forgot.

Life at the irrigation company in Kilinochchi had its dark side and difficulties. Aloof from the staff, Yoganathan was hassled by one among them, a bully who took every opportunity to taunt his brown-skinned junior. Months of this wore on, and one day, in the fury of an encounter, the bully threatened Yoganathan, not knowing that inside his younger victim a fire was smoldering. A fight ensued during which Yoganathan stabbed the aggressor. It was a terrible event, and Mr. Brown took it seriously. Yoganathan was ordered to serve six weeks of hard labor at the nearby Mankulam Quarry.

Meanwhile, Uncle Chinnaiya tried repeatedly to arrange a match for the young man, but Yoganathan wanted no part of it. He felt his path lay elsewhere. He spent his money on scriptures, books of hymns and stories of the Saivite saints. He studied these over and over again, never content until he could establish within himself the truth of the words he read. It awed him to think that life in this world could be lived with such purity and devotion. He knew the stories of the saints by heart and was forever singing their *Devarams*.

In order to study Sanskrit scriptures, he acquired proficiency in Sanskrit during these years as well. Kilinochchi afforded him the peaceful surroundings he needed for the study and worship he so valued. Yoganathan made good use of his time. He spent his days off alone in contemplative settings and was a constant visitor at all the nearby temples. People were amazed at how well and how deeply he knew the many scriptures of Hinduism. He could recite them page by page.

Mornings and evenings he meditated on what he read, and gradually he built up a daily routine of sadhanas. He added to these disciplines from time to time, and as his meditations deepened he took up various kinds of *tapas* as well. Sometime during his years in Kilinochchi, he took a formal vow of celibacy to affirm his commitment to the spiritual path and his decision, despite family efforts to the contrary, never to marry.

Inthumathy Amma notes:

Years later he told his devotees that he cultivated the habit of spending everything he earned in that month itself without saving anything for a rainy day. Except for his meager personal expenses, he spent the rest of the money on temples, friends, relations and the poor and needy.

While Yoganathan was employed at Iranamadu, a crucial event occurred that nurtured his inclinations to renounce the world. Ratna Ma Navaratnam wrote:

> At about this time, the triumphant return of Swami Vivekananda from the World's Parliament of Religions at Chicago created a stir in the hearts of the people enticed by alien culture, and his visit to Ceylon was acclaimed as a happy augury for the renewal of faith in Hinduism. The prophet of the New Age came to Yalpanam in 1897, and his elevating lectures at Hindu College, the Esplanade and the Saiva Pathashala at Columbuthurai made an undying impression on Swami.
>
> It is reported that when Swami Vivekananda was ceremoniously brought in a carriage drawn by the leading Hindu citizens to address the public at the present Hindu Maha Vidyalaya at Columbuthurai, he got down from the carriage at the junction where stands the *illupai* tree and walked up to the school. In his lecture, he reported that he was impelled to get down from the carriage, as he felt he was treading on sanctified soil and called it, prophetically, an oasis. This was the *illupai* tree under whose shade Swami would later sit in the sun and rain during his sadhana years. Columbuthurai was singled out as an attractive oasis when Swami in later years, too, hallowed this spot as his religious centre and ashram.

Inthumathy Amma adds to the chronicle:

> When Swami was working in Kilinochchi, Swami Vivekananda's visit to Ceylon took place (1897). Swami participated in the reception that Jaffna accorded to him with great enthusiasm. Swami also took part in the procession from the Fort to Hindu College, and later in the public meeting held at the Hindu College premises.
>
> The eagerness with which Swami later spoke of the topics discussed by Swami Vivekananda in those early days showed the great latent desire he had for the company of saints.

Yoganathan lived like a yogi in Kilinochchi, alone unto himself, immersed in his meditations. He spoke little, for his interests were not those of the people around him. He carefully protected his inner experiences. By his third year in Kilinochchi, he was well settled in his job, executing his duties quietly and well, letting nothing disturb his inner work. He frequently sat up late into the night studying scriptures, singing hymns or meditating by the light of a single oil lamp. He was in the world, but less and less of it.

One thought took root early on and eventually quelled all other plans—the desire to renounce the world and seek Realization of God undistracted. It made sense to him. Everything he had ever done, everything he had become, led in that direction. That alone intrigued and inspired him. But he knew he had to find a satguru, a jnani, to guide him. The scriptures are adamant: except through the grace of a living satguru, a man of Realization, the path to the Self is not seen in this world. Yoganathan didn't know anyone like that, so he hesitated, watching and waiting. It is traditional knowledge in Saivism that the guru cannot fail to appear when the disciple is ready, "ripe for grace."

Yoganathan knew this to his core. He had learned of the process in the hymns and life of Saint Manikkavasagar. At the age of eighteen Manikkavasagar was the Prime Minister of the Pandyan empire, young, brilliant and wealthy. Though he had everything, he yearned only for a guru to lead him from darkness to light. The moment he laid eyes on his teacher, he was powerless but to follow, as he recognized the object of his soul's search. He then abandoned all—family, friends, fortune and fame. Many such saintly lives Yoganathan had pondered, and he knew that finding a guru was not entirely in his hands. When he was ready, the guru would appear. He went on with his sadhana. He continued to work, and he prayed for a guru, prayed again and again.

Chinnaiya felt it increasingly urgent to broach the subject of marriage. Yoganathan understood the cultural pulls on him and avoided his uncle. He would find something to do elsewhere if he thought Chinnaiya might visit that day. Though he had long since decided to take sannyasa and thus enter fully the spiritual, monastic life he so admired, he hadn't mentioned this to his relatives. He was his usual, congenial self around them, though he was doing severe *tapas* of one kind or another every day.

In his private moments, sitting in the store, he sometimes found himself gazing through the open door, torn between staying or leaving that minute—walking away from the world, from Mr. Brown, from Kilinochchi, from everything. He yearned to be on his way, but something held him back, and in his heart he knew it was Siva's will. He endured by working harder on the inside, and his sadhana seemed to take on a life of its own. Every spare moment found him sitting quietly in his room or in a temple. He felt he had come to the end of everything, as if he had done all he could do. Sometimes he sat through the whole night in meditation, perfectly still, not moving once. On days when he was free, he would pick a far-off temple and walk there all the way from Kilinochchi without stopping, worship and walk back, singing hymns along the way. At Nallur Temple in Jaffna, he worshiped Lord Murugan, the first renunciate.

Meeting the Sage of Nallur

One day Vithanayar, his brother Ramalingam and Thuraiappah came to visit Yoganathan, and together they set out walking to Nallur. A man of similar interests, Vithanayar also did sadhana. In fact, being the elder of the two, he felt a certain duty to help Yoganathan forward on the path however and whenever he could. It was the day of the chariot festival in August, an auspicious time to worship Lord Murugan, who would be paraded around the temple in His elaborate chariot. They bathed at the well, put on holy ash and set out for Nallur. Vithanayar hoped they would see Chellappaswami as well.

On their way, Yoganathan told Vithanayar of an encounter he had with Chellappaswami many years earlier. He was about twelve at the time. Suffering from an infected cut on his foot, he was on his way to the doctor's hut in Jaffna town. As he passed by the *teradi* at Nallur Temple, a man shouted, "Come here! What do you want with medicine?" It was Chellappaswami, who beckoned him closer and had him sit down while he examined the wound, nodding his head like a doctor. Chellappaswami told him not to go to the ayurvedic doctor, but to mash a certain herb and apply it as a poultice to the wound. The foot healed in a few days. That was the only time Yoganathan had been near the sage as a child, though he undoubtedly saw him from time to time around Nallur Temple through the years.

It is said that at age ten or twelve, Yoganathan had also met Kadaitswami in Jaffna town, among the shops. The boy had a high fever and Kadaitswami just touched him, after which the fever gradually subsided.

A little before noon, Yoganathan and his friends reached Nallur and stepped into a huge crowd, a hundred thousand or more, gathered for the festival. Despite the sweltering midday heat, the temple compound was filled. Hundreds were moving about in front of the temple, awaiting a chance to get inside. Bare-chested men and boys rolled in the hot sand

· ·

It is said that Hindu holy men fall into two main categories: those who are pious, pure and of a saintly demeanor, and those who are sagely, homeless and even odd. Chellappaswami was more sage than saint, with his disheveled veshti, *his unkempt body and his strange behaviors. Still, he was known as a guru of the highest order.*

around its outer walls as a penance or sadhana, and devotees followed them singing.

A mingling aroma of incense and flowers perfumed the air, while a chorus of voices rose from the sea of umbrellas spanning the dusty square between the *teradi* and temple. In the tropics, umbrellas are not for rain alone, but more often to give protection from the penetrating sun. Out from the open doors of the sanctum came crescendos of shrill wood-winds, kinetic drums and bells, driven on by the chanting of the brahmins. Pujas had been going on from daybreak, and the air was intensely charged with Lord Murugan's presence.

The *mandapam* was packed with thousands of devotees, jostling and pushing to stand closer to the puja. Yoganathan and his three friends worked their way toward the *teradi*, where they hoped to see Chellappa-swami. Before they knew it, the crowd parted, and there he was, not three meters away, standing among the devotees, challenging and powerful. His gaunt figure stood out sharply against the crowd, seeming somehow taller than his five feet nine inches.

Everyone walked around him without coming near, intimidated by his striking appearance. He was barefoot, thin-bearded and burnt dark by the sun, wearing a single white cloth, wrapped once, from the waist down. Surveying the multitudes with transparent glee, he was talking aloud to no one at all, blithely unaware of the looks he drew. He carried himself with a lion's air of dominion and power. A penniless sadhu, he stood like a king, his posture at odds with his conduct and dress.

He spotted the four visitors just before they saw him and walked toward the *teradi.* They greeted him humbly. Yoganathan's friends had visited Chellappaswami many times, and Yoganathan could not help but be keenly aware of the majestic being; but now he was standing face to face with the great one.

After a few moments Chellappaswami dismissed the three household-ers, shouting, "Go and look after your families! You fellows are not fit to become sadhus." Yoganathan, on the other hand, he kindly invited to stay back: "I was awaiting your arrival here. I am going to have a coronation for you soon." Drawing Yoganathan to his side, he gave him instruction in spiritual values, then suddenly slapped him on the head with his right hand, exclaiming, "This is the coronation!" and voiced five momentous teachings:

Summa iru. (Be still.)
Eppavo mudintha kaariyam. (It was all finished long ago.)

Naam ariyom. (We know not.)
Muluthum unmai. (All is truth.)
Oru pollupumillai. (There is not one wrong thing.)

Yogaswami later wrote:

> Then and there I received divine grace. Once these words were
> imprinted in the heart of the devotee, Chellappah with his face blos-
> soming with grace said, "It is good, dear one; come, I have been wait-
> ing for a person like you."

That evening at sunset, still overwhelmed by the encounter, Yoganathan
walked back alone to his aunt's house. Those who recalled those times
said that following this experience the young man met often with Chellappaswami on weekend trips from Kilinochchi.

Moment of Truth

A subsequent meeting, which Yogaswami described years later in his
Natchintanai, was equally transformative. Yoganathan was walking along
the road outside Nallur Temple. Sage Chellappaswami shook the bars
from within the chariot shed where he camped and boldly challenged,
"Hey! Who are you?" *(Yaaradaa nee?).*

Yoganathan was transfixed by the simple, piercing inquiry. Their eyes
met and Yoganathan froze. Chellappaswami's glance went right to his
soul. The sage's eyes were like diamonds, fiery and sharp, and they held
his with such intensity that Yoganathan felt his breathing stop, his stomach in a knot, his heart pounding in his ears. He stared back at Chellappaswami. Once he blinked, in the glaring sun, and a brilliant inner light
burst behind his eyes.

> He revealed to me Reality without end or beginning and enclosed
> me in the subtlety of the state of *summa.* All sorrow disappeared; all
> happiness disappeared! Light! Light! Light!

Waves of bliss swept his limbs from head to toe, riveting his attention
within. He had never known such beauty or power. For what seemed ages
it thundered and shook him while he stood motionless, lost to the world.
He later described it as a trance.

> To end my endless turning on the wheel of wretched birth, he took

me beneath his rule, and I was drowned in bliss. Leaving charity and *tapas,* charya and kriya, by fourfold means he made me as himself.

The roaring of the *nada nadi* shakti—the mystic, high-pitched inner sound of the Eternal—in his head drowned out all else. The temple bells faded in the circling distance as from every side an ocean of light rushed in, billowing and rolling down upon his head. He couldn't hold on, not for an instant. He let go, and Divinity absorbed him. It was him, and he was not.

> By the guru's grace, I won the bliss in which
> I knew no other. I attained the silence where
> illusion is no more. I understood the Lord,
> who stands devoid of action. From the eight-
> fold yoga I was freed.

Yoganathan stood transfixed, like a statue, for several minutes. As he regained normal consciousness and opened his eyes, Chellappaswami was waiting, glaring at him fiercely. "Give up desire!" he shouted. People were passing to and fro, unaware of what was taking place. "Do not even desire to have no desire!"

Yoganathan felt the grace of the guru pour over and through him, all from those piercing eyes. Such elation he had never known. Dazed, he saw that the guru intended to dispel all darkness and delusion with his words, which were beyond comprehension in that moment: "There is no intrinsic evil. There is not one wrong thing!"

Yogaswami later wrote of this dramatic meeting in a song called "I Saw My Guru at Nallur:"

> I saw my guru at Nallur, where great *tapasvins* dwell. Many unutter-
> able words he uttered, but I stood unaffected. "Hey! Who are you?" he
> challenged me. That very day itself his grace I came to win.
>   I entered within the splendor of his grace. There I saw darkness

Yogaswami wrote often of the day his life was transformed. Passing the Nallur chariot house that morning, he was transfixed by Chellappaswami's holy presence. When the guru challenged, "Hey! Who are you?" the disciple was lost in an infinite light that engulfed him and changed him forever.

. . . .

all-surrounding. I could not comprehend the meaning.

   "There is not one wrong thing," he said. I heard him and stood bewildered, not fathoming the secret.

   As I stood in perplexity, he looked at me with kindness, and the maya that was tormenting me left me and disappeared.

He pointed above my head and spoke in Skanda's forecourt. I lost all consciousness of body and stood there in amazement.

While I remained in wonderment, he courteously expounded the essence of Vedanta, that my fear might disappear. "It is as it is. Who knows? Grasp well the meaning of these words," he said, and looked me keenly in the face—that peerless one, who such great *tapas* has achieved!

In this world all my relations vanished. My brothers and my parents disappeared. And by the grace of my guru, who has no one to compare with him, I remained with no one to compare with me.

As Yoganathan tried to comprehend the experience, his guru had already forgotten him there. Chellappaswami was scanning distant rooftops, mumbling to himself and nodding in accord with all he was saying, then began walking away. Yoganathan started to follow when the sage called back over his shoulder, "Wait here 'till I return!"

It was three full days before his guru came back, and the determined Yoganathan was still standing right where he left him. Chellappaswami didn't speak or even stop. He motioned for Yoganathan to follow, leading him to the open fire pit where the sadhu prepared his own meals. There he served Yoganathan tea and a curried vegetable stew, then sent him away.

He didn't welcome or praise his new disciple; he didn't say to come back or not to come back. He didn't have to. Yoganathan knew he had been accepted. And his training began—the first chance he got, he bent to touch Chellappaswami's feet, and his guru bellowed in dismay. Drawing back, the sage scolded him, "Don't even think of it!" Yoganathan was bewildered, but he obeyed, and his guru calmed down. "You and I are one," he said. "If you see me as separate from you, you will get into trouble."

Chellappaswami's insistence on the oneness of guru and disciple, in fact the oneness of everything, while strange to the average man, was a faithful expression of the ancient *Agama* texts, which decree:

"Siva is different from me. Actually, I am different from Siva." The highly refined seeker should avoid such vicious notions of difference. "He who is Siva is indeed Myself." Let him always contemplate this non-dual union between Siva and himself.

With one-pointed meditation of such non-dual unity, one gets himself established within his own Self, always and everywhere. Being established within himself, he directly sees the Lord, who is within every soul and within every object and who presents Himself in all the manifested bodies. There is no doubt about the occurrence of such experience.

He who is declared in all the authentic scriptures as unborn, the creator and controller of the universe, the One who is not associated with a body evolved from maya, the One who is free from the qualities evolved from maya and who is the Self of all, is indeed Myself. There is no doubt about this nondual union.

Sarvajnanottara Agama 2.13–16

Yoganathan was utterly devoted to Chellappaswami. In later life he expressed his profound reverence in many of his songs and writings, called *Natchintanai,* such as the following:

Come, offer worship, O my mind, to Gurunathan's holy feet, who said, "There is not one wrong thing," and comforted my heart. Come swiftly, swiftly, O my mind, that I may adore the lord who on me certainty bestowed by saying "All is truth." Let us with confidence, O my mind, hasten to visit him who at Nallur upon that day "We do not know" declared.

Come soon and quickly, O my mind, Chellappan to see, who ever and anon repeats, "It is as it is." Come, O my mind, to sing of him who near the chariot proclaimed, "Who knows?" with glad and joyful heart for all the world to know. Come now to Nallur, O my mind, the satguru to praise, the king of lions on *tapas's* path whom nobody can gauge. Come with gladness, O my mind, our father to behold, who of lust and anger is devoid, and in tattered rags is clothed.

Please come and follow me, O mind, to see the beauteous one, who mantras and tantras does not know, nor honor or disgrace. Come, O my mind, to give your love to the guru, free from fear, who like a madman roamed about, desiring only alms. Come, O my mind, to join with him who grants unchanging grace and is the Lord who far above the thirty-six *tattvas* stands.

Spiritual Work in Kilinochchi
After his life-altering experience, Yoganathan returned to his work at Kilinochchi, while pilgrimaging the full sixty-five kilometers to Nallur each weekend to be with his satguru, and again walking back in time to fulfill his morning duties on Monday. However, his heart ached to leave his job, to let go of the rope, to be with his guru at Nallur. The strenuous

effort he poured into his sadhana was all that allowed him to stick with the routine at Iranamadu.

No *tapas* was too harsh. One day, many years later, a young man came to visit the sage who had come to be known as Yogaswami. They talked for a few minutes, and the man mentioned that, to purify himself, he had been rubbing chili powder over his body and then sitting in the hot sun. Yogaswami's eyes lit up, "A fine *tapas!* I, too, have done that!" Ratna Ma Navaratnam, in *Saint Yogaswami and the Testament of Truth,* recounts:

> It is believed that at the beginning of this century Swami experienced spells of spiritual insights and felt powerfully drawn to his guru. During this time, a select coterie from Columbuthurai including the Vidhane Thirugnanasampanthar, Kadirithamby Vettivelu, Ponniah Upadiyayar, Sivagurunathar Thuraiappah and Thiagar Ponniah would visit Chellappar at Nallur quite frequently. Swami would join them whenever he came down from his sphere of work. He would at times recall how vigorously he used to walk all the forty-five miles from Kilinochchi to Nallur to meet Chellappar, for so great was his urge to be in the living presence of his guru.

At his workplace Yoganathan spent his free time during the week deeply immersed in his guru's teachings and in his sadhana. Inthumathy Amma describes those days:

> The Kilinochchi forest became an apt ashram for Swami to sit peacefully and cogitate and practice all that he had learned from Chellappaswami. By thinking deeply for long hours, by entering into deep *niddai* [a state of immersion in the Divine], by sitting in meditation and by following the yogic disciplines, he practiced all he had learned from his guru. His chief object was "to know himself." He studied the book that was within him carefully, with great alertness. He would look at his religious books only occasionally, and that, too, as a means of spending some leisure time. As he became more and more mature in his sadhana, he began to experience the treasure of being seated in yoga and the bliss of meditation.
>
> Swami always remembered Kilinochchi as his training ground to lead a life of happiness mingled with God. In later days, while traveling with his devotees through that area, he would point out the place where he practiced his yoga and say, "This place is extremely suitable for meditation."

Near the end of 1897, Yoganathan decided to quit his job to immerse himself completely in his guru's holy presence. S. Ampikaipaakan observed:

> In Swamikal's life the year 1897 was very important. It seems Swamikal quit His job at the end of that year and returned to Jaffna. Swamikal was about twenty-five years old. That was the time Swamikal progressed step by step in the religious life.

Inthumathy Amma writes of this transformative time:

> The insatiable love for Chellappa Desikar, the benevolent guru, full of grace, who was waiting to show him visions that were not visible, began to flourish in Yogamuni [a name for Yogaswami meaning silent sage]. He became astounded at Chellappa, the guru who taught him the path to knowledge and wisdom and who was the great knower "who knew and realized the *Veda* without any study." The repetition of his name became sweeter and sweeter. The form of Chellappa became the form he meditated on. His divine feet became the recipients of his worship. His nectaric words were mantric words. Just like a compass always pointing north, whatever work he performed, whatever hardships he endured—his mind was always focused on the chariot house. Yogamuni realized that it was impossible to have light and darkness at the same time and decided to renounce his employment and other worldly affairs. He realized that the company of good sages was better than relations, parents and siblings, and renounced his relatives. Thus he renounced his employment, kith and kin, and went to the chariot house, surrendering himself completely, and remained there at Chellappa's feet as his good devotee.

Yoganathan watched until Mr. Brown was in a good mood, then told him he was leaving. The stern Englishman was naturally unhappy about this and tried to dissuade him, but Yoganathan was firm. Brown then tried to postpone it for a year, and finally relented, saying, "If you desire to resign, at least appoint someone like you to take charge of the work."

Yoganathan agreed to that. He wasn't just leaving a job; he was renouncing the world. Brown didn't know that and wouldn't understand if he were told. Because Yoganathan didn't want to leave any upset or imbalance behind, he promised to stay on long enough to train a replacement. He recommended his cousin Vaithialingam, who was just 19. Ever the administrator, Brown promised to hire the youth only if he could perform as well as Yoganathan. Vaithialingam was happy to be offered the job and arrived a few days later. He shared Yoganathan's simple quarters and imbibed his years of experience during the weeks they were together.

Vaithialingam remembered well the time he spent with Yoganathan at the company store, and his recollections became the primary source of knowledge about this period in Swami's life. He was astounded at his cousin's firm habits and austere lifestyle. The whole family knew he was religious, but because he was living in far-off Kilinochchi, none understood the depth of his seeking.

Vaithialingam spoke of nights when he woke from a sound sleep to find Yoganathan sitting in yogic pose, pleading aloud for the grace of Siva. Oblivious to the room around him, he would pray to Shakti, the energy aspect of Siva, to rise within him and bring realization. Tears wet his face as he begged for grace, "O my dear mother! O my dear father!" as Vaithialingam lay awake, listening for hours. He said he saw there what the rest of the family had not—that Yoganathan could never be satisfied with an ordinary life in the world. He was determined beyond anyone's imagining to accomplish what he later said was the only work to be done on this planet—realization of Parasiva.

Throwing Down the World

The cousins worked together for some time until Brown was fully satisfied with Vaithialingam and told Yoganathan he was free to go. He left Iranamadu to undertake sadhana full time, renounce the world and be with his guru. He was ready. Lifetimes of preparation lay behind him. His *tapas* and meditations had already shorn the bonds of worldly life. Yoganathan returned to Aunt Muthupillai's house and received her permission to live in the hut on her land. She was surprised when he told her he intended to renounce the world, but accepted the idea when she saw how serious he was.

M. Arunasalam tells us about this time in his book *Sivayoga Swamiyar: Varalarum Sathanaihallum*:

From the year 1897 to 1900, Yoganathan's permanent base was the hut at Aunt Muthupillai's place in Columbuthurai area. From her residence, Yoganathan used to visit Nallur on some days and spend all the daylight hours with his guru, Chellappar. Sometimes Yoganathan would visit Nallur Temple with his friends (Vithanayar, Thuraiappa, etc.). Also during this period, Yoganathan used to walk up to

Kilinochchi and practice meditation in quiet areas under the trees. Then again he would walk back to Columbuthurai and stay for a few days, visiting his guru at Nallur Temple. This routine went on until the end of the year 1900. From 1901 to 1910 he underwent vigorous training and sadhanas given by his guru.

Aside from his jaunts to the hills of Kilinochchi, where he sometimes stayed the weekend with his cousin, Yoganathan's life was centered in Jaffna. Early each morning he would walk from his aunt's place to Nallur to spend the day with his guru. Sometimes Chellappaswami sent him away. Was Yogaswami permitted to stay at the *teradi* with his guru? He was silent on the matter, but some report that for a time, during the period between 1906 and 1910, he did camp with Chellappaswami at Murugan's chariot house, so that he could be ready early in the morning to set out walking with his guru. What *is* known is that they were seen each day traveling about and begging for their food. T. Sivayogapathy, son of A. Thillyampalam, narrated what he was told about Yogaswami's habits during this time:

> From early morning till late evening, he was always with his guru at the Nallur *teradi,* as well as in surrounding areas of Nallur, and at his guru's hut, too. Gradually, at the period of the peak of sadhanas, he used to accompany his guru to distant places and return to the *teradi,* all by walking. Therefore, Yogaswami was compelled to be at his guru's feet, since his guru had no fixed schedule, and might set out for some distant place quite early in the morning. So, mostly Yogaswami used to spend the night at the *teradi* steps. He seldom visited his aunt's place.

Yogaswami stood by, a silent witness, when he was with his guru. Though, if ever his mind turned to something else, if he thought, "Well, he surely isn't talking to me," Chellappaswami would say something to bring him back with a start and let him know that everything his guru did was worthy of his full attention. He always knew what his disciple was thinking, and no matter the time or place or who was around, if Yogaswami entertained a thought Chellappaswami didn't like, or did something that showed he had ceased to see himself and his guru as one, Chellappaswami would berate him so vehemently, it would have destroyed anyone else. Inthumathy Amma describes this difficult sadhana:

Chellappa remained the mystery of all mysteries. He would refuse even to look at the devotee who had just worshiped him. He would be angry like death and shout at the devotee who went to revere him with all love. Having been subject to this anger, the devotee would move away and wait with worry while Chellappa ignored him and spoke laughingly with the vagrants who went that way. The minute the devotee thought, "He is talking in jest," rare mantric [sacred] words would arise. If the devotee went near him, he would attack without any cause. If the devotee went further away, he would attract him. It became necessary to move with him like those sitting before a fire—"not to go too close and not to go too far."

The sadhu's life is difficult, unbroken by the solacing—Yogaswami would say distracting—pleasures ordinary people allow themselves. But there was one indulgence Chellappaswami allowed—their country lane walks. They would amble freely, stride powerfully, exploring their land as though time did not exist, as though they were its kings, roaming widely, unencumbered by even a destination. It was, for them, one of life's little celebrations.

Almost every day they were together, begging on village streets or meditating at out-of-the-way places only Chellappaswami knew. They made the rounds of rural shrines and temples in all the outlying villages, sometimes walking for hours to visit a certain one Chellappaswami had in mind that day. There they would sit in the shade and meditate together. But if the feeling wasn't just right when they arrived, if anything was amiss, Chellappaswami would keep going, to another temple somewhere else. It wasn't unusual for them to trek all day without stopping, sometimes as far as fifty kilometers. When they returned to Nallur, whether early or late, Chellappaswami would cook a meal for them.

Chellappaswami again made it clear that he would brook no show of reverence or devotion from Yogaswami. He never once allowed his disciple to serve him, to cook or clean or mend for him. He scolded in a shrill voice if Yogaswami tried to prostrate or even raised his hands in silent *namaskara* while Chellappaswami's back was turned. He would know, fiercely chastise and on occasion even kick him if he didn't stop soon enough. Yogaswami later wrote:

Hail to the feet of the true guru who took me beneath his rule and gave himself to me, saying, "Do not suffer by regarding me as separate from you!"

Hindu tradition urges the shishya to serve his guru night and day by every means, to wash his clothes, bring meals, run errands, anything to serve him as Siva in human form. Yogaswami knew this and longed to express the grateful love that filled his heart, but Chellappaswami was ruthless in denying him any expression of devotional dualism between guru and disciple. Yogaswami's training demanded much of him. He loved his guru dearly, but Chellappaswami was hard on the youthful shishya, bringing him slowly to patience, peace, service and spiritual maturity.

No matter where he was, Chellappaswami talked to himself constantly, as if he were the only person in the world. He rarely said *he, she* or *it,* never admitting a second. And he repeated the same obscure phrases over and over again for months on end. While Yogaswami was with him, Chellappaswami once repeated for a whole year, "There is nothing evil in the world. No evil in the world." Not all that the guru muttered was so exalted. Yogaswami later wrote that Chellappaswami's soliloquy was a stream of thought that transcended understanding, and one had to listen carefully in order to catch the gems that fell from those lips.

People who watched the two together wondered how the disciple understood anything at all from the guru. They observed no open exchange between the two. But Yogaswami saw through Chellappaswami's guise of madness and used every gesture, every word, every look from his guru to refine his own nature, to perfect his sadhana. All his life, Yogaswami marveled at Chellappaswami's absolute purity. He was so pure, Yogaswami said, that nothing impure could stand in his presence. In the following Natchintanai, "The Master of Nallur," Yogaswami gives a lucid description:

> He who both like and dislike has exterminated, the noble one who never forgets the holy feet of God, who that "there is not one wrong thing" has openly declared—'tis he indeed who has assumed the guru's splendid form! He who unceasingly proclaims that all that is is truth, the master who has passed beyond ideas of good and bad, he who sees and looks upon himself and me as one, out of love, upon my head has placed his beauteous feet.
>
> The exalted seer who by the name of Chellappan is called, who, ever and anon, "Who knows? Who knows?" repeats the madman who will never by the world be known; he will be seated every day upon the chariot-house steps. Dark as the clouds in color, he ever had the habit to sleep upon the earth; his pillow was his hand. In the form of the guru he lived with grace and honor at Nallur, where fresh

water and fertile lands abound. The mighty one who has declared for the benefit of all the great and blessed mantra "Nothing do we know," who delusion, lust and anger has banished from his heart—he bears the name Chellappan, and at Nallur he dwells.

The crowning jewel beyond compare, who always will repeat that it was all perfected ages long ago, that madman whom nobody is able to describe, in the presence of Lord Murugan he forever lives. At Nallur, where orators and poets bow in worship, my guardian, who made me his and ended birth and death, wears the divine and sacred form of holy Chellappan, who accomplishes his service at Kandaswami's shrine.

Inthumathy Amma gives form to Chellappaswami's formless teaching style in the following summary:

The sweet drops of honey gleaned from the sweet-scented flower Chellappar by Yogaswami flitting around him can be stated as follows. First, Chellappar taught the path of knowledge by the rare mantric words "Who are you?" *(Yaaradaa nee?)*. Then he taught the path to understanding this by delving deep within oneself with the words "Search within." *(Theydadaa ul)* and thus guided him.

The hindrance to search within was the attachment to the world; hence he said, "Abandon desire" *(Theeradaa patrai)*. He calmed the devotee who, while searching within, found everything enveloped in darkness and was shattered with the words "There is nothing wrong" *(Oru pollaappum illai)*.

When Yogaswami stood bewildered, not understanding the connotation of the words, "There is no wrong," the guru took him to the front of the temple of Kandan and, when the curtain was drawn, pointed to the spear *(vel)* of knowledge and explained the Vedantic truth that once the curtain of illusion is drawn, only Brahman remains. When the devotee was thinking of the mystery of maya, Chellappar gave the *mahavakya* "See it is as it really is" *(Athu appadiyeh ullathai kaan)*. And to explain that mystery, he said, "Who knows?" *(Yaar arivaar?)*.

After teaching the path to knowledge, he taught the path of yoga. Master the *vaasi* [pranayama: control of breath] *(Vaasi yogam theyr)*. Close the two channels *(Iru valiyai adakku)*—[the two channels are *ida* and *pingala*]; transcend the path to birth *(Karu valiyai kada);* concentrate on the tip of the nose *(Naasi nuniyai nohkku);* be single-minded in your thoughts; to the land of Kasi go; mount majestically on the fresh and lively horse *(Pacchai puraviyiley paangaaga ehru)* [a reference to the control of breath]. In the house that is not built by the carpenter [the body], tie the galloping horse *(Thacchan kattaa veettiley thaavu pari kattu)* [again a reference to control of the breath]. Chellappaswami, who knew without any study all the technical terms used in yoga, taught the nuances and details of the yogic path. He explained to the good acolyte Yogar the different signs and awakenings that occur as one progresses in the practice of yoga.

He further explained very clearly that once he had transcended the path of birth, the mind would be controlled; that if he concentrated on the tip of the nose and woke up he would see the cosmic dance, and that at another stage he would hear sweet musical sounds. He also encouraged Yogaswami not to abandon the path of devotion that he had practiced earlier, by saying words like, "Wear the rosary" *(Akku mani ani);* "Repeat the five letters" *(Anjeluthai ohthu);* "Let the heart melt and melt" *(Nekku nekku urugu).*

Guru and disciple were out walking the roads one day. As always, Chellappaswami walked boldly, his eyes gazing ahead, never watching the ground as most people do. It amazed Yogaswami that in the five years they moved about together his guru never stepped on even a single anthill, which were everywhere and which Yogaswami had to diligently dodge during their treks.

During this outing, Yogaswami noticed his guru was glancing back at him every few minutes. Had he done something wrong? He didn't think so. Chellappaswami quickened the pace as they approached a village and headed straight for the marketplace. He wandered among the stalls for an hour, pretending to shop and occasionally stealing a glance at Yogaswami. His disciple was quietly waiting.

They wandered around the village for a while longer, then took a cow trail through the fields. Chellappaswami walked quickly 'till they reached the road, then ambled along, talking to himself and watching his shishya. They turned left at the crossroads and hadn't walked six meters when the sage spun around, peering suspiciously at Yogaswami: "Why are you following me?" Was Chellappaswami subtly challenging his shishya to examine the deeper purpose of their relationship?

Chellappaswami was especially particular about his food. Nearly everything he ate he prepared himself, making sure the ingredients were clean and fresh. If anyone looked at his food while he was preparing it or even thought about him while he was cooking or eating, he would stop and discard the meal. His devotees often brought him yams, but he would never eat them. He dug holes in the yard and planted them instead. When the leaves began to appear, he would ask his sister to pick and cook them for him. Similarly, he was extremely sensitive to the vibrations people put into anything they offered him.

Among his devotees was the chief priest of the Nallur Kailasanatha Sivan Temple, an orthodox brahmin man who strictly observed the rules of his caste. His home was adjacent to the temple. One day, when he looked up to see Chellappaswami walking past his house, he called out and invited the sage to come in and share some milk rice he had just brought from the puja. He knew Chellappaswami's habits and was afraid he might refuse. To his surprise, the guru came inside to partake.

When the *pongal* was offered, Chellappaswami made a sour face and said he wouldn't eat leftovers. "Someone has already eaten from it." The priest said, "No, no, no. No one has even looked at it." He had brought it straight from the sanctum, he pleaded, where he had done the puja himself. But Chellappaswami insisted. The man called his wife, who had prepared the rice in the kitchen, and asked her if anyone had touched it. She was positive no one had, but just to be sure, she suggested they call their small son to see if he had somehow gotten into it before it went to the temple. When they asked him, he hung his head and confessed he had indeed picked a morsel from the dish before his father took it to offer during puja.

Most people in Jaffna were sure Chellappaswami was completely mad, or at least too wild a sadhu to approach for blessings. Yogaswami had seen through his disguise that first day at Nallur. That moment of recognition—the look in Chellappaswami's eyes, full of the intent to take this young man to the heights of realization—lived within him and was all the assurance he ever needed. To Yogaswami, everything he had ever wanted had already been accomplished in that moment. It was simply unfolding itself in the months that followed. His first year with Chellappaswami was the natural unfoldment of that first moment. He followed after the guru wherever he would permit, listening, watching, waiting for the quiet word or glance that would tell him what was wanted. Whether he was awake or asleep, Yogaswami's thoughts turned 'round his guru and the magic of his grace.

"You Haven't Caught Me Yet"

Chellappaswami rarely spoke directly to anyone. He never once told Yogaswami that he was his guru; he never talked to him like that. But he trained him, and Yogaswami adjusted everything about himself—his thoughts and feelings, his plans, his speech, the way he dressed—to blend his mind perfectly with his guru and thereby catch his veiled instructions.

Chellappaswami did the work without seeming to do anything. He trained Yogaswami to have one-pointed concentration at all times and took every opportunity to shatter even his most subtle habits and attachments—demanding his disciple's whole mind, his undivided attention, every moment they were together, even if nothing was happening. With Chellappaswami there was no routine, no rest, no slacking. A day in his company was worth a year of regulated life.

His constant babbling was not distracted chatter, but earnest, mindful statements—to him, anyway. Though he might repeat himself without apparent end or purpose, his voice and expression revealed the full force of his mind behind every word. It fascinated Yogaswami. Try as he might, he could never reconcile Chellappaswami's resonant, measured tones and luminous glance with the seeming nonsense that poured from his lips.

Yogaswami never tired of listening, for there would be a gem of purest jnana every so often amid the most whimsical prattle, priceless statements of supreme wisdom that only those close to Chellappaswami ever heard. Because he took in every word his guru spoke, sense and nonsense, Yogaswami caught these gems and used them purposefully to open his own inner mind. If these had been the only teachings Chellappaswami ever gave him, they would have been more than enough. In later years, Yogaswami passed these aphorisms on to his own devotees, calling them the *mahavakya,* or great statements, of his satguru.

In his poetic legacy, Natchintanai, Yogaswami summarized the four most pertinent statements: "All is Truth. There is not one wrong thing. It was all finished long ago. We know not." Yogaswami explained that these sayings, when reflected upon, penetrate the mind in such a way that they bring about profound insight into the mind itself. Such realization of the mind as an inherently dual and self-created principle leads, ultimately, through sadhana, to realization of That beyond the mind—Parasiva, the

. . . .

Chellappaswami was an enigma wrapped in a disheveled veshti. *Few realized that this solitary sadhu who mumbled philosophical adages to himself and cursed strangers was among the most illumined souls of the time.*

nondual Self, the Absolute. He told his closest devotees to use these sayings as keys to profound meditation. They are the deepest teachings that language can convey.

At a distance, Chellappaswami appeared to be just another sadhu around the temple. Only a few ever glimpsed the spiritual power and soul maturity he possessed. These became his staunch devotees, putting up cheerfully with any amount of ranting and mad talk. They knew it was not for them but was his way of chasing off the timorous and those who weren't ready for what he had to offer. Chellappaswami was unmoved by being misunderstood. Yogaswami explained this in a song called "The Madman:"

Clothed in rags, he stands in front of Skanda's holy temple. On those who come and go before him, my little treasure, he will shower abusive language as it comes. "It is as it is. It is all a juggler's trick," he'll say. He wanders here and there, my little treasure. You will see him seated near the chariot.

No caste has he, nor creed. He will not talk with anyone, my little treasure. People say he is deranged in mind. Justice and injustice have no place with him; nor does he conform to any pattern, my little treasure. He goes about like one insane. No holy ash or *pottu* does his forehead bear. He will not utter what has once been said, my little treasure. He has passed beyond the *gunas*.

He will not tell you to be calm and rid yourself of ego. He speaks in contradictions, my little treasure. Those hearing him will say he's lost his wits. Chellappan, my father, in vulgar language will revile all those who pass by in the streets, my little treasure. They will say that he is mad. With lordly gait he roams from place to place. But all of those who notice him, my little treasure, treat him with ridicule and scorn.

One report has him repeating again and again, "All the money in all the banks in the world is mine." Once he was introduced to a body builder, a man proud of his physique. As the man flexed his muscles and bulged out his chest, Chellappaswami pointed at him and shouted, "That body is mine!" The man, who had spent years developing his physique, was baffled and deflated by the advaitic claim.

Though his gruffness was what most who encountered him remembered, Chellappaswami was a free spirit. He walked about as though he owned the Earth and everything upon it, happy, radiating compassion and inveterately carefree, with a touch of regalness in his manner and his stance. He did not care to attract followers. He gave freely to all who were ready, accepting nothing in return. He worked in secrecy or not at all. His guise of madness, he confided, would spare him the curious, the magic-mongers and faint-hearted.

Most of his devotees were householders. He initiated only two renunciate shishyas in his lifetime, Yogaswami and Katiraveluswami. There had been others, young men who recognized Chellappaswami as their guru and had been accepted by him, but not in the way Yogaswami and his brother swami were. His method was stern, but they always felt his underlying and never-spoken care. They knew they lived under their guru's umbrella of grace.

Chellappaswami held Yogaswami so still, so awake to every experience and lesson, that he was gradually carried deep within, living for months at a time in perfect harmony with his guru. His mind and heart filled with light; he lived in realms the Gods hold dear. He rarely slept. If he wasn't with Chellappaswami, he was sitting alone somewhere, blissfully absorbed in the vast inner life his guru's grace had brought him. Yet, the purifying scoldings never stopped.

Chellappaswami harangued and swore at him for the least of faults, for no faults at all, taking everything away until nothing remained but the One Existence Chellappaswami knew. As long as Yogaswami possessed the least consciousness of anything other than That, of anything to get or give, to gain or lose, Chellappaswami would fume and glare. Just the sight of Yogaswami would raise the guru's ire. He let him know, whatever he had done, it was not enough; it was never enough. Yogaswami sang of the great sage and their relationship in "My Master:"

He is the master who bestowed the basic mantra's secret. He dwells within the minds of those with loving hearts. Laughing, he roams in Nallur's precincts. He has the semblance of a man possessed; all outward show he scorns. Dark is his body; his only garment rags.

Now all my sins have gone, for he has burnt them up! All powerful karma kindled in the past he has dispelled. His heart is ornamented with the love of God. He shines in purity, as a light well-trimmed sheds lustre. On that day at Nallur he came and made me his. He made me to be *summa* after tests.

Always repeating something softly to himself, the blessing of true life he will impart to anyone who ventures to come near him. And he has made a temple of my mind. All pomp of guise and habit he abhors.

When devotees with great love come to worship, he'll hiss at them and glower black as Yaman. Yet, artfully he drew me 'neath his sway. 'Twas he who made me; but if I approach him he will attack me— attack me without mercy. At me he'll look, and many words he'll utter. All aim and object did that look dispel!

He would not allow me to form any mental image. He would not allow me to offer any service. He would not allow me to know what was going to happen. And yet this God ingeniously fulfilled my heart's desire. To serve him was a pleasure, but he would not allow it. He would not let me know what his pleasure was.

He would not permit the gaining of pleasurable siddhis. Yet, thus did he befriend me. How wonderful was that! He would say, "There is no wonder!" And those who came in awe and wonder he would not suffer to approach him; he left them in perplexity. But his own devotees he permitted to pay homage—that teacher of true wisdom!

Enigmatic Lessons

On many of their morning walks, Chellappaswami led the way straight to a village marketplace about fifteen kilometers from Jaffna to buy eggplants for lunch. The farmers in that region grow the finest eggplants in all the island and sell them in the open market. As soon as Yogaswami appeared in his compound, Chellappaswami would have a few cents tied in a corner of his sarong and be in a hurry to get there before the best eggplants were gone. It was a two-hour walk, even at Chellappaswami's pace. Once there, Yogaswami would wait while his satguru went by turns to every stall in the market, soberly weighing the merits of dozens of eggplants before going back to finally buy one or two. Then they walked home to Nallur.

He would march up to his hut carrying the eggplants in both hands and without a pause sit down to cook, lighting a fire on the ground to heat water in a clay crock supported by three rocks. Chellappaswami was a masterful chef, even though he simply boiled everything together in one pot—rice, spices and vegetables. As Chellappaswami ate mostly what he cooked himself, Yogaswami was invariably left sitting by, watching his guru prepare and serve him lunch.

While the pot simmered, Chellappaswami would crush and add spices, then sit before the fire weaving palm leaves into bowls. He didn't talk unless to rebuke Yogaswami if he felt his mind had wandered. This was their meal for the day, and it deserved his attention. But

• •

Chellappaswami took care of himself, as bachelors must, and that included shopping and preparing his meals. Often he and Yogaswami would walk to the market, bargain for the freshest eggplants, then return to Nallur to prepare his famed Chellappa stew, in which all ingredients were cooked in a single clay pot.

if Chellappaswami sensed the least desire or attachment toward the food, should his own mouth even begin to water, he would stop where he was and break the pot on the ground. No lunch that day. They went on to the next thing.

It was the guru's way of disciplining his instinctive nature, keeping it reined in. He did this so often that the compound around his hut was littered with shards. Yogaswami later described his guru as "one surrounded by broken clay pots." Chellappaswami did this even before Yogaswami's time, smashing a steaming pot of food he had just prepared with the self-chastisement, "So, you want rice to eat!" Such was his renunciation.

While the common man saw a common beggar in the sage, to Yogaswami, everything Chellappaswami did revealed his infinite grace. For him there was only one goal in life, Self Realization, and to allow anyone to think that less was sufficient was out of the question. In "The Lion," Yogaswami captured his guru's unabating message:

Self must be realized by self. All must be pervaded by the Self. We must give up desire for wealth and woman, and shun the greed for

Trekking to the seashore one day, Chellappaswami and Yoga-
swami came upon a lady selling eggplants, Yogaswami's favored
vegetable. Knowing his disciple's penchant for brinjals, Chellappa
turned and walked away, not allowing the desire to be fulfilled.

Page 169
Chapter 10

ownership of land. We must guard dharma like our eyes. We must give worship to the lotus feet. All thought in us must die. O my great guru, thou mighty lion!

Free from ignorance must we remain. We must behold God everywhere. We must have knowledge of the truth and ever cherish it. Falsehood and jealousy must be expelled. We must transform and into blessings change the things which cause delusion and make us confused. O peerless guru, whom others hold in high esteem! O lion, who in my bondage takes care of me!

Perhaps it was precisely Chellappaswami's stringent restriction on anything smacking of gratitude and adulation that gave wings to Yogaswami's later poems, those odes to his guru that ring with the praise he felt but was forbidden to utter in Chellappaswami's presence. In another song, "The Cure for Birth," Swami extols Chellappaswami as the great soul who released him from the cycle of birth and death:

Lord of the devas with sweet-scented wreaths adorned, bounty's bosom, liberation's flame, the all-pervading consciousness who with form and without form stands, who is both here and there, who king and guru has become, at sight of Him my heart was calm.

My present birth he'll terminate; in all my births with me he stayed; to make me free of future births, on me his grace he has bestowed. He is himself his only peer. Throughout eternity he stands. For those who offer praise to him, no future birth or death will rise.

The Nallur Kandaswami temple is immensely popular throughout the peninsula, yet even today people may come there from distant villages perhaps only several times in their lives. Sometimes, without knowing why, such devotees would be called off the street by this eccentric rishi, then berated and abused for acts and thoughts they did not know were within them.

Perhaps it went right over their heads, but he made them sit still while he acted out some dramatic conflict they had no notion had anything to do with them; they just listened politely and waited to leave. When he sent them away, they were perplexed by the experience, having at the time no idea of the purification they had undergone. Many did not even know the name of the man who put them through the ordeal. But later, sometimes after years, they would meet a situation in their life, an experience would come, and they would feel a release from what might have been. Some would remember and trace that release to the scolding they received from the sage of Nallur. Bringing flowers or fruit, they might come see him again to make their pranams. He would invariably chase them away, cursing them for daring to worship him.

He was clever at avoiding or getting rid of people who wanted to drink the full measure of the guru's grace but were not ready to live with his intensity. He would scold them and chase them off to start. If that failed, he would hide from them. Whenever his sister let into her compound a person he didn't want to see, someone seeking to intercept him at his hut, he would stay away for days.

Chellappaswami always got his way in these matters, one way or another. No amount of devotion or pleading or persistence prevailed. Just before Yogaswami came to him, a young fellow had drawn near whom Chellappaswami seemed to have taken a liking to. Villagers assumed the guru was training him as his disciple. He was allowed to stay around the *teradi* each day, but never at night. Even though the youth had no relatives in Jaffna and no place to go, Chellappaswami chased him away every evening, no matter how much he begged to stay.

This went on for a few months until one day Chellappaswami told him to go live with a widowed merchant, a devotee who had opened a shop around the corner from the temple. He and his two children lived in a house behind the shop. There was plenty of room for the boy to sleep there, Chellappaswami said. It seemed a fine arrangement, but a few weeks later the aspirant approached him, standing in front of his hut one morning, and complained that there were just too many problems about living with the merchant. Would he please relent and let him stay with him instead? Chellappaswami inquired what the difficulties were.

The boy explained that the man had a daughter who managed the household in her mother's absence, and now people were talking about his living in the same house with her. That was the gossip going around, and it could have been avoided, he said, if he hadn't been sent there in the first place. By this plea, he hoped Chellappaswami would feel sorry and admit he had made a mistake. But without a moment's pause, the guru declared there was nothing to do now but marry the girl, and walked off to make the arrangements himself. A week later, the newlyweds were settled in their own home in Columbuthurai. Chellappaswami saw that everything went well for them thereafter, and they remained among his most faithful devotees.

In Chellappaswami's World

One morning during the hot season, Yogaswami was following his guru along a remote village path when Chellappaswami decided they should go to Keerimalai for a bath. There, as part of a complex of several temples near the ocean, one of which is a large Siva temple, are two walled-in, sunken tanks, fed by fresh-water springs, which people bathe in for purification. These pools are highly thought of, and people walk long distances to take the sacred bath. Adults and children joyously fling themselves into the crystal waters. Adults swim lengthwise and breadthwise. Children splash about and have their first swimming lessons here.

Off to Keerimalai they strode. Though it was an all-day walk to cover the twenty-one kilometers each way, which meant a late supper, Yogaswami couldn't help looking forward to a cool dip in the ocean-side tank. Such luxuries came all too rarely in his guru's company. Holding umbrellas aloft, they walked for hours in the parching heat.

Finally, below them they spied the famed seaside tanks. Only a few pilgrims were there ahead of them. The sun at its zenith sparkled on the cool blue water, and a gentle breeze reached them from the ocean beyond. Yogaswami sighed and smiled, savoring the salty air. Chellappaswami looked to the left and right, then announced, "We have bathed," and turned to go. A bit startled that he would not feel the cool waters, Yogaswami followed.

On the way back to Nallur, they observed that the chariot festival was in progress at the Mauthadi Vinayagar temple. Chellapaswami stopped, saying, "You need refreshments." He gave Yogaswami two cents to buy *pittu*. Yogaswami bought the sweet dish made of steamed rice flour and coconut and got some lime and jaggery water to go with it from the free refreshment tent. Chellappaswami, declining any food, stood by as his disciple enjoyed the snack. Just as Yogaswami finished the last morsels, Chellappaswami set out for home.

Yogaswami walked briskly to keep up, as the food sloshed in his gurgling stomach. Thinking, "I can't walk any more," he paused. Without turning around, Chellappaswami shouted, "Oh, come, come." It was not a comfortable walk. Back at the *teradi* in Nallur, Chellappaswami gave him a few cents for tea. Only then did he take anything himself. In one of his songs, Yogaswami alluded to such lessons about the body:

> Taking the body as reality, I am roaming like a fool. When the supreme and perfect one cured my delusion and made me his. That source of bliss—who graciously appeared, concealing the fair-tressed lady by His side—I saw at the city of Nallur, where *naga* blossoms fall like rain. When, through previous karma, my mind was in confusion and I was sorely distressed, God, of His great mercy, had the holy will to take me under his protection and come to Earth as the embodiment of grace. 'Twas Him I saw near the house of the chariot in the city of Nallur where the Goddess Lakshmi dwells.

One day, first thing in the morning, Chellappaswami took Yogaswami begging. They would, he said, get something from a rich merchant who ran a store in the Grand Bazaar, the main shopping district in Jaffna. Arriving while it was still cool, they stood outside the shop, waiting for an offering. This merchant was actually a poor prospect, and Yogaswami knew that Chellappaswami knew it—a miserly fellow who never gave or put up with "worthless beggars," as he called sadhus who approached him for alms.

The merchant arrived an hour or so after they did and—while he surely saw the swamis standing there—went inside, greeted his clerks and sat down at a table on the veranda, in plain sight, as if he hadn't noticed them. Business came and went as usual. He worked on his account books all morning, then closed the shop and went home for his bath and lunch.

The two sadhus sat through the hottest hours. Chellappaswami was in blissful soliloquy. Yogaswami was pensive. The merchant came back in the afternoon and returned to work. Hour after hour, they stood by, waiting for alms. It was nearing time to close the shop for the day, and Yogaswami was growing impatient. Chellappaswami was quiet. Finally, the merchant closed his ledger and stood up to go. As he did, the eyes of the beggars caught his. He motioned to his clerk, and sent him out to give them one cent. One cent! Chellappaswami proudly held up the paltry coin as if it were a treasure, declaring, "Good wages for a day's work!" Yogaswami wanted to speak his mind to the merchant, but Chellappaswami pulled him away, down the street and into a tea shop. He made him take the penny and buy himself a cup of tea.

At first Yogaswami refused, struggling still with the storekeeper's

. . . .

Yogaswami often told the story of the blisteringly hot summer day they walked the 21 kilometers from Nallur to the ocean at Keerimalai. Just as Yogaswami was ready to enjoy the cool waters, his guru turned, declared, "We have bathed," and marched back, teaching his disciple a lesson in detachment.

miserliness and not wanting to partake of any refreshment that his guru
was not also enjoying. But Chellappaswami insisted. As Yogaswami drank
the black tea, it suddenly struck him that Chellappaswami had begged all
day only for his disciple's benefit, thereby revealing his infinite patience.
That man gave a penny along with his spite, and the guru took them both
away. But Chellappaswami was ready to go, so he downed the last sip of
tea and followed the guru happily back to Nallur.

What passed between them was theirs alone. Chellappaswami rarely
spoke straight to his disciple; his method was indirect, yet Yogaswami
understood him perfectly. He didn't ask questions about the spiritual
path, about Siva, about the Saiva Siddhanta philosophy, about anything,
but simply remained open to all that Chellappaswami offered.

There was never a question of whether Chellappaswami would give.
He gave and gave and gave to all who could possibly receive. All his life
Yogaswami exclaimed in wonder that in the very first look he received
from Chellappaswami, all the effects due from his past actions, all his
desires and all his attachments to the world, were erased. This and more
he eloquently expressed in "Hail to the Feet of the Satguru," enumerating
the treasures that Chellappaswami bestowed upon him:

> Hail to the feet of the teacher, who gave initiation and made me his,
> saying, "You are not the body; you are the atma!" Hail to the feet of the
> able master, acclaimed as the great *tapasvin*, who gave the sweet and
> noble saying, "Be and see!" Hail to the feet of the satguru who came
> and guarded me like a mother so that I need not frequent the homes of
> the miserly and mean! Hail to the feet of the true guru who came like
> a madman and took in his hands my wealth, my body and my life—all
> three! Hail to the holy dancing feet that have become what is within
> and without, body and life, you and I! Hail, ever hail, to the anklet-
> circled feet of the revered and bounteous one who bestowed on me
> the priceless blessing of living as I please!
>
> Hail to the feet of the satguru who placed his feet upon my head,
> that I might not be bewitched by the beauty of ladies bedecked with
> blossoming flowers! Hail to the feet of the perfect one who gave me
> the grace to prosper, by looking at me, his slave, and saying, "Why
> do you have doubt?" Hail to the sacred feet of the great giver who
> dispelled my fears and made me his and, by one word, caused me to
> be as a painted picture! Hail to the holy feet of the good *tapasvin* who
> revealed the whole world within the one word *Aum* and told me, "It is
> I." Hail to the feet of the precious one who at the proper time took me

as his own and showed to me the glorious dance at beautiful Nallur!
Hail, all hail, to the feet of the gracious master who, by his laugh,
saved me from wandering here and there in search of food and money!

Yogaswami witnessed many times the power of the guru to expiate the effects of deeds and magnify the spiritual qualities in the disciple. Yet, he observed that precious few people ever suspected what Chellappaswami had done for them. The magic of the guru occurred daily around Chellappaswami, but always without his taking on the outward persona of guru. Only to Yogaswami and Katiraveluswami, and perhaps a few others, did the sage of Nallur show anything of his deepest self. Often, when his two disciples were with him, he would dance around laughing and tease them, "No, you haven't caught me yet! No, you've not caught me yet!"

On occasion Chellappaswami would go into a shop in Jaffna town and demand certain things—a few cents, a coconut or some bananas—always persevering until he got what he wanted. Once, when Chellappaswami was making such an ultimatum, a devotee was standing nearby. The shopkeeper was shouting back at the guru, refusing to give and ordering him to get out. Chellappaswami continued with accelerating insistence. Embarrassed by the exchange, the devotee offered to purchase whatever the guru wanted, anything in the shop. But the moment he spoke up Chellappaswami turned on him, chased him out of the shop, returned to the owner and barked, "I am doing a service for you, and for that I require payment."

One festival day Yogaswami stood on the Nallur path, awash in eternal bliss due to the contentment that everything was in his hands. The Deity was being taken in procession round the temple amid an enormous crowd of a hundred thousand or more. Yogaswami said, "They are not taking umbrellas. Today the Swami (the Deity) being taken in procession is going to get drenched thoroughly."

Almost before Yogaswami completed the sentence, his guru roared from the distance, "Many are the people who have said such things on this Nallur road." It was a not-so-subtle correction from his guru—and in a dismissive voice. Yogaswami was humbled. When the clear blue sky turned cloudy, and rain began to pour minutes later, Yogaswami was openly embarrassed to see his petty prediction come true. Then and there Chellappaswami had uprooted the shoot of miracle-mongering that had begun to sprout in the disciple.

"I Beheld the Sivaguru"

By the fall of 1906, Yogaswami's inner search had reached full stride.
For several years he had been with his guru. The young man who once
walked forth and back from Kilinochchi to Nallur was now gone. In his
place stood a veteran swami, robust and barrel-chested, in threadbare
white cotton *veshti,* his thick, grey-flecked hair wound into a knot at
the back, his forehead glowing with *vibhuti,* his stride powerful and
purposeful.

A thick, black beard framed his high cheeks and soft brown eyes. Their
steely calm gave a glimpse of the man—tempered by obedience and alert
to vast depths of silence within. Those who looked into his eyes seemed
to see the cosmos itself, so deep and serene. Yogaswami was like a young
lion. His eyes were as sharp as steel. His 34-year-old body was lean and fit.
Having found the treasure of treasures, his guru, he was more eager than
ever to pursue the demanding inner path ahead.

Yogaswami undertook a rigorous routine of sadhana and *tapas* under

To prepare Yogaswami for his initiation, Chellappaswami required him, along   Page 177

with a second disciple, to sit on a large stone slab. For 40 days the pair meditated   Chapter 10

and fasted. To end the fast, the guru prepared a meal, handed a bowl to each and

then kicked the bowls from their hands, declaring, "That is all I have for you!"

. . . .

the guidance of his satguru. One *tapas* he performed was to rub chili paste on his body and meditate bare-chested in the midday sun—and the sun in Jaffna is intense—or prostrate and roll around the temple in the scorching hot sand, as devout penitents still do today. Vaithialingam reported that Yogaswami rolled his body in this way the full three kilometers from Columbuthurai to Nallur two or three times.

Between Columbuthurai and Nallur there is a charming Ganesha temple, the Kailasa Pillaiyar Koyil, where guru and shishya would meet and sit for hours. The odd couple also visited the Panrithalaichi Amman Temple, where they would cook *pongal*, a sweet rice dish, make their offerings to Amman, pray and meditate, then enjoy the *pongal* as their lunch before returning by foot to Nallur Temple. This was their pattern until early 1910. Ultimately, they no longer moved as guru and disciple, but as one being. Chellappaswami's harshness had waned. He was still stern, and few of his ample eccentricities ever left him, but as he neared his seventh decade he softened and no longer pushed Yogaswami away. Swami shares glimpses into these momentous days in "Darshan of the Master:"

In Nallur's noble town, where dwell great sages who no second thing perceive, I beheld the Sivaguru, Chellappan by name, whose state is such that he cannot be enmeshed in the lustful net of women's sparkling eyes. "All is well, my son," he lovingly declared.

From time's beginning until now, all men have made inquiry as to whether it is one or two or three. He who beyond the reach of all philosophy remains came as the glorious guru of Nallur and upon me high dignity bestowed.

The taintless one, who air, fire, water and the mighty earth became, whom none can comprehend, as the satguru came there face to face, and, having banished all my doubts, took me beneath his sway. Then indeed I gained the state whereof the *gunas* I was free.

In the golden land of Lanka, where birds start at the sound of falling water, in Nallur's town, where the son of Him who holds the fire is pleased to dwell as the divine guru, to bestow true life upon me, he appeared and showed to me his feet and made of me his man.

Change was in the air. Yogaswami sensed it, and saw it in Chellappa-swami's sometimes searching glance, less stern than expectant, which said more clearly than words what was to come next.

"That Is All I Have for You"

Chellappaswami's second disciple, Katiraveluswami, was around through these years. Yogaswami saw him infrequently. Brothers though they were, forged in one fire, they were rarely seen in the same place, and knew little more than each other's names. Still, in one another they saw themselves. When they met they would know and nod. Chellappaswami seemingly went to any length to keep them apart, out of sight and away from people.

During the week of Skanda Shashthi, Chellappaswami called his two shishyas together and led them to a quiet place "to meditate." Under a shady ironwood tree, within shouting distance of Nallur Temple, was a long slab of flat, chiselled granite, abandoned there years before. Chellap-paswami seated them and ordered them to go inside until he called them out. They sat on the bare stone and closed their eyes. Nallur's sage quietly walked away.

Later in the day he brought them each a pot of water. It was several days before he came again, bringing tea, leaving it beside them without a word. He came and went in this way for several weeks, guarding and watching, careful not to disturb their vigil. He assigned a senior devotee to watch after the two *tapasvins* as well. They grew thin from the fasting, haggard and sunburned, but neither moved from his seat, except for nature's call. After a month, they received only water.

Chellappaswami would come and stand by for hours at a time, looking from one to the other. Finally, on the fortieth day (some say it was less than forty days), the guru approached, solemnly brewed tea on the open fire and filled their metal cups. As they feebly raised them to drink, he abruptly swung out, knocking the cups from their hands. They watched unperturbed as the tea spilled onto the dry sand, startled but accepting of the guru's gesture.

He glared at them briefly, then began cooking a meal. The two watched with interest—it was a scene they had witnessed many times. He wove eating bowls from palm leaves while the pot of rice and curry boiled, an inimitable concoction some called Chellappa Stew. When the food was ready, he ladled out small portions and handed a steaming bowl to each. As they began to eat, he kicked the food from their hands, shouting, "That is all I have for you! Go and beg for your food." Though it shook them both to the core, they knew this was a rare spiritual initiation, a sign that their

Following the initiation of his two disciples, Chellappaswami sent them off in different directions, declaring that you can't tie two elephants to the same post.

training was complete. "Two elephants cannot be tied to one post," he announced, releasing them from their austere vigil.

Not many days passed before Katiraveluswami disappeared. It is said he went to India. Yogaswami also went missing. He had returned to Columbuthurai to rest and recover from his arduous fast. After one week, he walked to Nallur to be with Chellappaswami. Blissful and eager to see his guru, Swami entered the compound.

During the few minutes they sat together, Chellappaswami blessed him with the following words, "Look here! Look here! The city of Lanka I have given, I have given. The king's crown I have given, I have given, as long as the world exists, as long as the seas exist." This final *diksha* took place on the second Monday of the Tamil month of Panguni (March–April) in the year 1910. It was witnessed by Thiagar Ponniah, a devotee of Chellappaswami and neighbor of Yogaswami. Ever thereafter, Swami observed that day as his *diksha* day, which he described as a coronation, like being crowned a king.

"Yoganathan Is Dead"

Afterhis *diksha,*Yogaswami immediately set out on pilgrimage to the South. Perhaps he sensed that his guru was severing the cord that had connected them so closely. Perhaps he remembered Swami Vivekananda's pan-Indian trek following the death of his guru, Sri Ramakrishna. Or perhaps he simply took Chellappaswami's words literally. For whatever reasons, he stood up and left the place. With only the clothes on his back, as a *parivrajaka,* "wandering monk," he set out on a pilgrimage to Kataragama, Lord Murugan's shrine in the remote south of the island. He told no one he was leaving.

Circling Ceylon on Foot

He walked along back roads and country paths, proceeding east to the coast, then south to Mullaitivu and beyond, going where he pleased, stopping often at shrines and temples to meditate for hours or days. He walked along the coastal belt that skirts the eastern region, through Trincomalee, Sittandi, Batticaloa, Tirukkovil and Pottuvil. With no place to be next, nothing to do, he strolled the roads through towns and valleys like a monarch in his private garden.

His practice was to see himself as everything, and everything as himself. Life flowed gracefully through him and around him—everything came of its own accord. He didn't need to plan or calculate. There was always a hut or a temple *devasthanam* waiting for him at the end of the day. When he was hungry, someone was there offering him food or inviting him to their home for a meal. He had nothing to do but his inner work, and wherever he found himself he went in and in and in.

Swami was a silent witness to the agrarian life that occupied most of Lanka's people in those days. Farming and fishing were the mainstays, along with celebrations, festivals, trials and tribulations. He saw a beautiful world filled with Siva, where everyone did their work and where everything is as it should be at every point in time. And all he saw he took as his own. The passage of life before him was instructive, contrasting as it did his own renunciation.

And Chellappaswami made no decree. This was a deeply inner pilgrimage, a time of reorientation after Chellappaswami's unexpected severance of their almost daily companionship. Yogaswami had to redefine

. . . .

Yogaswami visited Polonnaruwa, 140 kilometers north of Kandy, where the famed 46-foot-long reclining Buddha rests. It is said the carving depicts the moment Buddha entered nirvana.

his life in light of his guru's decree. All along the way, he prepared the ground for the work he would do in his lifetime, developing intuitive powers and immersing himself again and again in the Self, the Absolute Reality that was his formless home.

The majority faith on the island was Buddhism, then as now, and he encountered Buddhist people frequently during his travels, something that had rarely happened in the Hindu-majority North where he had lived his entire life. In later years, when Buddhists came to see him, he often spoke to them like a *bhikku,* quoting verbatim from Buddha's sermons.

On this pilgrimage, Yogaswami embraced the whole of Ceylon from the inside out. He fell in love with its tropical splendor, its geographical beauty and its human diversity. He saw and heard everything people did on his estate and ever after spoke of "my island," "my people," "my saints and sages."

In later years, if one of his devotees had some business to do with the government, Yogaswami would assure him, "No need for concern—my government, my Prime Minister, my Finance Minister." He sang:

Lanka is our land! There is no male or female, no sameness or diversity. Heaven and earth are one. This is the language of the great! Come now and be happy; we will rule the world!

If a man came to Yogaswami for blessings, having been transferred to some far-off province, Swami would tell him about the temples and shrines in that area. He knew the land, the legends and local people like he knew his own village. He would describe the shrines to visit, when to go and what kinds of prayers to offer. "I meditated there for several days," he would say. "You must go there often." Only gradually, through the years, did the great range and depth of experiences that his pilgrimage brought him come to light.

It was two months before he reached Kokkilai. He was in no hurry. Two weeks later he was in Trincomalee. From there he went inland to the hill country, to Polonnaruwa and Sigiriya, then out again to Batticaloa. He met many holy men along the way—saints, sages, fakirs. He sat with yogis living deep in the jungle or in caves in the hills. He visited Buddhist monasteries and met Sufi saints and Christian clergy. Everywhere, he felt at home; everywhere, he was welcomed.

On the road one day, he met a Muslim holy man. They walked together through the afternoon, and before they parted the saint sang for him a song in praise of God of such purity and beauty that Yogaswami never forgot it. He sang it often throughout his life. When he did, he would describe this saint to his devotees.

Near a crossing of the Gal Oya River he came upon seven fakirs who lived in huts in the jungle, practicing austerities to gain yogic powers. They invited him to join in their psychic pursuits, and performed several tricks to entice him, but he did not accept. A moment later, they materialized a huge, wild boar. Squealing and frothing, it charged straight at him, blood dripping from its jaws—he didn't have a chance to save himself. He didn't flinch; neither did he steel himself. He watched; and just as the beast barely touched him, it vanished as quickly as it had appeared. He thanked them for the fun and continued across the river.

Passing through a Muslim village in the Batticaloa district, he encountered an Islamic mystic named Thakarar who had divined Swami's inner thoughts and, desiring to honor the wandering holy man, invited him to a feast. Seeing the Hindu monk hesitate, he asked if he had any conflict with Islam. Remembering Chellappaswami's aloofness to caste and creed, Yogaswami joined the feast. Later he reported that, contrary to Islamic practice, the women joined with the men in hosting him. Thakarar gave him a bangle, saying, "Wear this amulet and go. You will not incur any difficulties." Years later Swami spoke of that incident: "So long as that bangle was on my wrist, the Muslims treated me very respectfully. One night I removed it and left it in the rest house where I stayed, thinking, 'Why do I need this?'"

Near Tirukkovil he met a lone fakir who lived in a cave. Taking shelter from the rain, they sat and talked for several hours. As Swami prepared to leave, the fakir presented him with a magical tin can, a symbol of what he had accomplished in the eleven years he had lived there. He told his guest, "Keep the can, and everything you want will miraculously come to you." Yogaswami graciously accepted the gift and went on his way. As soon as Swami was out of sight, he threw the can away.

In mid-July, about six months into his journey, Yogaswami reached the southern coast and began the trek inland to Kataragama—120 kilometers on harsh and difficult trails through the dense jungle of the Monaragala and Bibile area, which is home to the aboriginal tribe known as Vedda.

Yogaswami later narrated to Vallipuram, a schoolteacher in Jaffna, his experience about some of the trials he faced, which S. Ampikaipaakan captured in his biography:

I was walking towards Kataragama, and as I was approaching Mattakalappu suddenly I got fever. I could not bear the pain, so I rested underneath a tree and lay down on the ground with a stone as a pillow. In the morning the fever was gone, and there was a 25 cent coin on the stone pillow. I took that to a store, ate dosai, and continued to walk. Anaikutti Swami (perhaps Sitanaikutti Swami) saw me on the way. He came running and embraced me, saying, "Because I saw you, it will rain now." I responded, "Let the rain come after one hour." It rained indeed after one hour.

Later on the way I had to cross a river but it had flooded. Unable to cross, I made a shallow furrow in the riverbank sand and slept for three days. On the third day, some natives came to this side of the river on a catamaran. They cooked food for me and called, "O fasting nobleman," to wake me up. They fed me a meal and took me to the other side of the river with them in their boat."

Soon the trail was crowded with thousands of devotees on their way to Murugan's shrine for Esala Perahera, the annual fourteen-day festival that ends on the full moon night of July-August. Each devotee carried a bundle of supplies: food, camphor and simple bedding. Yogaswami carried only a coconut, the traditional offering every pilgrim brings. He slept in the open and ate nothing for the three days it took to reach the remote shrine. There he spent most hours of the night on the sacred hilltop in meditation and communion with Lord Murugan, and the daytime hours around the jungle shrine and ashrams.

Meanwhile, Yoganathan's relatives in Jaffna, frantic over his long absence, were making every attempt to find him. He was a sannyasin, so they were used to not seeing him for weeks at a time, but he had never left them for so long. Family ties are strong in Jaffna, and people keep track of one another no matter what they decide to do with their lives. Finally, after postponing it as long as he could, Chinnaiya arranged with one of Chellappaswami's oldest devotees to accompany him to Nallur. He thought perhaps "the mad one" might know the nephew's whereabouts.

They found Chellappaswami sitting alone on the *teradi* steps weaving fans, talking. Watching them come up the street, he put his work aside. They apologized for disturbing him, praised his fans, remarked on the weather, hemmed and hawed and then nervously asked their question, "Where is Yoganathan? We have not seen him for months." Chellappaswami shrugged and went back to weaving: "Oh, Yoganathan. He's

Yoganathan's aunt, Muthupillai, was shocked when Chellappaswami told the family he was dead. They held his funeral rites, only to later discover he was in fact alive.

dead." Realizing there was nothing more to that conversation, the family left in dismay. Badly shaken by the news, they tried to disbelieve it for a long time. Aunt Muthupillai took it especially hard. They waited several months, hoping Swami would appear, but they finally gave up; their nephew was gone. They performed what funeral rites they could without the body, and disposed of his personal effects.

Meanwhile, Yogaswami was wandering about the isle of Lanka, seeing everything for the first time. He said all his life that it was the finest of pilgrimages. Kataragama was all he had heard it to be. The spirit and power of the place at festival times is intoxicating. The shrine lies in a wilderness of nearly impenetrable jungle, but this only adds to its attraction. A sublime, solemn atmosphere hangs over this valley ringed by seven sacred hills. The name Kataragama is uttered with respect by Hindus, Buddhists and Muslims alike.

Empty and quiet much of the year, Kataragama erupts overnight at festival times into the most intense activity, then ending as quickly as it started. Filled with thoughts of the mercy and power of the Deity, people regularly perform special penances, receive blessings, make promises, take vows and attain to spiritual heights that don't seem possible elsewhere.

Swami spent an unknown time at the jungle temple—a few days, some claim, while others believe it was months. Here, at the Murugan Temple, he performed meditation and practiced "being still" *(Summa iru)*. Later he sang this brief song of praise:

O Murugan of Kataragama, playing with your upraised spear, rid me of that foe, my karma! To you, with faith, I now draw near. Our Lord with foot in dance uplifted, who has an eye upon His brow, you, as our God, to us has gifted. At your feet with anklets ringed I bow. Everywhere your holy faces, your eyes, ears, hands and feet, I see. O Lord who Kataragama graces, wherever you are, there I will be!

From Kataragama, Yogaswami headed west toward Colombo, following the coast, navigating through Magama, Hambantota, Matara and Dondra Head, Galle and Kalutara. He kept a leisurely schedule, walking through hundreds of villages, talking to people, watching life go on around him. He stopped less often here, for the South is a predominantly Sinhalese area, and there are only a few Hindu temples.

· ·

Just as Swami Vivekananda explored his beloved India, Yogaswami's 1910 adventure took him throughout the island, where he saw and celebrated the spirit of the people, the places of pilgrimage and the daily rhythms of life in Lanka's villages and fields.

Galle

Colombo

Matara

Adam's Peak

Maskeliya

Matale

Kandy

Caves of
Jailani

Hambantota

Bibile

Kataragama

Chenkala

Batticaloa

Tirukkovil

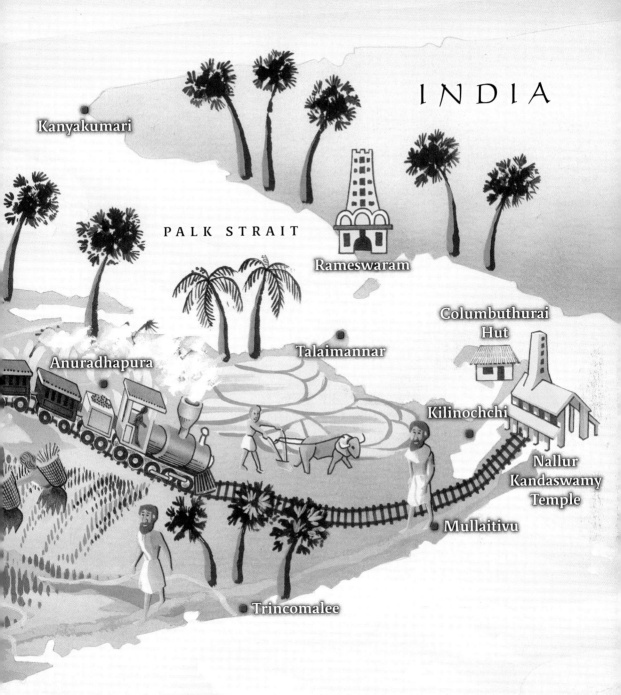

INDIA

Kanyakumari

PALK STRAIT

Rameswaram

Columbuthurai
Hut

Talaimannar

Anuradhapura

Kilinochchi

Nallur
Kandaswamy
Temple

Mullaitivu

Trincomalee

CEYLON

He stayed every night in a different village, invariably as a guest in a Tamil home. During his six-week return journey, he underwent severe hardship, surviving only on alms, walking through jungles and facing wild animals. Due to flooded, muddy rivers, Swami often did not have proper drinking water and fell sick with malaria. With great effort, he rose each day to march another twenty or thirty kilometers, forcing his body to perform its duty, ignoring its complaints.

Finally, with Lord Murugan's blessings, he arrived in the Colombo district, the bustling port capital of Ceylon. There, on the road, he received the blessings of one of Lanka's most renowned siddhas, known as Anaikutti Swami, "baby elephant," by virtue of his generous girth. Reaching out his arm, the siddha handed the weary wayfarer five cents, saying, "This is the trunk [of Ganesha] giving confidence to you!"

He stayed for a few days at Kochikade, where he begged for his meals and slept on the roadside along with the coal-handling railway workers. As a beggar, he approached the well-known Sir Ponnampalam Arunachalam, who gave him ten cents.

He spent one month in and around Colombo, the island's largest city, then several weeks inland between Kotte and Ratnapura. From there he took the rising roads to the mountainous town of Kandy and south to Nuwara Eliya, the hill country center of tea plantations. He walked along village paths and roads to Kurunegala and all the way to Puttalam, near the coast again. He stayed in Anuradhapura for several weeks, bringing all the threads of his pilgrimage together, then continued on toward Matale.

The night before Swami arrived in Matale, Tiru Saravanamuthu, overseer of the town's public works department, had a holy dream in which Lord Murugan appeared and instructed him, "Receive the saint who is returning by foot from Kataragama, famished and wearing tattered clothes. Give him all that he needs. Treat him well. We are one and the same. His return to Jaffna is a great gift to the people."

The next day Saravanamuthu met the mendicant who fit the description in his dream and, after inquiring as to who he was, invited Swami to his house with immense joy. He spoke excitedly about his vision as he practically dragged Swami inside. Yogaswami smiled, listened and let himself be hosted. Saravanamuthu gave him a new *veshti* and shawl and invited him to bathe. After a luxurious meal, Swami was shown the guest room, where he spent a restful, rejuvenating two days.

In the background, peeking out at Swami whenever he had a chance, was Saravanamuthu's nephew, a young boy who was so captivated by Swami's darshan on that fateful day that he served him with utmost devotion his entire life. It was A. Thillyampalam, who four decades later Swami assigned as the architect of his Sivathondan Nilayams in Jaffna and Chenkaladi.

Early in the morning of the third day, Swami decided to proceed the rest of the way to Jaffna by train. Declining the presents and a thick bundle of rupees his host urged on him, Yogaswami accepted just enough money for a train ticket. Yogaswami later remarked, "Lord Murugan was looking after me well through Saravanamuthu." As a parting gesture of gratitude, Swami sang the following verse:

Appanum ammaiyum neeye! Ariya sahothararum neeye!
Opil manaiviyum neeye! Otharum maintharum neeye!
Seppil arasarum neeye! Thevathi thevarrum neeye!
Ippuviyellam neeye! Ennai aandathum neeye!"

Father and mother are you. Dear brothers and sisters are you.
Incomparable wife is you. Precious sons are you. Royal potentates
are you. The devas and all Gods are you. This great Earth is
you; and that which guards and governs me is also you.

Under the Illupai Tree
The train ride to Jaffna took two days: back through Anuradhapura, then north the next morning 190 kilometers to Jaffna Station. Yogaswami arrived as he had left nearly a year before—with nothing but the clothes on his back. He walked straight to Nallur Temple and threw himself at the feet of Chellappaswami. Having completed his travels, Yogaswami was fulfilled, exuberant, his heart overflowing with love for his guru.

Now Chellappaswami gave his successor a new sadhana, "You go and hold the *illupai* root," "*Nee poy illupai verai pidi.*" Yogaswami was not eager to leave his guru, and he lingered awkwardly. Seeing Chellappaswami's clay meal pot which lay nearby, he thought, "What a great blessing it would be to have it as a sacred artifact." Suddenly Chellappaswami roared like thunder and scoffed, "So, this is your bondage?" He threw the pot on the ground, shattering it into pieces, a gesture taken as Chellappaswami's final sundering of the guru-disciple dualism that it represented to his shishya.

Following his guru's edict, Yogaswami returned to Columbuthurai, taking his seat three meters from a road crossing, at the base of a mature *illupai* tree (Madhuca longifolia), a hardwood species prized for its fuel oil and medicinal attributes. Its shade and protection from the elements would be important for him in the years to come. In pounding rain or scorching sun he sat immobile, immersed in his inner being, oblivious to the outside world. A Pillaiyar temple stands just across the road. From that point onward, from 1911 to 1915, Chellappaswami did not allow Yogaswami to be with him.

On one occasion Yogaswami visited Chellappaswami's hut. Suddenly the sage emerged, shouting and swearing at him to get out of there. Realizing that his guru was about to start throwing things, Yogaswami turned on his heels and retreated the way he came. "Stand on your own two feet!" the sage bellowed after him.

Chellappaswami would come to the *illupai* tree occasionally, observe his disciple and go. Once, when his guru came, Yogaswami stood up and went to worship him. Chellappaswami glared, scolding, "What! Are you seeing duality? Try to see unity." Chastened by these words, Swami remained rooted to the spot.

News travels faster than the wind in Jaffna. Before Swami had left Nallur Temple, his Uncle Chinnaiya and Aunt Muthupillai had heard from a dozen people about his reappearance. They were astonished, perplexed and happy all at once. They hurried to the *illupai* tree to see for themselves. There he was, in rapt meditation. They hardly recognized him at first; he had changed so much. They called out to him: "Yoganathan!" He did not answer, or even open his eyes. But it was him, alright. And he was very much alive.

They talked the matter over with friends and neighbors late into the night and decided that Chinnaiya, Muthupillai and her son Vaithialingam would return to the tree at dawn to speak with Yoganathan. When they arrived, he was still deep in samadhi. They left a tray of fruit for him and set off for Nallur by bullock cart to confront Chellappaswami again.

Chinnaiya ranted all the way about how strange and cruel it was for Chellappaswami to tell them their nephew was dead. He was bold in approaching the sage this time. He complained that they had conducted Yoganathan's funeral and finished the period of mourning, only to find he actually wasn't dead at all! They resented the lie. "How could you say that?" Chellappaswami rode out the storm. Holding his ground, he retorted stoically, "What I told you was not a lie. Yoganathan is dead."

That enigmatic response, delivered with such calm finality, left them speechless. Knowing that further discussion would be useless, they shook their heads in dismay and left. Pondering the sage's words for a long time,

. . . .

For years Yogaswami followed the difficult sadhana of meditating for three days at the base of an illupai tree in Columbuthurai. On the fourth day he would rest and move about, before returning for another round. In 1921, devotees cajoled him into taking up residence in a nearby thatched hermitage.

they slowly began to understand that he was referring to a spiritual transition rather than a physical one. With Chellappaswami's insight unfolding inside them, they perceived for themselves in the weeks and months ahead that, indeed, their nephew was a different person. And with his puzzling ruse, Chellappaswami had magically severed all remaining attachment they had for Yoganathan. He had renounced family life, and they had been forced to renounce him.

Adopting a Humble Hut

For some years Yogaswami made the *illupai* tree his preferred place of sadhana, his roofless roadside hermitage. Those who were alive in those days told of how he sometimes looked out from fierce eyes that struck people with terror. If anyone dared approach—and few did, they were so afraid—he would grab a stick and chase them away. When not immersed in his spiritual disciplines, he would wander the area around Jaffna and visit his favorite sites. S. Ampikaipaakan shares:

> For a long time Swamigal never went far from Jaffna after he came back from His walking pilgrimage to Kataragama. Swamigal used to say, "I don't have permission to go out of Jaffna Bay." As far as we know, only after 1928, Swamigal used to go to Kandy and Colombo. He took those journeys for the benefit of devotees living there. The advocate M.S. Elayathamby used to accompany him. Swamigal considered that he was the right person.

Just a year before Chellappaswami's mahasamadhi, Yogaswami moved into a hut in the garden of a home near the *illupai* tree. This hut, which would be his humble ashram for the next fifty years, was tied to the history of Nanniyar, the man who welcomed Kadaitswami on the island of Mandaitivu when Swami first arrived in Ceylon. Nanniyar had let Kadaitswami stay in this very hut, became a staunch devotee and maintained a shrine for the guru.

In Chellappaswami's day, Nanniyar, a large, muscular, slow-witted fellow, used the hut as a tea shop, not far from his temporary home in Ariyalai. He was devoted to Chellappaswami as well, but the sadhu ignored him, as he ignored everyone, whenever the shopkeeper came for blessings. Nanniyar remained determined to get what he wanted.

One day when Chellappaswami was walking by his shop, Nanniyar, drunk at the time, rushed out, grabbed the guru and dragged him, kicking and screaming, to the compound behind his shop, tied him to a post and threatened him with a knife, saying he would not free him until blessings were received. To Chellappaswami's horror, Nanniyar bathed him, managed to shave his head and with frenzied zeal conducted his guru puja, passing a flame of camphor before his captive to implore the master's grace.

All the while, Chellappaswami, not one to endure such things, protested vehemently in the strongest language—screaming, scolding and yelling for help. Finally, from inside her house on the same property, Mrs. Tangamma, the wife of Nanniyar's landlord, heard the ruckus and ran outside. The scene was as bizarre as it was farcical. Others gathered to see what was happening, and together the group, which by that time included Yogaswami, untied the captive guru. Chellappaswami fled, bellowing as he retreated indignantly. Nanniyar, it seems, was satisfied and didn't bother Chellappaswami again. In a way, Chellappaswami had met his match in Nanniyar. The guru, who had assiduously avoided being worshiped his whole life, lost on that day, and, as far as history knows, only on that day.

In 1914, Tangamma and her family noticed Yogaswami spending day after day under the *illupai* tree not far from the now-vacant tea shop, which was just a simple hut with mud walls, cow-dung floor and cadjan roof. Swami was there nearly every day, despite the hottest sun and driving rains. It occurred to them to invite him to move into the hut. They waited for a good time to approach the formidable sadhu. For days they read the subtle signs and studied his expression to ascertain if maybe it was the opportune moment to present their idea. Finally, they did.

Tangamma, her husband Thirugnanasampanthar, Tangamma's uncle Vallipuram and his wife Nagavalli together approached Yogaswami. Tangamma spoke: "How much longer are you going to sit at this junction, Swamigal?" Gesturing toward the hut, she bravely offered, "This hut lies vacant. You can stay there as long as you like in peace." Beseeching him with a pure and innocent heart, she recounted to Yogaswami the day Nanniyar had captured and worshiped Chellappaswami on that same spot and submitted how great a blessing it would be to the family if he would stay there now. He could make it his ashram. Everything he wanted and needed would be provided. They would see to his needs and stay out of his way when he wanted solitude. They referred to Nanniyar gingerly because, in a sense, they were trying to do the same thing he had done with Chellappaswami.

Yogaswami refused the offer for a time but finally relented, conceding he could use the hut when he was in Columbuthurai. From that day onwards, Tangamma, her son Tirunavukarasu, Mrs. Tirunavukarasu and their children performed selfless service to Yogaswami and all who visited his ashram. This humble hermitage became his abode until the day he attained *mahasamadhi*.

Many times during his life Swami declared, "I'm going away and not coming back to this place." Three or four days later he would be back. He once said, "Chellappaswami would not let me leave this place. He sent me back." He laughed, "Nanni's devotion to the guru has captured us here." He often spoke of it as "Chellappaswami's hut."

"A Miracle Will Happen Here Tonight"

In 1915, at age 75, Chellappaswami fell ill. When he developed a cold and consequent inflammation of the joints, his relatives treated him with herbal baths. He was sick for about two weeks. During that time, Yogaswami did not go to see him. That upset the devotees who were looking after Chellappaswami. For several years Swami had, from their point of view, been pushed to the outside of any circle gathered around Chellappaswami. Of course, his disappearance was by decree of his guru, but not all acknowledged that. Knowing that Chellappaswami was nearing the end of his life, they pestered Yogaswami to go see him, perhaps expecting some dramatic exchange that would indicate without a doubt that it was Yogaswami whom Chellappaswami had initiated as the guru to follow him.

One day, out of deepening concern, Yogaswami did go to Chellappaswami's hut. As Swami neared the compound, Chellappaswami roared, *"Yuuradaa padalaiyil?"* ("Who is at the gate?"), words not unlike the satguru's first statement to him, "Who are you?" Then he shouted, *"Paaradaa veliyil ninru"* ("Stand outside and be a witness").

Obediently, Swami left the compound and walked back to his hut. Intently aware that nations around the globe were locked in the bloody battles of World War I, Yogaswami reflected to others, "Many are the kings who are dying now," among them his spiritual king lying at death's door. Two days later, in the month of Panguni (March–April), on Ashvini *nakshatra,* the illumined sage and spiritual giant Chellappaswami attained *mahasamadhi*.

That morning he had told a neighbor who looked after his needs, "Tonight a great miracle will take place in this hut. Will you come?" But the neighbor did not go that night. The next morning he found Chellappaswami on the ground at the door to his hut. He had left his body in an unusual pose, one finger in his mouth and his legs frozen in a posture resembling Lord Nataraja's blissful dance, called *ananda tandava*. His

* * *

Chellappaswami invited people to his hut in 1915, telling them that "a miracle will happen tonight." That miracle turned out to be his Grand Departure. His body was cremated the following day.

Grand Departure that day was as strangely wonderful as his life had been.

Earlier he had ordered that his body be cremated, knowing that some would insist on interring him in a samadhi chamber, as is often done for enlightened saints and sages. His devotees carried out his instructions, scattering their guru's ashes in the sea at Keerimalai.

Without Chellappaswami, his followers felt helpless and lost. Many became despondent, discouraged. Everyone noticed that Yogaswami was not present for the last rites. Two of the men who helped with the cremation went drinking afterwards. The alcohol inflamed their anger toward Swami and made them bold enough to confront him. They gathered up their courage as they entered his compound, then one called out, "Our guru has left his body, and you did not even see fit to join us in our final respects to him!"

Yogaswami suddenly appeared in the doorway of his hut, picked up a stick and chased them out his gate and down the road. Running at full tilt, they took a turn into the village headman's yard and dove headlong into a stack of hay to hide. Yogaswami had since gone back to his evening. But their adventure was just beginning.

As they waited a moment until the coast was clear, suddenly the hay caught fire. They were both smoking cigars! They jumped up and scrambled to put out the fire. Neighbors came with buckets of water and extinguished the flames. The headman turned the two culprits over to the constable, and they spent the night in jail.

Such was Swami's inscrutable way. These men, like others who thought as they did, had no idea of what was going on in Swami's mind. He fully lived the spiritual life that pandits only talk about. He knew the secrets of life and death, knew that Chellappaswami was still very much aware in his inner world, that subtle world of light. Death was no end to things. He had simply discarded his old, used-up body.

That evening Swami sat in deep communion with his beloved guru, just as certainly as when they shared the *bilva* tree's shade at Nallur. Why attend the funeral? He had received no inner orders to go, and in fact Chellappaswami had asked him to stand apart. He was not one to do anything simply because social propriety dictated it. T. Sivayogapathy relates:

In the same spirit, Yogaswami never encouraged anyone to build a memorial ashram to his guru. Instead, he told his devotees to go to Sivathondan Nilayam meditation hall and meditate with devotion to enjoy the darshan of all gurus of the lineage. Yogaswami propounded: "Remain in one place with devotion," *"Onrai patri ohr ahatheh iru."*

Hence, no shrine was built for Chellappaswami during Yogaswami's lifetime. Later, devotees in the Nallur area built a simple shrine honoring the sage within the hut where he had lived and attained *mahasamadhi*. In 1982 Satguru Sivaya Subramuniyaswami had the hut rebuilt as a small, temple-like structure, with concrete walls and metal roof. After that, hundreds of people gathered there on special days, in the shadow of Nallur Temple, to sing the glories of the Kailasa Parampara.

God Realization

In the last half of 1915, in the wake of Chellappaswami's great departure, Yogaswami threw himself into a pattern of intensive sadhana. With his back to the giant *illupai* trunk, he would fast and sit in samadhi for days at a time. He slept without appearing to sleep, and on occasion it was noted that he spent nights meditating in the Columbuthurai cemetery, a common habit of the siddhas and Nathas. Of this spirit of renunciation he later wrote: "Let go the rope! Just go about here and there. See everything. Be a witness. Die before you die!"

Dr. T. Nallanathan, a strong Saivite and a close devotee, recalls Swami's comments to him about that period:

It was in 1922 that Swami told me for the first time how he attained God consciousness. His sadhana was indeed very strenuous. In a week, the first three days and nights would be spent in nirvikalpa samadhi; the fourth day was the only free day in the week, when he would have some food and talk to friends. The next three days and nights again he would be immersed in nirvikalpa samadhi. The culmination of this strict and strenuous sadhana was *sayujya* samadhi, perpetual God consciousness, even in the waking state. At the end of six months the heavenly joy temporarily disappeared and the mundane consciousness was indeed a step lower down. He gave up his regular sadhana and since then let this God consciousness trickle down to his physical brain in a natural way.

Yogaswami had joined that most elite of all groups, a handful of souls in each historical epoch who have realized Parasiva, the Absolute, the Self of all. Those who have had, and continue to have, the experience of Self Realization cannot explain it. Anything they say about the Self God does not satisfy them as true. Since the Self is beyond the mind, beyond even the most pure and refined state of consciousness, it is impossible to use the language of the mind to convey it. Most realized ones talk little about that experience, which is not an experience at all. One can feel them as different; the space around them is charged. Somehow they are not in the world in the same way that other people are. That darshan emanating from them is regarded by a Saivite as the truest guide on the path. The devotee opens himself more and more to the darshan of a great soul and, no matter where he is on the path, it carries him within.

Yogaswami's disciple, Sivaya Subramuniyaswami, who was not yet born, would later attempt a description of that ineffable reality:

The Self is timeless, causeless and formless. Therefore, being That, it has no relation whatsoever to time, space and form. Form is in a constant state of creation, preservation and destruction within space, thus creating consciousness called time, and has no relationship to timelessness, causelessness or formlessness. The individual soul, when mature, can make the leap from the consciousness of space-time-causation into the timeless, causeless, formless Self. This is the ultimate maturing of the soul on this planet.

The inmost center of consciousness—located only after the actinic forces dissolve concepts of form and even consciousness being conscious of itself—is found to be within the center of an energy-spinning force field. This center—intense in its existence, [with] consciousness only on the perimeter of the inside hub of this energy field—vitalizes all externalized form.

Losing consciousness into the center of this energy field catalyzes one beyond form, time, space. The spinning hub of actinic energy, recreating, preserving and dissipating form, quickly establishes consciousness again. However, this is then a new consciousness, the continuity of consciousness having been broken in the nirvikalpa samadhi experience. Essentially, the first total, conscious break in the evolution of man is the first nirvikalpa samadhi experience. Hence, a new evolution begins anew after each such experience. The evolutional patterns overlap and settle down like rings of light, one layer upon another, causing intrinsic changes in the entire nature and experiential pattern of the experiencer."

Stories were told that after Yogaswami first realized the Self he jumped up and ran forty kilometers in jubilant celebration of the tremendous energy of that breakthrough. Slowly, Parasiva became home base to him, as he returned to that ultimate reality day after day, letting that realization penetrate and infuse every atom of his body, every facet of his mind. No longer was he an outer person going into the Self; he was an inner person coming out of the Self and then going back in again. He was that Self, the All in all, and so was everyone else, even if they were unaware of it.

He came out of these spiritual reveries, walked, radiated the light that was so intense within him, and occasionally sat to write Tamil verses giving expression to his world of revelation and realization. In the years ahead he composed these profound verses in shrines and homes, and in the Columbuthurai Vinayagar Temple across the road from his *illupai* tree. He sang of his experiences in this Natchintanai:

> I climbed upon the platform of Omkara. There I saw nothing, Kuthambai; there I saw nothing, my dear. I was blessed with the bliss of sleep without sleeping. I remained *summa*, Kuthambai; I remained *summa*, my dear.
>
> Ego disappeared; happiness disappeared. I became He, Kuthambai; I became He, my dear. I have attained the flawless *nishdai* that ever stays unchanging. There is no "I," no "you," Kuthambai; There is no "I," no "you," my dear.
>
> I became like a painted image, Kuthambai; I became like a painted image, my dear, unable to say whether it is "one" or "two." I attained the feet of the Lord, Kuthambai; I attained the feet of the Lord, my dear, which cannot be described in terms of "good" and "bad."
>
> The Creator, Who is the Eye within the eye, I saw and rejoiced, Kuthambai; I saw Him and rejoiced, my dear. Whether macrocosm and microcosm are "one" or "two" I was unaware, Kuthambai; I was unaware, my dear.
>
> The six chakras and the five states of consciousness entirely disappeared, Kuthambai; they entirely disappeared, my dear. By seeing without seeing, the lotus feet I worshiped without worshiping, Kuthambai; I worshiped without worshiping, my dear.

Yogaswami, the Young Guru

By this time many people had taken note of Yogaswami, but a rare few knew of the spiritual power he carried. Chellappaswami did not make it known that he had ordained Yogaswami. He made nothing of it, thus allowing Swami the luxury of obscurity so he might unfold the power of that initiation within himself. But this secret, like so many, was hard to hide. Inthumathy Amma shares:

> In those early days there were still a few devotees who traveled from Columbuthurai to worship Chellappaswami. They knew through distinct signs that Chellappaswami had given all his wealth and blessings to Siva Yogar. Hence, even though they treated Siva Yogar as a colleague, they had great, deep-rooted devotion for him within their hearts. Like the great devotion they had for Chellappar, their great devotion to Siva Yogar was concealed in their hearts, and outwardly they behaved like friends. Among them there was one devotee, Thuraiappah by name, who could not conceal his eagerness. He was accustomed to singing *Devarams* in the Nallur Temple and at the steps of the chariot house. He began to come to the hut and sing *Devaram* hymns in Siva Yogar's presence. This was the first significant act in those early days to show that the hut was the temple of a living God.

Ratna Ma Navaratnam describes Swami's life during this period:

> From 1915 onwards, Swami led the life of a renounced recluse; he would be seen frequenting the *illupai* tree at the school junction in Columbuthurai, the Nallur *teradi*, the Ariyalai hermitage, the Thundi Crematorium, the Esplanade and the byways of Grand Bazaar. These were the years of gestation and samadhi experiences.

According to T. Sivayogapathy, son of A. Thillyampalam, Yogaswami met frequently with his strong devotees, such as M.S. Elayathamby, A. Ambalavanar, Mudaliyar S. Thiruchittampalam, M. Sabaratnasingi, V. Muthukumaru, Kalaipulavar K. Navaratnam, T.N. Suppiah, C. Mylvaganam and Pulavar A. Periyathambipillai, having discussions under the *illupai* tree or in his nearby hut. This began in 1916.

. . . .

Following his satguru's mahasamadhi, Yogaswami led a quiet life of sadhana and samadhi, years when he was seen but not known.

Jaffna had a long history of philosophical and devotional accomplishment, and those in the community who were both seekers and immersed
in spiritual literature gravitated to Yogaswami, who was well versed in
monistic Saiva Siddhanta. They found him a rare alloy of knowledge and
realization, and were inspired that he encouraged their intellectual and
teaching pursuits. Among them was a lawyer, Tiruvilangam, from Jaffna,
an authority in Saiva Siddhanta who met Yogaswami in 1920. He authored
several books related to *Sivajnanasiddiyar, Sivaprakasam, Tiruppugal*
and *Kandar Alankaram.* At the time he passed away in Colombo, Yogaswami ran out of his ashram and looked towards the sky and shouted,
"Tiruvilangam is now mixed with Sivasothy! ('Light of Siva')."

Another, Sri T. Kumaraswami Pulavar of Kokuvil, specialized in Saiva
philosophy, giving lectures and satsangs in temples and later authoring
a few books under Yogaswami's direction. Sri Somasunthera Pulavar of
Navaly, an authority in Hinduism and Tamil literature, similarly served
the Saiva cause.

Yogaswami loved the beauty and profundity of Tamil literature and
through these men was able to bring a small renaissance to the Jaffna
people. His own poems drew deeply on the ancient scriptures, while adding an illuminating directness that to this day commands the deepest
respect among Tamil literati.

Life at the Columbuthurai Ashram

One devotee fondly recalls Swami's early days in his hermitage:

> Even after devotees began coming in great numbers, Swami would
> become rapt in meditation at will, as though they weren't even there.
> On Sivaratri it was his custom to meditate through the night. A
> few devotees who had the good fortune to be with Swami at these
> times saw a light shine where Swami's body should have been. They
> believed that this was the divine light of his true, blemishless form.
> Even those who could not see this shining light were amazed to
> behold the erect, still form of Swami, seated like a statue. His golden
> form was as still as his umbrella in the corner. On one occasion when
> Swami sat so motionless during meditation, a crow came flying in,
> rested on his head for awhile and flew away.

That hut was an unimposing dwelling with mud walls, thatched roof and
a clay floor covered with cow dung, all set in a sandy compound. Inside
the single room, a low wall partitioned off a quarter of the space to the

right. Here Swami kept his meager possessions and food supplies. On the south side of the room, to the right as one entered, was a wooden plank on which Swami slept, meditated and also sat to receive visitors—a five-centimeter-thick plank of neem (*Azadirachta indica,* a species famed for repelling insects) that had small feet to keep it fifteen centimeters off the floor, away from crawling critters.

For a few years, there was a snake pit in the corner of the room where he slept, and others in the compound, not an uncommon thing in that arid region. In those days, Yogaswami slept on the dung floor in the small partitioned-off space. One night he awoke to find a snake by his side. Confronted with the deadly serpent, he made swift assurances, "It seems that you had best sleep here by yourself. I will go and occupy the other side." From that day onward, he slept in the main area of the room.

For some time Swami did not allow anyone to light a lamp inside the hut, though camphor was permitted to bring dim respite from the dark. And he never allowed anyone to modernize his hermitage, preferring its austere style, though every other year he allowed a few close devotees to re-thatch the roof, which they did within a day's time. He would be driven by car to one of his favorite places while they took off the old thatch and replaced it with fresh materials, then cleaned the entire interior and put all of Swami's things neatly back into place. By 6pm, when he returned, the work was done. In the early twenties he consented to cementing the floor of the hut due to the increasing number of snakes coming up through the floor.

The *illupai* tree was 40 meters east of his hut, on the other side of a small lane named Swamiyar Road. The north side of the hut bordered Main Road, on the other side of which stood Columbuthurai Maha Vidyalayam (school) and a Pillaiyar temple.

In an alcove in the boundary wall of the temple's garden, Yogaswami kept and worshiped the divine sandals of Chellappaswami. Later he installed his guru's *tiruvadi* inside the hut, in the northwest corner of the room, on a pedestal that also supported a small standing oil lamp which he kept constantly lit. Each morning after his bath at the well, he adorned the sandals with flowers and silently offered burning camphor to his satguru, the sage who taught him to see all as it is—as himself.

In front of his wooden seat and bed, on which he sat facing north to give darshan, he always kept certain items on the floor in front of him: a small camphor burner and a few camphor tablets, a brass pot of fresh water, which only he used, and a stainless steel tumbler for drinking, which served as a cover for the pot when not in use. Flowers from devotees were also placed on this spot.

Inthumathy Amma describes life at the ashram:

> In the blessed hut where Yogaswami sat, the Saiva personage M. Tiruvilangam, who was well versed in the *Shastras* and followed the precepts of Saivism, and other dignitaries, came and sat in silence. Sir Ponnambalam Ramanathan and other political leaders waited patiently in the compound of the ashram for the opening of the doors, with trembling and shivering hearts. Kalaipulavar Navaratnam and other educators began to move 'round Yogaswami. Tamil literary stalwarts, like Somasunthera Pulavar and Ganeshaiyar, stood with bowed heads in Swami's presence. Many who lived in Jaffna at that time, those who had studied thoroughly, ladies who were illiterate and who worked in the fields, those who drove bullock carts, in short all and sundry began to flock 'round Swami.
>
> Even atheists and those who could not give up their alcohol and cigarettes prostrated before him. Christians, Buddhists and those of the Islamic faith sought him. From early morning till midnight a stream of devotees came and went from that heavenly hut. From dawn to dusk one could see cars, bullock carts, hand carts all parked in a row on the road in front of the ashram.
>
> The only sounds in the early days were Thuraiappah's *Devaram* at dawn and dusk. At that time Mrs. Arunachalam, having completed a pilgrimage by foot to Kataragama, started the practice of lighting a lamp. Another devotee gathered the courage to light camphor and worship. The sweet sounds of *Devaram* and *kirtanas* [songs] began to

From 1914 until Yogaswami's mahasamadhi *in 1964, the little hermitage in Columbuthurai served as his abode and ashram. Devotees would gather daily to be with the guru, sing, receive his guidance on the path and enjoy his* upadeshas *and radiant spiritual presence.*

resound from the ashram. The delightful aroma of the objects of worship permeated the air.

Swami spoke to those before him so naturally. But even in those

simple words high philosophy echoed. Once Swami asked a devotee, "What news?" The devotee replied normally, relating some recent incident in the community. Swami retorted, "There is no news. Everything is as it should be."

At times, according to the needs of the devotees before him, sections from the *Vivekachudamani, Bhagavad Gita* and other philosophical works would be read. In order to give the true meaning of these readings, Swami would interrupt and comment on them, thus opening the eyes of the devotees. The *Sivapuranam* was chanted every evening. Devotees assembled in great numbers for the privilege of chanting in his presence, as he was seated there like Lord Siva, the object of the *Sivapuranam.*

Yogaswami often took refuge in Jaffna's Vannarpannai Siva Temple. He
would sit in front of the quiet shrine of the Goddess as Thaiyalnayaki
and there compose his mystic songs. He told devotees that one day
while meditating there he heard Her anklet bells as She danced in the
world of light. Thaiyalnayaki literally means "beautiful Goddess."

When the chanting was over, Swami gave prasadam to the devotees who were ready to go, saying, "Go and come again. But we do not go and we do not come." While walking away on the road, the devotees chattered appreciatively with pride, "He is pure soul who has no going or coming." Thus, in this way that ashram became a temple where a living God stayed.

T. Sivayogapathy shared:

Thuraiappah used to visit Yogaswami's Ashramam daily at 6:30 pm and sing the Parrot ("Killiye") Natchintanai. Thuraiappah's residence was situated just 100 yards from Swami's hut. On many early mornings they walked to the Columbuthurai beach for a stroll. My beloved father told me that Thirugnanasampanthar, Thuraiappah and Yogaswami went to Panrithalaichi Amman Temple every first Monday of the Tamil calendar month to offer *pongal* at the temple, worship and enjoy *pongal* as their lunch before returning to Columbuthurai Ashramam in the evening. They made the trip by bullock cart.

Gradually the hut became a regular place of pilgrimage for devotees from near and far. V. Muthucumaraswami, in *Tamil Sages and Seers of Ceylon,* tells what it was like to visit Swami's *kutir:*

In my late teens I remember visiting Yogaswami at his hut at Columbuthurai. There was the smell of incense and camphor. There were flowers of various hues, the shoe flower, the jasmine, the *mullai,* the red lotus, the *champaka* and more. There was a deer skin on which sat Yogaswami. The scene reminded one of Sage Vishvamitra or Sage Vasishtha, mentioned in the *Ramayana.* Yogaswami had a flowing beard, and his hair was silver. His eyes were magnetic. People came with various offerings: betel, areca nut, mangoes, pomegranates, pineapples, rice and vegetables. Some came with prepared food: *pittu,*

stringhoppers, *dosai, vadai, modakam,* etc. Yogaswami would ask the
people to be seated quietly, and a few devotees would distribute the
offerings to the rest.

Mr. Tamber, principal of Central College, paints a picture in S. Ampikaipaakan's biography of Yogaswami:

Darkness was setting in when we reached the junction of Columbuthurai and Swamiyar streets and we saw a divine being sitting under the
shadow of the street kerosene lamp. He was wearing white *veshti* and

Yogaswami's hermitage had the simple austerity of a monk's quarters. In the main room there was a neem-wood platform that was his bed at night and his seat during the day. Behind a curtain he kept the sandals of his guru, which he worshiped each day with camphor.

• •

sitting in *padmasana*. Swamigal was indeed magnificent looking, like one of those ancient rishis, with his lion look, his smooth skin, white beard and grey hair. When he emerged from his meditative state, his eyes were shining as a tiger's eyes reflect in the night. Then he started singing devotional songs as if a dam had opened into the ocean. For two hours it was like a hurricane blowing. Those songs came deep inside from his lungs. We and others were enchanted, and all stood mesmerized by his music. There was absolute silence and peace when he finished singing.

At the Marketplace Temple
In the early 20s, Yogaswami took to spending time in front of the Siva temple in Jaffna's Vannarpannai district, the same temple Kadaitswami had frequented. Boons and blessings flow so abundantly here, in the midst of Grand Bazaar, that the temple became the richest in all of Ceylon, overflowing with devotees' gifts of land, jewels and gold. Jaffna's goldsmith shops surround the site, bolstering the temple's staggering shakti. India and Ceylon worked almost as one nation in those days, and cartloads of flowers arrived daily, offered by devotees of this temple living in India.

Here Swami dissolved himself in the darshan of Thaiyalnayaki, Mother of the Universe, the Shakti of Siva. Her shrine was not far from Siva's, but more secluded, the *sannidhya* much softer, offering a protectiveness he loved. He found this quiet, unlit corner of the temple a special refuge where he could meditate, compose spiritual hymns and commune mystically with Chellappaswami.

In his reveries he said, "All one needs is to hear the jingle of Thaiyal-nayaki's anklets as she walks around the temple." He himself heard Her anklets jingling and shared the following verse with devotees:

O Mother Thaiyalnayaki!
This is an opportune moment, Mother!
World famous is the great city of Vannai
That You have come to, Vani! Sivakami!
Of whom Kandaswami was born
O Mother Thaiyalnayaki!
O Mother Thaiyalnayaki!

Though the temple was crowded with devotees, no one disturbed him. Worshipers revered his presence. Still, to one devotee, there was too much hustle and bustle for the inner work he sensed Yogaswami was engaged in. S.R. Kandiah watched and waited over a period of weeks, then approached Swami while he was walking about after a long meditation. "Vanakkam, Swamigal. Please forgive my boldness, but I have a storefront a short walk from here. It would be a great blessing to me if you would use it as your shelter."

Yogaswami accepted and was seen there often. He began teaching a little, too. Sitting on a simple wooden bench, he told passersby that the Mother's love is so powerful that it can dissolve you fully if you can hold yourself within it. Yogaswami was often seen around the nearby temple, worshiping Siva and Thaiyalnayaki Amman.

The Council of Rogues
In the 1920s and 30s several professional men drew near, whom Swami endearingly called "The Most Distinguished and Learned Council of Rogues." He met with this devout and educated group—teachers, lawyers, doctors and businessmen—roughly once a week at one of the members' large homes, built at the same time and in the same neighborhood as the Vannarpannai Sivan Temple. They were the core group of the future Siva-thondan Nilayam.

Swami was at ease with his Council of Rogues. In their company he could relax, and so could they. Often they took turns reading from Hindu scriptures. As they read, Yogaswami would stop them at crucial points to make comments. They valued these moments beyond measure. But he would not let them hold him or the saint whose words they read above themselves. "You must become the speaker of the words you read and hear. You are not who you think you are. You are the One. That is what you must practice."

Yogaswami sometimes spoke of Swami Vivekananda at these gatherings. He described the young swami, whose lectures he had attended in January 1897, as like a lion roaring, pacing up and down the platform, barely able to express all his perceptions and direct all the energies coming through him. At the outset of his talk, the 34-year-old Vedanta monk lamented, "The time is short, and the subject is vast." Swami reiterated that saying throughout his life.

This august assembly included Sir Vaithilingam Duraiswamy, Dr. C. Gurusamy, Mr. A. Thillyampalam, Mr. V. Karalasingam, Dr. V.T. Pasupathy, Pundit T. Mylvaganam (later Swami Vipulananda), Kalaipulavar K. Navaratnam, Mr. C. Mylvaganam, Mr. V. Muthukumaru, Mr. V.S.S. Kumaraswamy, Mr. T.N. Suppiah, Pulavar A. Periyathambipillai, Mr. R.N. Sivapragasam, Mr. M.S. Elayathamby, Mr. M. Sabaratnasingi, Mr. Tiruvilangam, Supreme Court judge H.W. Thambiah, Mr. M. Srikhantha, Mr. Kasipillai Navaratnam, Mr. T. Sinnathamby, Mr. K.K. Natarajan, Pundit A.V. Mylvaganam, and Justice of the Peace S. Subramaniam. Most remained Swami's devotees throughout their life.

Perambulations

Throughout his life, Swami talked openly with Chellappaswami as if he were there physically. Only in the later years did devotees learn that Swami had matured the siddhi of communicating with Chellappaswami in the period following his *mahasamadhi*. From then on, Chellappaswami guided him inwardly. Swami explained that this was also when he established connections with the transcendental forces of the universe, with the Gods, the devas and the Saivite saints.

As a young guru, Swami was often away from Jaffna for long periods. He would go to Colombo, or to the up-country, or possibly to a retreat place he had in the village of Poonagari, forty kilometers from Columbuthurai, out in the middle of rice paddies where there is a Ganesha temple and beside it a pool full of lotus flowers. On the other side of the temple stands a shady *kuruntha* tree, the tree sacred and revered by Saivites because under such a tree Saint Manikkavasagar saw Lord Siva as his guru. No one knew of this place, so Swami was not disturbed there and would stay for days at a time. It was peaceful, amid farmlands, with tireless farm workers all around.

Swami loved to walk and would cover great distances throughout the Jaffna peninsula. In later years, when droves of devotees began arriving at his gate, he would rise early before anyone appeared, grab his umbrella and take to the unpaved roads, walking for hours without respite, visiting the sacred spots en route and often stopping for lunch at a devotee's home unannounced, only returning to his hut when he knew no one was there, or only the most devout.

He was familiar with every street, every lane, every path. One day, in the 1940s or 50s, there was a terrible storm in Jaffna. High winds drove intense rain for several days without ceasing. Trees were blown down and roads flooded. After the storm, Swami asked one of his close devotees to drive him around in order to survey the damage. Whenever they came to a place where the road was impassable, Swami would navigate another route, down narrow lanes that only locals knew. When the devotee expressed his astonishment at his geographical acumen, Swami exclaimed, "This is my estate. I have walked every inch of it." No matter where he went, no matter how long he was gone, Yogaswami always ended up back under the *illupai* tree.

Swami was a stout man, five feet seven inches tall, an average height for Jaffna men in those days. Robust and strong, he could walk sixty kilometers in a day as a matter of routine, even into his seventies. And he was not averse to using his ominous presence and physical prowess to intimidate people he wanted to keep away. One devotee, Dr. S. Ramanathan, shares an unforgettable encounter:

> I went to visit Swami in 1920 with Advocate Somasunderam of Nallur. As a youngster, I was proficient in sword fighting and similar arts. As a result of these skills, I was a little arrogant. On my way to the ashram, Swami came to the middle of the road and felled me. I will never forget the incident. Even teachers of the martial arts cannot show that level of proficiency with their hands and legs. The only skill that gave me pride caused me to fall flat on the earth that day. Swami then took me to the ashram and showered me with love and affection. It was only in later years that I understood the divine sport that made me eat the dust on that road. Thereafter, whenever I traveled to Jaffna I went to the ashram and obtained his darshan. Sometimes he would scold and chase me away. Whenever I went with the sole purpose of seeing him, he would greet me and show great affection.

Most people kept their distance. If they saw Swami coming down the street, they hid or went the other way. People took long detours to avoid passing the *illupai* tree. Sometimes, though, a curious, unwary person would venture close. Yogaswami would scold in a booming voice. If that did not drive the intruder away, Swami would strike him to make sure his curiosity would not get the better of him again. Decades later, Satguru Sivaya Subramuniyaswami gave his insight on such outbursts of ire:

> They say that Yogaswami used to get angry at people. People couldn't stand his wrath, but afterwards they would say that they had been blessed by it. How does this differ from the ordinary person's fiery anger of blacks and reds with fire shooting out uncontrolled and uncontrollable? Yogaswami would send out white flames, lavender flames in his righteous indignation. For the devotee's own good he would say, "I am going to cut out all of this terrible stuff within you." He would have the appearance that he had lost control of anger, but it would not be the anger of the instinctive person. Rishis, they say, get very dominant and very angry. They use the word anger, but it would be more accurate to call it righteous indignation, a white flame. Then people feel that they are blessed, because afterwards they are totally free of what was bothering them before. It had been totally burnt out of them as a blessing.

In those days, his hut in Columbuthurai was far more remote and inaccessible than in later years. The road between Jaffna town and Swami's village was just a wide trail through overgrown bushes, and there were no houses for three or four kilometers. People feared robbers when they came that way at night, so Swami was spared the faint of heart. Only ardent, fearless devotees dared the journey from Jaffna in the evenings.

One night a few boys came. They had tried to catch Swami as he walked around Jaffna but could not keep up with his swift stride. By the time they arrived, Yogaswami was lighting oil lamps for the evening. Ignoring them, he sang the sacred songs he recited each evening. Then he invited them into his hut and asked why they had come. They explained that they had recently taken their graduation exam. If they passed, they would be able to go on to the university, maybe abroad.

The results had not been published, and they were worried. They had also begun feeling the weight of responsibilities they would soon assume as adults, and sensed that this night might be the proper time to make a pilgrimage to the sage of Columbuthurai and seek his advice. They knew of the power of blessings that could come from such a soul. Quickly Swami put the question of the exam results out of their minds. "You are bright boys and good students. Why do you worry? You must never base your actions on fear."

Swami knew they were at a point when they could stray from dharma, as so many do at this age. But with proper direction they could develop a deeper understanding of their life's purpose. He spoke forth strong direction for their lives, urging them to continue to obey their parents, to remain chaste and not be taken in by any of the fanciness of the world. He described the ideal perspective to hold throughout life:

> There is no one above us or superior to us. Good and evil cannot touch us. For us there is no beginning or end. We don't like or dislike. We don't desire material things. The play of the mind doesn't trouble us. Nor are we limited by place or time or karma. We simply watch that which goes on around us.

Rajayogi Prostrates
There lived a brahmin named Sankarasuppaiyar, respectfully known as Rajayogi. Born in Jaffna, as a young man he had left home for South India on a spiritual quest. For years he performed sadhana and received training in philosophy and public speaking. He matured as a brilliant, highly respected orator on Saiva Siddhanta. At Hindu temples on special days after the pujas, speakers and musicians perform in the courtyard. Rajayogi would speak at such occasions throughout South India, elucidating the fine points of Saivism, telling stories and explaining their meaning. People came from all over to hear his oration. In a dramatic, yet simple style, he made the inner significance of Saivite worship available to those who had been following the rituals without much understanding.

Sometime in the early 1920s, the prodigal son returned to Jaffna, where he was widely known and highly regarded, even though he had not been home for years. Many Sri Lankans pilgrimaging through South India had heard him speak at the ancient stone temples. At last, he was returning, a hero of sorts, to give a series of religious lectures. Rajayogi landed by boat in Colombo, spent several weeks enthralling audiences in the capital, then set out for Jaffna by train.

The whole community was excited. Such events rarely occurred in the quiet North. Representatives of the reception committee took the eight-hour train ride to Colombo to escort their celebrity home. The ladies decorated the train station in grand style for the reception, with thousands of flowers and palm leaves folded in decorative patterns. A new podium was built for the event, where dignitaries would give welcoming speeches and the pandit would offer his first address to the people of Jaffna. Each important religious and social group, and there are many in this region, brought lavish garlands with which to honor him. The air was thick with incense and the redolent perfume of roses and jasmine. As his arrival time neared, more and more people crowded onto the platform.

Meanwhile, on the train, Rajayogi was conversing with his hosts, noting how good it felt to be home again. But when the train stopped at Palai railway station, he suddenly fell silent, closed his eyes and entered a deep, blissful state. His face glowed with contentment. After a few moments he opened his eyes, clearly overwhelmed with his experience.

The head of the entourage asked, "What happened? Are you all right?" Rajayogi sighed, "I felt a great jyoti board at the last station. That light is pervading the train." He turned inward again, relishing that darshan for the rest of the trip.

At the Pungangkulam station just before the Jaffna depot, he felt the jyoti leaving the train. He asked his hosts who it was. One looked out the window and, seeing Yogaswami walking away, pointed him out to Rajayogi, explaining, "He's just an ascetic who lives in a village near here."

The train was ready to leave the station. Rajayogi insisted on getting off then and there. No reception would hold him. This was what was important for his life right now. He had to meet the being whose spiritual illumination he had felt so palpably.

His hosts stood confounded. Their duty was to get Rajayogi to the grand reception just a few kilometers away. Hundreds of people were waiting. They would be to blame if they were late or if anything went amiss. He understood their predicament, but still insisted on seeing Yogaswami. He urged, "Please just let me off the train. Simply postpone the reception until the evening, when I am scheduled to speak. I will take the blame." His hosts were just as adamant, promising they would cut the reception short and personally take him to see Yogaswami immediately afterward. Rajayogi relented as the train started up with a jerk and chugged forward to Jaffna.

Now the men had pause for thought. Why was the famous Rajayogi so enamored with Yogaswami? They had felt no special power from him all these years. To them, he was an enigmatic sadhu to be feared and avoided. Now here was Rajayogi ready to dispense with all the honors of friends awaiting him for a moment with a stranger. The reception would be the finest Jaffna had held in decades, and he wanted to push it aside to see Yogaswami!

As they pulled into Jaffna station, the platform was overflowing with

townfolk. Musicians were playing *tavil* drums and the *nagasvara* wood-wind in a frenzy of festive rhythms. Rajayogi was greeted in grand style. Garland after garland was placed on him, so many that they had to be removed quickly to make room for more.

In keeping with their promise, his hosts arranged, against stern objections, to postpone the main part of the reception until that evening. Rajayogi insisted they leave as quickly as possible. He gave a short, eloquent and humorous talk that satisfied the crowd, apologized for curtailing the program, then set out by car with his hosts to find Swami.

They squeezed into one of Lanka's ubiquitous black Ambassador

One day a highly respected pandit named Rajayogi was riding on a train from Colombo to Jaffna when he felt a great jyoti *nearby. He inquired about the source of this spiritual power, and a companion reported he saw Yogaswami disembarking at the station before Jaffna. Astonished by the shakti he felt, the pandit pursued.*

• •

sedans and headed for Columbuthurai. Reaching Swami's hut, Rajayogi, hands held together over his head in the highest form of namaskara, approached the sage and prostrated on the ground. He remained face down on the ground for a long time, then stood in speechless awe. Yogaswami greeted him warmly and offered a seat.

After a few moments of intense silence, Rajayogi spoke up, "I have never felt such peace as I do at this moment." Yogaswami responded, "What you feel is within you. I am within you." They talked together and sat for a time in intimate quietude. Then Swami announced that it was time for Rajayogi to go. Knowing that people would be curious, Swami advised that he not talk about their meeting. "Secret is sacred, and sacred is secret. You are the only one. Know that by keeping a secret."

That night, as he mixed with Jaffna's citizens at the reception, Rajayogi uttered nary a word of his encounter with Swami. But everyone knew. That's the way things are in Jaffna. His companions, unable to contain their enthusiasm, chattered about how their renowned pandit had recognized Yogaswami as his guru.

This was a turning point; others became aware of Swami's rare spirituality and began coming to him. Not in great numbers; he was so aloof, disengaged and difficult to approach. He lived an austere, reclusive life, constantly immersed in *tapas*, consciously cutting away every thread of attachment so that he could soar to the apex of existence, beyond time, form, space and any movement of the mind.

Working with Seekers

Chellappaswami had never allowed himself to be known as a guru. Yogaswami knew the wisdom of that position. He understood that those who open themselves too soon and take on disciples before reaching sufficient maturity and stability in the highest chakras may develop into proud, self-serving men. Reaching an intermediary plateau in their unfoldment, they open themselves prematurely, stop their *tapas* and spend all their time trying to bring others along the path.

No matter how noble their intentions, these swamis are brought into unexpected suffering by the crowds who gather around them. They have neither the humility nor maturity to deal with the adoration and adulation that come and carry these to the altar of the Supreme One within. Instead, they fall prey to spiritual pride and develop a new, worldly ego that closes the door to their own progress on the path and renders them useless in any effort to guide others.

Swami would not stumble into that abyss. Thus, during this time he strove to purify himself, to complete his transformation and establish himself so firmly in the Self that he could serve as a worthy channel for God Siva and all the Deities, devas and gurus living on the inner planes who assist and work through a satguru on Earth. He sat deep in samadhi, realizing the Self, Absolute Reality, again and again and again. He spent his time around holy places, communing with the transcendental forces or pilgrimaging from one place to another in obedience to inner orders.

Inthumathy Amma wrote of this period when more and more devotees began gathering around him:

In a short time there was a big change in Siva Yogar's attitude. Early morning one could hear the sounds of the compound in front of the hut. The floor of the hut was smeared with cow dung and appeared very clean. It was no longer a dilapidated hut where snakes dwelt. In the northern room the divine sandals appeared bedecked with flowers.

Whenever Siva Yogar was seen on the road, his glistening silver white hair was tied into a neat knot. The holy ash which he generously spread on his forehead shone in the sunlight. The shawl thrown over his shoulder dangled in a delightful way. He had in his hand an umbrella, a symbol of his protection to all.

At that time he frequented the then famous Shanmuganathan Book Depot. Those coming there in search of knowledge were attracted by Swami, the embodiment of wisdom. To those mature souls he would say, "Instead of delving deep into the sciences and arts, turn your mind within you and study the heart within you." Some of Swami's other favorite places were the Vivekananda Press at Vannarpannai and the Navalar Printing Press and Book Depot.

Rajayogi visited the sage at his hut and fell at the stranger's feet, acknowledging his greatness and thereby informing the world of Yoga-swami's stature. Because a pandit of his stature had prostrated, the entire community became aware of the great soul who was living in their midst.

Siva Yogaswami sometimes went to the house of the native physician Kasturi Muthukumaru, an ayurvedic doctor who not only treated the poor and needy free, but also gave them travel expenses if they came from far-off places. Those who went there not only received medicines from a famous physician but they also had the good fortune to receive the grace of Siva Yogaswami, who was the embodiment of compassion.

Mr. V. Rajasekharam recalled how word spread of Yogaswami's greatness in these early years of his four decades of spiritual prominence:

About the year 1925, many people from Jaffna began to utter Yoga-swami's name with great devotion and piety. People started to talk of him as a sage "who knows past, present and future." In the peninsula where there were no mountains, he was resplendent as a mountain of grace and compassion. Having heard these words, I too greatly desired to see him.

As word got around of Swami's yogic powers, people came to him as a soothsayer, astrologer or fortune teller. "Swami, I am considering a move to Colombo, where I have been offered a position at the University. What do you see in my future? Will it work out well for me?" Such queries— grounded in the fear that something might be taken from them or they might have a bad experience—were rejected and addressed with a fiery scolding. He invariably pointed out their blatant misunderstanding: "At no point in your life have you ever not had what you needed. All that we need is freely given to us. We only suffer because we are not aware that we need what we have received."

Swami was pointing out the importance of accepting each of life's experiences, whether seemingly harsh or happy, as our perfect next step on the spiritual path. Many who received such severe scolding, who endured Swami's reprimands, confided they were never afraid of any-thing else the rest of their lives. Swami had shaken them to the core as no mere change in fortune ever could. One close devotee, Dr. S. Ramanathan of Chunnakam, recounted:

Swami would explain the science of the movement of stars and zodia-cal signs. He would say that one of his students, Justice Akbar, knew this science very well. If anyone asked about astrological matters, Swami would say that he was not an astrologer. I saw the lines on Swami's palms; they were crystal clear. When I asked to examine his palm, he refused, saying "What use is there for astrology or the other sciences that predict the future to one who believes that all is Siva's doings and who does not worry about the morrow and is a witness to all that happens?"

As sincere devotees who were devout and grounded in the philosophy came for guidance, he took an active role in their lives. He would go to them, even pester them. Once Swami arrived at a devotee's home early in the morning, went inside and sat by the man's bed until he awoke from

. . . .

Devotees fell at Yogaswami's feet each day in the hut, while he took refuge in his guru's sandals, kept in a small shrine. Sometimes, in meditation, he heard the silver anklets of the Goddess as She danced in the Sivaloka.

sleep. As he opened his eyes, there was Yogaswami, demanding, "Where did you go in your dreams? I know where you went, and it was not where you should be going! You need only come to me from now on!" meaning that he should be as pure during his dreams as he tries to be in his wakeful hours. Then Swami watched as the man performed his morning puja, bluntly correcting him for any action he did carelessly or without devotion. Only after this puja to the Gods did he allow the man to worship him as the guru.

It was not unusual for Swami to focus on a devotee in this way for several days to convey personal, life-changing lessons, just as Chellappaswami had done with him. Now and again through the day, Swami would remind the devotee to be the watcher: "You are not your body. You are not your mind. You are not your emotions. You are the atma. That only is. Be that and be a witness!" To help devotees live such a detached life, he urged them to be like the tamarind fruit. As this fruit matures, it dries and shrinks, loosening itself from the hard pod in which it grows. When ripe, it is completely detached from the pod, touching it only at the point where the pod joins the tree.

Yogaswami was especially fond of Pundit K. Navaratnam, an effective school teacher who inspired the most unmotivated students to be attentive and strive to live informed, productive lives. Swami often arrived at his home early in the morning. They would sit together quietly for some time, then go on long walks before school opened. On occasion, Swami would wait in the park outside the school in case the teacher had some free time. While he sat there, people gathered around him and sang holy songs. The melodies would waft into the classrooms. The two sometimes sat with devotees in Muttavalli and read books by Swami Vivekananda and Aurobindo.

Swami encouraged Navaratnam's scholarly skills and brought books for him to read. One day Swami told him he should write books himself about Hinduism, to be read by those coming to Hinduism from the West. Hence, through the years Pundit wrote excellent books about many aspects of Hinduism, most notably *Studies in Hinduism*. Swami forbade him to mention his name, though, so the books mentioned many sages and saints, but not Yogaswami.

Pundit was a popular mentor for most of the principals and teachers of Jaffna schools. He was so respected by the Hindu community that he was given the title Kalaipulavar, meaning a master in poems and songs related to Tamil literature and Hindu philosophy. On the night of Mahasivaratri in 1927, he and Yogaswami sat together in meditation from 6pm to 5am.

Chellachi Ammaiyar

One of Yogaswami's contemporaries was a saint named Chellachi Ammaiyar, whose home had become like an ashram. She was born in 1863, the same year Swami Vivekananda entered this world. Devout from early childhood, she worshiped at the temple as often as her parents would take her and learned the Puranic stories and the hymns of the Tamil saints. She lived in Chunnakam, a farming and market village about twelve kilometers outside Jaffna Town.

In married life, Chellachi provided a good home for her husband and an excellent religious training for their two children. When their children were almost grown, her husband was offered a choice job in another province. He assumed his wife would move there with him, but she declined to leave their home. He relented, since it was not customary for Hindu women to travel about in those days. She stayed at their home, and he returned whenever he had leave.

After her husband took up his new post, Chellachi turned fully to temple worship. Her worldly duties were finished, it seemed to her. She no longer could take care of her husband, and her children were old enough to be her companions. She and her husband had lived chastely since the birth of their last child, as is the custom of Hindus of her upbringing, so it was natural for her to intensify the spiritual side of life. She frequented the temple more often than ever.

After a time, she began withdrawing into deep meditation in her home and is said to have never left her compound again. During one visit, her husband saw that she was now fully immersed in her spiritual quest. He respected this and no longer demanded any of the duties of marriage from her. He retired after awhile and died shortly thereafter. She had predicted the day of his death seven years before, saying that her inner voice told her to prepare him for that experience, which she did.

Hindu customs require a widow to withdraw for at least a year, to mourn and do special sadhanas. They wear white from that day and live a disciplined, unadorned, chaste life, apart from society. For a time they are not to even cook for themselves. On the day of his funeral she cooked her own food, defying that custom, declaring that she no longer belonged

• •

Among Jaffna's spiritual lights in the early 20th century was Chellachi Ammaiyar, a mystic and spiritual teacher nine years Yogaswami's senior. Toward the end of her life, she was so sensitive she could only eat food he prepared. He would cook a meal daily and carry it sixteen kilometers to her ashram, sometimes even feeding her if she was too weak.

to her husband, that she had fulfilled all her duties to him, and she now belonged to God.

From that day on, her spiritual life was her only life. She followed a strict discipline for several years of sitting in meditation every time the village temple bell rang at puja time—revelling in the shakti as it drew her deep into Siva consciousness. One day her inner voice told her to stop doing that and to sing certain songs to Lord Ganesha. After singing them for several months, she received the message that she should now perform a daily puja to Siva, using a Lingam to represent the Supreme Absolute. She was concerned because she did not have a Lingam in the shrine room and was not in the practice of leaving the family compound to search for anything. Later that day, while walking in the garden, she found a natural, Lingam-shaped stone under a bush. She cleaned it up and performed daily puja to it.

In time another inner message came: that her body would keep clean of itself, and she should not take a full bath again. She was not to go to the well and pour water over herself as she had done her whole life. She obeyed, never bathing again. Her gray hair, which knew no comb from that day, grew long and tangled. People who came to see her still remember the matted locks. Otherwise, she was perfectly clean and had a pleasant, radiant appearance.

Inner instructions came one day to stop performing the puja and to practice Sivadhyana, meditation on Siva as the Absolute. Siva puja had filled her with great joy during this period, and she saw no harm in worshiping the Sivalingam just one more time. The puja began, but Chellachi could not carry on. Devotees would later share her tale, that she was physically thrown six meters from the Lingam when her water offering touched the stone.

After that experience, Chellachi Ammaiyar followed her inner orders with renewed strictness. At one point, directions came that she should prepare to go into the deepest samadhi, God Realization, direct encounter with the Divine. Instructions came to tell all members of the household that she would be sitting in meditation in the shrine room for a long time and should not be disturbed for any reason. She carefully explained this to each one individually. Then, entering her shrine room, Chellachi sat in perfect stillness, controlling her breathing for several days. Sometimes she would breathe very slowly and quietly; at other times her breathing would stop altogether. For several days she sat in that profound state.

After three days of observing that Chellachi seemed to be not breathing at all, a relative grew concerned that she had died. For hours and hours—concerned that the body, if dead, be properly taken care of so that no disembodied entity could take it over—she watched for any sign of life and saw none. Finally, she cautiously approached Chellachi Ammaiyar, opened her mouth and pulled out her tongue to see if it exhibited the tell-tale signs of death. It was a fateful mistake and a startling intrusion for the Siva-immersed saint. Without warning, her samadhi was shattered and awareness was brought crashing back into body consciousness. Several days passed, as her nerve system reeled from the horrendous shock.

The disturbance of that unusually deep state caused a severe reaction that lasted for the rest of her life. She became so sensitive to light that she could not even stand direct exposure to moonlight. The darkened veranda became her favorite place. If anyone approached who was not pure minded or had selfish motives, her body would heat up to the point of causing her pain. Close devotees were nervously cautious about whom they allowed in her presence.

Chellachi neither blamed nor allowed others to criticize the well-intended relative. She believed her condition was arranged by the Gods as part of her mission on Earth.

A Spiritual Oasis

Her ashram-like home radiated peace and stability. Yogaswami visited there frequently beginning around 1914. She was his elder by nine years, and he regarded her as a spiritual mentor. She addressed him as Thamby, meaning younger brother. Once she told a devotee that only by virtue of that shocking experience of having her samadhi interrupted did Yogaswami come to take her farther within than she could have gone without his grace.

No one knows for certain in what way each influenced the other's spiritual work, but their mutual respect and reverence was undeniable. The informal meditation and satsanga gatherings, held randomly every month or so, were attended by Yogaswami and a few close devotees, including Kalaipulavar K. Navaratnam, Sir Vaithilingam Duraiswamy, and Dr. S. Ramanathan.

Chellachi became prominent in the community, in part due to her radical outlook advocating freedom for women, but more importantly for her pursuit of Hindu mystical practices. In those days, spirituality was considered a male preserve, but she felt no restriction and became revered as one of the gurus of the time.

Gradually people began coming to Chellachi Ammaiyar for advice, solace and just to bask in her darshan. Visitors took great care to inwardly prepare themselves before they visited. Upon reaching her cottage, they would sit outside for awhile until they felt in harmony with her vibration, lest she be disturbed by any residue of worldliness.

Everyone remarked about the serenity she emanated, a soothing, motherly energy. Oddly, the space around her was cool. Even on Jaffna's hottest days and warmest nights, here it was comfortable. She sang devotional hymns often, especially in praise of Lord Ganesha. Silence descended when she sang; the world disappeared, and only her beautiful, delicate voice remained, intoning the ancient Tamil hymns.

In her deeply introverted state, Chellachi naturally developed certain siddhis. One day a businessman arrived at her home, leaving his driver outside in the car. This was his first visit, and he was obviously testing Chellachi as he sat in her presence. He was rather agitated and preoccupied, and left before she was satisfied that he had gotten what he had come for. Returning to his car, he ordered the driver to go, but the engine would not start. As the driver tried and tried, the man grew exasperated, even angry, because the car was new and should have been in perfect condition. Finally, he barked to the driver, "Go find someone who can make the necessary repairs," then returned to the veranda to sit with the saint.

Now that he had nowhere to go, nothing to do, the sublime peace he had heard about flooded his being, washing through him like a gentle wave. After what seemed a long time, he heard her sweet voice, "You can go now." Refreshed and rejuvenated, he stood up and honored her with hands pressed together in *anjali mudra*. Floating down the steps, seeing that the driver had not yet returned, he got into the driver's seat and turned the key. The engine started on the first try.

Many who came sought to be healed. For such visitors, Chellachi had a special routine. She would observe a few moments of silence, as if sensing the ailment, then instruct the visitor: "Go to the well and drink some water" or "Go and bathe with the pure water from the well." A change in living conditions or diet was often part of her prescription. Many ailments, some quite serious, would vanish in the weeks to come. Family wells are outdoors here, an eight-foot-diameter hole, rock-clad, with a simple coconut tree log holding a wooden bucket that fetches the water from three meters or more below the ground.

Once a young village boy suffered from a raging fever. Unable to bring his temperature down, the doctors gave him up for lost, confiding to his mother, "It will be a miracle if he lives another day." Chellachi Ammaiyar's face flashed before the desperate mother's inner vision. Realizing that the saint was her last resort, she rallied the family to take the child to her house. Chellachi's remedy: "Pour three buckets of water from my well over him, then take him home."

Not without extreme hesitancy, since the prescription seemed unrealistically simple, they obeyed—one bucket, then two, then three, until he was completely soaked. Bare-chested in his drenched sarong, the deathly ill boy stood, hunched over, shivering in the evening breeze. Quickly drying him off, the family bundled him back into the bullock cart and took him home, hopefully for a restful sleep. By the next morning, to their amazement, the fever had broken, and the boy weakly asked for breakfast! In a few days he was back to normal, running around and playing with his friends.

One story shows how Yogaswami protected this fine saint from difficulties. One day, when he was on the veranda with Chellachi Ammaiyar, a group of people came for an audience with her. They had started an ashram and wanted to do sadhana, but they had no swami. Chellachi, they hoped, could be convinced to move there as their spiritual leader. Knowing this was not the right thing for Chellachi in her delicate condition, Swami suddenly lit a whole box of matches on fire. Because of her hypersensitivity to light, Chellachi went into a trance immediately and remained that way for hours. The visitors waited and waited, then finally left in disappointment. Soon after, she emerged from the trance.

Prior to this advanced stage, many people came to be with Chellachi. Some came only when they needed help. Others came more often just to be with her. A few came in search of enlightenment. She spent most of her time with these few. She gave them disciplines to follow and discussed profound topics with them.

C. Kandiah Chettiar was one of her disciples who sought the ultimate goal. He was a teacher of English hailing from Alaveddy village, a 30-year-old man of deep spirituality who would later in life introduce Sivaya Subramuniyaswami to Siva Yogaswami and thus secure a key link in the parampara's chain of succession. Ammaiyar trained him with bold strictness.

One of the special sadhanas she had him perform for years was to sleep on a narrow wooden bench. If he rolled over even slightly to the left or the right he would fall to the floor, so he learned to sleep the entire night without moving. One would see him lie down, fold his hands over his chest and immediately fall asleep. In the morning he would be in exactly the same pose.

One day Chettiar was transplanting a young palm tree near a temple. He had dug the soil out around the tree quite deeply, but was unable to uproot the palm. He just couldn't get enough leverage. It was nearing noon, and the scorching heat was almost unbearable. He was tired, sweaty and looking forward to lunch.

Suddenly, it dawned on him: he could tie a stout pole horizontally to either side of the tree, lash the poles together, then pry against a nearby short piece of log to wrench the tree from the ground. Rushing to the rear of the temple where supplies are kept, he spotted the two smooth *illupai*-wood poles that are used to carry the parade Deity on festival days. "Perfect," he thought, taking possession of the poles and some hemp rope.

He rigged the poles as he had visualized, placing the short log upright under one end of the pair of poles, then took hold of the other end and pushed up will all his might. It worked. With the extra leverage, he separated the root ball from the earth. Then, pulling on the poles, he dragged the palm to its new hole and set it in place. He then cleaned the poles and returned them to the temple. "Good work," he complimented himself, walking home for a well-deserved bath and rice and curry lunch that his wife had prepared for him.

The next day, when he went to see Chellachi, she greeted him with a thorough scolding. Why had he used the special poles for his landscaping—artifacts that have been held sacred for over a hundred years? What was he thinking? This was not good at all. "The poles were made for one purpose and should be reserved for that alone," she admonished. "By using them as you did, you desecrated them. They can't be used again in the temple until they are properly purified and reconsecrated," she said, and sent him away immediately to perform that duty.

"Make God the Center of Your Life"

Chellachi Ammaiyar was a gifted teacher. She spoke from her own experience about how important it is to follow the dictates of the divine voice within oneself and the divine laws that were perceived by the rishis. When people came to her who were having problems, she would always look to see where they were stepping outside the flow of life prescribed by the scriptures. She said:

> That is how the ego is born and gains its strength. When you begin to twist what you perceive, what you know from within yourself is right, when you step off the path of virtue, then you build up the "I," and that "I" separates you from all of life and from that which is the very spring of life.

She spoke in a quiet, thin voice, as though she were too sensitive to hear herself speaking. But it had a piercing resonance, and everyone took note of all she said.

> If you live life for its own sake, you have missed the purpose of living, for life is to be lived for the glory of God, and only God must be the center of life. Being obedient to the voice of the guru within yourself is more important than life itself.

Yogaswami often echoed those sagely words. "The spiritual path is a narrow bridge of hair over a river of fire!" was one of her well-known adages. It cautioned of the tenuous nature of the path and the abounding distractions that deter seekers. She taught that God will come in different forms, and that those forms change as you understand Him, love Him and follow His directions. "You will see more and more clearly, and finally you will be so pure that you will be only That."

During the first decade of his association with Chellachi Ammaiyar, Yogaswami was still hidden from public view. While in her company and in transcendental communication with Chellappaswami, he brought his teachings into articulation. Out of that all-important period of gestation, absorption and reflection came his emphasis on Sivathondu, "service to Siva," a potent term that embodied his compelling message to the Jaffna community and ultimately to all mankind: "Surrender totally in the pure act of service to God Siva. Be still. Know thy Self and serve the Lord who is All, in all." Two words would ultimately define his lofty public message: Sivathondu and Sivadhyana, service to and meditation upon Siva.

The following account by Chellathurai Swami indicates how Chellachi Ammaiyar and Yogaswami worked together to assist members of the community:

> A devotee went to Yogaswami's hut and complained about his wife's sickness. Another gentleman had gone to Chellachi Ammaiyar. As he left she asked him to carry a bunch of plantains to Yogaswami, so he delivered them to Swami. As he did so, Swami demanded, "Who asked you to bring these plantains?" Swami shouted and scolded some more, so the man went outside and placed the plantains on the ground. Swami called him back inside. After talking to him for a while, Swami turned to the man whose wife was ill and instructed him to take the plantains home for his wife. He took them and fed one each day to his wife. When the plantains were finished, she was in good health.

Toward the end of her life, Chellachi was so sensitive that she could only
eat food that Yogaswami prepared. He would make the meal at his com–
pound in the morning and carry it sixteen kilometers to her house each
day. She was too weak to eat, so he fed her. Her earlier reactions to visitors grew far more intense, so much so that the inflammation caused by
the presence of an impure visitor rendered her unable to breathe. Strict
screening of visitors, once a cautionary rule, became an urgent necessity.

On January 27, 1929, Chellachi Ammaiyar attained *mahasamadhi*.
Her family and some devotees planned to build a shrine and bury her
body there, as is often done for enlightened beings, rather than cremate
it. Yogaswami expressed his disapproval and emphatically said he would
have nothing to do with it. The matter was settled when her son went to
Yogaswami and agreed to cremate her body as Swami wished.

Her body was cremated on a sandalwood pyre. The arrangements were
carried out by Yogaswami, Sir Vaithilingam Duraiswamy and Doctor
Ramanathan. After Ammaiyar's passing, Swami, now age 57, was the sole
spiritual refuge and guide for many of the Jaffna people. He remained the
prominent spiritual light in that community for the next 35 years.

. . . .

The mystics of Jaffna—Chellachi Ammaiyar, Yogaswami and the rest—
were strict Saivites, monistic theists who understood God to be both
immanent and transcendent, form and formless. While others called
Him the God of Destruction, they knew Siva as pure light and love.

Yogaswami, Peerless Master

Time after time, Siva Yogaswami told his devotees that all that is needed is the darshan of the satguru, the being who knows and is That. "Chellappaswami was a mother and father and guru, everything to me," Yogaswami sang in one song after another. In Hinduism it is traditional to worship the feet of the guru, which are represented by his sacred sandals, called shri *paduka* in Sanskrit and *tiruvadi* in Tamil. Why? Some say that the power that resides in the guru's nervous system flows out through his hands and feet, and thus the feet are a way to connect with that pure power. Others see it more symbolically, taking the feet as the lowest part of the guru's body, and seeking to be worthy to touch even that most humble part of divinity. In this sense it is a surrender to the divine they themselves seek to one day become.

Yogaswami had a pair of his guru's wooden sandals enshrined behind a curtain in his single-room hermitage. To these, his most sacred possession, he offered worship each morning. His daily routine was to awaken early, bathe, pluck a few flowers and perform arati, passing burning camphor before them on a raised pedestal. These still remain today. It was his only personal worship, other than visiting certain temples. The sandals also reminded all who visited Yogaswami that, indeed, he too had a guru who had led him to the goal.

He was typically dressed in a white *veshti* that was forever and magically spotless, despite the dusty Jaffna roads. He often threw a white cloth of hand-woven cotton over his shoulders, his feet clad in simple brown sandals, worn from his incessant walks but well kept. A few of his personal items remain today. A stainless steel water cup and shower towel with colored stripes are kept on his altar at Kauai's Hindu Monastery, and the family of Ratna Ma Navaratnam, a close devotee, cares for his black umbrella. Dr. S. Ramanathan gave the following insights into Swami's daily habits.

Swami kept his body clean. He would not bathe for long hours, but always washed himself. A soft, sweet scent would always emanate from him. Early morning he would take a cup of tea with milk. At noon he would eat rice. The way he prepared rice was very clean, but

. . . .

Yogaswami was a mysterious medley: a solitary mystic who drew crowds to his feet, a loving guru who could speak harshly, a man with little education who wrote literately of the highest philosophy, a yogi who loved to drive through the villages, a simple man who confounded everyone who met him.

he never bothered about taste. By observing for many days the way he ate the rice, I deduced that he ate as a matter of habit and that it was not necessary for him to eat. When he ate, I always thought, "Salutations unto him who never ate and who never slept."

He would take tea in the evenings. If he was hungry, he would eat stringhoppers or bread at night. Swami did not allow others to wash his feet, let alone pour water over them. He would not allow others to remove the banana leaf on which he ate. He would dispose of it himself. He never liked a mattress on his bed. He did not like others to honor him as a swami. He would often say, "Do not make me a swami."

S. Ampikaipaakan provides the following details.

Swamigal was very particular in taking care of his body. He did not want to trouble others by becoming sick. He was careful in the food he ate. As he preached, he ate moderately, saying, "Even if God gives you food, do not eat when you are not hungry." Some days he did not eat all day, and sometimes he ate only a bun. Before he ate, he washed his hands, legs and face and applied holy ash to his forehead and body.

One day Swamigal saw a brahmin teacher in a restaurant sitting to eat after just washing his fingers. He admonished him, "You are a brahmin; you should know that one should wash one's face, legs and apply holy ash before eating. Since you are a teacher, you should be an example to your students."

Good Thoughts; Inner Orders

Siva Yogaswami taught each devotee the proper manner of worship, that would eventually empower him to see the divine within himself. And by talking or singing of his own guru, Chellappaswami, he also taught about worshiping the guru.

Often he would sing spontaneously. Sometimes he would arrive at a devotee's house with a song written down that had come to him from within. Invariably someone would write down what he was singing and hand the song around. Eventually a selection of songs and writings were published in a book called *Natchintanai* (a Tamil word meaning "good thoughts") in 1959, with a second, expanded edition in 1962.

Swami's teachings explore the mysteries of yoga, disclose the divine experiences on the path and praise Chellappaswami and the Mahadevas, especially the supreme Lord, Siva—avoiding the intricate complexities of the Tamil language, but instead using charmingly simple vocabulary

· ·

The legacy of enlightened souls often includes literary treasures and insights. Yogaswami left the world his Natchintanai, hundreds of spiritual songs.

and phrasing. In all, Swami's compositions consist of 385 Natchintanai songs, twenty letters, called *tirumuham*, and about 1,500 sayings, or *arul vachakam*. "Our Gurunathan," the very first song in *Natchintanai,* relates the teachings of Chellappaswami and projects to everyone who sings it the depth of Yogawami's affection for the soul who brought him into the light and into deeper realizations. It begins:

> He made me to know my self, our Gurunathan.
> On my head both feet he placed, our Gurunathan.
> Father, mother, guru—he, our Gurunathan.
> All the world he made me rule, our Gurunathan.
> Previous karma he removed, our Gurunathan.
> Even "the three" can't comprehend our Gurunathan.
> He sees neither good nor bad, our Gurunathan.
> As "I am He" he manifests, our Gurunathan.

Yogaswami worked intuitively, responding to those who came according to "inner orders." In explaining this process, he once said, "I do nothing. I can do nothing. Everything you see, that is done by what comes from within." Another time he said, "When you come here, what will happen was settled long ago. We go through it; you bring it, but it all happened long ago. Sit and be a witness." Swami explained the process: "When you are pure, you live like water on a lotus leaf. Do what is necessary, what comes to you to do, then go on to the next order you receive, and then to the next that comes."

He advised, "Boldly act when you receive orders from within. You need not wait until all details are in order. If you wait for everything to be worked out, you may miss your chance. Have faith and do the work that comes from within. Money will trail after you if you are responding to divine orders. Helpers will come. Everything will come. You have only to follow carefully that which comes from within."

When asked how to find one's inner voice, he said, "*Summa iru.* Be still! Be still, and what you need will come to you." "*Summa iru!*" was his constant command. He practiced it and heeded the answers that came.

Someone would ask him a question and he would wait to feel his orders. If he felt no orders, he would do nothing until orders came. Once a man drove up to Swami as he was walking through town and asked if he could drive him anywhere. "No orders," Swami replied and waved the man on. A few minutes later the driver came by and stopped again. "Now I have my orders," Swami said, and got into the car.

Sometime in the 1930s, two elderly German matrons set sail for India in search of truth, light and the good path. For months they endured arid austerities and boiled water as they searched out and spoke with every sadhu and holy man they could find. Their itinerary included Tiruvan-namalai, the popular destination for seekers, where the renowned mystic and master of Advaita, Ramana Maharishi, had lived for decades on the sacred Arunachala Hill in a humble ashram.

Traveling south, they eventually crossed the Palk Strait and entered Ceylon. From Colombo they made their way north to Jaffna where, it was said, one of the Great Ones lived. Locals stared unabashedly as the pair navigated dusty roads in long, frilly dresses, lace gloves and sun-thwarting parasols of dubious design. They found Yogaswami in his small thatched hut. Offering their obeisances, the two seekers sat on the woven mat he offered and drank dark Ceylon tea with the dark-skinned master who listened to the story of their pilgrimage and to their queries about the nature of Truth.

"So, you asked these same questions to others?" Yogaswami inquired. "Yes, Swami," they replied. "What did Ramana Maharishi tell you, then?" Intrigued that Swami knew of their visit, the elder responded, "His only words to us were 'One God. One World.'" "I can do no better than that. You may go," Yogaswami said abruptly. With that, the two departed, cherishing the darshan of one of their century's enlightened souls.

My Meeting with Jaffna's Sage

Dr. James George, former Canadian High Commissioner to Ceylon, was profoundly influenced by Swami. He wrote the following account.

The Tamils of Sri Lanka called him the Sage of Jaffna. His thousands of devotees, including many Sinhalese Buddhists and Christians, called him a saint. Some of those closest to him referred to him as the Old Lion, or Bodhidharma reborn, for he could be very fierce and unpredictable, chasing away unwelcome supplicants with a stick. I just called him Swami. He was my introduction to Hinduism in its pure Vedanta form, and my teacher for the nearly four years I served as the Canadian High Commissioner in what was still called Ceylon in the early sixties when I was there.

For the previous ten years I had been apprenticed in the Gurdjieff Work, and it was through a former student of P. D. Ouspensky, James Ramsbotham (Lord Soulbury), and his brother Peter, that, one hot afternoon, not long after our arrival in Ceylon, I found myself outside a modest thatched hut in Jaffna, on the northern shore of Ceylon, to keep my first appointment with Yogaswami.

I knocked quietly on the door, and a voice from within roared, "Is that the Canadian High Commissioner?" I opened the door to find him seated cross-legged on the floor—an erect, commanding presence, clad in a white robe, with a generous topping of white hair and long white beard. "Well, Swami," I began, "that is just what I do, not what I am." "Then come and sit with me," he laughed uproariously.

I felt bonded with him from that moment. He helped me to go deeper towards the discovery of who I am, and to identify less with the role I played. Indeed, like his great Tamil contemporary, Ramana Maharishi of Arunachalam, in South India, Yogaswami used "Who am I?" as a mantra, as well as an existential question. He often chided me for running around the country, attending one official function after another, and neglecting the practice of sitting in meditation. When I got back to Ceylon from home leave in Canada, after visiting, on the way around the planet, France, Canada, Japan, Indonesia and Cambodia, he sat me down firmly beside him and told me that I was spending my life-energy uselessly, looking always outward for what could only be found within.

"You are all the time running about, doing something, instead of sitting still and just being. Why don't you sit at home and confront yourself as you are, asking yourself, not me, 'Who am I? Who am I? Who am I? Who am I? Who am I? Who am I?'" His voice rose in pitch, volume and intensity with each repetition of the question until he was screaming at me with all his force.

Then suddenly he was silent, very powerfully silent, filling the room with his unspoken teaching that went far beyond words, banishing my turning thoughts with his simple presence. In that moment I knew without any question that I AM; and that that is enough; no "who" needed. I just am. It is a lesson I keep having to relearn, re-experience, for the "doing" and the "thinking" takes me over again and again as soon as I forget.

Another time, my wife and I brought our three children to see Yogaswami. Turning to the children, he asked each of them, "How old are you?" Our daughter said, "Nine," and the boys, "Eleven" and "Thirteen." To each in turn Yogaswami replied solemnly, "I am the same age as you." When the children protested that he couldn't be three different ages at once, and that he must be much older than their

· ·

Yogaswami dwelled in a simple hut, suiting a yogi's simple needs, without electricity or running water. Thousands of seekers came to him, and each took away the perfect message, full of spiritual insight that was often surprising.

grandfather, Yogaswami just laughed, and winked at us, to see if we understood.

At the time, we took it as his joke with the children, but slowly we came to see that he meant something profound, which it was for us to decipher. Now I think this was his way of saying indirectly that although the body may be of very different ages on its way from birth to death, something just as real as the body, and for which the body is only a vehicle, always was and always will be. In that sense, we are in essence all "the same age."

After I had met Yogaswami many times, I learned to prepare my questions carefully. One day, when I had done so, I approached his hut, took off my shoes, went in and sat down on a straw mat on the earth floor, while he watched me with the attention that never seemed to fail him. "Swami," I began, "I think…" "Already wrong!" he thundered. And my mind again went into the nonconceptual state that he was such a master at invoking, clearing the way for being.

Though the state desired was thoughtless and wordless, he taught through a few favorite aphorisms in pithy expressions, to be plumbed later in silence. Three of these aphorisms I shall report here: "Just be!" or *Summa iru* when he said it in Tamil. "There is not even one thing wrong." "It is all perfect from the beginning." He applied these statements to the individual and to the cosmos. Order was a truth deeper than disorder. We don't have to develop or do anything, because, essentially, in our being, we are perfectly in order here and now—when we are here and now.

Looking at the world as it is now, thirty years after his death, I wonder if he would utter the same aphorisms with the same conviction today. I expect he would, challenging us to go still deeper to understand what he meant. Reality cannot be imperfect or wrong; only we can be both wrong and imperfect, when we are not real, when we are not now!

The Master's Way

One devotee was in serious need of Yogaswami's help, but was afraid to approach him, fearing that his mind would be an open book to Swami. He was ashamed of the promiscuous thoughts that haunted him, but was an ardent devotee and couldn't keep away either. On his day off from work he made up his mind to go. He got up early, had his bath and put on clean clothes, saddened that his heart was not clean as well. Unable to control his mind he found himself descending further into sinful ways, with thoughts so despicable that he could not even discuss his problem with his friends, or his family, who would surely despise him if they knew. He decided to throw himself before Swami and cry his heart out.

On the way, he hoped that Swami would not be in meditation, because then he would surely perceive his crude fantasies. Entering the ashram, he found Swami happily conversing with some disciples. "I have escaped," the man thought as he prostrated and worshiped the satguru. With a wry smile, Swami looked straight into his eyes and said, "I know everything from your head to your toes. I know all your thoughts—not only yours, but everybody's. I am in everybody. You do not know this, because you think of yourself as separate from others. Learn to consider yourself as the same as others and not separate." Then, taking the camphor tray that was burning before him, he gave it to the devotee and said, "Take this light and, considering everyone here to be Siva, worship them."

It was Siva Yogaswami's habit to visit the homes of close devotees, usually without notice, but always to the delight of the family, who regarded even the shortest sojourn as blessings enough for a lifetime. He often arrived in the hours before lunch, and on rare occasions he would stay overnight. Some devotees, hopeful of such a visit, prepared each day's meal in the expectation, however uncertain, that Swami would arrive at their door. In her book *Saint Yogaswami and the Testament of Truth*, Ratna Ma Navaratnam tells of her family's association with Yogaswami.

> The meaning of Saint Manikkavasagar's famous plea—"Thou gavest Thyself to me, and takest myself to Thee. O Shankara, who hast gained more?"—dawned on us faintly, as we saw our parents revolve in the orbit of the guru's light. It was in the early thirties that, at our father's bidding, we took to the serious study of *Tiruvasagam,* which in turn served to illuminate the profound significance of the God-Guru in our spiritual quest.
>
> In all these early associations, Swami continued to be a distant star in the firmament of our lives till the last week of May, 1939, when he blazoned as a shaft of immense magnitude. Our father stumbled over a stone heap at the gate of his newly built house, called "Chelliam Pathi," and had a fall, but escaped any serious injury, except a sprain and strain of the ankle which confined him indoors during the month of April, 1939. After the observance of the Chitra-Purnima fast, he developed fever with slight digestive upsets, and after a fortnight his condition remained static. It did not improve nor deteriorate.
>
> Late in the evening of the 28th May, our father called for mother

and all his children, and asked us to switch on all the electric lights and spread a white cloth on the chair near his bed, and bade us sing. He also indicated that we should worship him who shall come, by prostrating at his feet. We did not understand the subject of his discourse. Though it seemed so enigmatic, we obeyed his injunction mechanically and awaited.

At the *sandhya* [dusk] hour, with the waxing moon of Vaikasi shedding its translucent light, he came with his umbrella tucked under his arm pit, and opened the garden gate. Swami's voice reverberated as he called out my father's pet name, Sinnathamby, and walked right up to his bedroom, ignoring midway my mother's prostrations amidst tears. Then was enacted a tuneful communion too sacred for communication.

At the sight of Swami, my father tried to rise up from his bed, but the guru took both his frail yet cooped hands and held them against his chest and sang. It was a song that conveyed the bliss which awaits the bondsmen of Siva! His voice resounded from time to eternity. Then he took the holy ash out of the conch shell on the bed table and placed it tenderly on my father's forehead. We saw our father's face gleaming in sweet communion:

It was not a parting. It was a promise fulfilled, an assurance of the certitude of Siva's beatific bliss! He arose and left us bewildered. It seemed to us, in passing, strange that Swami had not offered a word of comfort to any of the distressed inmates. It was his way. *Oru pollappum illai!* ["There is not one wrong thing!"] It was his will that we simply be, *summa iru*. We were merely spectators in this magnificent spectacle of the play of guru's grace! My father attained samadhi on the night of 30th May 1939.

Here was an introduction to increase our faith and clear all wavering doubts in the guru, whose Siva Jnanam, God-illumination, was a source of mystery as well as perennial attraction. It was the beginning of a new phase when, little by little, we learnt to draw from the guru's bank of grace. All resistance faded away. The magnet proved irresistible; and the realization dawned on us that the guru art all, after the agonising parting from a priceless treasure in our lives!

Subsequently Ratna Ma Navaratnam and her husband Thirunavukarasu became close devotees. Their home was a short walk from Yogaswami's ashram, which she would visit every day. Thiru was often Yogaswami's

Just as his paramaguru, Kadaitswami, loved to march through the marketplace, Yogaswami could frequently be seen in a 1940s black Ambassador exploring the entire peninsula or visiting a distant devotee's home unannounced.

chauffeur, and kept his black Ambassador polished and ready inside its small garage whenever called to duty. Ma, a brilliant author and educator, applied her linguistic skills to writing of her experiences with Swami and virtually every word she heard him speak. She would go to the hut mornings and evenings, sitting quietly in the back as the day's events unfolded. Once home, she would record conversations word for word, along with visitors' names, and, especially, Yogaswami's *upadeshas*.

Stationmaster S. Vinacithamby described his experiences.

Sometimes when Swami stayed in our house he would spend hours in deep meditation. Seeing him seated in the lotus pose as the Lord of Meditation on my return from work would enrapture me. Early morning when we would wake up, seeing Swami lying on the bed, he looked like the Lord of Serenity. On seeing that form I would sense that we were looking at God, thus proving the words of that rare mantra "I am He."

Even when Swami was not there, it was natural to recall his divine form and sagely words. I recollected that he once said, "You can see God only through God." As I remembered this, the certainty arose that there was no greater God than Yogaswami, who was constantly seeing God everywhere, within and without.

In this state of mind I went to the ashram at Columbuthurai to see Swami, who was seated amidst a few devotees. Without forethought, I fell at his feet and worshiped him. From that day onward, until he attained *mahasamadhi,* whenever I went to see Swami I worshiped him, despite his saying, "It is not necessary to worship in front of people. It is not necessary to fall on the ground. It is sufficient if you worship mentally."

One day he called me by name and queried, "What is the one thing God cannot do?" Hearing the question, I was shocked. When it is said that God is all-powerful, is there something He cannot do? Swami quietly said, "You need not answer now; you can give the reply when you come in two days' time." When I came home, the question kept resounding in my mind. I could think of nothing else. Then a section I had studied in the *Mahabharata* came to my mind. When Krishna asked what could be done to prevent the war, Sahadevan's reply was, "If I bind you straightaway, the war can be prevented." Krishna responded, "How will you bind me?" to which Sahadevan replied that he would bind his Lord with the fetters of love. This seemed to me a satisfactory answer to Swami's question.

Two days later, when I went to see Yogaswami, I gave my reply: "When God is captured by the love of the devotee, He cannot free Himself." Hearing my answer, he challenged, "How can that be? You can bind God by love only if love is different from Him. You cannot separate God from love. God is love." He continued, "The one act God cannot do is to separate Himself from us, even for a moment." By this device my guru impressed on my heart that God does not separate from us even for a trice and is always within us as the Soul of our souls. Now, since Swami is my God, I began to meditate on the fact he is the God who is inseparable from me. When a person seeking his blessing prostrated before him on the cow dung floor, Swami would often say, "Look, I am worshiping."

A devotee named Nagendran recalls when, as a boy, during the initial years of World War II, he observed Siva Yogaswami having lunch at his uncle's house near Colombo. He begins with a description of the state of affairs in those troubled days.

The Great War between England and Germany had begun in 1938. France and later Russia joined England in the war against Germany. Czechoslovakia, Poland, Holland, Norway, Sweden and Denmark were overrun by Germany and Italy. England and its Allies were fighting a strenuous rear-guard battle to save themselves and the rest of Europe.

Australia and Canada had sent forces and were fighting alongside England and its Allies. The English colonies of India, Ceylon, Madagascar and other colonies in Africa were all mobilized to support the war. The hard-fought battles and the routs of the Allied forces were headlines in the Ceylon daily papers. England had the full support of the people I knew in Ceylon. Hitler and Mussolini were detested names. Every evening my father and his friends would meet at the verandah of our house in Colpetty, near Colombo, to discuss and analyze the battles. The United States had just declared war on Germany, Italy and Japan and sent forces to Europe under General Eisenhower to fight alongside England and its allies.

My father would tell his friends, "You see, America has joined the war. It is a moving mountain. Germany and the Axis powers will now be crushed." His friends concurred. But the war had not as yet had much impact in Ceylon. As boys of seven and eight, we listened attentively, from behind the scenes, to these discussions among the adults.

Uncle Ramanathan was a vegetarian. Crisp and pithy sayings of

Hindu sages in large, green Tamil script were framed and hung in the drawing room. One of the scripts read, "Persons who have entrusted themselves to God should never let go of Him." During my visits there, I heard my uncle and other elders talk of Yogaswami in hushed and reverent tones.

I had my first glimpses of Yogaswami when he visited my uncle's house. Yogar was of medium height and build. His countenance was rugged and dark. Long, white-silver hair flowed back from the high forehead and was tied in a knot at the back of his head. He would occasionally untie the loosening knot and tie it firmly back in place. His forehead and body had no *tiruniru* [sacred ash], which was unusual for a holy man. No rudraksha necklace or garlands adorned his neck. He was a plain, unvarnished man. The significance of this simplicity only dawned on me much later.

Lunch would be served during his visit in the midst of devotees invited by my uncle. Woven mats were laid out on the floor, making a square in the large drawing room. A plantain leaf was placed first before Yogaswami and then the devotees. Steaming white rice and fresh vegetables, without chilis or other spicy condiments, were served on the leaves. Yogar would sprinkle a few drops of water on his leaf, utter a few words of blessing and commence his meal. Only when he had taken the first bite would the devotees begin their lunch.

His meal did not take more than a few minutes. He would then rise, go out with a *chembu* [a bronze vessel] of water and wash his hands in the garden compound. The devotees quickly finished eating and washed their hands as well. We always ate in the traditional way, using the fingers, after rinsing them first. Spoons and forks were never used to consume a meal.

The room was then cleared and swept. Yogar would seat himself on the mat with devotees gathered around to hear his words of wisdom. Such discourses were terse, and he would abruptly leave the house a short time later. During one such visit, we children were upstairs. We knew we would be a disturbance if we came down. No disciplinary steps were required to keep us upstairs. The atmosphere was such that we knew this was the behavior that was appropriate and required of us.

While Yogaswami respected all religions and never spoke critically of other faiths, he was strict in protecting and promoting the tenets of Saivism among the Tamil Saiva people. Dr. S. Ramanathan observed:

Swami was a staunch upholder of the Saiva customs and ways of worship. He taught that properly conducting pujas in temples and homes, and observing the festivals with faith and devotion bring benefits to the individual and the entire world. As an example, Swami once related the following episode. There was a Government Agent in Jaffna named Dyke. He went to Poonakari during the dry season. There were no irrigation facilities there. He asked the villagers, "Without irrigation, how do you cultivate?" Someone replied, pointing to the Pillaiyar temple, "If we pray to Lord Pillaiyar, we will get rain." The temple priest had a bath and, following all ritualistic details, went to the temple and prayed for rain. There soon was a huge downpour, which caused a flood. Dyke had to wait three days for the waters to subside before he could return to Jaffna.

Strengthening Saivism
Swami worked to encourage and revive the proper observance of traditional practices. In his own hermitage, most evenings at dusk, a sacred standing lamp would be lit and he would have devotees sit on the cow-dung floor in a semicircle facing him, loudly singing devotional songs, sometimes from texts like the *Tirumurai,* other times from his own Natchintanai lyrics. Swami insisted that all the children, especially those studying music, should learn the ancient hymns. He challenged, "What is the use in singing ordinary verses when it is so much better to study and sing the powerful *Tirumurai.*" S. Ampikaipaakan notes:

> Swami personally took many steps to promote Saiva religion including conducting Saiva Siddhanta philosophy classes and coaching classes for the proper manner to recite *Tirumurai* and also to teach and give new life to Puranic song and storytelling. Swamigal wanted to see that *Puranams* were read in the temples and ashrams regularly. Swamigal used to say that all miseries afflicting the Tamil community will go away by reading *Kandapuranam* and *Periyapuranam.*

V. Muthucumaraswami remembers another way Swami encouraged everyone to follow the Saivite saints:

> When Swami Vipulananda wanted to resuscitate the Vaidyeshwara Vidyalayam at Vannarpannai around 1945, it was Yogaswami who gave him the first donation of a rupee and blessed this move. This institution has now grown like a big banyan tree under whose shade

many youths enjoy a true education with a deep religious basis. Swami wanted to revive Hinduism by inspiring people to follow the real ideals of the four great Saiva saints. And great was his joy when he heard that the portals of the Sivan temple at Vannarpannai had been opened to the harijans.

S. Shanmugasundaram of Colombo shared:

Swami stressed the importance of a proper shrine room in every Hindu household. He suggested that a new and special shrine room should be included in every new house constructed. This bit of advice was well taken by Mr. Vairamuthu. In the year 1932, he constructed a new house for himself and his family in Colombo, making a point to include a large, beautiful shrine room right in the center of the house.

The construction was completed in due course and he was to move into the new house on a certain date. He had invited several friends and relations to a grand reception to take place at 6pm. By 3pm all arrangements had been completed and Mr. Vairamuthu sat in front of the house musing to himself, "What a glorious thing will it be if Siva Yogaswami would step in right now and bless the house."

Lo and behold! Just at that time, a car stopped in front of the house and Yogaswami stepped out. Mr. Vairamuthu ran to the car, welcomed the swami and brought him into the house. Swami barked, "I don't have much time to spare. I was passing this way and I thought I will drop in here for five minutes. Now show me your shrine room." He was taken into the shrine room, from where he blessed the whole house. He passed the camphor flame to Ganesha, Murugan and Siva and asked Mr. Vairamuthu whether he had any prasadam to offer him. Mr. Vairamuthu offered all that he had, but Swami took one item of each and remarked, "I have done the job for which I came," left the room and the house, got back into the car and drove away.

Swami opposed the ritual sacrifice of animals, which was the custom of the day at smaller, village temples. Dr. Ramanathan recalled how he spoke against it and brought about change.

There was an old Aiyanar temple amid the paddy fields in our village. Every year the people celebrated the Pongal festival there with a huge sacrifice. Goats and cocks were killed and offered to this village guardian Deity. One day Swami returned from Anunnakam, looked at me and said, "I saw many corpses in your village,'" referring to the goats and cocks that had been sacrificed at the temple. The power of Swami's compassion for those animals and birds eventually stopped this sacrificial practice. The temple authorities, who once refused to stop this practice, even when the people of the area arose in a storm of protest, now stopped it of their own accord.

Tolerance and Compassion

A strict vegetarian, Swami also abstained from alcohol, though he smoked cigars in his senior years. Still, he was not puritanical about life. A follower recalled:

> There were many devotees who participated actively in the prohibition movement in Jaffna. But one devotee had a large liquor store and traded in it. Swami saw nothing wrong in this, for he never considered anyone as a sinner. He considered all as different gems strung together on the chain that was Siva. One of Swami's close devotees learned that he should not differentiate even those who indulge in alcohol in the following manner.
>
> He was the principal of a school and was very friendly with a person who helped greatly in the development of the school. However, being an extreme disciplinarian, when he learned that his friend was a heavy drinker, he severed all connections with him. But when it was time to open a school building to which his former friend had made tremendous contributions, he was faced with a dilemma. With the thought of his friend worrying him, he went to Swami, who greeted him with the words, "Look here! We need drunkards, too. Even in a person considered to be a bad man may be some good qualities not found even in Mahatma Gandhi. Therefore, we should move with such people showing customary friendship and not discard them."

Swami urged devotees to not label people as good or bad:

> See everyone as God. Don't say, "This man is a robber. That one is a womanizer. The man over there is a drunkard." This man is God. That man is God. God is within everyone. The seed is there. See that and ignore the rest. Are you a good man or a bad man? Who is bad? There is no one who is bad in the world. No good man, no bad man. All are.

While Yogaswami accepted all people as they were, without discrimination, he was not passive about the problem of alcohol abuse in the community. In the 1950s he mobilized his devotees to campaign in favor of prohibition laws.

S. Shanmugasundaram recorded another incident that illustrates Swami's tolerant and compassionate outlook.

On one occasion there was a crowd of about twenty-five devotees in Swami's hut and everyone was listening attentively to his stories, which contained gems of spiritual wisdom. Suddenly Swami observed that one of the devotees was somewhat uneasy. He immediately called him forward, placed something in his hands and told him he could go. The man left the place happily but somewhat shyly.

Yogaswami then explained to the remaining devotees, "He is an attorney-at-law and a good devotee. Unfortunately, he has become slave to a bad habit—taking some liquor in the evening every day. He was getting uneasy because the pubs close at 6pm and he did not have enough time to go home to fetch some money and get back to the pub before it closed. So I gave him the necessary money and sent him away in good time. If he does not take his drink, he cannot eat and he cannot sleep."

This is an instance of Swami's love and concern for his devotees. He had a most sympathetic heart and before he tried to reform anybody, he captured their love and admiration through his benign care and concern. He did not attract devotees through magic and material gifts, but through love and sympathy.

Swami's Natchintanai "Call Not Any Man a Sinner" conveys his attitude:

Call not any man a sinner!
That One Supreme is everywhere you look.
Ever cry and pray to Him to come.
Be like a child and offer up your worship.
Forswear all wrath and jealousy;
Lust and accursed alcohol eschew.
Associate with those who practice *tapas*,
And join great souls who have realized Self by self.

. . . .

Every devout Hindu family hopes, one day, to feed the satguru,
and Yogaswami's devotees were always ready for his unexpected
knock on the door. A few of the ammas *were world-class cooks,*
and he stumbled upon their homes a little more often.

A story from S. Shanmugasundaram illustrates Swami's compassion, his close familiarity with the Jaffna people and his acceptance of the entire spectrum of humanity.

A close devotee of Yogaswami went to Swami's hut to have his darshan. Swami invited him to sit and then asked whether he had come in his car. When the devotee replied in the affirmative, Yogaswami said, "OK, come, let us go for a drive." He got in the car and asked the devotee to drive south. After they had gone about ten miles, Swami asked him to stop, turn and drive down a particular road. After about four miles, Swami said, "Your house must be somewhere here. Let us stop and go to see your sick wife."

The devotee was amazed. Swami had never visited his home, and he had never said where he lived. To his knowledge, Swami also did not know anything about his wife's illness. Lo, the spot where Swami ordered him to stop was exactly where his house stood. With awe and respect, the devotee got down and took Swami inside. The wife was bedridden, so Swami went into her room, had a close look at the patient, chatted with her for a few minutes. When he came out, he did not speak a word, and the devotee did not ask any questions.

At that time, somebody from the back garden shouted something and Swami asked who it was. The devotee replied, "That is my father-in-law, Swami; he is a peculiar type of man. He is not interested in religion or dharma. He is entirely self-interested and is only bent on making money all the time."

Swami then remarked, "This world is like an ornament worn on Siva Peruman's chest. That ornament is studded with various stones, like rubies, diamonds, sapphires and emeralds. Some of them may be white and some may be of various colors. Some stones may be bright and some may be not so bright. But all the stones join to make the ornament beautiful. Similarly, the people on this planet, who are stones on the ornament, cannot be all alike. If all are good, the world cannot go on. Therefore, there is nothing wrong in your father-in-law's attitude." When they were driving back, Swami told the devotee that his wife would have to continue in bed till her death three years later.

"The Day I Met Yogaswami"
Sometime in the late fifties, Sam Wickramasinghe of Colombo, a Sinhalese Buddhist, visited Yogaswami with a Tamil friend from Jaffna. Sam

was a sincere seeker who had heard much about Yogaswami but had never visited him. Sam had met his new friend one day while walking along the seashore in Colombo. Soon after they exchanged greetings, the elder began telling him about Yogaswami with great enthusiasm, then scolded him for never having visited Swami: "It is disgraceful that you haven't bothered to visit our sage who lives on this island." The man offered to pay Sam's train fare to Jaffna and invited him to live in his home in Tellippallai as long as he wished. Using the pen name Susunaga Weeraperuma, Sam recounted his experience in a small book he wrote in 1970, called *Homage to Yogaswami.*

Being a devout Hindu, my friend sincerely believed that it was necessary to purify me as a preparation for the forthcoming visit to Yogaswami. In the mornings before sunrise, his wife would recite hymns from the Hindu scriptures. Frequently I had to dress in a white dhoti with sandalwood paste and holy ash applied liberally on my body as a necessary requirement before entering certain temples. I did not quite see the religious or spiritual significance of these rituals, but perhaps they added a certain color to these otherwise drab and solemn occasions.

As the weeks passed by, much though I was enjoying the hospitality of my generous host, I was nevertheless beginning to feel rather impatient that we had not yet visited Yogaswami. Later I realized that my friend was sincere in his assurance that a preliminary period of preparation was absolutely essential before having an interview with Yogaswami. Nearly a month had passed and I was longing to return home to Colombo.

As I was fast losing my earlier interest in Yogaswami, I finally decided to leave Jaffna without visiting him. When I broke the news of this decision to my friend, he gleamed triumphantly. "Ah, I think the right moment has come. Now that you are losing interest in him you are in a ready state to see him. We shall go tomorrow." We decided to meet Yogaswami the following morning at sunrise, which was supposedly the best time for such a meeting.

It was a cool and peaceful morning, except for the rattling noises owing to the gentle breeze that swayed the tall and graceful palmyra trees. We walked silently through the narrow and dusty roads. The city was still asleep. We approached Swami's tiny thatched-roof hut that had been constructed for him in the garden of a home outside Jaffna. Yogaswami appeared exactly as I had imagined him to be. At

83 he looked very old and frail. He was of medium height, and his long grey hair fell over his shoulders. When we first saw him, he was sweeping the garden with a long broom. He slowly walked towards us and opened the gates.

"I am doing a coolie's job," he said. "Why have you come to see a coolie?" He chuckled with a mischievous twinkle in his eyes. I noticed that he spoke good English with an impeccable accent. As there is usually an esoteric meaning to all his statements, I interpreted his words to mean this: "I am a spiritual cleanser of human beings. Why do you want to be cleansed?"

He gently beckoned us into his hut. Yogaswami sat cross-legged on a slightly elevated neem-wood platform, which also served as his austere bed, and we sat on the floor facing him. We had not yet spoken a single word. That morning we hardly spoke; he did all the talking.

Swami closed his eyes and remained motionless for nearly half an hour. He seemed to live in another dimension of his being during that time. One wondered whether the serenity of his facial expression was attributable to the joy of his inner meditation. Was he sleeping or resting? Was he trying to probe into our minds? My friend indicated with a nervous smile that we were really lucky to have been received by him. Yogaswami suddenly opened his eyes. Those luminous eyes brightened the darkness of the entire hut. His eyes were as mellow as they were luminous—the mellowness of compassion.

I was beginning to feel hungry and tired, and thereupon Yogaswami asked, "What will you have for breakfast?" At that moment I would have accepted anything that was offered, but I thought of *idli* [steamed rice cakes] and bananas, which were popular food items in Jaffna. In a flash there appeared a stranger in the hut who respectfully bowed and offered us these items of food from a tray. A little later my friend wished for coffee, and before he could express his request the same man reappeared on the scene and served us coffee.

After breakfast, Yogaswami asked us not to throw away the banana skins, as they were for the cow. He called loudly to her and she clumsily walked right into the hut. He fed her the banana skins. She licked his hand gratefully and tried to sit on the floor. Holding out to her the last banana skin, Swami ordered, "Now leave us alone. Don't disturb us, Valli. I'm having some visitors." The cow nodded her head in obeisance and faithfully carried out his instructions.

Yogaswami closed his eyes again, seeming once more to be lost in a world of his own. I was indeed curious to know what exactly he did on these occasions. I wondered whether he was meditating. There came an apropos moment to broach the subject, but before I could ask any questions he suddenly started speaking.

"Look at those trees. The trees are meditating. Meditation is silence. If you realize that you really know nothing, then you would be truly meditating. Such truthfulness is the right soil for silence. Silence is meditation." He bent forward eagerly. "You must be simple. You must be utterly naked in your consciousness. When you have reduced yourself to nothing—when your self has disappeared, when you have become nothing—then you are yourself God. The man who is nothing knows God, for God is nothing. Nothing is everything. Because I am nothing, you see, because I am a beggar, I own everything. So nothing means everything. Understand?"

"Tell us about this state of nothingness," requested my friend with eager anticipation. "It means that you genuinely desire nothing. It means that you can honestly say that you know nothing. It also means that you are not interested in doing anything about this state of nothingness." What, I speculated, did he mean by "know nothing?" The state of "pure being" in contrast to "becoming?" He responded to my thought, "You think you know, but, in fact, you are ignorant. When you see that you know nothing about yourself, then you are yourself God."

Keerimalai
Springs

Gurudeva's Ashram
Alaveddy

Jaffna Town

Kadaitswami's Hut
Mandaitivu

KKS
Road

Kadaitswami's
Shrine

Nallur
Kandaswamy
Temple

Yogaswami's Hut
Columbuthurai

Chapter Fifteen

"We Know Not"

Siva Yogaswami's teachings, rife with esoteric insights about nothingness and not knowing, perplexed many an outsider. In life, the normal emphasis is on acquiring knowledge, or replacing a lack of knowledge on a subject with knowledge. We purchase a new computer. Knowing little about it, we read the manuals, talk to experts and end up acquiring enough information to use the computer. We have replaced a lack of knowledge with knowledge.

Yogaswami's approach, dealing as it must with spiritual matters, is the opposite. We start with intellectual knowledge about God and strive to rid ourselves of that knowledge. When we succeed, we end up experiencing God. Why is this? Because the intellect cannot experience God. The experience of God in His personal form and His all-pervasive consciousness lies in the superconscious or intuitive mind. And, even more cryptic, the experience of God as Absolute Reality is beyond even the superconscious mind.

Acquiring clear intellectual concepts of the nature of God is good, but these concepts must be eventually transcended to actually experience God. Sam Wickramasinghe recalls how Yogaswami drove this truth into one man's heart:

> The turning point in Swami Gauribala's life came when he returned to Ceylon and journeyed to Jaffna. A lifelong bibliophile, one morning he was browsing through the spiritual section of the Lanka Book Depot on KKS Road in Jaffna town when an old, white-haired and rather wild-looking stranger suddenly snatched the book from his hands and said, "You bloody fool, it's not found in books! *Nee summa iru!*" ("You be still!") This was his first encounter with Yogaswami of Nallur. His search was ended, and he accepted Yogaswami as his guru after many trials and chastisements.

One of the great sayings of Yogaswami's guru, Chellappaswami, emphasizes the same idea. He said, "*Naam ariyom,*" which translates as, "We do not know." Satguru Sivaya Subramuniyaswami, Yogaswami's successor, would later express the same idea in this aphorism: "The intellect

• •

Here we see Yogaswami with his back to us and (left to right) Markanduswami, and five of the six members of the Council of Cubs (the Kutti Kuttam): a Briton (Yanaikutti), a Tamil from Colombo (Pandrikutti), a Sinhalese (Pulikutti), an Australian (Narikutti), and a German (Naikutti).

strengthened with opinionated knowledge is the only barrier to the superconscious." He went on to explain that "a mystic generally does not talk very much, for his intuition works through reason, but does not use the processes of reason. Any intuitive breakthrough will be quite reasonable, but it does not use the processes of reason. Reason takes time. Superconsciousness acts in the now. All superconscious knowing comes in a flash, out of the nowhere. Intuition is more direct than reason, and far more accurate." One day Yogaswami exulted:

> I see God everywhere. I worship everywhere. All are God! I can say that because I don't know. He who does not know, knows all. If you don't know, you are pure. Not knowing is purity. Not knowing is knowing. Then you are humble. If you know, then you are not pure. People will say they know and tell you this and that. They don't know. Nobody knows. You don't want to know. I don't know. Why do you want to know? Just be as you are. You don't want to know. Let God act through you. Give up this "I want to know." Let God speak. This idea of knowing must be surrendered. Think, think, think. Then you will come to "I do not know." I don't know. You don't know. Nobody knows. It is so. Who knows? If I can say, "I know nothing," then I am God.

"Stop reading books," he told one disciple. "The greatest book is within you. That is the only book you should read. The others are just trash. Open the book that's within you and start reading it. Be very quiet, and it will come to you." Seekers were constantly making the spiritual path out to be arduous, convoluted and beyond their capacity, but Yogaswami repeatedly assured them that it was really not that way.

> So simple is the path, yet you make it hard by holding onto the idea that you are you, and I am I. We are one. We look at the sun and feel its rays. The same sun, the same rays, the same nerves doing the feeling. That also happens when we look within. We feel the darshan of the Lord of the Universe, Siva without attributes. The same darshan is felt by you and me alike. Not your Siva or my Siva; Siva is all. We must burn desire and let the ego melt in the knowing that Siva is all; all is Siva. There are millions of devas to help you. You need only implore them and keep yourself steady through sadhana. Then you will come to see all as one and will taste the divine nectar.

Chellathurai Swami summarized Yogaswami's approach as follows:

Spirituality is constant awareness of God or one's own Self. The *sahaja* state is one in which one is ever conscious of one's Self without any effort whatsoever. But to achieve this state, mighty efforts have to be made. Yogar Swamigal taught that this could be done by trying to remember God in all one's actions. He exhorted everyone to do everything as Sivathondu, which he knew would take one to the state where awareness comes about effortlessly. This, it is said, is the summit of spiritual experiences. To earnest seekers Yoga Swamigal has said, "Practice is greater than preaching," and "Let your Greater Self guide you;" for he knew that sadhana, or practice, with the Greater Self as guide would take them to the stage in which one truly feels that "Everything emerges from that great silence," and "everything is the perfection of that great silence." And these are the words which greet one as one climbs the steps leading to the Meditation Hall in the Sivathondan Nilayam in Jaffna.

Meditation on Siva

Thus, the gurus of the Kailasa Parampara emphasize that in order to realize God, we must go beyond the limitations of the intellect and its concepts. To guide seekers on the path to this experience, Yogaswami stressed the importance of meditation and formulated a key teaching, or *mahavakya: "Tannai ari,"* "Know thyself." This was a second dominant theme of his teachings. He proclaimed, "You must know the Self by the self. Concentration of mind is required for this…. You lack nothing. The only thing you lack is that you do not know who you are…. You must know yourself by yourself. There is nothing else to be known." Markanduswami, a close devotee of Yogaswami, would later tell visitors to his hut:

> Yogaswami didn't give us a hundred-odd works to do. Only one: realize the Self yourself, or know thy Self, or find out who you are. What, exactly, does it mean to know thy Self? Yogaswami explained beautifully in one of his published letters: "You are not the body; you are not the mind, nor the intellect, nor the will. You are the *atma*. The *atma* is eternal. This is the conclusion at which great souls have arrived from their experience. Let this truth become well impressed on your mind."

Knowing that most people are trepidatious about meditating deeply, diving into their deepest Self, Yogaswami gave assurance that inner and outer life are compatible. He counseled, "Leave your relations downstairs, your will, your intellect, your senses. Leave the fellows and go upstairs by yourself and find out who you are. Then you can go downstairs and be with the fellows."

One disciple was struggling to understand things Swami said to him. He went from one person to another for interpretations of the guru's advice. Swami heard of this happening and told him, "Stop running around from place to place like a lamb. Sit down and go within yourself. Meditate. Then roar like a lion."

The American Brahmin

Yogaswami met few Americans in his life, but one was soon to come to his humble hut. In 1947, 20-year-old Robert Hansen, traveling with a classical dance troupe calling itself the American-Asian Cultural Mission, disembarked on Ceylon. During his initial months on the island, Hansen gave dozens of dance performances. Here he learned the ancient, healing Manipuri dance and revived a type of dance indigenous to the area around Kandy—a colorful, bold and intricate art form. But the accomplished artiste had traveled to Ceylon to meet his guru and realize the Self.

Soon he began to encounter saints and sages, adepts of various yogic disciplines, masters of using the third eye, the science of tuning the nerve currents of the body, Hindu mysticism, controlling the forces of the material world and meditation. Each catalyst came to him at just the right moment. Robert felt that each of these meetings was auspicious. In each interchange he felt the pull of his guru. Every adept he met gave what he had to give. He obediently performed what he was told until he felt a release from that catalyst. Then the next teacher, the next swami, the next mufti, would come to open to him another realm of superconsciousness. As this was happening, Yogaswami kept himself veiled, always working through another person.

Robert had gone to the jungle caves of Jailani and fasted there until he realized the Self. He was continuing to follow a disciplined sadhana. In early 1949, the young brahmin from America, as he was called, met C. Kandiah Chettiar, the Hindu adept who would introduce him to Yogaswami. Kandiah lived in Alaveddy, a village not far from Jaffna town; he had been with Yogaswami for decades and knew him well. They had frequently talked in the streets and shops of Jaffna, and sat together many times in the ashram home of Chellachi Ammaiyar.

After spending several weeks together in Colombo, Chettiar invited the young man to travel with him to Jaffna. There, Robert stayed with Kandiah at his family home. The American brahmin was quietly eager to meet Jaffna's legendary "Old Beggar." Finally, the meeting was arranged.

When the 22-year-old American seeker finally met Yogaswami, they were, as the Jaffna saying goes, "Like milk poured into milk." They had deep philosophical discussions, and Yogaswami asked for fresh grape juice to be squeezed for his visitor.

· ·

Siva Yogaswami received the American seeker in his hermitage several times, spoke with him about yoga and things philosophical, gave him a Hindu name, Subramuniya, along with inner instructions, and initiated him with a powerful slap on the back, saying, "This will be heard in

America!" When Kandiah heard about the slap on the back, he knew what had occurred. He remarked to close friends, "Now it is finished. Swami has performed the coronation." The last time Subramuniya approached the hut, Yogaswami yelled out, "Go away. I am not at home." Yogaswami mentioned his American disciple only a few times thereafter.

In 1956, when Subramuniya had a climactic mystical experience in Denver, Colorado, Yogaswami said to Kandiah Chettiar's son Vinayaga-moorthy, "Hansen is dead. Hansen is dead." Everyone felt sad until they received a letter from Subramuniya, sharing that he had begun his teaching work in the West. Hearing that, the Jaffna Saivites understood what Yogaswami had meant. It was the same statement Chellappaswami had made about Yogaswami years earlier.

Later someone asked Yogaswami if he had left a guru. He replied, "Subramuniya is in America." Another time he said, "Oh, I have a man in America." One day Swami was giving some instructions to Vinayagamoorthy, going on about what he should do with his life. Vinayagamoorthy reminded him that he was taking care of Subramuniya's ashram in Alaveddy, and Yogaswami answered, "Oh, that friend of your father." But he later remarked to Vinayagamoorthy in an off-handed way, "So, you are helping us build the bridge." Subramuniya would later relate that "Yogaswami instructed me to build a bridge between East and West." It was a phrase Subramuniya would frequently reference, and a goal he never forgot.

During this period, Yogaswami urged people to build bridges to the West. He sent some to England and America to meet his close devotees. He told those going of the importance of their mission, and gave details on what they should say in bringing Saivism to various Western countries. He often talked about the spiritual power that would arise in America and envisioned the day when he would be known there.

The Council of Cubs

In the late 1950s a group of seekers, one from Ceylon and five from around the world, gathered around the gray-haired master. Haro Hara Amma, a mystic Muruga *bhakta* who lived on a tea estate near Adam's Peak, gave each a special name of a young animal, and so the group was also referred to as the *kutti kuttam*, "council of cubs." All were addressed as swami, though most were not initiated. They were a wild and diverse, free-thinking bunch, and the only thing they agreed on was that they were all disciples of Yogaswami. In 1956 these six men went to Kataragama to do *kavadi*, presumably with Yogaswami's blessings.

They were: Gauribala Swami (born Peter Joachim Schoenfeldt in

Germany in 1907), known as Naikutti (Puppy); Sam Wickramasinghe, a Sinhalese Buddhist, of Ceylon, known as Pulikutti (Tiger Cub); Barry Windsor of Australia, known as Shankarappillai Swami or Narikutti (Young Fox); Mr. Balasingham of Colombo, Ceylon, known as Mudaliar Swami or Pandrikutti (Piglet); James Herwald Ramsbotham of England, the 2nd Viscount Soulbury (whose father was Britain's last Governor General of Ceylon), known as Sanda Swami or Yanaikutti (Elephant Cub); and Adrian Snodgrass of the United States, known as Punaikutti (Kitten). The elder of the group, Gauribala Swami (popularly known as German Swami) was the only formally initiated sannyasin. He received that initiation in the Giri Dashanami order in North India prior to meeting Yogaswami.

During the annual temple festival at Nallur, Yogaswami could be found seated with his Council of Cubs in the chariot house where his satguru had lived and ruled. They were a motley crew, but they all understood the paramount importance of the guru and obeyed his every command. Swami made stern demands on them at times, swore and sent them running, but was also nurturing, giving each the subtle push needed to overcome the limitations of ego and proceed in his religious life, for each was intently striving for higher states of being.

Sam (Pulikutti) recalls, "He once said to me, 'The greatest scripture one can learn from is life. Learn from the book of life. Watch yourself and your reactions to externals. Don't suppress anything—go into every situation that strikes your path and watch mindfully, in joy or in sorrow, in anger or in love, then one day, quite suddenly, unexpectedly, the watcher who is watching all this and getting involved in all this will be seen!'"

T. Sivayogapathy shared some insight into the life of Sandaswami, who is considered one of Yogaswami's foremost brahmachari disciples.

German Swami is said to have lived in Jaffna from the early 1940s, predominantly in the Chelvasannathy Murugan temple at the northern tip of the island. He met Yogaswami in 1947, and introduced Sandaswami to Yogaswami in 1953. Three years later, Yogaswami initiated Sandaswami and assigned him to reside, meditate and serve at the KKS Road Sivathondan Nilayam, Jaffna. Yogaswami instructed Chellathurai, the Nilayam manager, to "be alert and not to allow German Swami to influence Sandaswami in a wrong direction." Devotees remember the English seeker as a serious, dedicated brahmachari who was often seen avidly studying books related to Saiva philosophy. Later, after Yogaswami's *mahasamadhi,* he spent twelve years in Batticaloa, managing the Sivathondan Nilayam in

Chenkaladi. In his later years, he returned to Jaffna and stayed for a few years with Markanduswami at his humble hermitage and ultimately returned to England and to his noble family. He attained *mahasamadhi* at the age of 92 on December 13, 2004.

Solace for All

Thousands and thousands of people approached him over the years, from all walks of life, from all corners of the Earth. Some visited him for purely worldly reasons, others for spiritual blessings, some to test him, some with medical ailments, some for visions of their future, others for blessings on undertakings. In the words of Sri Tikiri Banda Dissanayake, "To all stricken in body or weighed down by sorrow, he had a word of solace and a blessing. Everyone went away refreshed." Ratna Ma Navaratnam wrote:

> People of all faiths, men and women from different walks of life, seekers from all parts of the globe, east and west, north and south, the rich and poor, old and young thronged to him for succor, for they realized that they were in the presence of a great Master in whom conflicts and contradictions did not exist, and who radiated an abiding inward peace—*santam upasantam*.
>
> Swami's effulgent face, penetrating eyes, the white flowing beard, and the spreading forehead with the gleaming holy ash, his waist cloth of white cotton, and the hair knot on the crown of his regal head, altogether struck awe and majesty in the hearts of those who approached him with infinite reverence and humility.

S. Nigel Subramaniam Siva treasures this anecdote:

> One day, as usual, my father, Subramaniam, went to see Siva Yogaswami. Yogaswami told to my father, "I have to tell you some news." My father was very attentive to hear what Swami was going to say. Yogaswami announced, "God Siva really exists, and I have no news other than that."

One morning a man came to share his life's sorrows with Swami, complaining that he had several daughters and could not afford the dowries that would be required to get them married. Now one had received a proposal. Wordless, Yogaswami reached into his *veshti* (into that hip pocket that is really just the cloth folded in upon itself) and handed the man ten thousand rupees for the dowry. Other fathers he told not to worry,

Yogaswami often visited a devotees' homes without notice, sit in meditation, take a meal, sing a sacred song and, from time to time, spend the night. His closest devotees kept a special room for such a blessed visitation.

. . . .

that men would marry their daughters based on their merits. Invariably, it came to be. S. Shanmugasundaram recounts how Swami once called upon other devotees to assist a man with his daughter's dowry:

Yogaswami's heart was full of love and compassion for everyone. Whether he smiles at you or scorns you, whether he embraces you or kicks you, every act of his is an act of love and grace. Without any outward show, he would shower so much compassion on all beings. The care and concern he had for those in need was immeasurable. He never disappointed any sincere devotee who approached him with a problem. One fine morning, Yogaswami was seated in his hut with two devotees in front of him. He was chatting on various topics. An old man came there and stood outside the hut. Swami summoned him inside and asked, "How is everything going with you?" Without uttering a word in reply, the man broke down crying and sobbed for two or three minutes.

Then Swami spoke, "Don't worry. Siva will show you a way out of your difficulties. You may now go home in peace." The man left as directed and Swami addressed the two devotees who remained, "He is a good-hearted man. He is experiencing some difficulty in giving his daughter in marriage. She is 26 years old, and a cousin of hers is willing to marry her if the father will at least provide her with the minimum jewelry. Why don't one of you help him?" Immediately A. Thillyampalam offered to do the needful. Excusing himself, he ran after the man and got his name and address. The next day he went to his house and presented him with a gift of Rs. 5,000. The man was overjoyed. Without any delay, he got all the necessary jewelry made and gave the daughter in marriage.

Sometimes those who saw the great numbers coming to Swami wondered why he allowed so many, and why he did not refuse to see certain people, such as lawyers who came to him before arguing a case, knowing that just being with Swami for a few moments would help them. He once explained, "I see everyone, and everyone takes from me what they can hold. It is not my job to pick and choose, to say this one come and that one go." S. Kandiah of Ontario observed that those who came to Swami were of three categories.

The first were the exclusively spiritual, ascetic type. This was a very small number. Swami kept them aloof of the others, even visiting them instead of them coming to him. The second category were those living a worldly life, with all its enjoyments, but who had a touch of spiritual tendencies. The third were those mainly looking for worldly pleasures, positions, wealth, etc.

As I began to grow very close with the swami, all feelings of fear and stress gone, I one day asked him why he encouraged the latter hypocritical hangers-on around him. He gave out a hearty laugh that could have been heard a hundred meters away and asked me, "Do I have to make good men good, or bad men good?" In other words, all have a place with him, sinners as well as spiritual aspirants.

But he did chase some away in no uncertain terms, occasionally using the foulest language that had immediate effect but which devotees could never repeat. And he did refuse to see others. He explained that by chasing away or refusing to see someone, he was also giving darshan.

Once one of Swami's oldest and sincerest devotees visited, accompanied by his youngest daughter, who was getting married the next day. They came, of course, for Swami's blessings. Hearing them at the gate, Swami called out, "Who's there?" A devotee who was sitting inside went out to see, then reported back who it was. Swami responded, "Who is he?" Everyone knew that Swami knew him well. They also knew why he had come.

Swami was quiet for a while then said, "Tell him we don't want to see a stranger now. Tell him we can't see him now." A devotee conveyed the message. As soon as the car drove away, Swami sent someone out to see if it had gone. Everyone knew it had gone. They had heard it leave. But Swami wanted someone to check. As soon as that person came back to the hut, Swami started laughing. He laughed uproariously. Then he told those around him, who were deeply puzzled by his behavior, "It was settled long ago. Finished long ago." No one ever knew why he refused to see this devotee and his daughter, but they all sensed there was some spiritual purpose behind the scene they had witnessed.

A close devotee, a regular visitor to the hermitage, recounted one occasion when Swami told her to go away.

> Normally for Dipavali, a festival of lights that takes place in October, we buy new clothes for our relations or anyone to whom we want to give. So I bought a nice *veshti* for Swami. I went to Swami's place and waited, but he didn't call me in for a long time. Finally he said, "I don't want anybody to come in; all of you go away." I felt so sad, I cried. Then he said, "All right, don't bring your *veshti* in, but you can come in." I felt sad because Swami refused to take the *veshti* that I brought. He then quoted an example about a king called Janaka who was also a great saint. "Janaka's guru made him wait for forty days, and he was not perturbed. He just stood there. You, like a fool, you are crying for a little thing." Then he sent me away. "First obey, and then command," he used to say.

Once a man was inspired to open a bookstore, beginning with a collection of used books he had obtained. He wanted Swami to come and bless the store, but every time he saw Swami, the request slipped from his mind. Somehow, in Swami's presence, it didn't seem important enough to mention. He arranged to have a small ceremony at an auspicious time to mark

the opening. The time of the ceremony arrived, and still he had not invited Swami. Yet, at the exact moment the astrologer had set for the puja to
begin, Swami arrived. In time, the shop became the foremost bookstore in
Jaffna. The owner considered its success a direct result of Swami's blessing that day.

Hundreds of stories are told of Swami's answers to unspoken questions and fulfillments of impossible-to-know needs. If someone came
and had a significant experience with Swami, or received some important
help, he would forbid them to talk about it. "Sacred is secret, and secret
is sacred," he admonished. So carefully did people keep that advice, that
neighbors both might have visited Swami and not have told each other
about it. Many regarded it as amazing that such a secret could be kept in
Jaffna—where the breeze itself carries news.

Devotees came to see Swami either early in the morning or in the evening. He would awaken before dawn and meditate in his hut. The devout
would come and sit with him. After remaining in silence for some time,
Swami might start to sing. He had a rich voice, full and melodious. Once a
devotee asked him what a certain song meant, to which he answered, "Oh,
I didn't write that song; it came from within." He would also sing hymns
and scriptures composed by other saints. He would say they also came
from within: "I could have retrieved that song from memory, but I did not.
It came from within."

He might ask a devotee sitting with him to pick up a book and read
from it: the *Taittiriya Upanishad,* a work from the vast *Tirumurai,* Swami
Vivekananda's writings or some other holy book.

Whenever people sang for him or read, he would ask them—or even
scold them—to read not as if they were reading about some time and place
far away and removed from them, but as if they were Siva or Saint Manikkavasagar right at that moment. "That's the only way to understand these
words," he insisted. Swami challenged each one who approached him.

The only difference between you and me is that I know who I am. Can
I help you find out who you are? I can show you the way and light the
path, but you must stand on your own feet and do the work yourself.
Everything is within you. You have only to find it and claim it. I can
show you the way to go to Keerimalai or the way to Nallur. I know the
way. I've been there many times. But if you want to go there, you must
do the walking. I can't do the walking for you. It's the same with the
spiritual path.

Over the years, by his tireless efforts to uplift, inspire and assist each person with whom he came in contact, Swami built up a strong congregation of devotees. Inthumathy Amma writes:

By staying at the Columbuthurai Ashram and by going to the homes of devotees, Swami attracted a great following. Among those were some who were transformed into serving God by doing service to others, by taking and giving to others. Yet others, true to the words "Whoever thinks of me constantly, they are my good devotees," became devotees who thought of him constantly. Some entire families—husband, wife, parents, children, uncles and aunties—all became devotees as a group. Some of these families, disregarding the comments of others that they were mad, named their children Sivancheyal, Sivathondan, Yogaranandan, Yogaranban so that they could be constantly reminded of him. Yet others became karma yogis.

Some renounced and became acolytes, living near Swami. Even one who belonged to the nobility in England renounced everything and became Swami's devotee. Markandu Swami and other brahmacharis followed Swami's path of "Know Thyself," matured and became guiding lights to all the devotees of Siva. Swami's divine children, through religious knowledge and experience of dharmic conduct, strengthened by the disciplined life and observing the laws of celibacy, followed in his footsteps.

Some of Siva Yogar Swami's devotees were in government service. Those people who worked all over the country could not come to the ashram frequently. Hence, Swami went in search of them at their homes. Especially when they were in deep trouble and appealed to him with a broken heart, he would appear before them and bless them with divine grace. He went often to the postmaster at Mabale, and to Mr. Kandasamy's house, to the cottage of Mr. Veluppillai at Peradeniya, to the home of Dr. Ramanathan who worked at Gampola, and to other places. He also went to Mr. A. Thillyampalam's house in Ratnapura and to many peoples' homes in Nawalapitiya. In this way, Swami visited many devotees' homes all over the island. Those devotees maintained their shrine room with great care as Swami's own room. When they learned that Swami was at a particular home, they flocked there for his darshan.

For about twenty years, he went once a month to the Hill Country, to Colombo, to Trincomalee, to Batticaloa and other places and in this way brought up his devotees. All the homes that Swami visited began to flourish like temples. Then, in 1942, at age 70, he decreed, "There is no more going to outside places. Those who so desire can come here."

A devotee recounted the following anecdotes.

> One evening, when about fifteen people were gathered in the hut, Swami asked all of us how many were there. Nobody said anything. Then Swami said, "There is only one person."
>
> Swami often inquired, "If you are told you must not speak the truth, you must tell a lie, then what should you do?" One day Sandaswami was there, and Swami asked him this question. Immediately Sandaswami put his finger to his lips. He didn't speak. Later Swami told us, "He is a great man. So many people in Jaffna gave me all sorts of explanations; he just showed it in silence."
>
> One morning at about 5:30 or so, I went to Swami. As usual, he was sweeping the compound. He used to sweep the whole place every morning, heaping the dust on one side, the cow dung on the other. Then he stopped and shouted deliberately, "Who is there? Who has come?" Then he told me, "You know, all this time I was a lavatory coolie; now I am a swami." Then he went into the hut, took a small copper vessel and made a *kumbha* by filling it with water and placing a tumbler and some flowers in it. I think he meant he was purifying people's hearts. He would say, "There should be someone to turn people in the right path. Christ did that, Buddha did that. I am also doing that."
>
> One day I brought some tea to Swami in his hut when Sandaswami was there. He offered his cup of tea to Sandaswami, so I said, "Wait, Swami, I'll bring another cup for him." Swami responded, "Mind your own business; I know what to do," and gave the tea to Sandaswami.
>
> Yogaswami always wanted people to work. He emphasized work. "Work till you shed blood," he once said after sweeping. "Do your work. Do your karma. Don't expect any return. That is yoga. That is sannyasa." In other words, don't attach yourself to things.
>
> Once when we were all at Swami's place eating from plantain leaves, when everyone had finished dinner, a lady doctor who was there wanted to take Swami's leaf to throw it away. Swami said, "I can do my work. You do your work."

Swami opened the path of service to his devotees. "Work, work, work; serve, serve, serve." He always had a project going, something that seemed like more than anyone or any group of people could accomplish. And he demanded it be done to perfection, never allowing them to settle for second-rate performances. If it was a drama for a Hindu festival, he would boldly offer advice about the production. Swami might even act out parts of the pageant like a director, rehearsing scenes, stretching each participant a little beyond what he thought was his capacity. "You are more than you think you are," he would chide. Each one discovered new strength in fulfilling his expectations. A devotee recalls:

> If you were organizing a feeding for a thousand people at Nallur Temple, he made sure you had everything planned well so the event would go smoothly. He wanted to know precisely what curries you planned to serve, and might suggest substitutes or cutting back on the quantity. "Three curries is enough," he would direct.
>
> If you and other devotees were rebuilding a temple that had fallen into disrepair, he would get involved, making sure you rebuilt it properly and had the necessary ceremonies conducted for its reopening. He would even inquire if you had provided an adequate endowment to keep the temple functioning well into the future.
>
> If a devotee had accomplished something and came to Swami for praise, he would strip him down to size quickly. Sometimes he would ignore a devotee's achievement entirely and quickly guide his attention to another project that needed work. Or he would scold, "So, you think you have put on a good feeding? Was it you who put life into the food? Into those who cooked the curries? Who created hunger? Who discovered the way to satisfy it? My child, you must not think you have done anything. It is all the work of the Lord. When you know that, then you will know you have done nothing."

"Be like water on a lotus leaf," he urged. In other words, don't get attached; be free to move here and there with the feeling that nothing is happening. One time a devotee close to Swami had what he considered an extraordinary spiritual experience. He had encountered, in meditation, dimensions of consciousness that were remarkably new to him. In the street the next morning, Swami asked him what had happened. Without thinking, he blurted, "Nothing, Swami." "That's right," Swami affirmed. "Nothing happened."

Yogaswami knew exactly what each one who came to him wanted. People rarely spoke in his presence. It was against guru protocol unless he initiated the discussion, and most often they simply found themselves unable to ask questions. If they did, he would say, "Your ignorance is speaking! Send it home!" Usually he cleared up questions before they were voiced. One devotee thought, "Krishna showed Arjuna his divine form. I would like to ask Swami to show me his divine and resplendent self. How can I ask so that he will not scold me?" Right then Swami said,

> Some people wonder if I can show them my effulgent being, as Krishna showed His to Arjuna. That is easy. It will happen to each person when the time is right. But you must have no desires lurking in the corners of your mind. You must purify yourself of all desire. Sing hymns, chant "Aum Namasivaya, Sivayanama Aum," wear holy ash and practice any sadhanas that help you quiet desire. If you find desire, make your mind a funeral pyre and burn that desire. Burn it! Sit in meditation and watch it burn. Feel the flames. Then get up and wash and apply holy ash. And know that the ash is the ash of your desire.

Blessed Scoldings

Yogaswami closely watched how people revered him. One of his greatest teachings was to have devotees recognize within themselves what he represented to them. A person might worship him with the feeling that "I am so small and powerless and you are so great and powerful, let me enter your good graces so all the bad things I've put into motion, and that I'm sure are going to react back on me, just won't happen." Anyone coming to Yogaswami with such attitudes might be scolded and sent abruptly on his way. "Why are you worshiping me? I have two eyes, two ears, a mouth and a nose, just like you. Go do your own work. Stand on your own feet!"

Yogaswami was a great scolder. His scolding was more penetrating than fire. Years after Swami's *mahasamadhi,* his German disciple, Gauribala Swami, was told by his own devotees that he was a bit gruff and forceful. "Ha!" he chided, "I'm gruff? You couldn't stand for thirty seconds in front of my guru." Many are the stories of Swami's profane language, which he reserved for rare moments with devotees and as a useful way to ward off base strangers.

One man was constantly around offering to serve him, worshiping him with what seemed like true devotion. One day Yogaswami harshly lit into him, speaking the filthiest Tamil there was—language that could make a sailor blush. He kept at the man for over an hour for being afraid, for fearing what might happen to him, what he might have to go through. All the horrible things he had imagined, and some he had not, Yogaswami hit on, naming every one and scolding all the while. It was terrible. He finished, "If you think I'm going to protect you from any of these things, you're wrong. I don't even see them as real. You give them power; you get rid of them. There is nothing to fear, so stand on your own two feet and stop bothering me with your worries and fears, and get rid of them before you come to see me again."

In *Homage to Yogaswami,* Sam Wickramasinghe offered a mystical explanation for Yogaswami's responses to those who came before him.

A liberated mind has the advantage of being a mirror in which a non-liberated mind can see itself as it truly is. If Yogaswami seemed to lack an unchanging personality, it was presumably because his "personality" temporarily acquired the characteristics of his visitors. Not surprisingly, therefore, proud persons invariably found Yogaswami behaving arrogantly towards them. To those who were haunted by fears, Yogaswami's manner seemed timid.

A South Indian sannyasin recited a stanza from the *Bhagavad Gita* to Yogaswami. Thereupon, Yogaswami repeated the stanza with alterations and clever puns on certain words so that the sacred lines acquired an erotic significance. Yogaswami could not help doing that, for he was merely reacting to the hidden sexual imagery in the unconscious mind of that recluse. Consequently, this ascetic, like many other of Yogaswami's visitors, was not only irritated but embarrassed.

In a sense, Yogaswami was a Zen master who awakened people from their psychological slumber by shocking them without deliberately wishing to do so. The people of Jaffna regarded Yogaswami with a curious mixture of veneration, affection and fear. Some of his ardent admirers seemed more to fear than love him. To be received by Yogaswami, it was necessary to approach him without any ulterior motive whatsoever.

Yogaswami chased away most of his visitors. Many persons unfortunately regarded Yogaswami as a mere fortune-teller with the gift of making accurate forecasts. At one time Yogaswami had a stream of visitors every day from dawn to dusk. They came to him with various personal and other problems. Those who were privileged enough to be received by him usually regarded themselves doubly blessed. Some of those who were rebuked by Yogaswami regarded themselves spiritually chastised.

Seeing through the facades people presented to him, Yogaswami would rudely expose what was really on their minds. Mr. Nagendran shared this account.

It was the 1940s. I had just passed the Advocates Final Examination and was due to take my oaths at the Bar. I came back to Jaffna to spend a few weeks. Mr. Veerasingam, the retired principal of Manipay Hindu College, came to the house of my grand uncle Sellamuttu, where I was staying, and asked me to accompany him to Columbuthurai to see Yogar.

Before we reached Swami's hut, Mr. Veerasingam told me, "On the way to see a great man, we should not go with empty hands. We should take offerings." He stopped the car and purchased plantains, apples and other fruits, and had them wrapped up. As we reached the hut that evening, Yogar was seated on a mat covering a thin mattress on the floor.

Mr. Weeram, the Commissioner of Cooperative Development, my father's senior in the department, and other distinguished elders were seated in front of Yogar. As soon as he saw us enter his hut, Yogar said, "God is one, though sages call Him by various names." This phrase hit me, as these were the words painted on the wall of the shrine to Ramakrishna at the Mission Hall at Wellawatte, which I used to visit at that time. Has he, I wondered, divined my visits to the Ramakrishna Mission?

As was his usual practice, Yogar unwrapped the parcel which Mr. Veerasingam gave him and began distributing the fruits to the elders in front of him. Seated at the rear, I noted the number of fruits he gave each elder, wondering whether he would give me, a person not of the same status as the elders, the same number of fruits. While Yogar was handing the fruits to me, he remarked, "Everybody here gets the same number. See, even one of the fruits I am to give you has fallen because you had doubts." Yogar had read my mind. I was humbled.

In 1953 Swami Sivananda of the Divine Life Society sent a young sannyasin, Swami Satchidananda, to Ceylon to open a small yoga center in the hill station of Kandy. Charismatic and humorous, the dark-haired swami from South India drew crowds for his hatha yoga classes. One day he made his way to Columbuthurai for the blessings of Yogaswami. He described the meeting: "I entered the hut and prostrated. Immediately Yogaswami asked me, 'How many people do you have standing on their heads today, Swami?'" Satchidananda inferred that Yogaswami was encouraging him to use his considerable gifts for more than teaching the physical yogas to common crowds. Years later, Swami Satchidananda

. . . .

Singing the Tamil devotional hymns to Lord Siva is a strong part of Sri Lankan spiritual culture to this day. Yogaswami had devotees loudly and passionately sing Devarams *and* Natchintanai *whenever they visited his hut.*

ascended to fame when he gave a talk at the Woodstock festival in New York, and later founded the Integral Yoga Institute in the United States.

Siva Yogaswami's closest devotees longed for these scoldings and regarded them as a benediction. One day Yogaswami went to the house of a devotee named Kandan, taking another devotee, Arumugam, with him. Kandan was waiting in the yard when Swami arrived. Suddenly, Swami started pummeling him on the shoulders with both fists with all his might. Kandan stood still for it. When Swami was finished, Arumugam, somewhat aghast at the events, noticed that Kandan looked more blissful

than abused. Kandan, sensing his friend's puzzlement, sighed and con-fided, "I have been waiting a whole year for that blessing. Every three or four years I need a good, strong thrashing from Swami; then I'm fine."

He Who Knew All

When someone came to worship Yogaswami to change the part of him-self that Swami revealed for him, he was encouraged, given what he desired, and sent on his way. Such devotees did not have to say anything. He would just start answering their questions or telling them their next step. He also knew what people were thinking and what they wanted him to do for them. Who was coming and when they were coming and why they were coming were known beforehand. Sometimes he would say, "We must go now. So-and-so will be here in fifteen minutes and he mustn't find us here." Or, "Put a mat there and prepare some tea. So-and-so will be here within the hour and we must have everything ready for him."

Many people came with family problems, money worries, or other dif-ficulties. Sometimes he would scold them and send them off to solve their own problems: "You knew how to get yourself into that mess, so you must know how to get yourself out." Sometimes he would send them to the temple to do a special puja. "Do an *abhishekam* at the Ganesha temple near here. Then the answer to your problem will come." Sometimes he would ask another devotee to help. He would say to a third party, "Go and get five hundred rupees from so-and-so and give it to this man. His wife is sick and he needs help." Money would always come.

Hilda Charlton, who became a strong Muruga *bhakta* and helped establish the Bowne Street Ganesha Temple in Flushing, New York, found that her money problems vanished after her visits to Yogaswami. She wrote:

> He was exactly what you would think a yogi would look like—soft gray hair, gray beard, elderly, wonderful. When I used to go to see him, I would travel all night on an old train to Jaffna, where all the warfare in Ceylon is going on now. This one time I had brought some camphor. The day before, my friend had taken somebody there who wanted to know about a lot of worldly things. When this person went in there, the yogi asked him, "What have you got behind your back?" The man said, "Camphor," and the yogi said, "Burn it on your own tongue."
>
> Yogis could be tough, kids. Then he said to my friend, "Why do you bring people of that caliber here?" I came in the next day. I had some camphor behind my back. I had just heard this story. He asked, "What

have you got behind your back?" I said, "Camphor," and he said, "Come right in, come right in." See?

Every time I went there, he would say, "How much money do you have?" It was just like Yogananda with the food. I would think, "What kind of a person is this?" I would give no answer, and he would know I had no money. He would ask, "What is your salary?" Well, I didn't have any salary. So one day I was honest with him and said, "I don't have any money." He said, "Oh." He had a boy take a book and read, and as the boy read, the yogi sat there moving his hand a certain way.

The boy read, "There is an upper jaw and a lower jaw and the tongue is the conjunction. The tongue makes the sound, and the sound is prosperity," and the yogi asked, "What is that word? You mispronounced it. How do you spell *prosperity?*" The boy spelled it out. All the while the yogi was moving his hand, doing something. You understand? I never had money trouble after that.

Hilda Charlton wrote of another visit she made to see Swami:

The other day at 4am we went while it was still dark on a pilgrimage to see Yogaswami. As we sat listening to him in the flickering coconut lamp light, he sounded just like Mary Ellen. It could have been her talking. He was so simple, sweet, childlike, and his message was hers: that everyone is pure and perfect, only they don't know it. To love is the answer to all things. I came away with a spiritual intensification. It was really fine. He accepted nothing. He said, "I take nothing and I give nothing." But of course he gives a great deal. Though he sees few people, he talked to us for an hour.

Whatever was brought to Swami during the day he distributed by the time everyone left at night. He would give out the fruit and flowers offered to him, then start dismissing people. No one left his presence without his bidding, and no one stayed after being asked to go. Those with needs for which Swami could be of assistance were usually the last to leave. Then he might hand them money, food or cloth he had been given.

He did not always receive what was offered. He explained, "We never accept things from people who are trying to influence us or work their way up in the world or trying to buy a good conscience." He would leave such a gift untouched, or even throw it aside. Sometimes he even refused things offered by his closest devotees. "No orders," he would say.

One time a family of devotees who had stumbled on good fortune, which they attributed to Swami, arrived bearing a tray of gold sovereigns. There must have been a hundred coins in all. Swami said, "We cannot accept this. Take the coins back and find a good use for them. I'll just take a few." He took three or four. At the end of the evening, those coins were gone. A few fortunate visitors must have received them concealed in a handful of flowers or sweets.

There was a widespread belief that Yogaswami was partial toward wealthy and famous people who occupied high positions in public life or politics. S. Shanmugasundaram recorded Swami's views on this criticism.

One day a young devotee seated in the hut drew enough courage and posed the following question: "Swami, there is a misunderstanding among our people that you are friendly with only rich people, that you visit only their homes and that you do not care about the poor. Is there any truth in this?"

Swami smiled and replied: "People who have not been exposed to wealth, position and high life are generally good people. They are not a source of danger to the world. It is the rich and the high-society people who are full of bad ways and have qualities like selfishness, envy, greed, bad moral character, etc. If this latter category of people can be changed to live a better type of life, they can become more useful to their people and to the world. Fortunately, it is that class of people who come to me for the most part. What harm is there in my trying to improve their lot and through them improve the lives of hundreds of others?" Not only the young man who posed the question, but all the devotees present before Swami, were happy at his answer.

Many rich and famous people, in order to enhance their reputation further in society, try to strike a friendship with swamis, politicians, business magnates and popular film stars. There were a number of people who approached Yogaswami with such motives, but many of them found they could not withstand Swami's shouts and scoldings. However, a few reformed themselves, became good Hindus and lived useful lives after their association with Yogaswami. Many of them became great Sivathondars, changed to a virtuous life, gave plentifully to those in need, brought religion into their lives and continued to be ardent devotees of Swami.

It was Siva Yogaswami's dictum that "Man is one and God is One."

. . . .

One of Lord Siva's traditional forms is Ardhanarishvara, half man and half woman. In this form Saivites of Ceylon worship the unity of Siva and Shakti. Yogaswami sang, "O He who became both male and female, devotees offer their praise. O He who is heavenly. O He who has delivered and elaborated the meaning of scripture. O He who is She with the narrow waist on His left!"

Therefore, he loved and respected all beings. Swami used to say that if an animal is cruel, he will not do much harm to the world, because people know it is cruel and they can safeguard themselves. But if a man is cruel, he is capable of destroying a whole community. Therefore, if he came across people who were not true to themselves, who did not live virtuous lives, who paid obeisance to him only for selfish purposes, he scolded them properly, shouted at them and threw them out of his presence. This, too, formed part of Swami's grace, because there are many devotees who were able to reform themselves through this kind of treatment. However, due to this method of dispensing grace, many people feared to seek Swami's darshan.

Of course, not all who came to the ashram were of the educated and influential class, as S. Shanmugasundaram notes in this story:

One day, at about 12 noon, when the sun was unbearably hot, an old woman came into the hut, panting and perspiring. She appeared to have come a long distance, and she was carrying a large jak fruit, since it was known this was among his favored foods. She unloaded the burden in front of the Swami and sat down with a sigh of happy relief. Swami watched all this and addressed the woman thus: "Look here, are you mad? Why did you walk all this distance in this hot sun carrying this huge jak?"

The woman waited for two minutes and retorted: "It is I who carried it all the way for you. It was my pleasure; why do you reprimand me for that? I am not asking for anything in return from you. I wanted to bring it to you, and I have brought it. Now let me rest for awhile and get back home. You keep quiet." Thoroughly surprised at the woman's innocent admonishing, Swami told her, "You can have a fine rest and also a life of peace and joy." He had her served with a cup of coffee and told his devotees, "With one sentence she has shut my mouth. It was my fault to have blamed her." He then gave her an orange and sent her home.

Miracle Making

After Swami's *mahasamadhi,* many stories were told of how he had healed people and cured diseases. While he lived, no one dared to speak about these things. Swami did his work quietly and without show. Most often, if he knew someone was sick, he would send the ailing devotee to a doctor for medicine. As likely as not, he would arrive at the doctor's office at precisely the same time the patient did. He would often tell the physician exactly what medicine to give, then even make sure it was taken. Sometimes he would take the medicine from the devotee, carry it to his hut and put it under his pillow. "This way, it will work for you," he would say as he gave it back the next morning. S. Ampikaipaakan wrote of one such incident from 1936.

Mr. V. Duraiswamy, the leader of the ruling party in Sri Lanka, had been invited for the coronation of King George VI and to receive the honor of knighthood. He suddenly became ill when his travel arrangements to London were being made, and the physicians advised him not to go.

In those days, Swamigal sometimes stayed in Peradanai with Mr. Velupillai, brother of scholar Somasundaram. Swamigal felt Sir Duraiswamy's sickness from Peradanai and gave to Velupillai a list of medicines to buy. When Mr. Velupillai took the list to the store, the storekeeper warned him that the medicines were highly toxic. He conveyed that to Swamigal, but Swamigal said not to mind that and asked him to boil them. Mr. Velupillai made a decoction of the ingredients and gave it to Swamigal.

Swamigal consumed the mixture and a short time afterwards began to vomit violently and to suffer with severe diarrhea. Mr. Velupillai became afraid and started to cry. After some time Swamigal asked for some lemon juice mixed with salted soda water and drank it. A few hours later, he became well.

The next morning Swamigal announced, "Now Duraiswamy can go to London. The treatment for his illness has been done. It will be good for him and the Tamil society if he goes." Duraiswamy recovered, went to London, and received the title from the king.

. . . .

It was common for devotees to turn to Yogaswami when life was difficult or death drew near. He assured all that there was nothing to fear, that Lord Siva is looking after everything. Somehow knowing when a soul was about to depart, Swami would go to the home, apply holy ash to the forehead and thus bless the journey ahead.

Swamigal remained as though nothing happened even after this remarkable miracle, and Mr. Velupillai kept the matter secret and told me about it only after Swamigal attained *mahasamadhi*. What a difference there is between our Swamigal and those who announce every tiny accomplishment in glittering megalomaniac advertising.

Mr. Velupillai himself had a healing experience with Swami. S. Ampikaipaakan recorded it in his biography.

> One afternoon around 3 o'clock, I became dizzy and fainted. Lord's son sent two doctors, and they gave some medicine. I regained consciousness, but I was not able to get up, and I was also not clear what was happening to me. In the morning at 8 o'clock Swamigal came by coach and said to me, "I have brought three medicines for you. Coming near, he touched my head with his compassionate hands and intoned, "Sivayanama." Visiting again the next day, Swamigal said, "Look here, I will show Chidambaram darshan." He then danced as Nataraja for five minutes, with his loosened hair flying around. On the third day he gave me a medicine he had brought with him, mixed in warm water. I became well on the fourth day. I told of this miracle to the president of Kambala Hospital, Dr. Ramanathan, who exclaimed, "That dance was wonderful. It is called Mrityunjaya [defying death], a very effective cure."

As in the West, holy men in the East sometimes make claims of healing. It is a time-honored way to build large followings, capitalizing on the hopes stricken people have for miracle cures. Yogaswami pooh-poohed such outward, even ostentatious, displays of powers; but silently, when needed, he used his powers to both heal and console. Grandpa Chinnaya's relatives told the following story.

> Yogaswami had come down to Colombo from Jaffna. Many devotees in Colombo heard of his arrival and went to see him. One of these was Grandpa Chinnaya. He'd had to take a train to Colombo as his family lived out of town. Grandpa went to see Swami on behalf of one of his sons who was direly ill with double pneumonia. There were about thirty people sitting at Swami's feet, and one by one he dismissed them until only Grandpa Chinnaya remained. Grandpa told of his son's sickness, and Swami gave him a large bunch of grapes, telling him to take them home and give them to his son to eat.

Grandpa left, worried he might not catch the train back home, as it was getting very late. However, just as he arrived for the train, the train arrived, his timing perfect. He returned home to find his son seriously ill with a high fever. He sat him up and proceeded to feed him the grapes, one at a time. The son managed to eat half of them, then fell to sleep. The next morning the fever was gone and his son was well. Grandpa knew that Yogaswami's blessings cured his son.

S. Kandiah of Ontario shared:

My first experience with Swami's healing power was in 1949, when my wife's father was in Jaffna General Hospital, critically ill with tetanus. The doctors had given up all hopes of his recovery. My father-in-law was a devotee of Swami since early childhood, as Swami used to spend a week to ten days at a time at his family's home in Anuradhapura, in quiet meditation.

Unexpectedly, Swami came to the hospital ward accompanied by the medical superintendent, whereupon my mother-in-law fell at Swami's feet weeping. He consoled her, saying, "Go to Nallur Temple tomorrow, Friday, and perform an *archana* in the morning five o'clock puja." The doctors did not believe her husband would even last until that time; but he did. The *archana* was done, and no sooner was the holy ash applied to his forehead, his locked jaws opened and he spoke for the first time in three days. After ten days, he was back at home, fully recovered.

Swami was often seen in different places at the same time. He never spoke of this power, but people who had seen him at one place conferred with others who had seen him at the same time but at a different place. They had friendly arguments about who had really seen Swami. If he heard of the disagreement, he would laugh. Doctor K. Nithiyanandan tells this story:

My elder brother lived in England in 1938 and the early part of 1939 while attending to his higher studies. At that time the Second World War had just started in the Western countries. Hitler's activities were a great threat to the Allied Nations. The industrial towns of England were the target of Hitler's offensive. Hence, my father was terribly worried about my brother. One day he went to Swami wondering about all these worries. Swami looked at him and said, "Do not fear anything." My father feared as a result of the great dangers magnified in the papers. But other dangers that my father did not expect awaited my brother.

Swami's gracious words turned out to be words of assurance which protected my brother from all those dangers. One day, the heater in my brother's room burst and began smoking. My brother was stunned by this sudden incident and did not know what to do. As he sat there unable to do anything, he reached the state of unconsciousness. Then he heard Swami's voice say, "Thamby, break the windows." Swami's words, which were loud and clear, gave my brother new life. He broke the windows, came out and escaped the great danger he was in. The next day, early morning, when my father went to see Swami, he said, "I saw your son yesterday."

In *Tamil Sages and Seers of Ceylon* V. Muthucumaraswami recorded an unusual incident that was narrated to him by Dr. Francis Pillai.

The mother, a Christian, of an engineer who is now in the U.K. was deeply worried about her son, as she had not received any letter from him for a long time. She begged Yogar Swamy to find details about him. Yogar Swamy tried to dissuade her, but she persisted, so Yogar Swamy went into a trance and recorded what the engineer was doing. He found that he was in good health and good spirits. Then he came back from his trance and gave an exact description of her son, his friends, his room and what he was doing. The mother wrote a letter to her son about this and got a letter back, which exactly confirmed what Yogar Swamy had told her.

With just a slight change in his immediate environment he could make dramatic changes in the larger one. One day Yogaswami sat in his Columbuthurai Ashram with a few devotees, facing north as he always did. Oranges that a devotee had brought lay at his feet. Swami, who was engaged in eager conversation with his devotees, suddenly said, "Poor brahmin, the hermit." The statement was wholly irrelevant to the conversation. Saying that, Swami picked up an orange that had fallen from the pile and put it back in its place. He continued the conversation, and the devotees took little note of his statement. However, in fact, those were critical words of protection for the respected scholar and orator Rajayogi Sankarasuppaiyar. At the moment Swami moved the orange, the car in which the brahmin was traveling was saved from a tragic accident, the details of which Rajayogi himself related.

Once, after a lecture at the Sinthernkerny Mahaganapathy temple, I was returning to Nallur at night when there was a heavy downpour. At the bend in Seerani village, the drain had filled up, and the water was overflowing onto the road; the driver could not see the road. Suddenly a light appeared, illuminating the road, allowing us to avoid the drain and reach our destination safely. If not for the light, we would not have seen the deep trench and the car would have fallen straight into it. Many lives were saved due to the light. I later learnt from devotees of Swami how he had said, "Poor brahmin hermit" and placed the orange. What great compassion!

A devout Muslim man of Colombo, having heard about Yogaswami of Jaffna, persuaded a Yogaswami devotee he knew to take him to meet Swami. The man held the government post of Solicitor General, a post comparable to Attorney General in the US. The two made the trip to Jaffna by train and checked into a rest house. The next morning they bathed and approached Swami's hut in Columbuthurai.

As they were going in the gate, Swami shouted at the top of his voice, "Who is that? I don't want to see anybody today. Go away." The two stopped. After a moment of discussion, the devotee approached Swami alone and explained that the Solicitor General of Ceylon had come all the way from Colombo hoping to meet him. Swami shouted, "I don't care if he's the Solicitor General or a Supreme Court judge. I don't want to meet him today. Go away."

Deeply embarrassed, the devotee returned to his friend and advised that they not try anymore. Dejected, they returned to Colombo the same day. When the Solicitor General arrived at his home that evening, a letter from the government awaited him. It said that he had been appointed as a Supreme Court judge, effective immediately, and he must take up his duties the following day. With tears in his eyes, he recalled what the sage had shouted, and realized that if Swami had met with him, he would have stayed longer in Jaffna and would not have been able to act on this letter in the timely way it required.

The next week, he traveled to Jaffna to meet and pay his respects to Swami. This time, as he entered the gate, Swami greeted him with a big grin and said, "Well, hello, Supreme Court Judge. Nice to see you." As the years went by, the justice made it a point to come from Colombo to see Swami at least once a month. He served as a Supreme Court judge for twenty-five years.

One morning in the course of a lecture tour in Jaffna, Professor A.S.

Gnanasampanthan, an academic from Tamil Nadu, awoke to discover he had completely lost his voice. He was taken to a retired ear-nose-throat surgeon, who, upon examining him, informed him the ailment was serious and he must go to the hospital in Colombo for tests. Gnanasampanthan was downcast and fearful, as he depended on his speech to provide financial support to his family.

Just as he was getting into the car, the doctor rushed up to him, saying, "I know you are a devotee of Yogaswami; why not go and see him before you set off?" Mentally scolding himself for having not thought of it himself, Gnanasampanthan decided to go to Swami right away, despite knowing that devotees did not usually disturb him during the daytime. Swami greeted him saying, "Did you think the doctor was Lord Murugan? Why did you go there?" A tirade followed detailing his foolishness. Swami then beckoned the lecturer to sit down. A half hour passed in silence. Swami then ordered, "Go and give your talk tonight, then come back and see me."

Realizing that Swami had restored his voice, Gnanasampanthan responded weepingly, "I shall abide as instructed by Swamigal." When he returned after the lecture, he was confronted by Swami, who said, "We will cut and bury Kamban and Sekkilar." (Kamban translated the *Ramayana* into Tamil, and Sekkilar authored the *Periyapuranam,* in which he documented the life history of the 63 Saivite saints).

Gnanasampanthan claims that the voice he spoke with thereafter was that ordained by Swamigal, and from then on did conquer (cut and bury) the arcane subject matter. In the course of time, the professor produced thirty high-quality books, which he credited to Yogaswami's grace alone.

Sinnappoo Navaratnarajah narrated the following story.

My parents, having left me in the care of my grandparents, were away in Malaysia. I was said to be suffering from a peculiar ailment at the tip of my tongue. My grandmother, who could not bear to see me undergoing suffering, complained to Swami, stating that the family were greatly concerned over my illness, as their attempts to obtain medical treatment, Western as well as Eastern (ayurvedic), ended in failure to find a remedy. Swami did not say anything elaborate and, in his usual way of conversation, told them, "This is the present state of the problem."

Swami daily takes a trudge to Ariyalai, about two miles away from his ashram, passing my house. I used to run away from his sight when I saw him at a distance, because his body build and bearded face were scary. The distance of the Tamil school where I studied was about twenty-five yards from my house and necessitated my passing Swami's ashram, which was about five yards from the road.

One day when I was on my way to school, Swami opened his gate and as he emerged to the top of the road both of us met face to face, and there was no chance of my escaping from his sight. I stood still, in silence, and he ordered me to open my mouth. No sooner had I opened my mouth, Swami asked me if he could spit into my mouth, but just blew air three times over the affected part of the tongue, and it was completely cured.

Chellappaswami had taught him to avoid any semblance of supernatural powers, so he downplayed such mysterious events. Regarding this part of his work as incidental, he made everything miraculous seem ordinary, if it became known at all.

Seeing Death as a Part of Life

Yogaswami was also a great consoler when tragedy and the shadow of death loomed large and he knew someone's transition was imminent. Dr. Ramanathan wrote of his deep compassion in such times of distress.

Whenever we were stricken with grief and depression, Swami's divine words, full of affection, gave us great consolation. "Why are you frightened? Isn't there then One who directs everything? Surrender to Him and just be. There is no need for enmity. Forgive and forget the evil others do. The God who administers the world knows everything. Are you greater than that omnipotent, all-powerful one? What can you do?" With these words He graced and blessed us to live peacefully without losing self control.

When my brother-in-law lay on his death bed, Swami came, applied holy ash and sent him on his final pilgrimage. There is no doubt that he attained a good state.

Another devotee testified:

Once Yogaswami came by when our daughter was ill. We implored him to help. He said, "Don't worry, she is going to the feet of Siva Peruman." That night she passed on.

C. S. Dharmarajah wrote of Swami's knowledge of death:

Once a doctor holding a high appointment in the Health Department visited Swami, as he was wont to do whenever he went to the North. Swami said, "Now what you have to do is change your coat." A few days later, back in Colombo, the good doctor shed his mortal coil.

Ratna Ma Navaratnam shared the following insight on Swami's most transformative magic.

Swami attracted a great number of people from all walks of life, and to each one he revealed, according to his own measure of understanding, the fringe of his destiny. He was not an occultist nor a clairvoyant siddha who could prophecy a man's future; neither was he a supramental being who lived in the solitude of his powers. He was a man of God whose yogic wisdom made him touch some hidden chord in each one, so that he wielded a wondrous power to change people's inner nature by bringing up the secret chambers of their hearts to the surface, and expose to their gaze the bewildering reactions and hidden motives underlying their actions.

This was perhaps the reason why many people would shiver inwardly in his presence, or keep away from his penetrative eyes. They were afraid of exposure. Yet, so irresistible was his humanity that even his scorching onslaughts would act like the monsoonal showers of grace, and devotees would seek him in hours of tribulation and tension. In countless ways he alleviated their aches and pains, so that the faith of the multitude of people who sat at his feet towered as high as Mount Kailas, from where he brought forth the healing waters of the grace of Siva. Truly it was the descent of the divine Ganga!

Swami taught devotees to see beyond the realm of good and bad and strive to accept all that happens as just what is needed to further the soul's evolution. He explained:

We must not think that if such and such a thing happens, it is good; or if some other thing doesn't happen, it is bad. You must understand that all these actions that arise from maya are a help to realize the Self. By raising him up and bringing him down again and again, the Lord makes a man gain experience. You must get rid of all illusion. All tests are for good.

The Sivathondan Journal

In December of 1934 Swami had his followers begin a monthly newsletter called *The Sivathondan* (meaning "servant of Siva"), with articles on religious subjects, written in Tamil with a small section for English readers. Inthumathy Amma describes the enterprise:

> Its purpose was to encourage contemplation on Siva, since forgetting Siva is the cause of all woe, and the remedy is to repeatedly remind oneself to "contemplate, contemplate, contemplate the state of Siva." The publishing was done at the Kamalasani Printing Press, at Giragama Estate, Kaduganawa, near Kandy, and later at Peradeniya. Swami took a deep, abiding interest in the journal, tending to it as the eye is protected by the eyelid. He worked closely with the editor, Pundit K.K. Natarajan, and the printer, and ordered learned devotees to contribute articles, though no authors' names were ever cited. Swami even watched over the mailing, saying, "You must paste the wrapper around without concealing the *Siva* appearing on the cover. If the word *Siva* alone stays in the mind of those who see the journal, it will be a great achievement."

The motto he gave the publication was, "God resides in the heart of those who contemplate on Him." Each issue featured one of his Natchintanai songs. Yogaswami valued the publication so highly that he personified it as a small boy in one of his most inspiring songs, entitled "The Sivathondan:"

> O you servants of Siva! Know that it is your duty to gladden the heart of that small child, who to your noble courtyards comes Sivathondu to perform, and who the holy name of Sivathondan bears! That dear boy called Sivathondan, who worships the servants of Siva as Siva, has come on this earth for the happiness of all, in the auspicious month of Markali in Bhava Year. Though but a small child, because of his past *tapas* he is a master of great knowledge. He is one who knows the worth of taking a good deed, equal to a grain of millet, to be as great as a palmyra tree in size. He understands that everything is Siva's action. To him belongs the blessing of overcoming anger. He is filled with truth, forbearance and tranquility and is an adept in discerning the eternal from the passing. Transcending the path of the six *adhvas* [chakras], he has realized the state beyond the *tattvas*. Poverty will not disturb him, nor will prosperity elate him.

He is a pure soul, possessed of abundant patience. Not an inch from the path of dharma will he swerve, but will always go the way the supreme guru has declared. Honored by all the world, his nature is to live with hands engaged in work and thoughts engaged with God. Every month he will go with gladness to your home, from which the Goddess Lakshmi ne'er departs, bringing with him Good Thought and good religion, and the marvelous song of holy praise, and yoga expounded with deep learning.

The first Natchintanai that Swami wrote for *The Sivathondan* was "God Is Our All." It was later translated into English:

God is our life of life, so we belong and slave to God. All our movements are God's movements, and we cannot forget that at any time. We have nothing to grumble. We live always and everywhere. We know everything. Always we meditate on this and free ourselves from the lower consciousness and attain higher Divine consciousness.

As more and more devotees gathered around him, Yogaswami gave them assignments, such as translating into Tamil various works from Sanskrit or English.

Letters from Near and Far

For Yogaswami, everything was about knowing, or unknowing, who you are. "In the intensity of the moment, you will begin to know who you are." His flow of teaching this was incessant, no matter where he was. When traveling in India or remote parts of Ceylon, he sometimes sent hand-written letters to close devotees, beaming with insight. These were saved and treasured like gold. Many were published along with his songs in the book called *Natchintanai*. At the top of each letter he always scribed "Sivamayam" (It is all Siva). In a letter from the hill town of Kandy he wrote:

Sivamayam

I am here. The train from Colombo has come and is waiting at the station to go to its destination. The train from Badulai also has come and is waiting to go to its destination. All over is tea country. The planter is on his horse supervising the plucking of tea leaves. The nearby stream is trickling eagerly to join the main stream. The world is a wonderful place. Everybody is doing yoga. We are striving and quickening to reach [the goal].

One of his favorite penpals was Yogendra Duraisamy, a young man who would later become a Tamil leader in the nation. The letters to the boy Yogendra, then about 9, provide a charming summation of Swami's profound outlook. Here is one that brims with good advice.

Sivamayam

Letter to self, who is Yogendra, full of love:
I am with you and you are with me. You are I and I am you. What is it you fear? Look! I am you. Then what must you do? You must feel and show love. To whom? To everyone. In fact, your nature is nothing but love. Not only yourself, but all other things in the universe are overflowing with love. Not all other things, because you are the only one in existence. You are all things. Study well.

Siva does all. I am you.

Sivamayam

Yogendra!
This is the New Year's Day. You will prepare various excellent sweet meats. You will wear silk *veshtis*. You will whitewash your house. You will go to the temple. You will worship and give offerings. But I shall bathe in the waters of Peace, wear holy ashes which purify the mind, pray evermore for that great wealth known as Contentment, carry the shield of Fearlessness, and, having all these, I shall dance on the bosom of Subrahmanya.

Never forgetfully,
Yours ....

Yogaswami entitled the following letter, written on July 2, 1934, "The Best Kept Secret."

Sivamayam

We are all of the same race and religion. Within us there is no change. We are holy beings established in Divinity Itself. All multifarious changes represent the characteristic beauty of Reality. Great souls say that these are maya. This truth can be understood only by those who have grasped it through the magical charm of a life of rectitude, not by others. Because of that, sages have emphatically proclaimed again and again that it is necessary to love all existing lives as one's own. Therefore everything depends upon the practice of rectitude. By establishing ourselves in this path of rectitude and by constantly imagining that all are ourselves, we come, through wonderful experiences, to the understanding that we are not gross matter, but conscious beings.

He who never forgets.

Yogaswami would say, "If you are a king, will you have contentment? If you are a beggar, will you have contentment? Whatever your walk in life may be, you will only have contentment through knowing yourself by yourself."

One morning an old man came to visit Yogaswami who was Swami's same age and had known him for a long time. He was living in an old folks' home run by the government and subsisting on a small pension. Entering the hermitage, he placed a bunch of bananas at Swami's feet and prostrated. Swami was clearly happy to see him. This companion had come often, and Swami enjoyed his company.

"Good morning, old friend," Swami greeted him. Then they talked for some time about the man's situation. How had he been? Had he been enjoying good food? Finally, Swami asked him by what means he had traveled. "On the train, Swami," came the answer.

"But trains are crowded these days and difficult for an old man like you to climb on and off of. It's a great deal of trouble for you to travel on the train," Swami replied. "Oh, Swami, I only think of one thing when I set out to see you, and that carries me along. No difficulties at all coming here."

"I know what you mean," Swami replied, "but traveling is really too much trouble for you, and costly, too, these days. You needn't come, you know. There are other ways of visiting me." Swami fell quiet but his friend continued, "Oh, Swami, coming to visit you every few months gives my life a wonderful peace. It is worth any amount of trouble."

Swami kept his silence, allowing that conversation to die away completely, then spoke again. "Tell me, old friend, you have lived a long time now, and have lived a good life; do you feel at peace? What stands out in your mind as the most important thing in your life?"

"You know, Swami, I have given that question a lot of thought these days. Everything that I used to think was important is gone. My family is gone. My friends are gone. My home is gone and my work is finished. My body is old and feeble. Yet I go on the same. I always find love in my heart. I think that probably love is the most important thing in life." Swami was moved and pleased by the answer. "You and I are the same," he said. "That's what I find important, too."

After the man left, Swami told those who were gathered around that to have a simple heart, as this man did, is worth more than anything else. "Everything is so simple, but man with his monkey mind and his idea of

'I' and 'mine' makes a complex mess of it, then blames everyone around him because he cannot see the truth. This man will leave his body in a few days. It will be simple and natural for him. And he has something that he will carry on into his future lives: a fine and simple sense of life. Everything will be easy for him." The man died a few days later.

Anyone who came to Swami with an honest and simple heart was well received. When children visited, he would lift them onto his lap and tell those around him, "This child and I are the same age. We speak the same language. And we understand things the rest of you have forgotten."

Sometimes he would ask children to sing for him. They would sing the Natchintanai hymns he had composed, and he would join in, perhaps singing in a child's airy voice. As often as not, he would ask the child if he or she wanted anything, a toy, or something else. If a wish was expressed, he would send out for it immediately.

He was also stern with children. He told them that the most important thing to learn was obedience. Once he wrote a letter to a boy, advising: "Be obedient. Listen to the advice of your father, mother, elder sisters, younger brother, as well as your uncle, aunt and elder brothers. Always set an example in obedience. Siva does all." "Oh, it might seem hard," he would say, "But it is the best way of living in the world. Even I take orders. My orders come from within. Later you, too, will receive orders from within."

Most people came like children and were obedient to his orders. He was so close to his devotees that they would rush to tell him when a child was born, sometimes before they told the rest of their family. They would have a special offering ready to take to Swami so that when the child was born they wouldn't have to stop at a shop, but could go straightaway to see him and receive his blessing for the child.

Often he would greet these new fathers at his compound gate and shout at them with a twinkle in his eye, "Great news I have for you. A lovely girl named Thiripurasundari was born this morning. Come, let us celebrate." That, of course, was exactly the news the father was bringing, except that he hadn't yet named his daughter! Many people in Jaffna received their names from Swami in such ways.

One Day...

Yogaswami looked after everyone, and nothing was hidden from his inner vision. He knew exactly what was going on in his village, and all over Jaffna for that matter. Very little deserving his attention ever escaped it. A devotee recalls her time with Yogaswami during this period.

Yogaswami went about like a king. I came to know of him when I married into a family who had taken him as their guru. The first time I saw him was the day after my wedding on the 4th of September 1951. I had not yet met Swami, though he lived very close to our house.

We had returned from Malaysia after the Second World War. I first saw him on a visit with my husband and my father-in-law, Sir Vaithilingam Duraiswamy, who had known Swami since 1920. We took tea in a flask and fruits on a tray. It was about 7pm when we arrived at the small mud hut with roof thatched with coconut fronds. It was dark inside the hut as I followed my father-in-law and husband. There were no lights, only the camphor burning in front of Swami. When my turn came to fall and pray at his feet, I saw myself looking at a pair of eyes so powerful, as if they saw into you.

We sat opposite him. He spoke to my father-in-law for a while, then turned his eyes on me and asked, "Can you cook?" I replied, "Yes." He also gave me a *Devaram* book of Saint Tirujnanasambandar's songs. After that, I came to cook for Swami nearly every day. We would often visit him in his hut. He drank his tea from a coconut shell. The shell kept the heat in, and most Jaffna people had them in their house.

He also came for lunch the three years when my husband was stationed in Jaffna. My husband would read for him. He would say, "If Sorna reads, I can understand." He had named my husband Sorna and wanted his brothers and sisters to call him by that name.

The people of Jaffna treated him as their king. He walked about Jaffna, through the paddy fields and palmyra groves, visited houses and scolded people who had to be put right. In my father-in-law's house, his words were law. Most decisions to be made were put forth to Swami and his conclusion was carried out.

Swami encouraged everyone to go to the temple. Once on the morning of the annual chariot festival at Nallur Temple, my father-in-law was still asleep, and we could not leave without his permission. It was 7am, and at eight the Lord would come out of the temple. Suddenly we heard Swami shouting in front of the house, "What are you all doing there? Get out and go to the temple! Arumugan comes once a year to bless everyone. Go!" He was no other than Lord Nalluran Himself, ruling his people. He called everyone by name.

My mother was a great devotee of Lord Nalluran. As we lived close to Nallur Temple, she conducted her day according to the ringing of the temple bells. Getting up at 4am, she would say, "My Nalluran has gotten up." Swami would often come and sit on one of the verandah chairs. He would look at her as if to say, "Don't you know me? I am your Nalluran." He was a strength to the Jaffna people. He was their Nalluran.

Vithanayar lived near Yogaswami's hut and knew him his entire life. A sprightly man, he always joked lightheartedly with Yogaswami. "I was with Chellappaswami all those years," he said. "I saw him push Yoganathan to the side and chase him away. Now suddenly he has everything, and I must come to him!" Yogaswami loved Vithanayar and put up with his eccentric ways.

Occasionally, he refused to accept things, sometimes asking that food offerings be buried in the yard behind his hut. "Don't even let the crows eat it," he shouted. "It's not fit for the crows to eat!" One day a man came with a tray of offerings. In the middle of the tray was a bag containing five hundred rupees, a goodly amount in those days. Those around watched him present the offering, speculating within themselves what Swami would do, for they all knew the money came from a venture Swami was not in favor of.

Usually in such cases Swami would not accept it. To add force to the refusal he might even send the tray and its contents sailing through the air with a strong throw. But this time, to everyone's surprise, he instructed a devotee to distribute it to various people. Some should go to a poor family whose daughter was to be married soon—it would help with the wedding festivities. Some was to be given to an honest man who ran a tea shop. With that money he could add a buttermilk drink to his shop and expand his earnings. (He did just so, and his business grew considerably.) And, Swami instructed, "Save a hundred rupees and take Vithanayar to the doctor. I've heard he's ill. He won't want to accept the money, so tell him he can pay me back later. Then he will accept."

Entering the house, the devotee found Vithanayar sitting in the courtyard. Startled to see him appearing so fit, the man inquired about his health. Vithanayar said everything was fine, so the devotee gave him the money as Swami had instructed, which, true to life, was initially refused but finally accepted under the strict condition that it would be repaid.

A little unsure of what to do next, the devotee finally decided to return to Swami when Vithanayar's daughter motioned him aside and said that her father had a high fever and was quite sick, but was simply too stubborn to let on or do anything about it. Understanding this, he told Vithanayar that Swami had ordered him to take him to the doctor. He pleaded, "If you don't go, I'll be in trouble with Swami. And you know how that is." The devotee continued to beg, "Please come with me, just to satisfy Swami. Please come."

Vithanayar relented, and they set out to visit the doctor Yogaswami had specified. Examining Vithanayar, the physician scolded the devotee for even moving him, much less bringing him in a car. "He has double pneumonia," the doctor scolded. But when the man explained the circumstances, he understood. After administering some medication, he gave instructions to take Vithanayar home and put him to bed, adding that he would come by the next morning to check on him. The medicine, an expensive new antibiotic, cost almost exactly the amount Swami had allotted for the visit.

Swami arranged marriages, named babies, settled family arguments, helped devotees find homes to buy, got them jobs and generally mothered everyone. He kept all of Jaffna on its toes and made sure that people got what they needed and deserved. He gave and gave and gave and gave. He said, "We are in the tradition that gives. We give even to people who don't deserve anything, to selfish and jealous ones."

Inthumathy Amma recorded the testimony of Panchadeharam of Ariyalai, a school teacher who had gained much from his visits to Yogaswami through the years.

Even though a year had passed since our marriage, my wife and I had no children. Due to financial difficulties, we were not disappointed. Even after two years, we were childless. During this time when we went for his darshan, Gurudeva asked, "You have no children yet, isn't that so?" We replied, "Yes, Aasan." Then he plucked a big grape from a bunch, gave it to my wife and said, "Do not give this to anyone. You alone must eat it." My wife did accordingly. Next month we realized that she was pregnant. Because we had no children for two years, rumors were going 'round the village that we were sterile. Gurudeva realized this and gave us a remedy.

Whenever possible we went for Gurudeva's darshan. In those days, he would give us a reply both directly and indirectly for all our woes. The indirect replies came when he would talk about other matters. But there would always be an answer to our prayers. Gurudeva's darshan made us turn our direction little by little. We began to go to him desiring to traverse the abyss of birth and death and to seek the necessary control of the mind and gain peace.

In 1963, we had only two opportunities to visit Gurudeva. We went first in April. We then had two children and my wife was expecting the third. We entered the ashram with his permission and fell prostrate at his lotus-like feet. He invited us to sit and then asked the names of our two children. He then inquired, "Where is the other one?" We replied that we had only two children. He laughed with glee, saying, "The other chap is also here." Yes, the child we were expecting was a son.

Doctor K. Nithiyanandan tells this story:

A couple who were devotees of Swami had no children even after ten years of marriage. One Sivaratri day they sat in Swami's presence and observed the fast. Swami looked at the mother and mentioned a boy's name. Within a year, that lady gave birth to a boy and gave him the name Swami had mentioned.

Once a man found himself in serious trouble for embezzling money. For that he was standing trial and was also being charged with other crimes he had nothing to do with. He had spent all his money on prior legal fees and didn't have enough to pay the lawyer to argue his case, which was coming to trial the next day. In Ceylon, lawyers must be paid before a case is argued. Otherwise, they are not allowed to enter the court on a client's behalf.

Throughout the ordeal, his wife had remained faithful and kept the household running on practically nothing. Now, even her ability to do that was strained to the limit. She suggested they go see Swami. They went. When they entered the room, Swami ignored them. The evening went on and not a word or a look came from Swami to the couple. They were deeply concerned, but remained silent.

Finally, Swami began asking people to go. One by one, he called them to him or simply told them it was time to go. The couple eventually found themselves alone with him. Swami knew the whole story. He also knew the wife, a staunch devotee, was standing behind her husband to the end, true to the best of Hindu tradition. Calling her forward, Swami handed her a bundle of rupees wrapped in a banana leaf. It was enough to pay all the fees. The trial came, and the man won his case. This turn of events and his wife's benevolent influence caused him to change many of his errant ways.

The solace that Swami gave was often subtle and indirect. Sri M. Prasad told of how Swami helped ease his mind after an accident that some felt was his fault—a story told in *The Sivathondan*.

In 1952 or so when I was stationed in Jaffna as Government Agent, a great religious fair was held on the other side of the lagoon. People went to the fair in great numbers in a motor boat. At the time of the return journey, more people entered the boat than it could safely transport. The conductor in charge of the boat was helpless. Unfortunately the boat sank not far from the shore and several lives were lost. I did all I could to help those injured and offered my profound sympathy to the bereaved persons.

Some people alleged that the disaster was due to my neglect. I was in great agony of mind. A friend of mine advised me to go and pay my respects to Yogaswamiji. I did so a week after the incident. Swamiji must have known why I had come to him, but he said nothing till I was about to leave his ashram after about twenty minutes. Then he said, "Have no worry. I am your witness." I cannot describe how consoling and comforting those few words were to me.

Jananayagam from the UK, who had a lifetime of encounters with Yogaswami's magical ways, wrote:

According to the words of the great Saint Tirumular, "Absolute clarity is attained by seeing the guru, by reciting his holy name, by listening to his holy words and visualizing his holy figure." Guru Yogar Swamy was a legend known to myself and my predecessors for four generations. We are lost for words to describe our fortune to be under his holy surveillance.

Once, when Swamy was publishing his Saivite magazine, *Sivathondan,* he asked my mother to write articles and essays. Though the subjects for these articles were suggested or selected by Swamy himself, they subtly fitted the writer. One such article was titled "Once the river has burst its banks, it will not stop even if you cry." My mother wrote the article and submitted it to Swamy. He asked her to read it in his presence, which she promptly did. In a few days' time, my mother was pregnant. The entire family was delighted to hear the news and were looking forward to the new arrival after almost twelve years.

When the baby was born, according to our tradition, we took him to Swamy for his blessing. Swamy was roaming 'round his compound in the form of a ghost, making everyone shiver in anguish. We said, "Swamy, we were blessed with a baby boy and we have brought some sweets." At once Swamy said, "I will take none of them. Ask your mother to eat them instead." We returned home with shock, sorrow and disappointment added with fear. In about three weeks the baby died of diarrhea. The article Swamy had asked my mother to write was in fact a warning of what was to follow.

Sometimes Swami declined to help people and sent them away without even letting them see him. Consider the story of Master Rasiah, the burly police officer who became an ardent follower. Rasiah told of the day he took the train from Colombo to Jaffna, a common trek for Yogaswami's devotees who worked in the capital. Carrying a satchel of fresh fruits the entire journey, he got off at Columbuthurai and made his way to Swami's compound. Entering, he greeted his guru and placed the fruits at his feet, prostrated and was invited to sit. Nothing more transpired, yet suddenly Yogaswami ordered him, "Go away! Leave!"

Rasiah was stunned and physically paralyzed by the order, searching without finding a reason for this dismissal. Yogaswami—seeing no response to his command, and knowing that Sri Lankan policemen undergo a kind of military training—barked like a drill sergeant, "Stand up!" Rasiah obeyed. "About face!" Rasiah turned with practiced precision. "Left, right, left, right" Yogaswami called out the cadence, and Rasiah began marching out the door and into the compound. "Left face," came the order, "Left, right, left," as the march approached the gate. "Halt! Open the gate! Left, right. Halt! Close the gate! Right face! Left, right…" and as Yogaswami's voice grew fainter Rasiah found himself marching down the road, sent away by his guru in a manner that would always puzzle him. Hearing the story, others thought Yogaswami was teaching the disciple a lesson in humility, something they said was not the policeman's greatest strength.

S. Shanmugasundaram was close to Yogaswami for decades, an observant man who saw many come and go at the ashram. Years later in California he was asked to share the tales of those experiences with American devotees of Satguru Sivaya Subramuniyaswami.

Siva Yogaswami never made any distinction between the rich and the poor. The caste or religion of his devotees never bothered him. Nobody could predict how welcome or unwelcome he or she would be in his presence at any time. That remained a mystery. Receiving one with open arms or sending him away saying, "I don't have time to see you now" were daily occurrences, depending on Swami's mood. That mood changed in accordance with the purpose of each one's visit. The highest and the richest in the land as well as the lowliest and the poorest could be seen at Swami's ashram. Sometimes both categories

were driven away, even if they had come from distances of hundreds of miles, but there were also occasions when they were given a hearty welcome.

One day a man of the highest status, living in the Hill Country area about 200 miles away, came to meet with Swami. He was learned and wealthy. Maybe due to his wealth and status, he did not associate himself freely with others. But he was a devotee of Yogaswami, had visited Swami many times earlier, and Swami had gone to his place and stayed with him for one or two days.

On this day that man and his wife drove all the way to Jaffna and came to Yogaswami's hut with a large silver tray full of fruits and a variety of other gifts for Swami. They walked into the hut even before being welcomed by Swami and bent down and placed the tray at Swami's feet. Just at that moment the couple heard something like thunder.

Yes, it was Swami talking. With apparent anger in his eyes, Swami shouted at the top of his voice, "Take this away; we don't need any of these here. You can take them back. I don't have the time to see you now. Why are you waiting? When I say take them away, I mean it."

The poor folks did not expect such treatment. They were shivering with fear and too dumb to speak. They picked up their tray full of things and left the hut in utter silence and abject disgrace. The devotees in the hut felt sorry for them and sympathized.

After the couple left, Swami enjoyed a loud and hearty laugh. At the end of it he told the devotees, "These fellows came here to ask me to arrange a marriage for their daughter. They have hit upon a young man, but he is not agreeable to the marriage. So they expect me to intervene and finalize it. What a fine joke. I am not a marriage broker! Just see what things they brought to bribe me. They are educated fools."

Some went to the sage only once or twice. That was all they needed, for he gave them enough in those brief visits for a lifetime. One day a young man stopped at Nallur Temple on his way to see the man people called Yogaswami. After worshiping at Lord Murugan's shrine, he stood wondering

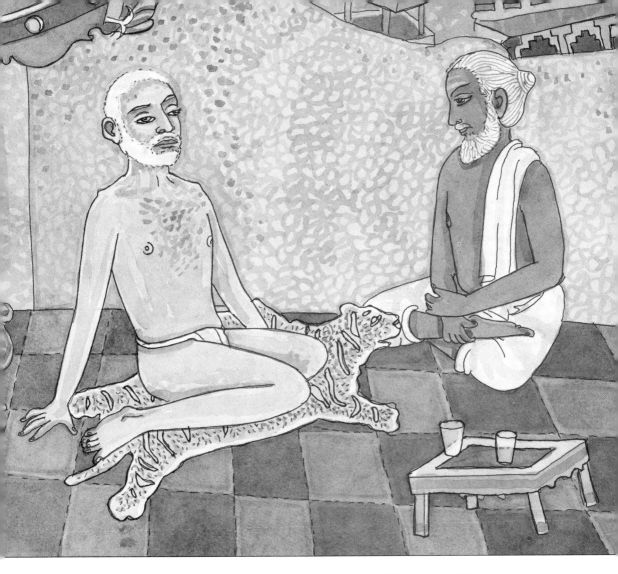

During a pilgrimage to India, Yogaswami visited Ramana Maharishi, the sage of Siva's Mount Arunachala who had become renowned. Their meeting was remarkable in its simplicity; neither spoke a word—two knowers of the Unknowable in perfect communion.

how he would get to Swami's hut, when Swami drove up in a car, stopped right by him, ordered him to get in, and drove to his hermitage. That day Swami revealed to this man his past, his present and how to live his life henceforth to build the best karma for himself. It was an intense encounter, more than enough for this devotee. For the rest of his life he relished the darshan of that day and followed Swami's advice to the letter.

Others were around Swami frequently—as much as possible. He was involved in the very fabric of their lives. Vithanayar was among those under his care. One day Swami heard that he was sick again, and now was

probably not strong enough to recover. Swami went to Vithanayar's house, sang an auspicious song, applied holy ash to his chest and forehead, then returned to his hermitage. Later in the day news came that Vithanayar had passed away.

Once, upon returning from a pilgrimage to India, Swami went to the home of a close devotee of Chellappaswami named Chelliahpillai, whose home Chellappaswami visited for meals many times. The man was on his

Three times Yogaswami took the ferry from Ceylon to India. From Kashi's Siva temples in the North to Tiruvannamalai and Madras in the South, he explored holy Bharat.

• • • • • • • • • • • • • • • • • •

deathbed, barely holding on to life. Swami teased him, "Sinnathamby ('younger brother'), why are you still here? You should have left long ago." Chelliah smiled, "I have my ticket and my suitcase is packed; the train is sitting in the station. I was only waiting for you to come and bid me farewell." Swami put sacred ash on his forehead, sang to him, then departed. That night the old man left his earthly frame.

On the Road
Swami moved about, by foot, car or train, all through his later life. He would go to Colombo, to the Eastern Province, or to the up-country to visit devotees. Wherever he went, many people would come to bask in his darshan. When it was heard that he was at this devotee's house or that, others would come with offerings—coconuts, flowers, fruit, money, books, clothing—anything they thought would please Swami or be of use to him. S. Ampikaipaakan observed, "When Swamigal visited a place, local and nearby people would come to see him. In the place where Swamigal stayed, usually a big *homa* was done."

One time he was visiting a devotee who worked as a foreman on a tea estate in the lush Ceylon hill country. The owner provided this man and his family a house. Although it was adequate, it didn't have its own toilet. In fact, the family had to go some distance to use one. The foreman had petitioned the estate manager, an Englishman, for permission to build an outhouse behind his home; but his petition had been refused. When the devotee told Swami the story, Swami knew the manager had refused because he feared the project would drain time and energy from the foreman's plantation work. He had not considered their comfort.

A devotee, the head of a road building crew, was present as they discussed the predicament. Swami asked if he could build a lavatory at the site in one day. The man, happy to be able to help, answered that he had many coolies working for him and access to all needed materials. If the foreman could pay the cost of materials and labor, yes, he could build the lavatory in one day. Swami chose the exact spot and asked that work begin the next day. That evening it was finished. The estate manager didn't even notice the little out-house, and nothing was ever spoken about it.

Swami journeyed by train frequently. Onboard, he would encounter many fellow travelers. His devo-tees claim that some of his best help was given as he moved through the coaches, meeting and talking with passengers.

One day he was on his way to Colombo. About halfway there the northbound train to Jaffna pulled into the station where his train was standing. Without explanation, he jumped off the southbound train and

boarded the train to Jaffna. He went straight to a man who had come to see Swami on several occasions and said, "You're surely in an ugly mood. I could feel your grim thoughts from the other train." The man confessed that he was thinking of taking his own life. He was besieged by problems and could see no way out other than suicide.

Swami laughed. "That's how much you know. That would only be the beginning!" Then he talked the problems out with the man and gave him some strong directives on how to reform his life. Swami's advice was so sound that, assured by the promise of a better future, the man's mood turned positive. Swami got down at the next station to catch the train to Colombo. Yogaswami checked on the devotee several times after that to make sure he continued to do all right and had no relapse of depression.

Scholar Padmasani Rasendiram recorded the following experience

Yogaswami loved to feed people: guests to his hut, sadhus at the temple, devotees celebrating a festival. He would shop and cook himself or give explicit instructions on what should be bought at the market, which was always full of the local farmers' fresh produce.

in *The Sivathondan* journal. It seems that Yogaswami, too, held at least one travel-study program, which Sivaya Subramuniyaswami would call Innersearch.

Once we wanted to travel to India, and with that desire we went to see Swamigal. Swamigal said, "Leave off India, we will go to some place for ten days." That evening we again went to see Swamigal. Swamigal said, we will just go and stay in a comfortable place. We set out for Ratinapuri and on the way visited a devotee's house for ten minutes. We did not spend a long time there, as after tea he wanted to leave. From there, we straightly went to Peliguloya. There an overseer had made all arrangements for us. We stayed in the Village Association Building. Devotees from Colombo, Palangotai, Ratinapuri came and assembled there. Both morning and evening we recited *Siva Puranam, Devarams* and *Tiruvasagam,* and at other times we listened to Swamigal's discourses. For ten days, there, it was very enjoyable. Swamigal gave advice to all according to their need and maturity."

At age sixty, in 1932, Yogaswami developed a small lump on his cheek. Doctors wanted to remove it, but Swami refused. Years later, he agreed to be tested, and the growth was found to be cancerous. The doctors urged him to go to the hospital in Colombo for radiation therapy and further tests. Swami refused. Instead he applied oil from crushed cotton seeds in the presence of Dr. S. Ramanathan, who was aghast: "Swami! Swami! It is poisonous. Why are you applying it on your cheek?" Swami laughed, "Doctor! The treatment is over and now I am OK." Yogaswami undertook a fast of milk and rice, and the combination of it all effected a cure.

There were other health issues in his life. Swami enjoyed an occasional short cheroot (the name of a non-tapered cigar that originally comes from the Tamil *suruttu,* and thence into French as *cheroute).* Beginning in the early 1940s, he smoked one each morning while using the latrine. He developed diabetes in the same decade. In the early stages, he took only herbal medicines. Beginning in 1950, he received insulin injections daily, administered by his devotee-doctors who came to his hut.

Yogaswami went on three pilgrimages to India, in 1934, 1940 and 1946, taking a few devotees with him each time. They went on the six-temple Murugan *yatra* in South India and to the massive, renowned Siva temples of Madurai and Chidambaram. They walked long distances together and met many spiritual luminaries.

On one pilgrimage, Yogaswami visited Sri Ramanashram in Tiruvannamalai to be with another great guru, Sri Ramana Maharishi, born in 1879, seven years after Yogaswami. Many people think of these two men as the greatest and purest of 20th century Hindu teachers. The two sat in silence for an hour in Sri Ramana's austere room near the holy mountain. Nor was a word exchanged when they met or parted.

After hearing that Yogaswami had visited Sri Ramana, people were eager to find out what had transpired. Swami told them, "We said all

· ·

Families felt blessed on those rare occasions when Yogaswami handed them a spiritual poem, often composed specifically for their spiritual guidance. These were dutifully saved over the decades, and later gathered into a book called Natchintanai.

there is to say." Later he added, "We did not go with any desire. *Summa* we went. We stayed for about an hour. He did not speak at all. He is a great hero *(mahaviran)*." By "*summa*," Swami meant "perfect stillness, communion in silence."

On each journey, after his fellow pilgrims had been with him for two or three weeks, Swami would send them back to Jaffna and continue on his own, traveling all over India. On the 1940 pilgrimage, he journeyed to Madras, Calcutta, Bombay, Benares and elsewhere with Station Master Rasiah of Nuwara Eliya. Benares, also known as Kasi, is sacred to Siva, located on the Ganges River. Hindus come here to die, be cremated and have their ashes consigned to this sacred river that is said to flow from the head of Siva. In Kasi, on November 3, Yogaswami penned the following letter.

After wandering far in an earnest quest, I came to Kasi and, lo, I saw the Lord of Kasi—Viswanathan—within my heart. Let not your hearts be troubled by wearisome pursuits. There is a fine saying that the herb that you have been searching for assiduously lies at your feet within easy reach. In this place, too, men live very much in the same manner as our people. There is nothing wonderful, nothing mysterious in this world. In this holy city of Benares, I have performed the rites and obsequies most solemnly for my countrymen who have lived in bygone yesterdays, and to those of today and even of the morrow. From henceforth, live in obedience to your inner spirit imbued with love for one another; and live in harmony with the world under the protecting shelter of His feet.

In the *Sunday Observer* (February 20, 1983), C.S. Dharmarajah wrote about Swami after that pilgrimage.

On his return, Swami—with his effulgent face, penetrating eyes, silvery, flowing beard, holy ash on his forehead, his waist cloth of white cotton, hair tied in a knot and an umbrella under his arm—could daily be seen leaving his ashram at the crack of dawn, trudging many miles, invariably declining offers of car lifts on the way, and returning to his abode in the evening.

There he sat cross-legged on a wooden plank, with devotees gathered in singles and in groups, in that room that accommodated only

· ·

Yogaswami's writings were a rare synthesis of simplicity and profundity, truth told in its simplest and most approachable form. Many times he simply spoke or sang them, to be captured by diligent devotees who recognized the preciousness of his utterances.

the few at a time, meting out his sanctifying grace with homely discourses that veiled his divinity, occasionally singing the praises of his guru—to each according to his need and understanding.

Swami never stopped traveling, even when he stayed close to home. He walked all over the Jaffna peninsula time and time again. This land of his is quite arid, and if it had not rained for a long time and the crops were suffering, people would come to him. "Swami, there has been no rain for

months. My fields are ready, but I can't plant my rice crop until we get some rain. It's nearly too late."

Soon Swami would be seen storming about the peninsula, striding through the dry rice paddies, shaking his fist at the clouds and scolding them for not releasing their gift of rain. "What are you doing, not raining? My people will starve, and you just sit up there doing nothing. My people need to eat; I order you to help them." Soon the clouds would darken and the life-giving rains would come. This happened not infrequently, and a certain amount of fame devolved on Swami for his uncanny ability to influence the forces of nature in this way.

S. Shanmugasundaram recounted the following story of rain-making in Batticaloa.

One fine day Swami motored to a town called Vavuniya, 90 miles south of Jaffna. As soon as he reached the town, he stopped at a restaurant for a cup of tea. Almost everyone in the area recognized him, and talk went around that Yogaswami was in town. Within half an hour, about one hundred people, all of them farmers, collected around him. They complained that they had not had the usual seasonal rain and their crops were withering. If they did not have a good shower in a day or two, the crops would die off.

Swami heard this pathetic story and meditated for a few minutes. Then he sang a series of Natchintanai hymns, starting with the words "*Nalla malai peiyyaatho, naadu siravaatho, ellorum inputtru vaalaaro,*" ("Won't there be good rain, won't this land improve, won't everyone live happily?"). At the end of the tenth verse, clouds gathered and rains started falling. In half an hour, there was such a heavy downpour that everyone felt happy and relieved.

· ·

The typical Jaffna home that Yogaswami visited was built for the tropics, with coconut tree beams, tile roof, dung or concrete floors, wood-burning stove and an open well in the back for water. Guests were frequent, showing up without notice and always looked after with unstinting hospitality.

Chapter Seventeen

Prescriptions for Sadhana

Swami spoke forcefully, artfully, but in everyday terms. Indeed, his language was incisively simple, and even his profound Natchintanai were couched in common vocabulary, unlike the classical verses of *Tirumurai* and earlier saints. Natchintanai is a personal diary of sorts, recording Swami's experiences, his realizations, his anguish and his hopes. The language and style are straightforward. His poems on Murugan and Siva have such a feel of familiarity that you could reach across the page and touch them. He talks to the lizard and the peacock with the confidence that they, too, can help his quest. He uses folk songs and dances, indicating that he was communing with the common man. He goads us on to the feet of the guru on the San Marga, reminding us often that is what a human birth is for.

Once a man highly educated in Siddhanta lore and philosophy came to him anticipating a philosophical discussion, hoping to employ all the pedantry at his disposal. At the same time, a simple man arrived. They both offered fruits and flowers, then prostrated.

Swami addressed the simple man who now sat before him next to the philosopher: "How have you been?" he asked. "I've been all right, Swami. Everything is coming along in a good way for myself and my family." "It's good to hear that your family is all right too. How many children do you have now?" "Three, Swami. Two boys and a girl." "And how much money do you make?" "Two hundred rupees a month, Swami." "Oh, that's not very much money for what you do, is it?" "No, Swami, but we get along all right. We have two cows, and we grow our own food." "That's fine, but you should get more money for your work." "I know, Swami, but what can I do?" "A man who works as hard as you do, and as well as you do, should receive more money. You should do something about it." "Yes, Swami."

Growing more and more impatient, the philosopher wondered, "When is Swami going to finish this tedious chatter and talk with me about things more in his realm?" Swami turned to him and rejoined sharply, "You should be paying attention to what we are saying. We're discussing profound spiritual matters."

In Swami's presence, such ordinary events seemed full of import and splendor, and little miracles seemed ordinary and natural. Usually

· ·

The Sivathondan Nilayam was built under Yogaswami's careful guidance as a center for meditation and service, though he entered it only rarely. From here, his monthly publication, The Sivathondan, *was issued, and here devotees gathered to celebrate festivals and perform puja to their guru, as they do to this day.*

someone would bring food each day, generally enough to feed six or seven people. Swami would ask that food be given to everyone, even if twenty or thirty were present. It would always reach around adequately without anyone asking how food prepared for a few could feed so many.

"Mother Earth Is Hungry"

Swami took great joy in feeding people. Often he would not allow a person to leave without taking a meal in his presence. Sometimes he would set about cooking large quantities of food in the middle of the day, sending out for fresh vegetables and asking for the big cooking vessels to be brought in from all over the neighborhood. He would build large fires in front of his hut and start cooking.

Some people thought he was crazy. It was no special occasion, and no one had been invited. What was he planning to do with so much food? But Swami went right on cooking, being careful that everything was tasty and well prepared. He would say, "There are so many hungry people. We must make sure they are fed. That is our duty." "But Swami," one would plead, "how will they know to come? After all, it is a rather odd time for a feast." "Don't worry," he said, "they will come."

Sure enough, when the food was ready, many people were there. Swami would sing and sing, then serve them all. Sometimes they would come for his *yagam* and stay until late in the evening.

Swami also gave food to the temple. He would buy huge sacks of rice and have devotees take them to Nallur Temple and distribute them—one measure of rice for each person. He also saw that each was given a handful of vegetables and a few coins. He said he could foresee a time when there would be little food on the Earth, and he wanted to do his part to alleviate the problem, if only in the microcosm.

Huge feedings for the less fortunate were held regularly, usually at temples, and regarded as especially meritorious, a good way to earn *punya,* or good merit. Yogaswami not only arranged these himself but urged his devotees to follow his example.

Fires were built in the sand, and heavy metal pots, one meter high and 15 meters wide, were set upon strategically placed rocks to boil rice and dal. All would sing Natchintanai as the eager guests, including indigent holy men and women, slowly gathered for what would be their one hearty meal in a week, or more.

When the food was ready, men with four-foot-long wooden shovels moved the rice onto large mats, swiftly making a soft, white mound as tall as a man. Thousands of sadhus and needy folks sat cross-legged on woven cadjan mats. There would be dozens of rows, with up to fifty in each—long, paired lines a couple meters apart facing one another. Those gathered would be served en masse with stunning efficiency—20 to 30 men rushing down the aisles, deftly dolloping steaming rice, dal and curry with big spoons onto the open banana leaves. Within minutes, thousands of meals were served. And as soon as the first sitting had finished, a second would take its place.

Afterwards, the banana leaves were fed to the cows, with families of crows snatching their lot between bovine bites. In this discipline of feeding, many of Swami's devotees recognized a sadhana he was developing for them. In the decades after his *mahasamadhi* they fed tens of thousands of hungry people at Nallur Temple and at other places around Jaffna, which they continued to do down the years.

On one occasion such a meal was planned by Swami at his compound. Devotees came early in the morning to start cooking. Others came to sit with Swami and sing with him. Lunchtime came, and he was still heartily singing, so deeply absorbed that no one wanted to disturb him. They all just sang. Others sat outside and listened. Everyone was satisfied. They were drinking in his darshan and no one wanted to disrupt that flow with matters so mundane as eating.

Hours after lunch should have been served, Yogaswami stopped singing and fell quiet for awhile. Just as one or two people were thinking of breaking that silence to suggest that Swami might wish to eat now, he asked several devotees to chant from the *Upanishads* in sonorous Sanskrit. They chanted and chanted and chanted, intoning the timeless teachings of the Self. Swami sat in silence, blissfully enjoying the fervor and serenity of the chanting—transported to the times of the rishis, he would say. Everyone felt his enstasy and, turning inward, touched into those sweet realms themselves.

At about four in the afternoon, the chanters paused, sensing that people were growing anxious about lunch. Not wanting to disrupt Swami's mood, they asked softly if perhaps they should stop chanting since many present did not understand Sanskrit. Swami decreed that it was not important for everyone to understand the words. The tones of the words and the consciousness of the chant would carry the teachings to all, whether they understood with their intellect or not. The mantras continued.

Finally, at about 5pm, he said, "Before we can partake of our *prasadam*, I shall ask eleven strong men here to dig a deep, square hole in the ground." They stepped forward and he indicated the spot where they should dig. Shovels were obtained from homes nearby, and the digging commenced.

All waited patiently for his will to be fulfilled, the stomachs growling, the mouths watering at the luscious fragrances of the hot *rasam* and the freshly-boiled rice, five perfectly spiced curries, chutneys, *kulambu,* yogurt and delicious sweet *payasam.* It was a real feast.

Finally, just before dusk, the pit was completed, and the great saint indicated that it was time to serve the food. "Come, children, surround this pit," he said. Two or three hundred people stepped forward and surrounded the ten-by-ten-foot hole. Women and children were sitting in the front and the men standing in the back, all wondering what he was going to say and hoping he would not delay any longer with the feast.

He announced, "Now we shall serve our *prasadam.*" He called forward two of the huskiest of the eleven men, the strongest and biggest, and commanded, "Serve the rice. Bring the entire pot." It was a huge brass pot containing nearly 400 pounds of rice. By this time, many had left, as they had been cooking all morning and singing all afternoon. Only the most devout had remained to see the outcome. When the day began, 1,000 had come. The preparations were for a very big crowd.

Now he said, "Pour the rice in the middle of the pit." Banana leaves had been laid carefully at the bottom of the pit to form a giant serving plate. The crowd was aghast. "Pour it into the pit?" "Don't hesitate," he commanded. Though stunned, the men obeyed Yogaswami without question, dropping the huge mass of steaming rice onto the middle of the banana leaves. He told one man, "Bring the eggplant curry!" To another he said, "Go get the potato curry! We must make this is a full and auspicious offering."

As all the curries were neatly placed around the rice, everyone was wondering, "Are we to all eat together out of the pit? Is this what the guru has in mind?" Then the *kulambu* sauce was poured over the middle of the rice. Five pounds of salt was added on the side. Sweet mango and ginger chutneys were placed in the proper way. One by one, each of the mouth-watering preparations was placed in the pit, much to the dismay of those gathered.

After all the food had been served, the satguru stood up and declared, "People, all of you, participate. Come forward." They immediately thought, finishing his sentence in their minds, "to eat together this delicious meal you have been waiting for all day as a family of shishyas." But he had something else in mind, and directed, "Pick up the eleven shovels, shovel some dirt over this delicious meal and then pass your shovel on to the next person. We have fed our Mother Earth, who has given so generously of her abundance all these many years to this large Saivite community. Now we are sacrificing our *prasadam* as a precious, heartfelt gift. Mother

Earth is hungry. She gets little back; we take all. Let this be a symbol to the world and to each of us that we must sacrifice what we want most."

In this way, Satguru Yogaswami began the first Earth worship ceremony in northern Ceylon. He taught a lesson of *tapas* and sacrifice, of fasting and giving, and giving and fasting. By now the hour was late, very late. After touching his feet and receiving the mark of Siva from him in the form of *vibhuti*, holy ash, on their forehead, the devotees returned to their homes. It was too late to cook a hot meal, lest the neighbors smell the smoke and know that mischief was afoot. We are sure that a few, if not many, satisfied themselves with a few ripe bananas, while pondering the singular lesson the satguru had taught.

Where All Words Are Silence
In May of 1953, Mr. A. Thillyampalam of Sangarathai Vaddukoddai gave his youngest daughter in marriage. Having completed his familial obligations, he submitted papers for early retirement from government service four days later. The following day, Swami visited his residence and thundered, "Thillyampalam! You are not to retire yet; you still have a vital task to perform! Go tomorrow to Jaffna and start the building planning and supervision of the Sivathondan Nilayam, with a proper meditation hall upstairs."

Earlier in the year, Swami had established a formal religious body, called the Sivathondan Society, holding the first general meeting to form a managing committee, nominated by Yogaswami, to manage the affairs of the Nilayam. Many of Swami's "council of rogues" were present. As became the pattern each month, puja and bhajan were held, then a meeting, followed by dinner served to all present.

In 1954, the facility was completed and ceremoniously inaugurated. Yogaswami's sandalwood *tiruvadi,* which he kept at his hut for two weeks for blessings, were installed in the Meditation Hall. Author S. Ampikaipaakan wrote:

It is apt that Sivathondan Foundation was located in Vannarpannai, the hub of many Saiva religious activities. We will understand the object for the Foundation if we look at the plot plan of the building. In the Sivathondan Foundation plan we see the Puranam Mandapam, Meditation Mandapam, rest rooms for the followers, kitchen and washroom facilities. In the Puranam Mandapam, *Puranam* story and music discourses, recitation of *Tirumurai* and memorization of Natchintanai were conducted. In the upstairs, in Meditation

Mandapam, puja for *tiruvadi* [holy sandals] is done. Silence is always observed there. At the time of Holy Feet Puja, the bell rings, camphor light showing and flower submission is done, and complete silence was observed throughout this time.

Swami strictly designated the Nilayam as a place of meditation and worship. Swami had three sayings posted on the wall, to be read as one climbed the steps to the Meditation Hall:

Sol ellam maunam. (All words are in silence.)
Seyal yavum maunam. (All doing is in silence.)
Ellam nann mauna niraive. (Everything is perfect within silence.)

And he posted (in Tamil) five rules of conduct:
1. Devotees should wash their mouth, hands and feet well at the inner entrance and apply *vibhuti* on the forehead before stepping into the prayer halls of the Nilayam.
2. Devotees should strictly confine themselves to their assigned duties in the Nilayam, without interfering with other devotees.
3. Devotees should maintain absolute purity physically, as well as wholehearted spiritual purity within themselves.
4. Devotees should maintain high discipline while the chanting of *Tirumurai* and *Puranam* is in progress at the Nilayam, without any form of disturbance to other fellow devotees.
5. Sivathondan Nilayam's main observances are Sivadhyana [meditation] and chanting, with discussions related to Saivism and Natchintanai only. Discussion of nonreligious and any other worldly matters is strictly prohibited.

Inthumathy Amma writes:

Swami was adamant that the rules be followed without fail to maintain the sanctity of the Centre. "If this Centre does not provide these blessings and deteriorates, then break it down; there is no loss by that action." He explained that the puja and chanting of religious songs in the Purana Hall creates the mood for meditation: "Singing and chanting are done because one cannot just be."

T. Sivayogapathy shares the following narrative about Yogaswami's hands-on management.

Yogaswami had enormous stamina and could walk all day in the scorching heat of summer. Jaffna residents knew him and feared him, perhaps knowing he knew the contents of their heart. He would rise early to avoid devotees and walk with an umbrella to keep the sun at bay.

When Sandaswami resided in the Sivathondan Centre, Germanswami and another European swami stayed with him for a few days. The conduct of the latter two was not in accordance with the rules of the Centre. Further, their association was detrimental to Sandaswami's religious practices. Hence, Yogaswami was boldly strict about getting rid of them from the Centre. Swami referred to himself as the watchdog of the Sivathondan Centre. Its meaning is clear in this and also many other instances.

To manage the Nilayam, Yogaswami assigned Mr. Chellathurai, the headmaster of the Madya Maha Vidyalaya in Navatkuli, Jaffna. One day in 1956, Swami stopped his car at the school and summoned Chellathurai to come and get in the car. Then he announced, "I am going to station you at the Sivathondan Nilayam. You are to be in charge as the permanent resident there, with immediate effect."

From then onward, Chellathurai served Yogaswami in that way, managing not only this center, but also a second Sivathondan Nilayam that the society established in Batticaloa. Taking up monastic life, he became known as Chellathurai Swami. He passed away in 2006 at age 92.

One day, when Swami was talking with Chellathurai, they were interrupted by a noise coming from the backyard. Realizing that it was a Sivathondan engaged in cleaning the toilet, Swami roared with laughter, saying, "Siva puja is going on there! He is the supreme Sivathondan who is washing the toilet for the comfort of the devotees of Sivathondan Nilayam!"

Swami stopped by often to give orders. With an umbrella under his arm and a cloth wrapped around his head to protect him from the tropical sun, arriving unannounced, he would call Chellathurai or others to come out, "Build this. Fix that. Publish this. Prepare rooms for guests from India." Having delivered his decrees, he turned and walked away, knowing all he had asked would be dutifully fulfilled.

Swami rarely entered the Nilayam himself, but at certain times, when it was quiet, he did go inside, and once, after his accident in 1961, he stayed there for three weeks. The bed that he used is still kept there.

He often advised people who visited him to go to the Nilayam and sing hymns or chant the *Vedas*, or to go upstairs to the meditation hall, the all-important Dhyana Mandapam where silence was, and still is, enforced. "Sit quietly," he commanded, "Then what you have come to me for will come to you." A plaque on the wall says it all: *"Summa iru."*

After the Sivathondan Centre was established, Swami often told devotees, "Why do you come to see me? Go to the Sivathondan Centre and meditate." He immortalized this message in the song entitled "Accept the Assurance of These Words:"

Go to the Sivathondan Home, and *mukti* win through meditation. Be at rest by keeping silent. Know this to be the mantra! Realize who is "this" and "that man;" know that the *atma* is eternal. Within you is bliss beyond compare. See that all that is is truth! Follow not the senses' path, but bring them under your control. Rid yourself of cruel hatred. Vedanta and Siddhanta seek to learn. Know that there is not one wrong thing, and "Om Sivayanama" pray. With melting heart true bliss attain. Accept the assurance of these words!

Swami insisted that pujas at the Nilayam be conducted in utter simplicity. In fact, they were done, and still are, in total silence, with no chanting whatsoever. Aside from *tiruvadi* puja held daily in a simple way, and elaborately on the first Sunday of each month, the only other events he allowed were Ardra Darshanam in December, when Lord Siva and the soul are seen to be one, and the annual festival of Mahasivaratri, when puja to the divine sandals is conducted in grand style. Swami admonished that no other days were to be observed.

Once when a member of the Sivathondan board expressed a desire to celebrate another festival, Swami said, "See, man, there is no permission," putting an end to the idea. After Swami's *mahasamadhi, tiruvadi* puja was also held monthly on Aayilyam (Ashlesha) *nakshatra* at the two *nilayams* and at his Columbuthurai hut. That was the same *nakshatra* on which he installed Chellappaswami's *tiruvadi* in his hut in the 1920s, and it was also the *nakshatra* of Yogaswami's *mahasamadhi.*

For special guests from outside Jaffna, Swami provided the Vannar-pannai Nilayam as a place to stay. From Tamil Nadu, three renowned scholars in the fields of Tamil language, English language and Saiva Siddhanta philosophy—Dr. T.M.P. Mahadevan, Dr. T.P. Meenatchisundaram and Prof. A.S. Gnanasampanthan—used to visit Jaffna frequently, via the 30-minute Trichy-Palaly air route. They came mainly to discuss philosophy with Swami at his hut, while also giving public lectures in the schools of Jaffna peninsula. They always stayed at Sivathondan Nilayam in Jaffna as Swami's guests, following his instructions.

A few years before Swami attained *mahasamadhi,* he prognosticated, "Difficult times are coming. It is going to be hard to even get liquid food. Take care in cultivating food and give food to all." Articles on the greatness of the gift of feeding appeared in many issues of *The Sivathondan,* and action was taken to procure good fields for cultivation to ensure that the project of giving food was successfully conducted. Swami indicated the need to distribute the produce of this cultivation to all, and to feed everyone.

Inthumathy Amma provides a glimpse of how, under Swami's direction, the Nilayam supported religious studies.

Three years after the establishment of the Sivathondan Centre, two
advertisements appeared in *The Sivathondan* journal. One was about
the Sivathondan Educational Fund and the other was about those who
obtained assistance from the fund. Those who obtained assistance
from this fund (and went to Indian universities to study *Devaram*
music, religious studies, etc.) were expected on the conclusion of their
studies to spend five years in the Centre doing service—and if they
so desired, to spend more time. This illustrates that the aim of the
Sivathondan Centre was to direct people in the high ideals of religious
knowledge. The Saiva Siddhanta taught by Swami, the lectures on the
Periyapuranam conducted in the temples by his devotees, the translation of the introductory chapter of Sir John Woodroffe's *The Serpent
Power* by Advocate Suppiah, the publication of books like *Vivekachudamani* (the advaitic text by Adi Shankara) and *In the Hours of Meditation* all show the spiritual ideals of the Sivathondan Centre.

T. Sivayogapathy provides details of Yogaswami's influence on some of the
spiritual heads of India's *mathas* and renowned religious scholars of the day.

Deivasigamani Arunachala Desigar Adigal (Kundrakudi Adigalar)
was the spiritual head of Tamil Nadu's Kundrakudi Aadheenam, an
ancient monastery-temple complex that is among the citadels of Saiva
Siddhanta. He made numerous visits to Jaffna and Batticaloa in the
1950s and 1960s to give lectures on Saiva Siddhanta in Saiva temples
and halls. One day in the late 1950s, when young Adigalar was in
Jaffna, Mr. A. Thillyampalam, my father, and Mudaliyar Sinnathamby
took him to Yogaswami's ashram, where Adigalar enjoyed a valuable
discussion with Swami. As a gift, Swami presented him a *Natchintanai* book. After leaving the hermitage, the young swami voraciously
read it from cover to cover. From that day onward, in all his lectures,
he praised Swami's songs as the cream of monistic Saiva Siddhanta
philosophy.

Dr. A. Lakshmana Swami Mudaliyar, former Vice Chancellor of the
University of Madras, upon visiting Swami in 1955, was enamored
with his uncanny ability to express complex concepts in everyday
language. The renowned educator told Thillyampalam that, even in
India, he had never met a saint of Swami's caliber, whom he revered as

"a treasure for humanity in this world."

Swami developed a close affinity for the Ramakrishna Mission, a relationship that began with his 1897 encounter with Swami Vivekananda. Swami Asangananthar, of the Colombo Branch, made frequent visits to Jaffna for Yogaswami's darshan. When the Ramakrishna Mission of Batticaloa was raising funds to establish a gurukulam at the Vannarpannai Vaitheeswaran Sivan Temple, Yogaswami made the first contribution. His blessed offering is still preserved by the Mission. Through the years, he encouraged men wishing to follow the monastic path to join the Mission, including scholar Pundit T. Mylvaganam and Swami Premathmananthar. While Yogaswami, for undisclosed reasons, disallowed anyone wearing the *kavi* robes to stay as a guest at his Sivathondan Nilayam, he made a standing exception for the swamis of the Ramakrishna Mission.

Only One Work to Do

Yogaswami often said, "There is only one work to do: realize the Self yourself. In other words, find out who you are. Or know thyself. How do you do this? You can't find the Truth in a thousand books or by listening to people talk. You must realize the Self by yourself. Go inside and remain there. Then you can come down and see the world." Yogaswami told seekers:

> There is a chair at the top reserved for you. You must go and sit in that chair. From there you will see everything as one. You will know no second. That is a state unknown even by the saints and celestials. Buddha attained that state and came down to help others. Christ knew that state and also tried to bring others to it. Many others no one has heard of have known that state. That chair is there, reserved for you. It is your job to occupy it. If you don't do it in this lifetime, you might do it in the next or in the next or in the next. It is the only work you have to do. There are those who can fly to the top like birds.

Swami was a reflecting pond to anyone who came to see him. To a simple person, he talked simply and directly. He related to educated people in terms familiar to them, whether Hindu, Buddhist, Christian or Muslim. He spoke to each through the context and vocabulary of his religion. He had a perfect command of Tamil, Sinhala and English.

When a Christian came, Swami might ask him to open the Bible at random and read aloud. Swami would interrupt to explain a passage, often relating it to the devotee's life and astounding him with knowledge of his past and future. His favorite section was the beginning of the Gospel according to John: "In the beginning was the Word. The Word was God. And the Word was with God." He would talk and talk about this teaching until he had completely unravelled it for his listener.

To Buddhists he would quote the teachings of Buddha and explain them as if he were the Buddha unfolding the path to nirvana. And to Hindus, no matter what path they followed, he would ground them firmly in the tradition they were used to. But to say that he would usually do one thing or another is not accurate. There was no "usually" about Yogaswami. He had no prepared responses or stock answers to questions, problems or situations.

Wisdom and divine sight were his guidelines and his tools. If he knew you one moment, he might ignore you the next or not even recognize you, not even know your name or face. Everyone who visited him got what he came for. Sometimes Yogaswami would just sit in silence, then after while announce, "Nothing is coming." He meant there were no inner orders, no spiritual directions from within.

One day around 1961 Yogaswami was alone in his hut when S. Shanmugasundaram, a close devotee, arrived from Colombo. Entering an empty room, the visitor wondered for a moment if Swami was away. Suddenly, Yogaswami came through the curtain, his long, white hair undone, not tied neatly as he always wore it. Without words, Yogaswami began to dance, his hair flying wildly with the vigorous movements of his body. Shanmugasundaram stood transfixed. He knew this was a special blessing. It was a blessing he never forgot, and when he spoke of it decades later, he surmised that Yogaswami was subtly guiding him toward Satguru Sivaya Subramuniyaswami, the dancer, for Shanmugasundaram later became a devotee of Subramuniyaswami, traveling to America and Mauritius and sharing Yogaswami's life and teachings there.

With Yogaswami's blessings, Markanduswami retired at age 60 to live a hermit's life. Yogaswami built him a simple mud and thatch hut and placed him there to live in seclusion. Yogaswami's love for his disciple was so great, he would prepare a meal for Markanduswami, carry it seven kilometers to Kaithadi and serve it with his own hands.

• •

"Just Be"

"I went to Nallur looking for God," explained Yogaswami. "I had only one desire: to know God. There I met my Chellappan, the man people called mad, the being who would not admit a second. Through his grace, I found out that he and I are one, and I, too, became one without a second."

He said that Chellappaguru took everything away from him—all desire,

Yogaswami had a vision for a spiritual center, not an ashram and not a monastery, but an agricultural community of young men who would follow the celibate life, work in the fields, in nature, growing food for pilgrims while following strict spiritual disciplines. The land was acquired during Swami's lifetime, but the center manifested in 1965, just after his passing.

all attachments, all ego—and that he then came to a state Yogaswami called *summa*. In Tamil that word means being still, not having any concern, not knowing. Once he translated it into English as "active awareness." *Summa* is the threshold of inner life. If there are desires and attachments, *summa* cannot be held for more than a few seconds, but once it has been touched, desires and attachments begin to dissolve and this state becomes easier and easier to hold: the mind's awareness is actively poised in stillness. Finally, when *summa* is held long enough, higher experiences begin to come and refine themselves until the Self only remains. Yogaswami had another way of pointing to the same result: "Meditate 'I am Siva,' then the state of Siva without attributes will come."

Swami gave different people different sadhanas, spiritual disciplines, they could follow if they wanted to attain the state of *summa*. Gauribalaswami (Germanswami) sat on the veranda of Sivaya Subramuniyaswami's ashram in Alaveddy and told this story to young seekers from America visiting Jaffna in the early 1970s. A natural raconteur, the white-bearded, cigar-smoking elder sat cross-legged on the concrete floor and told of his struggles with the intellect, and Yogaswami's constant efforts to get him to quiet his mind, to get him to reach into the depths of spiritual experience. But, he said, the mind has a way of its own. "I could not reach that thoughtless state my guru pointed to; I could not subdue the mental movements."

Saying that, he lifted his right arm, held it out at shoulder height for his young audience to see. There, on his forearm, was a one-inch high tattoo that read *"Summa iru"* in crudely drawn Tamil. *"Summa iru"* is what mothers say to silence their boisterous children, as English-speaking mothers plea, "Be still." "I put this tattoo on my arm to remind myself everyday of my guru's teachings, of my sadhana. Imagine the power of a master who can give you two words to follow, and you spend the rest of your life working to fulfill them. That was Yogaswami."

To one he gave the prescription: "The kingdom of God is within you. Meditate on that and go to the top." To another he said, "Work without working. Worship without worshiping. Eat without eating. Wash without washing. Walk without walking. When you can do that, then you will know *summa*, and everything else will come to you."

He spoke often of the importance of doing all one's work as an expression of service to God, which he called Sivathondu. "Let whatever work you do, my son, be an offering to the Lord." He would often end darshan sessions with a devotee or family with the admonition, "Now go and do your work!" He wrote:

> We are the servants of Siva. We are lacking in nothing. Our work is to do Sivathondu. It is for that alone that we are living in this world. The moon is doing Sivathondu. The sun and all the planets are performing the same holy service. In like manner, the devas, *asuras, kinnaras, kimpurushas* and *vihyadharas* are all ever doing Sivathondu.
>
> Everything is the work of Siva. Without Him not an atom can move. We lose nothing, we gain nothing. We are as we have always been. There is no one equal to us or superior to us. For us there is no good or evil, no birth or death, no like or dislike. We are free of desires for land and gold and woman. The devilish mind is absent for us. We are not concerned with matters of time and place. We live as the witness of everything. Om Tat Sat Om.

Sivathondu was one of two "medicines" he most frequently administered. Another was Sivadhyana, meditation on Siva. Yogaswami explains its importance in the following short *upadesha* called "Tapas."

> The senses drag down to unlimited depths even those who have done great *tapas*. Consequently, to overcome them you must practice Sivadhyana. Only by that means can they be brought under control. Therefore, do this meditation uninterruptedly.
>
> Whenever one dwells on sense impressions, attachment arises. From attachment springs desire; from desire, anger; from anger, delusion; and delusion causes one's downfall. Therefore, guard yourself by Sivadhyana.
>
> Because of our pettiness, our true nature is obscured and we stray from the path of dharma. To free oneself from error and to make oneself steadfast, Sivadhyana is the best means. Though we may possess great wealth in this world, and though we may have the power to make even celestial beings serve us, we still cannot control our senses. Therefore, invoking the grace of God, restrain the mind from

wandering along the path of the senses.

It is precisely this that great sages have called *tapas*. If this is neglected, even though you may perform ostentatious sacrifices and such things, you will never achieve firmness.

Yogaswami gave no formal classes, lectures or seminars, but he taught every day, spontaneously—at his hut in the mornings and evenings, in the bazaar or the streets, or at a devotee's home during a surprise visit. Usually his words were addressed to the needs and problems of one individual, but everyone present benefited.

Many came to Yogaswami wanting to renounce the world and go into the jungle to meditate. He only gave blessings to one or two of them, ordering all others to fulfill their *svadharma* in the world, commanding that they do the best they knew how, with detachment. His attitude was that all of life must be regarded as spiritual, knowing it is foolhardy to divide one's activities into sacred and secular. He would convey this strongly to the many souls who came seeking blessings to give up their jobs so they would have more time for spiritual life.

One day a young man came to him, beseeching permission to renounce the world and strive for God Realization. Yogaswami did not speak. He just sat there. The man pleaded and pleaded, saying it was the only thing in the world that he wanted to do and he needed the blessings of his guru before undertaking this mission. Yogaswami remained silent. The man begged insistently, desperately imploring that he could not live without the satguru's blessings. He would kill himself if Swami withheld his approval. He pleaded and begged for a long time. Swami did not respond, acting as if he were alone in the room. Finally, the man left.

Yogaswami later explained to the devotees present that the man's wife had just run off with another man, and he thought he could escape the humiliation he felt by retreating into the jungle. "If it had been his natural development, I could not have helped but give my blessing."

Whenever people were unduly hard on themselves, undertaking disciplines that were too severe, Swami would stop them. "The body is a temple, the mind is a sanctum. You must keep them pure and clear. You need them to do your work. Do not destroy them or harm them." Turning to a devotee sitting at his feet, he said:

As you walked into the room, it felt cool and fresh because you are on the path and have begun to feel the presence of the *atma*. Some people come and I feel hot, and there is no air in the room. That is because they are here to trick me and think they can cheat me out of something. You are searching and have no selfish motives. You come just to sit here. You can feel the same peace from me. That is why you come. It is good for people on the path to sit with one another.

More often than not I feel I am in the presence of God. You must treat that feeling you have of the presence of God as you would a little child. Nurture it. Give it everything it needs. If you see it as a child, you become helpless. You must obey its every wish and do exactly as it bids you. Just as a mother knows in every instance what to do for her child, knows the meaning of its cries and gives it what it needs, so does the Presence make itself felt to the devotee. You must carefully nurture the awareness of God that is growing within you. If you do, it will grow and grow, and without your knowing it, you will have disappeared and only That will be.

Time and again Yogaswami spoke of Siva, of worshiping the holy feet, of the path of spiritual discipline and love, as seen here in his song entitled "Worship the Feet of the Lord."

If you always offer worship to the Almighty's holy feet, then you will have peace. That will make you realize that all you see is transient. That will show the way to subdue the body. If you always offer worship to the Almighty's holy feet, then you will have peace.

That will make you rule the mind that treads the senses' path. That will daily repeat the letters five in your heart. If you always offer worship to the Almighty's holy feet, then you will have peace.

That will surely, by degrees, extirpate all anger. That will accept all mistakes as blessings in disguise. If you always offer worship to the Almighty's holy feet, then you will have peace.

That will remove and drive away all the three desires. That will reveal the holy feet, which neither come nor go. If you always offer worship to the Almighty's holy feet, then you will have peace.

That will keep you ever in the state of being *summa*. That will make you realize compassion for the poor. If you always offer worship to the Almighty's holy feet, then you will have peace.

That sets you in the open Void, and takes away all sorrow. That will see both Vedanta and Siddhanta as one. If you always offer worship to the Almighty's holy feet, then you will have peace.

That will control the fickle mind, which cannot be controlled. That will give the vision, where there is no night or day. If you always offer worship to the Almighty's holy feet, then you will have peace.

This song of Yoganathan will show the righteous path. It will nourish you with nectar for all the days you live. And to know "Aham Brahmasmi" is the crown that it will give. If you always offer worship to the Almighty's holy feet, then you will have peace.

Markanduswami, a close devotee of Yogaswami from the time they met in 1931, was a lifelong bachelor who wanted to renounce the world and take sannyasa in the middle of his career. Yogaswami told him to continue his profession as a surveyor. Finally, when Markanduswami's retirement came at age 60, Yogaswami surprised him by arranging for a *kutir* to be built among a small coconut grove in the village of Kaithadi, a hut with one room and an open porch, a concrete floor, with walls and roof of woven palm fronds. He settled his disciple there and looked after him for years.

His foremost sadhana, a difficult one they say, was to speak only the words of his guru, so everyone who spent an hour with him would hear, again and again, "Yogaswami said...." "Yogaswami taught us...." He was amazingly faithful to this discipline of not giving out his own wisdom, though he was deeply endowed. Standing on his porch or perched on a raised neem seat with four posts and a canopy, he would explain excitedly that Yogaswami gave him the following sadhana, his indirect way of inviting seekers to control their own minds:

Sit in one place. Do not move. Watch where your mind goes; watch the fellow. First, he'll be in Kandy, then go to Colombo, then to Jaffna, all in a fraction of a second. Keep track of every place he goes. If he goes one hundred places and you have caught only ninety-nine, you fail. As you progress in this sadhana, you will begin to pick up things coming from within. When you get messages from inside, you must deliver them to those who need to know. It will be a great help to them.

On one Mahasivaratri evening, Yogaswami paid a surprise visit to Markanduswami's hut and told the old sadhu, "We shall observe this Mahasivaratri *vrata* with meditation only." That night, for them, there were no pujas, no chanting of Natchintanai, *Agamas* or *Puranas,* only meditation in absolute silence. T. Sivayogapathy shared:

Markanduswami was a man of few words and avoided involving himself in the public life. He knew the whole corpus of Natchintanai songs by heart and always quoted Natchintanai when talking about Hinduism and spiritualism. Yogaswami is said to have told devotees, "Markanduswami is my compass to you all; he shall show you all the spiritual directions," this being an indirect reference to Markanduswami's career as a surveyor. Markanduswami attained *mahasamadhi* on May 29, 1984.

Yogaswami moved about as a beneficent sage, shopping for fresh food at the market, visiting devotees' homes, sharing in their lives, uplifting them with his blessings. T. Sivayogapathy tells of his experience from the 1950s and 60s:

Swami used to visit our residence, "Thillai Vasa" at Sangarathai, frequently and spend a full day there. He used to come early in the morning, after doing vegetable marketing, arriving at our place around 8am. Around 8:30, Swami, my beloved father and myself commonly took our Rover car to the nearest seashore, namely Tiru-vadi Nilai, and all of us would enjoy bathing in the sea and return home. On arrival at home, we would have bath again, with well water. Later, we all assembled in our large prayer room. Swami was seated at the center of the room, as we all observed prayers while chanting from *Sivapuranam,* as per Swami's instruction. In the meantime, my mother, Thaiyalnayaki, was preparing lunch for all of us, cooking all the fresh vegetables Swami had brought in the morning. Before the meal, Swami would chant the food blessing *(bhojana)* song, then we all sat with him and had lunch. After the meal, Swami would compliment my mother and bless her by saying, "Thaiyalnayaki Thaye! You have provided a full and tasty lunch for this beggar. Live well!"

The devout went to great lengths to assure Swami's visits. There was a famous V.S.S.K. Vegetarian Cafe situated just 200 yards from the start of K.K.S. Road. The owner, Mr. V.S.S. Kumarasamy, had been enamored of Swami, who frequented the cafe for coffee in the mornings or lunch at midday. Farther north on K.K.S. Road were the well-stocked herbal medical stalls, namely Subramaniyam Medical Shop (next to V.S.S.K. Cafe) and Nallathamby Medical Shop, where Yogaswami would stop frequently for casual chats.

Just before reaching Vannarpannai Vaitheeswaran-Thaiyalnayaki Sivan

Temple, on the same side of the road, stood the popular vegetarian cafe Thamothara Vilas. The founder, Thamothara Aiyer, encouraged Yogaswami to take his lunch here. He was clever in his approach. By the side of the cafe there stood a vacant shop owned by Mr. S.R. Kandiah, a devotee of Yogaswami who maintained the inside impeccably, complete with a simple bed, always ready for Yogaswami should he need to rest and relax during one of his daily treks, especially following a free midday meal at the cafe.

Close to the Earth

In 1960, Yogaswami expressed his wish to have a second Sivathondan Nilayam established in Chenkaladi near Sittandy, in the Batticaloa district. In 1910, during his pilgrimage to Kataragama, he had stayed in the town for three days at the home of Mr. Veluppillai, so the place had special significance to him. Whenever he was in Batticaloa, Swami visited the Sittandy Murugan temple. In accordance with his wishes, the Society established a center there in 1965. On the inaugural day, devotees carried a pair of his sandals 300 kilometers from the KKS Road Centre by foot in a parade. T. Sivayogapathy gives a glimpse of activities at the Nilayam.

> When Swami decided to have a Nilayam at Chenkaladi, some devotees of Swami donated land for it. Later, after the Nilayam was built, paddy lands were also gifted so that rice could be cultivated. Sandaswami managed the Nilayam and worked the paddy fields. He used to drive the four-wheel tractor through the paddy fields for ploughing. In the year 1967, I had a great opportunity to visit the Nilayam with my beloved father, A.Thillyampalam, and observed how active Sandaswami was in his daily Sivathondu. It was Yogaswami's intention that the Nilayam should cater food and provide shelter for pilgrims to Kataragama Temple, whom he held deep sympathy for, having suffered many hardships on his own journey to the remote jungle shrine in 1910. Srimath Sandaswami (Soulbury Swami) tried his best to implement Yogaswami's vision, but could not succeed due to poor response from the public. However, paddy cultivation was done for some years, due to the good efforts of Sandaswami, who served there from 1965 to 1977.

Like the Jaffna center, the Nilayam in Chenkaladi was established with the same strict rules of conduct as a place of meditation and prayer. But Yogaswami had specified for the Batticaloa center a stronger emphasis on service, and on cultivating food to feed those in need. Inthumathy Amma tells about Yogaswami's unique vision of this place.

Just as the Jaffna Sivathondan Centre is conducive to meditation, the Chenkaladi Sivathondan Centre is directed toward service. In the plan drawn up according to Yogaswami's wishes there was another temple-like structure on the western side. This was to be used to house celibate students and recluses. Recluses who had religious knowledge and knowledge of other arts, who were well experienced and of good conduct, were to reside there and teach others like them.

Fertile fields were obtained in which the acolytes were to work hard, cultivate food, and thus be useful to others. This Sivathondu would help in getting rid of their egoism, helping them to forget the "I" and live in unison with the "we."

Swami said that men who grow in this atmosphere will have bodies that exude good religious conduct and faces exuding the strength of mental peace. He visualized them meditating in the hall, under the trees, amidst the fields, guiding the world through their silence, while sitting, walking and working. The fulfillment of this idea of Yogaswami's depends on those who are prepared to sacrifice themselves fully in the pursuit of Self Realization. Yogaswami expressed that it is not the aim of the Sivathondan to indulge in propaganda, to press people or to go about lecturing.

Yogaswami's Final Years

During Swami's later years, in the early 60s, there was trouble between the two ethnic communities who live in Sri Lanka, the Tamils and the Sinhalese, between whom a rivalry has persisted for centuries. The Sinhalese Buddhists are a majority. At that time they were attempting to make their language, Sinhala, the official language of the country. Because of this effort and its implications, riots sprang up at different places all through the country. These conflicts came and went for years.

On February 21, 1961, Yogaswami had, as usual, left the ashram in the morning and walked to Vannarpannai. Passing the old Dutch fort, where people were fighting in the streets, he witnessed first hand the violence and bloodshed. Solemn and withdrawn, he walked back to his hermitage, reaching there around noon.

Usually upon returning to his hut, he washed his feet and gave his hands and face a scrubbing at the well on the other side of the road, where everyone washed before entering the compound. This day, however, he just got down from the car and walked directly through the gate past his hut and into the pasture, sixty yards or so, to the cattle shed where Valli, his cow, was tethered. He offered her a few bananas, as he often did, and petted her affectionately, despite the fact that Mr. Tirunavukarasu's daughter had warned him two days earlier not to go near "that Valli cow," due to her feisty demeanor the past few days. Suddenly Valli threw her head toward him, as playful bovines are wont to do, striking Swami with the strength of her thousand-pound frame. Eighty-eight years old and frail, Swami was thrown to the ground, unable to get up. He would later discover that his left hip had been broken by the fall.

Fortunately, Mr. Balakumar and his wife, who had come to visit Swami and were waiting at his ashram, witnessed the accident and came running to help. They called a neighbor and urgently told him to convey the news to Mr. Tirunavukarasu, who was at the bank where he worked, and to Mr. Thivendram at his book shop. Thivendram summoned Mr. K. Brahmananda, and they all rushed to the site.

Placing Swami on a makeshift stretcher, they carried him to Mr. Brahmananda's van and sped to Jaffna Hospital. Mr. A. Thillyampalam, who also had been alerted, joined them there and by phone conveyed the news

. . . .

For most of his life, Yogaswami wandered freely, often spending an entire day walking the lanes of his beloved Lanka. But a fall which broke his hip at 88 put him in a wheelchair, which meant devotees could visit him more readily.

to devotees in Colombo. The next morning, twenty devotees flew from Colombo, including two surgeons, Dr. V. Rasanayagam and Dr. A.J. Anthonis. Yogaswami was given a private room and the best of care.

The moment he entered the hospital, it turned into a temple. Devotees gathered around and waited for news of his condition, singing quietly his favorite songs from *Natchintanai* and *Sivapuranam*. That evening Dr. V. Rasanayagam, an orthopedic surgeon, operated on Swami's hip. He said afterwards that Swami would not be able to walk, though his hip would heal. During Swami's stay, five doctors looked after him in turns: Dr. C. Gurusamy, Dr. S. Ramanathan, Dr. V.T. Pasupathy, Dr. S.A. Vettivelu and Dr. N. Waloopillai.

"Some Day You Will Understand"

A concern arose that he sleep soundly and not move at all that night. The doctors gathered around him and explained how important it was that he

Yogaswami urged devotees to "Wear the body like a sandal," a call to not be overly concerned for their physical body, but use it well. One day while feeding his cow Valli bananas, she tossed her head, throwing him to the ground. His life changed, but his detachment never wavered.

• •

remain still so the healing could begin. Swami regarded the injury much differently than they did, saying, "Oh, you think it is important. To me it is nothing." Because of their concern and insistence, however, he agreed to receive a sleep-inducing drug. The doctors gave the injection, telling him it would make him sleep until eight in the morning. Yogaswami fell into a sound sleep right away, and the doctors thought they had achieved their goal. But at about four in the morning, he awakened.

Every morning after that he awoke early. By four o'clock he was sitting quietly, and people slowly gathered. Everyone came, doctors, nurses and devotees. From about 4:30 they were singing and chanting. Devotees burned incense and camphor. Sometimes Yogaswami spoke to them. Often he asked visitors to sing or chant from a certain scripture.

At about 5:45 he ordered everyone go to their work and asked his attendants to clean the room and straighten the sheets. At six each morning an English nun came in to look after his medical needs, and he wanted everything to be just the way she would expect it. He made sure the ashes from the incense were cleaned up and the bed was properly made. Greeting him, she would say, "Hello, Father. How are you today?" He responded, "Good morning, Mother."

One day he asked when she had time to pray. She answered, "My work is my prayer. What I do with my hands, Father, is my prayer." "We are also like that," he responded. "That way we stay pure so that God within us can work through us." When he mentioned God within, she held her hands over her ears, indicating that she just did not see God within and would not even hear of such an idea. Yogaswami laughed, "Oh, that's all right. Some day you will understand."

In the evening, after the main work of the hospital was finished, people again gathered in Swami's room to sing and sit within his darshan. They lit lamps and again burned incense and camphor.

Yogaswami had always been immediate and vibrant, a dynamic presence to all who came to him. Some grew fearful in that incredible presence. Others experienced it as a motherly compassion. He was aware of every aspect of their lives. After his accident, though, he spent more and more time within and was outwardly softer and remote. He had a luminance that made those around him feel as if he were in a celestial realm. Even those whom he had treated harshly before he now greeted with gentleness.

Sometimes Yogaswami would slip into contemplation and forget his body altogether. It was then that people began to realize that Swami had veiled his presence while he was with them as fully and as successfully as he said Chellappaguru had hidden his. Just from the way he was during these times, devotees could glimpse the true nature of the guru. Pointing to his body he would say, "You must not think of this person as the guru. The guru is vastly different from this."

A devotee wrote of visiting Swami in the hospital, recounting what Swami said about his injury.

> I went to see him in the hospital with my father-in-law. While in the car on our way, my father-in-law told me that Yogaswami's condition was deteriorating. I replied, "He is superhuman, and such incidents occur only to show the world how one should face any adversity in life." On our arrival, Yogaswami clasped the doctor's hand and said, "Rajah, you think that I am very ill, don't you? There is nothing wrong with me. The body which did the bad deed is paying the penalty." That he said with his leg in bandages, his mind so detached that his face was as fresh as a new rose!

In *Words of Our Master,* Swami elaborates on the above theme:

> This [illness] is a gift. Karma must be gone through. I have no connection whatever with this body. This body brought with it the seed of all else in life. Illness is part of it. People who understand the cause of this will merely note this as the end of all suffering and remain undisturbed. The ignorant become restless and sad."

When devotees anguished aloud about his condition, Yogaswami consoled, "Do you think you can forestall my karma?" They realized that from his perspective all was in perfect order and their best help to him was to be a loving witness to his condition.

. . . .

Yogaswami was a robust man, but he suffered from diabetes. From
the early 50s he received daily insulin shots from a doctor-devotee.

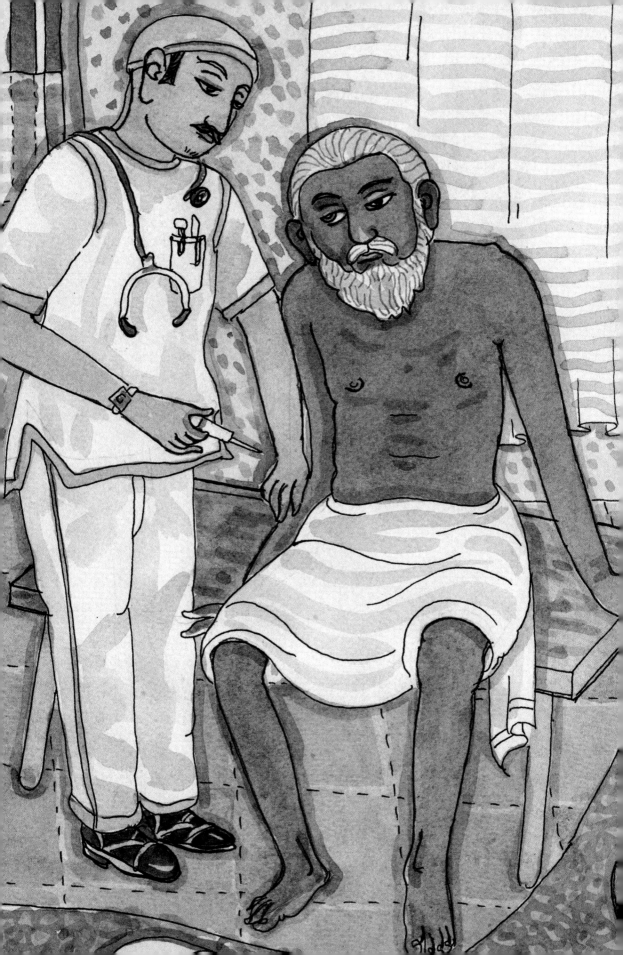

When people began blaming the cow, Yogaswami stopped them. "We put ourselves in Valli's way. It was not she who did what was settled in the beginning." Many devotees believed Swami foresaw that the Tamil community was going to face many problems and hardships in the future and through his injury intentionally took some of their suffering on himself in an effort to ease the horrific karmas he anticipated.

S. Shanmugasundaram said that, years earlier, when someone asked Swami why he didn't take medicine for his ailments, or why he got ill at all, Yogaswami replied, "I could die now if I wanted to, just close my eyes and in a short time be dead." But he said he had a few more things to do, and he still needed to overcome anger a little bit. He wanted to go permanently when he died, and not come back, so he was making sure he left nothing undone.

Swami gradually recovered his strength and began to move about in a comfortable wooden wheelchair and a walker. Sandaswami had air-lifted from the UK a modern stainless steel chair for him, but he preferred the old-fashioned one.

During his recuperation in the hospital, devotees worked day and night to build a new hermitage for him on the north side of his old hut. Similar in size to the thatched hut, it had concrete walls and floor, a clay tile roof, wheelchair access, indoor plumbing, electric lighting, a proper bed and other conveniences that Swami would need when he returned from the hospital. In fact, the doctors would not release him until the building was finished.

"We Learned Silence in His Presence"

In June of 1961, after three months in Jaffna General Hospital, Swami returned to Columbuthurai and moved into his new hermitage. People took turns caring for him. There was always someone on duty to look after Swami's needs, and Dr. Rajakaruna visited the ashram every morning to do physical therapy for Swami. In spite of this, he never regained the ability to walk.

As his strength returned, Swami would take excursions in his wheelchair. He was often sighted kilometers from his hermitage in his chair, pushed by Sivayogeswaran, nephew of Mr. Tirunavukarasu. He also moved about freely by car in the mornings. At noon, he would have lunch and then take a nap until 4pm. In the evenings he received devotees in the ashram.

A special activity each weekend was driving to the beach. He especially loved to visit the seaside in those days; it seemed to give him physical solace. A. Thillyampalam and his teenage son T. Sivayogapathy would arrive in their Rover with their driver at 4:30pm. The son's duty was to sponge Swami's body, dress him for the outing and ever-so-slowly move him into the wheelchair for the short ride to the road.

Swami sat in the front seat with the driver as they drove to the beach. Once there, they parked the car, with doors wide open and the skylight pulled back, so he could enjoy the sea breeze. From the seaside, Swami and his hosts proceeded to Sivathondan Nilayam, where, from the car, he would call Chellathurai over for a short talk.

Typically they proceeded to Nallur Temple. Parked at a distance in front of the *teradi*, Swami sang *Sivapuranam* and worshiped. Money, coconuts and camphor were sent inside the temple in a basket so that a special puja could be performed invoking the blessings of the Deity.

As sadhus and others invariably approached, Swami personally handed a plantain to each one, while, on the other side of the car, Thillyampalam reached into his coin purse, carefully prepared for just this moment, and gave each one a coin, ten or fifty rupees—a generous sum, as in those days an ample meal could be purchased with a single rupee. This remained the pattern until January of 1964.

People were no longer afraid of the once-fearsome sage, and many who had not dared approach him earlier now came. Often he sent them to the Sivathondan Nilayam.

Increasingly, efforts were made to ensure Swami's comfort. His legs were swollen with excess fluid, and it helped if someone rubbed them. He allowed only a few men to massage his legs, and they considered it such a blessing that they would have massaged forever if he had not sensed their fatigue and asked them to stop.

Ratna Ma Navaratnam gives us a glimpse into these final years.

Swami's sacrificial illness from 1961 to 1964 lit an unquenchable flame of devotion amongst his devotees, whence came the realization that even bhakti could be just as imperfect as karma or dhyana. We learnt to be silent in his presence and awaited the manna that fell from his lips. Day was indistinguishable from night, and the play of opposites preyed less and less on our captive minds, released to enjoy serene peace. Swami would take us backwards and forwards. He would recall many illuminating reminiscenses of Chellappaswami, his peerless Gurunathan.

The resonant voice of the guru became softened with love in his last days on Earth. He would call upon the Divine Mother, Devi Thaiyalnayaki, and avow that She abides in the conscious core of each one's heart, and would therefore know each one's pain and pleasure intimately, and would swiftly respond to the call of Her unswerving children. He would make us sing the four lines on Thaiyalnayaki for hours together. Was She no other than the beloved guru, the healer of all life's ills and forebodings? Can it be the Supreme Identity hailed by the sacred scriptures?

Doing pujas and *abhishekams* at Nallur Temple, and at the Vannarpannai Vaitheeswaran-Thaiyalnayaki Sivan Temple, was a prescription he often gave in these last three years at the ashram. Another was to conduct *padayatra*, pilgrimage by foot, from Sivathondan Nilayam to Nallur Temple and then to his ashram.

He told devotees to study the *Kandapuranam* in temples and in homes. As his *mahasamadhi* approached, Swami arranged for the study of the *Markandeya Padalam,* a chapter of the *Kandapuranam,* in a style of teaching in which one person sings the poet's verses and another sings the explanation in his own words. At that session, Thambaiyah, a teacher, rendered the explanations. Swami attended this kind of spiritual discourse off and on and encouraged others to do likewise.

One month before his *mahasamadhi,* foreseeing the hardships ahead, Yogaswami cried out in a loud voice, "O Thaiyalnayaki Amma! Please bless and save the Tamils from the hardships they will undergo in the future. They will find it difficult to have even a cup of rice porridge per person per day!" He decreed, "All Tamils must start paddy cultivation and agriculture to cultivate various grains in order to manage food during difficult times!"

That visit to the future proved uncannily accurate, as the entire Sri Lankan Tamil community learned twenty years later, when the ethnic war broke out, bringing with it thirty years of conflict, hunger and suffering.

Three photographs were taken of Yogaswami when he returned from the hospital, captured by a devotee who knew that soon he would no longer be on this plane. They were among a handful taken throughout his life, as he generally did not allow photos to be taken of him. Many people thought they had managed to get a photo, only to have the negatives emerge from the developing room blank. Only these taken as he sat on his bed and two taken by 19-year-old Sami Pasupati in 1951 had his blessing. These five, and one more taken as he walked away from the camera, umbrella held above his head, were the only known photos captured during his long life. In 2006, Sami Pasupati told of taking his photos.

At that time we had no photograph of Swamiji to pray to. Many people had attempted to take a photo and had failed. One day, while Yogaswami was staying at our home, my mother, Tamilammaiyar, said to me, "Tomorrow morning, when Swamiji is saying his prayers, why don't you take a photo of him." I was frightened that he might scold me. Mother said, "Don't worry, if he scolds you, I will take responsibility."

The next morning at 6:30, Mother woke me up saying, "Swamiji is praying now. You are not to go inside the room where he is meditating, but you can take the photo from outside." I took a picture. Later when he was having his breakfast, Swamiji asked, "Did anyone come into my room?" My mother responded, "No. No," and then kept quiet. Later, when we were seated with him outside, my mother said, "Swami, we have made a big blunder." Swami replied, "You couldn't have made a mistake." He had known her since she was a little girl. "We took a picture of you without your permission," she confessed. At that, Swami was silent, and we were a bit worried about what he would say. Then he burst out laughing, which greatly relieved us. Then I asked, "Swamiji, can I take another picture of you?" He answered, "You have already taken one; there is no need to take another." Having said that, a minute later he volunteered, "All right, you have taken one, no harm in taking another." So, while he was seated in the chair on the porch, I took a picture.

Every attempt to record his voice also failed. People would receive his blessings to record a song he was leading, and everything in the room could be heard in the recording except Swami's voice, even though he was singing the loudest.

"I Have Never Forgotten This, and Never Will"

Every once in a while, beginning in December of 1963, special alerts went out. One day Yogaswami said he saw the time coming when he would leave his body. He asked a close devotee to call the others. People came from Colombo and the Eastern Province, traveling long distances to be there for their guru's *mahasamadhi*.

The *Shastras* say that when a guru or a saint leaves his body he gives forth a shakti greater than at any other time in his life. So, devotees came anticipating extraordinary blessings. Also, they were deeply attached to him and came with sad faces. When a large group had gathered, Swami just looked at them and laughed and laughed, then sent them away.

After that he would be fine for days and weeks at a time and would go on long rides in automobiles. Mr. Thivendram, Mr. Kasipillai Navarat-nam, Mr. Kathirgesan and Mr. Rajendram, with their families, regularly brought their car to Columbuthurai to take Swami for rides.

When devotees came to see him at his hut, Swami asked them to sing, and he almost always joined in. His voice was still strong. Sometimes they sang for two or three hours. Once, upon arriving at a devotee's house, he asked that certain parts of the *Sivapuranam* be sung. They sang and sang, revelling in the presence of the guru.

Nagendran, a devotee who visited Yogaswami during his final months, offered the following narrative.

My Uncle Sivanathan and I went to Columbuthurai a few months before Swami's *mahasamadhi.* It was about 8pm and Yogar was seat-ed on a bed. A white shawl covered his loins. His upper body was bare. The silver hair was a bit rumpled. His face was gaunt and his eyes sunken. His two arms were placed behind him to support his weight as he leaned back. The room was flooded with electric light. I have a picture of Yogar from this day in my shrine room. As Uncle Siva and I paid our obeisances to him, devotional songs burst out of his lips. The songs were loud and clear and resonated around the room. He sang for about ten minutes. His eyes sparkled, and love poured out from them and suffused his face. I have never forgotten this and shall never will.

"Everything Is Golden"

Near the end of January, Swami became disinterested in going out to the beach, or anywhere for that matter, and limited his wheelchair travels to short distances. Ratna Ma Navaratnam shares:

It was during this period that he became accessible to all, being confined to his ashram. Devotees sought him in large numbers and, with infinite patience and love, he meted out inconspicuously his sanctifying grace. He extended his healing touch in his own peculiar technique of hot and cold compresses, and took upon himself the still sad music of humanity. He generated a force that never was on sea or land, and electrified all those who for one reason or other flocked to him by his soul-stirring Natchintanai songs and homely discourses. Thus his accident was looked upon by his devotees as an outlet for the outpouring of God's grace. In the last phase of his earthly life, Swami

. . . .

Devotees regarded Yogaswami's fall as a sacrificial injury, for it allowed them unfettered access to their beloved satguru. They gathered with devotion each day at the new hermitage, singing, meditating, listening to his wisdom and reveling in a closeness never experienced before.

taught the supreme sovereignty of the Lord's Will. "His will prevails within and without. Abide in His will" was his insistent plea.

He remained mentally alert. Just a month before his grand departure, he was visited by Mr. Ampikaipaakan. While approaching the compound, the former principal of Vaitheeswaran College mused that Swami's mental state must be sadly diminished and wondered how he would converse with him. Entering the hut, he heard Swami laugh heartily and call out, "Can you remember, Ampikaipaakan, fifteen years ago, when I shouted at that man, in your presence, just opposite the Vaitheeswaran Temple?" The principal was delighted that Swami was as keen as ever.

T. Sivayogapathy shares the story of the blessing his father received from Swami during this time.

Just a few weeks prior to the *mahasamadhi* of Swami, as usual, his devotee and confidant Mr. A. Thillyampalam visited Swami's hermitage. After they conversed for a while, Swami's tone turned serious: "Thillyampalam! There are many people in this world counting money day and night, calculating their respective bank balances and leading an unhappy life. But nobody in this world can touch or calculate your bank balance, because it is something unique, which is the value of your charity and large-hearted service to the community. Charity for the deserving is noble Sivathondu!" So saying, Swami blessed his devotee with a kind smile.

Swami seemed to assume that everyone was in the same realm as he was. That was the magic of the last days. He would talk to them and to unseen beings, the devas or even the Deities, as if they were all together on one plane of existence. He would tell a devotee to take an unseen being for a ride in his car. The devotee—accustomed to doing precisely what Swami asked of him—now just didn't know how. Feeling helpless, he would murmur, "Swami, I don't see anyone there." Swami would answer, "Surely you do. He's right there, standing beside you. Just take him on a short ride and bring him back."

The fellow had no choice but to take what he considered an imaginary being to his car, open the door for him, close the door, go around and get in the car and drive away. If he neglected his task in any way, such as not opening the door for the being, Yogaswami would shout out, "Well, you didn't open the door! He's standing in the road! Back up your car and let him in!"

Swami sent many devotees off with these beings. Once he sent someone to the cremation grounds with an invisible guest. The man had no choice but to follow Swami's bidding. If he did not, Swami would know and would send him off again to do so.

On one occasion he asked a devotee to take a deva home for tea. The man dutifully went to his home and, rather embarrassed, announced to his wife, "I have brought a companion for tea. Please prepare some tea for us." Sometimes people would lose courage and just drive around in their car for awhile and then come back. One man came back having done this, and Swami said, "He says you didn't give him any tea. You'd better take him again for tea." They were wonderful times, and everyone loved them, even if they were confusing.

Swami also seemed to be in the constant company of an unseen child. He would ask a devotee to take the child and walk it around. "Oh, this baby needs to go to sleep. Here, my son, take him, walk him to sleep." The devotee would hold out his arms and Swami would carefully hand the child to him. "Be very careful," he would urge. "Make sure he goes to sleep." Or he might ask someone to feed the infant. "He's hungry. See that he has a little cup of milk." When someone asked, "Swami, this is a soul child, isn't it?" or "Swami, this child is the infant Murugan, isn't it?" he would just ignore the query.

Swami engaged in planning a store during these final days. "We'll have a store. We'll give people everything they want, won't we? And we won't make a profit, not even a penny's profit, will we?" He spent days and days planning the store. When they asked, "Swami, is this a metaphysical store," he ignored the question. Their queries must have seemed as strange to him as his plans were to them. To him, the distinction between different realms of mind had faded. The veil between the inner and outer worlds no longer was perceived. All was one, right there, in the moment, completely available.

With just an oil lamp burning, the room seemed to glow with an inner light. And there was an inexplicable coolness in the air. At any moment, he might become transfixed, apparently oblivious to those around him.

Once while in this state, he talked aloud to Mother Thaiyalnayaki. His face took on the look of a small boy, radiant with the love that was coming from the Mother Spirit. He whispered his praise of that love and spoke elatedly of the energy he felt in Her presence. Then he was with Chellappaswami. He talked to his guru, telling of his work and saying that he wasn't ready to come with him yet. People who were with Swami at this time said that his face showed that he still assumed the role of disciple while with his Chellappaguru, open and receptive. For a long time he sat motionless, his expression blissfully effulgent. Everyone's ears rang with the highest inner sounds, penetrating yet gentle.

After awhile he came back into the presence of those sitting around him and asked if they had been with him. Had they seen what he had just seen? Then he told of that wondrous world: "Everything is golden. There is a soft and self-luminous light beyond anything you can imagine."

A few days before Swami's *mahasamadhi,* a devotee placed an offering of fruit and flowers at Swami's feet and worshiped him. Swami handed the offering to another devotee with instructions, "Take this and do an *abhishek-am* in the Nallur Temple."

Yogaswami Leaves His Body
Swami became confined to his bed on March 20, 1964, refused to drink or eat anything, and told doctors to stay away. An alarm went out that he was failing. He barely moved all day and when awake talked to himself in the tones of a child. Many people gathered around. Though emotionally distraught, they sang quietly or chanted. All were visibly saddened by Swami's imminent departure. The next three days saw a steady stream of devotees coming for his darshan, praying, seeking final blessings from their beloved master, knowing that he might leave his body at any moment.

Every so often Swami withdrew completely into his inner world. His temperature dropped and his pulse rate slowed, sometimes nearly stopping altogether, which alarmed the doctors. In this state he kept only a tenuous hold on his body.

On the night of March 23, about fifteen devotees sat quietly at Swami's bedside, singing in turns. At about 10pm, a devotee arrived who had always had a direct channel to Swami. It was Dr. S.A. Vettivelu, who had gone daily to the ashram to monitor Swami's blood pressure, as well as his blood sugar level and to give a daily insulin injection. Without hesitation, he approached and asked, "How are you feeling, Swami?" *"Ellam saree"* ("Everything is fine"), Swami answered in a full voice. Hearing these words, most of the devotees thought he had made a turn for the better and departed.

On the day he died, Yogaswami was carried on a palanquin through the villages to the cremation ground. The entire nation mourned, and tens of thousands joined the procession to honor the Sage of Ceylon who had touched so many hearts.

By 11:30 pm, five remained: Dr. S.A. Vettivelu, Mr. A. Thillyampalam, Mr. Kasipillai Navaratnam, Mr. K. Brahmananda and Mr. Tirunavukarasu. As soon as the crowd had departed, the feeling in the room changed from one of emotional upset to a peace hardly describable. Swami was quiet. At one point he spoke softly, indicating he wanted those around him to sing. They sang two songs Swami had always sung at profound moments: "Engal Gurunathan," written by Swami, and "Namasivaya Valka" an ancient hymn by Saint Manikkavasagar.

At 3:18 on the morning of Monday, March 24, 1964, Yogaswami released his body. Those present reported losing all consciousness and being consumed in a shakti so intense and pervading that it overshadowed every other experience of their lives.

Death's approach reminds us that life on Earth is temporary. All our possessions, power and ego will end. Seeing this truth, the Saivite Hindus of Jaffna were schooled to turn the mind toward God, toward life's ultimate goal, moksha, liberation, and toward the path of dharma that will take the soul there. They did this not in trepidation, but in assurance, faith and gratitude for the opportunity to progress spiritually in this physical incarnation.

Death is defined differently according to what people believe themselves to be. If they are only the body and brain (as with humanists or atheists), then death is the end of sensory experience, and thus of self. If we live once, death ends our only sojourn on Earth and is naturally dreaded. If we are born again and again, it loses its dread in light of the soul's pilgrimage to eternity.

No matter how ill, how infirm our condition, there is a serene and consoling center of our being to which we can adjourn, the Source within. It is more us than our body, more us than our mind and emotion. It will not die. It does not hurt or fear. As physical debility and death draw near, we seek this center, whether we call it Paramatman, God, Self or Divine Consciousness. In the *Katha Upanishad,* Yama, Lord of Death, explains: "Death is a mere illusion which appears to those who cannot grasp Absolute Reality. The soul is immortal, self-existent, self-luminous and never dies."

Sivaya Subramuniyaswami would later describe the process:

In Saiva Siddhanta philosophy, it is the soul's subtle body, *linga sharira,* that stores the "thought-energy" experiential impressions of life, called *samskaras.* When the body dies, this nonphysical sheath continues as a constellation of subtle elements—dispositions, memories, desires, etc. It is within this subtle body that the soul reincarnates, if necessary. Death, according to Hinduism, is not the contradiction of life. Death and birth are two sides of life's cosmic cycle. The culmination of that cycle is liberation. As Yogaswami taught: "By getting rid of desire, man can put an end to birth altogether."

Many who have had a near-death experience speak of having come back to complete unfinished obligations to children, parents or friends. It is a great blessing to know of one's impending transition. A Hindu approaching death works diligently to finish all his "business" of this lifetime, the allotted portion of his total karma carried into this birth to face and resolve. If death comes while loose ends remain—misunderstandings unresolved, misdeeds unatoned for or obligations unfulfilled—another lifetime may be required to expire that karma. Thus, it was not unusual in those and later days to see an aging or ailing Hindu going around to friends and enemies, giving love, help and blessings, working to resolve conflicts and differences, offering apologies and fulfilling all known obligations. In modern times he would also execute his own will, distribute his properties and duties to heirs, charities and endowments, not leaving such tasks to others.

That done, the soon-to-transition soul turns to God, reads scriptures, attends the temple and amplifies meditation and devotion. He may pilgrimage to sacred spots or retire to a secluded place to practice *japa* and yoga sadhanas. The family takes care not to disturb these efforts, nor his retirement from social obligation or interaction, realizing he has entered life's final stage, that of renunciation, or sannyasa.

Swami had given hints about the time of his death and shared thoughts about leaving this world. A devotee recalls:

> About three months before Swami's *mahasamadhi,* we used to go quite often to him, and he used to often ask the time, "Is it three o'clock? When it's three o'clock, I must get out, so tell me when it's three." He used to always leave at three o'clock. Someone's car would come for him at about that time, and he would go. One day he said, "I have done everything. Nobody must blame me. I have done everything for everyone. I have made arrangements for you all." And he made a bow, a sort of farewell gesture. Finally, it was at 3am that he passed away. Later only we connected the facts, his always asking for the time. He was preparing for the final journey.

Swami prepared everyone for his Great Departure, telling them that to him the body was unimportant. "Just throw it away when I have left it," he said to some. "I have done everything that I have to do for more than fifty years. I have said everything that I have to say. I have no regrets." He said he did not need his physical body to do his work or manifest his presence. And he told of a time when people all over the world would know him and feel the blessing of the guru.

The following account of the funeral was published in *Hindu Sadanam,* under the title "Light of Jaffna."

On Tuesday, 24-3-1964, devotees, school students and others paid homage to His Holy body in Columbuthurai Ashram. Devotees in groups sang *Tirumurai*, Tamil prayer songs and Natchintanai songs with melodious music. On 25-3-1964, Wednesday, early morning, about 5:00 they did *abhishekam* with devotion to Swamigal's body.

Swamigal's body was covered with pure white cloth and flower garlands. His body was carried in a square box decorated with flower strings. Devotees carried it through Columbuthurai Street to Thundi Cremation Grounds. The procession route was decorated with leaves and flowers. The people living in the streets paid homage with lighted oil lamps and water pots in front of their homes and sang bhajan songs.

About 9 o'clock the procession reached the funeral grounds. Thousands of people gathered to see the cremation. Volunteers arranged men and women to sit separately. There was silence, and it was peaceful. The body was placed on a wooden stack, which included one quarter ton of sandalwood. Everybody was meditating on the grace of Yoga Swamigal and their blessing to live in the same time as such a great siddha lived in this world. Kokuvil Mr. T. Kumaraswami Pulavar recited devotedly *Tiruvasagam* songs and one *Puranam*. Then the body was ritually lighted. Everybody loudly shouted, "Arohara" and worshiped the light.

Sinhalese brothers, Muslims and Christians also were there to pay their respects. Like this, everybody watched Swamigal merge with light. The place looked like earthly Kailas.

The following description was given by V. Muthucumaraswami.

Never did Jaffna see a larger crowd, so many devotees of various faiths coming to pay last homage to the Sage of Columbuthurai. Hundreds of devotees were in attendance. It seemed as if all of Jaffna was there. Many who had feared to visit him all their lives for what they thought he might expose to them now paid homage to the sacrificial life of this saint. It was a solemn affair. Many were unable to contain their emotion, even though they knew that the soul is immortal. From childhood, their scriptures and teachings had taught that there is no real death, that the soul merely passes from body to body on its pilgrimage to God. And they knew that Swami was surely enjoying the bliss of liberation from samsara. They were crying more for their loss of Swami's presence and the emptiness they felt.

Sri Ananda Pereira gave the following eulogy in *The Sivathondan:*

Most people are takers. Some, a very few, are givers. Yogaswami was a giver par excellence. His whole life was one long act of giving.

I had the good fortune to meet him in 1952 and again in 1963. Time and a sad accident had wrought their inevitable changes in the interval. He who had been strong and well was now weak and virtually bed-ridden, dependent on others for even the most elementary physical needs. The eyes that had been so bright and piercing were now dim. The voice had lost is resonance. The once-steady hands now trembled, and pain carved lines on the noble face. He was living proof of the law of change to which all beings, even the highest, are subject.

But I soon found that that flame of his heroic spirit still burned as brightly as ever. The dim eyes could still probe deep into the human heart. The voice had still the ring of authority. The trembling hands still held the scepter of true royalty. He was still the giver, and I the receiver.

What did he give? Peace, strength, hope, courage and many other gifts too numerous to mention. But, above all, he gave love. It radiated from him as light and warmth radiate from the Sun.

What did I receive? As much as I was capable of receiving. Take a little mug and stand under a waterfall. You emerge stunned by the impact of the water, but how much do you bring away? One little mugful.

Ratna Ma Navaratnam echoed:

For about ninety-two years, Swami was like a luminous ray reflecting the radiance of the Saiva saints down the ages. The Jaffna community in whose midst he lived and moved had grown imperceptibly to accept his presence as naturally as the beneficent sunlight, so that his *mahasamadhi* on March 24, 1964, created an unusual stir and sorrow among all ranks of people who had basked in his lustre from generation to generation. Swami was venerated as an illumined seer of the twentieth century, one who was God's witness on Earth, a saint in whom the sacred was secret; he was like the Triveni, a confluence where met the streams of past, present and future. He seemed to have held the whole world in the kinship of the supreme will of Siva. The Master Sivathondan blazoned the trail of service and renunciation, by his universal gospel of Sivathondu, service unto Siva. To live every split second as servitors of Siva was his clarion call to the modern man.

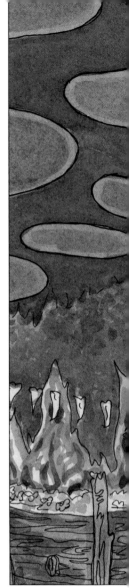

After the cremation, Swami's ashes were kept in the new ashram. Feeling that a proper samadhi shrine should be created, Mr. Tirunavukarasu, owner of the ashram land, consulted with three senior devotees of Swami, Dr. C. Gurusamy, Mr. A. Thillyampalam and Mr. Srikhantha, and they together decided to take down the old hut and designate the spot as a samadhi shrine. Funds were raised by the Sivathondan Society, and in the coming months work commenced on a new structure on top of the old concrete flooring. A large alcove was created in the perimeter wall on the west side of the building above where Swami's ashes would be kept in a crypt below ground, and a formal shrine, facing east, was established above it. The shrine was completed within a few months and the ashes were placed in the crypt during a small, informal ceremony.

There his sandals are kept and a priest does puja daily. The area where Swami used to sit, meditate and sleep is also a place of worship. Behind it, against the wall, a large photo of Swami is enshrined, the one that was taken of him meditating. The priest does puja here as well. The area where he sat is demarcated with white ceramic tile. There flowers are spread each day and offerings are made.

Swami Lives On

Some think that when a realized, liberated soul leaves his body, he is automatically released from further reincarnation on Earth. While this may be true for most, it is also said that liberated ones have a choice whether to come back again and serve. That possibility is suggested by the following story told by Yogaswami to a devotee.

Many years ago in Nallur, Chellappaguru's birth star happened to fall on the day before Mohammed's birthday, and Chellappar took Swami to Nallur Temple, ushering him to a tomb where a great Muslim guru had been buried at the time the temple was destroyed by the Portuguese. Initially a shrine had been built around his burial site; the

Yogaswami's body was consumed on a pyre that included pure sandalwood. Many experienced him in his subtle body in the years to follow, sensing his continuing presence in their lives and knowing that his death was not his end.

samadhi was reconstructed some time later. Yogaswami said Chellappar told him the Muslim saint who was buried there was Chellappar. In other words, Chellappaguru had held that body before as a liberated guru and had returned to Earth again as Chellappar. While narrating the story, Yogaswami looked his devotee in the eye and said, "That is the kind we are."

Even during Yogaswami's earthly life, many devotees saw him appear in his subtle body. After his passing, people in India and Malaysia, Sri Lanka and America had similar experiences. Since then, many have seen Swami's etheric form, as it was when he walked on Earth. Even those who never knew him in his physical form have experienced his unembodied darshan. Close devotees have seen him in quiet moments. He has manifested himself in their meditations, giving just the things they needed to keep focused on their spiritual work.

Several months after Swami's *mahasamadhi,* a man in Jaffna felt a subtle, inexplicable change in his home during the night. It was a feeling so strong that he could not dismiss it. He got up to investigate and, after checking several places, entered his shrine room. There was Yogaswami, just as in the famous photo, sitting in meditation, luminous and clear as day, one meter above the floor. The man worshiped, then went to call his wife and children to come. When they arrived, the figure was just fading into the wall, but they saw it, too. Other households had the same experience.

Devotees who knew Yogaswami have told of hearing his voice as clearly as when he was with them physically. One day, not long after his passing, a lady who had been close to Swami went to his compound and sat down in the simple hut. She missed him deeply and was sad over her loss. She began singing a song she had sung for Swami many times, to invoke the fulfillment she had felt when she was there with him. Part way through the song she stopped and sat quietly. Then she heard Swami speak, as clearly as ever before, "I am as I always have been. I am here, there and everywhere. Have no thought of sadness."

Swami often came to devotees in dreams during this time. Some who had problems that they would have taken to Swami for his advice had such dreams in which he gave the solution. In some dreams, devotees vividly experienced the intense presence of his shakti, as if they were sitting with him. These profound encounters inspired and gave them new direction.

Little by little, this kind of experience subsided. After 1968 he became less immediate and active. He now lives totally on subtle planes of the mind, emanating shakti. A person has to make a deeper pilgrimage to be with him.

In 1972, Satguru Sivaya Subramuniyaswami revealed from his mystical perspective in *Saivite Shastras* how Yogaswami "lives in a simple cavern, as that was his association with the inside of a small room in his ashram in Sri Lanka. He could make it larger with but a twinkling of the eye, but he sits there in deep samadhi, radiating darshan to the sanctified places that do puja in his name. When a puja is conducted in his name, his wall opens up and he is at the puja. He does not go to it; it comes to him, if the vibration of the puja penetrates deeply enough." Subramuniyaswami also encouraged his own disciples to learn and sing Natchintanai, often noting that Yogaswami attends in the inner worlds when devotees sing his songs.

All through his life, Yogaswami foresaw the emergence of monistic Saiva Siddhanta in the West, especially in the United States. He told close devotees that there had always been Siva worship on the American continent. He once explained that a group of ancient people living on the Colorado River basin, near the Grand Canyon, worshiped Siva with as much understanding as the ancient seers of India. Swami foretold of a time in the near future when many highly evolved Hindus would be born in America to restore the purity of ancient Saivite worship on Earth. Thus would be ushered in a new age of profound spiritual life on the planet.

During his life, Yogaswami purified the way called Advaita Siddhanta, or monistic Saiva Siddhanta. Where there were rough edges, he made the path clear and sharp. He embodied the beauty and the depths and the transcendence of Siva. Now, in Jaffna and in India, Yogaswami is remembered as the modern saint of Saiva Siddhanta, the being whose life harmonized the reality of ancient Saivite worship with the present era.

Swami would allow no fuss about the divine plan as it revealed itself before those who sat around him observing and enacting their parts in it. To him, it was completely natural and unworthy of special notice. To people who were astonished by what they saw unfolding in front of them he would say, "There is nothing amazing in the world. Your ignorance shows when you find this amazing. It all happened long, long ago." "What can be wonderful?" he would ask. "I am you and you are me. I am eternal, birthless, deathless, changeless, secondless."

One day a lady asked, "Swami, you are getting older now; are you going to make a guru to take your place?" Yogaswami answered, "Not a Jaffna man. I have a man in America."

Chapter Nineteen

Subramuniyaswami's Youth

The first mystical experience that I can remember was as a baby lying in my crib. It had little bars up so you couldn't fall out. All of a sudden, I was conscious of a tall, full-grown man standing over me in a serene, pale yellow robe. Then I became fully conscious of being this full-grown man looking down upon this little baby. Then I was conscious as the baby again, looking up into the face of this great soul. And then I was the tall person. Then I was the little baby looking at the tall person. It went back and forth and back and forth and back and forth. I realized that the tall man in the pale yellow robe was the body of the soul. I realized that as I continued maturing spiritually the soul body would finally fully inhabit the physical body.

That infant, Robert Walter Hansen, who would later become Satguru Sivaya Subramuniyaswami, was born at the Fabiola Hospital in Oakland, California, on January 5, 1927, to Walter and Alberta Nield Hansen. He was raised with his younger sister, Carol, in a cabin on the secluded, forested shores of Fallen Leaf Lake, near Lake Tahoe, California. Walter, a taciturn man, was a native Californian whose parents were both from Denmark, and Alberta was born in Kansas of an English-born father.

His mother and father were somewhat secretively involved with the medical school at Stanford University, though their life as caretakers of a remote log-cabin lodge gave little indication of why. Mysteriously, the medical school paid for all his mother's funeral expenses when she died. Robert was never privy to what happened at Stanford, as his description of those days would later reveal:

There's actually no proof of this, but I've always felt from different hints and things that were said that I was an experimental baby, which they used to call at that time a "test tube baby." I grew up with those thoughts in my mind. I believe that Grace Burroughs, who adopted me in dance and as a son, knew of my mother's cooperation with the research department of Stanford University Medical Center. Those were the days when artificial insemination or test-tube babies were only a concept and in the experimental stage. I remember at birth looking up at Dr. Chapeau, a Frenchman, a neighbor of ours, and to this day feeling him as being close to me as a father.

Lying in his crib only days after his birth, infant Robert Hansen had his first vision. Looking up, he saw the soul body of a tall, white-bearded man, and he knew instantly that this was himself in the fullness of maturity. Suddenly, he was the man watching the baby, then again the baby looking up at himself. Four times the observer changed.

He reflected, late in life, that his lifelong dispassionate nature, a powerful sense of detached innerness, might have been the result of the unemotional manner of his conception and birth.

Life was bucolic for the small family. The wild and remote Lake Tahoe area was one of America's most beautiful regions, and tourists flocked to the rough-hewn lodge in summertime. Walter and Alberta were the host-caretakers, looking after the guests and the upkeep of the resort.

But winters at 6,377 feet are severe; and the Hansens were alone for many months of the year, surrounded by old growth fir and pine trees and snow four to ten feet deep. They passed the seasons this way for years, far from the nearest neighbor, dependent on carefully garnered stores of canned foods and cords of firewood, stockpiled before winter set in.

Despite the desolate location, the children had lots of attention, gifts and toys. There were always huge piles of presents under the Christmas tree. At family gatherings they were surrounded emotionally by twenty or thirty relatives, and both children had photographs taken almost weekly throughout their early years.

Robert was three years older than Carol, and became her companion, caretaker and babysitter. He would make snowmen for her, instruct her in the fine art of snow travel on a wooden sled called Skootabog, down the gentle slopes behind the lodge, and teach her the ways of the forest which he had himself only recently learned. Brother and sister attended a one-room, log-built schoolhouse in which 23 students, of every age from six to sixteen, were taught by the same teacher. Their only wintertime connection to civilization was occasional mail and an old radio that brought them news and those sound-effects-laden soap operas sponsored by oil companies and Ovaltine.

Robert spent most of his time playing. His father tried to interest him in carpentry, building a table, obtaining tools, but he wasn't interested. He liked running barefoot in the snow, boating, skiing and snowshoeing in the winter. He played mostly on the trails and paths, or in the woods. In the summertime, Robert would swim out to a rock in the lake and meditate. He would stretch out on his back and go within until he felt he became the rock. Looking up, he would experience God pervading the sky and the rock, and all that was around him.

"I'm All Right, Right Now"

Among Robert's favorite radio shows was "The Lone Ranger," a serial adventure that was broadcast from 1933 to 1954. In the story, a heroic masked Texas Ranger gallops on his horse Silver to right injustices, helped by his clever Indian partner, Tonto. The weekly half hour was addictively popular with kids eager to be enthralled, among them the Hansen duo, who never missed an episode.

One cold December day in the early 1930s, Robert's father took his son on a supply errand to the village of South Lake Tahoe, three miles away, to pick up the mail and stock the family pantry. They had a custom-made truck—black in color, as all automobiles were in that day—that had two large skis mounted in front instead of tires, and dual-wheel metal snow tracks in the rear, so they could drive on top of the lightly packed snows without a need for roads. It had a fabric roof, no side windows and the back was an open flatbed for carrying supplies. On this day, father and son were running late, and that was not good. This was the evening "The Lone Ranger" would be aired, and it was unthinkable that an episode would be missed. But the unthinkable was happening. It was a moment the young boy would remember the rest of his life.

Quite often the snowmobile would become stuck in the snow. This might delay us an hour or two as my father worked to release it so that we could proceed. Each time we went to the village, on the way home I observed my thinking faculty being disturbed and worried for fear that we would not arrive home in time for me to listen to my favorite radio program. I hated to miss the sequence of the programs, such as "Captain Midnight," "The Lone Ranger" and "Jack Armstrong, the All-American Boy."

This was the first time I became aware in the area of the mind that always worries. There I was, though, and I didn't like it. I clearly remember mentally talking to myself and saying, "You are all right right now. We haven't gotten stuck in the snow yet! Have we?" At that early age, I actually saw awareness coming out of the area of the mind that always worries and entering a total consciousness of here and now. Then awareness would leave the now and go into the past, and I would begin to think, "Four days ago we were delayed in the snow for about an hour and my father had a very difficult time digging out the snowmobile." I saw my awareness travel into the past. Then I would repeat even more firmly to myself, "I am all right, right now. We are not delayed yet." And again, I actually saw awareness travel right back to the present moment.

This became one of my hobbies. The totality of the power of the eternity of the moment began to become stronger and stronger within me from that time onward, until whenever anything came along in the mind substance, I was able to handle it and work it out right from the now, instead of having my intelligence drift off into the future and try to work it out from that perspective or backtrack into the past and try to find a resolution there. All this and even more unfolded to me at that early age in such a beautiful and simple way.

Young Robert's mind seemed to take the best out of every experience, even then. But not all those early experiences were amenable to his gift.

Church-going was culturally mandated in those days, and the children were no exception. He would ask the minister questions, but the minister would not answer. "So, why should I go?" he challenged his mother. She talked to the minister, who obligingly conceded, "Please don't force him to come." The compromise of nonattendance seemed acceptable to all, and Robert's church and Sunday school days halted abruptly.

Orphaned

When Robert was nine, his mother, who had all his life been a vivacious and adventurous woman who loved nature and plucked herbs from her own garden, took ill. He helped care for her, even in times of delirium. In July of 1937, she came under the care of Dr. Malcolm Hadden in Berkeley. As the months wore on, her condition grew more grave, and by early November, she was admitted to an Oakland hospital. On November 11, 1937, Alberta died of cerebral arteriosclerosis and chronic myocarditis, leaving the children, 10 and 7, in her husband's sole care. She was cremated.

Grace Burroughs, an intimate friend of the family who lived nearby with her husband, took over the job of mothering the children. Walter, alone and burdened by his wife's death, raised Robert and Carol with Grace's help. Life in those backwoods parts is hard enough when shared by a fit couple, but overwhelming when one is left with all the responsibilities.

The family fared the winter as well as one might expect, but things were never the same. Walter grew morose, feeling the weight of his children's needs as any father would. He began drinking heavily, making the rounds of Nevada casino bars with his children in tow. This was to be Robert's first lesson on the powerful impact of sorrow.

One day, months after his wife's death, Walter was driven, for reasons unknown, to take a belt to his son. That beating would never be forgotten, and the two hardly spoke from that day, so traumatized was Robert by the cruel strapping.

On December 9, 1938, Walter left the home to drive into town with Bill Burke, a local stonemason. The weather was bad and their truck was side-swiped, forcing it off the road and into a tree. Burke was killed instantly, but Walter managed to drag himself away, his chest crushed and both legs broken. A neighbor carried Walter back to the cabin, and that night

• •

Robert made snowmen as he grew up in the woods. He discovered the eternal now at age nine, when he and his father got stuck in the snow in their half-track truck and it seemed he would miss his favorite radio show. He withdrew from his fear by assuring himself, "I'm all right, right now. It hasn't happened yet."

they drove him to a hospital in Reno. Doctors worked to heal his fractured legs and ribs; but as the days passed he began to fail, and finally succumbed to pneumonia on December 14, at age 50.

Walter's estate went into a trust for the children. The funeral was held in Auburn, California, where Walter's parents had been buried. Though the family begged him, Robert refused to attend. Days before his 12th birthday, he was an orphan.

> I can remember being hit twice in my life. Once with a ruler, two hits on the open palms. Then the father with a belt once. After that I would have nothing to do with him. I refused to go to his funeral.

Late in life, when asked about his youth by his monastics, he shared:

> As a boy, I was disappointed by adults and said to myself, "I'm never going to listen to anyone older than myself." And at that time being an orphan you could do whatever you want to—that's the one good thing about being an orphan, you don't have to listen to anybody. So, I listened to my own inner self and decided that I wanted to dance. And why was that? Because I was told God danced. Nataraja danced. I had already been taught pranayama, basic hatha yoga, when I was eight or nine years of age. Then during my teens, I learned attention, concentration and meditation.

He was referring to the summers he spent with Grace Burroughs at her school of dance at Fallen Leaf Lake, in which his father enrolled him during the summer following Alberta's death. Grace—an elegant, round-faced woman with an Oriental look born in Nebraska in 1895—had spent three years in the mid twenties touring the world with the Denishawn Dancers and a year or more in India as a palace guest of the Maharaja of Mysore, studying Indian dance, customs, art and philosophy.

"I Want to Dance"

Grace trained Robert in Indian and European dance, Indian culture and the fine art of meditation. This cultural discovery enchanted Robert, and the artistry and discipline of dance absolutely mesmerized him. It gave him a purpose, a goal, his first as a young adult, and he threw himself into it with all his heart. Decades later he recalled:

· ·

*Robert was introduced to Lord Siva through Nataraja, the
King of Dance. His teacher gave him a small Nataraja,
which he placed on a large rock altar with candles.*

About the age of ten or eleven, I became aware of what I wanted to do when I grew up. "I want to dance," I said. This came from deep within me. Music always moved the inner energy of the inner body and finally the muscles moved and the body would begin to dance. Dance, incidentally, in Hinduism, is considered the highest form of expression. That is why dance was used for worship in temples of ancient cultures. Through the esoteric forms of dance, you become acquainted with the movements of the currents of the physical body, the emotional body and the body of the soul. The meditating dancer, inspired by music, finds the inner currents moving first, and lastly the physical body. This releases his awareness into inner, superconscious realms of the mind in a smooth, rapid and systematic way. I started my life in the dance as the dance, and being the dance.

The young artist was eager to learn, and Mrs. Burroughs was thrilled to have a focused student. She decided to teach him the Manipuri dance of India, a traditional style that depicts the forces of the natural world.

Grace Burroughs, my first catalyst, was keenly interested in dance and in all the cultural arts of India. She was the first to bring an interest for Indian things to the West, mainly San Francisco, which was then a real center of culture. She brought artists over for concerts. She taught me the yogic and cultural practices she had been introduced to in India, in palace-like surroundings where religious Hindu music was constantly playing, meals served on trays, saris worn and the Mysore tradition carried forward, promulgated and taught in a royal and dramatic way.

By the time I was twelve years of age, I knew how to eat with my hands, how to put on a dhoti, how to wrap a turban; this was my dress for the year to follow. I learned how to dance; Manipuri dance was taught at that time. She also carefully trained me in concentration and meditation. We would have to sit for hours in her chalet and look at the calm, glass-like lake and equate it with the calm of mind devoid of thought. We would also meditate after the ceremony of lighting the lights that surrounded the fire altar that I was trained to dance before as fire itself moving to the music, as the wind and breath of air moved the fire. I was taught how to meditate on the cosmos (that was a big word for me in those days), the stars, the galaxy, Lord Siva, the

. . . .

His early mentors brought Indian culture into Robert's life, teaching him to wrap a turban and eat with his hands. His auntie took him to stage performances, modern and traditional, including psychic exhibitions where astral beings manifested using a substance called ectoplasm.

creator, preserver and destroyer of all mankind and all things—Lord Siva, God, raised foot, dancing to drums, the *tandava* dance that I had learned the last year.

I was introduced to Siva with Nataraja images. Those early impressions, you know, remain in your mind along with all the long stories and conversations about India and the culture of India. The school had large collections of Indian fabrics and saris and dhotis and artifacts and so forth that I was exposed to.

Grace taught him much. She took to softly disciplining the boy when needed, not directly, but by leaving handwritten corrections in an agreed-upon niche in the stone altar. Robert would go there now and again, read her note and adjust accordingly. All very civilized.

We never had a personal confrontation of correction. She always chastised me by leaving a note in a sacred place for me to read. Embarrassingly, I read it, took it within myself and corrected myself.

After his father died, Robert moved almost completely into Grace's world. Grace, an initiated Rosicrucian who knew much of the occult sciences, recognized the spiritual element in his dancing. In her presence Robert's unfoldment began. It was to be completely different from his earlier years. They understood each other. She was fantastically eccentric, a real-life Auntie Mame.

Grace wanted to become the guardian of the Hansen children, but the relatives, aware of the eccentricities of the artiste, would not hear of it. Instead, they appointed Robert's Aunt Helen, whom he liked. She was a refined lady, and a Christian Scientist. When Helen realized she did not have the means to raise them, she found a family from her church. The couple, Melville and Flora Hamilton, continued the children's upbringing in their Oakland Hills home, replete with beautiful gardens and a pond, from 1939 onwards. The children were given a background in Christian Science, and from it Robert learned of the healing powers of the mind, of the innerness of the spiritual path and of religious tolerance.

Nevertheless, Grace Burroughs was the most influential force in young Robert's life after his father's death. She whisked him away to spend summers at her dance school at Fallen Leaf Lake in a chalet she named Beau Reve, "beautiful dream." The rest of the year he could frequently be found at her place in Berkeley. She taught Robert Eastern dress and culture, as well as Manipuri dance and ballet, from age nine to fourteen.

Grace also trained me to be a teacher of small children—four, five, six and seven years of age—and behold! I was on the faculty of the Grace Burroughs School of Dance! I must say, at that early age, I taught them well. They responded beautifully from what they learned, and I learned in teaching them.

Finally, after I had absorbed everything I had to learn with my first catalyst, she introduced me to my second catalyst, Hilda Charlton, who patiently taught me how to center the whole being of the physical body, the emotional body and the spiritual body so that the inner light began to appear. With this catalyst, in Berkeley, California, I had my first inner light experience.

"Then I Am God"

Hilda Charlton was deeply devotional and meditated regularly. She was psychically awakened and had premonitions of Robert's going deeper and deeper into the teachings.

Shortly after they met, she asked the teenager, "Do you know who you are?" The question puzzled him, and after a while he had to admit that he did not. Then she said, "Next time you come back, I want you to tell me who you are."

After thinking it over for a few days, he decided upon an intellectual answer, taken from something he had heard in Christian Science. On his next visit he told her, "I am a part of God." She remained silent, then said softly and slowly, "If you were a bubble on the ocean—which would depict being a part of God—and the bubble burst, what would you be?" He knew the answer was "the ocean," but then the real meaning came to him with a burst of understanding from within, and he said, somewhat wondrously, "Then I am God."

I studied with my second catalyst twice a week during these two most wonderful years. Never asking many questions, I just obeyed what was told to me to the very best of my ability. I was taught this at a very early age not to ask any questions. I was told one must absorb inner teachings. One has to become aware of where the teacher is within himself and look at what he is saying from that perspective. This is the way that the student learns to absorb inner teachings. Then they awaken within him and he complements them with his own inner knowing. My second catalyst also taught me how to see into the akasha and view great, actinic, inner-plane beings.

My second catalyst was also well acquainted with various forms of mysticism, occultism and meditation. She taught me exactly how one leaves the physical body after putting the body to sleep. I learned of the astral body and how to work with and develop the experience of leaving the physical body in the astral body, while totally aware of the happening, turn around, look back at the physical body, see the silver cord which connects it to the astral body, and to travel astrally.

This catalyst taught me how the inner energies of the seven chakras function as the physical body moves and is inspired through the different types of music. She gave me a tremendous training and exercise in the free form movement of the dance, in which one experiences no inhibitions of any kind. This was extremely good for me, at the age of fourteen and fifteen, because it controlled and transmuted the energies of the emotional area.

Hilda Charlton drew Robert deeper into the mystical teachings, coming into his life at age 14. She was a deeply devotional person with natural mystical powers and premonitions. An exceptional teacher, she spent seven years taking the young seeker deeper into the disciplines of concentration and meditation, bhakti yoga and the art of giving. Later, she would travel with him to Ceylon.

In 1945, as soon as he turned 18, Robert left his foster home and moved to San Francisco. Carol, who died in late 2007, stayed on until 1948. Brother and sister did not connect thereafter, and it was not until he was giving a book presentation at a Borders store in Redwood City, California, in 2000 that they would see each other again and speak a few words. So complete was Robert's renunciation of his past.

"Even the Gods Will Obey"

Hilda Charlton introduced him to his third catalyst, her dear friend, spiritualist Cora Enright, known as Mother Christney, who would become the most influential teacher of his youth. In the years that followed, she brought him into karma, raja and jnana yogas, taught him obedience and service to others, selflessness and the inner light.

Standing just 5' 2", she did not quite reach Robert's shoulder, but she was larger than life, aristocratic and outspoken. With snow-white hair, a cherubic face and long, flowing robes, she looked, some said, like an angel or fairy godmother.

A kindly lady, she was also a tough teacher, demanding and sometimes domineering. She tested Robert severely and corrected him sternly, making him prove himself at every stage. He learned her ways and grew stronger in his spiritual commitments under her reign. She told her young charge, "When the spirit rises in command, even the Gods will obey." And she schooled him in the arcane arts of spiritual leadership. He told of her style:

> Mother Christney would test all who came to her, requiring proof of their sincerity. If a person approached her wanting to study, she would hand them a credit card with no explanation. If they held it a moment and handed it back, she would move forward with them. If they took the card, turned it over and looked at the reverse side, she would say nothing, but they would never be invited back. Mother Christney was like my *vishvaguru*, teaching me all the ways of the world.

Her Catholic background was completely unorthodox; at heart, she was a spiritualist, with immense psychic abilities. Though she had left the Church, she had frequent visions of the saints and often shared her otherworldly conversations. She could regale congregations and individuals with tales of psychometry, aura readings, Solar Biology, ectoplasmic manifestations and Christ consciousness.

Mother Christney followed a mystical form of Christianity, one considered heretical to most Christians. It was an attempt to weave mystical truths normally found in Eastern religions into the structure of the more narrow Christian faith. Such mysticism was alive quite early in the Catholic Church's history with the 3rd century philosopher Origen, and was reflected in more modern times in the Rosicrucians, Theosophists and Freemasons.

In the century before Mother Christney's life, Christianity had morphed in America, giving rise to new churches—the Mormons in 1830, Seventh Day Adventists in 1863, Christian Science in 1866, the Church of Divine Science in 1880, Unity Church in 1889 and Religious Science (also called Science of Mind) in 1927. These last three are part of the New Thought Movement, which emphasizes metaphysical beliefs concerning the law of attraction, healing, life force, creative visualization, personal power and the ideas that Infinite Intelligence or God is ubiquitous, spirit is the totality of real things, the soul is divine, high-minded thought is a force for good, all sickness originates in the mind and positive thinking has a healing effect.

Her Christianity was not the traditional one. She took Robert to seances where the dead talked to the living, to theaters where performer-spiritualists amazed disbelieving crowds by bringing disembodied souls onto the stage and conversing with them. Some of these spiritualists manifested gems or predicted the future. Others made it possible for the audience to hear faint voices from the spirit world, amplified through cone-shaped trumpets. It was another world, and she wanted the young seeker to see it all. He would never forget these scenes, and took his own followers to experience them decades later.

She was amazingly connected with the spiritual personalities of her day. In 1934 her home was the temporary ashram of a Sri Lankan guru, Dayananda Priyadasi (Darrel Peiris), who brought with him the Buddhist path of enlightenment. His ways charmed Mother Christney and inspired her to explore the Eastern path all the more, learning much she would pass on to her favorite student.

She also knew Yogi Hari Rama, who was then the rage. He had landed in San Francisco in 1924 and toured the US, demonstrating levitation and teleportation, something Americans had not seen. Though he showed these powers, he always stressed that they were not needed for deeper spiritual attainments. He taught yoga in her Oakland home and became her guru, bestowing on her the name Mother Christney.

Mother Christney was closely associated with Paramahansa Yogananda, serving on the board of directors of his Self Realization Fellowship. She studied Manly P. Hall and Edgar Cayce and met Indra Devi, who brought hatha yoga to Hollywood in the 30s. Mother Christney was impressed with Swami Bhagwan Bissessar, who came to America from Benares and who wrote the following affirmation for his devotees:

O Thou, the Absolute, the Infinite, the only Reality, give me wisdom and faith so I may open the portals to my illimitable powers. Om tat sat Om. The portal of my mind is now open to the inflow of spiritual knowledge. I am one with the Absolute, united and inseparable, and the help of the Elder Brothers is mine.

These Indian yogis and swamis brought with them the teachings of reincarnation, of an all-pervasive Divinity, of God within man, and man as being more of spirit than of body and mind. They taught the powers of pranayama and affirmation, the rigors of meditation and the elevation of consciousness. Mother Christney moved among them and absorbed the wisdom they brought from India and Ceylon, and that enabled her to ground her teenage prodigy in the subtleties of the Eastern path.

Their relationship would span the next 24 years of Robert's life, beginning with her mentoring him in her vast encounters with religion and mystical teachings, and ending with his looking after a frail friend. During the mid-60s, he stayed at her Oakland home on weekdays, helping with housekeeping and shopping, returning to San Francisco on weekends to manage his temple.

My third catalyst was wonderful and patient. She taught me the psychology of the vibratory rates of color and how to read an aura, understand the meaning of each color and combination of color within the aura and how to equate them with the moods and emotions and thinking faculty of the person. She taught me a method of character delineation in the understanding of human nature, the way people think, the way they act, and the inner, subconscious motivation.

She told me about the guru and said that one day I would meet my guru. But before I met my guru I would have to had realized the Self. She told me that I would find my guru on the island of Ceylon and that I must go there and study and that this was my next step. At that time, I was meditating two hours every day, right by the clock, just sitting there without moving, going in and in and in, trying to fathom the intricacies of what I had been learning and the purity and simplicity of the Self.

In the second year of training, I was intricately taught to understand the actions and reactions of people, how they moved, how they thought, how they acted. I was taught to be so observant with the powers of concentration that I would actually know by the movement of the mind or physical body of someone all about their inner attitudes and how they lived at home.

During the third year of training, I was taught how to test students inwardly and outwardly to determine if they were mystically inclined or just intellectually interested in the teaching. Then we went on into the study of thought forms and the feeling and meaning of various thought forms in meditation which one would see through his inner faculty. I began to know what a person was thinking about and his motivation for flowing awareness into that area of the mind where that collective thought substance occurred.

My third catalyst also advanced me through the study of great beings who live in the inner areas of the mind, beings so developed in their nerve system that they no longer need the use of the physical body to function and communicate with humans. Similarly, I studied great beings who have physical bodies but function deep in meditation, helping those who meditate as a kind of spiritual mission, as a

father and mother would oversee the emotional and physical maturation of their children.

My third catalyst on the path had a thorough training in mysticism from a very early age with the American Indians in Nevada, and then with Swami Bhagwan Bissessar from the Himalayas, Yogi Hari Rama of the Benares League, and from the wonderful being I was about to meet on the island of Ceylon, my fourth catalyst on the path.

All of this time I can't remember having asked many questions or entering into discussion. I do remember once, however, when I was a bit externalized and the subject matter was not quite clear to me, I did want to discuss it. I was cut very short with the statement, "There will be no discussion." I never did that again. When listening to inner teachings from a teacher who teaches in that way, if you miss a sentence or something is not quite clear, wait a few minutes and on the playback the clarity will come from deep within yourself. I learned this at a very early age. This is the way mystics are trained. There is no discussion. There are no questions. There is plenty of help on the inside from great unfolded souls, helpers on the path, enabling us to do this.

The San Francisco Ballet

At age sixteen, Robert entered the San Francisco Ballet School for an even more intensive training in classical dance. Within two years, he qualified himself as the premier danseur of the San Francisco Ballet Company,

Robert's performances were received with critical acclaim and popular applause. He would later relate that, looking out into the elite audience, he could see diamonds sparkling in the dark.

· ·

touring with them for two seasons throughout the United States and Canada. His training in yoga and meditation continued without a break. When in San Francisco, he would meditate two hours a day at the Presbyterian Church on Folsom Street, not far from the Ballet Company.

This was one of America's most prestigious ballet companies, and the competition was tough. Robert worked hard at his craft, driving his body for many hours a day to gain the strength and stamina a performer at that level requires. He worked out with weights and could bench-press 175 pounds at age seventeen, a necessity for lifting his partners aloft. Study, memorization, and practice, practice, practice. That was his day, his week and month.

To push his skills to their limit, he hired a trainer and asked him to critique his dance, quipping decades later that "I paid $20 an hour to have a man criticize me, not to point out what I was doing right, but what I was doing wrong." And that was when $20 was serious money.

The company traveled, as entertainers do, mostly by bus and train. It was here, he later said, that he acquired his love of travel and his military precision in packing for a journey, which he could do in minutes. He performed at local theaters and entertained the troops at USO shows. America during these years was deeply immersed in World War II.

The up-and-coming star ran with the best artists. No less than Ruth St. Denis and William Christensen choreographed his work, and he danced on stage with Italian divas and American stars. He moved with fine singers and musicians, and teamed up with opera singer Althya Youngman.

While the troupe was performing in Southern California, Robert took the opportunity to meet with one of the day's foremost gurus in America, Paramahansa Yogananda, at the Pacific Palisades center of the Self

Realization Fellowship. Robert met the Indian teacher about the time he published *Autobiography of a Yogi*. Yogananda was kind, and on each of the teenager's three visits thrust upon him an armful of literature and books. This was Robert's first direct encounter with the spiritual giants of the East.

Dance demanded most of his time and effort, but at night he turned inward. The world retreated and he meditated and studied the spiritual books he had, which were few. He was of a nature that mere reading was not rewarding—he would have to practice, explore, prove to himself the merits of what each teacher offered.

That proved challenging when someone gave him a copy of a petite book by Patanjali, *The Yoga Sutras*. He dove into it, unraveling its arcane language, following its subtle directions and practicing, practicing, practicing, as he had with the dance, the yoga disciplines described by the Indian yogi. It was his initiation on the yoga path and his first understanding of superconsciousness as seen by the Eastern masters.

Dance was flourishing in the young artist's life. He loved the drama of it all, the sophistication, the social interaction, even the pomp and glitter. But dance was much more to him. It was a study of energy, of the

At the height of a meteoric career, Robert's spiritual life called. At nineteen, he left the ballet company and sailed under the Golden Gate Bridge on a merchant marine vessel, voyaging to India and Ceylon in search of his guru.

· ·

mastery of life force, of how the spirit could move the material and thought could manifest action. He studied how the astral body moved first, and only then did the physical respond. He explored the life force in movement and the relationship of body and mind, a study that was not mere speculation but the science behind his artistry. Dance, to Robert, was the most divine of human expressions, the highest form of creativity. It was the only creation where the creator and the creation were truly one. The dancer was the dance just as the yogi is the cosmos. It was this inner aspect of dance that enthralled him even more than the stage lights.

Those stage lights. The young performer delighted in the audience. When called to bow for an encore, he would move out with his long-legged gait and graceful arms and hands, knowing the effect each move, each gesture had on the audience. Flowers would fly onto the stage, the roar of unbridled applause would fill the hall and he would stand, marveling at the wealth that sat before him, all those diamonds and sapphires, all those thousand-dollar gowns and hand-tailored tuxes. To young Hansen, raised in humble and isolated surroundings, this adulation seemed to be the highlight of his life. But he would receive still greater tribute decades later, during visits to Sri Lanka, India (especially Tuticorin), Malaysia, Mauritius and other countries.

He had reached the heights of dance. He had become the performer of classical solos and duets with ballerinas from Europe and South America, the headliner and star. He began talking of another journey, a journey to the East—the East that Grace Burroughs had intimated to him, the East that he saw in Swami Yogananda.

Mother Christney was part of those conversations, and she had contacts in Ceylon. She sensed he needed more advanced spiritual guidance than she could provide; and she felt that Dayananda, the Sri Lankan Buddhist mystic, could be his next mentor on the path.

Inspired by her encouragement, Robert started to ponder the practicalities of it. How would he get there? What would he do once he arrived? He knew no one and had little money, apart from a $700 a year stipend his parents had left him. The solution unraveled slowly. They would create the American-Asian Cultural Mission, touring India and Ceylon, singing and dancing and sharing their arts. He enlisted Grace Burroughs, singer Althya Youngman, composer-pianist Alva Coil and Hilda Charlton, dancer and mystic. As the plan solidified, Robert resolved to devote himself fully to its success. At the height of his career, only nineteen years old, he walked away from the San Francisco Ballet Company, never to return.

Right at the top of my dance career, I followed the advice of really professional people who said, "You should stop when you're on the top of your career." I was sent by one of my teachers to Sri Lanka to find my guru, because I was very anxious to find my guru. I was deep in the study of all of Vivekananda's teachings. I was listening to lectures at the Vedanta Society and meeting the swamis there and meeting Paramahansa Yogananda. I didn't find my guru in any of them.

Chapter Twenty

Finding God in a Cave

Robert's search for his guru took him across the seas on a merchant vessel to India and by train to South India where he caught a ferry to Ceylon, arriving in Colombo in March of 1947. As arranged by Grace Burroughs, he studied with Dayananda Priyadasi, a Sinhalese Buddhist teacher of meditation and occultism who had visited the US in the mid-1930s and captivated seekers there.

Dayananda proved a challenging teacher who confronted the young American with an onslaught of new ideas and personal ordeals. In the process, Robert learned the art of getting positive things done in the world, and he learned how demanding a spiritual teacher can be. The young seeker completed each assignment given him by his new catalyst, no matter how difficult. Within months of his arrival, he helped found

During the four-week voyage, the cultural troupe practiced   Page 391
on the ship's wooden deck and Robert enjoyed the first real
solitude of his life. They disembarked in Bombay.
· ·

two schools for village children, assisted in reviving the dormant Kandyan dance and introduced the use of power saws to carpenters, while still
finding time to tour the island performing with his dance troupe.

He was thrilled to be in a new land, with all of the discoveries and
surprises that brings. He loved the people, admiring their humility and
hospitable ways, learning from their subtle cultural instincts. But after
two years, all of this activity—and especially the never-ending litany of
projects and demands presented by Dayananda, many of them political—
was beginning to weigh on him. He was eager to help his teacher, eager
to fulfill his cultural mission, but never forgot his real purpose in coming to Ceylon: to realize God. He had always wanted to undertake serious
sadhana in a cave, and this desire loomed ever stronger in his mind.

> One day my training was completed. My teacher, Dayananda, flew off
> to attend a religious conference in Switzerland. I was alone in Ceylon. I
> thought about the cave again. One of my close Muslim friends, Anba-
> kara, who had Hanuman as his mentor, took me to the caves of Jailani,
> Kuragala, Balangoda, secluded caves naturally carved in solid rock in
> a mountainous valley deep in the central jungles of the island. There
> I met my fifth catalyst on the path of enlightenment. His name was
> Mustan.

The Jailani Caves are 150 kilometers southeast of Colombo, in the remote
jungles. It is to this day a holy site, and a gathering place for Sufi mystics.
The journey of several days wended through the nearly uninhabited central hills of Ceylon, with its tiny villages and dusty roads. Robert saw elephants bathing in the rivers and pulling logs on massive chains out of the
forests. It must have seemed a wonderland to the American, a Shangri-La.
One thing was for certain, it was far from the life he had been so actively
immersed in. It was the refuge he had longed for.

Up the hill Robert and Anbakara walked to the mouth of the rock caves
overlooking the Kaltota Plains. What they encountered is described by
R.H. Bassett in *Romantic Ceylon, Its History, Legend and Story,* published
in 1929:

The cave itself is a most interesting place. It is entirely natural, bearing
no signs of artificial excavations or of ritual adornment. The entrance
is situated in the face of a cliff a short climb down from the summit
where on entering there is a large "hall" from which two passages
lead off on either hand. The right hand passage is seen to extend for
at least 50 yards into the depths of the Earth before merging into the
general darkness of the shadows.

On the opposite side of the entrance hall, a narrow passage leads
out on to the meditation "ledge," a niche in the sheer side of the cliff,
some 6 foot by 4 foot with an overhanging roof of rock. Here seated
beneath a huge mass that towers fifty feet above on the edge of a
600-foot precipice, a hermit can find solitude indeed and food for
contemplation in the unbroken ocean of trees spread out below him.
Entering from a small hole in the rock, at the back an atmosphere of
complete detachment pervades the occupant of the tiny ledge. Earthly
considerations lose their importance before the uncomplicated
immensity of the colossal landscape and the fatality of the sheer abyss.

Robert was home. He was here to meditate until he realized the Self. But
his mind wandered to his lifelong ambitions for improving conditions in
the world by the power of spirit. World War II had just ended, and he had
the highest of hopes of a peaceful new age for humanity, as expressed in a
letter dated December 28, 1948:

Remember the day when evil forces held sway and how we did pray
to pen the way for Freedom of Nations through World Federation by
building this Nation in a cooperative way?

Evil forces are gone, we continue, March on and lead all these
Nations into the net of Universal Love for the masses irrespective of
classes, and release all from bondage, strife into new Life.

The Lord is on Earth in a practical way; a new system of finance
does now hold sway. Come on ye nations, Awaken today. Awake, alive
all beings united, the Life spark in man the Lord has ignited.

The Light shines so bright seven years from tonight. His Mission is
ended, organizations complete, the world now lies at his feet. All look to
Ceylon which now leads the way, a spiritual country in a practical way.

Freedom for Nations is well on its way, now He'll adjust. The Lords
Will holds sway. The spirit has risen, the Gods do obey. Their channels
are ready, to Earth do they come. The AUM is heard in a vibrant Hum.

· ·

*In a cave deep in southern Ceylon, Robert fasted and meditated, ultimately
realizing the Self beyond time, form and cause. One day a python slithered
across his lap, but he was so deep within he neither saw nor felt it.*

Souls reach perfection without delay. The last war has ended; TRUTH'S power has mended all hearts bound in war, and has made all beings pure like snow. The path clear, THE NEW AGE IS NOW HERE.

Jailani Caves

In a second letter to America, written from his aerie, Robert wrote of his aspirations:

> Off in the Jungle, so dear to my heart.
> I Darn't rest for a Moment, since we've given the start,
> To New Age Movements held long
> By one who is strong.
> He had others to help
> All turned Tail with a Yelp.
> I must develop more Will, and give these Movements a Push
> Sitting so still, Eyes turned in and up.
> I command forth Will enough to fill and make the Universe
> Quake and Shake, then Remain very still.
> Alone on a hill developing will,
> So as to fill and thrill
> Leaders to be in Lands O're sea.
> With Power so Great, Love so Grand.
> That they'll spread these Movements throughout their Land.
> Their Founder is strong. The Complete Master of Life.
> He knows how to Live. To give is to live.
> So he gives of Himself, a World to Create, an Order to
> Bring forth, that will Banish all Hate.

L'AMOUR UNIVERSAL IS THE WORLD'S FATE.
Bob AT JALANY CAVES ON RETREAT
for Ed. Munger, Esq., Jan. 9, 1949

Another mystic was living at Jailani, a wonderful Muslim called Mustan. Decades later, in relating the story to his monastics, he recounted:

> They say Mustan never took a bath, but he smelled as sweet as a flower. He was so old; he was so pure. We had a wonderful meeting. When he saw me he said, "I had a dream about you." Then Mustan pulled a little notebook out of his pocket. He said, "I wrote it down here where I write down all of my dreams." I said to him, through my

. . . .

Mustan, a mystic living near Jailani, seeing the seriousness of the American seeker, meditated with him and offered rare instruction about dreams and the third eye.

friend who translated from Arabic into English, "I had a dream about you, too," which I had just a few nights before. I had written it down also. I had been trained at that time to write down all my dreams. He said, "My dream was during the last full moon." We compared dates. We had both written down the same dream at the same time about our meeting together on the inner planes at night while we slept.

He began giving to me a profound training centered on the conscious use of the third eye. He explained and projected with his mind force the intricate capabilities, development and unfoldment of the faculties of this chakra. Mustan lived in a small cave with a little door on it. One had to walk many steps up the side of a hill to get to it. I lived in a nearby mosque at the foot of the path to his cave.

At night he took me out and meditated with me on wind-swept hills where yogis used to meditate hundreds of years ago. He made me sit perfectly straight for hours at a time. The wind was blowing hard against my body. It was cold. There, in the dead of night, he would say through my translator, "Did you see this? Did you see that? Are you seeing what I'm seeing?" He was revealing a form of mysticism taught in the Koran. He shared all of this with me. I learned some extremely intricate workings of the third eye and the psychic unfoldment of it through the faculties of the soul. This knowledge has become an extremely useful tool in my work today. I really appreciate my fifth catalyst on the path, Mustan.

He was an old, old soul, a rare being living a dynamic, spiritual life in that remote jungle. A Muslim saint named Abdul Qadir Jailani lived in the caves of Jailani, meditated and had a school of mysticism, hundreds of years ago. These caves were on top of a mountain about a mile from where we lived in the mosque. When penetrating deep into the cave, one can see light in the crevice deep in the center of the mountain. In the mysticism of Islam, this is thought to be a direct route to the inner planes, to Mecca.

The caves themselves are situated on a cliff that drops six hundred feet to a tropical jungle below, where wild elephants are often seen. I was taken there by my friend for a series of meditations. As I walked up the rugged dirt path, I realized that this was the cave in which I would one day realize the Self. For no particular reason, I felt it could be done here. It would be done here. That's how it is before you realize, you think there is something to do or something to get or become.

We stayed for a few days together, my friend, Anbakara, and I, sleeping on the stones just outside the cave, since they stayed warm during the night. We meditated long hours, silently penetrating deep into the mind. It was so quiet there. He told me one afternoon that as I sat above the valley in the lotus posture I always use, a large python had crawled over my legs, across my lap and back into the rocks. As the days passed I felt more and more blissful, drawn to the absolute center of myself, as if by a powerful magnet.

One morning I awoke and sensed we should leave the caves, that I should return alone to take the final steps. We returned to Colombo, where I completed several tasks for my former teacher, which inwardly freed me. When they were done, I returned by myself to the caves of Jailani. On the way back, I was determined. I vowed not to quit until I had the ultimate unfoldment of this lifetime. I had received outstanding training along the path up to this point. I had learned many things. Always the desire for the realization of the Self, *im kaif,* was paramount in my mind.

I was told by my teachers along the way that I had to get the foundation and the understanding of the various inner and outer areas of the mind in order to have strength enough to sustain the reaction to the realization of the Self. Each catalyst up to this point had helped me and introduced me in one way or another to my next teacher. This was not planned. I did not look for another teacher. I expected each teacher to be my last one. In fact, I didn't even think about it. Our meetings all happened in an easy, natural sequence of events.

Each teacher had his part in developing the memory faculties, one-pointedness, concentration, stimulating the meditation faculties, the willpower and the cognitive faculties—teaching me to see everything from an inner perspective and looking at the world as if one were the center of the universe.

There was just one thing lacking, however—and I had to find that myself—the ultimate goal, realization of the Self, God. It was with joy and a burning desire that I walked the ten or twelve miles from the nearest road to the caves of Jailani. I had absolutely no possessions with me. I had given all of my clothing away. I had given all of my money to the villagers along the road. I had nothing. I just went there to be alone.

I took no food, again vowing to myself, "I am going to fast until I find this realization that I so want and have wanted for such a long time. Now is the time." When I arrived late that afternoon, Mustan wasn't there. He had gone away on a pilgrimage. No one was there. There were no pilgrims. I was alone. I walked up and into the cave and

began to fast and meditate. I went in and in and in and in and then in and in again, and finally I went in and in until awareness became totally aware of itself, *kaif*, and into the control of the breath until the breath breathed no more, and then in from *kaif* to *ii kaif*—the most intense possible *kaif* experience wherein the brink of the absolute is felt—and then into the Self, Parasiva.

I came out again into the mind. Villagers had seen me on the cliffs from six hundred feet below. They thought I was some sort of holy man and brought food and drinks, all sorts of nice things. We had a big feast. I was hungry. They had come all the way up from the valley. They were so kind.

After several weeks, I returned to Colombo, the capital of Sri Lanka, a hundred miles away, with a Muslim man who also had come on a pilgrimage from a foreign country. He taught me a wonderful Islamic chant along the way. I never saw Mustan again. He taught me everything I needed to know to complete my training for the realization of the Self during my first series of meetings with him. It was intense. It was strong.

These mystics also connected Robert to inner-plane beings, especially a particular genie who worked with him to assist in his mission throughout his life, guiding potential disciples to the guru and often finding things that had been misplaced.

Discovering Hindu Temples
Still immersed in the radiant aftermath of his cave revelations, Robert took to the trail that led back to civilization, back to the capital of Colombo, back to another and lesser reality. This time he settled into the local YMCA, where he got a job teaching hatha yoga to pay for his room. He was between worlds. Freed from Dayananda and no longer obliged to the dancing mission which had split up, he began a new exploration which led him to the temples of the city.

Back in the city, nothing looked the same anymore. I was in another dimension. Everything was different. I had lost something: the desire for the realization of the Self. I felt complete. I felt alone. I spent several weeks in Colombo absorbing the darshan, the impact, of the cave experience. It was too vast to be understood, to be grasped by the intellect, so I enjoyed knowing that I knew something I could never

. . . .

Kandiah Chettiar befriended the American, taking him to the small, traditional temples in Colombo, where Robert discovered Lord Ganesha and other Gods of Hinduism. The two moved through the city like old friends.

adequately explain.

One night, just before sleep, I saw before me a vision of a tremendous peacock tail. It was fanned open in vivid colors, framing the screen before my eyes. In Hindu mysticism, Lord Murugan rides on a peacock through the akasha, the inner plane of consciousness inhabited by beings of very refined vibration. This is the way He travels in the inner area of mind.

In the Pettah district of Colombo, a Hindu enclave, Robert was drawn particularly to a Ganesha temple, a small, thoroughly traditional temple which had seen few outsiders within its walls. But within those walls Robert discovered an inner world hitherto unknown, even unimagined. It captured him instantly, and he began to visit daily.

The day after his vision of the peacock, Robert met Kandiah Chettiar, a businessman and English teacher from Ceylon's far north, where most of the island's Hindu community lived. Kandiah Chettiar was the quintessential Tamil—highly educated, English-speaking, spiritually awakened and philosophically astute. A man of 5' 8", he had a ramrod spine, and when he sat for meditation, it was as though he had turned to stone, the result of his years of discipline under Chellachi Ammaiyar. His encounter with the American mystic, newly arrived from the Great Beyond, was more than coincidental. Some thought that Yogaswami had sent him to fetch Robert, but there is no proof of that.

The next morning I met the sixth catalyst on the path, my next profound teacher, Kandiah Chettiar. He was a dark-skinned and broadly built Tamil man from the northern peninsula of the island. He was to take me to my guru, but I needed preparation first. He gave it to me. He took me deep into Hinduism.

Up to this point I had studied yoga and had a fine exposure to Buddhism in Sri Lanka, but had not been made aware of orthodox Hinduism. He brought me into Hinduism from a deep, inner-plane perspective, teaching me the mysticism and then the ritual. I began meeting the Hindu Gods, the Deities, inside the inner areas of the superconscious mind, and learned how to relate to them. They were kind to me. Chettiar patiently taught me all of the esoterics on Hinduism.

The two bonded at their first meeting, the towering foreign youth and the traditional local elder—each seeing himself in the other, each admiring the other's gifts. They formed a lasting friendship from the start. As much on his own inspiration as by Robert's insatiable curiosity, Kandiah set about instructing him in the esoterics and customs of temple worship as well as many of the occult laws at work within the rituals. Robert would later recount:

> For the first time, I experienced how Saivites worship the Gods, about puja and the priests, about the mysteries of the temple and their connection to the inner worlds. Now the pattern was complete. I had been taken into the Tamil Hindu community and was preparing myself to formally enter Hinduism when the timing was auspicious.

Somewhere in those first weeks of their friendship, which would span their lives, Robert began to intimate that he would like to be introduced to "a very pure priest," someone who could take him into the Saivite Hindu religion. Kandiah Chettiar knew well what he meant, but repeatedly dismissed the idea, knowing in his heart that the day would come if all was handled perfectly.

The two began to explore the temples in and around Colombo. Unlike most temple-goers, they explored the inner workings of the temple, and Kandiah instructed his charge in the inner and outer workings of their worship. Robert had awakened a sensitivity to spiritual vibrations, to the inner energies that are the essence of a Hindu temple, and he was driven to understand them, to know how they were generated by the priests, how they impacted the worshippers, what was their source. Kandiah Chettiar wrote:

> The young man was observed to be a man of character and ability to understand men and matters quickly and easily and was observed to be at some concentrated thought, though he was a member of many activities, such as the World Fellowship of Youth, World Fellowship of Artistes, Fellowship of Mothers and a host of other activities. His motto was "Art survives not by Mammon's Mammoth gold, not by titanic times' pyramidal remains, nor by ivory dreamers' gossamer tapestries, but only by the presence of the passionate votary at the altar of art's everlasting soul, from age to age."
>
> Every activity that he initiated progressed, but he had no attachment towards it and was often expressing that it was a duty to set it moving. A sort of non-attachment, like water on a lotus leaf, was seen in all that he did and spoke.

The Hindu temples of Sri Lanka are small by Indian standards. There,
the major temples are the size of a small town, with 12-foot-high walls
surrounding dozens of large shrines and smaller temples. But what Sri
Lanka's temples lack in size, they more than make up for in purity and
power. Pujas here are notoriously on time, and the entire space is clean
beyond imagination. There is a sense of closeness and shared community,
partly due to the presence of the majority Buddhists, a presence which
was not always friendly and which therefore tied the Tamils together for
self-preservation. The temples reflected that unity in an unusually stringent discipline and adherence to well-defined rules, including dress codes.
Women would never enter during their periods, and non-Hindus were
kept away. Men would never enter a temple except in their traditional
wrap, the *veshti*. Robert followed this most carefully. He knew his towering size and white skin made him the center of attention, and he wanted
to prove himself to the people he was learning to love.

Robert had been to the Buddhist monasteries and stupas throughout
the land, but it was the temples of Hinduism that captured him. Their
profound spirituality, made alive by Sanskrit chanting and rituals that
went back to the dawn of human history, moved him deeply. For the first
time in his life, within these holy chambers he saw true devotion, for the
Tamil people are profoundly devotional. Worship in the West is a shallow
thing by comparison. Here crowds move as one, and festivals are giant,
complex affairs that engage every man, woman and child in the area.
Devotion is not restrained, but let free, with tens of thousands of bhaktas
singing together, moving from shrine to shrine and suddenly shouting
"Haro Hara!" in a one voice that shakes the stones. Robert was enchanted,
and eager to know more. His teacher observed:

On hearing that the religious rites done in temples are so important
and create a devotion towards the Supreme Being, at first he
wanted as a matter of curiosity to pay visits to the temples; and
when once he started doing so, he felt a mental happiness and
ease that he was so highly pleased to pay regular visits to the
temples. Here he was observed to be forgetting himself from the
normal state of mind and enjoying a sort of trance and calmness
in the presence of images like Ganesha, Siva, Goddess Uma
and Subramaniya. Though he was not aware of the holy days
according to the Hindu calendar, he was asking whether a certain
day was a spiritual day for Lord Ganesha. It was exactly correct.

. . . .

When he wanted to attend the temple regularly, Robert was called before a council
of Saivite elders and interviewed in detail about his intentions and his understanding
of Hinduism. After assessing his sincerity, they allowed him to come freely.

Temples in Ceylon were not accustomed to Western visitors. For the most part, the British and others looked down on Hinduism and Buddhism, and kept a distance from the sacred sites. The young American's interest was welcomed, but it was also perplexing. The elders who oversaw the temple's affairs had observed the frequent visits by the Tamil Saivite and his charge. One day, they called Robert into their midst. Meeting for over an hour, they carefully interrogated him, inquiring into the nature of his interest and the depth of his knowledge. He was dismissed, as they discussed what to do.

A message was sent out to Kandiah Chettiar that Robert would be welcomed anytime into the temple. This careful scrutiny informed Robert of the privilege of his visits, and of the close security the community kept within the temples. He knew it was their way of protecting the sanctity, and in later years he would be similarly cautious with his own temples. Decades later he shared:

My sixth catalyst introduced me to the esoteric worship done within the Hindu temple. He told me why they ring the bells and blow the horns and beat the drums. He explained intricately the role of the priests and what they do, why they wear the holy ash, called *vibhuti*, on their forehead, arms and chest. All the whys and hows were explained to me. I saw it all from an inner perspective. I loved the temples. This experience brought the Gods to life in my mind, and we were like father and son. So we went everywhere together.

I became so sensitive to the vibratory rate of the astrological configurations of stars and the power that they effected upon the Earth during certain times of the year that I was able to tell my catalyst exactly what Hindu Deity would be worshiped at a temple and the very day that particular service would be conducted. I would tell him, "Come on, we have to go quickly to the temple. Lord Ganesha is being worshiped today."

My catalyst was amazed and enthralled that, without the calendar used exclusively by the priests, I could sense the vibration of the day accurately, thus proving that the old calendars establishing temple worship of the many Hindu Deities were superconsciously calculated thousands of years ago.

These are certain faculties one finds within himself. They are within every human being. I merely learned to use them, to be sensitive to what is already there. It came so easily. My experience at the caves of Jailani began to grow within me after subsequent experiences of the same type.

We, the catalyst and I, spent our time in conversation, meditation and traveling from temple to temple as he revealed to me the pure mysticism of Hinduism that one does not find in any books, for it is passed on from father to son, from teacher to disciple.

Elephant Pass

Robert had lived his whole life hearing of yogis and their magical powers, of Vedanta and its intellectual prowess. And he had spent the past two years among the Buddhists, for whom there is no Supreme Being, no God as such. While the Buddhist and Vedantin ideals of transcendence touched his deepest soul, there was in them little of the divine love, supreme devotion and sense of oneness with God as a real and present being, a feeling the temples and the Tamil people exuded without cessation. This combination seemed right to him, seemed a more complete concept of the sacred universe, one that his own meditations had revealed. The Saiva saints spoke a language he understood, though he had seldom heard it. The concept of God elucidated in Saiva Siddhanta—as the Supreme Being, who is immanent in His creation and yet transcends all time, form and space—mirrored Robert's deepest intuitions. He had found this completeness nowhere else and recognized Saiva Siddhanta as "the religion of my soul."

> I was happy to find a complete culture that accepted the monistic advaita of Vedanta and yet cherished and practiced the many other dimensions of life, celebrated festivals, valued the great yoga called bhakti, honored those who performed sadhanas, understood the way of kundalini yoga, knew the mysteries of penance, including rolling around the temple in the hot noonday sun, and lost itself—or should I say found itself?—in the chambers of the hallowed temples where darshan was sought out and the Gods were seen and felt as real beings when invoked by the magical priests to enter the temple at the height of the ceremony.

Each day the urge grew in Robert to go to the North. He knew the Tamils of Colombo were a tiny minority, and that the fullness of their culture was expressed only in the North, where their numbers were greater. So many stories were told of Jaffna, of its noble history, its rich culture and spiritual pride, its holy men and women. He begged Kandiah Chettiar to take him home. Chettiar later wrote:

The intimacy between us was so deep, sincere and true that we became two in one. His desire to go to Jaffna, my homeland, where the original ashram was started, was so great that I had to consent to his decision to go to Jaffna. He felt that he must be in my homeland once at least and I agreed for two reasons. One, to satisfy his desire, and two, to make him to meet a soul whom I love and regard and call "a speaking God."

The real start of religious life begins by meeting a yogi, who imparts the seed of holiness by a look, touch or word. In speaking about the greatness of this highly advanced soul, I used to describe him to my

Finally, Kandiah Chettiar drove Robert from Colombo to his home in the North. They stopped at Elephant Pass, where Saivites worship Lord Ganesha under a tree. This is considered the spiritual gateway to Jaffna, the stronghold of Ceylon's Tamil Saivite community.

· ·

friend, now Sri Subramuniya, as the "Yoga-swami," only "a typical beggar." Though this statement was made to Sri Subramu-niya at a distance of 250 miles, the advanced soul, jnani, on the first day of meeting, addressed himself a "typical beggar."

Chettiar was wise, and did not press the visit to the North. Instead, he continued to regale Robert with tales of Tirumular and Tiru-valluvar, ancient Tamil poets and yogis, and to intimate not infrequently how special it would be, how incredibly blessed it would be, for them to enter, one day, no hurry, Yoga-swami's mud hut.

Very carefully my teacher began tell-ing me about a "madman" in the area, a guru who was so powerful, so unpre-dictable, that people were afraid of him. He explained the nature of this man and how he had been the only disciple of the great Chellappaswami. I was told of his work in the Jaffna area. Carefully, my teacher described how one approaches such a being and how he attained Self Realization at forty years of age and ran for twenty miles on the power of it, he had worked for it for so long. He was so happy that he had finally achieved this great goal at forty years of age. I would be patient, and the subject would always come around to the guru of the area, Yogaswami. In this way, I learned of him and of his teaching. One day, my teacher invited me to his home on the Jaffna Peninsula in the North of Sri Lanka.

One day, when Chettiar sensed the time had come, the two embarked on the 250-mile cross-country journey, on unimproved roads through the Kandy highlands and then down into the arid northern plains to a place called Elephant Pass. All Hindus stop here, for it is regarded as the passageway into the Saivite peninsula. There is a small Ganesha shrine there, under a tree, where devotees light camphor on a coconut and then break it on the ground to beseech blessings from the Lord of Dharma before proceeding on the narrow, 3,000-foot-long isthmus that connects Jaffna to the mainland.

They stopped the car and worshiped Lord Ganesha. While meditating there, Robert inwardly saw a flame on top of his head. It appeared spontaneously to his inner sight and persisted for three or four days. Robert would forever feel that this was his formal entrance into the Saivite world. The name Elephant Pass was permanently etched in his memory.

At a Lord Skanda temple, Robert mystically absorbed a sacred form of dance, performed by Lord Nataraja, during a powerful darshan before the Nataraja Deity. In a profound vision, he saw Siva as the Cosmic Dancer animating all existence. It transformed him. What was unfolded to him in those sacred moments was a technique that employs a specific combination of 49 movements of feet and legs and 49 movements of hands and arms and 49 movements of head and eyes, shoulders, torso and body, in sequences of seven. The dance was a tool for throwing the shakti into distant places, as did Murugan aim and throw His *vel*. This was the purpose of this dance, which began on the rhythm, "*tye-ya tye-ya tye-ya ta—tye-taka tye-ya tye-ya ta.*"

As they left the temple that day, Kandiah Chettiar remarked, "You will never be the same after this." He remembered these days in a letter to America:

> The pleasure he took in standing before the images decked with gold and brilliants, which were more in the form of transmitters of power and knowledge, jnana, was highly appreciated and enjoyed by the young man. The priests in the temples were so highly taken up by the true devotion of a Westerner, with such a princely appearance, that they began performing pujas with special attention. I well remember a day, a Tirukarttikai Day, when my dear friend [then] stood before the golden statue of Lord Muruga (Subrahmanya) decked with brilliants and garlands, in a posture which I can never forget. Tears gathered in his eyes and he was in a trance with his hands bowing with

. . . .

For several weeks Robert lived with the Chettiar family, discovering their traditional lifestyle, being overwhelmed with their hospitality and learning the finer points of wrapping a cotton veshti, *which all Hindu men there wear.*

an expression that you (God) and I are one. It appears that a theoretical start of initiation has been started on this particular day.

Adopted by a Hindu Family

It was morning when the car pulled up in front of Kandiah's home in the village of Alaveddy. Seeing Kandiah with the unexpectedly tall Western guest, Kandiah's wife and son and daughter-in-law didn't know what to do. Their dwelling was humble—two small, adjacent houses made of earth and cadjan. As traditional villagers, they lived close to the earth, growing much of their own food, grinding their own flour and drawing their water from a simple well. They were struck by Hansen's presence; they had never seen anyone so tall, and they had never entertained a Westerner in their home before. Quickly, though, they were set at ease by his grace and simplicity. Kandiah Chettiar described the relationship:

> Our trip from Colombo to Jaffna was in a car, a new, comfortable Austin 12, and the whole journey was a happy one, because we visited a good number of ancient Hindu temples and were able to have concentrated religious practices.
>
> We arrived at our home, a humble mud house, at 5:30 in the morning, and the young man was introduced to the members of my family. The visitor felt himself quite at home. Food preparations in an Oriental style were served to him. He very much liked the mangoes in our grove and the jak fruits which we had in abundance.
>
> He loved me and the members of my family and started calling my wife "Mother Chettiar." The beauty in the love that existed between the mother and child was only expressed by kind smiles and looks, as he did not know Tamil nor she English. His expression of love and gratitude in all letters that he wrote from USA and her hearing it with pride and pleasure is worthy of comment.

Kandiah's son had just married, and his bride of just eighteen years had moved into his family's home. Decades later, Mrs. Sivayogam Vinayagamoorthy—that new bride—spoke of those days:

> When my father-in-law—who was staying with Robert at the Colombo YMCA and was impressed with his steady morning devotions—wrote home to inform the family that he would be bringing a young American to our home, all were horrified. The home was too

. . . .

When he sought more seclusion, the family took him to a nearby thatched hut they owned amid the brambles. Here he could meditate far into the night, freed from the bustle of village life, bathing at his own private well.

humble. To prepare for the guest, we decided that the family would move out of the house and give it entirely to Robert for his stay.

Upon his arrival we were astonished to see his great height. He was so tall he couldn't stand upright except in the very center of the house! After some hours, he was very close with us—like a brother to my husband. That evening my father-in-law took him to the Ganesha Temple. The priest asked his name, and my father-in-law said, "Thamby. We just call him Thamby ['young one']." He made everyone so comfortable, like part of the family; we all stayed in the house.

The home was on an unpaved road in the rural village of Alaveddy, in an area known for its agricultural bounty. There was no town there then, nor is one there now. The largest building, apart from the Ganesha temple 200 yards away, was a two-story shop across the street that would one day be Robert's ashram. Most of the surrounding area was peppered with the white tropical homes common of this desert climate, with their mud walls, windows covered with iron bars and open-to-the-sky interior courtyards which received the welcome, if infrequent, rains right into the home.

A few shops plied their wares down the road; a pen factory (if a cottage-industry-size business can be called that) was not far away, near a series of sheds where fifteen weavers at their hand looms wove loudly from dawn to dusk, making the *khadi* cloth that most Tamil men wore, 12-foot lengths of white cotton wrapped about the waist. The house was austere by Western standards, but immaculate, set in a three-acre compound full of coco palms, neem, *amla* trees and other edible species, surrounded by a natural fence of thorned bushes, and in a few places by woven palm fronds, called cadjan.

Fifty feet from the kitchen was the family well, an open *kinaru*, as the Tamils call it. Stone walls defined the eight-foot-wide well below ground, and above there was no wall, just a paved circular platform on which bathers stood. Water was drawn by hand, using a wooden bucket attached to a rope, attached to the small end of an 18-foot-long, 1-foot-thick coconut log set on a fulcrum, the other end of which had a net of stones to provide the needed balance. For bathing, Robert learned to wrap himself discreetly, for there was no fence to provide privacy. Each member of the house took turns, twice daily, at the well, the women bathing in full dress.

Meals were the central events of the day and took much of the women's effort, cooked as they were on open fires fueled only by wood. If a visitor even smelled the food, it was incumbent on the family to invite him for the meal. The community here was overwhelmingly vegetarian, and the cuisine was remarkable in its variety. South Indian rice and curry evolved further over the centuries in Lanka, including the unique Sri Lankan red country rice with its distinctive odors and lighter-than-air grains.

With no refrigerators, everything was bought and made fresh from the land; leftovers, along with the banana-leaf plate, were tossed over the fence for the cows to enjoy, eliminating much of the dishwashing. Nothing was wasted. When shopping, a family took its own basket to the market to gather the day's vegetables, legumes, grains and fruits; there was no food packaging. Milk was drawn directly into the pot it would be boiled in. The culture was so remarkably self-sufficient and Earth-friendly, there was no trash can in the home, no weekly garbage pickup and no landfills. The rare foreign pen that had broken had to be individually buried in the compound.

It was the first time I had been in an orthodox Hindu home. I was so at home there. It was wonderful. The northern part of Sri Lanka is quite different from the southern. It's like being in a different country. The religion is Hindu. In southern Sri Lanka, the religion is Buddhism. The North is dry, arid and very flat, not lushly tropical like the South and the hill country. I felt immediately at home. We lived quite humbly, bathing at the well and using Coleman lanterns when the sun went down. We walked or took a bullock cart when traveling to the temple or the open air marketplace.

Everybody was so simple there. They had no furniture in anybody's home; everything was all on the floor. And even if people could afford furniture, they wouldn't buy it because their opinion was that they would insult somebody who could not afford furniture. And since nobody used furniture anyway, they didn't need it. And there was no electricity either in most areas. So everything was very, very natural. And the temple is the center of each small community.

Taking our time, we visited fine temples of the area, the Ganesan temple, the Nallur Kandasamy Temple and many others. All the while I was absorbing the inner atmosphere and being blessed by the Gods themselves as electric vibrations would come forth from the temple and flow through my body. I felt wonderful. It was wonderful. I was there. I was expecting to become a Hindu, the peak experience of my life.

Privacy inside was a new experience for him as well. There were no doors on the rooms, just simple curtains, and no one knocked before entering. He was deeply impressed that things regarded as personal in the West were part of the family here. His mail could be opened and read without the slightest sense of intrusion. The consciousness of shared existence was a revelation to him.

The family loved their guest, and he adored them. They learned from one another and bridged their cultural differences. At one point, Robert sought more seclusion, and the family allowed him to stay for some weeks in a thatched hut about a quarter mile away. It sat in a sandy field, surrounded by nothing but sagebrush and coconut trees, but it did have a small well attached, and the aloneness there was conducive to his disciplines.

He would visit the Kumbhalavalai Ganesha Temple in the early hours of dawn, walking the narrow dirt paths that weave the village together, then return for a day of solitude and meditation. Kandiah Chettiar would check on him regularly, constantly worrying about the youth who was a stranger to his land and its manners. They spoke often of the inner life. It was something Kandiah could not share with his family, even with his guru, for that was a formal relationship. Here he had a fellow seeker to talk with, and both enjoyed the hours spent in spiritual conversation.

Meeting "the Old Beggar"

Robert felt so at home in this Saiva community, so at one with its culture, its people, its rich spirituality, that he wanted to formally unite with it.

> One day I said to him, "I want to become a Hindu. I feel like I am a Hindu already because that has been my training from a very young age up to this point, but how can you arrange it officially? Will you take me to a very pure priest, one who has Self Realization?" He responded, "There are no priests in our temples who have the realization of God of which you speak. Just wait. It will come. The time will come." He was destined to take me to my guru, but was waiting for the right time, watching for the signs.

Kandiah continued to play down the meeting. He would not let his American son, as he called him, go straightaway to Swami, but had him wait for the perfect moment. Finally, one day he announced, "It seems that today is a good day for you to meet Yogaswami." He did not go himself, but sent his son, Vinayagamoorthy, giving him careful instructions as to how they should go and who should take them.

That was May of 1949, an auspicious, festive time in Jaffna. Yogaswami's birth was celebrated in that month. There is also a special Muruga festival during the period. In the South, Wesak, the anniversary of Buddha's illumination, is celebrated, and mangoes, a fruit sacred to Lord Murugan and cherished by all, were ripening.

They started on their way at about three o'clock in the afternoon. There was a breeze in the air that cooled them as they walked to the next village, Mallakam, to catch the bus to Jaffna. At about 3:30 they reached that village. A bus came fifteen minutes later. Shortly after five, they arrived in Jaffna and went straight to the house of Kumar Surian, a barrister who Kandiah said would take them to see Swami. The proctor was happy to accompany them, but entertained them first with tea and stringhoppers while his servant prepared the bullock cart. Fifteen minutes later they were off, leaving the house in a wagon drawn by two handsome white brahma bulls.

The cart plodded first to Nallur Kandaswami Temple. Kumar suggested that they get down there and worship before going to see Swami. It was almost 6 o'clock, he said, and the puja would soon begin. They disembarked, washed mouth, feet and hands, and went inside the temple. In those days, devotees of the temple could worship closer to the sanctum than one can now. The three men stood just outside the sanctum for the ceremony, consumed in the intensity of the darshan.

It was about 7 pm when they arrived at Yogaswami's hermitage. The sun had set, and a full moon illuminated the landscape. The lamps were lit, and the evening had brought devotees to Swami. The atmosphere was electric—charged with the presence of the satguru. About fifteen people were sitting with him. No sooner had the screeching of the cart wheels stopped than Swami's voice from the hut was heard loud and clear, "Come, come, come. I am waiting for you." Vinayagamoorthy recalled:

> As soon as we opened the gate and entered the ashram, Yogaswami asked Robert in a loud voice, "Did you see me anywhere?" Robert replied, "Yes, at the Nallur Temple," and the following conversation took place. Yogaswami: "You are in me." Robert: "You are in me." Yogaswami: "I am in you." Robert: "I am in you."

The devotees present were astounded. No one had ever talked in such a way with Yogaswami since the days of Chellappaguru. Usually if he said to a devotee, "I am in you," the person would respond humbly, "Yes, Swami." Or he might begin singing a song that Swami had composed. No one ever responded the way Robert had. He spoke as confidently as Swami himself, and he echoed Swami's very words.

At that point Swami eased the intensity of the moment and asked his visitors to enter. "Come and sit with Jaffna's old beggar." Robert knew the protocol and once Swami was seated moved forward to prostrate. But Swami indicated he should not, and invited him to sit on a nearby mat that had been laid down for this unusual visitor.

Yogaswami was in a jolly mood that night, smiling and laughing as people came before him. It felt like a special holiday. There were large bunches of grapes on a tray in front of him. He called to a devotee, Pundit A.V. Mylvaganam, and asked him to take them and make some juice for the three visitors.

While awaiting the refreshments, Yogaswami asked his guest if he had read Patanjali's *Yoga Sutras*. In fact, he got the book down from his shelf, commenting that it was the only book he kept. Robert said yes, he had

• •

To prepare for meeting Yogaswami, Robert was taken to Nallur Temple to seek the blessings of Lord Murugan, enshrined as a vel. *Standing before the darkened sanctum, he had his first vision of the man who would be his satguru.*

read it. In fact, it was the only book he had really studied during his early training. He had read and practiced it for years. Yogaswami tossed a few penetrating questions about the pithy classic. Robert answered quickly and clearly. Recounting this experience later, he said that the answers came immediately, not as an intellectual memory, but from within.

Then Yogaswami asked about the difference between advaita and dvaita. Robert answered that both are true, depending on one's perspective. Yogaswami smiled, obviously enjoying the way in which the disciple had grasped that it is not one and not two. Swami, well familiar with the controversy between the two schools of philosophy, was satisfied. Dr. S. Ramanathan later provided the following insights:

During their conversations, Robert shared that he had established a small ashram in the village of Alaveddy. Yogaswami predicted it would one day be a three-story building.
. . . .

Swami once told me that the *mahavakya* "Aham Brahmasmi" is not correctly understood by people who criticize Advaita Vedanta. He had high regard for the Advaita Vedanta of Sri Shankaracharya as well as for the *Siddhanta Shastras*. One day when I was going to the ashram at Columbuthurai, I was thinking of the debate between Vedanta and Siddhanta. The minute Swami saw me he sang a line from the work of Tayumanavar: "We belong to the group of learned mystics who have understood the complete agreement and equality of Vedanta and Siddhanta." Then he placed his hands on his chest to indicate that it was the firm truth.

Their philosophical repartee lasted about twenty minutes. Finally the grape juice arrived and Yogaswami offered it to his guests. That ended all discussion for the evening. Swami told them to begin their trip home, as it was a long way.

Taking Swami's leave, they walked to the waiting bullock cart. The devotees, still entranced by the enigmatic encounter, also made their way off into the night. Kumar, the lawyer, an astute man, was impressed, and a little upset, too. He interrogated the guest, "Why did you tell Swami you saw him at Nallur Temple this evening? I was with you the whole time and I didn't see him." Robert replied, "I saw him in the inner sanctum during the puja. He was standing there, right in front of me." With that, the lawyer grasped the mystical nature of the relationship between Yogaswami and Robert.

Decades later, the American described his meetings with Yogaswami.

One day, I was invited to go to Yogaswami. Jnanaguru Yoganathan, affectionately known by the people of the area as Yogaswami, was a magnificent man. No one approached him unless they were in the right mood. Some were literally afraid of him. When within the radius of him, one could feel the atmosphere scintillating. One felt electricity in the atmosphere. Devotees would prepare themselves on the inside so everything was all right before visiting this guru. Just to take him a little bit of fruit, they would sometimes prepare themselves for three or four days. If asked when they would be seeing the guru, they would say, "Well, I'm not quite ready yet to see Yogaswami today, maybe tomorrow." Or, "I will go on a very auspicious day." This was because they didn't want him to look through them and point out something that they saw in themselves that they thought he might see. He always knew when people were coming to him before they arrived.

My meeting with him was unusual because I was introduced, and he said, "Come on in and sit down." Everybody else prostrated before him. In the Orient, devotees prostrate in front of a guru, placing the entire body face down on the floor. He said to me, "You come in and sit down. You don't have to do that. You and I are one."

Then he started asking me the deepest of philosophical questions. I must have given the right answer each time; he seemed very pleased. As soon as he had asked the question, without hesitation I spoke the answer. Then he gave me the name I hold today, Subramuniya. "You are white; Subramuniya [Lord Muruga] is white," he told me boldly. He was my guru, my master. *Subra* means "the light than emanates out from the central source." It just emanates out. *Muni* means a silent teacher, and *ya* means restraint. Subramuniya means a self-restrained soul who remains silent or speaks out from intuition, one who speaks out from the inner sky.

He showed me the book he had on Patanjali's yoga aphorisms. I had studied Patanjali, too. We had just a wonderful, deep and inner meeting. He treated me more like a brother. This did not surprise me, though, because I was so far within and not in the consciousness of being surprised, but it surprised everybody else. He made me eat food with him, and we parted. Before leaving, I mentioned to my guru that I had established an ashram in nearby Alaveddy and would like to have his blessings. He said, "Fine, good, it will one day become a three-story building, and you are going around the world, and you will feed thousands of people. You are going to build palaces."

He began giving me many different kinds of instructions, such as "You will return to America, and you will roar. And when you come back here, nothing will be gained and nothing will be lost." He

At the end of their third visit, Yogaswami followed his American visitor out to the gate. Coming up behind, he gave Subramuniya a powerful slap on the back that nearly toppled the taller youth. It was a spiritual initiation, one so potent that elders looking on stood perplexed.

said, "Now you go and teach the realizations that you have had." I was used to being told what to do by my six teachers on the path, so I was happy to have this positive instruction. After I left my guru's presence, everyone started relating to me differently.

On the second visit with my guru, we had a beautiful time together, just meditating and enjoying a beautiful flow. Many people came.

On the third visit, we had a beautiful conversation about the path. Then, as I was leaving his ashram and he was seeing me out, he gave me the hardest slap on the back that I had ever felt from any-body. With all his might he reached out and cracked me on the spine between the shoulder blades. It was tremendous. I would have fallen on my face if I had not been so tall. Some of the Hindu devotees were startled, too, because that is one of the most powerful ordination initiations ever given. After this initiation, he gave me some powerful instructions…. With this *diksha* he sent me as a sannyasin to America. I was 22 at the time, and he was 77.

The dozens of people at the hermitage that day began to regard the young American in a new light. Subramuniya later reflected:

> There are four ways that a guru will initiate or ordain. One is through talking, a very mild way. Another is by a look, and another is through thought. The most powerful initiation is through touch combined with the actual inner power, for through this contact, with intent, he begins to feed and transmit all of his inner knowing and inner power to the disciple. In this way, Yogaswami gave to me all his knowledge of how to be a guru. It later began to unfold within me from him, then from his guru and then from his guru's guru. This is how the spiritual power in a line of gurus is transferred and increased.

Of this, Vinayagamoorthy wrote:

> It is said that a guru initiates his disciple by one of the four ways— thought, word, look and touch. But, in Subramuniya's case we find that our Yogaswami knew of Subramuniya's presence at the Nallur Temple and gave darshan (thought); said, "You are in me. I am in you" (word); naturally looked at him (look); gave a blow on his back (touch) and hence showered and crowned him with all the blessings and power that has to be given by a guru to his disciple.

Yogaswami's giving Sri Subramuniya that resounding slap on the back surprised everyone present. They weren't sure what it meant. Kandiah smiled when he heard about it, saying, "Now he has performed the coronation." This was the young disciple's ordination, which would later be understood as Yogaswami's appointment of a successor. Justice of Peace Tiru S. Subramaniam witnessed the event, which he later described as "a transmission of Yogaswami's samskaras, or vital divine spiritual energies."

Yogaswami advised his young initiate, "When you're a guru, don't be like an American mother." Seeing his disciple puzzling over the meaning of his statement, he added, "You know, they wander about here and there while someone else takes care of the children. Stay in your ashram and be close to your students." As they parted this time, devotees heard Yogaswami tell his shishya, "Whenever you want me, I will be with you."

After Subramuniya left, Yogaswami quickly changed the tone of the gathering, leaving them no room to wonder or talk about what had happened. "He must be a dancer," he chortled, "He moves like a borzoi." Kandiah Chettiar later wrote in a letter called "Meeting the Speaking God:"

> From that day onwards Sri Subramuniya appeared as reborn and the mental calmness was very clear and visible. He was at the early stages observed to be interested in art, dance, music and other activities. Even in these worldly activities, where he had to be in the company of women, he trained them to partake in such activities to pronounce the word "Aum," which keeps humanity to have a control over the senses.

Subramuniya recalled that when he went the fourth time he found Yogaswami sitting alone, meditating deeply. As he approached the doorway, Yogaswami opened his eyes and roared, "I'm not at home." Startled, the youth turned to leave—but apparently not quickly enough, as Swami repeated, louder this time, "I am not at home!" The message was clear: their time together was finished; and the disciple left the hermitage for the last time.

Back in Colombo

In 1949, Subramuniya teamed up with Kandiah Chettiar to form the Ceylon Bureau of World Affairs, whose motto was "East has met West and all that has transpired has been for the best." They had also founded the Ananda Ashram. A Tamil-language newspaper wrote of such efforts in this report from May 22, 1949:

> Robert Hansen's Visit to Jaffna. One of the officers of the American Asian Cultural Mission has been in Colombo for the last two years. His name is Robert Hansen. He visited Jaffna last Friday. This young lad, who is interested in the soul culture, is studying the secrets of Hindu religion and the methods of worship with great sincerity. He very much appreciates the artistic activities here and the dances of the East. A center, called the Ananda Ashram, has been established at Alaveddy in Jaffna, under the patronage of the American Asian Cultural Mission. This ashram will promote spiritual and social progress. Any religionist can be a member of this institution. Mr. C.K. Chettiar,

who is a businessman, was instrumental in organizing the institution. His son, Mr. Vinayagamoorthy Chettiar, is working as the secretary. The first duty of the ashram is to spread universal love."

Subramuniya's stay in Jaffna would continue for some weeks, but everyone knew he would return to Colombo. By September of 1949 he was dancing again in the capital and taking the reunited troupe into the Kandy hills to continue the cultural shows. But it was never the same. His time with Yogaswami and with the Chettiar family had transformed him.

> I filed papers to become a citizen of Sri Lanka after being initiated and then adopted into Chettiar's family. I had burned all bridges of a career behind me and had nothing to go back to in the States. My visa was expiring, so I filed for citizenship. Chettiar took me into the office. I talked personally with the Prime Minister. Four months went by, and we didn't hear anything from the office.
>
> A friend of Chettiar's took us in to see about the status, and there the papers were, all by themselves on a shelf, unprocessed. That got back to Yogaswami, and he said, "Go build a bridge." So, I packed up, leaving everything I had in a big trunk and left the keys with Dayananda. I took the boat back to the US. It was a rough ride, too. I passed through the Suez Canal and landed in Boston, then took a propeller plane from there to San Francisco at a cost of $80. The ship cost was $400, all paid for by my inheritance.

Subramuniya's ship back to the US traveled through Port Said on December 14, 1949, sailing across the Atlantic to arrive in Boston on December 29.

Sadhana Years in America

I n March of 1950, Sri Subramuniya founded Muruga Ashram in Santa
Cruz, California. He was eager to bring the Hindu Deities to the West.
Advised by his guru to wait until he was thirty to begin his mission, Sri
Subramuniya spent the following seven years in contemplation and inner
pursuits, allowing his ordination and realization to mature.

> I followed Yogaswami's instructions and returned to the United States
> and settled down to unfolding more and more. Until his death, he
> communicated with me, year after year, through Kandiah Chettiar.
> Upon returning to the US, the first thing I did was to change my name
> legally to my new Saivite Hindu name [Subramuniya]. The judge took
> it in stride and quickly granted the request. Right after my ordination
> with Yogaswami, the book *Cognizantability* began to unfold from
> within me.

Little more is known of these years of contemplation, which were outwardly uneventful for the most part. Returning to Oakland, he connected
again with Mother Christney and in April began composing the first of
the affirmations that would later be published as *Cognizantability*.

He returned for at least two years to the world of dance, touring with
New York's Metropolitan Opera in their production of "Die Fledermaus,"
which opened in Boston then traveled through the East Coast and into
Canada. While with the Met, he made his first radio and television
appearances, performing bit parts, and became a member of the Screen
Actor's Guild and the American Guild of Variety Artists. He would speak
of his months of travel, living out of a suitcase, spending days on long
train rides through the countryside. Training, practicing, performing, and
earning $1,000 a month. He quit when the tour went to South America.

There followed what he termed "years of sadhana and solitude," spent
mostly in the Southwest: New Mexico and Arizona. He supported himself teaching Indian and Western dance, hatha yoga and Hindu advaita
philosophy; but his real work was the spiritual work, and he cherished
his aloneness.

In 1956 he migrated north into the pure mountains of Colorado that are

. . . .

*For two years following his return from Ceylon, Sri Subramuniya
returned to the stage to earn his keep. Though he toured the US
and Canada with the New York Metropolitan Opera company,
his heart was more interested in solitude and sadhana.*

today the refuge of seekers and modern-day mendicants. His meditations
deepened there. In Denver he underwent a tremendous spiritual experience during deep contemplation, as the last of the outer self was displaced
by the matured soul. He would later describe this event as "the full actu-
alization of the *svarnasharira* in which the soul body displaces the outer
self." At that time, the golden body of the soul completely inhabited the
physical body, concluding the long climb up the spine to its permanent
home in the crown chakra and the descent of the divine into the body. He
later wrote:

> The golden body, *svarnasharira*, is a body made of golden light.
> After many experiences of Parasiva, it gradually descends from the
> seven chakras above the *sahasrara* into the *ajna* chakra, which then
> becomes the soul's *muladhara,* then down into the *vishuddha* chakra,
> which then becomes its *muladhara,* and then down into the *anahata,*
> which then becomes its *muladhara.*
>
> All seven chakras above the *sahasrara* slowly come down and
> down and down until the entire astral body is psychically seen, by
> mystics who have this sight, as a golden body. The astral body slowly,
> slowly, slowly dissolves into the golden body. That is what I have seen
> happen. That is what our parampara and our sampradaya know from
> experience. Experience is the only true knowing—a knowing that can
> be verified in books, through others who have the same knowing, but
> a knowing that no others know who have not had the same experi-
> ence. To them it is only a concept, a nice one maybe, but just a concept
> or written off as an opinion.
>
> When the golden body fully enters the physical, having taken over
> the astral, the knowing that is known comes unbidden. It is beyond
> reason but does not conflict with it. It is a living scripture but does not
> conflict with those written by seers of the past who have seen and
> their records have become scripture. So great is the Sanatana Dharma
> that it defies all who doubt it, all who disdain it, all who disregard it,
> all who degrade it, with personal realization of its Truth.
>
> This golden body, which begins to build into a golden body after
> the experience of nirvikalpa samadhi, is connected to the *sahasrara*
> chakra. In other words, the *sahasrara* chakra is the home base in the
> physical body for the golden body. There are twelve basic unfold-
> ments to this chakra as the golden body grows. When the realized
> sannyasin travels in high states of contemplation, he moves freely in

• •

*In Denver in 1956 Subramuniya underwent a life-transforming spiritual
experience during which his golden soul body displaced his outer self. Soon
thereafter Yogaswami, thousands of miles away, announced, "Hansen is dead."*

his golden body and can help and serve mankind. Over time, he gains a conscious control of the *sahasrara* chakra as a force center which propels him into inner space.

It is this golden body, as it refines and refines and refines itself within the Sivaloka after moksha, that finally merges with Siva like a cup of water being poured into the ocean. That same water can never be found and put back into the cup. This truly is *svarnasharira vishvagrasa,* the final, final, final merging with Siva.

Two Superconscious Encounters

After the Denver experience, Satguru Yogaswami began telling people in Jaffna, "Hansen is dead." They thought it so until he wrote to Kandiah Chettiar from America a few months later to say that his mission had begun. Then the Jaffna Tamils understood that it was only his outer self that had died. Sri Subramuniya was alive and busy fulfilling the mission foreseen by Yogaswami.

It was in Denver, the mile-high city in the Rocky Mountains, that the commentaries [to *Cognizantability*] were written, seven years after the aphorisms were revealed. My external mind was learning to fully accept superconscious knowing, and the deeper inner mind was actively making itself the knower of the known.

Oddly enough, one day the inner said to the outer mind to number each aphorism, which are now Sections One and Two of *Cognizantability*, and place them all face down on the floor. I obediently did this. Then, one after another, the commentaries were revealed, three words at a time with a significant pause between. The superconscious would dictate word by word to the conscious mind to be written down. Amazingly, it proceeded to dictate the commentary to number seven, then number fourteen, and so on. When all were done, the natural impulse urged me to turn over the aphorisms that were still face down on the floor with a number on the back to see if the commentary matched the aphorism. It did! They all did! Truly, I became a more dedicated believer in the jnana *marga,* the aftermath of experiencing the beyond of the beyond of the beyond, which we call Parasiva, the

One day in the late 1950s, Subramuniya experienced the reality of the subsuperconscious mind: taking dozens of pieces of paper on which he had written mystical aphorisms, he wrote a commentary on the blank side of each that corresponded perfectly.

fulfillment of the yoga *marga.*

As the years passed by, one after another, this procedure of bringing unrehearsed wisdom through from the higher mind to the external became a natural part of my daily life, "one of the tools of the trade," I have often said. These psychic powers sometimes take years to develop. But under the right circumstances those carried over from a previous incarnation come immediately, of course, and are as much available as the ability to speak, listen and feel.

One of Sri Subramuniya's avid pursuits was the study of religious organizations—to determine the most stable and workable vehicle for Saivite Hinduism in Western culture and a technological age. He finally settled on the American church system.

I was told by Yogaswami, "Don't really start to do anything until you are thirty years of age. You have to be more mature." Until then I was to observe, have experiences and learn. So, I was sort of biding my time until I was thirty years of age. I went to Phoenix, Arizona, knowing that I would eventually get an organization going. Naturally, I wanted to know how to do that! So, I went around to all the other organizations—Vedanta Society, the Rosicrucian Order, Paramahansa Yogananda's organization—and I analyzed all their problems. You know you don't have to look at the successes, because you are successful if you don't have problems, automatically. I analyzed all their problems and all their faults and failings.

As I traveled through the United States from the age of 23 to 30, observing the various schools, philosophies and techniques given to aid people in philosophical and metaphysical thinking, I found that there was more philosophy and metaphysics than actual instructions on how to put it into action in your own life for spiritual awakening. The desire to fulfill that need directly began to grow and grow in me. I saw that the Western man needed a comprehensive, step-by-step, well-supervised method of study. This he was not getting. Those who did give a step-by-step training in metaphysics divided God and man and practiced techniques to put the pieces together again. This philosophical division led man more to an unsettled frustration than to bringing forth his inner security. Fine teachers from the East came and taught, but didn't remain long enough for a continued, positive, direct supervision of the individual's unfoldment, either on an individual basis or organizationally.

Finally, the time came to begin teaching, and I thought I would open the organization in Phoenix. So I went to the registrar of organizations and said, "I would like to open this organization. What shall I do?" He said, "The thing to do is to go to a sign maker and get a sign." I said, "Any papers to fill out or anything?" He said, "No, this state welcomes spiritual activity. Just go get a sign."

While I was waiting and deciding, I had another experience one

Driving one day in Phoenix, Subramuniya had an encounter with his inner voice. It instructed him to follow a convoluted route through a sprawling suburb, which he obediently did, only to be led, after two hours, right back to the beginning.

day while driving my small car. My inner self told my outer self, "Look at that sign." If any of you have been to Phoenix, you know it's totally a flat area, absolutely flat. There I was, driving around this big flat area where there were lots of houses and homes. "Look at that sign. Remember the sign." It was Spruce Street. I took note of the sign. Then I said, "Okay, I'm just going to get into my inner self." Inner self said, "Drive twenty blocks forward, turn left and drive ten blocks, turn right and drive five blocks, turn left, two blocks, turn around, back up, go ten blocks," and on and on like that for about two hours as I followed the instructions. Then it said, "Stop and look at the sign!" Spruce Street! I was a believer in myself, an absolute believer in myself.

After that I went to San Francisco and started the organization there. I had given a little talk and there were some people that were really interested. So I thought: "Well, how do I get it going? You need a lawyer." Because California was different. You had to have papers and everything, tax exemptions, and this and that. So where am I going to find a lawyer? I said, "I know." I went to the FBI. I knocked on the door and I said, "I'm getting this organization going. Can you direct me to an attorney?" They referred me to the man who would be our attorney for several decades. He had me develop a file of my work for the FBI, saying then they would never worry about me.

It was made quite clear to me that when I was thirty my students would start to come, so I waited. It happened just that way. This is how Himalayan Academy started in the United States in 1957.

Settling in San Francisco

For a short time after leaving Phoenix, Sri Subramuniya taught yoga classes to students in Los Angeles, but soon he moved to San Francisco. He held the first Applied Yoga class in a small Bush Street apartment in downtown San Francisco. A few stories above the clatter of a noisy street, the first few eager students began the study of themselves and awakened a new world of inner awareness.

He gave a talk at a small spiritualist church in the city to a group of elderly people, many of them women. In those days, yoga teachers were rare, and the subject was practically unknown. Theosophy was the fad of the day, and the healing work of Christian Science was in the ascendency.

On January 5, 1957, the occasion of his *jayanti*, they asked him sincerely when he would begin to teach them. "Right now!" he replied. He explained he would work with them for a few months and see how they did. If all went well, if they practiced and benefitted, he would continue.

The average age of that first group of students was fifty. For the most part, they were interested in psychism or spiritualism. Some had spirit guides and were interested in communication with the dead and other such phenomena. They were eager to know about healing with the mind, psychometry, alchemy and seeing auras. These areas, which he had been studying and experiencing his whole life, became the topics of many of his talks. He also spoke on the *Cognizantability* aphorisms, taught the basics of concentration and meditation, color psychology, breathing and the five states of mind, and gave instruction in hatha yoga and dance. His emphasis was always on Self Realization and the possibility of man's awakening his own superconscious state of mind. Of course, the term *superconscious* was practically unheard of in those days.

In April Sri Subramuniya gave his blessings for a permanent center. The Sutter Street Temple was opened that month, with Sri Arumugam, then Ceylon's Minister of Agriculture, attending as the guest of honor.

*During the seven years of sadhana before his spiritual mission began,
Subramuniya taught hatha yoga and dance to support himself.*

As a guru, I started with the basic philosophy of all gurus, "To do nothing is the greatest thing on Earth," simply responding to the needs of the students. I founded a temple, as it was needed at that time to harness the religious forces of those who were unfolding. The students were enthused and supported the temple. Later on, they asked for written materials, such as a course of weekly lessons of my inspired talks and teachings, neatly arranged for those who couldn't attend the temple. I also responded to the needs of those who wished to be monastics and founded a monastic order. The monastics printed the lessons which today are The Master Course.

During these formative years, Mother Christney brought her influence to bear. She dominated as a strong, elderly matron might, skewing the teachings toward her background, Christian spiritualism. As her long-time student, and her junior by 47 years, Sri Subramuniya supported her in this. He became the model of the spiritual leader she knew and idealized from her upbringing—preceptor, counselor, preacher, confessor. When she chose to name the institution the Christian Yoga Church, he understood her reasons.

Knowing the innate power of the press and having a lifelong affinity for the newest gadget and techie tool, he bought a mimeograph machine, which was used for printing schedules, talks and programs as well as the first editions of his books *Raja Yoga* and *Gems of Wisdom,* the Church's first publications. Sri Subramuniya learned to use the machine himself and then introduced it to his monks.

Mimeograph was the office printing technology that preceded photocopiers. It was a paper stencil duplication device invented in the late nineteenth century and used through the 1980s. He would later tell his monks of cranking out tracts and pamphlets late into the night, hands stained with the bluish-purple dyes of a messy, smelly technology. It was the beginning of his lifetime of publishing, the first glimmerings of what would become a major part of his mission.

The burgeoning group outgrew the Sutter Street building after two years and began looking for a larger place in the city for their chapel.

Then an anonymous somebody put a thousand dollars in the little offering box—a lot of money in those days. I had rented a little place in which I had a vision of Siva dancing on my head. I heard the drums and everything. And I saw a big door in that same vision. As soon as

· ·

A consummate communicator, Sri Subramuniya was constantly recording, lecturing and printing. In the early days he ran a mimeograph machine himself—an early, and messy, printing technology.

SAN FRANCISC[O]
HINDU TEMPL[E]

√[x̄ä̐ĵä̐π],
2··2

I saw the door on the Sacramento Street Temple, I knew that was the place. It was to become the first Hindu temple in the United States.

He used the $1,000 as a down payment on a building at 3575 Sacramento Street, a narrow, two-story apartment with a small garden in the back, not far from Park Presidio. The surrounding neighborhood, called Laurel Heights, was populated with apartments and small businesses, florists, restaurants and small stores. It had been used as a photography studio and was in unsound condition. To meet the city fire codes, the building had to be almost totally renovated. His students spent the next year or two in karma yoga on the building, several hours a day and late into the evenings after leaving their regular jobs. In the end, they had created the first public Hindu temple in America. On its opening day in 1959, the temple hosted the world-famous Kandyan Dance Troupe of Ceylon, then on tour in America.

An altar was established in the main hall, and two massive doors, in the form of an archway, were made. One entered from the street through the giant doors, past two purple velvet curtains and into the small main chapel, complete with wooden pews, a rock altar and waterfall and pulpit made of a single stone. From this pulpit each Sunday morning Father Subramuniya, as he was then known, gave sermons on yoga, the states of mind and Hindu thought. He spoke of how to live well, how to awaken the inner light, how to overcome instinctive emotions and habits, and of spiritualism.

Services were open to the public, though the upstairs was reserved for Father Subramuniya's residence and the Church offices. The first floor garden rooms were used for personal counseling with devotees, a small kitchen, recording sessions and for group activities.

When the congregation had settled in its new home, Sri Subramuniya put forth the first sacraments and initiations. He founded a yoga order and initiated the first monastics to serve the congregation. He stressed the importance of establishing a steady routine for mission activities in the years to come and stuck to that rule consistently, saying that would bring

Sri Subramuniya founded the first Hindu temple in America near the Golden Gate Bridge in San Francisco. Here he taught of the advaita path to the Self.

steady progress for everyone.

To set the example himself, in the fall Sri Subramuniya commenced the first sunrise service on Mount Tamalpais, a 2,500-foot peak in Marin County that offers a view of the northern San Francisco Bay Area. He took a vow to hold this monthly pilgrimage until his organization was twelve years old, at which time it would be well established.

On the first Sunday of each month, and on other auspicious occasions, his devotees met at the temple for a pre-dawn blessing and the lighting of 108 candles. Crossing the Golden Gate Bridge and driving part way up the mountain in a convoy of cars, Sri Subramuniya led the forty-minute hike to the summit for a sunrise sermon and meditation. He continued this monthly *tirthayatra* personally, rain or shine, for a dozen years, unless he was out of the country—a total of 154 pilgrimages in all.

Every Sunday we would make a pilgrimage there. We had a big rock on the mountain that we used to think of as the Sivalingam. That was a very routine time. It was easy for me to be routined because of being a disciplined person from the early ballet dancing training. I ran the institution consistently. Something was happening all the time, and it kept repeating itself.

Sunday morning, the big day of the week, found the half-dozen monks cleaning the temple and preparing for the 11am service. They would stock the shelves with books, incense and candles which congregants loved to buy and take home. The temple held about 50 people and was almost always full, with people standing and sitting in the hallways. Sunday service was also held at 8pm. Hymns were sung, mystical ones written by the monastics under Father's guidance.

He would enter the room through a door behind the altar, his tall frame and rich voice dominating the small room. He never spoke from notes. Not once. It was pure spontaneity, what he would call "from the inner sky." There would be a topic, written dutifully on the sign outside the temple for all to see, but it was often a mere hint of what he would discourse on that day.

Once he wrote the sermon's title "Was Christ a Yogi?" It brought a larger than usual crowd, all wanting to know the answer. He began the sermon that day, "Our topic today is 'Was Christ a Yogi?' Yes, he was. Now, let me talk about the yoga that brings you into the inner light." Not another word about Christ.

In fact, much of what he taught had to be filtered through the vernacular of the mostly Christian community. Many of those who came to listen called themselves Christian yogis. The United States then was a thoroughly Christian country. Hinduism was little known and even less understood. Therefore, almost all of the early students and members had strong Christian backgrounds. They were a breed of mystical Christian, those who did not follow the my-path-is-the-only-path philosophy, but instead believed in a greater spiritual reality that was inclusive and tolerant. They found those values in the San Francisco temple. They were quite comfortable learning about the Hindu religion.

In order to avoid confusion or opposition and to keep his Western devotees' transition into the Hindu religion gradual and rewarding, Sri Subramuniya kept the teachings simple and unramified.

The early years were a time of constant classes, lectures and counseling, for it was only through carefully educating the congregation that progress was made. There is a saying among the Buddhists of Sri Lanka: "The teaching not adapted to the needs of the taught cannot be called a

· ·

For twelve circles of the Earth around the Sun, Sri Subramuniya took devotees to the 2,500-foot summit of Mount Tamalpais. Arriving before dawn, they meditated among the redwoods and oaks, gaining what he called "a mountaintop consciousness."

teaching." The wisdom of such an attitude was self-evident in the founding years. Despite his eagerness to present Saiva dharma exactly as he had absorbed it while a member of the orthodox Saiva community of Jaffna, Sri Subramuniya was forced to be patient, carefully presenting through the years the universal principles of Hinduism through the teachings of advaita and the science of yoga and encouraging his devotees always in the practice of bhakti.

During these early years, I gave forth much of the teaching that's in *Merging with Siva:* "Life the Great Experience," "Love Is the Sum of the Law," "The Power of Affirmation" and "The River of Life." All those talks that some of you have heard for many, many, many, years started at that time. People started coming and going and going and coming. And I started seeing a new kind of life in the United States and adjusting myself to it.

Sri Subramuniya had regular hours for personal counseling with members and participated in the many regular activities, always available to teach and answer questions.

Gems of Wisdom, a book of his sayings, proved so popular that a second edition had to be printed in mid 1958. Sri Subramuniya oversaw this and was busy besides preparing the first Church Manual, a compendium of vows, vestments, sacraments, disciplines and schedules to guide the spiritual life of the congregation and monastics.

To embody the busy routine of classes and studies of devotees and members he founded the Yoga Institute, giving it several rooms in the San Francisco Temple. It was the forerunner of Himalayan Academy. He also initiated what came to be known as the Breakfast Club, a gathering held the third Sunday of each month, when devotees and members could be together with him amid informal surroundings to chat and enjoy each other's company. It was quite popular, and a productive spirit came of it. Above all, Sri Subramuniya saw to the smooth progress of his devotees in their devotions and spiritual disciplines. "Consistency is the key to the conquest of karma," was his refrain.

As his temple and activities thrived, challenges arose. Money was an issue. There was never enough. The consolidated financial statements for 1957 showed a total income of just over $3,000, not sufficient to manage such a growing institution. Yet he did manage.

At one point, unhappy with the way funds were being taken from one budget to pay for another, he initiated a paper bag system. At the beginning of each month, he pinned 20 paper bags on the wall of the upstairs offices. Into each he placed the cash that could be spent on the bag's hand-written category: food, candles, travel, rent, etc. No one could spend for any item except from its paper bag. It proved a dramatic way to teach frugality to all who were responsible to control the spending. Stories were told of how the food bag would be empty on the 26th of the month, and everyone would virtually fast until the first. Of course, the system was too simplistic to survive for long.

One of the students volunteered to take over the rudimentary accounting tasks. Soon, seeing how other churches supported themselves, Sri Subramuniya introduced the idea of tithing, which was shockingly new to yoga students who had become used to getting by with a ten or fifteen cent donation every Sunday in the plate. One day he put a sign on the front of the temple, "Charge a Tithe." Those were the early days of credit cards, and the idea was so creatively charming to popular journalist Herb Caen that he mentioned it in his "It's News to Me" column in the *San Francisco Chronicle.*

Of Monks and Sermons

The first few monastics took initial vows at the same time that the temple was opened on Sacramento Street. They continued to work in San Francisco at their jobs, tithing 25 percent of their income. After their job in the city was finished for the day, they would join their guru in the temple doing one thing or another until late in the evening, taking classes or helping with the public. In the 1980s the satguru commented:

> Our first brahmacharis and brahmacharinis began to appear in 1949 upon returning from Sri Lanka to America. However, no vows were given until 1957. This is when my *maha dashas* changed from Rahu to Jupiter, in December 1956. This began the Order in a very serious way. We purchased property at what is now the Palaniswami Temple. Prior to this time, I had been traveling some, lecturing and teaching Vedanta, Siddhanta and writing *Raja Yoga* [as *Cognizantability* was also known] and other works. Temple worship was unheard of in the West in those days, as the Catholic Church, as well as the Protestant churches, had much of the nation held into its belief patterns.

Sri Subramuniya's Sunday sermons, called inspired talks, were dutifully recorded, transcribed and printed each week by the monastics. After two years, the collected manuscripts were numerous, the basic philosophy and practices clear and the demand for a study course growing. In 1959, Sri Subramuniya and the monastics compiled and edited many of his talks into a course of lessons which could be issued by mail or in person. This was the first edition of his formal course of study called The Master Course. A decade later, speaking of his teachings during this period, he offered:

> The theme of all these years was to present the teachings and practices in such a way where man is able to bypass what he thinks he

is into that which he really is—to become conscious of the power within the spine and the refined energies within that, and that within that, and that within that, until he realizes the Self God—the underlying principle which cannot be described, which is at a higher velocity than energy itself. Working on the matter-antimatter principle is the closest that science has come to explaining the realization of the Self God as presented in the advaitist teachings and realized by myself and many of my close disciples.

Realizing that in the West this theme did not penetrate the Western mind, I worked for many years developing a comprehensive study program so that this theme could be brought out clearly and precisely—not intellectually, but in the actual experiential patterns of an individual's life.

Topics in those early lessons included the esoterics of man's bodies, the five states of mind, hatha yoga, mantra yoga, prana, concentration, meditation and more. Published under the title *World Fellowship of Yoga*, the lessons were issued free of charge, following the Eastern tradition. For the many students and members who lived too far from the temple to visit frequently, the lessons kept them in close touch and provided a way for their teacher to monitor their progress and offer guidance specific to their path. Sri Subramuniya often said, "The best of the East has met the best of the West," describing the nature of his work in the 50s. In 1971, he explained:

The best of the East is adhering strictly to the philosophy that the Self God is within man. Man can realize it fully within this life. That basically means opening the *sahasrara* chakra and having awareness escape through the door of Brahman, merging with the Self. Or the kundalini rising up through the various chakras through the spine, the pituitary and the pineal gland merging in power and awareness moving so deep within that it comes to the very core of Being itself. This is the fundamental philosophy of the great rishis of the East, the philosophy that I have lived with since my studies there and to this day.

Basically, the best of the West are the facilities for disseminating this teaching to the various levels of people on the path, the step-by-step organizational presentation leading one to his eventual goal without allowing him to digress in the presentation of the path.

Sri Subramuniya and the monastics traveled frequently throughout California, lecturing, teaching hatha yoga and *raja* yoga, the *Upanishads* and other Hindu scriptures and presenting the lessons of his *World Fellowship of Yoga* correspondence course that hundreds were enrolled in and studied daily. They spoke at colleges, in homes and often in Episcopal or Unitarian Church facilities whose doors were always open. They held summer camps for families and children and, in 1961, instituted a dynamic Prison Outreach program, visiting prisoners in their cells to teach Eastern ideals and the basics of yoga. Many inmates at Folsom, San Quentin, Vacaville and other institutions found solace and a new awakening to spiritual life through these efforts.

The Christian Yoga Church was formally incorporated in 1959. It educated members toward a progressively deeper understanding of Hindu beliefs and practices. At the same time, Sri Subramuniya trained the monastics in public speaking and had them give public classes in hatha yoga, the basics of meditation and beginning philosophy as soon as they took their vows. He also encouraged them in selfless service by having them visit hospitals in the community periodically, consciously carrying a spirit of blessing and upliftment from the temple to those in distress. Later he began Christian Yoga Study Groups that they oversaw, held in family homes throughout California.

On October 4, 1959, Sri Subramuniya flew to Hawaii, a personal retreat for himself and a forerunner of later Innersearch Travel-Study programs. He visited only the island of Oahu, a rare time alone that allowed him to become acquainted with Hawaii, though a local newspaper ran an interview with him about his spiritual work on the mainland.

On the eve of his departure from San Francisco, he gave an inspired talk in the temple to a small gathering of monastics and Church members entitled "The Self God," explaining the goal and purpose of religious life—a spiritual classic that was immediately published by the monastics. It remains to this day one of the most lucid and inspiring *upanishads* on the Absolute ever brought forth, a brief work that was lovingly known in Sri Lanka as "the Little Gem." Here are the first three paragraphs:

> The Self: you can't explain it. You can sense its existence through the refined state of your senses, but you can't explain it. To know it, you have to experience it. And the best you could say about it is that it is the depth of your Being, it's the very core of you. It is you.
>
> If you visualize above you nothing, below you nothing, to the right of you nothing, to the left of you nothing, in front of you nothing, in back of you nothing, and dissolve yourself into that nothingness, that would be the best way you could explain the realization of the Self.

And yet that nothingness would not be the absence of something,
like the nothingness inside an empty box, which would be like a void.
That nothingness is the fullness of everything: the power, the sustaining power, of the existence of what appears to be everything.

But after you realize the Self, you see the mind for what it is—a
self-created principle. That's the mind ever creating itself. The mind
is form ever creating form, preserving form, creating new forms and
destroying old forms. That is the mind, the illusion, the great unreality,
the part of you that in your thinking mind you dare to think is real.

For four years, the monks recorded Sri Subramuniya's talks on a second-
hand Wollensack reel-to-reel tape recorder—over 1,100 sermons and
interviews in all.

In 1960, he began a special series to be aired on the radio, focusing on
yoga in the West, positive attitudes and practices for the inner man. Time
was purchased from KBCO FM 105.3; and the talks, called "Temple of the
Air," were broadcast each Sunday at 10 am. Sri Subramuniya's persistent outreach efforts made the Hindu temple on Sacramento Street well
known throughout the Bay Area.

Laying Down the Law
The monks' training and service was going well as Sri Subramuniya nurtured discipline, detachment and relentless inner striving, balanced by
their service to others as priests in the temple and in various capacities in
the general community. He expected his monks to progress on the path
and in the process to get along with each other. He was a strict teacher,
and it became clear that he expected his directions to be followed.

> One day we were having a board of priests meeting and some of the
> monks began arguing back and forth. I warned them that we could
> not have this happening again. Then on another occasion they started
> up again. I said, "Look, if this happens one more time, I'm going to
> have to stop these meetings." I don't think the monks believed me, but
> the next time it happened, I said, "All right, that's it," and I never called
> another meeting of the board of priests.

One day it was discovered that one of the monks had taken a few dollars from the day's offerings. He had grown hungry, he confessed, due to
the sparse meals they could afford, and he had purchased extra food for

. . . .

*Every Sunday at his Sacramento Street temple, Sri Subramuniya gave discourses
on yoga, the Self, states of mind and practical applications of Hindu mysticism.
In a mostly Catholic city, he was among the first teachers of an Eastern path.*

himself. It was, for Sri Subramuniya, a minor tragedy which he would reference thirty years later as unacceptable behavior. He scolded the monk,
first alone, and then in front of the others, then required a severe penance
to be performed. It was made clear to all the monks that even their own
suffering was no excuse to break the bonds of trust. The order learned
many such lessons and grew in strength and maturity.

Some had difficulty obtaining the blessings or approval of their families to lead a renunciate life. A few families objected vehemently to their
son's joining a completely unheard of and seemingly exotic order. One
father stood knocking on the door of the San Francisco monastery, insist-
ing his son return home, calling him in a loud and desperate voice. In such
cases, Sri Subramuniya sometimes sent the monk back to live with his
family for a time. Others he would send on mission, "on the road," to be
alone and reflect on their commitments. One young man was instructed
to join the armed services for two years to work through his karmas.

There were women in the congregation who saw the spiritual progress of their counterparts and pleaded to also be taken into monastic life.
There were three of them in the beginning, and through gentle persistence they convinced Sri Subramuniya of their deep devotion. In late 1960
he initiated them into monastic vows as the Sisters of Devotion.

Like the monks, the nuns wore Western-style habits: austere, hood-
ed brown robes with a white rope tied at the waist. They shaved their
heads and looked much like the men, striving to be pure, spiritual beings,
beyond gender, by balancing their feminine and masculine energies. Some
mistook them for men. Their service revolved around the devotional services, the nurturing of families and their own spiritual disciplines. They
lived apart from the monks and came to the temple each day for classes
and service. These Sisters of Devotion—who cleaned and cooked, counseled the women, brewed tea for temple visitors, handled mailings and
stocked the little bookshelf—brought a tangible sense of caring, which
was called the Mother Spirit, to Sri Subramuniya's mission.

In 1961 the Church purchased a house in Glendale, a suburb of Los
Angeles, dedicating it as the Glendale Monastery for the three Mother
Nuns. Sri Subramuniya gave them the mission of service and silence.

To strengthen the families, Sri Subramuniya wrote the *Catechism of
the Christian Yoga Church,* outlining the fundamental principles of religious life and the philosophical and theological doctrines of the Church.
He began regular home services and meditations to be observed mornings
and evenings by the families in their shrine rooms. Seven Holy Weeks
were designated—seven periods around the year of special sadhana and

spiritual striving, fasting and reaffirmation of commitment to the inner path. Each Holy Week was dedicated to a great saint or important religious festival and corresponded to one of the seven chakras of the subtle body of man. These would become the annual focus of more intense spiritual work for all his followers.

Following on his study of the American church system and numerous religious organizations in the US, Sri Subramuniya decided in late 1961 that he would file for official designation as a church from the Internal Revenue Service. On February 12, 1962, the IRS sent formal approval of his church's tax exempt status. It was the first American church teaching Hinduism to be so acknowledged.

The Church summarized its mission in a press release: "Father Subramuniya's teachings have reached students in India, Ceylon, England, Germany, South America and even West Africa. He says, 'Christian Yoga answers the questions "Who am I? Where did I come from? Where am I going?" Members of the church learn how to explore the depths of their inner being to find these answers through concentration and deep meditation.'"

While his outer life was immersed in the founding of his mission and the training of his monks, Sri Subramuniya's inner life grew even more intense and profound. It would prove a challenge to him, to balance the two. He had come to this Earth, he would later say, to do the inner work of realization, and equally he had been prepared from childhood to lead a spiritual renaissance, to bring the mystical truths to those ready for them. But those two aspirations, each enormous, did not always sit well with each other.

There were times, he said, when he had to give a sermon on some mundane subject while his superconscious state of mind was soaring in another realm. To function in the outer world, he had to bring himself down to Earth, work hard to regain a "normal" perspective on life, so he could speak with others, guide them, inspire them. The reclusive, mystic yogi in him was, for a time at least, at odds with the founder of a spiritual institution. Through all that, he remained determined to make both of these goals work in his life.

Mystics do not always have an easy time living in the world. Functioning sometimes is extremely difficult, because though apparently they become sensitive, they also become stronger in all of their various other senses. Sensitivity cannot in any way be equated with being weak. Mystics do, however, become very different than other people.

In the early 1960s I went through a very difficult time functioning in the world because I was working intently with the unfoldment of a large number of students. Every time I picked up something that was heavier than a piece of paper, my arms and hands would turn to light, and instead of seeing the physical body, I would see the inner body. If I were to carry a book or a chair, first my hands would turn to light, then the light would creep up my arms and down my legs and the body would start fading away, invariably. This went on for about six years of my life. During this time, even a piece of paper was heavy. It was even difficult to wear a wristwatch because then that arm would turn to light. I would be more conscious of this beautiful light arm, that looked like crystal plastic, than I would be of other things. I would love to watch it, all scintillating in energy. It was just lovely.

Even while driving a car, it was great fun because each time I pressed my hands hard on the steering wheel, my whole body would start turning to light and I would start to see the most dense areas of the car in front of me, which was just the chassis part. All the top part and the people would fade away. I would only see the heaviest types of metal.

A mystic can really live in a wonderful world, if he prefers. Now I can be in this state if I want to. It is voluntary. It's not an involuntary state anymore. I remember once while in that state, I had to put the garbage can out on the sidewalk, and there was no one to carry it. I had a terrible time. I would get the can just so far and turn all to light and have to put it down again. Finally, with great effort, I got it out. It seemed like a long way. During this time, if the phone rang, it sounded so loud, and it was just a terrific thing to pull the physical elements together again so that I could answer it.

Mark Twain's Favorite Brewery

Following a 1962 summer retreat at Angora Lake, Sri Subramuniya visited nearby Virginia City, Nevada, to find a piece of property that could serve as a permanent retreat center. He didn't have to look far. About a quarter mile down the canyon from this legendary boom town of the Old West, he found a large, ramshackle brewery, originally built in 1864 on the site of the famed Comstock Lode Gold Rush. It was for sale.

Its austere Sierra Nevada mountain terrain, with its sagebrush and piñon pine landscape, something that might intimidate others, was appealing to him. It was yogic, almost desolate. It was a place where the

· ·

In the late 1950s, as he was establishing his spiritual mission, Sri Subramuniya had a vision of Siva dancing on his head. He could hear the accompanying musical instruments and in that same moment saw two unusual doors opening, doors he would discover were the entrance to his future temple.

inner was more important than the outer. His first thought, when he stepped inside, was, "What a wonderful ashram this would make!" He wandered through its cavernous rooms, on three floors, and, despite the dilapidated condition of the landmark, he arranged to purchase it.

The building, known as the Old Nevada Brewery, was the favorite haunt of American humorist Mark Twain. Samuel Clemens (Twain's real name) was first a writer and then the editor of the *Territorial Enterprise* in Virginia City from 1862 to 1864, a time during which he wrote his famed novel *Roughing It*. Each afternoon, it is said, he took refuge in the beer gardens of this biggest and most popular pub, telling tall tales to rowdy miners. And there were large crowds. In those days, Virginia City, with 30,000 people, was nearly half as populous as San Francisco, due to the gold rush which brought people from all over the world to the Wild West to dig into the sage-covered hills.

The landmark had been a silent memorial for half a century when Sri Subramuniya, the new owner, stepped into its brick and fancy-woodwork rooms. Its age was showing. The resident caretaker was a grizzled old prospector who kept his mule in the basement and a pig in the shower. He was hard of hearing and required more than a little convincing that his residence had indeed changed owners.

Church families adopted the ashram at once, like parents embracing an orphaned child, pouring their hearts and souls, and their money, into it the rest of that summer to bring it up to Sri Subramuniya's standards. Several monastics stayed as caretakers through the snow-throttled Nevada mountain winter, and plans for major renovations were made for the spring. The ashram became the Skandamalai Monastery (also called the Mountain Desert Monastery), reflecting Sri Subramuniya's insight that Murugan, Skanda, is the lord of renunciates, who would be its residents.

It would also be home of Comstock House, a major publication and printing facility, and the new center for the burgeoning Himalayan Academy courses and programs. For years, at this remote and desolate mountain aerie, 6,500 feet above sea level, Sri Subramuniya would train his renunciates and issue forth the teachings of Vedanta, Siddhanta and the Saivite religion through literature, travel programs, seminars and courses.

The Chemical Chaos of LSD

American television and magazines showed the world the first hippies and flower children in 1964, as the psychedelic movement and drug era reached its stride. Its Mecca was a tiny, previously unremarkable neighborhood in San Francisco called Haight-Ashbury, just over a mile from the Sacramento Street temple. Because of the nationwide news coverage given to the hippie movement and this district, young people from across the US began pouring into the area.

It was a curious feature of the birth of the drug era in America that no one quite took it seriously until it was almost too late. When Sri Subramuniya saw the number of youths arriving in the city and the continuing national news coverage, he arranged a meeting between the mayor's staff and representatives of the various religions and social workers who were ministering to the problem. As a result, the *San Francisco Chronicle* carried a series of stern articles by the mayor and others warning young people intending to migrate to the city for the drug culture to stay away.

In the early years of the hippie movement, no one in America knew quite what to make of it. Sri Subramuniya was well aware of its inner implications and dangers and spoke out against it, but even he had not foreseen how it would mushroom out of control across the country.

> The first time that I learned of LSD, shortly after it was discovered [by recreational users], I went to the Menlo Park Clinic to find out something about it. I talked with one of the psychiatrists there and he began explaining these different experiences one might have on this drug. I said to him, "Some of these experiences you describe— spiritual revelations, expanded awareness, blissful and brilliant inner experiences—are the ones I have had every day of my life for the last twenty years through the faculty of meditation." He responded, "Well, my, you are fortunate, aren't you?"

The crisis had its influence on the Church. As the year progressed, the number of odd-looking visitors to classes and services increased. For several years the American guru would counsel thousands of LSD users. His primary point was not that drugs are wrong, but that there is a better way, an ancient, natural and proven way, to achieve mystical experiences.

Gently, he encouraged young men and women to abstain from all drugs and, instead, to undertake the disciplines of yoga. The trouble with drugs, he told them, was that even if drugs stimulate such experiences, they provide no foundation or understanding of them, no way to repeat the experience or benefit from it. Nothing is gained for the damage done to the nerve system and mind. His words were never accusatory, and they had special power, for he knew personally the profound states of mind they had experienced and told him of. He had been there, they could see, so they trusted his counsel.

Sri Subramuniya's meditations on this social upheaval, whose epicenter was in his city, led to a talk in the temple called "Chemical Chaos," an exposition and criticism of the psychedelic movement and its philosophy. He directed the monks and adult counselors to do what they could to relieve the human suffering caused by the use of drugs, and he helped a great deal to spread an understanding of the nature of the problem among the city's ministers and others.

In the early 60s I became conscious that more and more of the people who came to me for counseling wanted to talk over aspects of their experience in higher states of the mind, states of the mind that had been opened through psychedelic experience. Their interest was in relating these experiences to yoga and the consciousness attained through meditation. These people were highly enthusiastic about their new world, for it seemed like sort of a canned meditation, something they could get very quickly without entering into the sometimes tedious yoga training that may take years to open the individual to the within of himself. People all over the nation now are becoming awakened to the world within.

I have interviewed seekers who have had a few psychedelic experiences and have come through them more vibrant, more alive, and more ready to face the challenges of a new world. I have met others who only stand and look at you blankly, who have lost their desire, even their self-respect. They have lost, shall we say, the structure through which their mind force previously flowed, and it has not been replaced.

I don't want to see a nationwide or worldwide movement built around a little bit of "acid." I don't want to see this, because of the young souls for whom this would be devastating. Some young souls who have been opened up without preparation stumble into psychic ability. They may read thought forms, see auras or travel astrally. In yoga we would say that this path of psychism must be avoided until you have attained Self Realization. This is because in opening up the mind to higher forces and beautiful experiences, we also open ourselves up to the unpleasant experiences of the shadow world of the chakras below the *muladhara* center at the base of the spine, areas of consciousness which we cannot control without preparation and training.

In yoga, the guru knows how to protect his students in the opening-up process by closing off the lower realms as the higher ones

· ·

In the 60s and 70s, America's time of foment, drug experimentation and spiritual questing, Sri Subramuniya undertook a series of lectures at major universities in America and Europe, teaching the advaita path to all who would listen.

open. He knows how to do this, but it is a steady training and does require time. I have met people who have had the psychedelic experience who cannot walk down the street past certain houses because they have become so sensitive to the contention, the negative force field, emitted from a certain home. Some of these people are opened up to the more subtle forces of the lower mind.

I believe that the gap which has been created between "turned on people" and "turned off people" can best be bridged through meditation, gaining control of the mind so that the individual can become master of himself. When you become master of yourself, you truly stand alone in completeness, not in loneliness. In doing so, you are able to bring forth knowledge and wisdom from yourself through the process of meditation, through being able to sit down and think through a problem, ultimately seeing it in full, superconscious perspective and bring forth an answer, a workable answer filled with life. Meditation is a dynamic process. It is much more than just sitting around and waiting. It creates a highly individualistic type of mind.

In early 1967 he arranged to meet with Dr. Richard Alpert, who, along with Dr. Timothy Leary, had become a kind of LSD evangelist, urging American youth to "Tune in, turn on and drop out." The meeting was arranged by a young monk, who accompanied Sri Subramuniya. Over a spaghetti dinner in a Berkeley apartment, they discussed the illuminating and sometimes devastating states of mind provoked by LSD.

Sri Subramuniya told him that the higher planes were open to souls who reached them through normal means, but when unqualified people began to show up astrally using drugs, the devas closed all doors. Sri Subramuniya alerted him to stop what he and Timothy Leary were doing, right away. Any souls using drugs would be caught in the lower astral plane, unable to expand their consciousness.

The errant former Harvard professor, who had taken LSD hundreds of times, leaned forward and listened most intently when, toward evening's end, Sri Subramuniya gave stern warnings of the karmas he was creating by putting all these young lives at risk. Alpert was entreated, firmly, to desist; and though he did not say he would, that conversation may well have led to his life-transforming journey to India—where he became a devotee of Neem Karoli Baba, who gave him the name Ram Dass—and his change of mind soon thereafter, when he publicly spoke against LSD.

Also in 1967, the founder of ISKCON, Vaishnava guru Swami Prabhupada, took up residence in San Francisco, establishing a small Krishna temple on Frederick Street, on the edge of the Haight-Ashbury district. Sri Subramuniya, as he always did, visited, welcoming the spiritual master from India and offering help getting established in the West. Members regularly took boxes of fruits and grains to help feed Swami Prabhupada's followers. He would regale Sri Subramuniya's followers with long stories from scripture, and he once visited the Sacramento Street Temple, giving a short *upadesha* and leading bhajan.

In other ways through the years, Sri Subramuniya assisted Hindu leaders seeking to establish themselves in America, such as loaning his attorney to Swami Chinmayananda when he needed help incorporating the Chinmaya Mission in the US.

Taking Charge

Through the 1950s and early 60s, Mother Christney played a significant role in the Church. At the Sacramento Street temple she served as head of the order of nuns and, as an elder, stood strongly behind Sri Subramuniya. One devotee recalls his own early days in the congregation:

> Mother Christney was then 83 years old. During Sunday Church activities, she attended by sitting in a little room behind the altar while Sri Subramuniya gave his sermons. At times she would lecture me and other newcomers about her life and times. She always supported Sri Subramuniya with such sayings as, "Obey your guru, obey your guru, obey your guru," and "Your guru will show you the way to your spiritual destiny."

At the same time, Mother Christney remained a bastion of Christian influence. As she grew more senior in years, and he came into his full authority as a Hindu guru, she attempted to make administrative changes in the Church. Her efforts failed; and in 1967, with the onset of senility, she left the congregation, retiring to live with her son. Sri Subramuniya, now solely responsible, set about removing all vestiges of her mystical Christianity from the order's teachings and redefining his organization as fully Hindu.

Chapter Twenty-Two

Moving to Nevada

O n March 24, 1964, the great Satguru Yogaswami of Jaffna attained *mahasamadhi*. Kandiah Chettiar sent photographs of the cremation rites within days, rites attended by enormous crowds. Sri Subramuniya was visited by Yogaswami inwardly. Soon thereafter a power swept through the American shishya, and he seemed to take on a new force of spiritual authority. His devotees saw what was happening and began calling him Master Subramuniya, a name he would make legal years later. He spoke of that time:

> Yogaswami passed from his physical body in March, 1964. After this happened, I began receiving letters from Ceylon saying, "You have to come back now, because we need you as the guru here," indicating that I was his successor. I felt that my mission was in the West.

Master named 1965 "The Year of the Academy." His mission was in the ascendency, and he longed to develop his property in Nevada as a remote retreat for himself and his monks. He began to make the four-hour drive from the San Francisco temple to the ashram more often, sometimes weekly. Seeing the need, members leased for him a black Cadillac. Nevada had no speed limits in those days, and he drove those remote roads himself, seldom exceeding 80 miles per hour. It was, for him, a meditation.

The Wild, Wild West

The Mountain Desert Monastery was to become Master's spiritual home and his publications center. It was just a quarter mile from the center of a cowboy town of 600 red-neck mountain boys and their families. The wooden boardwalks from 100 years earlier were still used, and the Bucket of Blood saloon opened early in the day. The heyday was long gone and the Opera House was a shell of its former self; but the town survived, barely, on a trickle of tourists who made the 24-mile drive uphill from Reno. They would gamble a bit, buy some trinkets, drink a beer and have their pictures taken in front of a wooden Indian.

The locals did not know what to think of Master and his San Francisco yogis who had bought the famed brewery. It took a year to get acquainted. Locals did this by crossing to the other side of the street whenever the monks came to town, which they did daily to fetch the mail from the

The guru purchased an abandoned three-story brewery in Virginia City, Nevada, as a summer retreat; but it soon was turned into a monastery for his growing order. For ten years his young monks served and trained in the remote, sage-covered mountains.

. . . .

post office. They did it also by racing their motorcycles past the ashram and screaming foul language to intimidate the monks. It was a clash of cultures. Master thought hard about how to make this work. In the end he bought cowboy boots, a hat and bolo tie, and worked to befriend the locals. He would visit their businesses, buy their services and talk their language. It worked, mostly.

Still, the raucous motorcycle welcome wagon continued. So he directed one of the monks, an ex-paratrooper with firearms training, to buy a shotgun. When the bikers made their next dust-cloud foray down Six Mile Canyon Road, the monk opened a second story window and let fly two 12-gauge shots over their heads. Communication is a wonderful thing. The drive-bys ceased, and a new respect for the monks seemed to emerge.

The monastery had to deal with another side of the local culture. Nevada is the only state in the union where prostitution remains legal, and the most famous brothel in the state was just a few miles away. More than once a shaven-headed monk would open the door only to be asked most embarrassing questions. They soon learned to discreetly direct inquirers "a little farther down the road."

Young men came from all walks of life, all parts of the country, to serve and learn from this living yoga master who understood the superconscious states of mind they had glimpsed. The monastery grew as the most ardent and qualified came forward, eager to follow the monastic path—twenty, then thirty and more. They slept on the dining room floor, the shed floor, in the hallways, the attic and the back porch—anyplace a sleeping bag would fit.

The guru welcomed them all, thereby setting himself an enormous work—for those young men, in their early twenties for the most part, came with all the things immature men have: bad habits, heavy karmas, personal preferences, combative natures, sexual longings, unfulfilled desires, experiences suffered, lack of discipline. So their guru began the work of training them: how to dress, how to walk and converse, how to work with others, how to eat at the table and answer the phone. He gave them projects to harness their youthful enthusiasm. For this, the publications served well.

Master bought out a printing business in Oakland and had all its equipment—a functioning shop—moved to Virginia City. There it was set up under the care of the monastics on the ground floor of the building, with the presses and paper cutter in the brick-walled room that had served as the town's Pony Express Station in the days of the Old West.

. . . .

Publishing continued to be a prime mission objective. The guru purchased state-of-the art printing equipment and set up Comstock House, his publishing arm, with monks printing and binding hundreds of thousands of spiritual books.

Monks were sent to printing school in Anguine, California, to become apprentice pressmen, typographers and darkroom photographers. By 1968 the ashram became a humming, productive, professional printing and publishing center. Master Subramuniya turned out one small book after another, and the monks worked day and night to print and bind them. When exhaustion came, they crawled into sleeping bags at the foot of a Heidelberg press, only to rise again in a few hours, brew a pot of coffee and print until the sun came up.

Master founded Comstock House, a publishing company; and through it the books swept across the nation, becoming some of the most popular spiritual writings of their time. *The Clear White Light, The Fine Art of Meditation, Everything Is Within You, On the Brink of the Absolute, The Lotus of the Heart*—one and then another came off those presses. Word spread of the monks' skills, and soon the Nevada casinos were offering printing work—keno cards, restaurant place mats, corporate stationary and more—which, accepted for a time, helped the monastery support itself.

Pushing the Monks to Perfection

Despite all the publishing activity, it was the inner work that was central at the monastery, and Master Subramuniya set a demanding meditation schedule. Four times a day—at 6am, noon, 6pm and midnight—he ascended the narrow wooden steps to the spacious third floor loft where the monastery temple had been established, and there, without fail, all the monks would assemble for a full hour's guided meditation. Babaji, the ashram's Golden Retriever, never missed a session, curled up at Master's feet. It was known to all that one could not miss a meditation. Master would be there without fail, and each and every monk would, too. The meditations were conducted in full lotus position, and it was unspoken but understood that no one was to move a muscle.

One monk had difficulty enduring these long sessions day after day. His legs would cramp, and he could hardly keep his mind on the meditation. So, one day before the hour was called, he reached down to untangle his legs and relieve the strain. Master said simply, "Don't," directing him to stay in the lotus position until the end. The next day and the next, the same thing happened, until the young monk began to silently weep as he fought to keep his body still.

Master took him aside and explained it was important for him to overcome this obstacle if he was serious, if he wanted a life of meditation. Master urged him to change his way of perceiving the pain, to see it as energy, as sound instead of pain. He said, "See yourself sitting on that sound as if sitting on a symphony. Try that." He did, and after some days the pain subsided, the body made the needed adjustments, and he could sit still without discomfort. Such calls for willpower, for overcoming difficulties, whether physical, emotional, intellectual or karmic, came often from Master.

Once, when trying to teach the monks how to control the heat of the body, he saw they were not getting it. So, he moved the 6am meditations outside. It was winter, and the high mountain snows drifted deep, so deep that in some years one could walk out a second story door onto the ground. That year was particularly cold. Each morning the monks followed their guru through the newly fallen snow to an open spot where they meditated together. They had only their robes and a woolen blanket to keep them warm, and these were pitiably inadequate.

As the morning winds swept snow and frozen air past their defenses, they sat, in full lotus, shivering and seeking the silence within. The guru would then guide them to warm their bodies with their minds, to bring up the heat of the body, which in his Shum language is called *alikaiishum*. The monks worked with feverish intensity to learn the art their guru had put before them. This was no longer an exercise; it was a matter of survival. After some weeks, most had learned to raise their body temperature mentally—not because they wanted to, but because they had to. Such was the way of the guru in those days.

Such training was intense for all the monks, as the guru took them through the personal transformations needed, the changes in their attitudes and their relationships, the resolutions of their past, the firming up of their work habits and meditative determinations. He taught them willpower, how to accomplish their goals, how to overcome obstacles, how to turn adversity and obstacles into success.

In everything they did, he asked 108 percent. One hundred percent, he often repeated, is not enough, is not what you are capable of. Under this intense scrutiny and guidance, the monks flourished in their inner and outer lives—so much so that, decades later, the satguru would wonder aloud whether monks of succeeding generations would develop the same tenacity and strength as his first group had.

From Virginia City, Master wrote this response to a seeker:

Namaste! Your lovely letter arrived just as I returned to the monastery today from our India Odyssey pilgrimage to my ashram in Alaveddy, Sri Lanka, and eight other countries. That good timing indicates that you are on an inner beam, no doubt from the efforts already expended in your spiritual quest. From your letter, it is certain that you have exhausted the many dead-end trails on the path. Your decision to be a renunciate monastic is a good one. It is a big step and I know you have thought it over well. Times are changing. Dedicated souls like yourself are needed as helpers on the path in our monastic orders to stabilize and teach those who are seeking. It is time now for the Western mind to rediscover the vast teachings of Saiva Siddhanta Hinduism.

I am going to give you the first of many challenges we may share together in this life. It is to meditate deeply every day for one full month on a talk I once gave to a small gathering of *mathavasis*, monks, at the San Francisco Temple. In fact, it was August 28, 1960. Like you, they were beginning to experience the blissful and peaceful areas of their inner being, and we spoke of enlightened insights one has on the very brink of the Absolute. You will be challenged by this assignment. Remember, the rewards are more than worth the effort required.

It is my duty as your spiritual teacher to assure you that there will be trials. The sannyasin's life is not easy. It will demand of you more than you ever thought possible. You will surely be asked to serve when tired, to inspire when you feel a little irritated, to give when it seems there is nothing left to offer. To drop out of this great ministry would not be good for you or for those who will learn to depend on you. A Hindu monastic order is not a place to get away from the world. You must teach us and yourself to depend on you, so that twenty or thirty years from now others will find strength in you as you fulfill your karmic destiny as a spiritual leader in this life.

Therefore, read carefully these words. Weigh your life and consider well where you wish to devote your energies. The goal, of course, is Self Realization. That will come naturally. A foundation is needed first, a foundation nurtured through slow and arduous study, through sadhana performed and the demands placed by the guru upon the aspirant. This is a wonderful crossroad in your life. Do not hurry into it. Do this assignment and, should you wish a more disciplined and intense training, do sadhana. Settle your affairs of the world. Then we can sit together. Love and blessings, Master.

There is a cave down Six-Mile Canyon Road, perhaps a mile beyond the monastery—one of the hundreds of abandoned silver mines that honeycomb the region's hills, but horizontally deeper than most. One can walk for half a mile into its chambers. When Master discovered the cave one

. . . .

Not far from the Mountain Desert Monastery lay an abandoned silver mine.
The guru would send young monks to live in this deep cave for days at a time,
teaching them how to see the inner light within the all-pervasive darkness.

day, he was thrilled, and immediately set up a program for his monks. Most often alone, but sometimes in pairs, he sent them to meditate in the dark chambers. Taking only water, no food, the monk would enter the cave, walk through the long tunnel, dodging the massive wooden supports that prevented cave-ins, until there was no light, then walk some more. Once inside the blackness of this space, he would settle down to stay for a day, for two days, as instructed, rarely more. He was to chant and meditate, nothing else—except, and this was the sadhana, to seek the light within, the clear white light of the mind.

Sometimes, when meditating, one does not know if he is seeing the inner light or perhaps seeing the luminous space of the room beyond his closed eyes. But in a cave, deep in the Earth, there is no peripheral light. There is blackness. There is silence. There is nothing else. Monks would dive into themselves in that cave, distracted at first with the random intrusions of recent experience, of their projects back at the monastery, the paucity of food, whatever. But as the hours flowed by, the silence grew, and that silence worked well to bring them into the light of the mind. And when you see light in a darkened cave, you know it's not coming from anywhere else; it is coming from you.

A few monks returned to speak of extraordinary moments when the light coming from within also illumined the floor and walls of the cave, brightly enough for them to discern details of the tunnel, bright enough for them to walk out without turning on their flashlight. Such was the way of the guru in those days. Master wrote about the inner light shortly after these cave experiences:

Remember, when the seal is broken and clear white light has flooded the mind, there is no more a gap between the inner and the outer. Even uncomplimentary states of consciousness can be dissolved through meditation and seeking again the light. The aspirant can be aware that in having a newfound freedom internally and externally there will be a strong tendency for the mind to reconstruct for itself a new congested subconscious by reacting strongly to happenings during daily experiences. Even though one plays the game, having once seen it as a game, there is a tendency of the instinctive phases of nature to fall prey to the accumulative reactions caused by entering into the game.

Therefore, an experience of inner light is not a solution; one or two bursts of clear white light are only a door-opener to transcendental possibilities. The young aspirant must become the experiencer, not the one who has experienced and basks in the memory patterns it caused. This is where the not-too-sought-after word *discipline* enters into the life and vocabulary of this blooming flower, accounting for the reason why ashrams house students apart for a time. Under discipline, they become experiencers, fragmenting their entanglements before their vision daily while doing some mundane chore and mastering each test and task their guru sets before them. The *chela* is taught to dissolve his reactionary habit patterns in the clear white light each evening in contemplative states.

Chapter Twenty-Three

Off to Europe

In the spring of 1967, Master Subramuniya embarked on a fourteen-week journey to Europe which he called the Actinics' World Tour. With three monks and five family members, he flew to Paris, bought a used Volkswagen van, and set out to visit fourteen countries. In each nation, they visited spiritual leaders; they met with monks in Swiss monasteries and priests in Roman theological seminaries. The budget for the tour was small—a mere $2 a day per person for room and board—so the group camped out, throwing their sleeping bags down in French wheat fields and bathing in streams in Germany's Black Forest. Twice the group checked into a rural inn and indulged in a hot shower.

It was a wild and wonderful adventure. They bargained for Persian carpets in the casbah in Tunis and, due to a breakdown in American-Algerian relationships, were taken off a plane and held hostage at gunpoint in an Algerian airport for 36 hours.

In Venice, Master spent three days exploring a previous life experience. With two monks, he walked around the entire city, occasionally hiring a gondola. He was consciously looking for a certain place, outside a theater, he said. He looked and looked for hours. On the third day, he suddenly exclaimed, "Here it is! This is the place where I was killed in a previous life. I was just leaving that small stage door over there after an opera performance when someone came up behind me, hit me in the head and threw me into the canal to drown."

Master mentioned later that night that he was always reluctant to sing in this life, and he attributed it to that horrible death long ago. He confided that it was hard to leave the body of that opera singer, because it was turning out to be such a nice life.

In Ascona, Switzerland, he spent two weeks at Casa Eranos, Carl Jung's charming summer chalet on the shore of Lago Maggiore, a massive mountain lake shared by Italy and Switzerland. Meditating, giving *upadeshas* and browsing through Jung's personal library, Master discovered the famed psychologist's penchant for Indian philosophy and his deep engagement with kundalini.

One morning a young monk asked the guru to describe the inner light. A few words of response came, but suddenly Master grew pensive, excused himself and retired to his room. After some hours, the monks

· ·

The travel-study programs in Europe took Innersearchers to the great historic places, such as the Parthenon in Greece. Wherever they went, Master spoke of the eternal Self within. It was the constant rock on which he sat.

knocked tentatively on the locked door to invite him to lunch, but he
told them he was busy. Hours passed, and again they knocked, with no response. Though they were loath to disturb him, this was so unusual the group began to worry aloud whether they should intervene.

While those deliberations were underway, Master unlocked and opened his door, calling them all to join him on the open stone patio that overlooks the lake. It was late afternoon. With them seated around, he brought out a yellow pad of paper, the kind lawyers write on. Beaming and clearly happy about something, he repeated the morning's question about the light, then revealed that he had "brought through" a small book during those solitary hours. He announced the title, *The Clear White Light*, then proceeded to read the manuscript, a profound explication of the mystical experience. Aside from *Cognizantability,* it was to be the only major work he ever wrote in his own hand, all others having his inspired talks and dictations as their source. Here is an excerpt.

It is a great new world of the mind that is entered into when first the clear white light dawns, birthing a new actinic race, immediately causing him to become the parent to his parents and forefathers. When living in an expanded inner state of mind, he must not expect those living in materialistic consciousness to understand him. On this new path of "the lonely one," wisdom must be invoked to cause him to be able to look through the eyes of those who believe the world is real, and see and relate to that limited world in playing the game as if it were real, thus maintaining the harmony so necessary for future unfoldments. To try to convince those imbedded in materialism of the inner realities only causes a breach in relationship, as it represents a positive threat to the security they have worked so hard to attain.

First we had the instinctive age, of valuing physical strength and manly prowess, followed by the intellectual age, facts for the sake of facts, resulting in the progress of science. Now we are in an age of new values, new governing laws, an actinic age, with new understanding of the world, the mind, but most of all, the Self. Understanding is preparation for travel, for it is an age of the mind, and in the mind, much more intense than the speed of light, exist spheres which seers are only willing to speak of to those who have the inner ear with which to listen.

. . . .

In 1967 Subramuniyaswami explored Europe with monks and family devotees. Traveling in a VW van, overnighting in fields in sleeping bags and eating on two dollars a day, the group brought advaita yoga to the continent. Master dictated "Yoga Letters" from the front seat while a monk in the back typed.

The mind of man tends either toward light or toward darkness, expanded awareness or materialistic values. Depending upon the self-created condition of the mind, man lives either within the clear white light of the higher consciousness, or in the external mind structure which reflects darkness to his inner vision.

Leaving Switzerland, the nine Actinics drove north, through Austria, Germany, Luxembourg, Belgium and Denmark. Master's purpose was to spread his Advaita Yoga teachings throughout Europe; and toward the end he lectured at Sorbonne University in Paris and sponsored the first-ever yoga conference in Amsterdam, bringing a hundred yogis and yoga teachers together from throughout Europe.

As they drove week after week through Europe, Master sat in the front seat of the Volkswagen, dictating the "Yoga Letters" to a monk sitting in the back with a portable typewriter. The van became a mobile writer's studio, and all enjoyed listening as the teaching of the day flowed forth in his rich voice. When one was finished, they would stop at a local post office and mail the typed papers back to the monks in Virginia City to be dutifully published so all at home could follow Master's journey. Here is an excerpt.

There is another great exerciser of the inner nerve currents, and that is using our willpower. This is where the term inner strength comes from. It is through practices such as finishing a job once started, doing each job perfectly, keeping promises and just living a life in accordance with one's highest ideals that these inner currents are strengthened. When a person has been using his inner willpower to accomplish his goals, you can feel his inner strength emanating from within him. When that person sits down to meditate, he will undoubtedly attack his meditation in the same manner, strengthening even further these inner currents.

The desire to meditate comes from positive accomplishments which have been gained through the practice of meditation itself. After a certain number of successful meditations, the subconscious begins to anticipate the next meditation until the mind is so conditioned that it constantly holds a meditative vibration. At this point, the desire for meditation is automatic and meditation becomes a way of life. Then, the energies and understanding of the fourth dimension are always available and are an ever-present part of a person's life.

"Shout It from the Rooftops"

Returning to America, Master dove into the spiritual regimens he loved so—Sunday sermons, monks' training, radio interviews, the long desert drives to his Nevada monastery. He had gained some fame as a yoga teacher and, to his surprise, was invited to be a guest professor at UCLA for a week, lecturing from The Master Course. He held a similar series at the International House in Berkeley for UC students, lectured at Stanford and traveled on an extensive speaking tour through Southern California, Colorado, the East Coast, British Columbia and Washington. In Seattle he gave talks on Hindu mysticism and esoterics at the Aquarian Foundation, a spiritualist, occult church established in 1955 by Rev. Keith Rhinehart, whom Master knew well.

It was a time of reaching out, taking the deepest teachings into the colleges and communities around America. It was not a time to remain silent about the Self, he would say, but to "shout it from the rooftops." American youth were remarkably open to this mystical message during those few years, as never before or since.

During 1968, Master Subramuniya lectured extensively in the Midwest for the first time and participated in a television series at San Francisco State College that featured dialogue with Zen Master Roshi Suzuki. Weekends were passed in San Francisco, but most of the week found him at the Nevada monastery, which became his primary home and new headquarters. His time was spent more and more with the monastics and with his published works.

Yoga and meditation were a vital part of personal, individual sadhana for all of Master's followers. Each was instructed to hold a fifteen or twenty minute meditation without fail after waking in the morning and before sleep. These inner explorations would become the anchor of their lives, giving them a security and insight that made each day joyous and each experience welcomed. Whenever their karmas became too intense and they came to him for relief, he would ask first if they were meditating regularly. Usually, for those whose balance had been lost, the answer was no.

The emphasis of Master's talks in the early 60s was on the awakening of the superconscious and the possibility of realizing the Self by clearing the subconscious. Encounter groups had gained popularity—therapy sessions where people shared things that were otherwise taboo and unspoken. Using the term Enter-In, Master implemented, for his monks only, group sharing.

To facilitate subconscious cleansing for his family members, he instituted the practice of confession, called Agni Yoga, personal sharing with

the guru of one's past, of those hidden repressions that hold us back on the path. Students with deep-seated repressions, painful memories and bottled-up character tendencies that they had never been able to confront or talk about would often come into their first inner light experience after going through a soul-searching series of confessions.

This was a major area of training for the early monks, as they listened, under Master's guidance, to hundreds and even thousands of confessions. He taught them how to take the energies of those personal revelations and draw them into the light where they would be resolved, not by analysis, not by any rational insight, but simply by being in the presence of the clear white light.

Birth of a Mystical Language

In July of 1968 Master led 32 students on a travel-study program called Innersearch Switzerland. He had long been dissatisfied with presenting the philosophy and concepts of Hinduism and yoga in English. The subtle states of meditation and intricate inner disciplines cannot be easily

On a small patio overlooking Lago Maggiore in Switzerland, Master taught his mystical Shum language for the first time. It would become his preferred way of sharing the penetrating, occult and subtle depths of the mind.

· ·

conveyed through the medium of an externally oriented language like English, he found. At Casa Eranos, Master went deep within, seeking a solution that would allow humanity better access to and understanding of the interior states of consciousness spoken of in Hindu sacred texts.

After a series of meditations, on the morning of July 28 the alphabet of the Shum language came forth from the inner mind, first one character, then another, as he sat in deep meditation clairvoyantly seeing and clairaudiently hearing the character's form and sound. When he had written them all down, he ran outside excitedly waving the paper in his hand. "I've got it! I've got it!" he said to one of the monastics passing by. He showed what he had done and dedicated much of the remainder of the retreat to bringing out more. An entirely new language of meditation—its basic alphabet, script, syntax and first vocabulary words, called pictures and portraits—was developed during the retreat.

In the summer of 1968, Himalayan Academy conducted an Innersearch Travel-Study Program to Ascona, Switzerland. I was working on a little book called *The Advaitin*. The book was about the refined states of experience deep within the inner realms of pure consciousness, just before one merges into the Self and after one comes out of that state. The little book was unfolding beautifully, but upon rereading what had been written, I thought, "This is very understandable to me, but would it be so to someone just beginning on the path? It's going to be so complicated, so difficult to understand, for what I wish to portray in words, there are no words in the English language." I then began to feel that what should be done was to begin using Sanskrit to provide the necessary, adequate words so that the inner and refined areas of the mind would have their own name in the same way emotions, physical things and so forth are named in English.

At our Ascona summer retreat, this theory that unfolded from within was going 'round and 'round in my mind, and I began looking through several Sanskrit dictionaries to locate certain words that could be used in *The Advaitin*. But in three Sanskrit/English dictionaries, each translator had translated each of the words in a different way. I threw up my hands at this and said, "This is going to make it more confusing for my beginning students than if we didn't use Sanskrit," simply because of the differing translations.

The feeling began to come that what was really needed was another language, a new, fresh language, one giving me a vocabulary that we could use to accurately describe inner states of consciousness. Two or three days later we traveled to Venice for a few days' excursion. This idea of a new language was still strong in my mind. It was in Venice that I decided to go deeply within and bring out a new esoteric language. So, I went deep within myself, and wrote down a message of instructions dictated by one of the Mahadevas to my outer self. The Mahadeva explained how and where to go within to be able to unfold another language. My instructions were, "You go within the *uda* current, which is found within the *sushumna*." That is the current of mind flow where language exists.

In following the instructions, my spine lit up in a beautiful, pale yellow and lavender light. The yellow and the lavender intermingled, one color coming in and out of the other. It was just beautiful! But I only found one end of the *uda* current, and did not have any results in Venice. Three days later, after returning to Ascona, Switzerland, while working within myself, I found both ends of the *uda* current. Then, in meditation, after coming out of nirvikalpa samadhi, I heard the tones of the *svadishthana*, the *anahata* and the *ajna* chakras. Within two hours, out of my inner mind came the script, the basic alphabet of eighteen sounds, the syntax as well as some of the basic vocabulary, like *simshumbisi, vumtyeudi, karehana*. The first word to be uttered was *Shum*.

Shum now names the mystical language of meditation. As fast as I could, I wrote it all down and ran downstairs to one of the monks, shouting, "I have it! I have it! Here is our language!"

Because of the immediate need for a vocabulary of fifty or a hundred words for me to work with during the Innersearch Travel-Study Program, I was eager to proceed in bringing through the new language. Shum started out in a very simple way. I thought, "Fine. Now we will have ten or fifteen or twenty or maybe a hundred more words eventually to work with, and they will be marvelous inner teaching tools." However, in the days to follow, this *uda* current became

. . . .

Sometime around 1968, following decades of sadhana, Sri Subramuniya had the experience of the kundalini coiling itself permanently at the top of the head.

stronger and brighter and brighter. I didn't tell anyone about it at the time except two or three of the Saivite monastics who were with me in Switzerland.

I began working day and night, and the structure and script for the language began to refine itself, and vocabulary started coming through, right from the inner light. I would see light within my head and see little images or letters in the Shum script drop down one after another and line up. Then I would read the word, like *shumsimnisi*, and know what it meant, and then write the Shum word with the meaning in English. Vocabulary flowed out like this for two or three weeks. In Nice, in Southern France, the whole concept of *liunasi*, the psychic nerve system, and *alikaiishum*, the warmth and psychic heat of the body, came through.

Then, later in our Innersearch, in Paris, more of Shum came through. Upon returning to the United States, I had a vocabulary of about 300 words, and every day more were coming to Earth. Finally, the images stopped dropping out of the inner light, and I would hear the meaning of the word clairaudiently, almost as if someone were speaking. Sometimes they would come in reverse—English first, Shum second. The vocabulary and the structure of the language developed quickly, but what is more important, the perspective of the Shum language was available.

In the Shum language, the perspective is deep within the mind. It is called *shumif*. From this perspective, we have the consciousness that we are the center of the universe. We see light within the spine as the central pole, and then open our eyes and look out into the world.

The following year, 1969, we returned to Switzerland and experienced the tremendous breakthrough of *mambashum*. These are Shum maps of areas of meditation that enable a devotee not only to map out his meditation before he begins it, but to make memos of the meditation as it progresses. Now devotees are able to go back to the same area of the inner mind, time and time and time again. By following the same *mambashum*, more than one person can go into the same area of the mind, time and time and time again. Mystical experiences began to develop between myself and the devotees, as we would go into the same area of the mind and experience, see and hear the same sounds, see the same colors—which is an event that is not made known in mystical and occult literature.

· ·

For thirteen weeks in 1969 Master Subramuniya guided 65 devotees around the world on the India Odyssey. It was his first return to India and Ceylon since 1949, and it began decades of interaction with those two nations.

Mutiny in the Mountains

Returning after the 1968 Innersearch to Nevada after four weeks in Europe, Master was faced with unfortunate consequences of his longer-than-usual absences. A small band of mutinous monks, led by the most senior, approached him with the outrageous suggestion that he retire; they would carry on the mission from now on.

Keeping his poise in the face of this challenge, Master invited the group to dinner at Miguel's, a Mexican restaurant in Reno, bringing along an equal number of monks who thought the brazen insurgence was preposterous. En route, he shared his strategy with those who were with him. They would listen to the rebels' reasons and ideas, learn more of their plans and remain nonresponsive.

During dinner, the rebels were disarmed by the lack of negative response and openly told Master that his absences from the monastery were too long and he was, after all, not getting any younger (at 41). They freely shared their ideas for the future, which amounted to transforming the monastery into an open institution, less strict and more New Age.

Master left the restaurant without directly responding and never spoke to the group again on the subject. In the days and weeks to follow he moved one monk, then the next, to another monastery, another mission, slowly reducing the responsibilities of those involved and dismantling the opposition. As the years rolled on, each of the renegades found the courage to leave the monastery. Years later Swami Satchidananda faced a similar takeover effort from his board of trustees, and Master sent his senior monks to help him successfully turn back his subversives.

In the months that followed, Master spent more time in his remote Nevada ashram, leading the monks in the regimen, followed in those days, of four one-hour meditations each day. The Shum revelations had intensified his mystical experiences. Of that time, he wrote:

> A sannyasin of attainment has had many, many lifetimes of accumulating this power of kundalini to break that seal at the door of Brahman. Here is a key factor. Once it is broken, it never mends. Once it is gone, it's gone. Then the kundalini will come back—and this gives you a choice between *upadeshi* and *nirvani*—and coil in the *svadhishthana, manipura, anahata,* wherever it finds a receptive chakra, where consciousness has been developed, wherever it is warm. A great intellect or a siddha who finds the Self might return to the center of cognition; another might return to the *manipura* chakra.

• •

During the 1970 Tahiti-Ceylon Innersearch, Master was regaled by the Saivite community of Ceylon. Tavil and nagasvara heralded his arrival in fifty villages, and miles of hand-woven cloth was laid on the ground for the holy man from the West to walk upon.

The ultimate is to have the kundalini coiled in the *sahasrara*. I personally didn't manage that until 1968 or '69, when I had a series of powerful experiences of kundalini in the *sahasrara*. It took twenty years of constant daily practice of tough sadhanas and *tapas*. I was told early on that much of the beginning training was had in a previous life and that is why, with the realization in this life, I would be able to sustain all that has manifested around me and within me as the years passed by. Results of sadhanas came to me with a lot of concentrated effort, to be sure, but it was not difficult, and that is what makes me think that previous results were being rekindled.

The Garden Island

There was a second Innersearch in 1968, this one to Hawaii in December, called Ashram Kauai. Master took 27 students to the Garden Island of Kauai, spending three weeks at a remote country resort called the Tropical Inn. They had the entire facility to themselves and turned it into an ashram. Situated four miles inland along the Wailua River, the inn, built in 1929, overlooked a lush river valley and offered a dramatic view of the island's extinct volcano a few miles away. It seemed like paradise.

> For years I had been looking for a new international headquarters through which I could expand the activities of my teachings and be more available to those around the world. I traveled through eleven different countries during the summer of the first Innersearch, and later many successive Innersearches around the world, covering 27 different countries in all, until I finally decided to establish my headquarters on the island of Kauai.

So much was everyone taken with the place that the devotees suggested it be purchased for the Church and optimistically took up a collection among themselves, the beginnings of a down payment. One morning they placed $480 in Master's hand, urging him to make this remarkable site his home. It was not for sale, but he set the money aside for its intended purpose.

The World's Finest Waiters

Returning to Nevada and San Francisco in early 1969, Master was challenged with the growth of his order of monastics. How could he support them, feed and house them, afford to train them? The monastics had, up to this time, lived in rented quarters in the neighborhood or in the temple building. In a new building he purchased for the monks, a new form of training was commenced, a program that had the monastics work in San Francisco restaurants. Master developed it to provide them skills of dealing with the public in busy situations, to mature their abilities to handle details and work with others, to help instill the spirit of humble service so essential to monastic life and to maintain the self-sufficiency of their order at a time when it had few other sources of revenue.

The goal was to become "the finest waiters in the finest restaurants in the world," which required the monks to exert maximum effort in personal discipline and deportment. To further their training, Master instigated an elaborate training program in fine waitering for the monastics, hiring professional maitre d's, sommeliers, chefs and restauranteurs of high standing in the city to instruct the monastics through lectures and demonstrations.

For years the monks worked anonymously in some of the city's finest restaurants, surrendering their earnings at the temple altar each night and spending their off hours and days in the monastery and with the guru. Master called the program Silent Ministry, as the monks went out incognito, carrying the vibration of the temple into the world to uplift and bless all those they served and worked with. It was an arduous sadhana, with long, late hours in intensely demanding conditions. For those who persevered, it proved to be a great training, one that strengthened the brotherhood and matured the young men. They did, in fact, become some of the finest waiters in some of the finest restaurants in the world.

An Odyssey to India
Master Subramuniya traveled again to Europe, this time with five monks and twenty-seven students in July and August on Innersearch Switzerland 1969. Portugal, France and Switzerland were the chief countries visited, with half of the month-long pilgrimage being spent in retreat at Casa Eranos. Here he again devoted his time to developing the Shum language, using its conceptual portraits to elucidate the Advaita Siddhanta philosophy. He sponsored at Casa Eranos a special training session for European yoga teachers living in Germany, France, Italy and Switzerland.

In October, along with twelve monks and fifty-four students, he undertook a thirteen-week pilgrimage to India and Ceylon. The pilgrimage, called the 1969 Indian Odyssey, visited France, Greece, India, Nepal, Ceylon, Singapore, Thailand and Japan, with the greater part of the time being spent in India, where Master's group was the largest tour ever to visit the country. It was large enough that the Minister of Aviation and Tourism, Dr. Karan Singh—who years later would visit Kauai and take

Master as his "Western guru"—helped with the arrangements person-

ally. In each country, the spiritual leaders were sought out—a master cal-
ligrapher in Japan, a Buddhist roshi in Thailand, and in India a galaxy of
yogis and great souls.

This was Master's first visit to India in two decades, and the first time
ever for the students traveling with him. India captivated, confounded,
challenged and uplifted. India was, they concluded, the last place on Earth
where magic lived on the streets and divinity lived in the eyes of the people.

One-week retreats were held in Darjeeling and Udaipur in the Himalayan foothills and at Ootacamund in the Nilgiri Hills of South India. One
day he took the pilgrims to a local theater to see the newly released movie,
"2001: A Space Odyssey." Shum was again a major study for the pilgrims,
and his devotees were introduced to orthodox temple worship. In Madras
he held the International Yoga Convention.

What was most dear to Master during this three-month odyssey
was his return to Ceylon, Satguru Yogaswami's home. Twenty years had
passed since he left the island, and he had longed to be back. The Saivites
of Jaffna received him with enormous respect, with pomp and ceremony
spiced with a little uncertainty. They knew Yogaswami had said, "I have
a man in America," and they could see that the American guru was a
remarkable soul, but there was resistance, a reluctance, to take a Western
man as spiritual master. It had never happened, and some were determined it never would. But Master paid them no heed. He had his mission
from Yogaswami and he would carry it forward, with or without them.

He sponsored special feasts and festivities centering around the Subramuniya Ashram and initiated a resident program for his monastics there,
whereby they would stay for extended periods at the ashram to broaden
their personal exposure to Hinduism and gather scriptures for publication in the West. Temple pujas, temple talks, cultural events and gatherings filled the days. With not a single hotel in the area, Innersearchers
stayed, in twos and threes, in the homes of Yogaswami's disciples, living the Saivite culture they had only heard tales of, learning the charms
and subtleties of the East and making the deep human connections that
would tie the East and the West together for decades.

Master was home. All could feel it. He stayed at the home of Kandiah Chettiar, who had introduced him to Yogaswami, and renewed their
connections. He wore a white *veshti* everywhere, to the surprise of all
who had never seen him in one. Feeling the time to be auspicious, he gave

. . . .

*During the 1972 Indian Odyssey, seventy-two Innersearchers circled
the globe with the satguru. In Palani Hills, Madurai Meenakshi-
Sundareshvara and other temples, crowds buried him under mountains
of garlands and heralded him as Hinduism's hope for a noble future.*

advanced *dikshas* to monastics and devotees and made plans for his Ala-veddy Ashram to expand its service to the Tamil community.

He worshiped at Nallur and Kumbhalavalai and at Yogaswami's hut, met with all the senior Sri Lankan disciples and visited an aged, wisp thin and white-haired Markanduswami in his thatched hut. To the amazement of everyone, Master prostrated to this solitary sage, something that never happened before, an act that was taken as his way, after all these years, of honoring the guru they shared. Nor did Markanduswami fail to enchant all present. As each Innersearcher entered, he was painstakingly careful to follow them with his eyes, and not go to the next until their eyes, and perhaps their souls, met. Not one was missed. Seated on a wooden bench in his pure white robes, barely in his body, his hair and beard wildly uncontrolled, he regaled his visitors with the great sayings of the illumined satguru who had died just five years earlier. The Innersearchers were transformed by it all as they shared in this joyous homecoming.

Master's entire mission was transformed by those weeks, by the profound encounters in India and Ceylon. Having visited Hinduism's source, worshiped at Chidambaram and immersed his followers in the ancient dharma, he would return many times, and he would bring forth like a river in spate all that he saw and remembered from his youth. No longer would India and Ceylon be a soft reference of the past. They would take center stage in his continuing efforts to bring the West knowledge of the Self and the beauties of Hindu culture.

During the pilgrimage, a daily diary was published to inform everyone back home of the events and experiences. These Odyssey Letters were mailed to Virginia City, printed and distributed from there to make everyone at home feel they were on the journey.

Kauai Calls

The staff were so exhausted by the journey around the world that Master delayed their return to San Francisco and flew them to Kauai, where he had held the Ashram Kauai retreat in late 1968. They checked into a hotel at Poipu for much-needed rest. But Master seldom did well at that, and he immediately undertook a project, to explore buying the idyllic Tropical Inn they had fallen in love with.

When Master asked a monk to inquire about such a purchase, the response came back, "But, it's not even for sale." "Never mind that," Master consoled, "just go there and ask." The monk dutifully drove the 45 minutes to the place and on his return reported that, "The owner said it's not on the market." "I see. Now go back and ask him, just theoretically,

In December of 1968 Master took 27 spiritual seekers on a three-week meditation retreat to a remote Hawaiian island. Kauai, half way between the East and the West, so captured him that in 1970 he established his headquarters on the Garden Island.

how much he would sell it for if it were ever to go on the market."

Back at the Tropical Inn the monk dutifully spoke with the owner, retired Col. Albert Roesch, asking for a what-if price. "As my manager told you twice, it's not for sale, young man." "Yes, I know. But if it were..." the monk sheepishly offered. Seeing there would be no respite until a number was forthcoming, Col. Roesch grumbled in a slightly threatening voice, "If it were to be sold, and I'm not saying it ever would, we would want no less than $300,000." Back at Poipu, Master heard the number and decreed, "Go back and tell him we can't afford that much, but we can offer him $165,000 right away. No more. Tell him that." "But..." "Trust me. Just go and make the offer." An hour later the monk stood before the man and made the counteroffer with great hesitation. "Hmmm! Let me talk with my wife," came the unexpected retort.

The offer, amazingly, was accepted and Master moved to the new property on February 5, 1970, spending the first night alone on the property to take psychic control before inviting the monks to join him the next day.

At Home on Kauai

Master named the lush seven-acre property Sivashram and made it his home, a courageous move in those days, leaving all past history and properties, moving thousands of miles away to a new land, a small island. Thus ended a long search for his spiritual headquarters.

> Years ago, we came to Kauai and finally never left. I chose Kauai, the world's most remote land mass, because I wanted to be close to my devotees in the East and close to my devotees in the West, while at the same time cloistered from the world at large. Yes, our inner life is more important than our outer life. If we were in San Francisco, New York, Singapore or New Delhi, we could not do this same work as a contemplative order of meditators and teachers, outreaching primarily through publications and the Internet. Kauai is a spiritual place, a vortex of healing energies emanating from its sacred Mount Waialeale, pristine air and ocean.

To keep in close touch with the careful planning needed to prepare for the upcoming Innersearch programs, he installed a teletype system between all three centers—Virginia City, San Francisco and Kauai. These large, metal typing stations brought great clarity to the pilgrimage planning and made communications across the sea and an overview of the many activities of the Church a much simpler matter. It was the email of its day, and could also serve as instant messaging if two or more were online together.

Master, whose Shum name was Mamade (pronounced "maʹ-ma-dee"), also sometimes called Madereh (meaning "satguru"), would sit and type long messages (only upper case was available) offline, onto a paper tickertape. Hundreds of feet of the tape, perforated with millions of tiny round holes, filled several forty-gallon plastic barrels. These were later fed back into the machine to transmit at 300 baud for hours, when the phone rates were low, to his monasteries, where they emerged from the machine on tractor-feed paper. Here is one of those messages to his monks, full of esoteric instruction in the Shum language for them to work on toward their goal of Self Realization.

. . . .

For weeks in 1970 Master sat in a wicker chair at his tropical Kauai monastery, spontaneously dictating twelve hours of mystical upadeshas that would become an audio edition of his primary teaching vehicle, The Master Course.

MESSAGE TO THE NATYA AT THE TEMPLE
SEPTEMBER 6, 1970
FROM MADEREH

I ARRIVED SAFELY IN LIHUE (THAT MEANS GOOSE PIMPLES IN
THE HAWAIIAN LANGUAGE) SAFE AND SHUMSIKA ABOUT ONE
OCLOCK OUR TIME YESTERDAY. IT WAS A LOVELY TRIP ON A
747 FROM SAN FRANCISCO. WE HAD A FINE SPIRITUAL TIME
TOGETHER. THE MEMORIES STILL LINGER. MERCI.

GOOD TO BEGIN PLANNING FOR THE BUSINESS MEETING FOR
THE FAMILIES ON THE FIFTEENTH. TODAY THERE WILL BE MANY
THINGS TO DISCUSS ABOUT THE NEXT LUAU, ETC., ETC., ETC.
BOTH THE BUSINESS MEETING AND THE LUAU WILL BE HELD AT
THE TEMPLE FROM NOW ON, SO WE CAN PLAN FOR THAT NOW.

BEST WISHES AND BLESSINGS FOR A WONDERFUL WEEK. WORK
HARD ON MOOLINGSHUM. EACH MAKE SOME SENTENCE
SKETCHES TO SEND ME SO THAT I CAN LEARN IT ALONG WITH
YOU, PLEASE.

IT IS BEAUTIFUL HERE TODAY. THE SUN IS SHINING. THE RIVER
IT IS FULL, REMINDING ME OF THE ABUNDANCE THE FAMILIES
WILL HAVE ON ALL PLANES IN THEIR FUTURE LIFE.

SHUMSIKA BIMAOO BASENAM SHUMMALE

STRIVE FOR EEKAEF OO EMKAEF. KEEP YOUR GOAL EVER IN THE
MEMORY CELLS OF YOUR IMMEDIATE DAILY AFFAIRS. KAEEF OO
EEKAEEF OO EMKAEEF.

LOVE, YOUR MAMADE

Globe-Trotting Guru

Though the transition from Nevada to Hawaii was all-consuming, Master continued the travel-study programs, taking 25 students to Switzerland in July and August, and 29 more to Tahiti and Ceylon during the month of November. This second visit to Jaffna deepened the ties with his Saiva roots and with Yogaswami's devotees, and those who traveled with him were immersed in Saivite temple worship and festivals. While in Colombo, he accepted an invitation from the Buddhist Meditation Center, where he spoke to over 700 Buddhists, partially in the Shum language and partially in English, the whole being translated into Sinhalese.

The year's third pilgrimage, a nine-day retreat held in December, included Kauai and the islands of Hawaii, Maui and Oahu. During the days at Sivashram on Kauai, he gathered the seekers each day in the Hibiscus Room. In his pure white outfit he sat in a large, elaborately woven wicker chair, recording hours of inspired talks that were later compiled, printed and packaged by his monks in Nevada into the sixth edition of The Master Course, twelve one-hour lessons on cassette tape that became his primary teaching instrument for many years.

While settling into his island home, Master continued to travel extensively, monthly to his other two monasteries and almost weekly to Honolulu to hold meditations and give public classes. A major renovation plan for the old inn evolved, and soon a group of followers flew to Kauai to undertake intensive remodeling of the 1929-vintage estate. For some three years the whining of saws and pounding of hammers became familiar sounds. He gave the new rooms exotic names: the Palace of the Noonday Sun, the Ryokan, Peacock Court and the Hibiscus Room. It was a heady time, full of travel, of new and constant publications and the establishment of his home. He always saw it as the guru's home, not an institution.

The monks planted tropical gardens and imported Toggenburg goats, the first in the state, for milk. Master bought horses and had the young monks learn to train and care for these intelligent creatures, advancing to equestrian jumping and barrel running. The virgin monks were commissioned to hire stallions for the mares and witness the breeding ritual and the birth, to enhance their understanding of nature's ways. Similarly, Gurudeva brought cows into the monastery to provide a touch of nature and, not insignificantly, milk and all of its gifts.

During the 1972 India Odyssey, 75 seekers traveled around the world with Master through Hawaii, Japan, Thailand, Sri Lanka (which became a republic and changed its name from Ceylon that year), India, Iran, Russia and France. More than before, he immersed them in the mysteries of Saivite temple worship and, as was his way when traveling, he took them to meet the spiritual lights of each nation they visited, Indian saints and yogis, the Dalai Lama in Dharamshala, Buddhist lamas in Nepal, Russian Orthodox priests in Moscow, Zen masters in Japan and imams in Iran.

Amid these serious visits, Master showed his easy humor. During the bus ride to Dharamshala to see the Dalai Lama, he led the Innersearchers in a long and rousing rendition of "Hello, Dolly!" After spending a day in Ganeshpuri with Swami Muktananda, he was on the bus returning to Bombay when a pilgrim inquired if he regarded the renowned swami to be enlightened. The philosophical exchanges at the ashram that day had been made through an unusually adept translator, Professor Jinendra Jain. Master thought for a moment, then offered, "Well, either he is or his translator is." Everyone on the bus roared.

In Paris, he met Swami Bua, a humor-loving yogi who would later visit Master's monastery often and live to be 120 by one calculation. There were remarkable encounters with Ananadamayi Ma, the senior Shankaracharya from Kanchipuram Matha, Maharishi Mahesh Yogi, Indira Gandhi, a saint named Pundiswami (since he lived in the village of Pundi), who never moved or stood and whose legs had completely atrophied, and others.

All across Tamil Nadu, Master visited the ancient Saiva *aadheenams*, eager to observe and absorb how these temple-monastery complexes operate, how they are organized, funded and administrated, the subtleties of how the gurus dress, talk, worship, live, their protocols for interacting with guests and junior swamis, their relationship with the surrounding community, the traditional ways in which devotees serve—to take it all back home to Kauai to continue building an authentic Saiva *aadheenam* of his own in the West.

These experiences would fructify over the ensuing two decades as he brought the sacred symbols of the spiritual office with him: the *shirobhashanam* (crown of rudraksha beads), the silver *danda* (staff), the *simhasanam* or "lion's seat" upon which the *aadheenakarthar* (pontiff) sits, the unique *kundala* (golden earrings) and the golden pendant he wears. He would bring all these Saiva insignia to Kauai, to the West.

One day in New Delhi he took an early walk during a quiet day. It proved to be a momentous one. He later described it:

> Having pilgrimaged with seventy-five monastics and devotees throughout India and Sri Lanka to saints and sages, ancient temples, dharmashalas, *aadheenams* and modern ashrams, I happened late one morning, during a spontaneous walk, upon an extraordinary Lord Siva Nataraja Deity at Nirmala's Copper Bazaar. I walked around the wondrous six-foot-tall bronze statue situated on the busy sidewalk and quietly said, "Hello!" It was the store's insignia and showpiece, too precious to sell, the owner declared, as no value could be attached. Bravely disregarding that fact, we bargained and traded through the morning hours and ultimately acquired it, and as evening approached arranged for its shipment to our distant Garden Island of Kauai.

At Mahasivaratri time a year later, in 1973, in the jungles of Kauai, our Kadavul Nataraja Deity, Lord of the Dance, arrived at Sivashram and was placed in the gardens overlooking the sacred Wailua River, where it was spontaneously decorated, bathed and worshiped. That night the exact location of the Deity's installation was chosen by Lord Murugan Himself when He appeared to me in an early-morning vision, upturned His glistening vel, His scepter of spiritual discernment, and powerfully pounded its point three times on the cement steps at the monastery entrance, marking the precise spot to place the Deity.

Lord Murugan's orders were obeyed. On March 12, the Deity was moved into place and worship began immediately. A rotating 24-hour vigil was established, and it has been maintained without a single hour's lapse to this very day. Under this strict monastery discipline, monks take turns every three hours in the temple, night and day, 365 days a year. During this vigil, they perform constant meditation, puja, yogas and chanting, quelling the mind and giving themselves in profound adoration, *prapatti*, to this remarkable icon. Thus the arrival of the Siva Nataraja Deity transformed our life, and from that day onward life in and around the monastery has revolved around His divine presence.

This establishment of Kadavul Hindu Temple on the lush, tropical Garden Island of Kauai, Earth's most remote land mass, at the base of Hawaii's oldest extinct volcano, known as Mount Waialeale, eventually was recorded in the State archives by the Governor as the first Hindu temple in Hawaii.

With the arrival of Lord Nataraja, thousands upon thousands of devas of the Second World and devas and Mahadevas of the Third World penetrated the inner atmosphere of the Lemurian mountaintop island of Kauai from several ancient temples—in Sri Lanka, the precious Kumbhalavalai Koyil, mystic Nallur and potent seaside Tiruketeeswaram, and in India, the mighty Chidambaram, Thanjavur's Brihadeeswarar, which I am said to have built in a previous life as Rajaraja Chola, according to several jyotisha *nadishastris,* and the sin-dissolving Rameswaram, overflowing in healing waters in twenty-two wells. The three worlds had at that moment become connected as one, and the Saivite Hindu religion began to flourish on this side of the planet.

Master had another vision of Lord Murugan, known in North India as Karttikeya, around the same time. One early morning in his small chalet next to the Tiruvadi Monastery in San Francisco, adjacent to the temple

on Sacramento Street, Master had a vision that brought Lord Murugan

even further to the forefront of his order's life. Suddenly, he found himself flying with a handsome, muscular being around the monastery room.
Master later told the monks that he had asked the powerful being who
he was, and received the reply, "If you don't know, who does?" He knew, it
was Murugan Himself.

Master was so inspired by that encounter, he planned to write a book
called *Flying with Murugan.* Though the book never manifested, Murugan's influence in and on the Order did, and Master always felt the first of
all sannyasins, son of Siva, was the tutelary head of his monastic community. Nearly every one of his monks was given a name of Lord Murugan
and taught to regard this mighty one as a personal guide and example of
purity, detachment, willpower and speed of accomplishment.

Books from the Inner Worlds
Kadavul Hindu Temple became the center of the monks' lives, and they
began years of training in the devotional arts of Sanskrit chanting and
puja. The Gods were introduced to them by Master, and they learned to
make them the center of life, their support and their friends.

Slowly, methodically, Master was, in a big way, bringing everything
of the tradition to the West, every monastic ideal, every temple protocol,
every yogic practice, planting them all in the fertile Hawaiian soil.

Each day he drove, with one or two monks, the five miles to the post
office, as in those early days there was no mail delivery to the rural areas.
Taking the day's correspondence to a table at the Coco Palms Hotel, he
would order a cup of coffee and, opening each letter, dictate his responses,
which the monks would type up and mail later that day.

On one such day, something remarkable happened. It had never happened before. It would last for months, and it would never happen again.
Here is Master's description of that morning:

Soon after we had placed the Nataraja Deity, my inner eye, within
the *ajna* chakra, was opened upon an array of great manuscripts, and
the inner library of Lord Subramaniam was seen. Upon each wish
and fancy, the librarian—a tall, fine, elegantly robed, bearded man—
would pull forth from one shelf or another great volumes and with
firm hands open and turn the pages to the proper place to be read. I
read these volumes one after another to the monastics at Sivashram

. . . .

While having morning coffee at Coco Palms Hotel, Master suddenly
encountered an astral plane librarian holding a large book with strange
scripts. He knew the meaning as his inner eye scanned each page. In
the months following, he dictated an entire book to his monks.

after this siddhi was obtained. They asked questions. The books were placed within the inner ether of my mind, the pages turned and read and enjoyed and understood. Thus, Siva's great diamond-dust-like darshan flooding out opened the inner door of our Lord Subramaniam's private library, which contains the records accrued since His arrival on this planet. Lord Subramaniam, the South Indian God also known as Karttikeya, Murugan, Skanda and Sanatkumara, has always been near and dear to us.

The venue of this remarkable clairvoyant happening was the garden restaurant of Coco Palms Hotel. As the librarian presented each volume and turned page after page, I dictated slowly to a sincere monastic scribe, who patiently and accurately wrote down each word. These were the days when cigarette smoke billowed forth from elite hotel guests at neighboring tables, clouding the atmosphere and creating an ambiance in which the akashic manuscripts could be clearly seen. The backdrop of Hawaiian music, the hubbub of people talking and the lower vibration of worldly feelings, too, helped screen out the conscious mind to make this clairvoyant siddhi a working reality.

On some days reams of pages were turned and read; on other days nothing was seen. Vigilantly, morning after morning, week after week, month after month, we sat waiting, while enjoying fruit, yogurt and coffee, for my inner eye to open on the inner-plane library. The restaurant was not in an ordinary location. Our table overlooked tropical ponds amid the island's largest coconut grove near the ocean on the east side of Kauai, the oldest and northernmost of the Hawaiian archipelago. Each day's writings, gleaned by my astral vision near the birthstone heiau, where royalty were birthed in olden times, were penned in letter-sized spiral notebooks. Before noon, we returned with them, following the sacred Wailua River four miles inland, to my ashram, now the site of Kadavul Hindu Temple.

What he returned with each day was a new chapter of the *Lemurian and Dravidian Shastras,* which was read only by the monks for twenty-four years before Master felt the world was ready and released it under the title *Lemurian Scrolls*. It was a revelation, a divine transmission that unfolded the early history of mankind in remarkable detail, how we came to this Earth four million years ago, the spiritual culture of early man, the mysteries of the kundalini and the Central Sun—focusing on the nature of life within ancient cloistered Saivite monasteries—how we lived in the

· ·

As Master reposed one morning, his third eye opened to see Lord Murugan, who lifted His Vel and struck it powerfully three times on a step, indicating that the six-foot-tall Siva Nataraja that had arrived from India should be placed "here."

ages now lost to human history.

Much of what was revealed to Master answered a need for traditional principles to effectively guide and govern his monasteries, provide a traditional pattern of Hindu ascetic life and catalyze his monks' spiritual unfoldment. These *Shastras*, along with the *Saivite Shastras*, an intimate

Meditating one morning at his San Francisco monastery,
Master Subramuniya suddenly found himself flying around
and around the room, with Lord Murugan flying at his side.
· ·

revelation that a group of devas wrote exclusively for Master's
monastic order, became a spiritual guideline that strengthened their faith and informed every dimension of their existence. The monks treasured the privilege and blessing of being
around Master as these superconscious revelations poured
through him each day, as the wisdom of the ages revealed
itself page by page by page; much like being with the rishis of
yore, they thought. Gurudeva told of those days:

The early revelations were enjoyed by *mathavasis* at Sivashram and shared with others at our branch monasteries via an
in-house teletype network, named *biniba* in Shum, our language of meditation. As the flow continued week after week,
mathavasis in San Francisco, California, and in Virginia City,
Nevada, gathered 'round to read the spellbinding messages
being clacked out on the piano-size communication devices.
The monks were able to type questions to me and receive my
responses in real time from Hawaii, thousands of miles away.
We enjoyed many philosophical discussions in this way.

As each volume finally drew to completion, it was typed
up by the scribe on an electric IBM typewriter, from which
a dozen or so copies were made and cased in plain, white,
softcover binding. One chapter was read daily at the meditation sessions to mold a new standard of selfless living in my
monasteries.

The devas said in their writings that there were many more
books to be read; but once the *Saivite Shastras* had been
completed, Master found it much more difficult to access the
library of Lord Subramaniam on the screen of his inner vision.
He struggled, in the face of external distractions, to keep this inner world
open to him.

Now we are starting our inner work in 1974 and I don't see a thing in
front of me on the screen. The devas must be off someplace. They are

finishing up their work with some of the students and devotees who visited Sivashram on the Ganesha pilgrimage. Now I'm beginning to see the glimmering light in the blue akasha, shimmering gold and silver lights reflecting off each other, dancing around in front of my forehead. This is seen with the third eye and I also see feelings, and entanglements, thoughts that have been blocking the vision due to the new guests and retreatants, who are fading into the distance as the shimmering lights take over. I have been working for three days now to get into this state, which was wide open for many months in 1973 when the shastric books were seen.

While Master's mystic explorations never stopped, they changed dramatically at this point. Rather than clairvoyantly reading akashic books, he communicated clairaudiently with three or four great devas to receive their advice and insights on current affairs that concerned him. These messages were vast and varied, from lofty dissertations on temple mysticism to earthy insights into the karmas of the newest monastic candidate.

Most central were the communications with an overlord who last lived on Earth as an aristocrat 10,000 years ago. When called upon, he provided guidance, especially about the future, pointing out the best direction to be taken and speaking, in transcendental tones, of the importance of the work in which Master was engaged. This rishi's messages, often the most profound and precious of all, were carefully written in a notebook or scribbled on a napkin in some tea shop in Japan, at a coffee table in Madras or in a cozy corner of Master's own office at the monastery.

During a session on Kauai on September 14, 1983, the monastic scribe asked how the devas work with the holy ash prasadam of Kadavul Temple that the monastery sends to devotees in the mail. The rishi responded:

With prasadam we are there, and with shakti we are there. The prasadam opens a channel, a long-lasting channel, between us at Kadavul and the devotee. The *vibhuti* especially holds the vibration. You have an open channel between you and certain temples in India. This is because the *vibhuti* from those temples is at the Aadheenam. Generously fill the homes with *vibhuti* from Kadavul, and they will draw on the shakti from Kadavul Nataraja and the open channel will remain wide and clear. Try to obtain your *vibhuti* from a certain place where it is made in the traditional way. The *vibhuti* is the voice of Kadavul. Give full amounts in your prasadam bags, not just a stingy little

• •

On rare occasions, Gurudeva received messages from the Gods of Saivism, poetic and sometimes cryptic verses from God Siva, Hanuman, Murugan and Ganesha. He dutifully wrote down and followed all such celestial decrees.

bit. And the guru's *vibhuti* pouches should be fat and overflowing.

The knowledge shared by Master's band of great devas was limited only by the quality and depth of the questions asked. It was not unusual, once a strong connection was made, for the devas to linger for an hour or more, and for Master to ask every now and again, "Any more questions?" The queries focused on current events, issues, people, philosophical queries and problems of the day. Master received invaluable, practical guidance for every aspect of his mission in these sessions, and the monks with him experienced a rare glimpse into another world, a world so familiar to Master, just as real as this world—more, he might say. He explained the way these beings of the inner worlds work to assist sincere aspirants who are incarcerated in physical bodies.

There are well-trained devas in the astral plane who work very closely to the Earth, seeing to the needs of all devotees worldwide. Devas who headquarter at Kauai Aadheenam's Kadavul Koyil attend the satsang *homa* held within the mission houses, dharmashalas and temples and monasteries of our members. This inner network of Mahadevas and devas, swamis, yogis, *natyams,* sadhakas, brahmacharis, brahmacharinis, mothers, fathers, children, in a divine way all work together. This is Saivism. This is Saiva Siddhanta. This is the Natha Sampradaya in action. This is how it was in the past when Saivism flourished all over this planet. This is how it is today. And this is how it will be in the future.

Fascinated with Master's helpers on the other side of the mind, the monks wondered what the rishi they had been hearing from looked like. One day in 1996 Master announced, "Rishi just appeared. I see him sitting there in white robes. He looks very nice. 'Greetings,' he said with a wave of his hand. Here is his message:"

It is time to be concentrated, precise and rigid. We have accumulated much, and more than is needed, knowledge for the future and all time.

Inner plane devas frequently guided Gurudeva, answering his questions and those of the monks, offering practical counsel and even helping to find lost items. He received their messages clairaudiently or by thought transference.

It has to be edited back, reexplained when necessary, and lived. (Master: "Different ones are lining up [to talk]. Any questions?" Master comments, "He looks a little younger," and the rishi responds:)

You are making me young by responding. It is lonely here sometimes in bliss. We have only the fullness of our Self, the company of our perceptions. Those in bliss don't talk to each other. There is no communication here. What is there to talk about when each of us knows what the others know? So, it is a welcome event to help out the unknowing. (Now he sits back and relaxes as if to say, "What do you want to know?" with a big smile on his face. "What *loka* are you in?" asks one monk.) In the Brahmaloka. And it is a nice place to be. Very active, harmonious, productive. Here everything that you have and use is conceived. This is the world of conception.

One of the strongest messages the *Shastras* brought for the monks was the value, meaning and absolute necessity of strict celibacy, brahmacharya, in monastic life. The devas gave detailed guidelines, including special sadhanas for those who had lived with women. Only those who had not lived too promiscuously could enter the swami order. Gurudeva addressed that theme in his Master Course trilogy, drawing a passage from *The Book of Virtue,* part of the shastric books he had clairvoyantly read.

Brahmacharya is holding the power of the Divine within the core of the individual spine so that, as Lord Siva sends His power through the five great winds of the astral body within the physical body, the winds adjust among themselves and emanate a shakti strong enough to adjust the five great psychic fluids within everyone around. This power of brahmacharya is accrued and disseminated through subli- mation, then transmutation, of the sexual force. Transmutation occurs automatically through regular daily sadhana, the rigors of positive living and adherence to the ceremonial customs of our religion. Ide- ally, brahmacharya begins at puberty for virgins and continues on until marriage. Otherwise, brahmacharya sadhana begins after the last sexual encounter with a member of the opposite sex has occurred and when a conscious decision is made to begin the practice of brahmacharya.

On rare occasions through the decades, Master blessed his monks with insights into their previous births, sitting alone with them for hours as the devas recounted in exquisite detail a series of lives the monk once lived, accomplishments made, and how the monk would contribute to Master's mission in this current incarnation. One learned of lives as a Chinese printer, an early American leader and an explorer.

While traveling with a swami on a month-long journey in India in 1982, Master brought through such knowledge one evening in New Delhi. At the dinner table, a deva made contact with Master, identify- ing himself as the muse of the hotel astrologer, and invited questions. For the next hour, Master unfolded details of three of the monk's past lives, guiding the session by explaining that the deva required that the monk write down each question he had. Then, standing behind the monk, the deva would read the question and respond, telling of previous lives as a sadhu in India and a merchant in Europe, and of his future in the Order. Master noted that the deva did not speak in words as some devas do, but rather projected his ideas as thought forms. The travelers from Hawaii had passed, several times, the doorway of the astrologer's office in the hotel, and been inexplicably attracted to the sign on the door. At the end of the evening, Master handed the monk fifty rupees and instructed him to slide the bills under the astrologer's door as payment for the reading, so that all the karmas of the interchange would be rightly balanced. For Master, it was money well spent.

These experiences with the devas built strong the faith of the monastics, helping them become strong, dynamic soldiers of the within. The devas themselves gave assurance in their messages that they were there to assist and empower them on the monastic path.

When a new *natyam* or sadhaka enters one of our monasteries, his life pattern is perceived, understood and digested. The *natyam's* or sadhaka's karma is absorbed into the total group karma of all the monasteries, missions and individual devotees. Once he has taken his vows, received sandalwood beads, each flower placed upon an altar, every camphor flame and act of religiousness performed by anyone of any mission or monastery any place in the world melts away some of the *natyam's* or sadhaka's karma. This is because of his supreme act of dedicating himself as a servant, a slave, a Sivanadiyar of the great Mahadevas of our Saivite religion. True, there will be things that come up within his personal life to be worked out, but there will be many helping hands from the Sivaloka, the Devaloka, Kauai Aadheenam, Kadavul Koyil, his own monastery in which he lives and from the surrounding mission, to help him through the turmoil.

One day at the monastery the monks who were growing food in the garden were invited to consult with the "garden devas." Here is an excerpt:

We have fun. If you want to work with us, just have fun. If you want to have fun, just work with us. Do surprises; we like that. Hiding an okra seed in a cabbage patch, now that's fun. And don't make everything the same, and don't eat the same food all the time. If all people were the same, that would be no fun. Don't line us all up the same in every line. Grow things in patches, slip in a few surprises, and we'll have a ball. As you find many varieties of people, so you find many plants in the garden.

Now, the lettuce, it doesn't like to be near the cabbage. Not even close. There's a whole group of cabbages, the cabbage family, that should all be stuck away in one corner of the garden, far from the lettuce.

Plant things in the lettuce patch that taste good with lettuce. Radishes and onions and lettuce—like that. Have fun with it, but keep the cabbage away from the lettuce. Lettuce has no taste, so grow what helps it taste good.

Master did not want the monks to make much of this side of his life—partly because he saw it as normal and unexceptional, the way a great artist takes his virtuosity for granted, and partly because he knew that devotees would focus on all that magical stuff instead of on their own spiritual growth through sadhana to the Self within. So, these little events, the common coin within the walls of his monastery, never were published, never were reported on the website. Each monk had the blessings of his encounters, to be kept sacred and secret.

Still, Master did openly, though sparingly, share his inner world with his dear monks, knowing it would be a source of inspiration to them, lifting the veil a bit, revealing another realm of human possibility that ordinary pilgrims on the path rarely get to visit. He would say these are the natural faculties of every human being, waiting deep inside to be unfolded. He would say such things are both our natural heritage and a troublesome distraction from the real work of Self Realization, a two-sided sword that can pull us inward if we accept it with tempered enthusiasm or push us farther from our goal if we become enchanted with the supernatural and the occult and take it on the ego. This balance was, for him, essential, for he was immersed in the supernatural from the beginning, and worked hard to not let it define him or his mission.

Chapter Twenty-Five

Building a Saiva Stronghold

T he power of the Kadavul Siva Temple became supreme following the installation of the Lord Nataraja Deity in 1973. The name *Kadavul*, from Tamil, is among the oldest names of Lord Siva, literally meaning "He who is immanent and transcendent" or "He who is within and without." Humble in its physicality, the temple had a life-transforming shakti from the start, the natural convergence of Master's vision, Siva's presence and Murugan's yogic thrust. It was, Master said, a fire temple, for fire is the element of change, of reformation and even annihilation. Some people entered the temple and began to weep uncontrollably. They would come in one state and leave in another, their lives changed in large and small ways. So potent its energies became that Master would in later years, just for a time, allow only vegetarians to enter, seeing that others were too overwhelmed by the energy, overcome by the transformative tsunami of shakti.

The monks found themselves awash in this new energy. Many were thrown into a turbulent time of discipline, change, inner purification and *tapas*, their tears watery testaments of the trials the guru set for them. This intensity launched a difficult time for the entire Order, a time of transition and of affirming commitments to their vows as Saivite monastics. It was a time of adjustment, as well, to the directions provided by the *Shastras* and to Master Subramuniya's stern demands, his uncompromising expectations of their ideal life, their most perfect dharma. "No one said monastic life would be easy," he would console.

He created a Flow Book which defined, in minute detail, how a Saivite monk should live, respond, learn, converse, cook, clean, perform chores, take direction, dress, eat, sleep, meditate, worship, surrender, get along with others. Each entry was signed in his own hand, to authenticate his acceptance. Every facet of life was described in the Flow Book, and the satguru's every guideline, called a flow, was to be followed—always and without exception, ever and without excuse.

The searing shakti of Kadavul Temple, the satguru's renewed call for

On Kauai island—which, he loved to quip, "is surrounded completely by water"—Master established Kadavul Temple, shipping in six-foot-tall granite murtis *of Ganesha and Murugan, a bronze Nataraja, a 16-ton Nandi and the world's largest crystal Sivalingam.*

. . . .

the elimination of habits and attitudes unbecoming of a Saivite monastic and the new requirement that all members of the Order be full, formal, proud Hindus all conspired to cause unprecedented uncertainties among the monks. Master made it plain that a total severance of all previous religious ties was necessary. This was to be an order of purely Saivite renunciates. It was an extraordinarily brave and demanding requirement.

Some may have come to be with a kind of Eastern messiah. Some may have thought themselves universalists beyond the pale of religion, any religion. Others may have simply discovered the limits of their will to change. Whatever the causes, many left. One and then another. Two and then three more, again and again—back to their families, back to their personal karmas, back to who they were before they entered the monastic path. It began first with the monks and then the members being

asked, "What religion are you?" and "What religion do you think Master is teaching?" This was a time of great upheaval, with half the monastic order leaving, and a similar percentage of lay members.

From a worldly point of view, the departures were catastrophic, like a devastating tornado sweeping through a neighborhood and blowing half the infrastructure to the horizon. All that training, all that dedication, gone. So what was Master's reaction to it? He rejoiced. He thanked Siva for sending all these men away, men who, with their doubts, would have brought the Order harsher karmas in the years ahead. With that prospect gone, he called for a party!

America's First Aadheenam

In the early hours of February 15, 1975, lying on a tatami mat in his Ryo-kan room, Master was having one of those profound sleeps that is neither awake nor full of dreams. In that clear space above physical consciousness,

On February 15, 1975, Master had a three-part vision of God Siva
which would culminate in the founding of his Iraivan Siva Temple.
In it he saw Siva walking in a valley with devotees, then he saw
Siva's face close up, then seated on a svayambhu *Sivalingam.*

Page 511

Chapter 25

. . . .

the 48-year-old satguru experienced a threefold vision that would be the spiritual birth of the great Siva citadel called Iraivan Temple and its surrounding San Marga Sanctuary.

> I saw Lord Siva walking in the meadow near the Wailua River. His face was looking into mine. Then He was seated upon a great stone. I was seated on His left side. This was the vision. It became more vivid as the years passed. Upon reentering Earthly consciousness, I felt certain that the great stone was somewhere on our monastery land and set about to find it.
>
> Guided from within by my satguru, I hired a bulldozer and instructed the driver to follow me as I walked to the north edge of the property that was then a tangle of buffalo grass and wild guava. I hacked my way through the jungle southward as the bulldozer cut a path behind me. After almost half a mile, I sat down to rest near a small tree. Though there was no wind, suddenly the tree's leaves shimmered as if in the excitement of communication. I said to the tree, "What is your message?" In reply, my attention was directed to a spot just to the right of where I was sitting.
>
> When I pulled back the tall grass, there was a large rock—the self-created Lingam on which Lord Siva had sat. A stunningly potent vibration was felt. The bulldozer's trail now led exactly to the sacred stone, surrounded by five smaller boulders. San Marga, the "straight or pure path" to God, had been created. An inner voice proclaimed, "This is the place where the world will come to pray." San Marga symbolizes each soul's journey to liberation through union with God.

That vision must have wrought profound changes in Master's interior world, for it certainly was the seed of profound changes on the outside. Immediately he embarked on a long journey that would bring Saivism deeply into the lives of his followers and build not only a temple to honor his life-changing vision, but a traditional *aadheenam* like the great ones he had visited in South India just three years before.

Master had observed there was no such temple/monastery complex in

all of the West for Hindus and threw himself into its creation. With no
authorities to guide, he searched within for the systems of spiritual and material management and crafted an astonishing set of procedures and flows to guide every aspect of his several institutions, and to inform the monks' lives and relationships. At this point Master changed the name of his headquarters from Sivashram to Kauai Aadheenam, which, for the sake of local islanders, he also called Kauai's Hindu Monastery.

His travels diminished as he began to set roots deep in the Kauai soil. Under his instructions, the senior monks began a thorough study of Saiva Siddhanta and its relationship with and difference from Adi Shankara's Advaita Vedanta. Rishi Tirumular's *Tirumantiram* and Saint Tiruvalluvar's *Tirukural,* the seminal spiritual texts of Saiva Siddhanta, were translated, memorized and commented upon in his inspired talks. He commissioned the carving of life-sized granite murtis of Tirumular and Tiruvalluvar in South India and brought them to the monastery, giving visual form to their psychic and theological presence.

Late in the 1970s Master had two magnificent, six-foot-tall murtis, the portly Ganesha and the noble Murugan atop His peacock, carved by renowned master architect Nilamegam Sthapati in Mahabalipuram. In February, 1979, they arrived from India, and Master had them installed in Kadavul Hindu Temple on June 1. On a remote American island, Saivite Hinduism was being fully grounded in the West, every aspect of it—not a modern American version of Hinduism, thought by some to be a logical, even inevitable, evolution, but the complete, unabridged Hinduism that has been followed for millennia.

A 32,000-pound black stone Nandi was also brought to Kauai to sit outside Kadavul Temple in perpetual adoration of Lord Siva, making TV's Channel Nine news, which opened the piece with the tongue-in-cheek headline "16 Tons of Bull." The enormous sculpture, ordered in 1976, took four years for Nilamegam Sthapati to complete, arriving finally on August 16, 1980. He confided to the monks that Nandi, the "joyous one," ranked among the finest creations of his lifetime. The huge granite bull—six feet tall, nine feet long and five feet wide—was the largest carved in India in the 20th century and among the five largest ever carved.

For the next decade Kadavul Temple pulsated with a palpable shakti that sustained the monastery and changed the lives of all who visited. With the basic elements of the temple in place, Master allowed no further construction until the fall of 1984. Then he marshalled a major construction effort reminiscent of the early 70s, landscaping around the temple,

· ·

Convinced he could find the Sivalingam that had appeared in his vision, Master hired a bulldozer, instructing the driver to follow him into the dense undergrowth, carving a trail through the trees that would become the San Marga path.

putting in hundreds of feet of concrete paths, lining Kadavul's bare concrete block walls with lava rock inside and out, tiling walls, floors and ceiling and installing shelves for the 108 bronze *tandava* murtis, depicting Siva in 108 dance poses, that he had specially cast in South India.

March of 1985 marked the traditional twelve-year point in the life of Hindu temples when refurbishing and repairs are permitted, prior to a grand reconsecration ritual. You might call it a full restarting of the system, in which the energy is actually removed from the temple during extensive *homas*, and then placed back inside once physical improvements are complete. Master tried it out, this one time.

Two priests, one from Madurai and another from Bangalore, performed elaborate rites that took the power of the temple Deities into special *kumbhas*, which were then transferred to a temporary *yagasala*

If a Christian asked to be his devotee, Master would send that person back to his church elders for their blessings and a formal release. Stealing from religious flocks was such an anathema to him that he created an ethical form of conversion.

Page 515
Chapter 25

. . . .

constructed under a nearby banyan tree.

The effect of the three-day ceremony was not subtle; it was as if the Earth had slipped off its axis. The feeling was eerie, unsettled, downright spooky. The temple, emptied of is spiritual potency, felt like an abandoned warehouse, a feeling Master and the monks did not enjoy. The weather went wild with horizonal rains, thunder, lightning and howling winds. The monastery was upset as never before. Master vowed to never do this again, even though it is traditionally required every twelve years. It took months until the *sannidhya* was restored.

Building a Yoga Order

Naming each year had long been Master's way of setting a direction for everyone. He called 1974 "The Year of the Guru" and 1975 "The Year of the Monastics," his way of informing one and all that all would be working on the guru-shishya relationship. Training and more training. The monks did everything themselves, as was once done in India, where today much of a matha's care is given into the hands of overseers, cooks, groundskeepers, carpenters and accountants. Not at Kauai Aadheenam. Virtually every task was done by the monks, who took great joy in the ideals of self-sufficiency and the diverse skill set that emerged. It was hard work.

The monks were challenged and corrected, not always softly, and were expected to respond, expected to receive the correction in a nondefensive spirit and use it to change and improve their lives. Those who threw it back, who cried, "Unfair," soon learned that such tactics did not work. Obey the guru; that worked. Eschew self-defense and stop blaming the blamer; that worked. Change yourself and don't demand others to do the same; that worked, too.

Years later Master would smile while explaining that the monks were all soft and gentle, harmonious and kindly, and that they had gotten that way in much the same manner a jeweler polishes gems. Rough gems are thrown into a turning vat and allowed to tumble for days against one another, each being an agent of abrasion for all the others, each losing its own sharp edges by constant collisions. In such a way, the monks—living together, working together, struggling and learning together, meditating and worshiping together under the guru's direction—each slowly became a polished gem. Differently faceted, of different colors, but all gems. All due, they knew, to the guru's grace.

These years of working with the monks led Master to stress the artisan-apprentice system of training. Older monks, with their accumulated skills, were assigned to train the younger ones, and the younger to serve and learn under their elders. In time, this evolved into what Master called the *kulam* system, the overall architecture of monastery management of duties and responsibilities. *Kulam* means "family" in the Tamil language and, by extension, describes a group of monks in the same field of expertise and service. Five *kulams* emerged, each called by one of Lord Ganesha's names, each an independent team responsible for an aspect of the monastery's daily routine: temple/kitchen (Lambodara); members' nurturing/teaching (Ekadanta); administration/finance (Pillaiyar); buildings/grounds (Siddhidatta); and publications (Ganapati).

The monks were sent to India and Sri Lanka for longer periods during this time, to absorb, learn, immerse themselves in Saivism and in the worship of God Siva at His great temples. Master had them work on the scriptures, learn Siva puja from the Sivacharyas, experience the magic that is India—and the culture, which he regarded as the world's most sublime. With the monks well established in the faith, he made another major move.

The Conversion Conundrum

"I have paid my debt to my countrymen. Henceforth, I live in service to Tamil Saivites throughout the world." With these words, spoken to all assembled in the San Francisco Temple on January 5, 1977 (his 50th *jayanti*), Master Subramuniya formally and finally retired from public ministry in the West. He knew from experience that commitment to a single spiritual path is essential to the deepest goals of life, and those who waffled or straddled or hedged would not get far. So, he determined not to be guru to the curious and the uncommitted, choosing to dedicate the remainder of his lifetime in service to the Saivite religion and the greater glory of God Siva, the Gods and his satguru, Siva Yogaswami. No more public lectures. No more explaining for the umpteenth time what yoga means.

Again, some of the monks, even some who had been close for decades, left the Order, unable to follow where Master was leading. Though initially it was one of his rare disappointments, this winnowing process proved part of a larger plan. Those who stayed were whole-heartedly dedicated to fulfilling Master's mission. This created a harmony and one-pointedness that could not previously have been achieved, or even imagined. The lesson was not lost on the monks: the strength of an organization depends on its members' level of commitment; in more general terms, quality is more important than quantity.

For the last two decades Master had taught the highest truths of advaita, the Self God, to students with non-Hindu backgrounds. The real-world trials and tribulations through the years had convinced him that in order to have these lofty teachings bear fruit in his students, they must fully embrace the Hindu religion and culture, eschewing all others. He saw the power of one-minded commitment to a path, and the infinite distractions that face anyone who has not the strength of such focus. The loftiest of human spiritual summits was only for the strong and the sure-footed.

For years Master had seen the effects of divided loyalties, those who kept their Christian names and a few beliefs while adopting a Hindu lifestyle and nickname. It did not work; it divided the person, evoking a religious schizophrenia. One should decide who one is, fully and forever, as he had done. Never mind what family or community might think.

Thus, in 1977, he intensified requirements for his Western devotees to sever all prior religious, philosophical loyalties, legalize their Hindu names and formally enter Hinduism through the name-giving rite, upholding the same standard that he required of his monks. To exemplify the ideal he was asking of them, he dropped the name Master and adopted a traditional Hindu name for a spiritual preceptor: Gurudeva.

This all went against the grain of many in the Hindu world, who cringed at the word *conversion.* But he explained that conversion is nothing new for Hinduism. The advent of Jainism and Buddhism in India in 600 bce resulted in the conversion of millions of Hindus. Centuries later, revivals resulted in the reconversion of millions of Jains and Buddhists. In modern times, conversion to or from Hinduism remains a major issue, often resulting in extreme disharmony within families and towns. We have Hindus switching as a result of enticement or deception. We have Indians who converted wanting to return to Hinduism. And we have non-Hindus from lands outside India requesting formal entrance into the faith, including those who have married a Hindu.

Gurudeva addressed each of these issues, ultimately formalizing his experience and suggestions for "ethical conversion" in the book *How to Become a Hindu.* Most conversions in religion, he observed, are forced or wrongly motivated. Catholics stealing from the Jewish flock, Muslims converting from among the Baptists, Mormons and Pentecostals harvesting souls—that awful phrase—aggressively from them all. Gurudeva thought religions should respect each other. If, say, a Jewish boy wanted to convert, he should be encouraged by his new spiritual advisors to seek the blessings of his rabbi, not run away from the synagogue in the dark of night.

As with his approach to most topics, he started with a mystical insight. In ancient times, people tended to reincarnate right within the same village and religion time and again. "Now," he said, "with modern-day travel and worldwide communication, this tightly knit pattern of reincarnation is dispersed, and souls find new bodies in different countries, families and religions which, in some cases, are foreign to them."

For such a person, the "Eastern soul in a Western body," he proposed a thoughtful and peaceful method of self-conversion. He required his devotees wanting to convert from a previous faith to study that faith and explain convincingly, point by point, why they no longer held its beliefs. He sent them back to their churches, synagogues, even previous Hindu gurus, to attend services for a while and speak with their ministers. Every chance was given for them to change their mind, or to have someone change it for them.

If they passed this test, they were required to demonstrate their knowledge of Hinduism through a series of exams, legalize their new Hindu first and last name, then enter the faith formally through the name-giving rite, *namakarana* samskara, in an established temple. The name was important to Gurudeva, and he insisted his shishyas put their legal name on all documents—passport, driver's license, bank accounts, everything—a requirement for Church membership to this day. Seeing the tendency of many groups to keep the birth name and informally adopt a Saivite Hindu name, and the dual identities provoked by toggling between the two, he insisted on a single, formal, legal Saivite name, and would settle for nothing less. In early years he had long-time members help newcomers make this transition, but eventually he required those interested in his teachings to do it all on their own strength and motivation.

There were many among his devotees who had no previous religion, even though they grew up in the West. These seekers were allowed to adopt Hinduism as their first religion, through the study of it and the name-giving ceremony, without the need to convert. Gurudeva strongly enjoined Hindus of the broader community to welcome sincere Western converts and adoptives into their midst and not shun or ignore them, as is often done.

. . . .

The great debate of the 80s centered around the two schools of Saiva Siddhanta. Gurudeva's own realizations were in consonance with Saint Tirumular, who spoke of the nondual union of Siva and the soul, while many Saivites took the side of Saint Meykandar, whose pluralistic teachings decreed an eternal separateness of God and soul.

Those who undertook this serious conversion to Hinduism went through a great fire which transformed them forever, hardened their commitments, purified their loyalties and made them some of the strongest Hindus in the world. This strictness was radically different from the stance of all other Hindu and quasi-Hindu groups, most of which required little or nothing by way of real change or commitment. Gurudeva would jest that they abhorred "the C word," that today's seekers are deeply committed to remaining uncommitted. This would set his followers apart and make them leaders. Years later, Hindu philosopher and writer Ram Swarup, who met Gurudeva and his shishyas and contributed articles to HINDUISM TODAY, wrote of them in *The Observer,* New Delhi, 1998:

> They are not NRIs. They are mainly white Americans—converts, Hindus by choice, and some are sannyasins at that. Those of us Hindu by birth tend to take Hinduism for granted and neglect its deeper, spiritual categories. But it is different with those who embrace it after much reflection and self-searching. They are seekers and sadhakas; they are interested in the problems of God, of Self, of inner life, of dharma and mukti.

The year 1979 began with a whirlwind week of Guru Jayanti celebrations that included over twenty *namakarana* samskaras conducted in Kadavul Hindu Temple. Devotees receiving this name-giving sacrament, marking their entrance into the Saivite Hindu religion, had studied for several years with Himalayan Academy. Many had completed arduous severance procedures from their former religions. It was a landmark event in American history.

In the coming years, after hundreds of self-conversions and *namakarana* samskaras, Gurudeva became content with his fellowship, proud of its strict adherence to dharma. Thereafter, he only reluctantly took others into the faith—and only if they knocked the door down with their urgent sincerity. He had crafted a Hindu community in the West, built it from scratch, and spent the rest of his life from within the confines of Hinduism with little connection to the merely curious, giving his energies to those who had made a full commitment to the Hindu dharma.

The vision of the future was clear in Gurudeva's mind. In it, Saivite Hinduism held a place of honor alongside the other faiths. Hindu families in the West were strong and integrated, supportive of one another and firm in their spiritual commitments. Working toward that future, he assembled all of the elements, one by one, giving large tasks to his monks.

Under his direction, they developed family codes of conduct and discipline, ministerial guidelines, children's study courses, Hindu hymnals and rites of passage to guide Hindus from conception to death. He crafted certificates to qualify lay chaplains and school teachers, developed a Saivite homeschooling program and wrote lessons to guide teens through their difficult years. The Hindu Businessmen's Association was created to bring stability to Hindu entrepreneurs and the Hindu Women's Liberation Council to give a forum to women.

His vision encompassed the East as well, for he saw a lack of training there, too, especially for children. In Alaveddy, Sri Lanka, his Subramuniya Ashram initiated a highly successful series of classes in spoken English for children, along with classes in music, dance, art, *Tirumantiram* and *Devaram* hymns.

He propounded the need for national and even international councils of Hindu organizations to aid in forwarding and sharing the knowledge of experience and experiment among the thousands of Hindu congregations that he saw would one day dot the landscape of the United States, Canada, Britain, South Africa, Europe and Asia. While no such communities existed at the time, his vision would manifest in a mere thirty years. To tie far-flung groups together, Gurudeva worked hard to reestablish the monastic printing facilities, bringing equipment from Nevada to Kauai and founding a newspaper, *The New Saivite World,* which gave news of Saivism around the world.

In doing this work, Gurudeva had precious little help. Those who knew the tradition were on the other side of a non-Interneted world and not much able to guide. This drove him within, to seek the guidance of Yogaswami; and in dozens of crucial moments, that guidance flooded forth. Gurudeva would frequently tell the monks that Yogaswami visited in a vision or meditation, gave bold instructions to do this, to avoid that, to initiate a project or let another go. Yogaswami was his connection to the true Saiva path, and Gurudeva assiduously followed every hint, however subtle, that came from his guru.

One day, Gurudeva reported, Yogaswami gave a three-word order with no explanation: "Don't be equivocal!" Gurudeva asked the monks, "What does equivocal mean?" Hearing that it means to be uncertain and full of ambiguity, he immediately undertook a style of expression that was direct, firm and clear, without possibility for misinterpretation or unclarity. His closeness to the guru who had left his body some fifteen years earlier was a lesson to the monks, and an inspiration.

Two Tamil Treasures

By the late 70s Gurudeva, the white-haired American Hindu mystic, had effectively established an *aadheenam,* a traditional Tamil Saiva monastery-temple complex, the first ever in the West. He was officially the pontiff, the *mahasannidhanam,* of Kauai Aadheenam, and he took it as his charge to rearticulate Saiva Siddhanta for a new era, using modern English. In doing so, he rejected Puranic stories and the epics, which he, perhaps alone among Hindu leaders, boldly decried as philosophically inconsistent and mistakenly elevated to the status of scripture.

He must have felt the authority of this spiritual seat, for he spoke with imposing certitude, and each of his declarations and edicts rang true to all who were with him. The works he produced in this period were full of fire and force, pure expositions, mystically authentic expressions of his guru's religion. In a flattering twist, his writings found avid friends among the Tamil Saiva elite and were translated into Tamil, propounded as the clearest articulation of Saiva Siddhanta in modern times in any language. Dr. B. Natarajan, S. Ramaseshan, S. Shanmugasundaram and others were among the translators.

Gurudeva promoted the yogic perspective of monistic theism, the religious theology, also known as panentheism, that embraces both monism and theism, two perspectives sometimes considered contradictory or mutually exclusive. He brought uncommon clarity to the pivotal Hindu concepts of karma and reincarnation, affirming that all souls are intrinsically good, that all karmas can be resolved, that Realization, as he had experienced it, can be attained, and that liberation from the cycles of birth and death is indeed possible.

He propounded Saiva Siddhanta's four-stage path to God, consisting of charya (service), kriya (worship), yoga (meditation) and jnana (wisdom). These stages, he said, are successive and cumulative, each one preparing for the next. He extolled temples and elucidated proper ways of worship. He also laid out in detail the disciplines of monastic and family life, including specific instructions about the control of sexual force. So that people could "catch the overview" of the world's oldest religion, he summarized Hinduism in nine beliefs and Saivism in twelve. He put forward the *Vedas* and *Agamas* as Hinduism's primary and revealed scriptures, but also acknowledged secondary scriptures like the *Tirumantiram* by Tirumular and the *Tirukural* by Tiruvalluvar (both ca 200 bce).

In India during Tiruvalluvar's time there was neither paper nor pens, so writing was accomplished with a stylus, the characters being scraped or scratched into a specially prepared leaf, called an *olai* leaf. Many ancient scriptures and literature were produced in this manner, and it is amazing that some of the original writings so made still exist today. Certainly no modern-day paper would have withstood the centuries so well!

Again and again, he brought forward the traditional path of Saiva Samayam, and taught his monks, and later the lay families, the nuances of that path, its vocabulary and theology. Clearly, he wanted Yogaswami's path to be deeply imbedded in his shishyas. Introducing the two life-sized statues which he had installed on the monastery grounds, Gurudeva described his view of these two cardinal scriptures in glowing terms.

The statue of Saint Tirumular shows him sitting in the lotus posture, deep in meditation, while Saint Tiruvalluvar is seated with a small writing table on his lap composing his sacred verses with stylus in hand. His *Tirukural* speaks on virtuous living. It gives us the keys to a happy and harmonious life in the world, but it doesn't give any insights into the nature of God, whereas, the *Tirumantiram* delves into the nature of God, man and the universe in its depths. Taken together, they speak to all Hindus and offer guidance for every aspect of religious life, the first addressing itself to the achievement of virtue, wealth and love, while the second concerns itself with attainment of moksha, or liberation.

The *Tirumantiram* is a mystical book and a difficult book. The original text is written in metered verse, composed in the ancient Tamil language. Saint Tirumular is the first one to codify Saiva Siddhanta, the final conclusions, and the first one to use the term "Saiva Siddhanta." It is a document upon which the entire religion could stand, if it had to. It is one of the oldest scriptures known to man. I was very happy to find that all my own postulations, gathered from realization, are confirmed in this great work. That is why this book is so meaningful to me—as a verification of personal experience and a full statement of the philosophical fortress erected and protected by our guru parampara.

His 1978 talk, "*Tirumantiram*, Fountainhead of Saiva Siddhanta," excerpted here, is a glimpse into his emphasis on this sacred text:

One of the oldest of the preserved theologies of Saivism available to us today is that of Saint Tirumular. Of course, his was not the first theology, just one of the oldest to be preserved. He did not start anything new. His work, the *Tirumantiram*, is only a few hundred years older than the New Testament. He codified Saivism as he knew it. He recorded its tenets in concise and precise verse form, drawing upon his own realizations of the truths it contained. His work is not an intellectual construction, and it is not strictly a devotional canon either. It is based in yoga. It exalts and explains yoga as the kingly science leading man to knowledge of himself. Yet it contains theological doctrine and devotional hymns. It is the full expression of man's search, encompassing the soul, the intellect and the emotions.

Saint Tirumular was a Himalayan rishi, a siddha, sent on mission to South India to spread the purest teachings of Saivism to the people there. Hinduism is a missionary religion. Everyone within it, myself included, is on a mission or is purifying himself through sadhana enough so that he can be given a mission for the religion from some great soul, or a God, perhaps. This is the pattern within Saivism, and Saint Tirumular's mission was to summarize and thereby renew and reaffirm at one point in time the final conclusions of the Sanatana Dharma, the purest Saiva path, Saiva Siddhanta.

Today we hear the term *Siddhanta,* and various meanings of the word may come to mind. For some, perhaps their immediate thought would be Meykanda Devar and his interpretation of Saiva Siddhanta. For others, some concept of a philosophy halfway between Advaita-Vedanta and Dvaita, a vague area of unclarity, and for others various literal translations of the word such as "true end," "final end" or "true conclusion."

The term *Siddhanta* appears for the first time in the *Tirumantiram*. The word *anta* carries the connotation of goal/conclusion, as does the English word *end*. Tirumular's specific use of the word was "the teachings and the true conclusions of the *Saiva Agamas*." And these he felt were identical with Vedanta or "the conclusions of the *Upanishads*." In fact, he makes it very clear that pure Saiva Siddhanta must be based on Vedanta. Siddhanta is specific, giving the sadhanas and practical disciplines which bring one to the final Truth. Vedanta is general, simply declaring in broad terms the final Truth that is the goal of all paths.

There are those who would intellectually divide Siddhanta from Vedanta, thus cutting off the goal from the means to that goal. But our

. . . .

Here is depicted the human spiritual path, with Saivite, Vaishnavite, Buddhist, Sikh, Christian, Muslim, Jewish, Jain and Taoist seekers. All these and more faiths are respected by Saivism, which sets no limits for its tolerance.

guru parampara holds them to be not different. How can we consider the mountain path less important than the summit to which it leads us? Both are one. Siddhanta and Vedanta are one also, and both are contained in Saiva Siddhanta. That is the conclusion of scripture and the conclusion of my own experiences as well. The Suddha Siddhanta of Saiva Siddhanta is Vedanta.

Vedanta was never meant to stand alone, apart from worship, apart from religious tradition. It has only been taken in that way since Swami Vivekananda brought it to the West. The Western man and Western-educated Eastern man have tried in modern Vedanta to secularize traditional Sanatana Dharma, to take the philosophical conclusions of the Hindu religion and set them apart from the religion itself, apart from charya and kriya, service and devotion. Vedantists who are members of other religions have unintentionally sought to adopt only the highest philosophy of Hinduism to the exclusion of the rich customs, observances and temple worship. They have not fully realized that these must precede yoga for yoga to be truly successful. Orthodox Hindus understand these things in a larger perspective. These same problems of misinterpretation must have existed even in Saint Tirumular's time, for he writes that "The pure and illustrious Siddhanta is Vedanta" (Verse 1422). "The bhakta of the eulogized Suddha Saivam is the eternal one. He is the blemishless jnani and ruler of radiant jnana. He is the truly liberated, in whom wisdom has dawned and who is stable in the middle position of the Vedanta-Siddhanta teachings" (Verse 1428).

It may be that Saint Tirumular pioneered the reconciliation of Vedanta and Siddhanta. But what is the Vedanta that Tirumular was referring to? Shankara, with his exposition of Vedanta, was not to come for many centuries. Thus, concepts such as Nirguna and Saguna Brahman being two separate realities rather than one transcendent/immanent God, the absolute unreality of the world, and the so-called differences between the jnana path and the previous stages had not yet been tied into Vedanta. The Vedanta that Tirumular knew was the direct teachings of the *Upanishads*. If there is one thing the *Upanishads* are categorical in declaring it is Advaita, *"Tat Tvam Asi*—Thou art That," *"Aham Brahmasmi*—I am Brahman." And when Saint Tirumular says that Siddhanta is based on Vedanta he is using Vedanta to refer to this Advaita, which according to him must be the basis of Siddhanta. This is perhaps one of the most important essentials of

. . . .

To bring the pure path of Saiva Siddhanta to Kauai, Gurudeva introduced the Tirukural *of Tiruvalluvar and the* Tirumantiram *of Tirumular to his monks and shishyas, commissioning life-size granite murtis of the two Tamil saints.*

Tirumular's Siddhanta to be brought forward into the Siddhanta of today, for it did, in fact, stray from the rishi's postulations.

That is why we occasionally use the term "Advaita Saiva Siddhanta." It conveys our belief in the Siddhanta which has as its ultimate objective the Vedanta. It sets us apart from the Dvaita Saiva Siddhanta school of interpretation begun by Meykanda Devar which sees God and the soul as eternally separate, never completely unified. It is not unusual to find two schools, similar in most ways, yet differing on matters of theology. In fact, this has been true throughout history. It has its source in the approach to God.

On the one hand you have the rishi, the yogi, the sage or siddha who is immersed in his sadhana, deep into yoga which brings forth direct experience. His conclusions will always tend toward Advaita, toward a fully non-dual perception. It isn't even a belief. It is the philosophical aftermath of experience. Most satgurus and those who follow the monastic path will hold firmly to the precepts of Advaita Saiva Siddhanta.

On the other hand there are the philosophers, the scholars, the pandits. Relying not on experience and ignoring yoga, they must surmise, postulate, arrange and rearrange concepts through an intricate intellectual process in an effort to reason out what God must be like. These are not infrequently the *grihasthas* and their reasoning leads them to one or another form of Dvaita Saiva Siddhanta. These are both valid schools. They are both traditional schools, and comparisons are odious. But they are very different one from the other, and it is good that we understand those differences.

We must understand the difference between the Self-God, Parasiva, and the soul. Many people think that the Self is something that you get. You pursue it and after a while you get it, like you get something in the world. But the Self is not separated from you by even the tiniest amount. You cannot go someplace and get it and bring it back. The formless, transcendent Self is never separate from you. It is closer than your heartbeat.

God Siva is called the Primal Soul because He is the perfect form, the original soul who then created individual souls. The individual soul has a beginning, and it has an end, merging with God. It has form as well. All form has a beginning and an end. The Absolute Self, Parasiva, is formless, timeless, endless and beginningless. All things are in the Self, and the Self is in all things. Many people think of the Self as an object to be sought. You start here and you go there, and you get the Self. You pursue it today; and if you don't get it today, you try again tomorrow. It's different than that. It comes from within you more as a becoming of your whole being than something that you pursue and get. And yet you seem to pursue it, and seem to get it. It is very difficult to explain.

The individual soul is different. The soul has a form. The soul is form, a very refined and subtle form, to be sure, but still a form and form obeys the laws of form. The soul has a beginning in Lord Siva and an end in union with Him. The purpose of life is to know God, your very Self. This is the end of all religions, of all religious effort. This is why we say that religion is this process of lifting ourselves up, attuning our minds to the laws of life so that we become stronger and more mature beings. We become higher beings, living in the higher chakras, and we come closer and closer to God. God doesn't come closer to us. How will God come any closer? He is closer to you right now than your own thoughts. He is nearer than breathing, closer than hands and feet.

I shall explain the soul in yet another way, for I see a questioning look in some of your faces. Man has five bodies, each more subtle than the last. Visualize the soul of man as a light bulb and his various bodies or sheaths as colored fabrics covering the pure white light. The physical body is the outermost body. Next comes the pranic body, then the physical body's subtle duplicate, the astral body. Then there is the mental or intellectual body in which one can travel instantaneously anywhere.

Then comes the body of the soul, which I term the *actinodic* body. This is the body that evolves from birth to birth, that reincarnates into new outer sheaths and does not die when the physical body returns its elements to the Earth. This body eventually evolves as the actinic body, the body of light, the golden body of the soul. This soul body in its final evolution is the most perfect form, the prototype of human form. Once physical births have ceased, this soul body still continues to evolve in subtle realms of existence. This effulgent, actinic body of the illumined soul, even after nirvikalpa samadhi, God Realization, continues to evolve in the inner worlds until the final merger with Siva.

I like to say, "God, God, God." There is one God only, but man's comprehension of That is helped by consciously exploring the three aspects of the one Divine Being: the Absolute, Pure Consciousness or the Self flowing through all form, and the Creator of all that is.

Lord Siva is the Absolute Self, Parasiva, the timeless, formless,

spaceless Reality beyond the mind, beyond all form, beyond our subtlest understanding. Parasiva can only be experienced to be known,
and then it cannot be explained. Lord Siva is pure consciousness, the
substratum, or Primal Substance of all that exists. He is the Energy
within all existence. He is Satchidananda, or Truth, Consciousness
and Bliss, the Self that flows through all form. Lord Siva is the Primal Soul, Maheshvara, the original and most perfect Being. He is the
Source and the Creator, having never been created. He is the Lord of
all beings. He created all souls out of Himself, and He is ever creating,
preserving and destroying forms in an endless divine dance. When I
was nine years old, I was taught that Lord Siva is God—God the Creator, God the Preserver, and God the Destroyer. To this day I know and
believe that Siva is all of these, Brahma, Vishnu and Rudra. These are
the final conclusions of Saivism, the Sanatana Dharma.

You must all study the great scriptures of our religion. These divine
utterances of the siddhas will enliven your own inner knowing. The
Tirumantiram is similar to the *Tirukural* in many ways. You can teach
them both to the children and apply their wisdom to everyday life.
You can use them for guidance in times of trouble and confusion, and
they will unerringly guide you along the right path. You can read
them as hymns after sacred puja in your home shrine or in the temple
precincts. Each verse can be used as a prayer, as a meditation, as a holy
reminder of the great path that lies ahead.

It is a difficult work, but don't be discouraged by that. Just understand that it could easily take a lifetime, several lifetimes, to understand all that is contained in this scripture, that it is for those deep
into their personal sadhana. It was given by the saint to those who
fully knew of the *Vedas* and the *Agamas*, and to understand it you,
too, will have to become more familiar with these other scriptures,
slowly obtaining a greater background.

It is interesting to reflect on the parallels, how Saint Tirumular was sent
by his Himalayan guru to the South to spread Saiva Siddhanta to the generation of his day, and how Gurudeva, sent back to the West by Yogaswami to build a bridge between the East and the West, did much the
same work for today's Saivite seekers around the globe. Both men took
Saivism's cultural and spiritual treasures from one culture and one language to another, drawing upon their deepest realizations to unravel,
summarize and explain, bringing Saivism forward in a new era.

Gurudeva's love of Tirumular and his deeply mystical verses derived in part from the saint's uncompromising philosophy of oneness and in part from the bold Saivism expressed. In every talk for years he would quote Tirumular and, with a wry smile, note how happy he was to find a scripture that was in consonance, perfect agreement, with his own realizations. Here are some verses from the *Tirumantiram.*

> In the distressed world existing in the midst of the ocean,
> Seeking the lustrous inner light residing in the body,
> One can experience in the waves of the expanding sea,
> The inner Lord placed in the body.   3028

> Being the inner light of the three great lights [Sun, Moon and Fire],
> The Lord of the celestials stands as their intelligible bodies.
> Leaving the great lights, in the limited space
> He follows in compassion as the minutest of all.   3029

> He is the consciousness; He is the life;
> He is the embracer and He is the act of sulking.
> He is the imponderable; yet one can think of Him;
> He is akin to the pollen of a flower.   2857

> The Lord with flowing matted locks bedecked with konrai flowers,
> Is mingled everywhere as the subtle being;
> The eight cardinal directions, the worlds above and below
> Are centering 'round Him in this manner.   3042

One day in 1977 he called a few senior swamis to his office and asked them to read to him from another South Indian scripture, the *Tirukural.* He knew Yogaswami had given great import to this text by the weaver saint of Mylapore. It was a Tamil masterpiece, full of insights into the human condition and lifestyle principles, learned by schoolchildren even today; but its content was not much known in English. The swamis showed him a new translation of the classic into British English. It sounded quaint and artificial to his ears. He took the book, read several verses aloud and paused on one to comment, "It's nice, but what does it mean exactly?" The meaning was discussed. Tamil dictionaries were consulted, and after half an hour an attractive rewording of the rather turgid prose translation was achieved.

Gurudeva was so delighted to have the meaning succinctly given that he gave two swamis the mission of translating the entire *Tirukural*

from the original Tamil into modern American usage, striving for perfect clarity of expression. They began that same day, as was Gurudeva's
style. Though a relatively small work, just 1,080 couplets (the monks did
not translate the final 250-verse section, which is a mildly sensuous love
poem that seems to have been added later by another author), the ancient
text was technically and linguistically complex; and it was twenty-two
years later, with long interludes, that the full work was completed and
published. In 1999 *Weaver's Wisdom* was finally published, with its
straightforward American English. Gurudeva's summary at the end was,
"We are actually living all the things Tiruvalluvar wrote about. His ideals
have become our way of life."

He called for a comparison of the verses with previous translators, and,
placing them side-by-side, smiled as if to say, "We did it." For example,
verse 15 speaks of the importance of rain. In 1886 Rev. G. U. Pope rendered
it: "'Tis rain works all: it ruin spreads, then timely aid supplies; as, in the
happy days before, it bids the ruined rise." Gurudeva's swamis, adhering
to the terse and direct Tamil, wrote: "It is rain that ruins, and it is rain
again that raises up those it has ruined." Verse 252 on meat-eating provides another example. In 1962 K. M. Balasubramaniam translated it as
"The blessings of wealth are not for those who fail to guard. The blessings
of compassion for the flesh-eaters are barred." The swamis translated it
as "Riches cannot be found in the hands of the thriftless, nor can compassion be found in the hearts of those who eat meat."

Saivism Finds a Modern Voice

In 1978, after a hiatus of several years when his time was consumed with
establishing the Kauai headquarters, and now free from outside influenc-
es that had demanded so much of his time and netted so little in return,
Gurudeva took again to prolific publishing. It started with a simple series
of pamphlets, which he called Prasada, or grace-filled gifts. Then came
the booklets, called Inspired Talks, published in the same style as the publications done in Virginia City. Though the monks printed these 16-24
page booklets from his *upadeshas*, which was his life-long manner of
conveying his teachings, he wanted them to be elegant, and so asked that
they be professionally typeset in Honolulu.

It worked, until the invoice for phototypesetting came. Astonished by
the $700 bill, Gurudeva refused to pay another nickel for type. Instead,
he asked the publications team to explore ways they could produce their
own phototypesetting in house. The timing was perfect, for the first
such device had just been released, and Gurudeva flew to Oahu with

the monks to secure the purchase of a Quadritek 1200 phototypesetting machine. This tool transformed the way the monks were to publish in the years ahead, putting into their own hands the ability to set type in any font, any style, and for a reasonable cost.

The effect was galvanizing. Type began to flow in streams that swelled to rivers. The immediacy of it inspired Gurudeva. Each time he saw a talk he gave one day typeset the next, he went right back to work to produce another and another. This cycle was different than before, in that the teachings were purely Saivite. From his return to Lanka in 1969, 1970 and 1972, he had meditated on Saiva Siddhanta, talked about Saiva Siddhanta, lived Saiva Siddhanta. Now that which had been within him began pouring out in a hundred ways.

Titles included *Free Will and the Deities in Hinduism; The Hand That Rocks the Cradle Rules the World; Protect, Preserve and Promote the Saiva Dharma; The Two Perfections of our Soul; The Meditator,* and more. Among the most popular and controversial was *Hinduism, the Greatest Religion in the World.* From the title, some feared it was a bigoted diatribe by a zealous believer claiming the superiority of his faith. But inside was a balanced summary of Sanatana Dharma, including a poignant statement on Hinduism's innate and unique tolerance for other faiths, listed among many facets of its greatness. Here is an excerpt:

> Hinduism has been called the "cradle of spirituality" and the "mother of all religions," partially because it has influenced virtually every major religion and partly because it can absorb all other religions, honor and embrace their scriptures, their saints, their philosophy. This is possible because Hinduism looks compassionately on all genuine spiritual effort and knows unmistakably that all souls are evolving toward union with the Divine, and all are destined, without exception, to achieve spiritual enlightenment and liberation in this or a future life.
>
> Naturally, the Hindu feels that his faith is the broadest, the most practical and effective instrument of spiritual unfoldment, but he includes in his Hindu mind all the religions of the world as expressions of the one Eternal Path and understands each proportionately in accordance with its doctrines and dogma. He knows that certain beliefs and inner attitudes are more conducive to spiritual growth than others, and that all religions are, therefore, not the same. They differ in important ways. Yet, there is no sense whatsoever in Hinduism of an "only path." A devout Hindu is supportive of all efforts that lead to a pure and virtuous life and would consider it unthinkable to

dissuade a sincere devotee from his chosen faith. This is the Hindu mind, and this is what we teach, what we practice and what we offer aspirants on the path.

Gurudeva developed *A Catechism for Saivite Hindus* and *A Creed for Saivite Hindus,* condensed summaries of the faith that he considered among his most important works. The catechism consists of questions and concise answers about life according to Saivism, and the creed consists of twelve beliefs summarizing the philosophy. Every word was carefully chosen, discussed with the senior swamis of the Order, explored and crafted so as to carry the force and spirit of Saivism into the minds of future generations. The work was ready a few days before Mahasivaratri, March 7, 1978. He then distilled the creed into an affirmation of faith, which was the shortest summation possible of the Saiva Siddhanta beliefs, to be repeated each day by his followers. It simply says, "God Siva is immanent love and transcendent reality."

The several stages of monastic life were documented and formalized for the future during this time, an ongoing effort of the senior swamis of this theological seminary, working closely with Gurudeva. From this work came the Aspirant, Supplicant and Postulant vow books of the Church. In April Gurudeva commenced the preparation of a definitive document for the lifetime vows of a Saiva sannyasin, this to be called *The Holy Orders of Sannyas.* It was the first time that the oral transmission of the dharma for the Saiva renunciate was ever assembled in a concise yet comprehensive document to guide the monks' life and clearly delineate their ideals, disciplines and lifestyle. Gurudeva took this opportunity to have all of his sannyasins reaffirm and sign their vows in the new booklet, including a formal oath of entrance into his Saiva Siddhanta Yoga Order. He had first founded the yoga order in the late 50s, and now it was becoming the core of his work and mission.

For ten years, from 1970 to 1980, we had lived upon this island of Kauai with no members, no students and no visitors. The only visitors were my shishyas on pilgrimage and close special guests of high calibre who enhanced the spiritual lives of the young monks, such as swamis, pandits, scholars and the like. During this period, the monks spent their time in scriptural research for our publications, including a deep study of the two schools of Saiva Siddhanta, the six schools of Saivism, the four denominations of Hinduism, and all the major religions of the world. They supported themselves in rescuing a failed beekeeping industry, which they regenerated from 300 to a total of 3,000 colonies all over the island. This gave them a wonderful means for developing relationships on the island at a grassroots level.

Though rife with complex thought and mystical overtones, Gurudeva's teachings were as simple as sand. He spoke of man as not being the body, the mind or the emotions; and brazenly declared, as had Yogaswami before him, that man is not man, man is God. Again and again he drilled into all who would listen that the inherent nature of the soul is divine, existing in perfect oneness with God. This identity of the soul with God always exists, ever awaiting man's awakening into realization. Each of us is a perfect soul, he assured, living in a perfect universe. All of this, articulated now in the disciplined language of Saiva Siddhanta, had been said by him decades earlier when he gave his 1959 talk called *The Self God*. How far that talk went is another story, told by Gurudeva.

In the years that followed, tens of thousands of copies of the little booklet called *The Self God* were printed in America and in Asia and have been widely distributed. To show just how widely, one day our car experienced a flat tire on a road outside a remote village in South India. As it was being repaired, we wandered about. People were passing by now and again. After a while, an elderly villager noticed us and inquired as to our "native place." I handed him a little pamphlet to be polite. He looked at us, refused my offer and pulled a little booklet from his shirt pocket, saying, "I am in need of nothing more. I have all I need right here." He held up my *The Self God* booklet. Having made his point to these strangers, he walked on, not knowing he had been speaking to the author. In India and Sri Lanka, it is often referred to as "the little gem," and is highly regarded as an explanation of the inexplicable nirvikalpa samadhi.

Chapter Twenty-Six

Standing Strong for Hinduism

As though operated by unseen stagehands in a cosmic play, doors began to open in the early 1980s for Gurudeva's mission to expand powerfully beyond American shores. After an initial visit to Malaysia with two swamis, a twenty-something group of Master Course students in Kuala Lumpur urged him to visit their country again. This journey was arranged as part of the 1981 Indian Odyssey to Malaysia, Sri Lanka and India. Thirty-three devotees, accompanying Gurudeva as Innersearchers, became witness to what was unfolding in Malaysia—something historic, the introduction of an American guru to a country that had over a million Hindus desperately seeking spiritual guidance while living in the midst of twenty million Muslims.

Gurudeva's visit was widely publicized as he met with the Hindu leaders of the nation and spoke to tens of thousands of Hindus in a dozen temples in and around Kuala Lumpur. Gurudeva's Western origins and ways of expressing Saiva Siddhanta, which is the major tradition followed by Hindus in Malaysia, made it easy for them to relate to him. It galvanized especially the youth, woke them from a kind of hibernation and brought them together in a spiritual fellowship that would help shape the next few decades of Saivism in their nation. In the years to follow, Gurudeva returned again and again to personally direct their spiritual progress.

Everywhere Gurudeva was greeted and honored with elaborate receptions by local religious groups and societies. At all public gatherings he would introduce the *Catechism* and *Creed* to cheering crowds. He spoke with pride of the Saivite religion, telling them they were the inheritors of the most profound religion on the planet. They were accustomed to something different, to having their ancestral faith demeaned and belittled. Here was a guru from the West, tall, leonine, hazel-eyed and wearing hand-woven swami robes telling them the opposite, telling them they could—no, *must*—be proud of their religion and shout its virtues from the rooftops. At public meetings Gurudeva gave such assurances they would never forget, gave them a new vision of themselves and a new courage to express that vision.

How startlingly new this was to the Malaysians, who lived in the shadow of Muslim and Christian influence, is hard to imagine, but they caught

. . . .

Again and again Gurudeva traveled to India, Sri Lanka and Malaysia, giving outspoken discourses in hundreds of temples. In every talk he called for Saivites to rediscover their ancient faith, to be strong in the face of opposition, to realize the profundity of Siva's path to liberation.

his spirit, and their lives, and those around them, changed forever.

"Hinduism is the greatest religion in the world!" Gurudeva thundered from podium after podium during three consecutive annual pilgrimage tours to India, Sri Lanka and Malaysia in 1981, 1982 and 1983. "Stand strong for Hinduism! Be proud to be a Hindu!" he commanded to applauding audiences. All along the way he would speak to standing-room-only gatherings at temples, ashrams and public halls, each pilgrimage carrying a specific message. It was a mission to "convert Hindus to Hinduism," as described by Gurudeva's spiritual brother and fellow worker for the Hindu renaissance, Swami Chinmayananda, characterizing his own aims.

A Hindu Renaissance

Historically, the modern renaissance of Hinduism began in the 1800s with the missions of Dayananda Saraswati, founder of the Arya Samaj; Ramakrishna and his disciple Swami Vivekananda, founder of the Ramakrishna Mission; Kadaitswami of Jaffna, in Gurudeva's own lineage; Sivadayal of the Radhasoami Vaishnava sect; Arumuga Navalar of Jaffna and Ramalingaswami of Tamil Nadu. It included Eknath Ranade, whose social reform thinking inspired Gandhi; Sri Aurobindo, who sought to advance the evolution of human consciousness; Swami Rama Tirtha, who lectured extensively in America; Sadhu Vaswani, Ramana Maharshi and many more. They were dedicated to bringing Hinduism out of centuries of oppression into its rightful place in the modern era.

For all the progress made by these great men, and dozens more since, there remained in the 1980s serious obstacles to a true Hindu renaissance. At a time when the "brain drain" was drawing India's best and brightest to America, perhaps it required Gurudeva—one of America's best and brightest—to travel the other way and remind Indians that they had something money couldn't buy: Hinduism, the greatest religion in the world. It was to be a tough mission. First, many Hindus wouldn't even admit they were Hindus. In a lecture in Sri Lanka, he described the problem:

> Today there are many Hindus who when asked, "Are you a Hindu?" reply, "No, I'm not really a Hindu. I'm nonsectarian, universal, a follower of all religions. I'm a little bit of everything, and a little bit of everybody. Please don't classify me in any particular way." Are these the words of a strong person? No. Too much of this kind of thinking makes the individual weak-minded. They are disclaiming their own sacred heritage for the sake of money and social or intellectual acceptance. How deceptive! How shallow! The word should go out

loud and strong: "Stand strong for Hinduism, and when you do, you will be strong yourself."

Closely related to this lack of self-identity as a Hindu was the popular notion that "All religions are one." Hindus don't need to claim to be Hindus, went this line of thought, because it doesn't really matter what religion you follow, since all are the same. This Hindu universalism was rampant, and its followers took every opportunity to deprecate traditional Hinduism as unnecessarily narrow. Furthermore, they argued, Hinduism is more lifestyle than religion. Gurudeva countered:

> All religions are not one. They are very, very different. They all worship and talk about God, yes, but they do not all lead their followers to the same spiritual goal. The Christians are not seeking God within themselves. They do not see God as all-pervasive. Jews, Christians and Muslims do not believe that there is more than one life or that there is such a thing as karma. They simply do not accept these beliefs. They are heresy to them.

Going against a common trend, he preached the merits of sectarianism, of each of the great traditions of Hinduism—Saivism, Vaishnavism, Shaktism and Smartism—retaining and valuing their unique features. The watered-down, homogenized Hinduism which some were advocating, he warned, would not sustain the individual sampradayas, spiritual teaching traditions, which are Hinduism's core strengths.

One of India's leading thinkers, Sita Ram Goel, wrote, "Gurudeva's greatest contribution has been to rescue the word *Hinduism* from being a dirty word and restore it to its age-old glory. He made Hindus everywhere to see themselves as a world community and as inheritors of a great civilization and culture." Swami Advaitananda of the Brahma Vidya Ashrama in India put it this way: "In the present days, when Hindus are ashamed to call themselves so, it has been his work and teachings that have propelled faith and infused dynamism among the millions who lovingly addressed him as Gurudeva."

When speaking to Saivites, Gurudeva would extol the greatness of their denomination and declare that Saivism is the religion of the New Age:

> Here in Sri Lanka and India there is some misconception that in order to progress, in order to move into the age of technology, we have to abandon our religion, give up our culture. This is a false concept.

Religion does not conflict with technology. It enhances it, gives it balance and purpose. Our religious teachers are beginning to teach the fact that Saivism is the one religion on the planet best suited to this great age, which agrees most closely with the most advanced postulations of modern science, yet is itself even more advanced.

Speaking at receptions in Saivism's most venerated temples, in assembly halls and at village podiums throughout Malaysia, India and Sri Lanka, Gurudeva stirred his fellow Saivites into action. Newspaper coverage of the tour was extensive, and in the South of India a taped radio program of his talks was broadcast on All India Radio.

What to Do About Christian Infiltration?

Gurudeva was astonished at the pervasive Christian influence in India, even though just two percent of Indians were Christians and even though the British had left fifty years earlier. He found those in India educated in Christian schools to be anemic Hindus, their faith undermined by the years of study under nuns and teachers propounding an alien faith. One Catholic priest in Colombo told him straight out, "The Hindu children that pass through my school may never become Catholics, but they certainly will never be good Hindus."

Gurudeva had nothing against Christianity, or any other religion. He came, after all, from a country where Christians are in the majority. Only rarely in his years of ministry in America did he experience any Christian interference. In his early years, he studied with deeply mystical teachers of several religions, including Buddhists, Muslims and Christians. He knew the finer side of each faith.

What he saw at the Christian schools was bad enough, but the methods of Christian missionaries—trickery, enticement, intimidation—incensed him. He opposed this devious side of Christianity wherever he found it and told Hindus worldwide to stand by their religious rights as Hindus. "When an elephant is young," he said time and again, "the mahout, trainer, can control it with a small stick, and the elephant learns to fear that stick. When the elephant is big, he still fears the stick, even though he could pick it up and the mahout, too, and toss them far away."

By this same psychology, Gurudeva said, Hindus had become meek and submissive under years of Christian rule and unwilling now to mount serious protest to continued Christian oppression, even when the political power which made it possible in the first place was gone. His advice was not to attack the Christians, but to disengage from and ignore them.

He told crowds of thousands of Hindus to take their children out of Christian schools and to close their doors on Christian missionaries who came to their homes to proselytize.

> You can remember this when a missionary comes to your door: Welcome him with "Namaste." Tell him that we have a Catechism of our own. We have a Creed and an Affirmation of Faith in our religion, too. We have our scriptures—our Holy Bible of Saivite Hinduism—the *Vedas, Agamas, Tirukural, Tirumantiram* and so many sacred texts. We have religious leaders and a tradition that is vastly more ancient than any other. We have our holy temples and our great Gods. We are proud to worship God and the Gods. We have all this and more. Thank you very much. And then close the door!

As Gurudeva ended each section of his talk to a crowd, there would be a soft murmuring of acknowledgement from those few who spoke English fluently enough to follow his complex thoughts. A translator would then come to the microphone to repeat it all in Tamil, and, when he finished, a roar would fill the temple or hall chambers—sustained cheers of appreciation, joyful applause as the crowd experienced the presence of an eloquent spiritual leader whose courageous words, especially about conversion and anti-Hindu campaigns, had often been whispered among them but never thundered from a public podium.

Doubtless, few had the courage to follow his advice. A handful of Hindus opposed him, unsure of what he was trying to do, or feeling perhaps that their turf was being encroached upon by an outsider. In 1999, he told his monks on a cruise ship during the Alaska Innersearch program about this time: "We did not fight them—'them' is 'us'—but let them find out that we were all working for the same thing, the upliftment of Hinduism." And over the years they did, ultimately causing Gurudeva to humorously lament, "I am so disappointed in my enemies. Not one has ever been able to stay mad at me."

Gurudeva's renaissance message to the Saivites of Malaysia, Sri Lanka and India included Hindu pride, clear and public religious identity, correct religious understanding, reverence for scripture, respect for religious leaders, home worship, opposition to conversion, preservation of traditions, harmonious working together, interfaith harmony, Lord Siva as the God of Love and Hinduism as best suited of all religious for the modern, technological age. He dispelled many myths and misunderstandings about Hindus among Hindus and non-Hindus alike. He advocated a strong and loving Hindu home, encouraging mothers to not work but raise their children full-time and for parents to not use corporal punishment on children. He projected this message with clarity, boldness, love and humor, and he made a difference, redefining our modern Hindu world. Here is an excerpt from those talks:

> In looking back on all the wonderful aspects of Hinduism that have been spoken of tonight on the beautiful island of Sri Lanka, it is clear that Hinduism is the answer for the future generations on this planet. It is the answer for the New Age, for the dawning Sat Yuga. The gracious Sanatana Dharma, our great religion, has all the answers. It has always had all of the answers in every age, for there was never an age when it did not exist. The time has now passed for many and is quickly passing for everyone when they can deny their Hindu heritage, when they can be afraid to admit their belief in Hinduism or even the simple fact that they are a Hindu. The time has come for Hindus of all races, all nations, of all cultures, of all sects to stand up and let the peoples of the world know of the great religion of which they are one of the staunch adherents. Take courage, courage, courage into your own hands and proceed with confidence. Stand strong for Hinduism.

It had been four years since Gurudeva had announced that he had settled his debt to his countrymen by teaching the truths of advaita to non-Hindus, and henceforth was turning his attention toward the Hindu community and to non-Hindus who wished to follow him fully into the depths of the world's most ancient faith. When speaking from podiums throughout South India and Sri Lanka, he urged devotees to not allow their practice to be diluted by putting the icons of other faiths on their altars, a puzzling phenomenon he encountered in home shrines and even recently established temples.

> In order to really meditate to the depth of contemplation, and not merely to quiet mind and emotion and feel a little serenity, you have to be a member of a religion that gives the hope of nondual union with God, that teaches that God is within man, only to be realized. Meditation, if it is to lead to jnana, must begin with a belief that there is no intrinsic evil and encompass the truth of karma, that we are responsible for our own actions. Such meditation must be undertaken by a member of a religion that gives a hope of a future life and does not threaten failure with eternal suffering should failure be the result.

Such meditation is possible, in fact required, of those who follow the Hindu Dharma. Hence, the practice of yoga is the highest pinnacle within our most ancient faith.

If you go through the entire holy scriptures of Saivism, you will not find our saints singing hymns to Adonai-Yahweh, Buddha or Jesus. Our saints told us to worship God Siva, the Supreme God, to worship Ganesha first before worshiping Siva, to worship Lord Murugan. In the old days, there were millions of Siva temples, from the Himalayan peaks of Nepal, through North and South India, Sri Lanka and what is now Malaysia and Indonesia. Everyone was of one mind, worshiping Siva together, singing His praises with a one voice. As a result, India was spiritually unified. It was then the wealthiest country in the world. The worship of Siva will give you wealth. The worship of Siva will give you health. The worship of Siva will give you knowledge. The worship of Siva will fill your heart with love and compassion.

The Saiva Samayam is the greatest religion in the world. The Saiva Samayam is the oldest religion in the world. The Saiva Samayam has yoga. It has great temples, great pandits, rishis and scriptures. All the saints who sang the songs of Siva told us how to worship Siva and how we should live our Saivite lives. We must all follow those instructions. In singing those songs to Siva, Siva will give you everything that you ask for. He will give you everything that you ask for, because Siva is the God of Love. Our saints have sung that Siva is within us, and we are within Siva. Knowing that, fear and worry and doubt are forever gone from our mind.

When the mind has resolved all of its differences through worship, penance, *dharana,* dhyana, then the inner, which is stillness itself, is known. Then the inner is stronger than the outer. It is then easy to see every other person going through what has to be gone through during his or her particular stage on the path. Opposites are there, but no opposites are seen. This is why it is easy for the wise—made wise through spiritual unfoldment—to say, "There is no injustice in the world. There is no evil, no sin."

We only see opposites when our vision is limited, when we have not experienced totally. There is a point of view which resolves all contradictions and answers all questions. Yet to be experienced is yet to be understood. Once experienced and understood, the quiet comes. The karmas are quiet. This is the arduous path of charya, kriya and yoga resulting in jnana. This is the path of not only endeavoring to unfold the higher nature but, at the same time and toward the same end, dealing positively and consciously with the remnants of the low-er nature. Following this spiritual path, we find ourselves effortlessly replacing charity for greed and dealing with, rather than merely sup-pressing, the instinctive feelings of jealousy, hatred, desire and anger.

The Primacy of Initiation

Continuing his stress on bringing souls deeper into the Saivite religion, Gurudeva made arrangements to give Saiva *diksha* in the 1,000-pillared hall of Chidambaram Temple, initiating fifteen men and women as mem-bers of Saiva Siddhanta Church. As all the Saiva gurus before him had done, Gurudeva gave pride of place to *diksha*, initiation. He wrote:

Initiation is the goal of all Hindus, and an absolute must for all Saiva souls. This is why they seek out a guru. This is why they manifest in their lives all the good that he would approve. This is why they strive and strive and strive to fulfill, even better than he would expect, all of his expectations. *Diksha* from a satguru is nothing that can be erased, nothing that can be altered, nothing that can be described. This is why initiation is given—at an auspicious time, in a spiritual mood, at the right moment in the karma of the soul's long journey from con-ception in Siva's all-pervasive shakti to manifestation in the current incarnation. *Diksha* is a pathway to moksha in this life or a future life. There is no alternative way. There is none. There is none.

Diksha provides the spark to clear barriers. It is the satguru's bless-ing and inner sanction for further sadhana. Giving *diksha* may be likened to planting a seed. Fruition, growth and ripening come with time and naturally depend on the shishya's sincerity and personal effort to perform the sadhana given with the *diksha*, or to fulfill the assigned *prayashchitta* [penance] to compensate if the sadhana is not performed. The fellowship of initiates are the core of the Hindu Church of the noble Kailasa Parampara. They are truly stalwart and dedicated, having carried the banner of dharma through the thick and thin of their many lives.

Samaya diksha, also called mantra *diksha*, is the fundamental Saiva initiation, for through it the devotee is formally connected to a par-ticular lineage by virtue of the preceptor's spiritual power and author-ity. All initiates instruct newcomers, not just intellectually but more

. . . .

Nothing is more important than initiation, rites whereby the power is passed from guru to disciple. Here a guru has brought young seekers to the banks of a river, blessing one by holding both hands on his head. The Vedic homa *ritual has been completed, and two assistants hold the orange robes and rudraksha malas that will be given to the new swami following the sannyasa* diksha.

by example. Novitiates are instructed in how to transform themselves by themselves through daily puja, temple worship, attending festivals, tithing, vegetarianism, pilgrimage, scriptural reading, Ganga sadhana and more. *Samaya diksha* is the blessing and empowering to enter the kriya *pada* and perform certain daily sadhanas, including chanting the Panchakshara Mantra, "Aum Namasivaya," each day at least 108 times on a mala of rudraksha japa beads.

This mantra quiets the mind, harmonizes the nerve system, bringing forth knowledge from within, reminding the shishya of his purpose in life and relationship with Lord Siva. Namasivaya literally means "adoration to God Siva." The symbolism of each of the five letters is: *Si* is Siva; *Va* is His revealing grace, *Ya* is the soul, *Na* is His concealing grace and *Ma* is the world. Namasivaya is the gateway to yoga. The secret of Namasivaya is to hear it from the right lips at the right time. Then, and only then, is it the most powerful mantra of Saivism for you.

Dr. Anandanatarajah Deekshidar, a senior priest at Chidambaram Temple who Gurudeva had been close to for decades, related the following story:

There was one time Gurudeva came to Chidambaram with a group of pilgrims. I was waiting for him at the hotel entrance with a man who is a millionaire. Gurudeva got off the bus and we greeted him and started to talk to him. A few minutes later an old beggar lady came up to us asking for money. Gurudeva turned to her and gave her some money and started to talk to her. He made her feel welcome and did not chase her away. I have seen so many swamis and other people who would have ignored the poor lady and entertained the wealthy man. Gurudeva is the only person I know who truly saw Siva in everyone. He treated everybody the same.

Gurudeva was faithfully following the Natha way, mixing freely with all castes, all social strata, all races, seeing no differences and showing no preferences.

Deekshidar had brought Gurudeva to his humble home a number of times for tea or lunch, and they knew each other well. The priest shared another story with one of Gurudeva's monks:

Whenever a puja is performed to Lord Nataraja in the Chidambaram temple, it is traditional that the priest who is doing the Siva puja makes the *naivedyam* [food offering] and brings it to the shrine

In every nation, city and village he visited, Gurudeva met with priests and pandits, aadheenakarthars, yogis, philosophers and theologians, sharing the principles of Advaita Siddhanta and urging them to work as one spiritual family.

himself. All my life I have been on time in preparing the *naivedyam* at home and have brought it to the shrine before I begin my puja. But once, on my birthday, I was late. I started preparing the *naivedyam* but could not get it ready in time for the puja. I had to begin the puja; then half way through I stopped to go get the *naivedyam*. I felt bad about this and never told anyone about it.

Some years later, when Gurudeva came to Chidambaram, I was talking to him, and he suddenly said to me, "So, on your birthday you didn't get the *naivedyam* ready in time for your Siva puja." It always amazed me how he knew about it when I had never told anyone.

A Flood of Inspired Talks

During the late 1970s and early 80s Gurudeva gave a steady stream of talks, urging Hindus to stand strong for their faith, expounding the glories of Hindu culture and elucidating the subtleties of Saiva Siddhanta philosophy. In speaking of the mystical within, Gurudeva was precise and explicit, able to speak of the ineffable, to make the deepest truths meaningful to others. On May 18, 1981, he spoke to his monks on the two perfections that lie at the core of every soul:

> Parasiva, the Self God, lies resident at the core of man's existence, far beyond the reach of the external phases of consciousness; yet these

Gurudeva loved a procession, and none was so splendid as in Tuticorin. Over 300,000 welcomed him, showering baskets of flowers from the rooftops as they paraded the Hawaiian satguru and his 70 devotees through the streets for three hours.

. . . .

exist only because That exists, the timeless, causeless, spaceless God Siva beyond the mind.

The other perfection inherent in the soul of man is Satchidananda—Being, Consciousness and Bliss. When mind force, thought force and the *vrittis*, or waves of the mind, are quiescent, the outer mind subsides and the mind of the soul shines forth. We share the mind of God

Siva at this superconscious depth of our being. In entering this quiescence, one first encounters a clear white light within the body, but only after sufficient mastery of the mind has been attained through the disciplined and protracted practices of yoga.

Hearing the vina, the mridangam, the tambura and all the psychic sounds is the awakening of the inner body, which, if sadhana is pursued, will finally grow and stabilize, opening the mind to the constant state of Satchidananda, where the holy inner mind of God Siva and our soul are one. I hold that Satchidananda—the light and consciousness ever permeating form, God in all things and everywhere—is form, though refined form, to be sure. Satchidananda is pure form, pure consciousness, pure blessedness or bliss, our soul's perfection in form. Parasiva is formless, timeless, causeless, spaceless, as the perfection of our soul beyond form.

Though it is supreme consciousness, Satchidananda is not the ultimate realization, which lies beyond consciousness or mind. This differs from popular interpretations of present-day Vedanta, which makes these two perfections virtually synonymous. Modern Vedanta scholars occasionally describe Satchidananda almost as a state of the intellect, as though the perfected intellect, through knowledge, could attain such depths, as though these depths were but a philosophical premise or collection of beliefs and insights. This is what I call "simplistic Vedanta."

To understand how these two perfections differ, visualize a vast sheath of light which permeates the walls of this monastery and the countryside around us, seeping in and through all particles of matter. The light could well be called formless, penetrating, as it does, all conceivable forms, never static, always changing. Actually, it is amorphous, not formless. Taking this one step farther, suppose there were a "something" so great, so intense in vibration that it could swallow up light as well as the forms it permeates. This cannot be described, but can be called Parasiva—the greatest of all of God Siva's perfections to be realized. This, too, can be experienced by the yogi, in nirvikalpa samadhi.

Thus, we understand Parasiva as the perfection known in nirvikalpa samadhi, and Satchidananda as the perfection experienced in savikalpa samadhi. By the word formless I do not describe that which can take any form or that which is of no definite shape and size. I mean without form altogether, beyond form, beyond the mind which conceives of form and space, for mind and consciousness, too, are form.

Marching Through Sri Lanka and South India

The 1982 Indian Odyssey and the all-island tour of Sri Lanka that followed had no precedent in history. No one, not even S. Shanmugasundaram, the liason officer for the Church in Sri Lanka who had done the groundwork for the journey, had an inkling of the overall magnitude of the receptions that awaited Gurudeva there.

It was unprecedented precisely because religious followings in Asia remain exclusive, and the followers of one teacher or guru do not attend the lectures of another. When a Ramakrishna swami travels, for example, his audience is, for the most part, Ramakrishna Mission members, plus a few uncommitted seekers. But here was a rare soul, a guru, not from India, but from the Wild West, from America, who had no local following and posed no threat to any movement. After all, he would soon return to his land and not draw devotees away from the local ashrams. Everyone was, therefore, free to attend his talks, and they did in numbers that had not been seen since the legendary saints of yore walked these same lanes to speak similar thoughts to devotees centuries before.

In this remote part of the world, the village was still the center of life; and when Gurudeva rode through a village, by car or carriage, it came alive. Thousands of Saivites lined the lanes of Alaveddy, Kopay, Karainagar, Batticaloa, Hatton, Kokuvil and elsewhere to honor and revere the satguru and affectionately greet the Saiva pilgrims from the West. A holiday was declared in Kilinochchi so all the school children of the district could join in the parade, which wound a full sixteen miles through the region and took an entire day.

From 9am to 5pm Gurudeva was seated on a tall chariot made for the occasion, drawn through the crowded streets by hundreds of men pulling two long, stout ropes. At the gate to each family compound, typically just off the road, nearly every household had set up an elaborately decorated greeting altar, with brass oil lamps called *kuttuvilakku* and a *kumbha*. Standing around the altar, the entire family (often three generations) would greet the tall, white-haired, orange-robed, rudraksha-bedecked satguru with flowers, rosewater, holy ash and arati.

For most, he simply passed by and they rushed forward to throw their garland into his hands. Now and again, the procession halted, and Gurudeva got down, approached the family's altar and allowed them to pass the lighted lamp before him, to pour water on his dusty feet, place the red *pottu* on his forehead and garland him. He looked like Siva Himself, they whispered to one another, so divine, so full of light and love. For these families, stories would echo for generations.

Processions continued for miles and miles in the hot sun, village after village. As he approached the outskirts of a village, you could hear the distant, welcoming roar of hundreds of voices intoning "Aum Nama-sivaya" with heartfelt fervor. Kids set off firecrackers and lit sparklers. Those with more ingenuity had set nets of flowers high in the trees, and as Gurudeva walked beneath, they tugged on ropes to release showers of blossoms. Each procession had its destination, a temple usually, for this is the common gathering place for Saivites and saints, but sometimes it was a hall or a schoolyard.

The last few hundred meters, sometimes the last mile, men would scurry in front of him, in teams of eight, to place on the ground newly woven white *veshti* cloth in ten-meter lengths so the satguru's feet, bare as he approached the temple, would not have to touch the Earth. Walking before the satguru, there was always a team of nagasvara and *tavil* musicians and a flock of young girls in white dresses tossing rose petals beneath his feet.

Arriving, Gurudeva was escorted to the Deity's shrine for a brief puja, then to the stage for the obligatory oratory by local politicians and village elders, which, if allowed, would eclipse the real purpose of the day. Toward the end Gurudeva decreed that his talk would be first and the introductions would follow. Amazingly, it worked; and his connection with the audience came to life, absent the hour-long soporific speechifying by others.

It is customary, for guests of such stature, for the community to prepare a beautifully composed and framed document, a kind of certificate of praise, which is read aloud then gifted to the visitor. Hundreds of these were given to Gurudeva, each a work of art which someone spent days writing and typesetting. Some were poems in Tamil and English, some were spiritual manifestos and others were outpourings of love for the swami whose noble presence was a promise that Saivism has a future as grand as its past.

Here are excerpts from two of dozens of welcome addresses that were lovingly presented to Gurudeva by representatives of Saiva institutions of Malaysia, Sri Lanka and India during the 1982 Innersearch Odyssey. This one is from the Saivaits' Sabba, Sri Somanatha Swami Temple, Arumuga-neri, India:

The devotees of Sri Somanatha Swami Temple at Arumuganeri deem it a privilege to welcome Your Holiness and the enlightened disciples who accompany Your Holiness in this pilgrimage. The debut of Your

Holiness at our village is really a palliative unto the ardent Saivites. Being dedicated to Saiva philosophy and faith, Your Holiness is an exemplar to devotees of this village, who long for a spiritual message. It is a soothing solace to our mind that Your Holiness has been giving bone and flesh to Saiva Siddhanta at the ripe time after becoming a sage in the East. While most of the people in the East have ceased to have the Saiva symbols on their foreheads out of changing fashions and culture, the timely message from Your Holiness to possess them is welcomed and hailed by us.

The pilgrimage undertaken by Your Holiness and devoted disciples may enlighten the people and help them fasten to the fold of the time-immemorial Saivism. We earnestly beg the blessings of Your Holiness and pray that the endeavors shouldered by Your Holiness in the rejuvenation of Saivism may open a new page in the annals of Hindu religion. Let Saiva dogma flourish bounteously all over the world!

Sri Subramuniya Ashram, Alaveddy, January 14, 1982:

Your pilgrimage is unmistakenly a divinely inspired one undertaken to dispel the gathering darkness of intense materialism in this wide world by proclaiming and reaffirming the eternal message of the most ancient faith of Saivism. The origin of Saivism is beyond the ken of historical research, lost in the mists of time. Was it not the omnipresent and omniscient God Himself who assumed the enthralling form of Dakshinamurti, the Supreme Preceptor, and revealed to the four immortal sages the eternal verities of Sanatana Dharma and the luminous path to Reality as enunciated in the Saiva Siddhanta philosophy? Has He not, out of His infinite grace, sent down His emissaries of saints and sages to redeem mankind whenever virtue subsides and vice prevails? It is the appearance of these saints and sages which has illuminated the otherwise dark history of humanity.

Humanity is now on the brink of cataclysm of war, having forsaken dharma and faith in Providence. It is at this critical moment of history that God has chosen you, Gurudeva, to preach and propagate the endless glories of Saivism and the Vedic religion as the sure means to salvation and unalloyed happiness. Your lucid expositions of the Saiva religion in all its aspects have reawakened the faith of Saivites in their own religion and rekindled in their hearts a burning desire to live more fully the Saivite way of life. You have not only forged a marvelous unity among Hindus all over the world but also won the staunch following of thousands of erudite Americans and created a beautiful array of American monks of unsullied purity. You have thus engendered an infinite spiritual power to liquidate the forces of materialism and reestablish dharma and lasting peace on this Earth.

You have now come down with a majestic group of pilgrims, like the Great God Siva surrounded by His *ganas,* to lose yourself in the stillness of communion with God in the grand temples of South India and Sri Lanka, and involve His unfailing grace for the fulfillment of your mission. May the whole world hearken to the voice of God reverberating through you, Gurudeva, and attain the four *purusharthas* of life. Om Shanti, Shanti, Shanti.

At each venue, schoolchildren came forward to dance and sing for their guest, then institutions, one by one, approached with offerings of flower garlands. Such garlands they were, giant garlands, some a full foot in diameter and nine feet long, carried by two people to the stage—fragrant garlands, simple and fancy garlands, tens, then scores, then hundreds of garlands. Two men would be fully occupied for thirty minutes removing the flowers from Gurudeva's neck, always leaving just enough so he could see over and into the crowd. The heat of that burden was only known to those close to Gurudeva, and the monks took turns fanning him when he began to perspire.

At the end, a pile of garlands four feet tall sagged the plywood stage. Finally, Gurudeva strode to the podium to deliver his talk. Day after day it went thus—morning, afternoon and evening processions, morning, afternoon and evening talks. Gurudeva covered much of the 25,000-square-mile nation, driving the back roads from Jaffna to Kilinochchi, from Kandy to Batticaloa, from Colombo to the mountainous tea country.

The turnout, in terms of sheer numbers, coupled with the deeply devotional spirit that arose from the hearts of the Sri Lankan Saivites for this occasion, exemplified an abiding reverence for the satguru. It is estimated that during those three weeks, Gurudeva trekked to every major Saivite center in Sri Lanka and over 300,000 came to see and hear him, to touch and be touched by him. S. Shanmugasundaram commented:

Not since the days of Saint Tirujnanasambandar, 1,200 years ago, has there been such devotion shown, where crowds of thousands would greet, follow and attend the words of a *jivanmuktar,* a liberated soul.

· ·

During Gurudeva's many journeys to India and Sri Lanka, hundreds of thousands came forward for blessings. Following a temple talk, he would typically sit for hours as, one by one, people came forward to greet him. Each would receive a smile and a mark of holy ash on the forehead, delivered with his right thumb.

As one of the Church's senior swamis observed:

> The state of Saivism in Lanka is like a blazing fire that has burned
> down to smoldering embers. All that is needed is to fan the embers,
> put on some wood and the roaring fire is there once again. Gurudeva
> is simply fanning those embers, and the fire is blazing forth.

Gurudeva must have stopped four or five hundred times on this trip.
Every time he headed toward an event, there was a great jockeying of
families and institutions urging him to stop at their place, which was
always, they said, on the way: "It's just for five minutes, Gurudeva, I promise. People have been waiting all day for your blessings. You can spare just
five minutes." This happened so frequently that the monks developed the
FMS Theory, the "five-minute-stop theory."

A typical FMS began with Gurudeva's team relenting, "OK, we will
stop for just a quick darshan." Reaching a crossroads, they stepped into
a crowd of a thousand people, cheering, elbowing for a view, holding
homemade banners aloft welcoming the "Saint of Saivism," offering arati.
Suddenly the mass of people would be on the move, pushing Gurudeva
forward, sweeping him into a hall where another twelve hundred people
waited, singing and chanting and begging Gurudeva to say a few words.
But first, a little introduction by the local elders! Forty-five minutes later,

During the 1980s Gurudeva visited all of the Saiva mathas *of South India, connecting with their abbots. The traditional culture he observed in these ancient monastery-temple complexes guided his development of Kauai Aadheenam.*

with military precision, the team would forcibly extract Gurudeva, retreat to the white van in which he and his five-man staff (two of his swamis, one sadhaka, a lay minister of the Church and the driver) were traveling, and escape, until the next FMS. In that way, to go twenty miles sometimes took three or four hours—not a happy thing for those waiting for the official event down the road.

In one place villagers heard that Gurudeva was not stopping, so they felled a large tree and put it across the road. He got down there, so sincere was their devotion, so desperate their tactics.

Similar receptions happened during the Innersearch in India. In the city of Tuticorin, Tamil Nadu, 80,000 people turned out in 1981 for a two-hour welcome parade down the main street, with joyous citizens showering Gurudeva with baskets of flower petals from rooftops as he and his followers rode by in decorated rickshaws and horse-drawn carriages. The sight of Western marching bands next to *tavil* and nagasvara players drove home the cultural interplay. The only parallel, one Innersearcher offered, was a ticker-tape parade down New York's Fifth Avenue for returning astronauts. From the temples of downtown Kuala Lumpur, to school assembly halls in Jaffna, to the *aadheenams* of South India, these gatherings of Western and Eastern Saivites set new patterns and established connections that would span generations.

Somehow Gurudeva had been warned that an ethnic war would break out the following year in Sri Lanka, a war that didn't end until 2009 and ultimately killed as many as 100,000 and drove hundreds of thousands of Tamils from their beloved homeland. His message to the people was a

preparation for the worst: "Hold tight to Siva's Feet and don't be afraid." Two and a half million Tamil Hindus lived in the Jaffna area at that time. They were afraid of the future, and Gurudeva was working hard to quell their fear, telling them to have courage and not forget God and guru.

He also spoke boldly about another battle that was being waged, the battle for their souls, driven by the armies of Christian conversion:

> If you love Siva, you don't fear death—and you don't fear those who live in fear, be they a Christian missionary or anyone else. In Hatton, I saw posters on the walls of buildings offering one hundred rupees to anyone who converts a Hindu to Christianity. How disgusting that all of the Tamils have bounty money on their heads. That means if you convert somebody, the Christians will pay you one hundred rupees, just as in the old, Wild West days the sheriff would pay a bounty for bringing in a bank robber.
>
> These conversions are all very shallow. They do not change anybody's belief structure or anything of that nature. They are just promising worldly benefits, you know: "You can get medical attention if you convert; otherwise, just go over there and die." Such cruel tactics—probably very much unbeknownst to the headquarters in the United States, because it is being done by Tamils who have converted to Christianity. There are no governing rules, and that's how the local missionaries get money from the United States, by giving a list of names of those they have "saved."

Saiva Siddhanta Finds a Hero

From his days with Satguru Yogaswami, Gurudeva held and taught that Saiva Siddhanta is essentially monistic, though of a different breed than the well-known monism of Adi Shankara. But there was another, quite prominent Saiva Siddhanta view that he learned of in Sri Lanka in the late 40s and was now about to face in a personal way.

> I first became aware of this perennial debate in 1948 while performing sadhana, living in little mud huts with cow dung floors, in Jaffna, Sri Lanka, prior to my initiation from my satguru, Siva Yogaswami. I learned that various pluralist adherents in the area were not pleased with this modern mystic's monistic statements and conclusions.
> Siva Yogaswami asked me which of these schools of thought was

· ·

In Malaysia, Fiji, Trinidad, Europe, Sri Lanka, India, Mauritius and more, devotees took special joy in receiving the tall satguru who looked like Siva, spoke like Siva and radiated a palpable love that transformed their lives. During grand processions, they placed white cotton cloth on the ground for him to walk on.

the right one. I told him that both were right in their own way. It all depends on whether you are on top of the mountain looking down or at the bottom of it looking up. He smiled and nodded. Jnanaguru Yogaswami taught that monistic theism is the highest vision of truth.

In my life, the issue again came into prominence in the early 80s after my recognition by the world community of Saivites as Guru Mahasannidhanam of Kauai Aadheenam and Jagadacharya of the Natha Sampradaya's Kailasa Parampara.

While visiting the 1,400-year-old Dharmapura Aadheenam, Gurudeva made note of the abbot's massive earrings. The monastery head called for two gold earrings and ceremonially fit them on his guest.

. . . .

In the early 1980s Gurudeva produced hundreds of thousands of pamphlets that circled the globe, proclaiming the oneness and ultimate unity of God and soul. These provoked some interesting responses from those who hold that God and soul are eternally separate and who refer to themselves as pluralists. He described the fundamental difference between the two views:

In the monistic view, God Siva is everything; even this physical universe is a part of Him, though He transcends it as well. In the pluralistic view, God Siva animates and guides the universe, but it is not a part of Him. The crux of the difference, then, is whether there is one eternal reality in the universe or three, whether the soul is eternally separate or is, in essence, one with Siva.

For the most part, monists and pluralists within Saiva Siddhanta are of one mind. These are not diametrically opposing philosophies. They share more in common than they disagree about. In fact, between these two schools there is ninety-five percent agreement and only five percent dissidence.

At first, letters from the pluralists were tame and kindly, if a bit patronizing. They softly reminded the satguru in Hawaii, as an adult might correct an unknowing child, of the eternal, separate existence of God, soul and world, and hinted he might want to revise his books, and his creed, to accommodate this truth. Back went the responses, assuring the concerned elders that he had it right, that his teachings were in concert with Yogaswami's and Saint Tirumular's, and the other form of Saiva Siddhanta was a modern divergence from that tradition.

That did it. Off went the gloves as pandits and swamis from several nations barraged the little Kauai monastery with ontological assaults, tendentious arguments and petty criticisms. It was important for them to sway the guru in Hawaii, for he had a presence on the global stage that they did not enjoy; and just as they had embraced him for bringing Saivism back to life in the modern age, they were now compelled to distance themselves from his errant beliefs.

All efforts to persuade Gurudeva only elicited affection from him, and support for his position from authentic sources, not the least of which was Justice Maharajan of Madras, regarded as the world's foremost authority on the *Tirumantiram* and an avid supporter of Gurudeva's views.

The pluralists grew insolent and mean, launching a campaign of name-calling and put-downs, all couched in the subtle slurs that only well-read men are capable of. They thought to isolate Gurudeva from the Saiva Siddhanta mainstream by suggesting he had formed an aberrant, contemporary Siddhanta. Disparagingly, they called it "Hawaii Saivism."

To no avail. Gurudeva would not budge. Instead he reached out to them and invited a debate of sorts, through the mail. He traveled to the Saiva centers, where he made the case for monistic Saiva Siddhanta, drawing deeply from the *Tirumantiram,* the spiritual well of Tamil scripture that had fed Saiva mysticism for centuries. At first, the pandits cried foul, accusing Gurudeva of having his translators skew the English to support his interpretation. But when other equally competent Tamil translators were marshalled to the task, the pluralists saw that Gurudeva was right: the great *Tirumantiram* indeed spoke boldly of a monistic view. The pandits did what any desperate debator does; they tossed out their own sacred text, averring, "We have been drinking at a poisoned well." A shocking gesture, but their only viable tactic, since their own scripture indicted their cause.

In July of 1983 a conference on the issue, which had spread to every learned Siddhantin in the world, was convened in Kuala Lumpur. Six hundred attended the two-day event, during which both sides presented their views. Between the plenaries, tedious sessions were held in the library as text after text was marched onto the battlefield of belief. It was an historic two days, and if anyone left with a single impression it was this: Gurudeva stood staunchly for monistic Saiva Siddhanta, and no one was going to change his mind.

Seeing this, and no doubt partially persuaded by the mountain of evidence that Gurudeva and his monks presented, the opposition softened, concluding finally something Gurudeva had offered as the solution months before: that there are indeed two schools of Saiva Siddhanta, the

original monistic school of Rishi Tirumular and the subsequent pluralistic school founded by Saint Meykandar. This brought peace to a tense
situation and allowed both sides to work again together for the future of
Saivism. Gurudeva later recollected the resolution:

> The monism/pluralism debate, rekindled by our statement that there
> can be only one final conclusion, was resolved in the understanding
> that within Saiva Siddhanta there is one final conclusion for pluralists
> and one final conclusion for monistic theists. This occurred in Febru-
> ary of 1984 at the South Indian monastery of Sri la Sri Shanmuga Desi-
> ka Gnanasambandha Paramacharya Swamigal, 26th Guru Mahasanni-
> dhanam of the Dharmapura Aadheenam, at a meeting of professors,
> advocates, theologians, academicians and pandits on the issue.
>
> Thus the spirit of Sanatana Dharma that is modern Hinduism
> bound the monistic school and the pluralistic school into a productive
> partnership for the good of all, working together in the great Hindu
> renaissance, which is surging forward as a result of the global Hindu
> diaspora, and spawning an indomitable Hindu front. We are happy
> to say that peace, tolerance, forbearance and mutual respect now exist
> between these two schools.
>
> We feel that the foundation for this coexistence of love and trust
> was made on January 30, 1981, when we met with His Holiness for
> the first time. I was on a holy pilgrimage to Saivism's most sacred sites
> with my entourage of forty Eastern and Western devotees when mes-
> sengers from His Holiness invited us to visit his ancient Dharmapura
> Aadheenam.
>
> Together we sat in the inner chambers of his palatial spiritual ref-
> uge, built by maharajas in the sixteenth century. It was quite a spec-
> tacle—Eastern pandits with their guru, and Western mystics with
> theirs, discussing the philosophical enigmas that have perplexed
> the mind of man from the dawn of history. Through our translators,
> we spoke of God, of the soul and the world, and of the dire need for
> Saivite schools in South India, and around the world, to pass this great
> knowledge on to the next generation.
>
> After our lively discussion, a special lunch was served. Later, one of
> our swamis casually inquired of His Holiness about his large golden
> earrings, wondering where such a pair might be obtained for myself.
> Without hesitation, the guru summoned an aide and whispered some
> instructions. Moments later, a pair of earrings identical to those he
> was wearing were placed in his hands. His Holiness indicated that

these were for me. Joyfully shrugging off our objections that he was being too generous, he immediately set about placing them in my ears with his own hands, enlarging the existing holes to accept these massive gold rings which are the traditional insignia of a *paramacharya guru mahasannidhanam aadheenakarthar*. Then he presented new orange *kavi* cloth to me and to my accompanying swamis.

We gratefully accepted the *sannidhanam's* unexpected and generous gift as a gesture of goodwill to help us on our way of spreading the message of Saiva Siddhanta. Perhaps even more importantly, it was to us a sign of cooperative efforts between two great monasteries, one firmly teaching pluralistic Saiva Siddhanta in the East, and the other boldly promulgating monistic Saiva Siddhanta in the West. We thought to ourself that all that transpired after this would be for the best. To the onlooking pandits, this presentation of the acharya earrings meant that all knowledgeable Hindus would know that the Guru Mahasannidhanam of Dharmapura Aadheenam and the Guru Mahasannidhanam of Kauai Aadheenam would work together for the future of Saiva Siddhanta.

Later the same day, Mahasannidhanam asked me to address several thousand people who were seated in the giant inner hall overlooking the large temple tank. I spoke of the greatness of Saivism and Saiva Siddhanta and the effects of its spreading into the Western world. The day culminated when His Holiness handed me an ornate silver casket, in which was kept a precious scroll honoring our work in spreading Saiva Siddhanta.

Later, after being engraved with words of acknowledgement, the casket was officially presented to me at the 1,000-pillared hall in Chidambaram Temple just before the sacred Bharatanatyam performance by premier dancer Kumari Swarnamukhi, a state treasure of Tamil Nadu, which we arranged as part of our Innersearch Travel-Study Program. This was the first dance performance within the temple's precincts in over fifty years, since the Anglican British outlawed the dancing of *devadasis* in temples. More than 15,000 devotees were packed into the viewing area while 300,000 more, we were told, filled the 40-acre temple complex. The entire city of Chidambaram came forward, as well as neighboring villages, for this historic presentation of all 108 *tandava* poses, a magnificent event held on the temple's most popular evening, establishing once and for all that, yes, dance could again be held in Chidambaram. This tradition, once banned, now continues at Siva's most hallowed sanctuary.

So, dancing with Siva began again on that historic day—a dance that never ends. We look forward to the day when dance in each and every Saiva temple in South India and around the world is a vital part of worship. That day is not far off, for temple congregations in Europe, Australia, Canada and the United States already take great joy when their girls and boys dance for God and the Gods. That dance is the perfect metaphor of Siva's gracious presence in the world He created!

Chapter Twenty-Seven

The Mission Goes Global

Gurudeva's global travels brought home to him the fact that Hinduism was a fragmented religion, each group isolated from every other group. He realized that this prevented Hinduism from realizing its inherent strength. As was his way, when he saw a need, he took well-planned steps to fulfill it. In 1995 he wrote:

> It was during a world tour through Singapore, Malaysia, Mauritius, Reunion, Africa, India, Nepal, Sri Lanka, Europe and other countries that I realized Hinduism had no global voice and no network of communication. The Hindus in Durban had no idea what was happening with Hindus in Colombo. Those in London had no connection with Hindus in Canada. Thus, I was divinely directed by inner orders from our Yogaswami Kailasa Parampara, by my satguru in this life, to fulfill the crying need to create an international network that would interconnect all Hindus into one invincible front.
>
> When I decided to launch HINDUISM TODAY in 1979, my thinking was: to make Saivism strong, we have to make all the other three main denominations strong. Because our philosophy is being devoted to Siva in everyone, we support every Hindu sect equally. Our strength is in having oneness with all the Hindus around the world, even though our philosophical, doctrinal and cultural approaches may differ somewhat. This is for the benefit of the overall Hindu renaissance, which is gaining in power as the century turns, for as each becomes strong, that strength benefits the overall body of Hinduism, giving pride, stability and courage to proceed with confidence. This is Hindu solidarity, one of our heartfelt commitments. The other is monistic theism—Advaita Ishvaravada—of Saiva Siddhanta.

In June, 1980, Gurudeva and two swamis visited Malaysia for the first time. During their stay, several elders told them of a prophecy made almost 30 years earlier by a Malaysian sadhu named Sri Jeganathaswami that an American swami named "Subramaniam" would come to Malaysia to spread Saivism and Hinduism. Gurudeva didn't suddenly take Malaysia by storm. In fact, he never took any place by storm. He sought no self-promotion, but rather worked to support and strengthen local religious

. . . .

As Gurudeva began to craft a global fellowship of Saivites, the Hindus of Malaysia came forward powerfully. He visited often, guiding their spiritual learning and practice, giving diksha *to the worthy.*

leaders and institutions, according to their needs and not his ambitions.

Malaysia's Hindu leaders had been feeling increasingly challenged on two fronts: the government of this predominantly Muslim country had been placing increasing restraints on their religion, while their youth had become fascinated with the Western lifestyle. The leaders were beginning to awaken the general Hindu community to these threats to their identity and future. Gurudeva gave form, style and impetus to this awakening as he traveled through the country and visited the major Hindu institutions—the Malaysia Hindu Sangam, the Kuala Lumpur Maha

Mariamman Temple, the Ceylon Saivites Association, the Ramakrishna Mission, the Divine Life Society and others—to make friends. Especially drawn to him were those of the Tamil community. Many of Sri Lankan descent, particularly those who knew Yogaswami, made an easy connection. He was the guru they had been waiting for, one grounded in their Saiva heritage but totally at home with Western ways and idioms.

The situation of Malaysian Hindus, just eight percent of the country, is different than that of Hindus in India. Government policies favor Islam and the *bumiputras*, Muslim native Malaysians, over the Indians and Chinese. As a result of this inequity, many Hindus—especially among the youth—had turned to their religion to strengthen self-identity.

Malaysia was the first place in the world, for example, that Gurudeva ever met a youth group attached to a temple. This fine group of young men all wore jackets with "Siddhi Vinayaga Temple" on the back and worked as a team in selfless support of the temple's care and management. Gurudeva was received enthusiastically by the younger generation, and he counted that a good sign. To his delight, they were ready to follow directions, a rarity among modern youth, and many were seriously committed to spiritual progress.

Over the next few years, Hindus attracted to Gurudeva's teachings held after-hours classes in Hinduism at local public schools. These popular seminars and the widespread distribution of HINDUISM TODAY magazine had a huge impact on Hindus in Malaysia. Many became dedicated members and, through the years, disseminated Gurudeva's clear Hindu teachings to the youth. He spoke to their souls as no other had, to their contemporary ideals of religious life and service. Their own disciplined and successful lives served as a model; and more came, relieved to be part of a dynamic institution that instilled pride in the Hindu religion.

He sent one of his monastics to teach classes all over the nation for nearly a year. In 1986 his devotees conducted successful Hindu youth camps in Malaysia, inspiring other Hindu organizations to put more emphasis on youth camps. When Gurudeva returned to Malaysia in the 1990s, his lectures were packed; and at his last book signing there, in 2000, over 800 people showed up, exceeding the hall's capacity. Appasamy Kuppusamy writes:

Once upon a time Gurudeva was ignored by many Hindus of Malaysia because he was white. But after getting to know him, the same people praised him for his services to Hinduism worldwide.

At a national level, the cumulative impact of his work has been a dramatic increase in the pride of Hindus.

Gurudeva's publications have always been popular in Malaysia. In the 1980s, local devotees requested Gurudeva to write a book on Lord Ganesha, to explain this elephant-headed God to Hindus. They wanted it right away, to distribute at an upcoming festival; so Gurudeva and his monks created the entire book in eight days. That was a twelve-hour-a-day effort by a dozen monks; and the resulting book, *Lord Ganesha, Benevolent Deity for a Modern Hindu World*, was a success. The title alone was an inspiration to people. Later it was expanded into the even more popular *Loving Ganesha*.

Each time Gurudeva visited Malaysia, he stopped in Singapore, where he nurtured a small group of followers and encouraged Hindu temples and organizations. His Malaysian and Singaporean devotees are among his staunchest and most active. Mr. Kuppusamy shared this testimony of Gurudeva's impact on his life:

> At the beginning, I was not very serious about doing the sadhanas, the religious practices, but later I did do them seriously. I learned the *atmartha* puja for home worship and taught it to others. I and my wife, along with our ten-year-old son and twenty-two-year-old daughter, all became vegetarians without any reluctance. Gurudeva made me realize my mistakes, my bad karma done earlier in this life, and had me correct it through penance, *prayashchitta*. After that difficult penance, I am relieved and happy that this karma is gone.
>
> I thank Gurudeva because he changed our lifestyle. He taught us Hinduism. He taught us discipline. He made us see God everywhere, within and outside. He taught us to do *thondu*, religious service, all of which I am doing my level best to follow.

Gurudeva spoke often on these topics, urging people to see God everywhere as a first solution to many of life's problems:

> God has no names, but all names are the names of God. Whether you call Him this or that, He remains who He is. God is both within us and outside of us. Even desire, the fulfillment of desire, the joy, the pain, the sorrow, birth and death—this is all God, nothing but God. This is how God can be seen everywhere and in everyone. He is there as the Soul of each soul. You can open your inner eye and see Him in

others, see Him in the world as the world. Little by little, discipline yourself to meditate at the same time each day. Meditate, discover the silent center of yourself, then go deep within, to the core of your real Being. Slowly the purity comes. Slowly the awakening comes.

When problems come in the family or workplace and emotions arise, it is only natural to forget God. It's so much easier to be involved in twoness rather than oneness. It takes a lot of inner strength to remember God all of the time, to keep the love for God flowing. We forget. We get involved in ourselves and others. It is impossible when our ego is attacked or our feelings hurt. So it's easier, much easier, to forget God and even regard Him as a God to be feared; whereas it is our own instinctive mind and our pre-programmed, nonreligious intellect that should be feared. That's the demon in our house, the mischief-maker who causes all the trouble. If you want to remember God, then first learn to forget yourself a little.

It is natural to forget about God, but there are many helpful ways that we can avoid distraction, that we can remember to keep seeing God everywhere. One of the practical ways to bring God into the midst of all this is to keep repeating His name. Do japa when you find your-self forgetting, when you just can't see God at all, let alone everywhere. When life becomes difficult or strained, mentally put it all at His feet.

See Him in everyone that you meet or confront, regardless of the circumstances. He is there as their life force, but you just need to quiet the mind to see. Smile when you feel unhappy with someone and say to yourself, "How nice to see you, God, in this form." Animals, beggars, princes, politicians, friends and enemies, holy men, saints and sages are all God to the soul that loves God. He smiles and thinks to himself, "How nice to see you, God, in this, another of your many forms."

God is love and nothing else but love. He fills this universe with love. He fills you with love. God is fire. God is earth. God is air. God is water. God is ether. God's cosmic energy permeates everything and gives light and life to your mind. God is everywhere and all things. God is your small, insignificant worry, the concern that you have been holding in your mind for so many years.

In His own way, He is bringing you into realization, into knowledge of yourself and of Him. He has given you the world of experience. Study your experience. Learn from your experience. If it is painful, that is also good. In the fires of experience, which are both pain and pleasure, you are being purified. In doing so, you must go through much pain, through much joy. Both register on the scale as the same intensity of emotion. It is what caused it that makes one more pleasurable than another. Don't be afraid to live with God and go through your experience joyfully. Go through it with courage. Don't try to avoid it.

Saiva Periya Sangaratna Tan Sri Somasundram, president of the Malaysia Arul Neri Thirukkootam, wrote:

> Gurudeva avoided arguing the philosophies of the various sects of Hinduism. He showed the importance of religion, but not the arguments. He was not only the guru for a particular group of Saivites; he was accepted by all of us as a guru. If we are to respect him, we must live according to his teachings, to have peace in the world, peace at home, peace between husband and wife, peace everywhere.

Mauritius: Island Jewel

For some unknown reason, Gurudeva's influence had disproportionate impact on islands. It began in Sri Lanka, then extended to Kauai, Fiji and Trinidad. Mauritius, an island nation of one and a half million, of which fifty-two percent, including the ruling elite, are Hindu, would feel the grace of his holy feet.

He was invited there by a Tamil elder and leading writer and thinker, Retnon Velvindron, who wrote to Gurudeva in 1981 saying he feared for the future of Hindu youth. They were being systematically converted by two other faiths, and their numbers were eroding at a fearsome rate. The Muslims had taken to converting those in financial straits, helping the jobless find work, helping the mortgage-challenged to keep their homes, all at a price. Salut et Guérison, the Mauritius mission of the Assembly of God, worked on those with health issues. They approached Mauritian Hindus who were sick or dying, befriended them and promised to pray for their recovery. If they did get better, bonds had been forged and friendships made, and formal conversion was soon to follow. The Tamil community of the nation was being particularly targeted, and Tiru Velvindron sought Gurudeva's help to turn the tide.

Gurudeva responded swiftly and with full force, flying with two swamis to the island nation in early 1982 after the India Odyssey. The receptions, while less populous than those that greeted him in Sri Lanka and South India weeks earlier, were equally loving and appreciative. His message was more bold than the normal Mauritian defenses of faith: Hinduism is the greatest religion in the world, the temples are the homes of the Gods and it is alright to turn missionaries away from your door and not let them in. In all nations, Hindus feel duty-bound to be hospitable even to those who would tear their families apart. The tall, white-haired guru from America made it okay to say no.

Again in February of 1983, he flew there with two monks. This time he stayed a full month, one of his longest sojourns. A small guest house had been built especially for him at the Sri Sockalingam Meenakshi Temple in Port Louis. Gurudeva visited virtually every major Hindu community on the island, speaking with large crowds at temples, awakening the Mauritian youth to the grandeur of their religion. It was a turning point in the nation's spiritual evolution. Gurudeva introduced his French-speaking monastic to one and all and arranged for him to remain in the country and teach Saiva Siddhanta classes for six months. These seminars were a grand success, leading eventually to the growth of Church membership and the founding of a seven-acre Spiritual Park and monastic center in the country.

The Mauritius Spiritual Park started with a vision, which Gurudeva described in the following account.

In 1986 I had a powerful vision of Lord Ganesha while I was here in Mauritius looking for property for Saiva Siddhanta Church. Lord Ganesha was walking from His temple attended by two priests. He was about to take a bath in the beautiful Indian Ocean in the country of Mauritius where the river meets the sea. I was standing in the water with several sharks swimming around me. Lord Ganesha, accompanied by two priests, looked at me and said, "Just rub some oil on their noses and they will not harm you."

The vision led me directly to this special land by the Rempart River and its lagoon. The Spiritual Park is a fulfillment of that vision. I see it combining environmental and architectural beauty that will give spiritual peace and mystical knowledge to visitors for many generations in the future. It is destined to become a pilgrimage site of great renown in the Indian Ocean area. Hindus from Malaysia, Singapore, Indonesia, Africa and India will come here.

While looking for property for a center in Mauritius, Gurudeva had a vision of Lord Ganesha and a shark which took place in a river near the ocean. That vision guided him to the seven-acre, ocean-side parcel that would become the Spiritual Park.

Today thousands of Hindus attend the monthly *homa* at the Spiritual Park, burning their prayers in its magical fires. Outside the wooden, Kerala-style thatched pavilion, they crowd together in the shade of mango and sacred konrai trees to worship the nine-foot-tall black granite murti of Lord Ganesha with five faces and ten arms. In this way, Gurudeva's mission took root on the tropical island that enchanted Mark Twain when he visited in 1896 and wrote, "You gather the idea that Mauritius was made first, and then heaven, and that heaven was copied after Mauritius."

Mauritius, basking peacefully in the Indian Ocean, is a land of pious temple worship for the general Hindu population. Almost every family there has been associated for generations with one of the thousands of local temples. Hindu celebrations like Mahasivaratri and Tai Pusam are grand events that often stop traffic with magnificent processions of thousands of people. For the average Hindu, basic religious obligations are fulfilled by participating in these festivals.

An understanding of the significance of the Hindu guru was almost nonexistent in Mauritius until the 1980s, when Gurudeva first set foot upon this island. This spiritual innovator redefined the concept of Hinduism for many on the island. In the Mauritian nomenclature "Hindus" were the North Indians; the "Tamils" were regarded, and looked upon themselves, as a separate religious group. Gurudeva explained they were all Hindus, and these were just ethnic/linguistic divisions. This simple change of identity vitalized the inspiration of sincere seekers and began a new era in Mauritius—the era of Hindu unity and cooperation. Rajen Manick told of Gurudeva's influence on his family:

> It was at this time that I first met Gurudeva. Although I had been studying his teachings through a correspondence course and writing for HINDUISM TODAY, my first encounter with him in person was a memorable experience. I could see immediately that he was not an ordinary man.
>
> He changed my life. The girl I was lucky enough to marry was also one of Gurudeva's students. We were the very first of his devotees to be married in Mauritius. This happened in 1985. Our greatest joy has been to serve Gurudeva by imparting his teachings on the island of Mauritius, which we first did by organizing classes at local temples.
>
> After ten years of marriage we despaired of having children. Gurudeva taught us to face our karmas gracefully and to be humble in difficult situations. Shortly thereafter, most certainly with the blessings of Gurudeva, we had two children.

During this time there was a regular flow of monastics traveling from Kauai Aadheenam to the monastery in Mauritius. Under Gurudeva's direction they established the Spiritual Park and held retreats and seminars for thousands of youth around the island.

Meanwhile, Gurudeva advised his family members on the island to use ayurvedic medicine and adopt a healthy diet, including raw sugar, brown rice and whole grain bread in place of white sugar, white rice and white flour. He encouraged followers to wear Hindu dress at home, in the temples and during festivals, even at work if employers allowed.

•••

Seeing a dearth of Hindu missionaries during his wide travels, Gurudeva trained teachers and leaders to pass Saivite Hinduism on to the next generation. In Malaysia and Mauritius especially, his followers undertook to speak regularly to groups and families in temples, ashrams and homes.

Mougam Pareatumbee, a retired hotel chef, now manager of his own catering center, remembered how life was hard during the early days of his marriage, when his wife's health seemed unfavorable for childbirth. One day, Gurudeva called from Hawaii and said, "I am with you. Don't worry!" Soon his wife, Amutha, gave birth to two beautiful daughters.

Accountant S. K. Moorghen remembers that prior to Gurudeva's arrival in Mauritius, the importance of the home shrine was not fully understood. "Now," he says, "even nonfollowers of Gurudeva make it a must to keep shrines in their homes, and they are proud of it."

Politicians like Anil Baichoo, Minister of Transport, affirmed that Gurudeva's teachings in Mauritius helped to harmonize the various ethnic groups of the island:

> Gurudeva's approach to Hinduism is not based on ethnicity or language. This has helped to build up more Hindu solidarity between Hindus of both North Indian and South Indian origin. Also, conversion is less of a problem in Mauritius, all due to the influence of Gurudeva and the Sai Baba groups.

The story of Gurudeva's influence on individuals, leaders and entire communities in Mauritius happened in other nations as well during these two decades, his years of strengthening Hindus worldwide. Similar tales are told by Hindus in Fiji and Germany, Trinidad and South Africa, Canada and Australia, Malaysia and the United States.

Guiding an International Congregation

By the mid 1980s Gurudeva had established a strong international congregation of men, women and children, the members of Saiva Siddhanta Church, striving for personal, spiritual transformation while living and working in the world, tithing on their income to support the Church, conclaving in local mission groups and gathering in homes to worship and perform karma yoga.

From the early days Gurudeva was strict with himself and his monks and shishyas, and that strictness called for everyone to take vows. Vows, to him, were a way to build discipline and character and master the forces of mind, body and emotion, giving strength to face the future and holding the individual firmly on the path of sadhana. First there was the tithing vow. In the 80s vegetarianism was also required, and in the early 90s he added the vow of loyalty to the guru lineage. A few years before his passing, after discovering that some followers were still using physical

Gurudeva brought large murtis *of Ganesha, Muruga and Siva to the Spiritual Park, and inspired Mauritian Hindus to learn and faithfully follow their religion. The pride he awakened forestalled Christian conversions and changed the island nation forever.*

· ·

punishment to discipline their children, he imposed a fourth vow, to be taken by all current and prospective members: the ahimsa *vrata*. Gurudeva explained the need and efficacy of vow-taking:

Wholeheartedly accepting four vows—Ahimsa, Parampara, Shakahara and Dashama Bhaga—is essential to any aspiring student. The devonic adepts take these vows very seriously, knowing that once a vow is taken at an auspicious moment in life, the karmas yet to come change slightly to the positive side so long as the vow is upheld. But when vows are neglected, the full force of the held-back karmas

not previously dissolved, mostly the bad ones, comes as a blow to individual, family and friends. So it is imperative that those who have taken these four first vows—Ahimsa, Shakahara, Parampara and Dashama Bhaga—receive help when needed from our *mathavasis* in fulfilling them.

Because it has always been our aim to build a harmonious, productive, dynamic global fellowship, new candidates for membership and initiation are carefully screened and required to adjust themselves to the cultural standards, beliefs and attitudes that prevail at the time they seek entrance. They must be loyal and dedicated to our philosophy and goals, willing to blend their energies with the existing group of initiates to advance their own religious life and further the broader work of the fellowship. We are strict and demanding in order to build and maintain a core mission group.

Moreover, steady improvement is expected from each member through the years. Each has come to me as a shishya for the sole purpose of performing sadhana. None is allowed to lose sight of his or her

Children were dear to Gurudeva, and he worked hard to guide their upbringing, provide them with religious texts and protect them from harm. Thousands would grow up immersed in his teachings.

Page 579

Chapter 27

original intent. Initiates appreciate their life–changing moments and strive hard to keep up with the pace.

Gurudeva summarized the path of these tried and tested souls:

> If both husband and wife are on the spiritual path, the householder family will progress beautifully and deeply. Their love for one another and their offspring maintains family harmony. However, the nature of their sadhana and unfoldment of the spirit is different from that of the sannyasin. The struggle to maintain the responsibilities of the home and children while simultaneously observing the contemplative way, in itself, provides strength and balance, and slowly matures innate wisdom through the years.

It is this balance that Gurudeva taught his householder devotees to accomplish, in his conversations with them and in *Living with Siva,* where he addressed every issue that arises on the family path, from the spiritually subtle to the most mundane. Deva Seyon, who lives near the monastery on Kauai, observed:

> Gurudeva brought the true and ultimate meaning of *gotra,* or family lineage, to his initiated devotees. While Gurudeva was the supreme monastic, he was never at a loss in advising on the business, social or intimate, personal problems of his initiated families, down to the smallest detail. He knew every family shishya on a deep, personal level—their hopes and dreams, fears and shortcomings—and never tired of guiding, helping and serving his congregation.

Deva Rajan of California recalls just such an encounter:

> In the early 90s, we were having some financial difficulties in our business, Canyon Construction Company. I told Gurudeva about it and asked for his advice. He said. "Let's go over to your office and you can tell me all about it."
> It was a Sunday, so no one was there except us. He sat in the big

swivel chair with a high back at my desk. I handed over the books of the business and he asked a few key questions. I showed him how we had borrowed over $140,000 from our business credit line just to pay bills, make payroll and taxes. Competition had driven our profit margins way down, and economic constraints at that time were not encouraging to clients. New projects seemed few and far between. I had no foreseeable way to pay off the debt.

Gurudeva looked over everything closely and then with a warm smile of confidence, our business books in his lap, simply said, "Well, let's just turn things around." Then with a swift kick, he spun my chair around several times. Round and round he went, smiling all the while. Sitting on the floor in front of him, I pushed myself back, stunned and transfixed by the magic of these moments.

When he finally came to a stop, he asked the monastic accompanying him to do a little puja and office blessing. The priest went around to every room and corner, clearing our business space with the wave of a bell, lamp and incense. At each window, he left a piece of fruit on the sill, asking any resident *asuras* to please enjoy the fruit, but also to please leave this office forever.

Meanwhile, Gurudeva gave me some specific instructions about the business, ending with much encouragement and the words, "Proceed with confidence."

Within a few months, everything began to change for the better. Job after job came in. We expanded our business, hiring more personnel. Our debts were quickly erased, and profits began to accumulate such that we could continue to expand and grow out the business.

After a few years, large, multi-million-dollar projects were knocking at our doors. We couldn't seem to do anything wrong. At one point, a multi-millionaire invited us to build his $14-million estate on a 40-acre hilltop in nearby Oakland, California. Initially I turned him down, explaining that it was too big for us and that we had little experience at that level. He kept coming back, so I called Gurudeva to talk it over.

Gurudeva was delighted with the prospects for our business and again poured on the encouragement to proceed with confidence. After we had signed the contracts, I called him with the good news and a question, "I've never built for such a rich man. What should I do?" Gurudeva said simply, "Just do what he says."

Those instructions may sound too simplistic, but I discovered them to be an essential key to working with this highly successful businessman and subsequently with all our clients. In our weekly meetings with him, I used to secretly take notes on every little thing that he or his wife would mention. I made sure that our management immediately fulfilled these requests and reported back to our clients that changes had been made or that specific instructions had been carried out. I watched as his architects would argue with him over design details. They were later fired. I instructed our management team and some eighty subcontractors working on the project to never argue or try to change the mind of our client. "Just do what he says," I told them.

During a thirty-year period, Gurudeva moved us from a small, struggling company to one of the most successful and respected contracting businesses in the San Francisco Bay Area. We took quantum leaps at times, to new levels of management and capacity, all the while under his guidance. He continually encouraged me to "reach for the stars," sweeping away self-doubt and fears of failure. Yet, his advice was always rooted in simple basics.

Though scattered across the globe, Gurudeva's followers found themselves no less connected than if they lived in a single village. One example is the cross-national marriage that brought together the Deva Seyon family of Kauai and the family of Manon Mardemootoo, a leading lawyer in Mauritius. In 1991, Kavita, Deva's daughter, married Sivakumaren, Manon's son. Though half a world away, the two families merged like milk poured into milk. Deva recalled:

> Gurudeva's constant blessings and loving care for the needs of our family led us to love and trust those who also loved him. His international global spiritual family became our family, as we shared the same goals and priorities in life. In amalgamating our two families, all the big issues regarding the future of our children were already settled, as we shared the same *kulaguru*.

Gurudeva required his Church members to live strictly by the traditional, time-tested protocols of Tamil Saivite culture, which he detailed in his 365 Nandinatha Sutras in *Living with Siva*. Association with orthodox Saivites of India and Sri Lanka allows Westerners to absorb the subtleties and depths of this refined culture, and Gurudeva encouraged it at every opportunity.

Succinctly, boldly, these Nandinatha Sutras describe how people lived and interrelated with one another when life was simpler, when families and villages were close-knit, and love and peace, respect and wisdom prevailed. There is no new knowledge contained herein. Each sutra proclaims an ancient wisdom and protocol which, when followed, brings that same simplicity, community support, peace, harmony and refinement of enduring relationships into daily life. Each of these 365 sutras, one to be read each day of the year, is a thread of purity, many from the historic past into the present, some from contemporary times. Even today, in the fifty-second Hindu century, these precepts define the daily life of hundreds of millions of well-bred and well-raised Asian people.

While they are law, these sutras are not commandments. They simply describe what devout Hindus do. Naturally, my expectations are that my close followers will heed and earnestly try to put into practice all 365 sutras. Many who read these sutras will wonder to themselves or even among friends, "Why do we need to follow such strict traditions and disciplines? Aren't they a bit old-fashioned?" My answer is: before the two world wars, many traditions similar to these were followed even in the United States, regarding raising of children, man-and-wife relationships, women rarely working outside the home, and thus not neglecting their children, etc. It was during World War II, when women began working in the world, that the breakdown of traditional culture occurred, setting a trend that is now being followed in almost every nation.

The nonculture, or the destruction of culture which is nonculture, has become the "culture" which everyone follows. Hence the avalanche of promiscuity, divorce, suicide, various excesses and abuses—murder, theft, wife-beating, drug abuse, unstable, ever-shifting cohabitation as a substitute for marriage and the shameful neglect of children. Everyone's security is threatened.

When my satguru, Sage Yogaswami, was asked half a century ago why we should follow the old ways, he answered simply, "The railway engine pulls many coaches. Can it do so if it runs off the track? No. Great people have shown the path. We must follow it." Though perhaps challenging, the disciplines and guidelines described in the

Following the daily pre-dawn meditation, it was common to find Gurudeva walking along Siva's garden paths, coffee in hand, greeting monks and visitors alike, reminding one and all of their innermost Self.

sutras create happy individuals, harmonious families and secure nations. When you take them as a total whole, you will glimpse the ideal community. Such a community is able to work together, love together, trust together, create together, serve Siva together, worship together, live together in a productive harmony and ongoing creativity, as they each experience birth, life, death and birth again.

Hindus have spread throughout the world, relocating themselves because of employment opportunities, ethnic disputes, violence and economic deprivation within their homelands. Because of this

diaspora, it has become necessary to restate the law of the culture, the protocol and modes of behavior that their forefathers knew and lived so well.

The Saivite Shastras, revealed to Gurudeva in 1973, explain, "The guru worked with the families in the same way he worked with a single monastery." Deva Seyon elaborated on that relationship between the monastery and family homes:

> The monastery and the families of Saiva Siddhanta Church work closely together on many levels in fulfilling Gurudeva's directives, both within the Church missions and with the public at large. The families learn by watching the monks—their attitudes, their commitment, their selfless service.

This relationship is born out of the love of striving through daily religious disciplines, such as meditation and scriptural study, that Gurudeva nurtured in all of his devotees.

Gurudeva urged the families of the Church to forge frontiers in passing on the traditions of the Hindu religion by worshiping daily together in the home shrine, wearing Hindu clothing, raising children nonviolently, holding daily family meetings and spending an evening together at home at least once a week. He taught groups of families in each area to collaborate and help each other live a meaningful Hindu lifestyle in many ways, such as homeschooling their children together, hosting pilgrims and special guests and going on pilgrimage together to temples in South India and to the Aadheenam in Kauai.

Gurudeva put great emphasis on establishing a lay ministry, designating one or more couples in each Church mission as a *kulapati* family. Much of his work with the congregation, and with spiritual initiatives in many nations, was channeled through this hand-picked, highly trained group, his missionaries in the field whom he called upon almost daily.

Manon Mardemootoo eloquently summarized Gurudeva's impact on the lives of householder devotees:

> Gurudeva has exposed us to a way of life conducive to peace, love and harmony in and outside the home. He has given us the tools to be peacemakers, to shine as examples of good family people, and as elders who have been endowed with wisdom, able to stand as respected leaders even in the most difficult times. He has taught us

. . . .

Gurudeva was available to devotees night and day, taking calls anytime of the day to discuss their health, family, jobs and meditations.

by his own life how to be strong in our beliefs and values and succeed in life by planning carefully and living fully in the present. If we now enjoy daily the wonderful experiences of extended and joint families, and if we know how to protect and keep our culture and religion alive and prosperous, it is all thanks to our satguru.

Gods in Exile

Gurudeva taught Hinduism to Hindus from the inside out, beginning with explanations of the deepest spiritual world.

> The Third World is where the highest beings, such as Lord Ganesha, Lord Murugan and our Great God Siva, exist in shining bodies of golden light. This Third World is called the Sivaloka. The Second World of existence, or astral plane, is called the Devaloka. The great Gods have millions of helpers in the Devaloka who help each and every one of us. One or more of them is assigned to personally help you in this First World, which is the world of material or physical existence, called the Bhuloka.

He would then explain how the devas can see the sacred ash upon a person's forehead, how they and the Gods can hear the Sanskrit chanting of the priest in the temple and how the stone icon of the Deity in the temple sanctum is like a telephone connection to the Third World of the Gods. A precious few in his audiences had heard such explanations from their grandmothers or grandfathers, but it was quite a different matter to hear Gurudeva teach from his own realization.

He addressed a special part of his message to his fellow Saivites to dispel the common misconception that God Siva should not be worshiped in the home, and that the worship of Siva, who is incorrectly seen by many only as the God of Destruction, will make one poor. "Nonsense," he retorted, "Lord Siva is the God of Love!" He explained that worship of Siva—the Creator, Preserver and Destroyer—will bring every benefit, including wealth. Thousands of Saivite families who, succumbing to the local superstitions, had been afraid to bring a simple Nataraja into their home, boldly brought the God of Love into their puja rooms.

Gurudeva wanted all the Gods brought "out of exile" and encouraged Hindus of each sect to make their home shrine the most beautiful room in the house. He reserved a special censure for those Hindus who put their shrine in the closet, to be easily hidden when a guest visited. "Closet Hindus," he would chide. For his followers, the house should proudly and openly reflect the religion and culture of its residents. It should be, in his words, "...an absolutely breathtaking home shrine, used solely for meditation and worship of Sivalingam, Nataraja, Murugan, Ganesha and the satguru's *tiruvadi*. This is the home's most beautiful room."

He began emphasizing the daily performance of puja in each and every home, in addition to meditation, which for decades had been the mainstay of his prescription for spiritual living. For those in the West, as well as the East, he had his monks put into writing the traditional home puja, which he had arranged for them to learn in the late 1970s. He published it as the *Saiva Atmartha Puja*—likely the first time it was ever made widely available—presenting the ancient Sanskrit chants, and providing English and Tamil translation and transliteration.

Thoroughgoing in everything he did, Gurudeva drew deep from the well of Saivite liturgy to bring the ancient priestly magic into his own sanctuaries in 1982, asking Subramania Gurukkal to do something unheard of—convey the arts of temple puja, Saiva Parartha Puja, to his monks, which he did, in Alaveddy at the Sri Subramuniya Ashram. In 1985 Gurudeva had that knowledge bolstered by B. Shanmugam Sivachariyar, who flew to Kauai from South India to teach the monks the *homa* rites and patiently wrote out by hand the Parartha Puja in Devanagari and transliterated English. This was done with the blessings of Sambamurti Sivachariyar, head of the Then India Archaka Sangam.

During the 1981 India Odyssey, while talking with an elite group of Tamil elders in Tiruchendur, Gurudeva said, "If you give up your temples and your religion, you will, within 50 years, lose your race." On that same Innersearch, Mr. A. Gunanayagam, president of the Eelathu Thiruneri Thamil Mandram, gave a talk on behalf of the Mandram at the Saraswati Hall in Colombo, enumerating the activities and accomplishments of Saiva Siddhanta Church and lauding its service to Saivism:

When the apostles of different faiths left the Western world in the 15th to the 19th centuries for the shores of the East, they believed they were following the true course of the river of spirituality, which to their mind was flowing from the West to the East. They genuinely felt they were carrying the torch of spiritual enlightenment to those that needed it. But the emergence of Swami Vivekananda set them thinking. Was not the flow of the river really from the East to the West?

Now has come a third stage, with the blossoming of the Saiva Siddhanta Church of Hawaii. Is it not a near miracle being enacted before our very eyes? Has the river started to flow backwards? What we

mean is, the once spiritually glorious East has dried up into insig-
nificance except for a few oases here and there. The East has become
insensitive to changing times and has failed to keep pace with the
technological age. Lethargy and indifference have overpowered the
rightful heirs of a golden heritage. It has therefore fallen to the lot of the
Saiva Siddhanta Church to stand up for the greatest religion on Earth,
both by precept and example. It is carrying aloft the torch of Saivism.

An earnest seeker cannot but sit at the feet of the Church to regain
something of the glorious Saiva past. Such is the silent revolution that
is being enacted in Hawaii. Otherwise, how can a 16-ton granite Nandi from Mahabalipuram be installed in the holy precincts of the Saiva
Siddhanta Church in Hawaii? How can the six-foot Lord Nataraja take
abode in the Kadavul Temple of Hawaii?...

An early adopter of new technologies, Gurudeva was fond of tools that
helped him capture and communicate ideas and writings—miniature
recorders for voice notes and portable computers, like the innovative
1980 Sony Typecorder that recorded text to a cassette tape.

Page 589

Chapter 27

• •

It is not only the ritual and ceremony concerning these that alone are fascinating, it is the underlying philosophy which the Church so assiduously puts across which is most inspiring. We lift our hands in homage and gratitude to you, Gurudeva, as the God-sent dynamic ambassador of Saivism, to the dedicated and selfless band of swamis and to the Saiva Siddhanta Church, with a prayer in our heart, that the great and good work of the Church may continue to edify and enlighten all mankind!"

Defending the Word *Church*

Back in 1975, Gurudeva had officially changed the name of his organization to Saiva Siddhanta Church, having recognized, through his years of study, the strategic value of that legal form of religious institution in the United States. It was not a popular choice for some. Objections came from many sides, especially, and understandably, from Hindus in Asia who did not like the association with the Catholic and Anglican churches, which they saw as the nemesis of Hinduism. But Gurudeva held his ground, and spent decades defending his decision.

Ultimately, he would be proved right, but it was not an easy campaign. Members left him on this issue. But then, members also left him because they refused to stop smoking or refused to have their wives stay home and raise the children, or refused any number of the requirements he placed on dedication. In *Saiva Dharma Shastras, the Book of Discipline of Saiva Siddhanta Church,* composed in the early 90s, Gurudeva explains:

The name of our Hindu church is Saiva Siddhanta Church, meaning "sacred congregation of Supreme God Siva's revealed Truth." These two Sanskrit words and one English word we consider to be our international trademark.

No other terms should be substituted for the word *church* when writing or conversing in English. The word church may be translated into other languages for purposes of conversation. It may also be so translated for legal documents, such as for registration of mission groups, as deemed preferable by the parent Church. Such translations

shall always use the official terms approved by the Church. In such translations, based on the pattern of well-established local churches, we choose words that most strongly convey this meaning: a one-minded, hierarchical body of devotees, following a single doctrine of belief, with strict codes of conduct, an initiated priesthood, ministry and missionaries, well-defined sacraments, shared scriptural authority and exclusivity of membership free of other alliances.

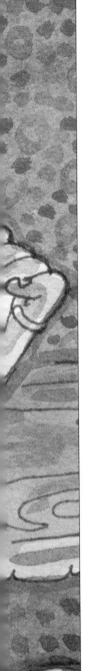

In 1979 Gurudeva founded the magazine that would later be called Hinduism Today, *telling his monks that its purpose was not to promote his mission, but to strengthen, connect and inform Hindu communities around the globe. He called it "the prow of the ship."*
· ·

We know that the term *church* will, in some communities, carry great respect and power, and in other communities it may be demeaned and belittled. Knowing theirs is the world's first Hindu church on the planet, our members use the name Saiva Siddhanta Church (or its equivalent as traditionally rendered in the world's many languages) boldly in all instances, defending its use when needed. Finally, it must be emphasized that while we adhere strongly to the institutional structure of church, we do so to most effectively convey the pure, traditional Sanatana Dharma as expressed in the *Vedas.* As one of the world's most orthodox congregations, our use of this institutional structure should never be misconstrued as carrying or even implying any Christian or Western religious content.

While the Greek-based word *church* is most commonly understood as a place of worship, the full meaning encompasses the religious congregation and organization on many levels of activity. *Church* takes on special importance in legal and governmental discussions, where matters of church and state are frequently focused on. In more and more nations, in federal and state governments, religion is defined as church, and the separation of church and state is respected and constitutionally enforced. Such protections, grounded in the concept of church, are crucial to the rights of all religious groups. These include protection from government and from other religions which may seek to dominate faiths with less political power.

Gurudeva was clear on cardinal guidelines in administering his institution. First, the satguru and his monastics would be completely in charge; there would be no family involvement of any sort in the running of the Church. Second, no relatives of the guru or the monks would have any special access, privilege or participation in the administration. Third, the Church would not support itself through running businesses but rather

be supported by donations. Fourth, his monasteries would be strict cloisters for men only.

Publishing Goes Digital

Late one afternoon in 1985 Gurudeva entered a little computer store in
the historic town of Kapaa. After playing with a state-of-the-art Macintosh for a while, he bought one for himself. Computers had never much
interested him, but this one seemed different, friendly, approachable. For
a week he experimented with it, calling the monks into his office every
time he discovered a new feature.

The guru and his shishyas learned the computer together, side by side.
Seeing its potential, he ordered one for each of his monks, instructing
them to adapt their various services to this new tool. And did they. From
that day forward, the monks saw that their satguru always had the newest,
fastest, sleekest Macintosh on his desk; and from the release of Apple's
first PowerBook, fellow airline passengers would gaze covetously at the
holy man's cool laptop.

Going headlong into the world of computers to do the work of dharma proved a strategic move of prodigious proportions. In order to fully
embrace the new technology, Gurudeva decided that his order of monks
would need to sell the 2,500 colonies of bees, since the small publications
team, which was doing both, had limited manpower. The monks had
managed the bees island-wide for ten years on Kauai as an agricultural
endowment, much like the farming enterprise Yogaswami had started in
Batticaloa, Sri Lanka, for his young men followers.

One of Gurudeva's most strategic and looked-forward-to duties was
writing his Publisher's Desk column for HINDUISM TODAY, which for
many years was monthly. Frequently he addressed matters that were
brought to his attention through his personal ministry with devotees,
students and members around the world.

In 1983 he came upon a way to solve the problem that Hindus throughout the diaspora were having with Christmas. Hindu kids were upset, and
their parents were in a quandary. And no one in the Hindu world was
providing a viable answer to the annual torture. In one Publisher's Desk,
Gurudeva announced the inauguration of a modern Hindu holiday, to be
called Pancha Ganapati. It was five days of worship, sharing and gift-giving, celebrated from December 21 to 25, focusing on Lord Ganesha's five
shaktis, which bring harmony in the home, among friends, in the workplace, in the community and the boon of religiousness and refined culture

· ·

Each month Gurudeva sat with his HINDUISM TODAY *editorial
staff. As publisher, he guided the content of the magazine, defined
its goals, set policy and helped with distribution strategies.*

that this harmony brings. Now when children asked mom and dad, "Why don't we get presents during Christmas?" they could answer, "We do, and not on just one day, but on five days." Gurudeva wrote:

"Daddy, why don't we have Christmas?" That question was heard in so many Hindu homes we visited that, in cooperation with scholars and elders, an alternative for Christmas was conceived. It's interesting that in 1966 the Afro-American community created Kwanzaa, a social, Black-identity, earth-based festival celebrated each year from December 26 to January 1. Our own Pancha Ganapati is a festival to the five-faced elephant God. It is five days of gift-giving and festivities within the home, especially for the children. There is no need for a tree (eco advocates appreciate this), nor wreaths, nor a Santa. Lord Ganesha does it all, in five days of merriment and mirth.

Those who have taken up this home festival from December 21st through the 25th have enjoyed it year after year. It can include outings,

picnics, feasts, exchange of cards and gifts with relatives, friends and business associates. Each day a tray of sweets, fruits and incense is offered to Pancha Ganapati, often prepared and presented by the children. Chants, songs and bhajans are sung in His praise. After puja, sweets are shared as prasadam. Each day gifts are given to the children, who place them before Pancha Ganapati to open only on the fifth day. Greeting cards are exchanged, always offering Hindu wisdom or verse from scripture.

As HINDUISM TODAY became his central outreach effort, Gurudeva focused his editorials on issues that were generally shrouded in silence, using his journal to guide the modern Hindu mind in how to dharmically approach matters like spousal abuse, suicide, adultery, pornography, mixed marriages, organ transplants and human cloning. The latter led to an invitation from President Bill Clinton's Blue Ribbon Committee on human cloning for Gurudeva to define the Hindu view for legislators confronting the issue. Years later, the Texas Medical Association asked the magazine to write a chapter in their book on medical ethics to guide US doctors in their care of Hindu patients.

Gurudeva took special delight when the editor of *Christianity Today* approached the editors of his journal to develop an article that would inform Christians about Hinduism. It was something of a dream he never had: *Christianity Today* working with HINDUISM TODAY to better understand their respective faiths. He guided the development of the article in every detail. In fact, that was his way with almost every article, which he kept close to through detailed and frequent discussions with his monks.

In late 1996 Gurudeva transformed HINDUISM TODAY from its original newspaper format into a magazine, a quantum leap that extended its global reach and impact in Hindu communities. In 1999 he described his vision for this unique journal:

Who could ever conceive of a journal founded to help everyone, to support every sect? For a long time it was a mystery to everyone, until the realization came that this was our public service. Most monasteries, or mathas, have established feeding centers for the poor, orphanages, schools and hospitals as their way of paying back for the privilege of being allowed to live aloof and apart from the world. Ours is HINDUISM TODAY: a much-needed service as we march boldly into the 21st century.

Timeless Legacy

I n the spring of 1987 Gurudeva's vision for Iraivan Temple was evolving from a mystical revelation to a real-world plan. Working with sacred architects in South India, he was defining its physical form, establishing the principles of its creation and considering the style of the massive stone edifices built during South India's Chola Dynasty a millennium ago. The big question was still pending: What form of Siva would inhabit the inner sanctum? It was a meditation that continued for months, for he knew the relevance of this decision. It would define the temple more than any external style. It would be its life and essence, the most holy and powerful force around which all else would circle.

A Clear Crystal Vision

One day, in an early-morning vision in his private quarters, Gurudeva saw the future, as he would later say. In fact, he often said, if you want to know what you should do, do this: In your mind, travel into the future, and from there look back and witness what happened. The present-day decision will be obvious.

In this vision of the yet-to-be, Gurudeva saw a massive crystal Siva-lingam shining brightly in the sanctum of Iraivan Temple, radiating out to the world. It was a titan among crystals. In fact, it seemed in this first see-ing impossibly large, fantastical and beyond reality. Perhaps, he thought, it is merely the spiritual form of the Sivalingam and not the physical one.

Downstairs a few hours later, he shared this vision with the monks, letting them know he had his answer as to which form of Siva that Iraivan Temple would embody. It would be a crystal Lingam, known in Sanskrit as *sphatika* Sivalingam. In the ancient texts it is said that a Lingam, which is the aniconic form of the Creator-Preserver-Destroyer of the universe, is the highest of worshipful icons. It represents That which is beyond representation, beyond form and even imagination. It is the All in all, the Self beyond time, form, space and cause.

The *Agamas* say one can worship this Great God Siva in the form of a Lingam made of mud or sand, of cow dung or wood, of bronze or black granite stone. But the purest and most sought-after form is the quartz crystal, a natural stone not carved by man but made by nature, gathered molecule by molecule over hundreds, thousands or millions of years,

....

An early morning dream of a perfect crystal Sivalingam led Gurudeva to a giant, six-sided, single-pointed sphatika. *Unearthed by miners in 1975, the same year as his vision of Iraivan, it arrived on Kauai in 1987.*

grown as a living body grows, but infinitely more slowly. Such a creation of nature is itself a miracle worthy of worship.

The monks were delighted to hear of their guru's revelation and imagined the meanings behind it. Kadavul Temple already housed God Siva as Nataraja, the divine dancer who creates and inhabits every atom of the cosmos, and Iraivan Temple would host Siva as the transcendent Beyond, immanent and transcendent, form and formless. It was perfect. But the monks were not at all prepared for what would happen next.

Gurudeva paid a visit the next day to the Crystal Journey shop at Kilohana on Kauai. He was there looking at the wares, asking the proprietor about crystals, looking for a large one he had visualized. She did not have such a crystal, but eagerly shared her own similar vision of a giant crystal.

Some weeks later, she called requesting to meet with Gurudeva, arriving at the monastery mid morning. She was a kind of mythical character, a child of the 70s, a cherubic, intelligent lady about 40 years old. In her long dress, looking a bit Roma, her round cheeks pink with the pleasure of her visit, she shared that she had an important message for him. She was taken to Gurudeva's office, where he listened to her tale. "Gurudeva, I had a dream last night. In my dream I saw, even more clearly than before, a giant crystal. Very tall and perfectly formed, just like the one you described. Not only that, I saw where it is. If you will allow me, I want to go there. I want to find the crystal and bring it to you. Will you buy me a ticket?"

Never in his life had Gurudeva bought a ticket for a near stranger on a dream-induced mission. But this was different. Gurudeva then told the visitor of his own dream that same morning, of how he had seen the giant crystal, too, but never imagined someone else might have the same dream at nearly the same time. He took it as a sign, and did the unthinkable—bought her a round-trip ticket to Arkansas, the Natural State.

Soon she was on a crystal quest. Having never visited Arkansas, she took the logical course and began visiting the various mines in the area. Along with Brazil, Arkansas is the world's most productive crystal source, and there were dozens of mines to be tracked down at the end of long, unpaved roads.

Ultimately she found the crystal at the mines of one James Coleman, a hard-scrabble man dressed in denim with a scrappy beard and callused hands, whose father and grandfather had mined crystals and who knew the business like none other.

Ambling to his Jeep, the taciturn miner motioned to her to get in. Off the two drove, about a mile on a pitted coral path some called a road that ended at an old wooden warehouse. Getting down, Coleman walked through the double doors and headed to the back of the open space, stopping at a pallet in a dark corner. On it was a musty mattress, worn and worthless, rolled in a circle and tied with a hemp rope.

Without so much as a word, Coleman cut the rope with a pocket knife and threw open the mattress. There lay the huge, milky white, quartz crystal. It was a marvel to behold, a perfect thing that could be an artifact in a museum of art or a masterpiece in the foyer of a billionaire's mansion. But it was here, not far from nowhere.

His customary reticence overcome by the urgent need to relate his story, Coleman turned to the woman, who stood speechless, with happy tears washing down her cheeks.

In 1975 my brother and I were digging for crystals. Below these hills there are honeycombs of caves where our rocks are harvested. We were 65 feet under that day, when we found our way into a new cave. Nothing unusual about it at first; it was some twenty feet across and five feet high, all dark and dank. But then our light fell on this crystal. It had fallen and lay on its side, broken away from the cave floor. Around it on three sides was a colony of smaller crystals, ten or so, which were all still intact and growing. This one had stopped growing, of course. As you can see, it has six sides and is perfectly pointed, and its surface feels like cool ice, day and night. We went up to get the mattress and wrapped the crystal in it, dragging it inch by inch to the surface. Took all day.

It was, to both of us, an amazing discovery. Though our family has been mining crystals for three generations, no one ever heard of such a gem. My brother and I knew it was one of a kind, and we both sensed it had a destiny, though we didn't know what that might be. Something extraordinary. We kept it in the mattress and brought it here, out of sight, vowing not to tell a soul about it. But somehow you saw it. How else would you know? We figured that one day we would learn what the crystal was meant for. I think it was meant to go with you, to Hawaii, and to be with that holy man who saw it. The crystal has been waiting, and I'm glad you came to get it.

The crystal seeker was exultant. She called Gurudeva, who asked for photos to be sent. When he saw them, he said, "Yes, that's it!" She arranged for the purchase and packing of the crystal, then flew home. The 700-pound, 39-inch-tall *sphatika* Sivalingam arrived at the monastery on August 14 and was formally installed in front of Lord Kadavul Nataraja two days later, awaiting the day Iraivan Temple would be completed. Gurudeva's morning vision had manifested in a magical way.

One afternoon years later, a deva with whom Gurudeva often communicated signalled that he was present and asked if there were any questions. The monk with him asked about the significance of the huge crystal. With the same ease that ordinary people listen to a friend speak, Gurudeva clairaudiently heard the inner-plane deva's answer and dictated it, in two- and three-word volleys, to his amanuensis of the day.

> Now, the large crystal we have is very special, having been especially prepared for its mission as a relay station for peace on Earth, harmony, contentment, healing and patience, freedom and goodwill and close cooperation among the life forms and humans beings on this planet. It is at this very moment relaying trillions of messages through every crystal on this planet, energizing and educating even the smallest insect.

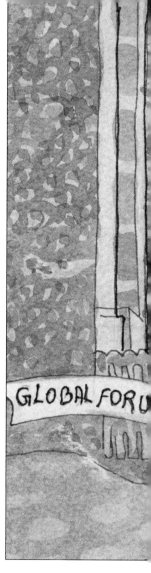

Fighting for Peace and Human Survival

Gurudeva's global renown grew steadily. In 1986, the World Religious Parliament in New Delhi named him one of five modern-day *jagadacharyas,* world teachers, for his international efforts in promoting a Hindu renaissance. That award and other messages made it clear to Gurudeva that he was being embraced by the East. In fact, he was being anointed as the first Western person ever to be regarded as a satguru, that highest of spiritual offices, heretofore reserved, even guarded, for men of Indian origin. It was an honor; but more importantly, it was a responsibility, one that he never took for granted. It was also a double-edged sword, for there was a conservative coterie of Indians who could never accept the idea of a non-Indian rising to prominence as a guru, whose feet they were obliged to touch. They kept their distance, holding a critical watch.

Gurudeva only occasionally attended conferences, though he was often invited. He found a handful deeply significant: the Global Forums of

HUMAN SURVIVAL

For five days in 1988 Gurudeva met with spiritual and political leaders at Oxford University, bringing the tolerant, all-embracing message of Hinduism to a forum that included the Dalai Lama, the Archbishop of Canterbury, Cardinal Koenig and leaders of every major faith, joined by ranking politicians, media and scientists.

Spiritual and Parliamentary Leaders on Human Survival in Oxford (1988), Moscow (1990) and Rio de Janeiro (1992), the Parliament of the World's Religions in Chicago (1993) and the Millennium World Peace Summit of Religious and Spiritual Leaders, held at the United Nations (2000).

If man finds the fear of his own death difficult to confront, consider the possibility that the human race itself is in mortal danger and could perish forever. That was precisely the enterprise for which approximately 140 of the most influential men and women from sixty nations gathered at Oxford University in England from April 11 to 15, 1988. Astrophysicist Dr. Carl Sagan, biologist Dr. James Lovelock, Soviet nuclear scientist Dr. Yevgeny Velikhov and other preeminent experts in population, media and education presented a litany of ominous threats. Humankind had awakened to the terrible revelation that the Earth and its tiny cargo of living things are vulnerable—that unless something is done soon, one day man himself, like tens of thousands of species disappearing each year, may become extinct.

Not since the Middle Ages had legislators and spiritual leaders met at such a level, and then it was limited to European statesmen and Christian leaders. The 1988 Global Forum brought together representatives of five major faiths—Hinduism, Buddhism, Christianity, Islam and Judaism—as well as African and American Indian religions, Jainism, Sikhism and Shintoism.

What are the problems that endanger us? In no particular order: war, hunger, poverty and inequity of resources, debt, drugs, desertification, illiteracy, population growth, religious fundamentalism, global warming, disintegration of ecology, loss of species and social injustice.

As the five days unfolded, it was evident that delegates shared the urgency voiced by Austrian Cardinal Koenig: "We have come together to find ways out of crisis. There is only one choice: to survive or perish together." To this Robert Runcie, Archbishop of Canterbury, added: "There are two qualities for survival, reverence and cooperation. We need to control our spiritual hubris. We need to cease believing this is a cheap, throw-away universe in which everything but human life is expendable." Africans stressed the vast schism that exists between rich and poor nations, decrying "excess materialism and unbridled consumption."

The Dalai Lama's presence caused the biggest stir, partly because his unadorned talk of love and compassion cut to the core of the human dilemma, pointing to the heart as the place to transform both self and world. His message of mutual respect and understanding, of resisting the urge to propagate one's faith and to replace it with a desire to contribute usefully to humanity as a whole were messages needing to be heard. For this, the exiled Buddhist god-king was the perfect spokesman.

Gurudeva created quite a scene when one of the religious leaders was slighted at a plenary session opening blessing. After an eloquent African priestess concluded the prayer, the panel moderator said, "Now let's get on to the real business of the day." Gurudeva boldly stood among them and took exception to this remark, telling the organizers that they had invited the spiritual leaders to work with the political leaders, but instead had them come up and give some little prayer, then insulted their presence and diminished their participation. "This priestess is the real business of the day," he scolded them, his long arm held aloft, "as much as everything else, and you've really offended every spiritual tradition by pronouncing that we're just here as wallpaper to your meeting. That's not why we came here." The chairperson apologized, first from the podium and the next morning in person. She and others realized he was right, and they had met to change their habits. It was a crucial moment in the conference, and the rest of the week spiritual leaders were eagerly brought forward and properly honored.

In 1990, Gurudeva again joined the world's religious and political leaders, this time for a seven-day sojourn where ice and snow were the prime physical reality and the sun was never seen. Imagine a room roughly the size of an airplane hangar filled with 1,400 beautiful and colorfully-costumed souls from every corner of the globe, all discovering their shared cosmology, all remembering that this fragile Earth is our only home, all learning how we have foolishly polluted our only sanctuary and all determined to protect it. Imagine that, and you will have a good idea of what the Global Forum experience in Moscow was all about.

> We were invited to the Global Forum of Parliamentary and Religious Leaders in Oxford, in Rio de Janeiro and also in Moscow. All of our invitations were handled in this way: "If you want us, we're ticketless travelers. We are renunciate monks and don't have a travel budget. Send tickets and we'll be there." It seems they wanted us there so badly, for some reason, that tickets arrived. The tickets either have to be first class or business class, because I don't fit into those little seats anymore. They're getting smaller and smaller and smaller every year.

The strong delegations of indigenous peoples there—from Africa, North America, Hawaii and elsewhere—reminded Gurudeva of how valuable these traditions are and how much they are still ignored and abused. They are like fragile cultural gene pools, seeds of an earlier wisdom that mankind once amassed, then squandered and now needs to sow again. One elder rightly suggested that we are all Earth's indigenous people. It was clear to Gurudeva that Hindus are the natural allies of these traditions, and that we should, without imposing, offer them resources they might find useful and speak up on their behalf.

The Global Forum in Moscow, funded by the Russian government, was also about learning that man has become the major predator on the Earth, so much so that he is preying on himself in an unnatural cannibalism. Unless the present course is altered, scientists urged, we may be responsible for a kind of unintentional suicide. What Gurudeva heard in Moscow could be summarized: If we don't change our attitudes, if we persist in our present habits and practices, we will not thrive, we may not even survive. It can be said even more simply: Change or perish. The Earth will heal once we stop hurting it. Wars, pollution, species extinction and fundamentalism will cease when they are no longer acceptable to human conscience. And they will no longer be acceptable the minute we understand their terrible results.

Gurudeva loved his days in Moscow, even the awkward evenings when he and the swami with him were asked to join, in their simple, unsewn monastic garb, a concert and cocktail party in the dazzling 150-year-old Kremlin reception hall and hobnob with the leaders of the world.

On one evening toward the end, the Russian government held a grand ball in the Kremlin, inviting business and cultural leaders to join the men and women who had come from other lands to face the future of humanity. Interestingly, as each of the earlier days had unfolded, religious leaders had vied to give the opening blessing, fighting, sometimes furiously, to be chosen. All but the Hindus, who stood aside, witnessing this jockeying for pride of place. After five or six days, all of the major religions had had their turn, except the Hindus. So, a Hindu leader was selected for this night, which turned out to be the most important of them all.

It was to be Swami Paramananda Bharati, a Shringeri monk who had been a physicist before renouncing the world. Swami approached Gurudeva during lunch, concerned that his message might not be fully understood by this diverse group. Gurudeva gave him courage to speak out boldly to the world, assuring him that the message would be clear to all present.

That evening, dressed as Adi Shankara himself had dressed, *danda* in hand, three stripes of *vibhuti* on his arms and forehead, a picture of purity and simplicity in that formal room, Swami removed his slippers, strode to the podium under the gaze of 300 TV cameras from all over the world and began his invocation.

We are in an age of disillusionment, confusion and panic. We do not know from what point to commence our journey to enlightenment, in what direction and at what speed. Fortunately, there exists one course of knowledge which determines all of these parameters. That is the immortal *Veda*. Here I give two hymns from the *Veda*. These are

· ·

In the frigid winter of 1990, as the USSR was breaking apart, Mikhail Gorbachev invited 700 politicians and 700 spiritual leaders to Moscow for a week-long forum. Gurudeva was among the Hindu leaders.

prayers to the Gods pervading the various celestial bodies like the sun, the moon, the stars—nay, all the five elements of the environment. Herein we pray for shanti, that is for peace in the kingdom of the animals, like cows, peace in the kingdom of the humans. Let this shanti, this peace, descending by the grace of God, reverberate in the depths of our hearts to give each one of us everlasting bliss. Let it augur peace and prosperity to the leaders and to the people of this great nation, our host country, to the rest of the world and to the Global Forum.

Swami then chanted, his sweet Sanskrit filling the Kremlin Hall. He closed by asking all present to join him in saying aloud "Aum," the all-encompassing sound, three times. Swami chanted "Aum" and lifted both hands to invite all to join. A deep, resonant Aum filled the chamber. A second time and then a third the Swami chanted and the audience responded, each time more forcefully. It was a powerful moment, as though the whole world was chanting together, sharing a language that all understood, that transcended their differences and arose from their

Indigenous peoples held a special place in Gurudeva's heart. He met with Brazilian and African tribals, invited Inuit elders to help him found a temple in Anchorage and visited with Hopi elders in Arizona, putting their sacred texts online to help preserve a fading culture.

· ·

underlying oneness. Gurudeva later said that, mystically, the "Aum in the Kremlin" was the force that let loose the remarkable changes in the USSR that, unbeknownst to all present, were soon to follow. He told of the experience in HINDUISM TODAY:

> Who could believe it? Over two thousand spiritual and political leaders and guests, seated in Lenin's Kremlin, Khrushchev's Kremlin and now Gorbachev's Kremlin, all hearing a shanti chant from the *Vedas* and all chanting "Aum" aloud together, led by a swami from India. That Aum was a war–shattering cry for peace, but sadly it was ignored in the US press, except for a trivial reference in *Time* magazine. So many

important and high-minded people were there—including Gorbachev and Scheverdnazy, including the world's most influential rabbis and imams, priests and swamis, monks and theologians, not to mention politicians from the parliaments of 57 nations, scientists and environmentalists, artists and media pandits. It was perhaps the first global council for the human race, all working for peace, all chanting the sacred Aum mantra of Universal Oneness in a single, melodious voice.

Having the opportunity to meet many young Soviets in their early thirties and even in their teens, we observed a surprisingly mature interest in yoga, meditation, the occult, mysticism, crystalogy and clairvoyance. Many people don't know that Soviet scientists and Hindu yoga adepts have been collaborating for the past two decades in mental telepathy and other extraterrestrial sciences to increase the communication faculties of the human migration into space (and for less noble purposes, too).

Despite the -10°F winter (for which our hand-woven cotton robes were not designed) my personal experience in Moscow was warm, vibrant and full. I enjoyed attending Russia's first public Christmas celebration in seventy years. I also enjoyed speaking with the spiritual old friends we had made at the Oxford Global Forum in April of 1988. The spirit was one of hopeful eagerness.

As a species, we have essentially proven ourselves fully capable of seeking pleasure, of lack of concern for others and a general disregard for the concerns of the day until the reality of some emergency is upon us. The two global forums laid out the entire emergency that humankind is facing on this planet, factually and without exaggeration. It is a sad list of problems, but the spirit in man is more powerful than any challenge it ever faces, and I found hope in seeing these eminent world leaders tear themselves away from pressing responsibilities to fly to Moscow in the middle of winter and spend seven days living together, eating together, talking together, liking and learning to love and trust each other, listening together, questioning, sharing knowledge. Both the seriousness of our plight and the sincerity of people to cooperate in resolving things emerged. Because these are the leaders of humankind, their voices will be heard back home. Every member of their parliaments or their congregations will know and understand the message, and the scientists who were present will share it with all their colleagues.

The truth, without exaggeration, finally came out, and the solution

· ·

At the 1992 Global Forum in Rio de Janeiro, Gurudeva was pleasantly startled to hear the world religions all saying, "Everything is divine. We are all one." Brazilian tribals wanted their picture taken with the tall swami from Hawaii.

was clear. They say when a problem is adequately explained and understood, the solution is self-evident. The solution is simple, and it rests on the shoulders of each human: think globally, act locally to restructure one's own home, one's own values, one's relationship to nature for a purified, sustainable environment.

We took our own message to Moscow, of course. It was a plea for the world to rediscover the ethic of nonviolence, called ahimsa in Sanskrit. We need to be very practical and not just philosophical about this. World peace begins in the home. Families must learn to be peaceful, to settle all arguments and contention before they sleep at night, even if they stay up for three days, so the children can see that peace can be attained and then maintained through the use of intelligence. It is up to the parents to create the peacemakers of the future. And we teach children in only one way—by our own example.

Parents must teach children to appreciate those who are different, those who believe differently. Teach them the value of human diversity. Give them the tools to live in a world of differences without feeling threatened, without forcing their ways or their will on others. This is the way of dharma.

I also spoke about how we should bring the mother spirit forward and seek out the guidance and intuitive knowledge of our women. If the Hawaiian mothers, the African mothers, and all the mothers of the planet come forward, then we can realize a global peace. We are too deep into the Kali Yuga for men to make a difference. They tried. The mothers, daughters, sisters and wives—who have a great ability to heal, to harmonize and influence—will bring us into the Golden Age. Give them more power in the struggle for peace.

Nonviolence should be redefined to include not only killing, but also causing injury physically, mentally or emotionally, even in the most subtle ways. We can injure ourselves, we can injure our environment, we can injure nature's other creatures and thus be a source of pain and sorrow. Or we can live a harmless life and be a source of healing and joy.

The sages and illumined ones knew all about karma. They full well knew that what we have done to others will be done to us, if not in this life then in another. They knew that violence which one commits will return to him by a cosmic process that is unerring.

There was a strong influence of Eastern thought and perception in Moscow. While a few Semitic leaders spoke about man's relationship to the natural order as one of dominion, the Buddhists, Jains, Sikhs

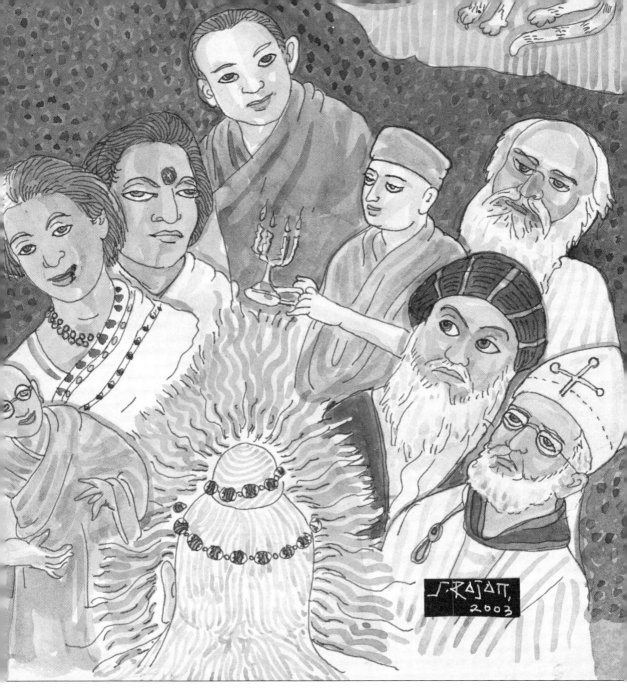

Everywhere he traveled, Gurudeva sought out leaders of all faiths, making connections to strengthen tolerance and understanding—from the Dalai Lama to the Grand Mufti, from Anandamayi Ma to Pramukh Swami to Chandrashekharendra Saraswati.

and Hindus came forward and spoke of the wonderful oneness that makes up life. They explained that a sense of domination offends the oneness and perpetuates wrongful and harmful action. From the Eastern viewpoint, everything exists within a divine law and order,

At the 1993 Parliament of the World's Religions in Chicago, which marked
one hundred years since Swami Vivekananda's powerful message to
the West, Sivaya Subramuniyaswami, Swami Chidananda and Mata
Amritanandamayi were elected the principal representatives for Hinduism.

Page 613

Chapter 28

and no creature has more right to life than another. They said it is for us humans to adjust to being a part of the greater whole which sustains life, which is intricately interwoven and interdependent.

On the final day, Gurudeva was dining in one of the dozens of restaurants in the Rossiya Hotel. The staff all knew this was the Forum's last day, so everyone was flying home. The waitress glanced again and again at Gurudeva's warm, gray boots, which he had brought in anticipation of the frigid winter. When offering the check, she boldly shared that her family was suffering. In broken English, she softly asked if she could have the boots for her husband. Gurudeva, seeing her noble desperation, removed them and asked the monk traveling with him to remove his, handing two pairs of boots to a thankful waitress and walking back to his room in his socks.

While he found value in these major conferences, Gurudeva also found the meetings inefficient, boring, repetitive and woefully lacking in follow-through. He complained about meeting the same people time and again, making the same well-meaning resolutions, then forgetting all about it. After the 1993 Chicago Parliament of the World's Religions, he tried to keep the group of twenty-five "presidents" of religion going, of which he was one of three Hindus. He felt this group could occasionally make strategic statements on important issues. But there was little interest beyond his own efforts, and nothing came of it. It made him wary of future involvements of this kind.

Dr. Kusumita Pedersen, a devotee of Sri Chinmoy on the staff of the Global Forum, Parliament and Millennium Summit at the UN, commended Gurudeva's participation at these international conferences for "his powerful spiritual presence and his great clarity and commitment in engaging the issues. Also, his behind-the-scenes contribution has made a little known but historic difference to the development of interfaith work in the last generation."

When the third Global Forum for Human Survival was announced, a wealthy Hindu, realizing his faith yet had no substantial representatives, sponsored Gurudeva's 1992 trip to Rio de Janeiro. This was a smaller event, about seventy-five religious leaders in a dialog with three hundred parliamentarians. Apart from the usual things you would expect from such a gathering, something quite unusual, maybe even extraordinary, took place there. Gurudeva was not really prepared for it, nor was it on anyone's agenda. But it happened.

From the opening address by a US Senator to the closing remarks by religious leaders three days later, virtually everyone acknowledged the sacredness of existence. It was not just the Hindus, Jains and Sikhs who were saying these things. It was everyone. Politicians propounded it. Business people professed it. Priests preached it. Musical poets praised it. It ran like a golden thread through every speech, through every call for a change in human behavior.

Gurudeva was amazed and thrilled by this common mantra. Such a thing had not happened at previous Global Forums. In Rio it was being said loud and clear: Nature is sacred. Life is sacred. It is a desecration to destroy this precious and holy creation. It is a sacrilege which, if continued, will surely end in our own death as a species.

Senator Al Gore, who approached Gurudeva and shook his hand, spoke of the wrongful "assumption that we are somehow separate from nature." Brazilian Archbishop Camara made this rather stunning statement: "We are inside God. How can I hate if I am part of God? This is incredible, but true. If God is everywhere, it means we are inside God, and we have God inside ourselves." India's Bishop Gregorius spoke of "immanence and transcendence." African priestesses shared the vision that life is sacred, plants are sacred, animals are sacred. Jain leaders called for reverence of all forms of life. Jewish theologian Dr. Susannah Herschel noted, "Too many religious leaders present God as remote and transcendent." Acharya Sushil Kumar led a meditation, "Go deep and deeper. Feel oneness with all living beings."

It was a virtual assumption in Rio: "God is everywhere. Life is sacred." This will seem a normal insight to our readers, and on an individual level it is. But coming from every corner in Rio, it took on the empyreal visage of an Earth-wide revelation, the gospel according to everyone, the new spiritual consensus. No one really commented on it. It was one of those things too obvious to speak of. Like the air, it was everywhere, its invisible presence firing the furnaces of confabulation—unnoticed.

Spirit of the Guru

When hundreds of thousands of Sri Lankans were driven from their homeland by civil war in the 1980s and 90s, Gurudeva reached out to assist and guide their lives in new nations. As they had fallen at Yogaswami's feet during earlier ethnic crises, Sri Lankan Tamils shared their woes with Gurudeva. It was a difficult work, listening to thousands of tragic stories, answering again and again the question "How could God allow such things to happen?"

Throughout it all, Gurudeva never avoided a call, never failed to give all the time necessary to a family in need, whether they had lost their son, watched their home being burned to the ground or been compelled to flee their homeland and begin a new life in a strange place. Their calls to Gurudeva were a lifeline, and he knew it. The calls, continuing for two decades, came from India, Canada, America, Germany, Denmark, Sweden, Norway, Finland, Africa, Australia, New Zealand, England and France. The massive racial riots and ensuing civil war between the Tamil Hindus and the Sinhalese Buddhists in Sri Lanka ultimately caused an exodus of 700,000 Tamils.

By divine grace Gurudeva had traveled throughout the Hindu areas of Sri Lanka in 1983, only months before the killings began. In fact, he was in Anuradhapura when a bomb went off at Elephant Pass, the narrow causeway between the Jaffna peninsula and the Sri Lankan mainland. He and the monks were supposed to leave for Jaffna that morning, but Gurudeva kept delaying the departure. They finally left about noon, arriving at the bomb site later in the day to encounter intense scrutiny by the Sinhalese army. Had they left on time, they may have been in the area when the blast occurred. And, if the bomb had actually hit its target (no one was hurt by it), the riots which occurred a few months later could have started then and there. His message, given in dozens of temples, would fortify Sri Lanka's Hindus in the trying times ahead: "Stand strong for Hinduism!" "Fear neither death nor those who live in fear."

In 1985, following some particularly horrific happenings in and around Jaffna, Gurudeva gathered his monks together to create the Sri Lanka Refugee Relief Fund, raising critical financial support from Tamils in the West to help the homeless victims of war. He spent months on this project. As funds began flooding in, he watched as each transfer was made, to assure it would actually go to the needy. His initiative inspired others to

Almost daily at Kauai Aadheenam, visitors would meet Gurudeva in the Guru Pitham, sharing their life's purpose and problems, receiving spiritual counsel and leaving with a book and life-affirming blessing.

collect donations and send financial aid to the island nation.

Soon after the conflict started, Gurudeva closed his ashram and school in Alaveddy. A decade and a half later he remarked:

Learning of the imminent conflict by listening to the elders, we closed all our activities in Sri Lanka and centered our work outside of the United States in the country of Mauritius. Then we found out from the elders that the place Sri Lankans were wanting to reincarnate was Mauritius. So, the Sri Lankans are reincarnating in Mauritius. They

Each year during the July festival of Guru Purnima the monks and devotees paraded Gurudeva in a chariot down the San Marga path to the Svayambhu Sivalingam where pada *puja was performed.*

· ·

are probably fifteen to eighteen years of age now. I sent two swamis to Mauritius to conduct youth camps. Our missionaries there are family men and women, and every member of the organization is connected to a missionary family. Everybody watches after everyone else.

The Tamils who began settling in the West appreciated Gurudeva's commanding presence, traditional ways and clear guidance. Rather than lamenting their losses, he showed them their opportunities, enjoining them to settle down and become contributing members of their new countries. His simple words to many were, "Unpack your bags." Most had not committed to their new country and were living as if waiting to catch a flight home to Sri Lanka. He gave insights into integration, citizenship, public relations and more, urging each group to start a temple, saying that the culture and religion comes from the worship and they need temples close by to preserve their heritage and pass it on to their children. He unstintingly gave them his personal cell phone number, knowing that calls would come anytime, day or night.

In 1995, with two monks at his side, Gurudeva undertook a 21-day

On every continent, Gurudeva worked with communities to   Page 621
build Hindu temples, to guide their trustees, even to raise funds   Chapter 29
for them. In all, he helped build 37 temples during his life.
• •

European tour, covering Germany, Denmark, Switzerland, Austria and the UK. He visited all of the Tamil Hindu communities in those countries, had a street parade of 11,000 in Hamm, brought converts into Hinduism, revisited Ascona, where Shum came through in 1968, and uplifted the thousands of Tamil refugees in these nations.

Everywhere he encouraged them to pray for peace by chanting "Aum" and sending energy to loved ones still in Sri Lanka. He repeated the message he had given since 1983 and taught them ways to endear themselves to the local community:

Your karmas brought you to this country, and you have more opportunities here than if you went to the University of Colombo. Educate your children, learn the local language and settle down. When permanent peace comes to Sri Lanka, then you can go back.

I think we all appreciate what the governments have done. There are many ways we can pay back. One way is to smile at everybody you meet. You smile, and then they smile, and pretty soon the whole country is smiling, just because you smiled. To be happy yourself, you have to make someone else happy.

Mrs. Puvanesam Veeragathiyar shared:

He visited a boys' refugee house in Berlin, talked with the officials and saw to the boys' material needs. He then met with a group of mothers and told us that what was lacking in these boys' lives was a mother's love. He encouraged us to invite the boys and other refugees to our home for meals and make them feel part of our family. Most of us are still doing this today.

Many tell of the special magic held by Gurudeva's business cards and photos, which he gave out by the hundreds of thousands during his travels. Some reported easily passing through Sri Lankan military checkpoints after showing Gurudeva's picture. M. Elangovan of Italy related:

In 1990, when I was 14, I left Sri Lanka in a fishing boat to India. The only picture I had in my wallet was Gurudeva's. That picture helped me through difficult times. Even today I have the same picture in my wallet. Gurudeva has always been with me, helping and guiding me.

Gurudeva showed up for the Tamil people of Sri Lanka in even deeper mystical ways, including simply being there for them on the astral plane as many passed away during the hostilities. When his monastics at his Kauai monastery noticed him taking naps during the morning hours, they asked him if he was feeling alright. He assured them that he was fine; he was spending this seemingly idle time quite actively in the inner worlds, blessing souls who had recently died in Sri Lanka, placing the mark of *vibhuti* on their foreheads as they came to him in long lines. He would visit his shishyas in far-off places on the astral plane, working with their lives and karmas, providing solace, guidance, protection.

Thiru Satkunendran of Toronto, Canada, recalled:

Gurudeva was not only our spiritual guide, but also a highly respected mentor, for both the young and old suffering from culture shock. Every occasion that I met Gurudeva, he was keen to know of progress made towards peace in Sri Lanka. He was always prepared to offer his services as mediator. Such is the love of this great guru towards the island and people, where he found his satguru, Yogaswami. We are certain that he is working for peace even now, from the inner world.

Gurudeva explained some of the challenges of that time:

During that time, we were getting the Sri Lankan devotees settled down as best we could. It was very difficult, because everyone was migrating here and there and everywhere. In Germany we had what were called "container boys." They would get smuggled into Russia, and in Russia they would get put in containers and be smuggled into Germany. Many died of suffocation. But most arrived in pretty good shape. We encouraged Tamil families to take them in. The German government was extremely compassionate and kind.

"Build Those Temples!"

Throughout his adult life, Gurudeva recognized the need for the Hindu temple as the center of religion and culture. He was involved in the planning, building or consecration of 37 temples on several continents. He

At temples in Sri Lanka, Fiji, Texas and elsewhere, Gurudeva poured the sacred kumbha *over the tower during the* kumbhabhishekam *ceremony.*

knew that for Hindus to truly feel at home anywhere on the globe, they needed temples nearby, temples that gave devotees access to their God and the Gods. And he assured one and all that the Gods are actual inner-plane beings rather than just symbols as is sometimes claimed. From his own experience, he colorfully described the beings who live in the heavenly realms, what they do and how they can be of practical assistance to devotees requesting their aid.

My devotees wisely settle in areas where Ganesha, Murugan or Siva temples exist for their frequent pilgrimage, worship and spiritual security. None should live farther than a day's journey from such sacred sanctuaries. It is in the Hindu temple that the three worlds meet and devotees invoke the Gods of our religion. The temple is built as a palace in which the Gods reside. It is the visible home of the Gods, a sacred place unlike every other place on the Earth. The Hindu must associate himself with these Gods in a very sensitive way when he approaches the temple.

The weekly homa *in Kadavul Hindu Temple became a central rite for the monastery and devotees. Afterwards he would give a discourse, answer questions from CyberCadets and bless all who attended.*

Page 625

Chapter 29
· ·

You can go to a Hindu temple with your mind filled up with worries, you can be in a state of jealousy and anger, and leave the temple wondering what you were disturbed about, completely free from the mental burdens and feeling secure. So great are the divine psychiatrists, the Gods of our religion, who live in the Third World, who come from the Third World to this world where our priests perform the pujas and invoke their presence over the stone image.

In this he was unique, as most swamis were not enthusiastic about temples, preferring to focus on social upliftment, philosophical teachings and yoga. Gurudeva described his approach:

In the 1980s, Hindu Indian community elders of newly forming temple and cultural societies approached me to help them make the final leap in establishing temples in various states of our country. We accomplished this by gifting them large murtis, always of Lord Ganesha, to begin the worship. These were times of fostering and inspiring temple groups throughout North America. In case after case, within two years, million-dollar facilities to house the other Deities were built as funding began to flow in the wake of satisfaction experienced by *dadis* and *dadas*, *appas* and *ammas* and their coming-up generation. This brought us into a new area of seva, service, to the Hindu public.

At the same time, we were encouraging getting temples started in Europe. We visited one small group that was conducting pujas in a basement. I gave fifty dollars, saying, "We're going to start a temple." Six months later they had rented a large warehouse and built a temple inside it—a really nice temple, with a priest from Sri Lanka doing the pujas. I was invited back and was paraded around the temple with ten thousand people participating. The police had blocked off the entire area. It was quite a scene.

Arumugan Saravanapavan, one of the founders of the multi-million-dollar Murugan Temple of North America in Maryland, a few miles from America's Capitol, recalls his experience of Gurudeva's temple-building thrust:

We wanted to build a temple in our area. Since we didn't have land, or a clear idea of how to proceed, someone suggested we see Subramuniyaswami in Hawaii. The next week my wife and I went to visit him, in 1982. I explained the problem, and the next day he presented us with a three-foot-tall Ganesha. He said, "You take Pillaiyar with you, and He will show you the way to build the temple."

As instructed, they began the worship of Lord Ganesha, first in homes. The community's devotion came to the fore. Gurudeva visited several times, helped with the planning and personally blessed the land they purchased. When Gurudeva spoke at that blessing, recalls Mrs. Guruswamy,

Each day Gurudeva shared lunch with all the monks, his seat flanked by two
teak elephants. The monks sat below, on the brick floor, eating with their
hands in traditional style and sharing news with their guru and brothers.

Page 627

Chapter 29

• •

wife of the temple's first president, "The children were carried away. He
was able to explain our religion in a way they could understand." In 1999
Gurudeva was the honored guest at the temple's *mahakumbhabhishekam*.
A newsletter from the temple expressed gratitude:

> With his monks, Gurudeva helped every step of the way in building
> the Murugan Temple, from the community to the structure. As busy
> as he was, he made time to take phone calls from the temple devotees.
> He inspired the young and grew himself in many of our hearts.

In 1982 he visited Chicago and met with a group interested in starting
a temple. Previously, one of the trustees, Dr. N. Janakiraman, had visited Kauai. They were having a great number of problems, Janakiraman
explained, and couldn't agree on what to do next. They did, however, agree
to do whatever Gurudeva told them to do. Gurudeva told them to start
the worship of Lord Ganesha. "After receiving Gurudeva's blessings," said
Janakiraman, "we returned home and, to our utmost surprise and ecstatic
joy, Lord Ganesha had already arrived at the O'Hare airport." Gurudeva
had expedited the delivery as a surprise gift.

A handful of devotees greeted the 2,000-pound statue and decided to
start the worship in Mr. Rajagopalan's home. The house soon proved too
small to accommodate the crowds, so they moved Ganesha to an industrial complex in 1983. Gurudeva assigned one of his local devotees, Dr. Dev-
ananda Tandavan, to work with the community and keep him in touch
with the progress. Thus was born the Hindu Temple of Greater Chicago.

Gurudeva was a great fund-raiser for temples. He attended a few fund-
raising meetings as the guest of honor in Chicago and gave an inspiring
discourse each time, telling those gathered to get out their check books
and write down a number—then "add a few more zeros."

When he visited one temple being renovated in Singapore, the trustees
explained their fund-raising strategy to sponsor each square foot of the
new temple for $100. Immediately he reached in his bag, took out a $100
bill and bought one sponsorship. It was likely, judging from the trustees'
astonished look, that he was the first visiting swami to ever contribute to
their temple fund. Then he appealed for funds to the temple congregation

during his speech. "I gave $100," he said, "because I need the good karma of that gift to come back to me one day, maybe in the form of $500."

The same promotion was repeated to bolster temple fund-raising around the world. People were impressed to see him raise money like this for others, without saying a word about his own fund-raising needs. He told his monks often that by strengthening others, they would become strong; by helping others build their temples, his temple would manifest. In the years that followed, many he helped in their time of need turned their generosity toward him.

In a similar way, Gurudeva was directly involved in three dozen other temples in the United States, Canada, Guadeloupe, Denmark, England, Fiji, Germany, Mauritius, New Zealand, Reunion, Russia, Sweden and Sri Lanka, giving each community or temple a granite murti and guidance when needed. He helped many more with direct advice, often dealing

Dikshas *marked key milestones in the monastic fellowship.* Page 629
From his traditional lion seat Gurudeva would offer blessings, Chapter 29
sandalwood paste, vibhuti *and home-grown rudraksha malas.*

· ·

with fund-raising, zoning, community relationship building,
priestly staff, debt management and more.

The Maha Ganapathy Temple in Edmonton, Canada, is one
of many that he guided closely. In addition, he helped this
temple's first priest immigrate from Sri Lanka. This was Sub-
ramanya Gurukkal, who had known Yogaswami as a young
boy. Aran Veylan, an attorney in that community, recalls:

The conception of the Edmonton temple came right from
Gurudeva. It gives the temple a special power to be connected to Gurudeva in that way. He brought the whole community together. He defined the community as "Tamil Hindus,"
because in the early 70s, the Tamils were a Tamil cultural
group—Christians and Hindus together. Now the community has matured into a Tamil Saivite community, and that is
all because of Gurudeva's influence.

The community went so far as to make the constitution of
the temple state that one has to be a Saivite Hindu to be a
member. Because of this, according to D. Selvarajah, one of
the founding members, the temple now has a very clear and
strong power. People from all over Canada come to this temple and have
told Selvarajah it is the best temple in Canada and an example for them to
follow. He recalls:

Gurudeva told us in the beginning, "You have all built temples in Sri
Lanka. Now, because of the children, you have to teach them what
you know. The temple is what will bring the families together and the
children together."

In Denmark, Gurudeva helped establish the Abirami Amman temple.
The priestess, Sri Abirami Upasagi, is deeply psychic. While in trance, she
channels the Goddess to heal and bless people. In the beginning she was
criticized. In 1995 she had appealed to Gurudeva, as she felt these chan-
nelings were good and caused no harm. He assured her that what she was

doing was correct and, giving her a Ganesha Deity, put her under his psychic protection. The icon arrived on the Ganesha Chaturthi festival day in August. They commenced the worship that same day, and milk began dripping from Ganesha's eyes.

A month later the famous "Milk Miracle" happened around the world, and this tiny statue began drinking gallons and gallons of milk offered before it with a small spoon. For many days after, hundreds of Hindus and local Danes came to feed Ganesha, including national television reporters.

In 1995 Gurudeva met with 89 Adisaiva priests in Mumbai to discuss their Page 631
future and offer his support. Throughout his life he gave prominence to Chapter 29
the priests and taught others of their importance in the community.
• •

No one could explain the phenomenon witnessed by so many.

A few months later, Gurudeva sent a three-foot-tall Goddess Amman Deity to that temple. With Gurudeva's support, the priestess became a respected spiritual leader. In August of 2001, after leading a travel-study program through Northern Europe, Gurudeva laid the five traditional bricks to begin her new temple with his own hands.

Now that hundreds of temples have been built all over the world, many trustees have asked, "What's next?" Gurudeva gave the answer:

> I want to see the stewardship of each temple take their leadership responsibilities seriously. The temples are built, the temples are dedicated, the Deities are there, the priests are there, the congregation is there. It is up to the core elected leadership, the trustees of the temple, to actually become full-time spiritual leaders and make a difference in the lives of the parents and children and change the community into a model community.

"Stop Bashing the Priests!"

Gurudeva stood ready to defend the priesthood who serve in the Hindu temples around the world. Especially in the early 90s he campaigned for fair treatment of temple priests. Not surprisingly, the priests, who had few champions for their cause, adored Gurudeva, invited him always to their temples and called upon him from time to time.

The leader of the Adisaiva priest community, Sivasri Dr. T. S. Sambamurti Sivachariyar, wrote, "His support for us was great. At a time when many organizations and even governments were discouraging us, he always raised his voice on behalf of us around the world at difficult times." In one of his HINDUISM TODAY Publisher's Desk columns, Gurudeva wrote:

> Hindu priests, known as *pujaris*, are being bashed—physically, emotionally and mentally—by temple managers, trustees and sometimes even the devotees. We know that this is not right. Still, no one, well maybe a few, is objecting, except the priests themselves. Their objections and efforts to provide for their own security go largely unheard,

as they are looked at by management as uneducated, simple people who perform rote rituals.

Priest bashing is a popular sport outside of India. Priests have their *sanga* and elders back home in India to stand up for them. When a priest goes into disfavor, the slightest excuses are used to hurt him, such as wrongdoing in handling money—that is a favorite and usually the first to be used. The list goes on, giving management the permission to yell at him, push him, ignore his needs, embarrass him in front of his peers and sometimes the public.

Yes, Hindu temple priest bashing is a worldwide tragedy, and those who perpetrate these acts are also bashing the Sanatana Dharma. Abusing priests is not to be taken lightly. Those who can invoke blessings from the Gods can also invoke curses from *asuric* forces of this planet for their own protection when angered, embarrassed and deeply hurt. This very thing happened in Hawaii when the Christians were converting all the followers of the powerful native kahuna priesthood. Some angered and became some of the best black magicians, feared to this day. They now live in the *pretaloka*, the astral plane close to Earth, afflicting wrongdoers and helping the faithful. It did not have to happen this way, but it did.

Hindu temple priests deserve the richness of their holy profession, the dignity of their office, and this should not be interfered with. They have earned the same respect that any professional in "the real world" enjoys.

The time has now come for Hindus to change our attitudes about temple priests. This will require temple managers to adjust their thinking. It will also require the international priesthood of the Sanatana Dharma to take a firm stand against their molesters and refuse to submit themselves day in and day out to harassment or to the humiliation of janitorial work and the handling of shoes. Some work fourteen hours a day and more. They are considered servants of the manager rather than the temple Gods. Their final justice may not be found in man's law. It may be more mystical. They may decide to go to God's unfailing law or, if so inclined, to the darker realms for relief.

Beware! Their mantras are powerful. History shows entire societies that have gone down with their priesthoods. Let's not have this happen again.

While supporting legitimate priests, he criticized those who claimed social superiority by virtue of merely being born into the priestly caste:

I don't understand how some people claim they are brahmins because their fathers are brahmins. They don't know the religion, and they can't do the worship. It's like someone saying, "My father is a doctor, so I'm a doctor. Let me operate on you." No way.

In Europe and America he advocated proper treatment of the priests, especially that they be given decent salaries, proper working conditions, reasonable hours and good housing. He wanted them to be represented on temple boards and be given the respect and position that priests and ministers of other faiths enjoy, akin to that of a doctor or a lawyer. It wasn't his most popular suggestion, especially to temple boards comprised of brahmins who were doctors or engineers. As an alternative, he encouraged priests to start their own temples, which a few have done and more plan to in the future.

Turning Conflict into Cooperation

Gurudeva preached—and practiced—cooperation among Hindus. He said that three harmful habits stand in the way: attacking leaders, tolerating detractors and disharmony among boards and committees.

It is important that you refrain from the pattern that if one person in the community comes up, cut him down, malign him, criticize him until all heads are leveled. In modern, industrial society everyone tries to lift everyone else up. People are proud of an individual in the community who comes up, and they help the next one behind him to succeed as well. They are proud of their religious leaders, too.

Not so here in India, because if anyone does want to help out spiritually they have to be quiet and conceal themselves, lest they be maligned. Nobody is standing up to defend the religion; nobody is allowing anybody else to stand up, either. This has to change, and change fast it will.

"Swami bashing" was another sport Gurudeva would not tolerate. Its origins were easily detected: Christian missionaries on one side and communists on the other, each for their own reasons wanting to discredit the swamis. Gurudeva later said, "When swami bashing was in vogue years ago, swamis took it seriously. They got to know each other better, stood up for each other and put a stop to the nonsense." Gurudeva made a point of meeting as many of the swamis of India as possible. He stayed in contact with them, too, especially through HINDUISM TODAY, and gathered

their views on dozens of issues to formulate an all-Hindu stance and to empower spiritual leaders.

At a time when vocal advocates of a militant Hinduism arose, Gurudeva stood firm in defense of ahimsa, nonviolence, as an essential principle. Yet he was not a pacifist. He endorsed the right of nations and individuals to self-defense. But he could foresee the negative karma and endless cycles of retribution in store for those who advocated violence, taking the law into their own hands to achieve their goals or to right past wrongs. This was not always the popular stance; but with scripture and the majority of swamis backing him up, one heard fewer and fewer Hindus advocating violent solutions.

Zero Tolerance for Disharmony

While other leaders, even great ones, aspire for complete harmony while conceding its impossibility, Gurudeva knew it was achievable and held that ideal so firmly that his monastics learned to believe it was possible. He spoke often of "zero-tolerance for disharmonious conditions."

As was his way, he went beyond the idea by giving tools for its accomplishment. His rule: if one monk upset another, even inadvertently, the two could not sleep until the matter was resolved. They were expected to sit together, make amends and apologies until both felt the matter was settled and the pranas between them were fully harmonized.

Thus little hurts and entanglements never were left to fester and burrow themselves into the subconscious mind. Young monks might spend hours resolving a contentious encounter in this way, while veterans learned the art of settling things swiftly—and more importantly, learned how to avoid contention altogether. Gurudeva described his stance in *Living with Siva:*

> In our fellowship all work stops and the problem is attended to at once. It is each one's responsibility to follow this wisdom. Nothing could be more counterproductive and foolish than to continue work, especially religious work, while conflict prevails, for demonic forces have been unleashed that must be dispelled for any effort to be fruitful and long lasting. Any breach in the angelic force field of the home, monastery or workplace must be sealed off quickly.
>
> Our approach is simple. We are all committed to the shared sadhana that all difficult feelings must be resolved before sleep, lest they give rise to mental argument, go to seed and germinate as

· ·

For most important discussions about philosophy, spiritual training and monastic life, Gurudeva would meet with his acharyas, share his views and seek theirs, then wait for a unanimous nod on how to proceed.

unwanted, troublesome *vasanas,* subconscious impressions, that cannot be totally erased but only softened and neutralized through the
mystic processes of atonement.

Governing by Consensualocracy

In a similar departure from institutional politics, Gurudeva created a governing style he called consensualocracy. Actually, there were two forms of
government in the monastery. One followed the tradition that says the satguru's word is law. But he used that power rarely, and even gave it a place,
the Guru Pitham (a meditation room containing his guru seat). When
he sat there on the seat of authority as Guru Mahasannidhanam, his
words were edicts, not suggestions or ideas to be debated and discussed.

Elsewhere, he chose to give the power of decision to the group—not
the entire monastery, but to those involved in a project, an innovation, a
meeting. In such cases he never allowed a vote, which to him was the tyr-
anny of the many over the few. In place of a vote, he asked for unanimous
concurrence. If a single voice objected, no decision could be reached, and
further discussion was needed. Everyone at every meeting knew his own
voice was all-important. He could stall a project, even when ten others
were eager for it to proceed. Each learned to not abuse that privilege.

The monks soon discovered the dual wisdom of this system. First, while
the process was sometimes tediously slow, it meant that every decision
made had the full force of the entire group behind it, without a single dis-
senting monk pulling against it. This gave its execution a power and clarity that only shared commitment can bring to a group task. Second, there
would be times when the minority in a group had some special insight.
While the majority might be eager to move swiftly on something, one or
two monks might have a more profound, nuanced view, something not
uncommon in a spiritual community, where intuitions are highly honed.
Plus, consensualocracy assures that no one is left behind, overridden, out-
voted or ignored. In the conclusion of *Lemurian Scrolls,* Gurudeva wrote:

> There is a higher form of government that we might call consensual
> governance. This is a style of rule that has neither a single person nor
> a majority as the controlling force, but which embraces all its peoples,
> needs and constituents in a special way at every meeting. Ironically,
> such a system could not evolve on its own, but only under the special
> circumstances of a spiritual leadership, provided by great beings of all
> three worlds, as described in these scrolls.
>
> Under this system, there is deference to seniority and special care

and nurturing of the youngest. Under this system, there is no voting, no rule of the majority and thus submission of the unenfranchised or the outnumbered. All have a voice; all have an urge to sacrifice their needs to the greater good of all others. In this system, major decisions are ratified not by vote but by a consensual process that brings all parties together to find a unified agreement as to the best course of action for the highest good of all. Its process may be slow, even tedious when new members are involved who do not understand its subtle ways, yet in the long run it accrues a great power, the power of 100 percent heartfelt support of all members for all decisions. Inspiration flourishes. Consensual governance is a difficult form of governance, but worth the effort to achieve.

Thus, we have government by chaos (anarchy), government that gives permission for guerrilla force (terrocracy). This is government that incites deadly acts of terrorism to gain its ends. Then we have government by one ruler's force (autocracy), government by military force (dictatorship), government by social and financial force (oligarchy), government by statist force (socialism), government by numerical and emotional force (democracy), government by kings and queens (monarchy), government by religious leaders supported by the inner worlds (theocracy), and government by shared soul force (consensualocracy).

This is a form of government based on Sanatana Dharma. It is a rule that values intelligent cooperation and is pranically binding on all concerned. It is the exact same way that divine souls in the Second World and highly evolved beings in the Third World get things done, by managing to keep the actinic pranas flowing in the right direction, first with impulse, the birth of an idea, then pulse, the development of a plan, and creation, the totality of the group vision and effort, leading to its manifestation into astral or physical reality. Thus, consensualocracy is what the *Vedas* record. It is how the great cultures existed. It is the method of government that large, joint and extended families and tribes have perpetuated for generations and use to this very day.

Consensualocracy is a most compassionate form of governance, well suited for spiritually dedicated groups, highly ethical and dedicated communities with a singular vision and purpose. In it, all concur as to the goals, the methods to be employed to achieve those goals and the day-to-day activities that implement those methods. It is, simply put, management by intelligent cooperation.

Chapter Thirty

Harnessing a Hurricane

On September 11, 1992, Hurricane Iniki struck a direct hit on the island of Kauai. The eye of this Category 4 hurricane went right over the monastery. Great damage was wrought by that storm. Three monastery buildings were destroyed, along with 10,000 trees and plants. It was months before electricity and running water were restored. That was a great challenge to the monks. But Gurudeva took it all in stride. He saw Siva at work even in this tragedy. He had the monks bake bread each day and take it, along with fresh cow's milk, to the neighbors, who were stranded at home since all the roads were blocked. Gurudeva laughed and made the experience a positive one, which was amazing since the destruction and the disruption was so severe. It was a lesson to all the monks, a reminder and a living example of Gurudeva's teaching that it is not what happens to us in life that matters, it is how we react, how we respond. And he responded to disaster with grace, turning the devastation of the monastery he had worked a lifetime to create into an ingenious way to preserve it forever.

It happened like this. When, months later, the monastery received the woefully inadequate insurance check for $300,000, Gurudeva refused to cash it, but kept it in his room and meditated on its best use. After a few days, he told the monks that he was putting it all in the bank, and that not a penny would be spent. That fund would earn interest that could be used to repair the damaged monastery. It might take ten years, he said, but at the end of that time all the facilities would be restored, and the $300,000 would still be intact.

It was a brilliant move, and it taught the monks about the power of endowments. Gurudeva worked with Paramacharya Bodhinatha, his senior disciple, to create a unique financial institution, Hindu Heritage Endowment (HHE), officially founded in 1994. As of 2011, HHE has over 80 funds and $10 million in assets, helping orphanages, temples, swamis, ashrams and publications around the world. Turning a natural disaster into a global service institution typified the way Gurudeva worked with energy, transmuting it for a higher purpose.

Gurudeva was engaged in every aspect of his mission, knew every detail, approved every budget. He held weekly stewards' meetings with his senior monks, often at seaside hotels, to keep an overview of his global mission.

As I see it, everything that was strong survived, and everything weak was destroyed in the face of wind gusts measured at 194 miles per hour at the Kauai NASA station. The whole island was engulfed and few escaped damage.

What is to be done with all this energy? From a mystical point of view, external or internal, negative or positive, energy can be run through the converter named jnana (wisdom) and turned into a creative force. At our spiritual center, we put most of ours into newer and bigger and better publications, including HINDUISM TODAY.

The scriptures say adversity makes strong men stronger. It is always best to face adversity and success in equanimity, and we have to confess we enjoyed fetching water in buckets, beating our clothing on a rock by the river and cooking over an open fire. All these simple joys reminded us of the many times that our swamis lived the village life on the Jaffna peninsula.

Gurudeva founded Hindu Heritage Endowment as an independent public service trust to provide Hindu institutions with permanent, growing income through charitable endowments. He secured from the IRS a special ruling allowing that beneficiaries can be anywhere in the world. This enables wealthy Hindus in America to support their village temple in India, for instance, and receive a US tax deduction. He was not planning just for his own institution's future, but the future of every Hindu institution in the world.

Each quarter from 1994 to 2001 Gurudeva met for a day at the posh Princeville Hotel with HHE's monastic stewards to monitor the funds, expand their capacity and refine their uses. HHE ultimately became a primary supporter of his monastic order and Iraivan Temple, fulfilling Gurudeva's vision of self-sufficiency.

All the guardian devas of all the people in the beneficiary organizations and of all those who set up the endowment are involved in the HHE. It is a devonic creation, not forged by us, but bequeathed upon us from the Devaloka and the Sivaloka to fulfill a need. The guardian devas of each organization have a personal interest in Hindu Heritage Endowment because they are putting all their energy and thought into creating for each Hindu organization a permanent financial abundance so that its leadership can concentrate upon fulfilling its goals rather than on constant fund-raising and basic concerns about money.

Power of the Press

From the beginning, writing and publishing were the cornerstone of Gurudeva's spiritual mission. He understood the staying power of the written word and knew that every spiritual tradition rests on a bedrock of holy texts. But the extensive travel of the late 70s and early 80s had kept him on the road and away from the philosophical writings that he so loved. His work with HINDUISM TODAY magazine never ceased, though; and his marvelous *upadeshas* given all over the globe during this hiatus were captured and saved for future publication.

The late 1980s and the 90s were that future—a return to earlier times when he published with great energy and enthusiasm. But technology had evolved; and he inspired his team to immerse themselves in state-of-the-art digital publishing, including multimedia CDs, audio, video and computer graphics. He introduced his daily Hindu news service, called Hindu Press International (HPI), using the Internet to connect and inform Hindus. By then he had become accustomed to the radical conceptual change that the Internet had conjured.

With the help of that marvelous technology, Gurudeva developed an editing style that was ingeniously, perhaps uniquely, collaborative, using networked Macintosh computers. Each afternoon, 365 days a year unless he was traveling, he met with a team of two, and later three, monks between 3 and 7 pm. The team's portable Macs were connected so that the same document, say a chapter of *Loving Ganesha*, was displayed simultaneously on all monitors. When any member of the team made an alteration, all monitors were updated instantly, in real time. No more scribbling down dictation on paper, to be typed up and brought back for review the next day.

Gurudeva never wrote a book in the usual way. If he wasn't working from the transcript of a talk he had given, he would come to the table with a topic he had meditated on that day, and typically begin by dictating a page or two as one of the monks captured it onscreen. Then he would invite them to dive in and edit the pages. "Open season," he would announce, and together they would all work on bringing it, as Gurudeva often said, "from talkenese into the English language"—though all this was done with the greatest caution to preserve the power of the original expression. When working with talks that were given in the 50s, 60s and 70s, from which many chapters of his Master Course trilogy were sourced, every effort was made to undo unnecessary editing that had occurred in earlier days and restore the original *upadesha*.

It often took hours to edit just a few sentences. But as in all he did, Gurudeva never rushed, never felt the weight of time. He was after quality; and if it took three hours to craft a sentence, he would rejoice in the accomplishment at the end. In the creation of the 365 sutras of *Living with Siva*, an average of two or three sutras were edited, discussed and finalized each afternoon—though even those crafted to perfection were often re-edited a week later, and again the next month.

In writing *Dancing with Siva*, the challenge was to condense oceans of information into a single page for each topic. Gurudeva took special delight in following his self-imposed discipline for the pages of this book,

which decreed that the questions and answers be exactly the same length,

each character of each word fine-tuned so that every *shloka* and *bhashya* fit in exactly the same amount of space.

Adding to that challenge, a workflow evolved in which the team researched, wrote and refined the text, then—when it seemed as though it were perfect and complete—asked, "What more needs to be explained here?" If they unearthed a vital addition, even one that seemed impossible to incorporate, they would churn and distill the words down even further, to the most condensed summary imaginable, magically adding perfection to perfection. It was not easy, but these requirements brought forth an uncommon clarity and a density of meaning rarely achieved, except by gifted poets.

Gurudeva looked forward to these sessions every day, preparing subjects and calling upon the inner forces, his team of devas, to assist in bringing forth the powerful, insightful writings that would guide devotees into the future of futures, writings that would last for millennia.

Every word, every phrase, every punctuation mark passed by his careful eye; and only when he was truly satisfied would the team move on. Though he typed only occasionally in those sessions, he would freely break in to type or voice a clarification or answer a question about the wording of a passage. This often led to unpredicted new insights. If research was required, as it not infrequently was, he directed the swamis to gather information during the next day for their afternoon session together. In these days before Google, this entailed old-fashioned forays into the monastery library or emails to knowledgeable sources.

So disciplined was Gurudeva's editing routine that Church members in the neighborhood could look out their window at exactly the same time each afternoon and see their satguru heading off for his editing session. For years, he worked in several of the coastal hotel lobbies. The staff loved him dearly and always felt special blessings were in store for the evening if he came to their place. They did not know his reasons for leaving perhaps the most beautiful place on Kauai to meet at their hotel. He had tried to edit in his office, but his mind was not free, and the interruptions were constant.

When asked if the many sounds around him in the bustling restaurant area were disturbing, Gurudeva responded, "Not at all; noise makes me quiet!" It did perplex some of the monks how noise could make one quiet, how being in the rather worldly vibrations of a hotel lobby could be a catalyst for creative, inner writing. It was no mystery to the master. Like Yogaswami, who almost daily walked the swarming streets of Jaffna,

. . . .

Gurudeva loved to meander in the monastery's sacred gardens. These solitary walks almost always had a purpose, and he often returned with new insights, ideas and plans for the future to share with the monks.

and Chellappaswami, who lived for years in front of a tumultuous temple, Gurudeva had experienced the effect of contrast, the clash of the inner and the outer states of consciousness which, for him, brought forward the subtle in contrast to the gross, shone a light on light, exactly because of the surrounding shadows. Without the grounding, the anchor which the noises and the people and the swirling karmas provided, the inner states of mind dominated and he grew too remote, too refined to bring the teachings forth.

Here, near the ocean, he could work for hours with few intrusions, unencumbered by the weight of his many responsibilities as satguru and the minds of hundreds of devotees. The most innocuous five-minute disruption at the monastery could result in an hour of thought about the

For a few years Gurudeva did his daily editing near the ocean in a specially outfitted Winnebago Rialta. The editing team, working at a table in the back, had a view of turtles and whales.

Page 645

Chapter 30

. . . .

issue. His seaside work was efficient, focused and free-flowing. A glass of wine or two through the afternoon made for a relaxed and joyful session and, as Gurudeva said, subdued the conscious mind, allowing the super-conscious mind to flow through and guide the work. He reflected that this was akin to great Japanese poets for whom sake is a linguistic elixir.

When Hurricane Iniki shut down all but two of the island's four dozen major hotels in 1992, Gurudeva flew to California with the editing team and continued the work in hotels there for three months. Before returning to Kauai, he went shopping one afternoon for a used RV. He found one he liked, a 1979 Winnebago, and had it shipped to Kauai for the afternoon sessions. Refurbished by the monks, it became his creative headquarters on most days, parked twenty yards from the sea at Kealia beach. In the winter months, he enjoyed watching the whales and green turtles frolicking off the reef. On the day he completed *Dancing with Siva,* a massive male whale breached a hundred yards off shore, then forcefully flapped his twelve-foot-long fin twenty-seven times on the water, as if celebrating the event. Seeing this, Gurudeva commented that the book's creation was driven by "whale power."

An early adopter of cell phones, Gurudeva kept his on the table during every editing session. His close devotees around the world all had his personal number, which spelled out "New Deli." Hardly a day would pass without a call from some far land—someone's father had died, someone was elected to parliament, a baby was born that morning. Gurudeva never once hesitated to interrupt his session to take a call. If it was a serious one, he would get up and walk in the hotel garden as he counseled and consoled his shishyas. Then he would return and invariably know the next word of the next sentence on the screen.

When he dictated, and sometimes he did the typing himself, it was often as if he were hearing an inner voice. When the monks with him complimented the wondrous words that had poured forth during those surges, he would quip, "I have good writers upstairs." During this torrential, two-decade-long, computer-assisted transmission of spiritual insight, Gurudeva methodically assembled the fruits of fifty years of sadhana and ministry to create his philosophical, cultural and spiritual legacy.

His books were vast, diverse and always focused on deepening everyone's understanding of Hinduism, and always in an approachable and practical idiom. In his last ten years the book effort took on a new momentum as more and more people realized their preciousness. Spanish-speaking readers wanting to share the teachings received permission to translate the works. A team in Russia published editions, as did others in Sri Lanka (Tamil), Mumbai (Marathi), Kuala Lumpur (Bahasya Malay) and elsewhere. Motilal Banarsidass, Munshiram Manoharlal and Abhinav, three of Delhi's foremost publishers, vied to reprint his books in India. Each firm was given rights to certain books.

A Heart for Art

Gurudeva understood the importance of art in communicating ideas and uplifting the human spirit, and he regarded Hindu art as itself sacred. During his travels, he noticed that art, like so many other aspects of Hinduism, was waning, with unappreciated artists urging their sons to be engineers. In response, he sought out the finest artists and commissioned them to do major works in traditional styles, paying them well for their gifts. Artists in India, Bali and North America took on creative projects, some involving years of painstaking work on a single canvas, others requiring hundreds of large paintings illustrating Hindu motifs.

Art is more than painting, and Gurudeva retained bronze and stone craftsmen to produce Saiva saints, Siva's 108 dance poses, a 32,000-pound Nandi and a 12-foot Dakshinamurti. Artists were awed by the Hawaii swami's interest in their skills. Traditional artists A. Manivelu and S. Rajam spent years of their lives illustrating his publications. After Gurudeva purchased his lifetime collection, which was decaying in a Madras closet, the elderly S. Rajam wrote, "To take my 400 paintings to his ashram in Hawaii is something that opened my heart, to know there is a future for my paintings. Above all, his very majestic personality reminds artistes like me of old-time rishis and religion-makers."

Writing a Modern Shastra

Having completed, with his editing team, the Nandinatha Sutras, answering in writing, once and for all, the many questions he had been asked over and over for decades by followers wanting to know his views on myriad life issues, Gurudeva devoted the full year of 1994 to what he humorously called "the world's most boring book, or the best remedy for insomnia:" *Saiva Dharma Shastras, The Book of Discipline of Saiva Siddhanta Church.*

He carefully timed its publishing to coincide with the date of the retrospective perspective the devas took when writing *The Saivite Shastras*, which he clairvoyantly read in 1973 from the oversized, white inner-plane book that a group of three devas wrote to guide his order into the future. They had done this by projecting themselves into the future to the year 1995 and writing their superconscious history of what Gurudeva and his order did, or would do, up until that time. Like the words of fortune tellers, the pages of their book not only painted a picture, they carved a path, influencing and coloring for Gurudeva and his monks what was to come, what they would do and how they would do it. For 25 years he had followed that angelic prophecy, and now it had arrived.

Gurudeva shared his perspective in the book's introduction:

As this year, 1995, unfolds, the past has met the present, and it is truly a glorious time, because I can now add to the great inner-plane manuscripts first read from the akasha in 1973 these *Saiva Dharma Shastras,* the story of our contemporary Church's ideals, day-to-day customs and procedures. *Lemurian Scrolls* and these *Saiva Dharma Shastras* are the legacy I leave my acharya successors, their guidelines and firm laws, their commission to follow and fulfill, along with The Master Course trilogy—*Dancing, Living* and *Merging with Siva,* and Shum, the language of meditation. Our pattern has been completed, the prophecy manifested better than any of our expectations. We are eternally grateful for the untiring help the Gods, devas and rishis have provided ever since the *Lord Subramaniam Shastras* were revealed, a profoundly needed message from the past for the present, now preserved for the future.

Saiva Dharma Shastras, the seventh or eighth church manual Gurudeva had written, drawing on aspects of the American church system, was crafted to assure his organizations' social viability and structural integrity. In its pages he finalized patterns for the future, including the extended family structure for his missions, and he designated as his successors three of his senior monastics: Acharya Bodhinatha Veylanswami, to be followed by Acharya Sadasivanatha Palaniswami and then Acharya Sivanatha Ceyonswami.

My acharya successors will have a momentous task, to be sure. They who have striven so hard to fulfill their holy orders of sannyasa will have these *Saiva Dharma Shastras,* the *Lord Subramaniam Shastras* and the *Mathavasi Shastras* as their discipline, their sadhana and,

yes, sometimes their *tapas.* As the future is based upon the past, this recorded past within these *Shastras* releases new energy.

As predicted in *The Saivite Shastras,* by 1995, the year we are in now, our pattern is set, and constant preservation and perpetuation is commissioned by me and by the inner worlds for its fulfillment generation after generation for over a thousand years into the future of futures, for ever and ever. Yea, much longer than that, much longer than forever, for these *Shastras* give the explanation of life as it is to be lived and has been lived by a healthy, happy, spiritually productive, small inner group and larger outer group, both ever growing in strength and numbers.

For decades Gurudeva worked closely with his senior acharyas to guide the Church's global mission. In 1995 he declared they would succeed him in order: Bodhinatha Veylanswami, Sadasivanatha Palaniswami and Sivanatha Ceyonswami.

• •

A South Indian Temple in Hawaii

Sivalaya Dipam in 1991 proved prophetic. On that rainy December afternoon, the monks and two dozen members held a *homa* in the Agni Mandapam. As decreed by tradition, an enormous fire was built in an open field nearby where the far-swirling sparks from bamboo and logs could fly freely and safely, an intense bonfire to represent God Siva as a pillar of flames. Gurudeva arrived after dark in his Winnebago Rialta, having just come from his afternoon editing session. It had been raining for days, and

the ground was so soaked that it couldn't hold another ounce of water.

As Gurudeva descended from the vehicle in his dapper, orange Indian kurta outfit, monks and devotees huddled under umbrellas greeted him warmly. But instead of sitting for the rites as he did each year, he slowly trudged around the blazing fire, as if entranced, then stopped in his tracks and prostrated in the mud, worshiping the fire that stood for the infinite Siva. It was a rare thing to see the satguru on the ground, prone, out in a field. No one knew in that moment that this would be the exact spot on which Iraivan Temple would rise. Superconsciously, Gurudeva must have known, though he never spoke of it.

It would happen again. In 1994, in Edmonton, Alberta, Canada, Gurudeva was visiting the committee of an incipient Ganesha temple. Four years before, he had instructed them to buy a "beautiful piece of land, at least five acres, with a knoll and a stream on it." They since had found the land, and Gurudeva was setting foot on it for the first time.

Instead of entering the little house where Lord Ganesha was temporarily enshrined, he walked around the structure and then, to his hosts' puzzlement, headed out into the pathless woods. Followed by less fleet devotees, he strode through brush and brambles with an intent that defied reason. Suddenly he halted, and they caught up in time to witness him prayerfully holding a handful of flowers with which they had greeted him. Placing the flowers on the ground where he stood, the satguru prostrated in the woodsy dirt.

The significance was not lost on the temple hosts, who the next day hired a surveyor to mark the place where those blossoms were offered. In the coming years, the Edmonton Maha Ganapathy Temple was built upon that now holy site. Twice Gurudeva prostrated on virgin land, and twice temples arose on the spot.

Between 1975 and 1990 Gurudeva had been working to bring Iraivan Temple to the Earth plane. Roads were built, lands cleared, mortgages paid, the crystal Svayambhu Lingam acquired and master plans drawn by architectural firms. In 1982 Gurudeva visited the famed Mahabalipuram College of Architecture and Sculpture and met the rising Sri V. Ganapati Sthapati, who would soon become one of Bharat's foremost temple architects. Honored with the coveted Padma Bhushan award in 2009, in recognition of outstanding civilian service to the nation, this gifted master builder would design Iraivan in the style of his ancestors.

It would be a granite edifice, in the tradition of the ancient citadels of Tamil Nadu's Chola Dynasty, famed for their elegant beauty and

. . . .

Throughout the 90s Gurudeva visited India often, working on the ever-evolving Iraivan Temple details. On December 21, 1990, he chipped the first stone in an elaborate ceremony at Kailash Ashram in Bangalore.

remarkable sculptural craftsmanship. Its name, too, harkens back to that era. *Iraivan* is an ancient Tamil name for God, an endearing appellation that describes Siva as "He who is worshiped." In this Hawaiian home for God Siva, every stone would be sacred, each piece a part of the body of God, carved in the old ways, by hand, by craftsmen of an art that was on the verge of dying out, like many in our modern age.

By decreeing that this temple be made without the efficiencies of electric or hydraulic tools, Gurudeva assured two things: first, that it would reflect the best of human skill, since hand sculpting is vastly more refined and subtle than works crafted by modern machines; and, second, that at least one more generation of stone carvers would become proficient in the craft, which is passed down from father to son, artisan to apprentice.

Even in India nowadays, temples are rarely built entirely of stone, and never in this time-consuming and expensive, traditional manner. Modern contractors opt for concrete and brick for structural work and power tools for stone shaping, which cannot compare to carving. It may well be, and only history knows for sure, that Iraivan Temple, carved between 1991 and 2017 in Bangalore, India, is the last temple created completely by hand in India, with a primitive coke-burning forge and just two simple carving tools—a bamboo-handled hammer and hand-forged chisels of mild steel.

Gurudeva worked daily on the details of the temple. He also engaged his monks and all of his shishyas in its creation, knowing that this massive undertaking would define their shared goals and bring them together. He often described its import:

> As I look into the future, I see Iraivan, fully completed, as a center where devotees will come to find the center of themselves. We will preserve it and maintain it so that it is the way Rishikesh used to be, a proper, pure, quiet place where devotees can go within themselves through the practice of yoga. There are very few such places left on the Earth now. Kauai's Hindu Monastery is one of them. I see Iraivan as a yoga citadel, a place of pilgrimage for the devout, sincere and dedicated. I see Iraivan as India's message to the world on visitors' day, when Hindus and non-Hindus alike come to admire the great artistry of the *silpi* stone carving tradition. I see Iraivan as a fulfillment of our lineage, our scriptures and our monastery. This is a place where you do not have to invoke God, for God is here, for this is where heaven meets the Earth.

· ·

Artist S. Rajam envisions the auspicious day when thousands gather on Kauai for the consecration of Iraivan Temple. As holy waters are poured over the vimanam, *Gurudeva blesses from his world of light, surrounded by the gurus of the Kailasa Parampara.*

Help from His Indian Brothers

Faced with the daunting task of constructing a granite temple in India and having it shipped to Kauai piece by piece, Gurudeva made inquiries as to who in that great land might facilitate the effort for him, 8,000 miles away, where a contract is less the end of negotiation than the beginning of further discussion. Who had the experience, expertise and grassroots contacts that would be needed? He was directed to Tiruchi Swami, who not only agreed to meet with Gurudeva but insisted on hosting at his ashram for two days the thirty pilgrims who were traveling with him on the 1990 Indian Innersearch.

Tiruchi Swami was a white-robed saint based in Bangalore, a rare mystic, born in 1929, just two years after Gurudeva came into this world. The story is told that, while traveling in Kanyakumari in South India, his parents were informed by a stranger near the Devi temple, "By the grace of the Divine Mother and Lord Subrahmanya, a glorious son will be born to you. He will be a teacher and benefactor for all mankind." The prophecy proved true. In his twenties, around the same time Gurudeva received his ordination in Sri Lanka, the young seeker trekked to Nepal where he was initiated. Sri Tiruchi Mahaswamigal (1929–2005), or Tiruchi Swami, as he is known, was instructed by his guru, Shivapuri Baba, to return to India, propagate dharma and build a temple. Before returning, Swamiji went to Mount Kailash. There, he had a vision of Goddesses Durga, Lakshmi and Saraswati, who told him to go south, to Karnataka.

In 1960, while traveling, Swamiji had a divine vision that inspired him to start an ashram and temple near Bangalore, three years after Gurudeva founded his first center in San Francisco. His Kailash Ashram and Rajarajeshwari Temple, where Gurudeva would sojourn many times, were the fulfillment of those inner orders. These two great gurus and their successors would be profoundly connected, their lives interwoven.

With Sri Tiruchi Swami's guidance and practical engagement, the plan solidified, obstacles were overcome and Gurudeva chipped the first stone for Iraivan in a grand ceremony at the Rajarajeshwari Temple. With that, Gurudeva flew back to Kauai, leaving two of his swamis in India to complete the protracted contract negotiations with Ganapati Sthapati.

Earlier, while the Innersearch pilgrims were in Madras, Gurudeva rode by car with three of his monks to personally carry the blueprints of Iraivan Temple to another of India's greatest saints for blessings. Arriving in Kanchipuram, they waited in the standing queue for darshan of Sri la Sri Chandrashekharendra Saraswati, then 97, the senior pontiff of Kanchi Kamakoti Pitham. Devotees filed by, receiving blessings from the

Sitting on the banks of the Wailua River, Iraivan temple's golden towers would, in the years to come, draw devotees from around the world. The 12-foot-tall stone Dakshinamurti sits silently nearby as the monks approach in procession with drums and conches.

. . . .

frail sage who, drifting in and out of consciousness, lay on a simple white canvas cot. At his side, assisting in this sacred daily routine, was his successor, Sri Jayendra Saraswati, shaven headed, graying, intense and serious. Alerted to Gurudeva's impending visit, he greeted the tall, orange-robed American sage with respect and asked to see the temple plans. Quickly they were rolled open on the table that separated the Vedanta monks from the line of devotees. Jayendra Saraswati then whispered in the ear of his senior, "The swami from Hawaii has arrived."

Suddenly the sage became conscious, wide awake, and asked to be propped up on the cot. His big doe eyes met those of Gurudeva. Moments passed. The sage saw the papers, placed his hand on them, then eased back down on the cot and closed his eyes. Jayendra Saraswati asked about the temple and listened raptly as one of Gurudeva's monks who spoke Tamil gave details of the project. Jayendra Saraswati, too, blessed the plans, then posed for a photo with Gurudeva, whom he had met twice before. "The deed is done," Gurudeva remarked as they exited the ancient stone chamber and reemerged into the light of day.

Back in Bangalore, discussions centered on a carving site, for a Hindu temple made of stone is built in a special and unusual way. An entire village would have to be created, including housing for 75 sculptors and their families, gardens for their food, wells dug for their water, blacksmith forges and carving sheds, plus facilities for managers. Where would all this happen?

Fortunately, Sri Balagangadharanathaswami of Adichunchanagiri Mahasamsthana Math, who received his training at Kailash Ashram, was told of the need and offered eleven acres of arid land for the project, at no cost. It was an enormous boon, and within months the worksite that would continue for several decades was completed. Having the carving site near Bangalore was critical, as the Indian swamis there could keep close watch over the construction process as Gurudeva's representatives. They looked after his project as if it were their own, and looked after him with unfettered affection and unlimited assistance. They were, to be sure, the key to Iraivan's manifestation.

Five Holy Bricks

Iraivan Temple, Gurudeva proclaimed, would be India's gift to the Western world. Gurudeva named 1995 the Year of Iraivan Temple. To rally the forces necessary for this prodigious effort, he flew the monks from outlying monasteries to Kauai, bringing his entire order together for the first time in forty years.

The event that catalyzed the monks' homecoming was the elaborate two-day Panchasilanyasa Puja, a ceremony to sanctify the foundation and begin the building of Iraivan Temple. About 200 devotees from around the globe came to witness the placement of five bricks in an underground crypt, along with a cache of gems and other treasures. Warm Hawaiian breezes enveloped the faithful in a gentle embrace. Camphor, incense and

. . . .

When a North Indian Narmada Lingam was gifted to the monastery, Gurudeva invited pilgrims to perform abhishekam *on the sacred stone and occasionally bathed the Sivalingam with stream water himself.*

flowers spoke to their senses, as did the tintinnabulation of bells and the sonorous Sanskrit chanted loudly by *vibhuti*-smeared priests. Deva Rajan shares his experience of the event:

> Many priests were there from Chennai for the *homa*, including the respected Sivasri Sambamurti Sivachariyar, who officiated the Hindu rituals, along with architect V. Ganapati Sthapati. A four-by-four-by-four-foot square pit had been dug at the northeast corner of the future inner sanctum of the Iraivan Temple. In the pitch black of the hours before dawn, no one could tell if we were in India or in Hawaii. With great ceremony, my Gurudeva, the Hindu priests, the architect and others installed sacred substances into the pit—gems, gold, silver, rare herbs and other auspicious items. Tray after tray was carried by the monks to be placed. At one point, a large pot of *vibhuti* was poured into the pit; hence any further offering drew clouds of *vibhuti* floating out of the hole, blessing us all.
>
> Under the tranquil light of the moon, Sambamurti Sivachariyar, together with Gurudeva, frequently waved the glowing camphor flame. In bursts of powerful sacred chanting, the pit was consecrated. Master architect Ganapati Sthapati placed five sacred bricks engraved with the letters *Na Ma Si Va Ya* in Tamil.
>
> After these rich and abundant blessings, Gurudeva directed a few of us to seal it all off with concrete. As the crowd dispersed, we mixed several wheelbarrows of fresh concrete and poured it into the pit. When the task was complete, with joyous hearts we drifted away, knowing we had participated in a rare and magical event that would stay with us forever.

In the years that followed, Gurudeva met a thousand times with the various teams building the temple, following every detail. He would live to see only the first three courses of the sanctum in place.

Kinship with a Vaishnava Order

In 1995, while traveling for three months in India with two of his swamis, Gurudeva was invited to give the major speech to 50,000 devotees in Mumbai at the 75th birthday celebration for Pramukh Swami Maharaj, the preceptor of the Bochasanwasi Akshar Purushottam Swaminarayan Sanstha (BAPS), a huge, Gujarat-based Vaishnava organization.

The scene could have been right out of Vedic times, with dozens of

· ·

Gurudeva described God Siva as "the architect of the universe,
with a beautiful human-like form which can actually be
seen and has been seen by many mystics in visions."

orange-robed sadhus gathered around to catch a glimpse of the two gurus as they sat in mostly silent communion. Both taught a path that encompassed devotion and meditation, that insists on the strict and traditional rules of monastic life and that holds the guru essential to spiritual advancement. Both orders shared a distinctive mix of orthodoxy and progressiveness, of ancient ways and high technology, coupled with a guru-centric ethic where monks and householders work for a common goal.

In the six-sided pavilion under a sprawling mango tree outside the publications
facility, Gurudeva met with visitors, answered their questions and signed books.   Page 661
Chapter 30

Gurudeva immediately sensed how profoundly these monks regarded their own guru by the loving reception they accorded him.

Gurudeva wanted to see how the BAPS monks were trained, answer questions they might have for him, and most importantly, inspire and encourage them in their chosen path, which he so admired. So he was whisked to their sadhu training center in Sarangpur, several hours away. The village itself sits upon the flat plains amidst farm country. The center is a modern complex of two-story buildings that houses more than a hundred monks in training—each one an avid reader of HINDUISM TODAY.

One of the BAPS monks asked, "Gurudeva, people call us fanatics. How should we respond?" Gurudeva turned the criticism around, "Take it as a compliment. They are only saying that because they are envious of your dedication and enthusiasm."

Later, Gurudeva told them to be faithful to their vows, not thinking of women, even in their dreams, and boldly offered advice that they knew in their hearts but, due to modern Indian sensitivities, they had never heard: "There is only one duty of the disciple. Obey your guru! Obey your guru! Obey your guru!" When he said this, the room erupted with the applause of 250 elated sadhus.

After the meeting, each of the monks came forward to receive a handful of flowers from Gurudeva. It was a memorable visit, and uplifting for both monastic orders. Gurudeva later commented, "I have never seen such a training center for Hindu monks anywhere in the world."

Several years later, one of the BAPS senior monks was sent into the 2001 Gujarat earthquake disaster that killed 50,000 people. Pramukh Swami instructed him to direct the relief work for the people. "It seemed an impossible task, " he told Rajiv Malik, who was writing a story on BAPS for HINDUISM TODAY, "like the story in the *Upanishads* of the disciple being sent to the forest with 400 sick cows and told to return only when the herd had reached 1,000. But I recalled Gurudeva's words, 'Obey your guru. Obey your guru. Obey your guru.' and proceeded with confidence." To this day, whenever BAPS monks meet monks from Kauai, they relate the story of Gurudeva's powerful message and the transformative impact it had on their order, essentially giving them permission to be openly at the feet of their beloved guru.

Gurudeva moved freely with monks of all sampradayas, feeling them to be his brothers in the great work of enlightening mankind. Every visit to an ashram or matha was an opportunity for encouragement. Sri Bala-gangadharanathaswami of Bangalore wrote:

> In many ways Gurudeva has been of great influence both on me as a person and to our institution. When he visited our educational institutions, he told me that education should not restrict itself to academics like a government program. He said we should teach our scriptures, our traditions and values as well. On his advice we have incorporated this, setting aside time for spiritual items.
>
> Sivaya Subramuniyaswami was pained to hear that female infanticide and abortions were being carried out in our hospitals, and he advised me that we should stop this practice. He was truly a messenger of peace. I was impressed by Sivaya Subramuniyaswami's forthrightness. He would speak directly about issues relating to dharma and religion. I was deeply touched by his concern for society, especially issues concerning family and children.

Visiting brother monks was often a time for adopting new ways of doing things. From one South Indian *aadheenakarthar* he got the style of his swamis' earrings and the color of their robes, and from another an introduction to the *Tirumantiram*. In the wake of an earlier visit with the BAPS sadhus, he dove into their guiding principles, 212 couplets on how to live—strict principles that are followed by tens of thousands of families. Gurudeva drew on this body of work, called the *Shikshapatri,* when writing his own 365 Nandinatha Sutras.

Spiritual Toolbox

Thousands of people came to Gurudeva for spiritual realization, hoping for some magic pill of enlightenment—and solutions to their problems in the bargain. They had grown up on stories of how the touch of a peacock feather had brought a total stranger to the path to Siva's feet, and they hoped for a swift journey to the land of light for themselves.

Gurudeva knew such happenings, while not impossible, were impossibly rare. As he grew older, he increasingly withheld the deeper practices, even prohibiting meditation at times, until devotees proved they were living a pure life, that they were worthy to practice yoga. He hoped to ensure that they would not be disappointed when success in meditation eluded them—as it ineluctably would, because of their impure lifestyle and unwholesome karma, their meat-eating, their lustful thoughts, bad habits, deep-seated resentments and unresolved hurts and fears. The strictness of his system of rules formed his first line of defense.

Those not willing to adjust themselves were automatically kept away. To those who persisted, he offered not a magic mantra or a set of orange robes but tools for self-transformation that addressed the most basic levels of personal life, starting with learning to be a good person. He knew that spiritual attainment is hard work, and to achieve the summit of Self Realization requires more discipline, more commitment and training, more change in lifestyle and attitude than climbing Mount Everest requires. Only those with these qualities will succeed. Though not all understood this, he continued to press his shishyas on every front, his underlying hope being they would transform themselves inwardly and that transformation would usher in the spiritual illumination they sought but had no idea how to achieve.

At no time in his ministry was he interested in creating a movement with thousands of followers. Always he preferred quality to quantity. He was so serious about only working with those who were willing to work on themselves that when devotees brought problems to him that clearly resulted from not following his advice or from neglecting their sadhana, he chided, "What am I to you, just a picture on the wall?"

But no one, not even the most sincere and serious, came to him without at least some baggage, some blind spots and areas of their life that needed fixing. In his latter years, Gurudeva grew weary of fielding the same questions that he had heard for decades and giving the same advice—advice that was not always, even often, followed. The human condition was now an open book to him; he had heard it all—confessions of every transgression imaginable, every predicament and problem. The load of hearing all this and taking on the karma was heavy, requiring quiet moments each day to absorb it, lest it back up on him and disturb his nervous system. It was, he explained, his task to take them in and project them up through the top of his head and dissolve them in the inner light.

He learned that it was more effective, and less troublesome, to put the work back on the devotee, to give a remedy, a penance, which he called *prayashchitta*. The goal and purpose was to unburden the subconscious mind of unresolved hurts and resentments, fears and repressions and the guilt of past transgressions. He gave a mystical explanation of penance:

The inner process of relieving unwanted karmic burdens occurs in this order: remorse and shame; confession (of which apology is one form); repentance; and finally reconciliation, which is making the

situation right, so that good feelings abide all around. Therefore, each individual admission of a subconscious burden too heavy to carry must have its own reconciliation to clear the inner aura of negative samskaras and vasanas and replenish the inner bodies for the struggle the devotee will have to endure in unwinding from the coils of the lower, instinctive mind which block the intellect and obscure spiritual values. When no longer protected by its ignorance, the soul longs for release and cries out for solace. *Prayashchitta*, penance, is then the solution to dissolve the agony and bring shanti.

There are many forms of penance, *prayashchitta*, such as 1,008 prostrations before Gods Ganesha, Murugan or Supreme God Siva, apologizing and showing shame for misdeeds; performing japa slowly 1,008 times on the holy rudraksha beads; giving of 108 handmade gifts to the temple; performing manual chores at the temple for 108 hours, such as cleaning, making garlands or arranging flowers; bringing offerings of cooked food; performing *kavadi* with miniature spears inserted in the flesh; making a pilgrimage by prostrating the body's length again and again, or rolling around a temple. All these and more are major means of atonement after each individual confession has been made.

Devotees were amazed at Gurudeva's ability to translate abstract philosophical principles into simple language—then go one step further to conceive specific sadhanas designed to put those principles into practice. The mystical axiom of "clearing the subconscious," so essential in yoga, provides an example.

The subconscious mind is the storehouse for the conscious mind. All the happenings of each day and all reactions are stored up there. When the subconscious is in control, the control is at one rate of vibration. When the subsuperconscious is in control, after the subconscious has become understood, concentrated and cleared of all confusion, the vibratory rate is higher.

It is one thing to know there are unresolved memories, feelings and experiences that need to be released; it is another to have a means to accomplish this. Faced with so many devotees needing release from the past, he evolved, through meditation, a simple but profoundly effective technique that anyone could use. Most did, and it proved crucial for their spiritual

· ·

He had chosen Kauai for its remoteness, yet visitors discovered the monastery and came from all corners of the globe to be with the satguru, hear his talks and worship in Kadavul Temple with its giant murtis and crystal Sivalingam.

progress. Gurudeva called it vasana *daha* tantra, "purification of the sub-conscious by fire."

He instructed devotees to take their conflicts and pains, their confusions and negative experiences and write them down, bring them from the deep subconscious into the conscious mind, and intentionally, consciously, burn them up, both physically as the paper turns to flames and ash, and psychically, through seeing the physical representation of the problem being incinerated.

> Mental impressions can be either positive or negative. In this practice, we burn confessions, or even long letters to loved ones or acquaintances, describing pains, expressing confusions and registering grievances and long-felt hurts. Writing down problems and burning them in any ordinary fire brings them from the subconscious into the external mind, releasing the suppressed emotion as the fire consumes the paper.

He counseled those practicing this tantra to burn their problems in a common fire, making sure they distinguished between a sacred fire pit into which prayers are offered and an everyday fireplace or cauldron where trash is burned. The process was so effective that Gurudeva developed a system for methodically going back through one's entire life in this way.

The Forgotten Foundation of Yoga

Nearly one third of Gurudeva's third book of the trilogy addressed the ancient *yamas* and *niyamas*, which he called the Cardinal Virtues of Hinduism. He pointed out that these twenty restraints and observances are a necessary foundation for the practice of yoga. Without them, no spiritual pursuit would bear lasting results.

Dr. S.P. Sabharathnam Sivachariyar, a *Saiva Agama* scholar, observed that this was just one example in which Gurudeva had, like a true rishi, brought forth the wisdom of the *Agama* texts without having ever read or known of them. After reading Gurudeva's explication of the *yamas* and *niyamas*, Sabharathnam commented, "The observation that spontaneously dawned in my heart was: Here has come the true acharya who could shape well the modern community, who could perfectly guide humanity, being tuned to the true spirit of guruhood."

He noted an uncanny similarity in Gurudeva's words to those of a verse from the *Sukshma Agama,* which reads: "The system of yoga in which

On every full-moon day in July, the monastery celebrates Satguru Purnima, worshiping the guru's feet at the site of the Svayambhu Lingam. In worshiping one's own guru, all preceptors are honored.

. . . .

yamas and *niyamas* are not practiced is as fragile as the mansion without foundation, as vain as the flower without fragrance and as imperfect as the knowledge not centered on the oneness of Siva and soul." Sabharathnam also observed:

> Gurudeva's explanations on the real nature of the shaktis of Mahadevas living in the inner Third World, on the invincible *vel* of Skanda, on

the five states of mind, on the nature of the twenty-one chakras—seven in the upper realm, seven in the middle realm and seven in the lower realm—on the significance of temple, temple rituals and mantras, on the role and significance of colors and such other elucidations are the undistorted and clear reflections of the verses of the *Saiva Agamas.*

Gurudeva was the first yogi I know of who dealt with the chakras lying below the *muladhara,* which have been mentioned in the yoga section of the *Sukshma Agama* only.

The crowning revelation is Gurudeva's Shum language of meditation. In the *Sukshma Agama,* Lord Sadasiva reveals the finest and highly transcendental disciplines of Sivayoga to the much advanced Sivayogis. At one point He stops the instructions and says: "Enough with these directions. There are many more subtle and transcendental aspects of this *sarvatma-nada* yoga. These will be revealed to the competent Mahayogis in due course of time. Not now." I was reminded of these lines when I came to know that the Shum language of meditation was unfolded to Gurudeva at Ascona, Switzerland, in 1968.

"Stop Abusing the Children"

In the late 1990s, Gurudeva learned that many of his devotees, even long-time shishyas, were using corporal punishment on their children. Shocked and hurt by this revelation, he demanded an abrupt change. No more hitting, pinching, ear-twisting, slapping, beating or pummeling; no more verbal abuse, humiliation and use of shame and blame.

To help parents compensate for past misbehavior, he required them to perform penance. First, they had to sincerely apologize to their children and perform specific practices, such as standing in front of a mirror while slapping themselves five times for every time they slapped a child. Second, he instructed them to hold classes in Positive Discipline in their community. Positive Discipline is a system developed by California educator Dr. Jane Nelsen, and presented in a series of books and lectures showing how to raise children with encouragement, love and respect rather than blame, shame and pain.

Manon Mardemootoo, a long-standing devotee of Gurudeva and a prominent attorney, was among many on the island of Mauritius who wholeheartedly undertook this mission. He said, "To take these teachings of ahimsa into the public and make them a living reality is the present sadhana of Gurudeva's devotees here in Mauritius." Thus, in 1998 Gurudeva began an ardent campaign for the right of children to not be beaten by their parents or their teachers, and helping parents raise children with love through Positive Discipline classes taught by his family devotees as their primary community service. A devotee in Singapore explained:

> Gurudeva advocated abolishing corporal punishment in homes and schools, directing his devotees to teach classes for other Hindu parents in nonviolent means of parenting and to change school policies regarding corporal punishment of students.
>
> In the last few years, Gurudeva's devotees have waged a campaign against corporal punishment in Singapore's homes and schools. They made substantial progress in the local schools, which were already tackling the issue, by seeing to it that teachers still using corporal punishment were reprimanded and retrained in better methods.

Always Now

Aside from what Gurudeva did, how he helped others and who he was known to be, there was something intangibly magical about him. Because he lived at the center of himself, the Self of all, everyone felt close to him and loved him dearly. For them, his life was like a magnificent rainbow, arched high above the woes of the daily norm. Gurudeva emanated a sense of being ever youthful, unencumbered, innocent, open and always in the now.

> To have the feeling of being in one place, and that everything is happening around you, like a maypole—this is how I feel these days. I watch the cycles of life as they flow one into another. The physical-plane cycles flow into the astral-plane cycles which flow into the superconscious-plane cycles and back to the physical-plane cycles again as men and women unfold on the path. This state is what I call "doing nothing." Just watching, watching, watching.

He was, despite the most serious challenge or calamity, ever poised, centered, detached. Whatever he was doing–discovering Shum at Casa Eranos, laying the first stone of Iraivan Temple–he maintained an effulgent joy that knew no suppression, a boundless love that made everyone around him feel he regarded them as special.

He imbued his monastics with this magical quality as well. Coupled with the unfoldment of their decades of brahmacharya, it gave them an abiding joy that made visitors remark, "Everyone here seems so happy!" It was true. Happy, inspired and driven to perform sadhana and to serve— these were irrepressible qualities that lived on in his order even after he

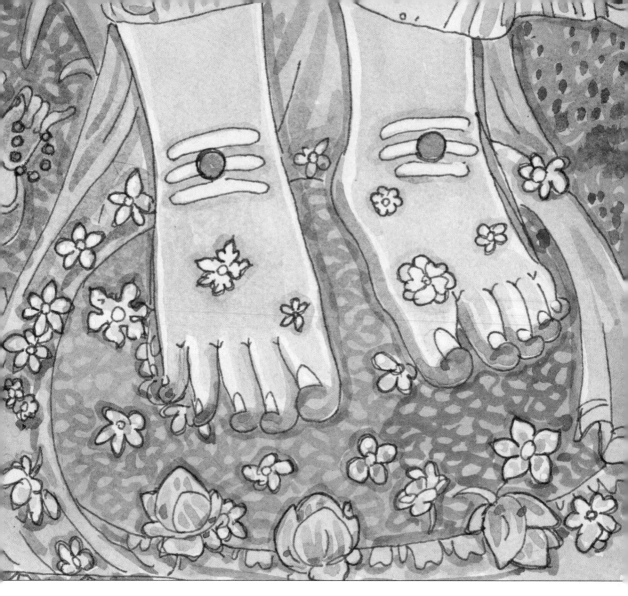

left his Earthly frame.

He had an uncanny power to attract and continually train and intrigue—with his mystic, otherworldly insights into the nature of reality—a strong group of monks and family people around him. He trained these dedicated souls carefully, cultivating the abilities of each so he could delegate increasing responsibility to them. This enabled him to accomplish what no single person could have done in one lifetime. Though some of his devotees—monks as well as lay members—found their personal karmas would not allow them to follow where he led, the rest worked unceasingly to fulfill the mission that he, and they, were born to carry forth. In earlier years, he coined the term *soldiers of the within* to name those who had gathered around him for this inner work. "Born for the job," he often commented.

The Kularnava Tantra *proclaims, "At the root of meditation is the form of the guru. At the root of puja are the feet of the guru. At the root of mantra is the word of the guru, and at the root of all liberation is the grace of the guru."*

• •

It was, no doubt, Gurudeva's keen centeredness that made all his efforts so successful. He approached every project and responded to each need and problem with acute attentiveness, daily assessing his strategy, consulting with his senior monks, and at each day's end summing up the progress and noting areas of concern. He was capable of a kind of detachment seen in a good general on the battlefield who sees soldiers fall, yet, while it is painful, keeps the strategic overview and does not get caught up in the immediate tragic loss. Gurudeva could do that: keep a remarkable detachment from events of the day, always seeing a larger field of view, a longer immediacy.

"Is This Legal?"

In the mid 1990s, the popular mind started to embrace the World Wide Web. The monks were monitoring the beginnings of this amazing phenomenon, little knowing that the web would change the way the monastery, and the world, would work. It was new, exciting, confusing and not a bit user-friendly. Still, the monks began to cobble together incipient uses, and showed them to Gurudeva. Soon his basic publications were online for all to read, and unlike any other distribution system in history, it seemed to be free.

One morning the monks connected his computer to the Internet with a dial-up modem. After surfing around the web for a while, he turned to ask seriously, "So, who pays for all this? Is it legal?" Turns out, it was legal, though no one present could quite explain how. Within months the Internet became a major place to publish his many works: HINDUISM TODAY, *Dancing with Siva*, a page of Aum graphics and more.

As the monks' skills matured, Gurudeva was generous in sharing their expertise with others, such as designing a website for the Hopi Indians to help them archive and preserve their tradition. Even the office of Kauai's mayor turned to the monastery for help with this new media.

One day in the summer of 1998, he gathered his nerd herd in the Cedar Room, a conference room in the publications center, and asked if it would be possible to share with the world the daily happenings at the monastery, thus bringing his global spiritual fellowship together each day, digitally. From that request grew "Today at Kauai Aadheenam," or TAKA, a mix of news, audio talks, photos, spiritual quotes and tidbits about his mission at the monastery and members' activities around the globe—perhaps the world's first blog.

Almost daily for three years, he addressed pilgrims and seekers on the web, speaking on dharmic subjects or answering their spiritual inquiries. He coined the word *CyberCadets,* his name for visitors to the website, and invited them to send in questions by email. His answers were recorded and posted to TAKA, usually the same day they were spoken; these may have been the world's first podcasts. Hundreds of these CyberTalks accrued, and for the first time in history anyone with a computer and an Internet connection could hear the satguru speak to real people about real life issues in near real time, for free.

There was a small downside to TAKA, Gurudeva discovered. When traveling, his common pattern for decades had been to share with devotees in each city his experiences over the past few days. Arriving in Malaysia, he would give a news update of his stay last week in India and Mauritius. Now, in 1999, he found everyone in these audiences looking distracted, almost disinterested. He asked why, only to be told, "Gurudeva, we saw all that on TAKA yesterday." That moment he realized that TAKA had truly tied his shishyas together, and it was his cue to find new subjects to talk about during his travels.

The Internet would continue to evolve, and the monastery website would become one of the leading Internet repositories in the Hindu world. Gurudeva would see this when searching for some Hindu custom or fact only to have the search engine of the day deliver links to his own writings. Even years later, the monks would marvel at how their resources were consistently near the top of Google search results for "Hinduism."

The 1995 Journey to India

From December 1995 to February 1996, Gurudeva traveled through six nations and throughout India, where he was greeted with overwhelming affection in every town. Many of his initiatives were advanced during this journey, but it proved a major turning point in another way. Late one afternoon toward the end of the journey, something unexpected happened on a flight from the South to the West.

A crowd of 5,000 was waiting in Ujjain, an historic Saiva Siddhanta center. Elephants stood ready at the airport to lead the world-famous satguru from Hawaii to the sacred centers of the city, including the famed Siva temple, Mahakaleshwar. But on the Mumbai-bound plane, Gurudeva experienced a seizure, falling unconscious in his seat for some two minutes. Stewardesses leapt to his aid and a doctor seated just in front provided some counsel, taking his pulse and shrugging off the episode as a non-event. Gurudeva was unfazed and insisted on continuing with the arduous itinerary, giving a major speech in Ujjain the next day and then traveling on to Malaysia and Singapore.

There were more seizures in the days ahead. The two swamis with him were terrified by the powerful convulsions, even fearful for his life, but his own experience was simply of waking from a sleep, and he would inevitably ask, "Did you smell that sweet fragrance? How long was I out?" Learning that it was a minute or more, he still insisted that the journey continue. The episodes continued on occasion until his passing in 2001, though they grew milder in later years.

Back on Kauai, his doctors insisted on an MRI, anxious to discover the underlying cause of the seizures. "No, never," was Gurudeva's firm response when the monks broached the idea, "I don't want to get under the thumb of the doctors. They will fill you with fear, take control of your life, drive you into bankruptcy. It never ends once it begins. That's no way to live." No tests were allowed.

Fully aware of the gravity of the matter, Gurudeva took days to meditate on the course of action he would take. One day he shared with a few monks that he would be observing a three-year sabbatical, staying on Kauai and not traveling. It was a radical shift from the rigorous schedule of dynamic journeys he had been on. Days later he announced to all the monks his resolve to take a self-imposed retreat on Kauai in order to work on his legacy to the world, The Master Course trilogy, consisting of 1,000-page editions of *Dancing with Siva, Living with Siva* and *Merging with Siva*. It was a brilliant example of how he could take the energy of any situation and transform it into something positive, utilize a setback to create something extraordinary that never would have otherwise existed.

Reaching the Summit

From 1996 to 1999 Gurudeva centered his life at the monastery, working more than ever with the monastic *kulams*, pushing projects through. A special group invited him to join their small and elite circle. Called Vision Kauai 2020, it was composed of the island's leaders: political, business, educational, agricultural. Gurudeva was the sole spiritual leader on this council, and he brought to their table his gifts. Mayors and former mayors, journalists and thinkers all came together each month to imagine and articulate the future of the island and her people, and to hear what Gurudeva had to offer. He and his monks became the driving force for the group, and much was accomplished during these years. Ron Kouchi, then the County Council head, told the monks, "The only reason I attend these meetings is to see what Gurudeva will do next! He's the most amazing person I have ever met."

Progress on the trilogy was intense. Every day, without fail, Gurudeva would board his RV and head for the ocean side with his editing team. Even on days off, even on festival days, this was an appointment he never failed to keep. It was, for him, the purpose of his *vrata* to stay on the island, and he was determined to complete the work.

He and the editing team completed the fifth edition of *Dancing with Siva* in 1997, then dove into *Merging with Siva*. Gurudeva took special delight in this book, for it was his mystical and metaphysical summation, an opus that would contain and thus preserve a lifetime of insights, lessons, talks and recorded moments. He subtitled it "Hinduism's Contemporary Metaphysics," for metaphysics were, to him, the bone of life on which all else finds its support.

He named 1998 the "Year of Merging with Siva." Day after day he sat in the cramped end of the RV, with windows looking out on the Pacific Ocean, whose waves crashed on the rocks just a few yards away. Day after day he crafted the chapters, tweaked the language and offered new writings to fill a discovered lacuna. Month after month he muscled the writing forward, reviewing galley after galley as each section was brought back to the table for review. It became his great joy to share chapters with the monks as they were finished. After a full year of assembling, editing, illustrating and polishing, *Merging with Siva* was released. A few months later, Gurudeva described it for the world:

Every word of every publication was meticulously reviewed by Gurudeva at the editing table. He stressed working collaboratively and loved the technology that allowed his team to work on the same document from four different computers—something new in those days.

• •

Merging with Siva is a book unlike our other books. It's a book all about you; about the inside of you—how your mind works with your emotions, your emotions with your physical body, and the real goal of life, which is Self Realization. My Sri Lankan devotees in Canada, in Sri Lanka itself, in Europe and scattered out among the world because of the war have found it a very useful book to help get a new lease on life, a new self-image that we are a soul living in a physical body,

For five years Gurudeva met monthly with the business, educational,
media and political leaders of the island, their sole purpose being
to map out a spiritual vision for the future of Kauai.

Page 677

Chapter 31

living in an astral body, having an intellect, but we are a pure soul—
untarnished, unblemished—living through the karmas of this life.

Unlike other metaphysical books, which take you away from the
world into high philosophy, *Merging with Siva* (which also does that)
provides techniques and sadhanas for making you successful in the
world so that you can move the forces of the world because you control your awareness that flows through the mind like a traveler that
travels around the world, from city to city, state to state, from place
to place. We celebrated our fiftieth anniversary of my ministry and
teaching of philosophical subjects and metaphysical sadhanas by
releasing *Merging with Siva* in five countries.

One day Gurudeva drove to the sea, only to discover that his favorite
ocean-side parking spot had been blocked off with giant boulders—part
of a project to create a bicycle and walking path near the beach along
the east side of the island. Unable to return to that magical spot, he soon
bought a condo right on the ocean, not far away, which from 1998 on
served as his editing headquarters. This spacious new facility allowed
him to take an afternoon swim in the ocean before each session and even
to stay overnight if he was so inspired. He called it Hale Makai, his "home
by the sea." Like Yogaswami, he loved the daily excursion to the ocean. For
safety, he and his trio of editors held hands to keep from falling as they tra-
versed the treacherous coral to enter the warm waters. Gurudeva loved to
watch the tropical fish and to float on his back, buoyed softly by the waves.

On January 5, 1998, the monks surprised Gurudeva with a birthday
party, given in part to ease his rock fever (the island variety of cabin fever)
and because his birthday had never been celebrated by the whole island.
After months of secret planning (the monks knew he knew everything,
but neither they nor he uttered a syllable), he was cajoled, though he did
not know the destination, to board a helicopter that was waiting in an
open meadow on the monastery grounds.

Three minutes later the craft circled Kilohana Mansion, a famed Kauai
estate, then landed amid a jubilant crowd to begin an amazing night of
recognition and joy. Four hundred island people who had grown to love
Gurudeva greeted him. Hawaiian dancers and chanters led the elegant

satguru to the hall where everyone was gathered to surprise him.

That night he danced with the Mayor, Maryanne Kusaka, she leading him in a hula and he leading her in a Manipuri dance on stage. That night his Church members placed him on a giant makeshift scale, adding gold-colored bricks until the other side balanced, then writing a check for nearly $900,000—the price of his weight in gold—and offering their pledge to raise that amount for his Iraivan Temple, which they did in the months ahead. That night his life was reviewed, gifts given, memories recounted and appreciations offered for his contributions to the island. He felt and looked like a monarch that night, surrounded by so much love and gratitude for his life.

Never, several said later, had such a diverse group of islanders gathered under one roof, noting Gurudeva had touched every stratum of the community, from top to bottom. It was officially his 71st birthday, but he thought of it as his 72nd, following the Indian system in which conception marks the beginning of life. Age 72 is recognized in Hinduism as a major milestone, marking the beginning of life's fourth stage, the sannyasa ashrama, and it was important to Gurudeva.

Exploring Inner Worlds through Shum

Throughout his life Gurudeva had an inner and an outer existence, the two having little communion. While on an Innersearch, he would retreat into his meditations when rare free moments presented themselves. During a typical day, he would have work to do psychically, always being ready, when the external mind called, to come to lunch, join his editing team or see a pilgrim.

During the 1990s, those precious hours of inner work revolved around Shum, his language of meditation. He would rise at two or three in the morning to work on Shum before the day started, refining and organizing the vast Shum database and lexicon that he had developed through his inner explorations over the decades. Several monks were assigned various tasks to assist his efforts. But for Gurudeva, it was all about describing the subtle world that was, he assured, more solid than this plane.

He was, in a sense, like an explorer who daily visited a land no one else saw, returning again and again to describe and map that magical territory for others, excited to tell them that there was such a land and that they could also visit it one day. In later years he explored the dimensions of the mind, describing fourteen worlds containing, or more exactly constructed of, unearthly colors and forms and sounds. Here he describes the intuitive realm, or fourth dimension.

The fourth dimension then is the subsuperconscious faculty of man. It is a beautiful place to be, and you can be there all of the time by feeling the power of your spine. The minute you feel that radiant energy in the spine, you are disconnected from the third dimension and soar into the fourth.

Artists are in the fourth dimension. Each time you designed or created anything, you were bringing the beauty of the within through your nerve system into manifestation. Didn't your whole nerve system feel good? That was the subsuperconscious fourth dimension of you. It finds expression in the creative intellect that wants to know for the good of the other fellow, that seeking to know.

We say a person is open-minded, more willing to listen than to banter back his own ideas at you, he is conscious in the fourth dimension. He's a new age person. When he says something, it's because he has something to say, and generally his perspective of looking at the world is quite different from the material attitudes of people around him. He is able to see all four sides of a subject at the same time and to understand what people mean even if their viewpoint differs from his own. He is inspirational. He has and enjoys happiness. He is creative, unique, and works out of the box. He is independent, relying on himself and the power of his spine. He is quick to help others but slow to get entangled with their third-dimensional forces. He is highly motivated with well-defined purposes and goals. He expends his energy well, not wasting or draining the power that propels him onward and inward. He is enthused, charmed with life, charged with great desire to pursue the spiritual path.

That's the fourth dimension of the mind—a wonderful place to live and to bring through inner unfoldment, for you then have the continuity of creative thought. From the fourth dimension you can see the panorama of life unfolding flawlessly day to day. You can look deeply into the subconscious, cognize and understand the chemistry of feeling, thought and reaction. You can look into the magnetic force fields of the third dimension and comprehend the processes by which different people relate to one another.

It's very easy to get into the fourth dimension, very easy. It's a little more challenging to hold that detached perspective when things are not going as well as we would like, but then its easy to return when the forces smooth out.

A Typical Day at Home

Gurudeva loved to travel. Except for his three-year retreat, he was away from the monastery some two or three months a year—called to open a temple, visit his initiated members, attend a conference. At home, his days were richly filled with a mind-numbing to-do list, which, harnessed by good habits, he met with elan.

On most days, he rose even earlier than the monks, showered and walked downstairs to his Mahogany Room, the office finished in that hard wood for him when he renovated the old estate house. After he had been working at his desk for some time, a monk would arrive with hot tea or coffee. Gurudeva would chat with the early visitor awhile about inner things or a vision that occurred last night and then dismiss him, turning to his computer to sort through the first emails of the day, check the calendar and, twice a week, prepare for his temple talks. These were quiet moments he cherished, the lull before the day began, a time often for his Shum work, which was not work for him at all but a consuming passion where hours spent seemed like moments.

Sharp at 5:15 he took the short walk to Kadavul Temple, where the monks gathered each day for Siva puja. He would greet Siva with hands pressed together, then walk through the temple's main hall to sit in the back corner in a tall-back wicker chair.

As the monks gathered before the puja, each would offer him a flower, lovingly touch his feet, prostrate and then sit nearby to enjoy a few informal moments together with their guru. At 5:30, Gurudeva would stand for an arati for Ganesha and Murugan before walking up to the inner sanctum, taking his special seat just a few feet away from Siva Nataraja. There he sat erect, immersed in what he called "outer worship." "First external worship, then internal worship," he smiled, noting that both are essential for an ego-negating immersion in true Saiva Siddhanta, which sees God within man and man living literally within the being of God, as the world.

At 6:00 the puja ended, and he would stand and thread through the temple catacombs to the adjacent Guru Pitham. He always brought a flower from the Siva sanctum to offer at the small Yogaswami shrine, worshiping his guru alone each morning, before the monks gathered, just as Yogaswami had worshiped Chellappaswami in the form of his sandals.

Taking his seat cross-legged on the traditionally designed *simhasana,* "lion seat," he would sip a little coffee brought by one of the monks as the others arrived and took their yogic seat in four neat rows on the floor before him. Gurudeva chanted "Aum" to set the day in motion; then the

. . . .

Each morning before dawn, Gurudeva sat on his lion seat in the Guru Pitham. With the monks seated facing him, he would guide their yogic meditation for an hour, all in the Shum language.

monks chanted the Guru Mantra together in Sanskrit and recited, twice, the cadenced affirmation he had created as the monks' mission statement, expressing their shared purpose and goals.

An acharya led the preparation for meditation, a 15-minute quieting of the mind and systematic going within. When that reached a crescendo, Gurudeva led the final ascent, in Shum, taking his monks to the top of the mountain. It may well have been the only such perfectly synchronized

Gurudeva made a pact with the devas, arranging for written prayers to be transmitted through the sacred fire. Each week he would consign to the fire a basket of prayers sent in from devotees around the world. He explained that their astral double would appear in the Second World to be read by the devas, who could help answer each prayer.

• •

meditation on the planet, with all following the same inner trajectory, guided by the guru and his Shum language.

As some monks fought to fend off what was playfully called "snormadhi," the veterans among them dove into the light and the Self. Gurudeva sat ramrod straight, so at ease with the discipline that challenged others, so poised and clearly in-turned. His body itself was radiant in those sessions, a testament of divine transformation and a constant inspiration of the possibilities of kundalini yoga for all his monks, the only ones privileged to attend this daily deep-see dive into the divine. After an hour, the meditation was concluded.

Gurudeva usually spoke after the meditation. Sometimes he would say a few words about the day, preparing the troops for the morning-to-evening march, noting the arrival of guests or a project that would involve everyone. Sometimes he spoke of inner effort, of sadhana. About this time he began a long series of *upadeshas* directed toward the monks and their life. He called these talks his *Mathavasi Shastras.* They ranged from two to forty-five minutes long, and each was laser-focused on the ideals of a monastic, the dos and don'ts of living in his monastery. Here is one he dictated which he called "Obedience and the One Mind:"

At Kauai Aadheenam everyone is obedient to their vows; so, then, they are obedient to everyone else. We have one great intelligence here; we don't have a lot of people here. There is no individual person here; it's just one intelligence. A lot of people blending their minds together with a lot of other people makes a one big mind. That's why we can influence people through HINDUISM TODAY and our publications, because someone reading one of our publications tunes into this one big mind. We have up to twenty-five minds blended together—merged together—in obedience to their own inner self and cooperation with one another for the greater good.

Now, if we had a situation here where everyone had their own preferences, "I want to do this, and I don't want to do that," and, "I would rather be doing something else. But do I have to do this?" Then we would have a lot of people here—people who would read our publications, and say, "Well, that's really nice, what they're doing; the pretty pictures are nice." There would be no magnetism to tune into. But because we have isolated ourselves from the world and the family community, because we isolated ourselves by blending our minds together as a one group (we're not blending our minds with the family group, we're blending our minds with our own group), we have become like a big person, one big mind with a whole lot of bodies.

So, someone reading *Dancing with Siva*, reading HINDUISM TODAY, tunes into this one big intelligence and becomes a part of it for the short time they are reading what we have given from this great intelligence. That's all from the vow of obedience.

He was bold in those moments, addressing issues that were typically not discussed aloud, certainly not in such a general setting. When they were all spoken, these talks stood as an amazing body of spiritual insight and principle, systematically articulated and carefully recorded for future generations. It was to be a final call to his soldiers of the within, those in the room and those who one day would be, his warning of the perils of weakness on the path, his praise of the powers of living a strong renunciate life, his instructions for how to live dynamically and harmoniously together. He would even scold monks mildly during these sessions, pointing out little things they should do better and praising small accomplishments that were, to him, signposts of progress on the path.

Then, when the crescendo was reached, he would smile broadly and wish each one a good day before beginning the singing of "Aum Namasivaya," which all would chant as they came forward, one at a time, in order of seniority, to kneel and touch his feet, receive a daub of holy ash on the forehead from his right thumb and leave the Guru Pitham on their way to perfection.

The first to arrive, Gurudeva was always the last to leave the meditation, often staying on for a few minutes to meditate a while longer or talk with a monk who had something on his mind to share.

A short morning walk in the garden often followed, then breakfast served in his Mahogany Room—fruits and yogurt, or his favorite: mung beans and spicy coconut chutney, Jaffna style. On most days, breakfast segued into a rainbow of duties that he loved, for each of them was a small part of the mission he had spent his life building. If he had major issues on his mind, he would call a meeting of the monks involved. He seldom delayed in handling issues, preferring to mount an immediate assault and resolve them right now.

Absent such a meeting, his habit was to turn to the list of the day, editing a Publisher's Desk editorial, emailing responses to his shishyas around the world who might be asking about a new name for their baby, advice on a business decision, what to do with grandma's ashes or how to avoid a threatened divorce. The list went on, hour after hour—preparing for stewards' meetings, resolving petty conflicts between monks, communicating by phone and email with shishyas, satsang groups and branch monasteries, and guiding thirty or more *kulapati* families and a half dozen Church missions in several countries.

When that was done, there was more: resolving financial and legal issues, guiding temple boards of trustees, gathering with groups of monks handling projects, fielding editing questions, publishing questions, public relations questions. He kept close to the business of the monastery, signing all contracts and bank loans and each and every check. In the midst of all this were spontaneous meetings with the monks throughout the day. His door was always open, and "no one need make an appointment to see the guru."

This all came to a temporary halt whenever pilgrims were waiting for his darshan. He loved visitors and considered their arrival to be the arrival of Siva Himself. Greeting pilgrims was a central duty, and he told the monks, "The only reason for anyone to visit the monastery is to have darshan with the satguru." Informed of pilgrims' arrival, he would swiftly, without any sense of disturbance or interruption, walk the fifty feet to the Guru Pitham and sit with a family for as long as they needed him, giving advice, blessings, sometimes a gift of one of his books that was relevant to their path, or a shawl to bless two newlyweds or a couple celebrating their anniversary.

That done, he might take to the garden paths for five minutes, striding off to the Orchid Mandapam and back, to stretch and enjoy the beauty of the monastery. More often than not, a monk would see him afoot and join the walk, eager for a few informal minutes of the guru's time for some essential project question or just to enjoy his darshan.

Back to the Mahogany Room, Gurudeva surfed the next wave of issues: *kulam* planning, answering monks' philosophical and meditation questions, making plans for travel, resolving intransigent budget issues, including approving (or not approving) purchase order requests. Midmorning he would go to his quarters for a "yoga break," a quiet time all his own.

He often used this break to psychically check up on shishyas around the world. On one occasion a monk came up with hot tea, but saw Gurudeva was lying on his couch. He quietly put the tea down and was starting to leave when Gurudeva said, "Don't go. I'm not sleeping. I'm practicing seeing the devotees in Kadavul Temple by looking through the *maha sphatika* Lingam." Then Gurudeva described a lady sitting closest to the step on the Ganesha side who was wearing a red dress and asked the monk to go to the temple and see if she was actually there. Sure enough, she was just as he described.

On other occasions while Gurudeva was taking this break on the couch he described various devas who would come and offer food, sometimes putting it directly into his mouth.

Within half an hour he was back in his office, addressing questions about local politics, Iraivan Temple design and production, policy discussions, cats and cows and birds and fish, wild pigs and corn, diet and neighbors, art and architecture, scriptures, intruders and VIP visitors, a new car purchase, a new computer purchase, an upcoming Innersearch, the next Hindu Heritage Endowment meeting, renovations, repairs, safety concerns, monk candidates, resident guests, farming and garden issues, updating the three-year plan, assigning temple duties, planning festivals, conceiving publications, HINDUISM TODAY planning meetings, video and audio recording sessions, arranging marriages, preparing members for *diksha*, giving sadhanas and *prayashchittas,* taking a congratulatory call from another swami, helping a monk through a minor crisis.

Sharp at 12:30 he would adjourn to the Peacock Court. The monks would be gathered there for lunch, seated in rows on simple mats on the red bricks. He would lead the traditional Sanskrit food-blessing chant and then invite one *kulam* each day to share with the group its progress for the past week. This was Gurudeva's way of keeping everyone informed of everything that was going on.

That done, he would give his own short report on upcoming travels or some accomplishment members had made in Malaysia, Mauritius or elsewhere, always eager for the monks to know the daily details of their worldwide mission. To signal the end of lunch, he picked up a large wood-and-fabric mallet and struck the 36-inch Balinese metal gong behind him, its resounding crescendo sending all off to their forest *guhas* for a short siesta, and him to his Ryokan quarters upstairs.

Early afternoon found him back in his office for a phone call or two;

then sharp at 3pm he met his editing team and took the 14-minute ride down the hill to the ocean. Without fail, the afternoon was dedicated to his books and publications, for he considered this communications and teaching ministry central to his work. By 7 or 8, depending on the intensity of the session, he would call it a day and drive up the hill to the monastery, joining his family of monks in the Sun Palace, a vaulted, second-story gathering room, for what he humorously called "a few minutes of bad TV." But even here Gurudeva offered the monks a mystical perspective from which to experience and gain from the mundane:

> Television has afforded us the ability to work through our karmas more quickly than we could in the agricultural age. On TV, the "other people" who play our past experiences back to us, for us to understand in hindsight, are actors and actresses, newscasters and the people in the news they broadcast. Saivites know nothing can happen, physically, mentally or emotionally, but that it is seeded in our *prarabdha* karmas, the action-reaction patterns brought with us to this birth. Therefore, on the positive side, we look at television as a tool for karmic cleansing.

This informal, end-of-the-day time with the monks was vital to him and rarely missed. The young ones would bring him some light dinner—*dosai* and *sambar,* soup or salad. At 9pm sharp, not 9:01, he would rise, open his arms wide and embrace each one in turn, then, with a big smile, say a sweet "goodnight" and close the redwood door to his quarters with a flourish, disappear and retire, sleeping, as all his monks still do, on a simple futon on the floor.

Taking to the High Seas

By early 1999, the three-year self-imposed retreat on Kauai was nearing an end; and the monks, sensing Gurudeva's growing rock fever, stumbled on a plan to end the incarceration. They suggested a special, never-done-before Innersearch on a cruise ship to Alaska. Gurudeva delighted in the notion, sharing that ever since an earlier trip to the Land of the Midnight Sun was forestalled by the Great Alaska Earthquake of 1964, he had wanted to go. And go he did.

From June 18 to 25, 1999, he, four monastics and thirty-eight pilgrims spent a week aboard the Holland America Line's MS Noordam, cruising the seas from Vancouver to Valdez. He had lived for seven decades; so for each day of the cruise, he met with the Innersearchers in the starboard-facing Hudson Room and shared one decade of his life, connecting his spiritual quest with theirs and bringing them deeper into Saivite Hinduism.

In Anchorage on June 25, Gurudeva formally founded the state's first Hindu temple, a sanctuary to Ganesha. Gurudeva wanted temples of the Hindu diaspora to be accepted in the local communities, especially among the indigenous Inuit people, so he insisted that the blessings of the Alaskan native spiritual leaders and elders be obtained. The Pipe Carriers, as the chiefs there are called, joined the rites, honoring the Anchorage Hindu community with songs and chants. They shared the peace pipe with Gurudeva and gave him a sacred drum. Gurudeva similarly invited native Hawaiian priests to bless the Iraivan Temple site at Kauai Aadheenam.

Along the way, he began three years of bookstore visits, where he would speak with some fifty to eighty readers, answer questions and sign books. Gurudeva loved the bookstore signings, not because he sold a lot of books but because it gave an opportunity to meet new seekers. Anyone could come and interact with the author in an informal setting, and from this interaction some became devotees.

This became a new note in his travel symphony, and everywhere he went the books were his gift, his message, his panacea for all the problems people brought before him. "That's a great question," he would grin, "and the answer you are looking for is here, in this book." His guru Yogaswami had scoffed, "It's not in books, you fool!" But he didn't have these books!

The cruise was a great success, connecting as it did his love of travel and Innersearch, the opening of new temples and the chance to go backstage on the ship to meet with the evening's performers, a flashback to his own days in dance.

Following his mariner's call, Gurudeva set sail again the following year. From March 25 to April 4, 2000, five monks and forty-nine Innersearchers sailed from Fort Lauderdale, Florida, south to St. Kitts, Martinique, Trinidad, St. Thomas, Dominica and Half Moon Cay. The Caribbean had called him many times. Hindus there are far from the rest of the world, and swamis seldom make the distant trek.

Gurudeva knew his presence there would resound throughout that part of the world, and so off he went, this time on the MS Volendam, a new and immense vessel that nearly dwarfed the islands it docked at. Reaching Trinidad & Tobago, the farthest islands, Gurudeva met with 4,500 Hindus, encouraging them as no guru ever had to meet the special challenges they faced.

During the Innersearch cruise in 1999, Gurudeva founded Alaska's first Hindu temple, inviting native Inuit elders to join in the homa. *A cruise with 54 devotees in 2000 through the Caribbean did much to fortify Hindus, especially in Trinidad.*

"Make it Last a Thousand Years"

Iraivan was an improbably difficult project. It had such difficulties built into it—a global logistical nightmare, a budget that such a small group of renounced men would never voluntarily undertake, a level of shastric expertise that would require much learning and guidance, and exacting rules of construction, such as it must be entirely hand-carved—as to make it nearly unthinkable. Did Gurudeva put this on his Order's shoulders knowing this generation of monastics would have to be a team to accomplish it, that it would require them to sacrifice, to cooperate, to stretch and grow? Yet he would only see the initial parts of its earthly manifestation, such as the all-important foundation.

Many were the long and involved discussions, beginning with the geological differences between an ancient India and a young Hawaiian island. Some seventy million years have passed over India, eroding many meters of soil and exposing the bedrock. Everywhere you can see bare rock jutting out from the earth, humongous stones, entire hills and ranges of hills. India is seasoned and settled. It is upon this bedrock that Indian temples have been built for some five thousand years, and it is because of that unmoving and unmovable foundation of rock that they still stand, unfazed by earthquake or flood, unintimidated by time.

Kauai is everything India is not—young, vulnerable, slathered with a skin of clay and loose rock. Being a mere five million years old, the island's bedrock lies far below the surface, 80 to 120 feet. The soft subsurface is no place to build a heavy temple, and certainly not the gravity-held structure the Cholas designed. Granite, that crystal-rich, dense and super-hard rock that builders love for its durability and strength, has a weakness: It has little tensile strength, so it cannot tolerate even the slightest bending and torquing without shattering. It is structurally brittle. Should a 12-foot-long roof beam be bent just ⅛th of an inch along its length, it would crack and fail, bringing down the roof.

This zero tolerance for movement of the temple foundation was an early challenge. After abandoning the idea of installing enormously long pilings deep into the earth, engineers finally came up with a clever solution—they would build the foundation as a single, monolithic concrete island, which they call a raft. This man-made rock would mimic the real bedrock back in India. If an earthquake or other force of nature should sink one end of the temple half an inch, the raft would move as a whole, keeping the same relationship among all the pillars and beams and averting disaster. This stone island literally floats on top of the clay soil below.

To create the raft foundation, designs were evolved that echoed volcanic-ash technologies of the Roman era and heralded a new interest in high-density, fly-ash concrete. The guru of that technology turned out to be a Saivite Hindu engineer at the University of California at Berkeley, and it was this innovative soul, Dr. Kumar Mehta, who brought together the knowledge and the elements for what was in 1999 the largest fly-ash pour in modern times, an event that would put Iraivan on the cover of *Concrete Today* magazine.

Gurudeva took every opportunity to insist on the longevity of the temple. Even before construction had begun, he was already looking at the endgame. It must last 1,000 years and more. Every detail, every plan, every decision consulted this touchstone. Perhaps it was his way of saying that his work, and that of his Order, was destined to persist beyond a lifetime or two, a call to his monks to set their sights on a more-than-your-lifetime horizon.

Inside the monastery, that one decree had a powerful impact, widening the scope of the monks' minds and plans, engaging them in a future that would be for others and not themselves. The thousand-year rule would be applied to the endowments, to the publications and more.

In Gurudeva's trips to India, he had seen many majestic temples that had fallen into neglect, with too little funding to maintain them, staffed by an inadequate handful of underpaid priests. Determined that Iraivan never suffer that fate, Gurudeva established a permanent maintenance endowment, stipulating that half of every dollar donated go into that endowment. In this way he ensured that Iraivan Temple will continue to flourish into the far future. So central was this idea to his planning, he decreed that the temple could only be consecrated once the endowment reached $7.2 million, an amount equal to the estimated cost of the project. This endowment was designed to provide sufficient income that the monks will never again have to raise funds to care for the temple.

On August 21, 1999—24 years after his threefold vision of Lord Siva—Gurudeva witnessed the pouring of his temple's foundation. In an all-day effort, a forty-man team poured a two-foot-thick base of concrete. One week later, the second two-foot layer was added. Visitors from the island joined Gurudeva to watch the thrilling sight as 20 trucks in 108 round trips placed the 56-foot by 117-foot by 4-foot-deep high-density plinth for Iraivan Temple.

Gurudeva stood at the far end of the foundation during those days, his arms outstretched ecstatically, smiling the smile men have when they know they have done something amazing. In early November of that year, he emailed all the monks this inspiring message received from the devas:

Iraivan's foundation is coming alive. Light is vibrating through it. It is a remarkable sight to behold. Something we never expected or anticipated. What is happening is yet to be known. Seemingly, it is of itself a Being, beautiful to behold, to be approached with awe. Yet, its only form is the form of itself, radiating light in billows and rays, as of many-colored rainbows.

After curing, the foundation was carefully inspected, and Dr. Mehta's

controversial technique was vindicated. For the first time in 2,000 years, a massive concrete slab had been placed without rebar, and there was not a single crack—not even a hairline fissure!

Following the foundation pour, Gurudeva began a new pattern. After the monastery's weekly *homa* in Kadavul Temple, he would have the monastic priest light a camphor flame from the *homa* fire, and all would join in a grand parade out to the Iraivan Temple site. Gurudeva conducted a brief *homa*, started from that flame, in the *yagasala* just north of the Iraivan foundation. Then, using the *kumbha* that was blessed at the *homa*, Gurudeva would lead everyone in circumambulating the temple foundation three times while sprinkling the *kumbha* water here and there, all the while visualizing Iraivan Temple rising on the spot in the years to come. He was plying his mystic skills to nourish the budding temple as one might nurture a young plant.

It was the next development in a routine he had followed for four years prior to the foundation pour. Periodically after the early morning puja in Kadavul Temple, he led the monks and members out to the Iraivan Temple site and offered the arati to a tiny Ganesha embedded in the banyan tree behind where Dakshinamurti now stands, just north of the temple, then led a procession around the heart of Iraivan, the below-ground crypt that marked the future position of the Sivalingam. In these holy excursions he was consciously transmitting the spiritual power of the long-established Kadavul Temple to the future Iraivan, training his shishyas to manifest

Throughout the 1980s and 90s, Gurudeva traveled frequently to all corners of the world, greeted by each nation's Hindu communities, speaking at temples and inspiring students and members.

Page 693

Chapter 31
· ·

the temple that would one day stand there. "Visualize, materialize," he loved to say to everyone. To him, it was as real in its inchoate state as it would one day be on the physical plane.

In May of 2001 Gurudeva participated in the ceremonial placement of the first block of stone. Chief architect V. Ganapati Sthapati, who was flown from India to officiate, spoke to the large gathering after the rituals:

> Years ago Gurudeva invited me to come to the US. I had never been here before.... He told me I should come and help build the Hindu temples in North America.
>
> Now I wish to relate to you a true story. You may know about the famous *Nadi Shastra* readers we have in India. They have large libraries of *olai* leaves with prophecies. Before I met Gurudeva I went to one of these. He read my *nadi* leaves and said: "The great King Raja-raja Chola has been reborn; he is a tall man with white hair, and he will soon come to ask you to go to the West and build temples there." And I tell you it was only later that I met Gurudeva and realized that he was the reincarnation of Rajaraja Chola. So this temple has special significance. It is one of only three sacred temples that face south. This means the temple has the power to grant liberation, moksha.

Recognition, Local and Global

In September of 1999 Gurudeva traveled to Mauritius, Malaysia and Singapore, meeting members who had not seen him for eight years. He met with national leaders, ministers and VIPs and on Ganesha Chaturthi opened the new Panchamukha Ganapati Mandapam, the centerpiece of his Spiritual Park that would grow to be the premier spiritual nexus of Mauritius.

A year later, at the end of August, Gurudeva received the U Thant Peace Award from Sri Chinmoy in the Dag Hammarskjöld Auditorium at the United Nations headquarters. This honor had previously been bestowed on the Dalai Lama, Nelson Mandela, Mikhail Gorbachev, Pope John Paul II and Mother Teresa.

A few days later, Gurudeva and three monks traveling with him attended the Millennium World Peace Summit of Religious and Spiritual

Leaders, held in the United Nations' General Assembly Hall. At the nearby Waldorf-Astoria Hotel, Gurudeva addressed the 1,200-strong spiritual assembly from all faiths, speaking on "Forgiveness and Reconciliation" and offering a summary of his UN message "For World Peace, First Stop the War in the Home."

Upon his return to Kauai, 350 citizens and county and state officials gathered on October 18 to herald his accomplishments on the island and beyond. Mayor Maryanne Kusaka and County Council Chairman Ron Kouchi arranged a luncheon at the Terrace Restaurant at the Marriot Hotel. Island leaders and Hawaii Governor Cayetano's representative Roy Nishida spoke eloquently of Gurudeva's remarkable effect on their lives and on this island, the many ways he had influenced them. Ron Kouchi gave an amazing talk on prejudice, confiding, "When I first met the monks, with their strange clothes and long beards, I didn't know who they were or why they were on the island, and furthermore I didn't want to know. Then through the vision group I came to know them, to see how Gurudeva works, how he brought us all to think of ourselves as Kauaians; and now, four years later, I can say he has changed my life, has become the most influential person in my adult life."

The leaders of the island appreciated Gurudeva's firm policy of being politically neutral (his monks never vote, but support whomever is elected) and his instructions to his monks and family members to be good citizens, never asking for or expecting special favors from the government, always contributing and never taking.

Who would have guessed that a hazel-eyed American guru would establish a traditional monastery in Hawaii that the whole Hindu world would look up to as a source of knowledge, authority, influence and inspiration? Kauai's Hindu Monastery had become something of a legend, attracting the praise of the greatest of Hindu swamis, leaders and thinkers, all of whom who were charmed by its unlikely existence and impressed by its purity and authenticity. Gurudeva's monastery and order are held up as an example of how Hinduism might survive the traumas of the past. If the Sanatana Dharma could thrive in Hawaii, people thought, might it not also survive in India? There were apocryphal tales of his past life as Swami Vivekananda or Rajaraja Chola, and hints that Siva Himself had incarnated to save Saivism. Gurudeva smiled to hear such accolades.

Jayendra Puri Swami, head of Sri Kailash Ashrama Mahasamsthana Math, Bangalore, observed:

• •

The United Nations' Millennium Summit in 2000 was history's largest gathering of world leaders, and the first time that religious leaders joined in the General Assembly Hall. Gurudeva gave a talk on peace to 1,200 leaders and received the prestigious U Thant Peace Award from Sri Chinmoy.

This birth of Sivaya Subramuniyaswami is a very rare birth. To learn and practice a religion that did not belong to your land; being an outsider and contributing so much to Hindu religion is amazing. He has been able to teach Hindus how to be a Hindu. My guru, Tiruchi Swami, a realized jnani himself, has repeatedly said more than a hundred times that Sri Sivaya Subramuniyaswami is an avatar of Lord Karttikeya, the Commander in Chief of the divine army. Tiruchi Swami said of Gurudeva's books, "No one in India has been able to do such tremendous work."

Swami Paramananda Bharati, attached to Sringeri Pitham and famous for chanting Aum in the Kremlin at the Moscow Global Forum, echoed:

No one could equal Gurudeva in inspiring Hindus all over the world. He was a Siva bhakta to the core, but without a trace of fanaticism. His vision of Hinduism was total, his approach rational and his love universal, pure, soothing and irresistible. I have never seen a person who is so integral.

Swami Bua Ji Maharaj of New York declared:

The sublime substance of Saiva Siddhanta was succinctly spread all over the world by this saint. How was this possible for somebody who was born and brought up in a totally different culture? It could not be anything other than an unbreakable bond from the previous birth, *purva janma bandham*. The spiritual awareness brought about by him among the Hindus of Western countries is just amazing. Gurudeva's unique method of explaining the most complex principles in the simplest way was astounding. The most complicated philosophies appeared as the simplest and easiest messages in his hands, but with the same power and essence.

Painful Karma

On December 5, 2000, Gurudeva and three of his senior monks hiked to the top of a nearby hill to see the new lands the monastery had acquired across the river. The hill was steep, and on the way down Gurudeva slipped. Though he did not fall, the force of the movement badly injured his lower back. He was in severe pain, and asked to stay at Hale Makai, the monastery's beach-side retreat in Kapaa. For the next four months he

. . . .

Gurudeva worked hard on his books and knew they were without equal. Bookstores like Borders and Barnes & Noble knew, too, and invited him to introduce the books to readers at book signings all around the country.

stayed there, 150 feet from the ocean and five miles from the monastery, preferring to heal away from his normal onslaught of duties, and closer to the doctors and therapists who would attend him. Each day at lunch and dinner two or three monks drove down from the monastery with a hot meal for him and his three monastic caregivers, to be with him, talk story and enjoy some personal time with their satguru.

Knowing that the European Innersearch was just months away, he set a major recovery plan and worked powerfully each day to heal his body. His Pilates therapist would later confide that he had never seen such an amazing healing take place, never seen an injury that would debilitate most people for years resolve itself in mere months, even in young athletes he had worked with, let alone in a man of 73. The x-rays were almost unbelievable, when before and after were set side by side.

Gurudeva did more than just heal during those months. He kept his mind active, working with his editing team every day. The goal he set was to complete *Living with Siva,* the third and final book of his Master Course trilogy, before the Innersearch departed in August—not a small paperback, but another 1,000-page masterwork. His willpower was astonishing during those months. As he pushed his body and his mind, the goals toppled before him, the book going to press in July and his body ready to travel the world by August.

Sailing the Seas of Northern Europe

Innersearch Europe followed on August 10-22, 2001, with seventy-two Innersearchers sailing through Northern Europe on yet a more massive ship, the 780-foot, 2,000-passenger MS Amsterdam, then the largest and newest in the fleet. Before the cruise, Gurudeva visited London and Germany, connecting with the Tamil communities there. Groups of seekers were waiting at each port to greet the guru from afar, in Helsinki, St. Petersburg and Warnemunde. In Oslo and Stockholm, small Tamil communities brought Gurudeva to their temples to give talks. Gurudeva brought Russian followers aboard the ship and conducted a *namakarana* samskara for one in the Neptune Lounge.

The international group of Hindus and *ardha*-Hindu seekers who gathered for this journey stood out on the ship, all those elegant saris and *veshtis* moving toward the meditation hall while everyone else was there to eat and gamble, swim and shop and sit for hours on the sunny deck.

On his last and longest Innersearch cruise, with seventy-two devotees, Gurudeva visited a dozen nations in Northern Europe and Russia, giving talks to Hindu communities and laying the foundation stone for a major temple in Denmark.

• •

Gurudeva was the center of attention, especially at night. He loved to enter the five-star dining room, walking down a two-story staircase followed by his entourage of monks. Each night as this little drama unfolded, the noisy background sounds of the diners would turn silent in an almost startling way as a thousand passengers stopped eating to watch the elegant, saffron-clad guru descend into their midst, nudging each other as if to say, "Look. Who is that man?" Once he settled, a percussion of clatter would break the silence as, all at once, knives and forks went back to work on expensive china. One day he was challenged, "Why do you go on these five-star cruises?" He quietly retorted, "Because they don't have six-star cruises yet."

After the cruise ended in Copenhagen, Gurudeva and his monastic staff flew in a prop plane to Denmark's far north, where he laid the foundation stone for an Amman temple in Brande and joined the Hindus of Herning for a festive ceremony in their remote Ganesha temple. It was a challenging journey for Gurudeva, due to his debilitating back injury and the illness he did not know he had. Still, he strode through nation after nation, never complaining, always cheerful and ready for the next experience. No one knew, not even he, that he had just a few months to live.

In his daily classes in the Hudson Room, Gurudeva covered a stunning array of subjects, including gratitude, seeing God everywhere, the *yamas* and *niyamas,* sadhana, family togetherness, the spirit of the guru, the Nandinatha Sutras, zero tolerance for disharmony, growing old, the need for religion, the power of penance and standing strong for Hinduism. He loved the question-and-answer times and patiently fielded everyone's queries and concerns. In his cabin he kept close to the monks and kept the monks close, coordinating details of the day, adventures on land, changes in the plans, waiting, without saying a word, for a monk to offer to rub his weary feet.

Life's Most Exalted Moment

On October 6, 2001—just weeks after Gurudeva returned from that arduous, multi-nation trek through Northern Europe—he was admitted to Wilcox Hospital for severe anemia. During a three-day stay, doctors discovered he was harboring advanced stage cancers in his colon, small intestine and brain. Gurudeva returned to Hale Makai; and over the next week, teams of doctors on Kauai, in California and in Seattle pored over test results and confirmed that he had not long to live.

On October 16, after a few days of reflection, he gathered the senior monks to inform them of his decision to fast to death. He had taught the traditional way of leaving the body, called *prayopavesha,* and now he would follow that difficult regimen, preferring the conscious departure of the yogi to weeks or months of medical intervention and systemic deterioration leading to loss of consciousness. He had always spoken of death as life's most exalted moment, so the monks were not surprised by his decision. They remembered that other great souls, like Ramana Maharishi, who also had cancer, had left life consciously in this way.

Gurudeva was matter-of-fact in his decision. He asked how long it would take, and after hearing some stories about others who had fasted in this manner, said, "So, in about twenty-four days it will be over and I will be on twenty-four-hour service." That theme was repeated, as he sought to console the monks that now he would be with them around the clock, not just during sixteen waking hours of the day. "It's a good time now, while you are all young," he observed. Still, the monks' lives were dramatically changed, their world turned upside down, in those critical few days.

On the evening of the 16th he returned to the monastery, where the monks had set up a special bed in his Mahogany Room. In the ensuing weeks, his own departure was not the most onerous work. It was the sorrow in the hearts of his monks. Hoping to heal their hurt, he assured them, caressed them, offered encouragement and solace. Not a syllable of complaint was uttered. At one point he whispered, "Everything that is happening is good. Everything that is happening is meant to be."

From his fasting bed he gave guru initiation to his three successors and signed a few critical documents that such circumstances require. But mostly he was working to leave the body—not an easy thing to do, it turns out. The approach of death held no fear for him, but it did focus him, as he undertook this last great sadhana, diving into the transition with the same fervor that defined all of his works. When monks would come to commune, he would softly instruct, "Sit in silence and we will communicate." There was work to be done, and it was not to be interrupted by chatter about the past or the future. The work was before us now. His work: to resolve all karmas and depart through the crown chakra. The monks' work: to aid his transition and prepare for a life without him.

One evening after asking if the monks had had dinner, Gurudeva sat up, pressed his palms together in namaskara and in a weak voice offered the following message:

> People say, "I sleep eight hours a day, and that is a fact of life." They say, "I eat three meals a day, and that is a fact of life." You say, "You are the Self," and they say "That is not a fact of life." That is ignorant, erroneous thinking that blocks you from knowing the Self. Those blocks come from Western concepts.

When one of the monks asked for advice about realizing the Self, Gurudeva responded:

> You have to realize that you already have it. It's not something you are going to get or that is out there in time. You already have it. So, you think on that. First admit to yourself that the Self is in you. The end of the light is *im kaif*. Admit that the Self is not apart from you. It

pervades everything, creates everything and destroys everything. You
are the Self right now. Get that strong in your mind and write down
and burn up everything that is opposite to that, then you will be the
Self all the time.

First, accept the fact that you are the Self already. Then, the end of
the "eee" is *im kaif*. Realize the Self. Whatever comes up in your mind
to keep you from the Self, write down and burn. That's all you have
to do. It's very simple. You have all the tools. The only thing then is to
realize the Self again.

A senior monk placed the Self God talk, in Gurudeva's handwriting, in his
hands and asked if the monks could read it aloud. "Yes," was his simple
reply. Taking turns, each monk read a few lines. In the dim light, the room
bristled with shakti. Those profound words spoken in those varied voices
in this timeless moment were mesmerizing. After the reading, Gurudeva
commented, "So, the Self God was true in the 50s and it is still true in the
2000s." All present laughed in acknowledgment that the Absolute Truth
is always the same, always true, transcending life and death.

One day Gurudeva was greeting astral guests. Sitting up in bed, he
would raise his hands in namaskara, acknowledging each one. At one
point, in the dark of night, he told the monks that Yogaswami had come
to him and said, "Everything is finished. All is complete. I will be back."

Devotees poured in from around the world to be near their satguru in
these final days, though he had requested only the monks should enter
his room or see him. But his noble shishyas were there, in love and appreciation for his gifts and guidance. He had transformed their lives and had
taught them the importance of being in close proximity to the satguru
during *mahasamadhi,* the shakti of which tradition says is greater than a
thousand dips in the river Ganga, a thousand pilgrimages to Mount Kailas,
a thousand grand yajnas.

At 11:54pm, during Chitra *nakshatra,* November 12, 2001, after fasting for 32 days, Gurudeva attained *mahasamadhi,* minutes before the
dawn of Dipavali, Hinduism's festival of lights. A lifetime of courage and
willpower was crowned by a noble departure which showed the world,
and all who suffer their final days, the continuing relevance of an ancient
approach to death. An hour later all the monks assembled in the monastery's Guru Pitham, as he had decreed, to install his designated successor, Satguru Bodhinatha Veylanswami, the order's senior monk, and to

. . . .

*Learning of his incurable cancer, Gurudeva declared he would fast
to death. For 32 days his monks stayed at his side, finally carrying
his body on a palanquin to the cremation fires. A mystical puja
called all the past gurus to come and escort him to Siva's abode.*

prostrate to him for the first time, thus beginning a new era—the era of the next preceptor in the age-old Kailasa Parampara.

As a youth of 21, while still studying at the University of California at Berkeley, Bodhinatha first met Gurudeva in a brick-walled room at the Mountain Desert Monastery in Nevada. Joining Gurudeva's order in 1965, he was the guiding administrator of Gurudeva's institutions for decades, overseeing their legal and business matters. In the 1970s, Gurudeva sent him to the Big Island of Hawaii, there to live alone in a crude thatched hut on the ocean sands for nine months. Gurudeva would fly to Kona to visit and guide Bodhinatha's sadhana and meditations. Such service and sadhana had prepared Bodhinatha for the momentous responsibilities placed on his shoulders. When Gurudeva stationed him in Sri Lanka for six months in 1972, Yogaswami spoke into his right ear, saying, "I am preparing you for your/my mission." With the humility that defined his monastic life, he ascended the *pitham* and became the next in a long succession of Nandinatha satgurus.

The following afternoon the monks and shishyas carried Gurudeva's body in procession to the monastery entrance. Unexpectedly, a police escort, arranged by the mayor who loved him so, sped the entourage to the crematorium, with police cars stationed at every intersection of the 20-mile ride, stopping all traffic along the route, as though Kauai's favorite spiritual master must get to Siva's feet without another moment's delay. Hundreds of people were there to say goodbye at an emotionally charged memorial service, replete with a Hawaiian hula halau offering mystical chants and dances in a riveting outpouring of love until the senior monks, chanting "Aum Namasivaya," carried his body on their shoulders the last few feet to the modern pyre. *The New York Times*, CNN and others announced his passing.

At dawn the next day, the monks gathered his ashes and brought them to the monastery, placing them, as he had instructed, in the wall of an underground cave behind the Guru Pitham. From that day forward his life and legacy have been honored at a monthly guru puja on the day of Chitra *nakshatra* at a shrine the monks built in the main *mandapam* of Kadavul Temple, on the spot he sat hundreds of mornings to give spiritual guidance to his devotees. Jai Gurudeva!

. . . .

Satguru Bodhinatha Veylanswami was installed on November 13, 2001, as the Guru Mahasannidhanam of Kauai Aadheenam. His earlier life as a monastic teacher and accountant and a meditating sadhu would change as he set forth to represent the Church and perpetuate Gurudeva's life work.

Conclusion

A parampara is like a mighty river, its waters ever fresh, its vitality unremitting. Branching out and winding through the centuries, through many nations and cultures, the Kailasa Parampara brings life-giving waters to all who thirst for Truth.

We have glimpsed seven lives in this story—seven great beings who strode the Earth, who spoke of the inseparability of man and God, the unity and perfection that pervades every atom of the universe, seven satgurus who realized God and exemplified spiritual life as few have. What we have not seen is their yet-to-be-known impact: the illumined satgurus of millennia to come, who will meet in wisdom challenges these seven did not know would exist; and those who, upon encountering monistic Saiva Siddhanta, will fall at their feet, only to learn that they are the All in all. They are the Truth they seek.

No one can say how a guru should initiate another. In some traditions, such as the Dashanami orders, sannyasa *diksha* is a formal ritual following rigid protocols. In others, such as the Natha orders, it is usually more spontaneous and unstructured, a potent awakening that can be transmitted by a thought, a word or a touch. The Kailasa Parampara gurus commonly pass on their spiritual power through touch. Kadaitswami was touched by the rishi and passed his power on to Chellappaguru by placing a large rupee coin in the disciple's open palm. At the auspicious moment, Chellappaguru knocked a cup and a bowl out of Yogaswami's hands. Yogaswami nearly knocked Gurudeva to the ground with that resounding slap on the back at his compound gate. By such otherwise mundane gestures, spiritual power is transmitted from one generation to the next.

That special touch, full of purpose at the crucial moment, acknowledges the realization and maturity already unfolded in the disciple and confers upon him the mantle of spiritual authority of the parampara, much as a father might pass a family business to a worthy son. The full weight of this responsibility is assumed only when the initiating guru leaves his physical body.

To assure the continuity of the parampara, each successor leaves the lineage in the illumined hands of the next, thus fulfilling his part in a chain extending from the grace of Siva, a chain that began with man's first search for the realization of the Absolute and will continue ineluctably to the end of time, and a few days beyond.

Image Gallery

Photos from the lives of Kadaitswami, Chellappaswami, Siva Yogaswami and Sivaya Subramuniyaswami

கடையிற் சுவாமிகள்

சமாதி **13-10-1891**

அச்சளிப்பு:
கடையிற் சுவாமி கோயில் பரிபாலனசபை

(clockwise from left) The *teradi* at Nallur Temple, in which the tall chariot is stored and where Chellappaswami often lived. Inset: the *teradi's* enclosed chamber where Chellappaswami stood and shook the bars when Yogaswami first was immersed in the light. A woman worships the *bilva* tree under which Chellappaswami ate and meditated. Sketches of Chellappaswami and Kadaitswami made by their own devotees. Kadaitswami's samadhi temple. Insets: yellow pillars inside the temple, with the Sivalingam under which Kadaitswami's body is interred in a crypt; bronze image of Kadaitswami with his trademark umbrella.

Realms of Kadaitswami & Chellappaswami

(clockwise from above) A typical Jaffna market. Cadjan, the ubiquitous palm-thatch, fencing along a Jaffna trail. Rice paddy, banana and palm trees near Point Pedro. The fresh-water pool at Keerimalai where Chellappaswami and Yogaswami often went for a dip. Nallur Temple in the early days, before it was renovated. The Sivathondan Nilayam building on KKS Road built by Yogaswami for devotees. Chellappaswami's small samadhi shrine at Nallur. Inset: A man worships Chellappaswami inside the shrine.

Jaffna

(clockwise from upper left) Photo of Yogaswami meditating in the home of a devotee in 1950. Yogaswami's hut at Columbuthurai. Inset: Yogaswami walking with an umbrella to protect from the torrid sun. Markanduswami's hut at Kaitatadi. Inset: 1960 photo of Germanswami (Gauribala), far right, with Sandaswami of the UK, Narikuttiswami of Australia and one other. Markanduswami addresses visitors in 1969. Yogaswami after his fall, with devotees gathered near. The wall surrounding his hut, where Subramuniyaswami received the slap on the back.

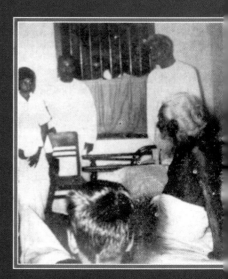

Siva Yogaswami

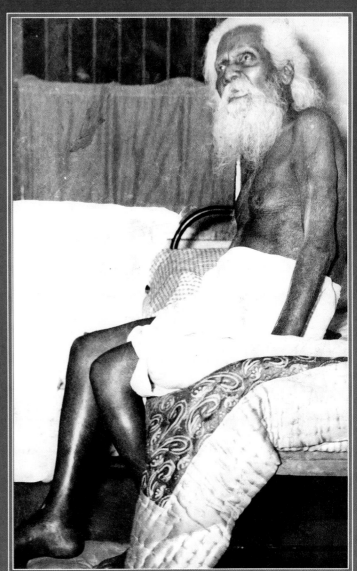

(clockwise from far left) Yogaswami on the porch of a devotee's home around 1950. Devotees prostrate before the shrine in Yogaswami's hut, where his ashes are kept (they were spread to several places). Yogaswami on the hospital bed after breaking his hip. Yogaswami on his funeral bed. His body being carried on a palanquin to the cremation grounds, March 24, 1964.

FALLEN LEAF LODGE.

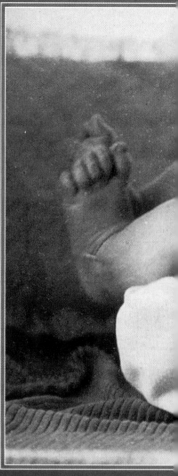

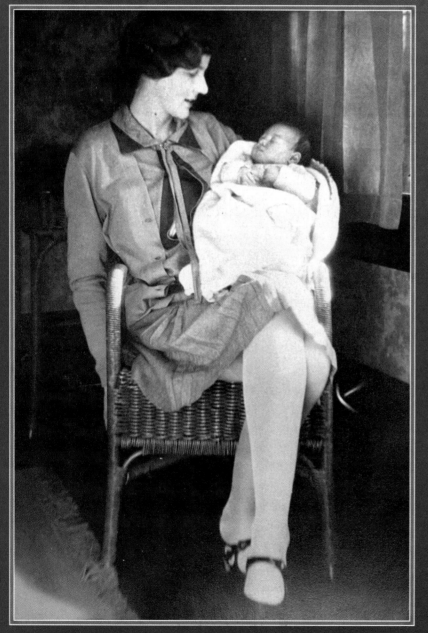

(clockwise from top left) The wooden lodge at Fallen Leaf Lake where Bob Hansen was raised. At three months old. The snow truck with skis and tracks that took the family to town in winter. Young Robert at six. A view of Fallen Leaf Lake in California, just south of Lake Tahoe. Infant Robert in the arms of his mother, Alberta.

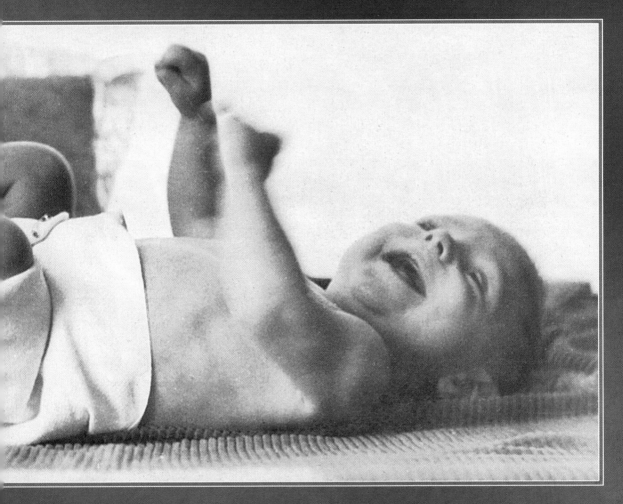

Subramuniyaswami's Childhood

(clockwise from left) Robert at the one-room schoolhouse (second from left, back row, arms crossed). With his mother, father and little sister Carol. Mother Christney, an early and influential catalyst. Chalet Beau Reve, the lakeside home and studio of Grace Burroughs where Robert studied dance in the summer. Dancing on stage. Portrait as a teenager.

Ceylon Calls

(clockwise from top left) Photo that appeared in a Colombo newspaper on March 26, 1947, the day after he arrived in Ceylon, with Alva Coil, left, and Hilda Charlton. The Colombo YMCA, where he stayed after his retreat at Jailani Caves. A view of the entrance to Jailani Caves, where he fasted and realized the Absolute Truth. An all-stone Siva temple in Colombo that he visited. At the gate of the Chettiar home with Vinayagamoorthy, left, and wife during his first return in 1969. Robert's 1947 passport, showing his 1949 return to the US via Boston.

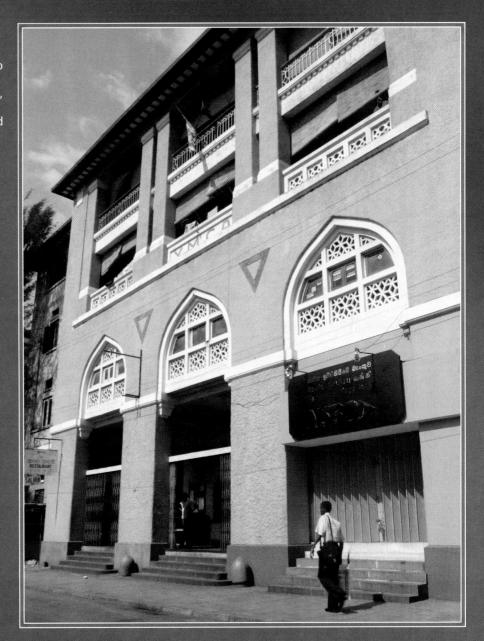

DARRELL PEIRIS
(Ananda Priyadarsi)

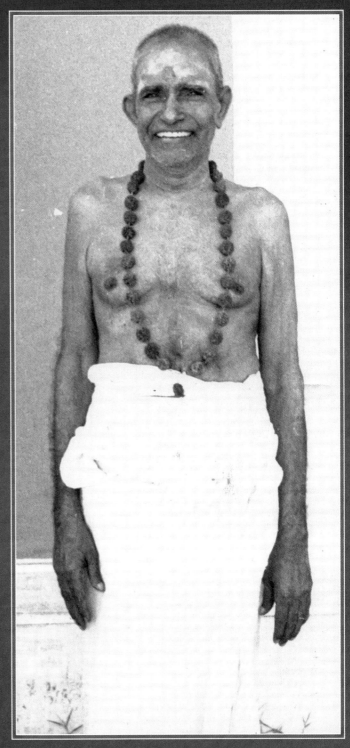

(clockwise from above left) Beturbaned, from a Sri Lankan poster announcing the East-meets-West dance and musical program they performed throughout the country. Robert in a white kurta onstage. Kandiah Chettiar, the English teacher who brought him to meet Yogaswami. Robert learned Manipuri, a traditional dance form from the northeastern Indian state of Manipur. Amma Vinayagamoorthy points to the jungle near her home where Gurudeva did sadhana alone in a hut. Dayananda Priyadasi (Darrell Peiris), mystic and mentor, taught him the Buddhist ways.

San Francisco & Virginia City

(clockwise from top left) At the airport for his first flight to Hawaii in December of 1959. The archway doors at the San Francisco Temple on Sacramento Street. Posing in his kurta outfit not long after returning from Ceylon. Sunday brunch was a popular event in the late 50s. Every Sunday, without fail, Sri Subramuniya would lecture on the path to the Self, on the Divinity of all, on the life of dharma. The Mountain Desert Monastery in Virginia City, Nevada, where his young monks were trained in the 60s and 70s.

(clockwise from upper left) The 1969 Indian Odyssey, a 13-week, around-the-world spiritual adventure. Teaching Shum on the banks of Lago Maggiore in Switzerland, July, 1968. Inset: Ascona, the nearby town on the lake. On the dock during the March-April 2000 Innersearch cruise to the Caribbean. Gurudeva was greeted in hundreds of homes in Asia. Recording the audio Master Course in Hawaii in 1970.

Innersearch

(clockwise from upper left) Jaffna musicians escort the American satguru and his followers from the train station through the streets in 1982. The 1972 Indian Odyssey stopped in Moscow for a few days. With Swami Muktananda in Ganeshpuri. Leading a meditation in Sandakpu, Nepal, at 13,600 feet in the Himalayas. In Kopay, Sri Lanka, 1982, a Morris Minor is outfitted with ropes, and Subramuniyaswami is pulled through the villages. Taking devotees to meet with Maharishi Mahesh Yogi in Rishikesh in 1969.

India & Lanka

(clockwise from above) At a temple in India, N.K. Murthi translates Gurudeva's talk into Tamil; Gurudeva gave thousands of such talks, calling on Hindus to worship Siva, live strong and be proud of their faith. Visiting a temple in Tamil Nadu. At Nallur Temple in Sri Lanka, parading to the next talk, and the next and the next. A public talk at Colombo's Saraswati Hall, with his monks on stage. Performing arati during a visit to Nallai Aadheenam in Sri Lanka. With Tamil elders in front of his ashram in Alaveddy. Everyone was mesmerized by the tall sage from Hawaii and eager to hear his wisdom, always unscripted, always articulate, always uplifting.

A Friend to Hindus Everywhere

(clockwise from above left) Meeting in Mumbai with 89 temple priests in 1995; he was the priests' greatest ally. Taken on a chariot through the streets of Malaysia. Paraded through the streets of Alaveddy with schoolgirls strewing flowers; he could connect equally to every generation. Through the years, tens of thousands of Hindus, like this family, flew to Kauai for his darshan and counsel. Visiting with the spiritual head of the Madurai Aadheenam, one of many mathas he collaborated with.

Global Conferences on Human Survival

(clockwise from top) April of 1988 at the strategically important Global Forum for Human Survival at Oxford, five days of meetings with spiritual and political world leaders. On an Oxford panel. At the United Nations in 2000, speaking to 1,200 religious leaders on "Stop the War in the Home." After receiving the 2000 U Thant Peace Award at the U.N. in New York. In Rio de Janeiro in 1992, addressing the assembled leaders. Bundled against the winter's cold during the December 1990 Global Forum for Human Survival in Moscow.

Iraivan Temple Is Born

(clockwise from above) Iraivan Temple, which Gurudeva envisioned as America's only hand-carved Agamic temple. Meeting with the master architects and *silpis,* stone sculptors. On the day of the installation of the first temple stone in Hawaii. In Bengaluru, India, reviewing architectural plans with the designers. At the village worksite he built, standing between two unfinished pillars. December, 1990, carving the first stone at Kailash Ashram to mark the official beginning of the temple-building process. August 21, 1999, Gurudeva stands before the temple foundation.

Power of the Press

(clockwise from upper left) Gurudeva editing on his first Macintosh in 1985. Releasing his two newest publications in Kuala Lumpur, Malaysia, in 2000. At the editing table near the ocean in 2000; the four laptops were connected wirelessly, enabling the team to simultaneously edit the same document. At a school in Fiji, giving away his children's course on religion. Holding an issue of his flagship publication, HINDUISM TODAY magazine, which he called "the prow of the ship." After working for years to create each masterpiece, Gurudeva signed his books with great joy.

At Home on Kauai

(clockwise from above) Kauai, the Hawaiian island Gurudeva lived on for over 30 years. Each week Gurudeva presided over the sacred *homa* rites, burning prayers to the devas. Every week after the *homa* Gurudeva spoke in Kadavul Temple to the monks, families and visiting pilgrims, inspiring and guiding their spiritual life. Holding his *danda* and a cup of coffee, Gurudeva takes a morning walk. Before dawn each day the monks gathered in the Guru Pitham, where Gurudeva guided the meditation in Shum, then spoke extemporaneously. With his successor, Satguru Bodhinatha Veylanswami.

adheenam: ஆதீனம் A Saivite Hindu monastery and temple complex in the South Indian Saiva Siddhanta tradition. The *aadheenam* head is called the *guru mahasannidhanam* or *aadheenakarthar.*

abhisheka(m): अभिषेक "Sprinkling; ablution." Ritual bathing of the Deity's image with water, curd, milk, honey, ghee, rosewater, etc. A special form of puja prescribed by Agamic injunction. Also performed in the inauguration of religious and political monarchs and other special blessings.

Absolute: Lower case (absolute): real, not dependent on anything else, not relative. Upper case (Absolute): Ultimate Reality, the unmanifest, unchanging and transcendent Parasiva. See: *Parasiva.*

acharya (āchārya): आचार्य A highly respected teacher.

actinic: Spiritual, creating light. Adjective derived from the Greek *aktis,* "ray." Of or pertaining to consciousness in its pure, unadulterated state. Describes the extremely rarefied superconscious realm of pure *bindu,* of quantum strings, the substratum of consciousness, *shuddha* maya, from which light first originates. Actinic force is the superconscious mind and not a force which comes from the superconcious mind. Commonly known as life, spirit, it can be seen as the light in man's eyes; it is the force that leaves man when he leaves his odic physical body behind. It is not opposite to odic force; it is different than odic force as light is different than water but shines through it. Actinic force flows freely through odic force. See: *kosha.*

actinic body: The soul body or *karana sharira.* See: *soul.*

actinodic: Spiritual-magnetic. Describes consciousness within *shuddhashuddha* maya, which is a mixture of odic and actinic force, the spectrum of the *anahata* chakra, and to a certain degree the *vishuddha* chakra. See: *actinic force, odic force, tattva.*

advaita: अद्वैत "Non-dual; not twofold." Nonduality or monism. The doctrine that Ultimate Reality consists of a one principal substance, or God. Opposite of *dvaita,* dualism. See: *dvaita-advaita, Vedanta.*

Advaita Ishvaravada (Advaita Īśvaravāda): अद्वैत ईश्वरवाद "Nondual and Personal-God-as-Ruler doctrine;" monistic theism. The philosophy of the *Vedas* and *Saiva Agamas,* which postulates the ultimate oneness of all things and in the reality of the personal Deity.

Advaita Siddhanta (Advaita Siddhānta): अद्वैत सिद्धान्त "Nondual perfect conclusions." Saivite philosophy codified in the *Agamas* which has at its core the nondual (advaitic) identity of God, soul and world, with a strong emphasis on internal and external worship, yoga sadhanas and *tapas. Advaita Siddhanta* is a term used in South India to distinguish Tirumular's school from the pluralistic Siddhanta of Meykandar and Aghorasiva.

Advaita Vedanta (Advaita Vedānta): अद्वैत वेदान्त "Nondual end (or essence) of the *Vedas.*" The nondual final conclusions of the *Vedas.* Commonly names the various Indian monistic schools, most prominently that of Shankara, that arose from the *Upanishads* and related texts.

Agama (Āgama): आगम The tradition; that which has "come down." An enormous collection of Sanskrit scriptures which, along with the *Vedas,* are revered as shruti (revealed scripture). The primary source and authority for ritual, yoga and temple construction.

Agastya: अगस्त्य One of eighteen celebrated Saiva siddhas (adepts), and reputed to be the first grammarian of Tamil language. He is said to have migrated from North India to the South. His name appears in the *Mahabharata, Ramayana* and the *Puranas* and was known to ancient Indonesians.

agni: अग्नि "Fire." 1) One of the five elements, *panchabhuta.* 2) When capitalized, the God of the element fire, invoked through Vedic ritual known as yajna, *agnikaraka, homa* and *havana;* the divine messenger who receives prayers and oblations and conveys them to the heavenly spheres.

ahimsa (ahiṁsā): अहिंसा "Noninjury," nonviolence or nonhurtfulness. Not causing harm to others, physically, mentally or emotionally. See: *yama-niyama.*

ajna chakra (ājñā chakra): आज्ञाचक्र "Command wheel." The third-eye center. See: *chakra.*

akasha (ākāśa): आकाश "Space." The sky. Free, open space. Ether, the fifth and most subtle of the five elements—earth, water, fire, air and ether. Empirically, the rarefied space or ethereal fluid plasma that pervades the universes, inner and outer. Esoterically, mind, the superconscious strata holding all that exists and all that potentially exists, wherein all happenings are recorded and can be read by clairvoyants.

all-pervasive: Diffused throughout or existing in every part of the universe.

anahata chakra (anāhata chakra): अनाहतचक्र "Wheel of unstruck [sound]." The heart center. See: *chakra.*

ananda (ānanda): आनन्द "Bliss." The pure joy—ecstasy or enstasy—of God-consciousness or spiritual experience.

aniconic: "Without likeness; without image." When referring to a Deity image, *aniconic* denotes a symbol which does not attempt an anthropomorphic (humanlike) or representational likeness. An example is the Sivalinga, "mark of God." See: *murti, Sivalinga.*

anjali mudra (añjali mudrā): अञ्जलिमुद्रा "Reverence gesture." Also called *pranamanjali.* A gesture of respect and greeting, in which the two palms are held gently together and slightly cupped. Often accompanied by the verbal salutation "namaskara," meaning "reverent salutation." The *anjali* mudra has various forms, e.g., near the chest in greeting equals, at eye level in greeting one's guru, and above the head in salutation to God. One form is with the open hands held side by side, as if by a beggar to receive food, or a worshiper beseeching God's grace in the temple.

antyeshti (antyeshṭi): अन्त्येष्टि "Last rites." Funeral.

anugraha shakti (anugraha śakti): अनुग्रहशक्ति "Graceful or favoring power." Revealing grace. God Siva's power of illumination, through which the soul is freed from the bonds of *anava,* karma and maya and ultimately attains liberation, moksha. Specifically, *anugraha* descends on the soul as *shaktinipata,* the *diksha* (initiation) from a satguru.

arati (ārati): आरती "Light." The circling or waving of a lamp—usually fed with ghee, oil or camphor—before a holy person or the temple Deity at the high point of puja. The flame is then presented to the devotees, each passing his or her hands through it and bringing them to the eyes three times, thereby receiving the blessings. *Arati* can also be performed as the briefest form of puja. See: *puja.*

archana: अर्चन A special, personal, abbreviated puja done by temple priests in which the name, birth-star and family lineage of a devotee are recited to invoke individual guidance and blessings. See: *puja.*

ardha-Hindu: अर्धहिन्दु "Half-Hindu." A devotee who has adopted Hindu belief and culture to a great extent but has not formally entered the religion through ceremony and taking a Hindu first and last name. Also refers to Easterners born into the faith who adopt non-Hindu names.

ashrama (āśrama): आश्रम "Place of striving." Hermitage; order of the life. Holy sanctuary; the residence and teaching center of a sadhu, saint, swami, ascetic or guru; often includes lodging for students. Also names life's four stages. See: *ashrama dharma.*

ashrama dharma (āśrama dharma): आश्रमधर्म "Laws of life development." Meritorious way of life appropriate to each of its four successive stages (ashramas), observing which one lives in harmony with nature and life, allowing the body, emotions and mind to develop and undergo their natural cycles in a most positive way. The four stages are: brahmacharya: studentship, from age 12 to 24; *grihastha:* householder, from 24 to 48; *vanaprastha:* elder advisor, from 48 to 72; and sannyasa: religious solitary, from 72 onward.

ashramas (āśramas): See: *ashrama dharma.*

ashtanga yoga (ashṭāṅga yoga): अष्टाङ्गयोग "Eight-limbed union." The classical raja yoga system of eight progressive stages to illumination: 1) yama: "Restraint." Virtuous and moral living. 2) niyama: "Observance." Religious practices which cultivate the qualities of the higher nature. 3) asana: "Seat or posture." 4) pranayama: "Mastering life force." Breath control. 5) *pratyahara:* "Withdrawal." Withdrawing consciousness from the physical senses. 6) *dharana:* "Concentration." Guiding the flow of consciousness. 7) dhyana: "Meditation." 8) samadhi: "Enstasy," "sameness, contemplation/realization."

astral body: The subtle, nonphysical body *(sukshma sharira)* in which the soul functions in the astral plane, the inner world also called Antarloka. See: *soul.*

astral plane (or world): The subtle world, or Antarloka, spanning the spectrum of consciousness from the *vishuddha* chakra in the throat to the *patala* chakra in the soles of the feet. In the astral plane, the soul is enshrouded in the astral body, called *sukshma sharira*. See: *loka, three worlds*.

asura: असुर "Evil spirit; demon." (Opposite of *sura:* "deva; God.") A being of the lower astral plane, Naraka. Asuras can and do interact with the physical plane, causing major and minor problems in people's lives. Asuras evolve and do not remain permanently in this state.

asuric: Of the nature of an asura, "not spiritual."

atma(n) (ātman): आत्मन् "The soul; the breath; the principle of life and sensation." The soul in its entirety—as the soul body (*anandamaya* kosha) and its essence (Parashakti and Parasiva). One of Hinduism's most fundamental tenets is that we are the atman, not the physical body, emotions, external mind or personality. See: *Paramatman, soul*.

Atmartha Puja: See: *Saiva Atmartha Puja*.

Aum: ॐ or ओम् (Tamil: ஓம்) Often spelled *Om*. The mystic syllable of Hinduism, associated with Lord Ganesha, placed at the beginning of sacred writings. In common usage in several Indian languages, *aum* means "yes, verily" or "hail."

aura: The luminous colorful field of subtle energy radiating within and around the human body. The colors change according to the ebb and flow of one's state of consciousness, thoughts, moods and emotions.

Auvaiyar: ஒளவையார் A saint of Tamil Nadu (ca 800 ce), a contemporary of Saint Sundarar, devotee of Lord Ganesha and Karttikeya, or Murugan, and one of the greatest literary figures in ancient India. Her Tamil primer is studied by children to this day. An earlier traditional date for Auvaiyar, 200 bce, is from a story about her and Saint Tiruvalluvar.

awareness: Individual consciousness, perception, knowing; the witness of perception, the "inner eye of the soul." *Sakshin* or *chit* in Sanskrit.

ayurveda (āyurveda): आयुर्वेद "Science of life." A holistic system of medicine and health native to ancient India, seeking *ayus*, "longevity," and *arogya*, "diseaselessness," to facilitate spiritual progress. Focus is on balancing energies through methods suited to the individual's constitution, lifestyle and nature.

ayurvedic: pertaining to ayurveda.

Bhairava: भैरव "Terrifying." Lord Siva as the fiery protector. He carries and is represented by a *trishula* (trident), a symbol often enshrined as guardian at the entrance to Siva temples. See: *Siva*.

bhajana: भजन Spiritual song. Individual or group singing of devotional songs, hymns and chants.

bhakta: भक्त (Tamil: *bhaktar*) "Devotee." A worshiper. One who is surrendered to the Divine.

bhakti: भक्ति "Devotion." Surrender to God, Gods or guru. Bhakti extends from the simplest expression of devotion to the ego-decimating principle of *prapatti*, which is total surrender. Bhakti is the foundation of all sects of Hinduism, as well as yoga schools throughout the world.

bhakti *yoga*: भक्तियोग "Union through devotion." Bhakti yoga is the practice of devotional disciplines, worship, prayer, chanting and singing with the aim of awakening love in the heart and opening oneself to God's grace. Bhakti may be directed toward God, Gods or one's spiritual preceptor. Bhakti yoga is embodied in Patanjali's Yoga Darshana (philosophy) in the second limb, niyamas (observances), as devotion (Ishvarapranidhana).

bhashya (bhāshya): भाष्य "Talking over, discussion." Commentary on a text. Hindu philosophies are largely founded upon the interpretations, or *bhashyas*, of primary scripture.

Bodhinatha Veylanswami (Bodhinātha Veylanswāmī): போதிநாத வேலன்சுவாமி "Lord of Wisdom, Holder of the Vel." The current preceptor of the Nandinatha Sampradaya's Kailasa Parampara, and Guru Mahasannidhanam of Kauai Aadheenam, ordained by Satguru Sivaya Subramuniyaswami in 2001.

Brahma (Brahmā): ब्रह्मा The name of God in His aspect of Creator. Saivites consider Brahma, Vishnu and Rudra to be three of five aspects of Siva. Smartas group Brahma, Vishnu and Siva as a Holy Trinity in which Siva is the Destroyer. Not to be confused with Brahman. See: *Brahman; Parameshvara*.

brahmachari (brahmachārī): ब्रह्मचारी An unmarried male spiritual aspirant who practices continence, observes religious disciplines, including sadhana, devotion and service and who may be under simple vows. Also names one in the student stage, age 12 to 24 or until marriage.

brahmacharini (brahmachāriṇī): ब्रह्मचारिणी Feminine counterpart of *brahmachari*.

brahmacharya: ब्रह्मचर्य "Divine conduct." Controlling lust by remaining celibate when single, leading to faithfulness in marriage. See: *yama-niyama.*

Brahmaloka: ब्रह्मलोक The realm of the *sahasrara* chakra, it is the highest of the seven upper worlds. See: *loka.*

Brahman: ब्रह्मन् "Supreme Being; Expansive Spirit." From the root *brih,* "to grow, increase, expand." Name of God or Supreme Deity in the *Vedas,* where He is described as 1) the Transcendent Absolute, 2) the all-pervading energy and 3) the Supreme Lord or Primal Soul. These three correspond to Siva in His three perfections. Thus, Saivites know Brahman and Siva to be one and the same God, being both Nirguna Brahman and Saguna Brahman. Nirguna Brahman is God "without qualities" (guna); the formless, Absolute Reality known as Parabrahman or Parasiva, totally transcending guna (quality), manifest existence and even Parashakti, all of which exhibit perceivable qualities. Saguna Brahman is God "with qualities;" Siva in His perfections of Parashakti and Parameshvara: God as superconscious, omnipresent, all-knowing, all-loving and all-powerful. The term Brahman is not to be confused with 1) Brahma, the Creator God; 2) *Brahmana,* Vedic texts, nor with 3) brahmana, Hindu priest caste (English spelling: brahmin). See: *Brahma.*

Chakra: चक्र "Wheel." Any of the nerve plexuses or centers of force and consciousness located within the inner bodies of man. In the physical body there are corresponding nerve plexuses, ganglia and glands. The seven principal chakras are situated along the spinal cord from the base to the cranial chamber. Additionally, seven chakras exist below the spine. They are seats of instinctive consciousness, the origin of jealousy, hatred, envy, guilt, sorrow, etc. They constitute the lower or hellish world, called *Naraka* or *patala.* Thus, there are fourteen major chakras in all. The seven upper chakras are: 1) *muladhara* (base of spine): memory, time and space; 2) *svadhishthana* (below navel): reason; 3) *manipura* (solar plexus): willpower; 4) *anahata* (heart center): direct cognition; 5) *vishuddha* (throat): divine love; 6) *ajna* (third eye): divine sight; 7) *sahasrara* (crown of head): illumination, Godliness. The seven lower chakras are 1) *atala* (hips): fear and lust; 2) *vitala* (thighs): raging anger; 3) *sutala* (knees): retaliatory jealousy; 4) *talatala* (calves): prolonged mental confusion; 5) *rasatala* (ankles): selfishness; 6) *mahatala* (feet): absence of conscience; 7) *patala* (located in the soles of the feet): murder and malice. See: *Narakaloka.*

charya (charyā): चर्या "Conduct." Service and character building. See: *pada, Saiva Siddhanta.*

charya *marga* (charyā *mārga*): चर्यामार्ग Same as charya *pada.* See: *charya pada.*

charya *pada* (charyā *pāda*): चर्यापाद "Conduct stage." Stage of service and character building. The foundation for all further spiritual progress. See: *pada.*

Chellappaswami (Chellappaswāmī): செல்லப்பசுவாமி "Wealthy father." Reclusive siddha and 160th satguru (1840-1915) of the Nandinatha Sampradaya's Kailasa Parampara, he lived on Sri Lanka's Jaffna peninsula near Nallur Kandaswami Temple in a small hut where today there is a small samadhi shrine. Among his disciples was Siva Yogaswami, whom he trained intensely for five years and initiated as his successor. See: *Kailasa Parampara, Natha Sampradaya.*

Chettiar: செட்டியார் A particular clan or caste group of South Indian origin, predominantly a trading and agricultural group. In the varna system, they belong to the Vaishya clan. In Tamil Nadu 14% of the population belongs to the Chettiar community, which includes more than a dozen subgroups, such as the Nattukottai, Nagarathar and Senaithalaivar Chettiars. *Chettiar* is the third most dominant clan and surname in Tamil Nadu.

clairaudience: "Clear-hearing." Psychic or divine hearing, *divyashravana.* The ability to hear the inner currents of the nervous system, the *Aum* and other mystic tones. Hearing in one's mind the words of inner-plane beings or earthly beings not physically present. Also, hearing the high "eee" sound, or *nadanadi* shakti, through the day or while in meditation.

conscious mind: The external, everyday state of consciousness. See: *mind.*

consciousness: *Chitta* or *chaitanya.* 1) A synonym for mind-stuff, *chitta;* or 2) the condition or power of perception, awareness, apprehension.

contemplation: Religious or mystical absorption beyond meditation.

cosmos: The universe, or whole of creation, especially with reference to its order, harmony and completeness. See: *loka, three worlds.*

crown chakra: The *sahasrara* chakra. The thousand-petaled cranial center of divine consciousness at the crown of the head. See: *chakra.*

Dakshinamurti (**Dakshiṇāmūrti**): दक्षिणामूर्ति "South-facing form." Lord Siva depicted sitting under a banyan tree, silently teaching four rishis at His feet. See: *Siva.*

danda (daṇḍa): दण्ड "Staff of support." The staff carried by a sadhu or sannyasin, representing the *tapas* which he has taken as his only support, and the vivifying of *sushumna* and consequent Realization he seeks. *Danda* also connotes "penalty" or "sanction."

darshan(a) (darśana): दर्शन "Vision, sight." Seeing the Divine. Beholding, with inner or outer vision, a temple image, Deity, holy person or place, with the desire to inwardly contact and receive the grace and blessings of the venerated being or beings. Even beholding a photograph in the proper spirit is a form of darshana. Not only does the devotee seek to see the Divine, but to be seen as well, to stand humbly in the awakened gaze of the holy one, even if for an instant, such as in a crowded temple when thousands of worshipers file quickly past the enshrined Lord. Gods and gurus are thus said to "give" darshana, and devotees "take" darshana, with the eyes being the mystic locus through which energy is exchanged. This direct and personal two-sided apprehension is a central and highly sought-after experience of Hindu faith. Also: "point of view," doctrine or philosophy.

dashama bhaga (daśama bhāga): दशमभाग "One-tenth-part." Tithing. The traditional Hindu practice of tithing, giving one-tenth of one's income to a religious institution. It was once widespread in India.

Deity: "God." The image or murti installed in a temple, or the Mahadeva the murti represents.

deva: देव "Shining one." A being inhabiting the higher astral plane, in a subtle, nonphysical body. *Deva* is also used in scripture to mean "God or Deity."

Devaloka: देवलोक "Plane of radiant beings." A synonym of Maharloka, the higher astral plane, realm of the *anahata* chakra. See: *loka.*

Devaram: தேவாரம் The collected devotional hymns composed by Saints Tirujnana Sambandar (ca 600) Tirunavakarasu (Appar—a contemporary of Sambandar) and Sundaramurti (ca 800). These make up the first seven books of the *Tirumurai.* See: *Tirumurai.*

devasthanam (devasthānam): देवस्थानम् A facility offering food and lodging to religious pilgrims, usually for little or no charge.

devonic: Of or relating to the devas or their world.

dharana (dhāraṇā): धारणा "Concentration." From *dhri,* "to hold." See: *ashtanga yoga.*

dharma: धर्म From *dhri,* "to sustain; carry, hold." Hence dharma is "that which contains or upholds the cosmos." *Dharma* has manifold meanings, including: divine law, ethics, law of being, way of righteousness, religion, duty, virtue, justice, goodness and truth. Essentially, dharma is the orderly fulfillment of an inherent nature or destiny. Relating to the soul, it is the mode of conduct most conducive to spiritual advancement, the right and righteous path. There are four principal kinds of dharma, known collectively as *chaturdharma,* "four religious laws." 1) *rita* dharma: "Universal law." The laws of being and nature that contain and govern all forms, functions and processes, from galaxy clusters to the power of mental thought and perception. 2) varna dharma: "Law of one's kind." Social duty. Varna can mean "race, tribe, appearance, character, color, social standing, etc." Obligations and responsibilities within one's nation, society, community, class, occupational subgroup and family. 3) ashrama dharma: "Duties of life's stages." Human or developmental dharma, fulfilling of the duties of the four stages of life—brahmacharya (student), *grihastha* (householder), *vanaprastha* (elder advisor) and sannyasa (religious solitaire). 4) *svadharma:* "Personal obligations or duty." One's perfect individual pattern through life, according to one's own particular physical, mental and emotional nature; the application of dharma (dependent on personal karma) reflected in one's race, community, physical characteristics, health, intelligence, skills and aptitudes, desires and tendencies, religion, sampradaya, family and guru.

dharmashala (dharmaśāla): धर्मशाल "Abode of righteousness." A monastery or ashrama, offering religious training for monks and in some cases lay persons on pilgrimage or religious retreat. In Saiva Siddhanta Church, it also refers to branch monasteries of Kauai Aadheenam.

dhoti (dhotī): धोती (Hindi) A long, unstitched cloth wound about the lower part of the body, and sometimes passed between the legs and tucked into the waist. A traditional Hindu apparel for men. See: *veshti.*

dhyana (dhyāna): ध्यान "Meditation." See: *ashtanga yoga.*

diksha (dīkshā): दीक्षा "Initiation." Solemn induction by which one is entered into a new realm of spiritual awareness and practice by a teacher or preceptor through bestowing of blessings. Denotes initial or deepened connection with the teacher and his lineage and is usually accompanied by ceremony. Initiation, revered as a moment of awakening, may be bestowed by a touch, a word, a look or a thought. Most Hindu schools, and especially Saivism, teach that only with initiation from a satguru is enlightenment attainable.

Dipavali (Dīpāvalī): दीपावली "Row of Lights." A very popular home and community festival in October/November when Hindus of all denominations light oil or electric lights and set off fireworks in a joyful celebration of the victory of good over evil and light over darkness.

dualism: See: *dvaita-advaita.*

dvaita-advaita: द्वैत अद्वैत "Dual-nondual; twoness-not twoness." Among the most important categories in the classification of Hindu philosophies. Dvaita and advaita define two ends of a vast spectrum. **—dvaita:** The doctrine of dualism, according to which reality is ultimately composed of two irreducible principles, entities, truths, etc. God and soul, for example, are seen as eternally separate. Here are four related terms. **—dualistic:** Of or relating to dualism, concepts, writings, theories which treat dualities (good-and-evil, high-and-low, them-and-us) as fixed, rather than transcendable. **—pluralism:** A form of nonmonism which emphasizes three or more eternally separate realities, e.g., God, soul and world. **—advaita:** The doctrine of nondualism or monism, that reality is ultimately composed of one whole principle, substance or God, with no independent parts. In essence, all is God. **—monistic theism:** A dipolar view which encompasses both monism and dualism.

Enlightenment: For Saiva monists, Self Realization, samadhi without seed (nirvikalpa samadhi); the ultimate attainment, sometimes referred to as Paramatma darshana, or as atma darshana, "Self vision."

enstasy: A term coined by Mircea Eliade to contrast the Eastern view of bliss as "standing inside oneself" (enstasy) with the Western view as ecstasy, "standing outside oneself." A word chosen as the English equivalent of *samadhi.*

evolution of the soul: *Adhyatma prasara.* In Saiva Siddhanta, the soul's evolution is a progressive unfoldment, growth and maturing toward its inherent, divine destiny, which is complete merger with Siva. In its essence, each soul is ever perfect. But as an individual soul body emanated by God Siva, it is like a small seed yet to develop. As an acorn needs to be planted in the dark underground to grow into a mighty oak tree, so must the soul unfold out of the darkness of the *malas* to full maturity and realization of its innate oneness with God. The soul is not created at the moment of conception of a physical body. Rather, it is created in the Sivaloka. It evolves by taking on denser and denser sheaths—cognitive, instinctive-intellectual and pranic—until finally it takes birth in physical form in the Bhuloka. Then it experiences many lives, maturing through the reincarnation process. Thus, from birth to birth, souls learn and mature. ¶Evolution is the result of experience and the lessons derived from it. There are young souls just beginning to evolve, and old souls nearing the end of their earthly sojourn. In Saiva Siddhanta, evolution is understood as the removal of fetters which comes as a natural unfoldment, realization and expression of one's true, self-effulgent nature. This ripening or dropping away of the soul's bonds *(malas)* is called *malaparipakam.* The realization of the soul nature is termed *svanubhuti* (experience of the Self). ¶Self Realization leads to moksha, liberation from the three *malas* and the reincarnation cycles. Then evolution continues in the celestial worlds until the soul finally merges fully and indistinguishably into Supreme God Siva, the Primal Soul, Parameshvara. In his *Tirumantiram,* Rishi Tirumular calls this merger *vishvagrasa,* "total absorption." The evolution of the soul is not a linear progression, but an intricate, circular, many-faceted mystery. Nor is it at all encompassed in the Darwinian theory of evolution, which explains the origins of the human form as descended from earlier primates.

Ganesha (**Gaṇeśa**): गणेश "Lord of Categories." Or: "Lord of attendants *(gana)*," synonymous with *Ganapati.* Ganesha is a Mahadeva, the beloved elephant-faced Deity honored by Hindus of every sect.

Ganesha Chaturthi (Gaṇeśa Chaturthī): गणेश चतुर्थी The birthday of Lord Ganesha, a ten-day festival of August–September that culminates in a parade called Ganesha Visarjana. It is a time of rejoicing, when all Hindus worship together.

Ganga sadhana (Gaṅgā sādhana): गंगासाधन A practice for unburdening the mind, performed by releasing the energy of unwanted thoughts. An internal cleansing sadhana of sitting quietly by a river or stream and listening to the Aum sound as the water flows over the rocks. When a thought arises, it is mentally placed into a leaf held in the right hand, then gently tossed into the water. Then a flower is offered to thank the water for carrying away the thought. This is a subconscious cleansing process of letting go of hurts, anger, problems or whatever it is that rises in the mind to disturb the meditation.

God: Supernal being. Either the Supreme God, Siva, or one of the Mahadevas, great souls, who are among His creation.

Goddess: Female representation or manifestation of Divinity; Shakti or Devi. *Goddess* can refer to a female perception or depiction of a causal-plane being (Mahadeva) in its natural state, which is genderless, or it can refer to an astral-plane being residing in a female astral body.

God Realization: Direct and personal experience of the Divine within oneself. It can refer to either 1) savikalpa samadhi ("enstasy with form") in its various levels, from the experience of inner light to the realization of Satchidananda, pure consciousness, or 2) nirvikalpa samadhi ("enstasy without form"), union with the transcendent Absolute, Parasiva, the Self God, beyond time, form and space. Here, the expression *God Realization* is used to name both of the above samadhis, whereas *Self Realization* refers only to nirvikalpa samadhi.

Gods: Mahadevas, "great beings of light." Here, the plural form of *God* refers to extremely advanced beings existing in their self-effulgent soul bodies in the causal plane.

Gorakshanatha (Gorakshanātha): गोरक्षनाथ Profound siddha yoga master of the Adinatha Sampradaya (ca 950). Expounder and foremost guru of Siddha Siddhanta Saivism. He traveled and extolled the greatness of Siva throughout North India and Nepal where he and his guru, Matsyendranatha, are still highly revered.

grace: "Benevolence, love, giving," from the Latin *gratia,* "favor," "goodwill." God's power of revealment, *anugraha* shakti ("kindness, showing favor"), by which souls are awakened to their true, Divine nature. Grace in the unripe stages of the spiritual journey is experienced by the devotee as receiving gifts or boons, often unbidden, from God. The mature soul finds himself surrounded by grace. He sees all of God's actions as grace, whether they be seemingly pleasant and helpful or not. Grace is not only the force of illumination or revealment. It also includes Siva's other four powers—creation, preservation, destruction and concealment—through which He provides the world of experience and limits the soul's consciousness so that it may evolve. More broadly, grace is God's ever-flowing love and compassion, *karunya*, also known as *kripa* ("tenderness, compassion") and prasada (literally, "clearness, purity"). The concealment power is known as veiling grace, God's power to obscure the soul's divine nature, or *tirodhana* shakti, the particular energy of Siva that binds the three bonds of *anava*, karma and maya to the soul. It is a purposeful limiting of consciousness to give the opportunity to the soul to grow and mature through experience of the world.

grihastha (gṛihastha): गृहस्थ "Householder." Family man or woman. Family of a married couple and other relatives. Pertaining to family life. The purely masculine form of the word is *grihasthin,* and the feminine *grihasthi. Grihasthi* also names the home itself.

guha (guhā): गुहा "Cave."

guna (guṇa): गुण "Strand; quality." The three constituent principles of prakriti, primal nature. The three gunas are: 1) sattva: Quiescent, rarified, translucent, pervasive, reflecting the light of Pure Consciousness. 2) rajas: "Passion," inherent in energy, movement, action, emotion, life. 3) tamas: "Darkness," inertia, density, the force of contraction, resistance and dissolution.

guru: गुरु "Weighty one," indicating an authority of great knowledge or skill. A teacher or guide in any subject, such as music, dance, sculpture, but especially religion. Often preceded by a qualifying prefix. Hence, *kulaguru* (family teacher), *vinaguru* (vina teacher) and satguru (spiritual preceptor). In astrology, *guru* names the planet Jupiter, also known as Brihaspati. According to the *Advayataraka Upanishad* (14–18), *guru* means "dispeller *(gu)* of darkness *(ru)."*

guru *jayanti* (guru *jayantī*): गुरु जयन्ती Preceptor's birthday, celebrated as an annual festival by devotees. A *padapuja*, ritual bathing of his feet, is usually performed. If he is not physically present, the puja is done to the shri *paduka*, "revered sandals," which represent the guru and hold his vibration.

guru *mahasannidhanam* (guru *mahāsannidhānam*): गुरु महासन्निधानम् The spiritual head of a traditional *aadheenam*. See: *aadheenakartar*.

guru *parampara* (guru *paramparā*): गुरुपरंपरा "Preceptorial succession" (literally, "from one to another"). A line of spiritual gurus in authentic succession of initiation; the chain of mystical power and authorized continuity, passed from guru to guru. See: *sampradaya*.

guru *pitham* (guru *pīṭha*): गुरुपीठ "Seat; pedestal; foundation." 1) A religious seat, such as the throne of the abbot of a monastery. 2) An *aadheenam*, ashrama or matha established around such a seat of spiritual authority.

guru-shishya system (guru-śishya system): गुरुशिष्य "Master-disciple system." An important education system of Hinduism whereby the teacher conveys his knowledge and tradition to a student. Such knowledge, whether it be Vedic-Agamic art, architecture or spirituality, is imparted through the developing relationship between guru and disciple.

Hanuman (Hanumān):** हनुमान् (Hindi) From the Sanskrit *Hanumat,* "Large jawed." The powerful monkey God-King of the epic *Ramayana* and the central figure in the famous drama *Hanuman-Nataka.* The perfect devoted servant to his master, Rama, this popular Deity is the epitome of *dasya* bhakti, "servant's devotion."

hatha yoga (haṭha yoga): हठयोग "Forceful yoga." A system of physical and mental exercise developed in ancient times as a means of rejuvenation by rishis and *tapasvins,* used today in preparing the body and mind for meditation.

Hatha Yoga Pradipika (Haṭha Yoga Pradīpikā): हठयोगप्रदीपिका "Elucidation of hatha yoga." A 14th-century text of 389 verses by Svatmarama Yogin that describes the philosophy and practices of hatha yoga.

Hindu: हिन्दु A follower of, or relating to, Hinduism. See: *Hinduism*.

Hinduism (Hindu Dharma): हिन्दुधर्म India's indigenous religious and cultural system, followed today by nearly one billion adherents, mostly in India, but with a large diaspora in many other countries. Also called Sanatana Dharma, "Eternal Religion" and Vaidika Dharma, "Religion of the *Vedas.*" It is a family of myriad faiths with four primary denominations: Saivism, Vaishnavism, Shaktism and Smartism.

homa: होम "Fire-offering." A ceremony of offering oblations to the Gods through the medium of fire in a sanctified fire pit, *homakunda,* usually made of earthen bricks. *Homa* rites are prescribed in the *Vedas, Agamas* and *Dharma* and *Grihya Shastras.*

Iccha shakti (icchā śakti):** इच्छाशक्ति "Desire, will." One of Siva's three primary shaktis.

ida nadi (iḍā nāḍī): इडानाडी "Soothing channel." The feminine psychic current flowing along the spine.

im kaif (īm» kaīf»): ⌐◙┬ ⌐◘ ┬ (Shum) No awareness, state beyond that of singular awareness. Not a word for Self Realization, but the entry into that nonexperience. Pronounced *eem-kaw-eef*. See: *Shum*.

instinctive: "Natural" or "innate." From the Latin *instinctus,* "impelling, instigating." The drives and impulses that order the animal world and the physical and lower astral aspects of humans—for example, self-preservation, procreation, hunger and thirst, as well as the emotions of greed, hatred, anger, fear, lust and jealousy.

instinctive mind: Manas *chitta.* The lower mind, which controls the basic faculties of perception, movement, as well as ordinary thought and emotion.

internalized worship: Yoga. Worship or contact with God and Gods via meditation and contemplation rather than through external ritual.

Iraivan: இறைவன் "Worshipful one; divine one." One of the most ancient Tamil appellations for God. See: *San Marga Sanctuary.*

Iraivan Temple: See: *San Marga Sanctuary.*

Jagadacharya (*jagadāchārya*): जगदाचार्य "World teacher."

japa: जप "Recitation." Concentrated repeating of a mantra, silently or aloud, often counting on a mala or strand of beads. A cure for pride and arrogance, jealousy, fear and confusion.

jayanti (*jayantī*): जयन्ती "Birthday." See: *guru jayanti.*

jiva (*jīva*): जीव "Living, existing." From *jiv,* "to live." The individual soul, atman, during its embodied state.

jivanmukta (*jīvanmukta*): जीवन्मुक्त "Liberated soul." One who has attained nirvikalpa samadhi—the realization of the Self, Parasiva—and is liberated from rebirth while living in a human body. (Contrasted with *videhamukta,* one liberated at the point of death.) This attainment is the culmination of lifetimes of intense striving, sadhana and *tapas,* requiring total renunciation, sannyasa (death to the external world, denoted in the conducting of one's own funeral rites), in the current incarnation. While completing life in the physical body, the *jivanmukta* enjoys the ability to re-enter nirvikalpa samadhi again and again.

jnana (*jñāna*): ज्ञान "Knowledge; wisdom." The matured state of the soul. It is the wisdom that comes as an aftermath of the kundalini breaking through the door of Brahman into the realization of Parasiva, Absolute Reality. Jnana is the awakened, superconscious state (*karana* chitta) flowing into daily life situations.

jnana *shakti* (jñāna *śakti*): ज्ञानशक्ति "Power of wisdom." One of Siva's three primary shaktis. Also a name for Lord Karttikeya's *vel.*

jnana *pada* (jñāna *pāda*): ज्ञानपाद "Stage of wisdom." According to the Saiva Siddhanta rishis, jnana is the last of the four successive *padas* (stages) of spiritual unfoldment. It is the culmination of the third stage, the yoga *pada.* Also names the knowledge section of each *Agama.* See: *pada.*

jnani (jñānī): ज्ञानी "Sage." Possessing jnana. See: *jnana.*

jyoti: ज्योति "Light." In this text, an illumined being.

jyotisha: ज्योतिष From *jyoti,* "light." "The science of the lights (or stars)," Hindu astrology, analyzing events and circumstances, delineating character and determining auspicious moments, according to the positions and movements of heavenly bodies.

Kadaitswami (Kadaitswāmī): கடையிற்குவாமி "Marketplace swami." The 159th satguru of the Nandinatha Sampradaya's Kailasa Parampara. Born ca 1810; attained mahasamadhi October 13, 1891. Renouncing his career as a judge in Bangalore, South India, Kadaitswami became a sannyasin and trained under the Rishi from the Himalayas, who sent him on mission to Sri Lanka. For decades he spurred the Sri Lankan Saivites to greater spirituality through inspired talks and demonstrating siddhis. He initiated Chellappaswami as the next satguru in the parampara. Kadaitswami's initiation name was Muktiayanandaswami. See: *Kailasa Parampara, Natha Sampradaya.*

Kadavul: கடவுள் "Beyond and within." An ancient Tamil name for Lord Siva meaning, "He who is both immanent and transcendent, within and beyond." See: *Siva.*

kaif (*kaīf»*): ௐ ௧ Pure awareness aware only of itself. It only takes a moment to become aware of being aware; but to hold this state for any length of time, preparation has to be made.

Kailasa (Kailāsa): कैलास "Crystalline" or "abode of bliss." The Himalayan peak in Western Tibet; the earthly abode of Lord Siva, a pilgrimage destination for Hindus and Tibetan Buddhists.

Kailasa Parampara (Kailāsa Paramparā): कैलासपरंपरा A spiritual lineage of 163 siddhas, a major stream of the Nandinatha Sampradaya, proponents of the ancient philosophy of monistic Saiva Siddhanta. The first of these masters that history recalls was Maharishi Nandinatha (or Nandikesvara) 2,250 years ago, satguru to the great Tirumular (ca 200 bce) and seven other disciples, as stated in the *Tirumantiram.* The lineage continued down the centuries and is alive today—the first recent siddha known being the "Rishi from the Himalayas," so named because he descended from those holy mountains. In South India, he initiated Kadaitswami (ca 1810–1875), who in turn initiated Chellappaswami

(1840–1915). Chellappaswami passed the mantle of authority to Siva Yogaswami (1872–1964), who in 1949 initiated Sivaya Subramuniyaswami (1927–2001), who in 2001 ordained the current preceptor, Satguru Bodhinatha Veylanswami (1942–). See: *Natha Sampradaya.*

Kali Yuga: कलियुग "Dark Age." The Kali Yuga is the last age in the repetitive cycle of four phases of time the universe passes through. It is comparable to the darkest part of the night, as the forces of ignorance are in full power and many subtle faculties of the soul are obscured. See: *yuga.*

***karehana* (ka-reh-ā-na):** ௘⌒ா௭ The psychic current within the spine, called *ida* in Sanskrit, that is pink in color and flows downward, ending on the left side of the body. Feminine-passive in nature, *karehana* is the physical-emotional energy within the being.

karma: कर्म "Action," "deed." 1) any act or deed; 2) the principle of cause and effect; 3) a consequence or "fruit of action" *(karmaphala)* or "after effect" *(uttaraphala),* which sooner or later returns upon the doer. What we sow, we shall reap in this or future lives. Selfish, hateful acts *(papakarma* or *kukarma)* will bring suffering. Benevolent actions *(punyakarma* or *sukarma)* will bring loving reactions. Karma is threefold: *sanchita, prarabdha* and *kriyamana.* **—sanchita karma:** "Accumulated actions." The sum of all karmas of this life and past lives. **—prarabdha karma:** "Actions begun; set in motion." That portion of *sanchita* karma that is bearing fruit and shaping the events and conditions of the current life, including the nature of one's bodies, personal tendencies and associations. **—kriyamana karma:** "Being made."

karma yoga: कर्मयोग "Union through action." Selfless service.

Kauai Aadheenam: Monastery-temple complex founded by Sivaya Subramuniyaswami in 1970; international headquarters of Saiva Siddhanta Church.

***kavadi* (kāvadi):** காவடி A penance offered to Lord Murugan-Karttikeya, especially during Tai Pusam, consisting of carrying in procession a heavy, beautifully decorated, wooden object from which pots of milk hang which are to be used for His *abhisheka.* Often the penitent's tongue and other parts of the body are pierced with small silver spears or hooks.

***kavi* (kāvi):** காவி "Ocher-saffron color." A Tamil word for the color taken on by robes of sadhus who sit, meditate or live on the banks of the Ganga. Hence the color of the sannyasin's robes. The Sanskrit equivalent is *kashaya.*

khadi (khādī): खादी "Cotton." Indian handspun and hand-woven cloth. In today's use, khadi raw materials may be cotton, silk, or wool, which are spun into threads on a spinning wheel called a charkha.

kirtana (kīrtana): कीर्तन "Praising." Devotional singing and dancing in celebration of God, Gods and guru. An important form of congregational worship in many Hindu sects.

kosha (kośa): कोश "Sheath; vessel, container; layer." Philosophically, five sheaths through which the soul functions simultaneously in the various planes or levels of existence. They are sometimes compared to the layers of an onion. The koshas, in order of increasing subtlety, are as follows. **—annamaya kosha** ("Sheath composed of food"): The physical or odic body, very coarse in comparison to the faculties of the soul, yet indispensable for evolution and Self Realization, because only within it can all fourteen chakras fully function. See: *chakra.* **—pranamaya kosha** ("Sheath composed of prana"): Also known as the pranic or health body, or the etheric body or etheric double, it coexists within the physical body as its source of life, breath and vitality, and is its connection with the astral body. Prana moves in the *pranamaya* kosha as five primary currents or vayus, "vital airs or winds." *Pranamaya* kosha disintegrates at death along with the physical body. See: *prana.* **—manomaya kosha** ("Mind-formed sheath"): The lower astral body, from *manas,* "thought, will, wish." The instinctive-intellectual sheath of ordinary thought, desire and emotion. It is the seat of the indriyas—the sensory organs *(jnanendriyas)* and the motor organs *(karmendriyas).* The *manomaya* kosha takes form as the physical body develops and is discarded in the inner worlds before rebirth. It is understood in two layers: 1) the odic-causal sheath (buddhi) and 2) the odic-astral sheath (manas). **—vijnanamaya kosha** ("Sheath of cognition"): The mental or cognitive-intuitive sheath, also called the actinodic sheath. It is the vehicle of higher thought, *vijnana*—understanding, knowing, direct cognition, wisdom, intuition and creativity. **—anandamaya kosha** ("Body of bliss"): The intuitive-superconscious sheath or actinic-causal body. This inmost soul form *(svarupa)* is the ultimate foundation of all life, intelligence and higher faculties. Its essence is Parashakti (Pure Consciousness) and Parasiva (the Absolute). See: *soul.*

kovil: கோவில் Tamil word for temple (the formal spelling).

koyil: கோயில் Informal, colloquial spelling of *kovil.* See: *kovil.*

kriya pada (kriyā pāda): क्रियापाद "Stage of religious action; worship." The stage of worship and devotion, second of four progressive stages of maturation on the Saiva Siddhanta path of attainment. See: *pada.*

kriya shakti (kriyā śakti): क्रियाशक्ति "Action power." The universal force of doing. One of Siva's three primary shaktis.

kulaguru: कुलगुरु "Family preceptor" or "family teacher." The *kulaguru* guides the joint and extended family, particularly through the heads of families, and provides spiritual education. He may or may not be a satguru.

kulam: குலம் "Family" or "clan." Here, one of the five monastic "family" groups at Kauai Aadheenam, each with specific areas of service and responsibility, that collectively encompass all the needs of the monastery.

kulapati: कुलपति "Family head." The title of a male family leader, or missionary, in Saiva Siddhanta Church, the head of an extended family of members and students assigned to his oversight. His wife's title is *kulamata.*

kulapati family: The extended family of Church members and students headed by a particular *kulapati,* or missionary, of Saiva Siddhanta Church.

kumbha(m): कुम्भ "Jar or pot; water vessel." *Kumbhas,* usually metal or clay, are used in temple pujas and *homas.*

kumbhabhisheka(m) (kumbhābhisheka): कुम्भाभिषेक "Water pot ablution." The formal consecration of a new temple and its periodic reconsecration (usually at twelve-year intervals) following renovation and renewal. The rites culminate with the priests' pouring sanctified water over the temple spires, which resemble an inverted pot, or *kumbha.*

kundalini (kuṇḍalinī): कुण्डलिनी "She who is coiled; serpent power." The primordial cosmic energy in every individual which, at first, lies coiled like a serpent at the base of the spine and eventually, through the practice of yoga, rises up the *sushumna nadi.* As it rises, the kundalini awakens each successive chakra. Nirvikalpa samadhi, enlightenment, comes as it pierces through the door of Brahman at the core of the *sahasrara* and enters. Kundalini shakti then returns to rest in any one of the seven chakras. Sivasayujya is complete when the kundalini arrives back in the *sahasrara* and remains coiled in this crown chakra.

kundalini yoga (kuṇḍalinī yoga): कुण्डलिनीयोग "Uniting the serpent power." Advanced meditative practices and sadhana techniques, a part of raja yoga, performed to deliberately arouse the kundalini power and guide it up the spine into the crown chakra, *sahasrara.* In its highest form, this yoga is the natural result of sadhanas and *tapas* well performed, rather than a distinct system of striving and teaching in its own right.

kutir (kuṭīr): कुटीर "Cottage" or "hut."

kuttuvilakku: குத்துவிளக்கு A standing metal lamp kept in the temple, shrine room or home, with several wicks fed by ghee or sesame oil.

Liberal Hinduism: A synonym for Smartism and the closely related neo-Indian religion. See: *neo-Indian religion, Smartism.*

liberation: Moksha, release from the bonds of *pasha,* after which the soul is liberated from samsara (the round of births and deaths). In Saiva Siddhanta, *pasha* is the threefold bondage of *anava,* karma and maya, which limit and confine the soul to the reincarnational cycle so that it may evolve. Moksha is freedom from the fettering power of these bonds, which do not cease to exist, but no longer have the power to fetter or bind the soul.

Linga(m) (Liṅga): लिङ्ग "Mark." See: *Sivalinga, svayambhu Linga.*

liunasi (līūnasī): ᤢᤱᤠ (Shum) Feeling life force flowing through one's nerves within the physical body and subtle body; becoming aware of the energy flow within and around the body.

locavore: Someone who exclusively (or at least primarily) eats foods from their local area (commonly either 100 or 250 miles, depending on location). By eating locally, most locavores hope to create a greater connection between themselves and their food sources, resist industrialized and processed foods, and support their local economy.

loka: लोक "World, habitat, realm, or plane of existence." From *loc,* "to shine, be bright, visible." A dimension of manifest existence; cosmic region. Each *loka* reflects or involves a particular range of consciousness. The three primary *lokas* are 1) Bhuloka: "Earth world." The world perceived through the five senses, also called the gross plane, as it is the most dense of the worlds. 2) Antarloka: "Inner or in-between world." Known in English as the subtle or astral plane, the intermediate dimension between the physical and causal worlds, where souls in their astral bodies sojourn between incarnations and when they sleep. 3) Sivaloka: "World of Siva," and of the Gods and highly evolved souls. The causal plane, also called Karanaloka. Existing deep within the Antarloka at a higher level of vibration, it is a world of superconsciousness and extremely refined energy. It is the plane of creativity and intuition, the quantum level of the universe, where souls exists in self-effulgent bodies made of actinic particles of light. It is here that God and Gods move and lovingly guide the evolution of all the worlds and shed their ever-flowing grace.

Mahabharata *(Mahābhārata):* महाभारत "Great Epic of India." The world's longest epic poem. It revolves around the conflict between two royal families, the Pandavas and the Kauravas, and their great battle of Kurukshetra near modern Delhi in approximately 1424 BCE. The *Mahabharata* is revered as scripture by Vaishnavites and Smartas.

Mahadeva (Mahādeva): महादेव "Great shining one;" "God." Referring either to God Siva or any of the highly evolved beings who live in the Sivaloka in their natural, effulgent soul bodies. God Siva in His perfection as Primal Soul is one of the Mahadevas, yet He is unique and incomparable in that He alone is uncreated, the Father-Mother and Destiny of all other Mahadevas. He is called Parameshvara, "Supreme God." He is the Primal Soul, whereas the other Gods are individual souls.

maharishi (maharshi): महर्षि "Great seer." Title for the greatest and most influential of siddhas.

mahasamadhi (mahāsamādhi): महासमाधि "Great enstasy." The death, or giving up of the physical body, of a great soul, an event which occasions tremendous blessings. Also names the shrine in which the remains of a great soul are entombed.

Mahasivaratri (Mahāśivarātri): महाशिवरात्रि "Siva's great night." Saivism's foremost festival, celebrated on the night before the new moon in February–March. Fasting and an all-night vigil are observed as well as other disciplines: chanting, praying, meditating and worshiping Siva as the Source and Self of all that exists.

mahavakya(m) (mahāvākya): महावाक्य "Great saying." A profound aphorism from scripture or a holy person. Most famous are four Upanishadic proclamations: *Prajanam Brahma* ("Pure consciousness is God"–*Aitareya U.*), *Aham Brahmasmi* ("I am God"—*Brihadaranyaka U.*), *Tat tvam asi* ("Thou art That"—*Chandogya U.*) and *Ayam atma Brahma* ("The soul is God"—*Mandukya U.*).

Maheshvara (Maheśvara): महेश्वर "Great Lord." In Saiva Siddhanta, the name of Siva's energy of veiling grace, one of five aspects of Parameshvara, the Primal Soul. Maheshvara is also a popular name for Lord Siva as Primal Soul and personal Lord. See: *Parameshvara.*

mala: मल "Impurity." An important term in Saivism referring to the three bonds, called pasha—*anava,* karma and maya—which limit the soul, preventing it from knowing its true, divine nature.

mala (mālā): माला "Garland." A strand of beads for holy recitation, japa, usually made of rudraksha, *tulasi,* sandalwood or crystal. Also a flower garland.

mambashum (mambashūm): ꓷ◌◌⁻ (Shum) A map or diagram written in the Shum language, designating specific areas of the mind to explore in meditation.

mandapa(m) (maṇḍapa): मण्डप From *mand,* "to deck, adorn." Temple precinct; a temple compound, open hall or chamber. In entering a large temple, one passes through a series of *mandapas,* each named according to its position, e.g., *mukhamandapa,* "facing chamber."

mantra(m): मन्त्र "Mystic formula." A sound, syllable, word or phrase endowed with special power, usually drawn from scripture.

matha (maṭha): मठ "Monastery." See: *monastery.*

mathavasi (maṭhavāsi): मठवासि "Monastic; monastery dweller." See: *monk.*

maya (māyā): माया "She who measures;" or "mirific energy." In Saiva Siddhanta, the substance emanated from Siva through which the world of form is manifested. Hence all creation is also termed maya. It is the cosmic creative force, the principle of manifestation, ever in the process of creation, preservation and dissolution.

meditation: Dhyana. Sustained concentration. Meditation describes a quiet, alert, powerfully concentrated state wherein new knowledge and insights are awakened from within as awareness focuses one-pointedly on an object or specific line of thought.

mendicant: A beggar; a wandering monk who lives on alms.

mental plane: Names the refined strata of the subtle world. In Sanskrit, it is called Maharloka or Devaloka, realm of the *anahata* chakra. Here the soul is shrouded in the mental or cognitive sheath, *vijnanamaya* kosha.

metaphysics: 1) The branch of philosophy dealing with first causes and nature of reality. 2) The science of mysticism.

Meykandar: மெய்கண்டார் "Truth seer." A 13th-century Tamil theologian, author (or translator from the *Raurava Agama*) of the *Sivajnanabodham*. Founder of the Meykandar Sampradaya of pluralistic Saiva Siddhanta.

mind (five states): A view of the mind in five parts. **—conscious mind** (*jagrat chitta,* "wakeful consciousness"): The ordinary, waking, thinking state of mind. **—subconscious mind** (samskara *chitta,* "impression mind"): The part of mind "beneath" the conscious mind; the storehouse or recorder of all experience, whether remembered consciously or not. The holder of past impressions, reactions and desires. Also, the seat of involuntary physiological processes. **—subsubconscious mind** (vasana *chitta,* "mind of subliminal traits"): The area of the subconscious mind formed when two thoughts or experiences of the same rate of intensity are sent into the subconscious at different times and, intermingling, give rise to a new and totally different rate of vibration. **—superconscious mind** *(karana chitta):* The mind of light; the all-knowing intelligence of the soul. At its deepest level, the superconscious is Parashakti, or Satchidananda, the Divine Mind of God Siva. **—subsuperconscious mind** *(anukarana chitta):* The superconscious mind working through the conscious and subconscious states, which brings forth intuition, clarity and insight.

mind (three phases): A perspective of mind as instinctive, intellectual and superconscious. **—instinctive mind** (manas *chitta*): The seat of desire and governor of sensory and motor organs. **—intellectual mind** (buddhi *chitta*): The faculty of thought and intelligence. **—superconscious mind** *(karana chitta):* The strata of intuition, benevolence and spiritual sustenance. Its most refined essence is Parashakti, or Satchidananda, all-knowing, omnipresent consciousness, the One transcendental, self-luminous, divine mind common to all souls.

moksha: मोक्ष "Liberation." Release from transmigration, samsara, the round of births and deaths, which occurs after karma has been resolved and nirvikalpa samadhi—realization of the Self, Parasiva—has been attained. Same as *mukti.*

monastery: "Place of solitariness." Matha. The age-old tradition, carried forward from Lemurian times into the Hindu culture of India, a sacred place where those of the same gender go through their birth karmas together toward realization of the Self. Living under strict vows, they thrive. Most monasteries are cloisters for men, though monasteries for women, headed by female ascetics, also exist in the Hindu tradition. Male and female monasteries are traditionally situated several miles or more from one another. Monasteries, in the correct sense of the word, are for individuals on the path of enlightenment who have arrived at a certain subsuperconscious state and wish to stay there. Therefore, they release various interactions with the world, physically and emotionally, and seek to remain poised in a contemplative monastic lifestyle. The intention of monastic life is to put oneself in a self-imposed intensity where unfoldment of the spirit can be catalyzed more quickly and more fully than in family life, or in a commune or coed ashram situation where the two genders live together. In monasteries, residents are dedicated to transmutation of the sexual energies, therefore celibacy is strictly upheld and there is no fraternizing with the opposite sex.

monism: "Doctrine of oneness." 1) The philosophical view that there is only one ultimate substance or principle. 2) The view that reality is a unified whole without independent parts. See: *dvaita-advaita.*

monistic theism: Advaita Ishvaravada. The doctrine that reality is a one whole or existence without independent parts, coupled with theism, the belief that God exists as a real, conscious, personal Supreme Being—two perspectives ordinarily considered contradictory or mutually exclusive, since theism implies dualism.

monk: A celibate man wholly dedicated to religious life, either cenobitic (residing with others in a monastery) or anchoritic (living alone, as a hermit or mendicant). Literally, "one who lives alone" (from the Greek *monos,* "alone"). Through the practice of yoga, the control and transmutation of the masculine and feminine forces within himself, the monk is a complete being, free to follow the contemplative and mystic life toward realization of the Self within. Benevolent and strong, courageous, fearless, not entangled in the thoughts and feelings of others, monks are affectionately detached from society, defenders of the faith, kind, loving and ever-flowing with timely wisdom. A synonym for *monastic.* See: *sannyasa.*

mridanga(m) (mṛidaṅga): मृदङ्ग A South Indian concert drum, barrel-shaped and two-headed.

mudra (mudrā): मुद्रा "Seal." Esoteric hand gestures which express specific energies or powers. Usually accompanied by precise visualizations, mudras are a vital element of ritual worship (puja), dance and yoga.

mukti: मुक्ति "Release," "liberation." A synonym for *moksha.*

muladhara chakra (mūlādhāra chakra): मूलाधारचक्र "Root-support wheel." Four-petaled psychic center at the base of the spine; governs memory. See: *chakra.*

murti (mūrti): मूर्ति "Form; manifestation, embodiment, personification." An image, icon or effigy of God or a God, into which the Deity's presence is invoked during worship.

Murugan: முருகன் "Beautiful one," a favorite name of Karttikeya among the Tamils of South India, Sri Lanka and elsewhere.

Nada *(nāda):* नाद "Sound; tone, vibration." Metaphysically, the mystic sounds of the Eternal, of which the highest is the transcendent Soundless Sound, Paranada, the first vibration from which creation emanates. Paranada is so pure and subtle that it cannot be identified to the denser regions of the mind. From Paranada comes Pranava, Aum, and further evolutes of *nada.* These are experienced by the meditator as the *nadanadi* shakti, "energy current of sound," heard pulsing through the nerve system as a steady high-pitched hum, much like a tambura, an electrical transformer, a swarm of bees or a shruti box. Listening to the inner sounds is a contemplative practice called *nada upasana* (worship through sound), *nada anusandhana* (cultivation of inner sound) or *nada* yoga (union through sound). Subtle variations of the *nadanadi* shakti represent the psychic wavelengths of established guru lineages of many Indian religions. *Nada* also refers to other psychic sounds heard during deep meditation, including those resembling various musical instruments. *Nada* also refers to ordinary sound.

nadanadi shakti (nādanāḍī śakti): नादनाडीशक्ति "Energy current of sound." See: *nada.*

nadi (nāḍī): नाडी "Conduit; river." A nerve fiber or energy channel of the subtle (inner) bodies of man. It is said there are 72,000 *nadis.* These interconnect the chakras. The three main *nadis* are *ida, pingala* and *sushumna.* 1) The *ida nadi,* also known as *chandra* (moon) *nadi,* is pink in color. It flows downward, ending on the left side of the body. This current is feminine in nature and is the channel of physical-emotional energy. 2) The *pingala nadi,* also known as surya (sun) *nadi,* is blue in color. It flows upward, ending on the right side of the body. This current is masculine in nature and is the channel of intellectual-mental energy. 3) The *sushumna nadi,* pale yellow in color, is the major nerve current which passes through the spinal column from the *muladhara* chakra at the base to the *sahasrara* at the crown of the head. It is the channel of kundalini.

nadi jyotisha: நாடி ஜோதிடம் A form of astrology practiced in Tamil Nadu based on the belief that the past, present and future lives of all humans were foreseen by rishis in ancient times and recorded on palm-leaf manuscripts (*nadi* shastra, or *nadi* grantha) in an ancient Tamil script. To do a life reading, a *nadi* astrologer, or shastri, locates the appropriate leaf based upon the person's thumb print and other factors. Then he interprets the etching on the leaf. This art of divination was made famous by *nadi* shastris around the Vaitheeswaran Temple, near Chidambaram; the astrology is centered there to this day and practiced by their descendants.

nadi shastra: நாடி சாஸ்திரம் See: *nadi jyotisha.*

nadi shastri: நாடி சாஸ்திரி See: *nadi jyotisha.*

naga (nāga): नाग "Serpent," often the cobra; symbol of the kundalini coiled on the four petals of the *muladhara* chakra. See: *kundalini, muladhara chakra.*

nagasvara (nāgasvara): नागस्वर "Snake note." A double-reed woodwind about three feet long, similar to an oboe but more shrill and piercing, common in South India, played at Hindu pujas and processions with the *tavil,* a large two-headed drum.

naivedya(m): नैवेद्य Food offered to the Deity at the temple or home altar. An important element in puja. See: *prasada, puja.*

nakshatra: नक्षत्र "Star cluster." Central to astrological determinations, the *nakshatras* are 27 star clusters, constellations, which lie along the ecliptic, or path of the sun. An individual's *nakshatra,* or birth star, is the constellation the moon was aligned with at the time of birth.

namakarana (nāmakaraṇa): नामकरण "Name giving."

namakarana samskara (nāmakaraṇa saṁskāra): नामकरण संस्कार "Name giving rite" and formal entry into one or another sect of Hinduism, performed 11 to 41 days after birth. The name is chosen according to astrology, preferably the name of a God or Goddess. At this time, guardian devas are assigned to see the child through life. One who converts to or adopts Hinduism later in life would receive this same sacrament.

Namasivaya (Namaḥ Śivāya): नमः शिवाय "Adoration (homage) to Siva." The supreme mantra of Saivism, known as the Panchakshara, or "five syllables."

namaskara (namaskāra): नमस्कार "Reverent salutations." Traditional Hindu verbal greeting and mudra where the palms are joined together and held before the heart or raised to the level of the forehead. The mudra is also called *anjali.* It is a devotional gesture made equally before a temple Deity, holy person, friend or even momentary acquaintance.

Nandikeshvara Kashika (Nandikeśvara Kāśikā): नन्दिकेश्वरकाशिका The only surviving work of Nandikeshvara (ca 250 BCE). Its 26 verses are the earliest extant exposition of advaitic Saivism, aside from the *Saiva Agamas.*

Nandinatha Sampradaya (Nandinātha Saṁpradāya): नन्दिनाथसंप्रदाय See: *Natha Sampradaya.*

Narakaloka: नरकलोक Abode of darkness. Literally, "pertaining to man." The nether worlds; a gross, hellish region of the Antarloka. Naraka is a congested, distressful area where demonic beings and young souls may sojourn until they resolve the darksome karmas they have created. Here beings suffer the consequences of their own misdeeds in previous lives. Naraka is understood as having seven regions, called *talas,* corresponding to the states of consciousness of the seven lower chakras.

Nataraja (Naṭarāja): नटराज "King of Dance" or "King of Dancers." God as the Cosmic Dancer. Perhaps Hinduism's richest and most eloquent symbol, Nataraja represents Siva, the Primal Soul, Parameshvara, as the power, energy and life of all that exists. This is Siva's intricate state of Being in Manifestation. The dance of Siva as Natesha, Lord of Dancers, is the rhythmic movement of the entire cosmos. All that is, whether sentient or insentient, pulsates in His body, and He within it. Both male and female elements are depicted in this icon—as they are in Ardhanarishvara, the "half-female God," symbol of the inseparable nature of Siva-Shakti.

Natchintanai: நற்சிந்தனை The collected songs of Siva Yogaswami (1872–1964) of Jaffna, Sri Lanka, extolling the power of the satguru, worship of Lord Siva, adherance to the path of dharma and striving for the attainment of Self Realization.

Natha (Nātha): नाथ "Master, lord; adept." An ancient Himalayan tradition of Saiva yoga mysticism whose first historically known exponent was Nandikeshvara (ca 250 bce). *Natha*—Self-Realized adept—designates the extraordinary ascetic masters (or devotees) of this school.

Natha Sampradaya (Nātha Saṁpradāya): नाथसंप्रदाय "Traditional doctrine of knowledge of masters," a philosophical and yogic tradition of Saivism whose origins precede recorded history. This oldest of Saivite sampradayas existing today consists of two major streams: the Nandinatha and the Adinatha. The Nandinatha Sampradaya has had as exemplars Maharishi Nandinatha and his disciples, Patanjali (author of the *Yoga Sutras*) and Tirumular (author of *Tirumantiram*). Among its representatives today are the successive siddhars of the Kailasa Parampara. The Adinatha lineage's earliest known exemplars are Maharishi Adinatha, Matsyendranatha and Gorakshanatha, who founded a well-known order of yogis. See: *Kailasa Parampara.*

natyam (nāṭyam): नाट्यम् Literally, "divine dancer." Here, a Sanskrit and Shum word naming a monk who is a sannyasin or is training to become one.

neti pot: A small vessel used to pour a saline solution into the nose in order to flush out the nasal passages. Typically it has a spout attached near the bottom, sometimes with a handle on the opposite side. Neti pots are traditionally made of metal, glass or ceramic. *Jala neti,* "nasal cleansing," is an ancient hygienic practice integral to ayurveda and yoga.

New Age: According to *Webster's New World Dictionary:* "Of or pertaining to a cultural movement popular in the 1980s [and ever since] characterized by a concern with spiritual consciousness, and variously combining belief in reincarnation and astrology with such practices as meditation, vegetarianism and holistic medicine."

nirvani & upadeshi (nirvāṇī & upadeśī): निर्वाणी उपदेशी *Nirvani* means "extinguished one," and *upadeshi* means "teacher." In general, *nirvani* refers to a liberated soul, or to a certain class of monk. *Upadeshi* refers to a teacher, generally a renunciate. Here, these two terms have special meaning, similar to the Buddhist *arhat* and *bodhisattva,* naming the two earthly modes of the realized, liberated soul. After full illumination, the *jivanmukta* has the choice to return to the world to help others along the path. This is the way of the *upadeshi* (akin to *bodhisattva*), exemplified by the benevolent satguru who leads seekers to the goal of God Realization. He may found and direct institutions and monastic lineages. The *nirvani* (akin to *arhat*) abides at the pinnacle of consciousness, shunning all worldly involvement. He is typified by the silent ascetic, the reclusive sage.

nirvikalpa samadhi (nirvikalpa samādhi): निर्विकल्पसमाधि "Undifferentiated trance, enstasy (samadhi) without form or seed." The realization of the Self, Parasiva, a state of oneness beyond all change or diversity; beyond time, form and space. See: *samadhi.*

niyama: नियम "Restraint." See: *yama-niyama.*

Odic force: Spiritually magnetic, of or pertaining to consciousness within *ashuddha* maya, the realm of the physical and lower astral planes. Odic force in its rarefied state is prakriti, the primary gross energy of nature, manifesting in the three gunas: sattva, rajas and tamas. All matter—earth, water, fire and air, as well as thought—is composed of odic force. It is the force of attraction and repulsion between people and between people and their things, and manifests as masculine (aggressive) and feminine (passive), arising from the *pingala* and *ida* currents. These two currents *(nadis)* are found within the spine of the subtle body. Odic force is a magnetic, sticky, binding substance that people seek to develop when they want to bind themselves together, such as in partnerships, marriage, guru-shishya relationships and friendships. It, of itself, is stagnant and unflowing. Odic energy is the combined emanation of the *pranamaya* and *annamaya* koshas. See also: *actinic, kosha, subtle body, tattva.*

Pada: पद "Step, pace, stride; footstep, trace."
pada (pāda): पाद "The foot (of men and animals); quarter-part, section; stage; path." Names the major sections of the Agamic texts and the corresponding stages of practice and unfoldment on the path to moksha. According to Saiva Siddhanta, there are four *padas* (charya, kriya, yoga and jnana) which are successive and cumulative; i.e. in accomplishing each one the soul prepares itself for the next. **—charya pada:** "Good conduct stage." Learning to live righteously and serve selflessly, performing karma yoga. **—kriya pada:** "Religious action; worship stage." Stage of bhakti yoga, of cultivating devotion through performing puja and regular daily sadhana. **—yoga pada:** Having matured in the charya and kriya *padas,* the soul now turns to internalized worship and raja yoga under the guidance of a satguru. **—jnana pada:** "Stage of wisdom." Once the soul has attained Realization, it is henceforth a wise one who lives out the life of the body, shedding blessings on mankind.

pādapūjā: पादपूजा "Foot worship." Ceremonial worship of the guru's sandals or holy feet, often through ablution with precious substances and offering of fruit and flowers. After the ceremony, the water of the bath, the fruit and other precious substances are partaken of as prasada by the devotees.

padmasana (*padmāsana*): पद्मासन "Lotus posture." The most famous hatha yoga asana, the optimum pose for sustained meditation. The legs are crossed with the feet resting on the thighs, close to the body, with soles upward, resembling a lotus flower. In this pose the intellectual-emotional energies are balanced and quieted.

paduka (*pādukā*): पादुका "Sandals." Shri *paduka* refers to the sandals of the preceptor, the traditional icon of the guru, representing his venerable feet and worshiped as the source of grace.

panentheism: "All-in-God doctrine." The view that the universe is part of the being of God, as distinguished from pantheism ("all-is-God doctrine"), which identifies God with the total reality. In contrast, panentheism holds that God pervades the world, but is also beyond it. He is immanent and transcendent, relative and Absolute. This embracing of opposites is called dipolar. For the panentheist, God is in all, and all is in God. Panentheism is the technical term for monistic theism. See: *dvaita-advaita, monistic theism.*

papa (*pāpa*): पाप "Wickedness or sin;" "crime." 1) Bad or evil. 2) Wrongful action. 3) Demerit earned through wrongdoing. *Papa* includes all forms of wrongdoing, from the simplest infraction to the most heinous crime, such as premeditated murder. Each act of *papa* carries its karmic consequence, *karmaphala,* "fruit of action," for which scriptures delineate specific penance for expiation. Those who have awakened psychic sight can clearly see *papa* in the inner subconscious aura of a person as a colorful, sticky, astral substance. *Papa* is seen as dark, unrelated colors, whereas its counterpart, punya, is seen as pastels. The color arrangements are not unlike modern art murals. *Papa* colors can produce disease, depression, loneliness and such, but can be dissolved through penance *(prayashchitta),* austerity *(tapas)* and good deeds *(sukritya).*

Paramatman (Paramātman): परमात्मन् "Supreme Self," or "transcendent soul." Parasiva, Absolute Reality, the one transcendent Self of every soul. Contrasted with atman, which includes all three aspects of the soul: Parasiva, Parashakti and *anandamaya* kosha. See: *Parasiva, Self, soul.*

Parameshvara (Parameśvara): परमेश्वर "Supreme Lord or Ruler." God Siva's third perfection, Supreme Mahadeva, Siva-Shakti, mother of the universe. In this perfection, as personal, father-mother God, Siva is a person—who has a body, with head, arms and legs, etc.—who acts, wills, blesses, gives darshan, guides, creates, preserves, reabsorbs, obscures and enlightens. In Truth, it is Siva-Shakti who does all. The term *Primal Soul,* Paramapurusha, designates Parameshvara as the original, uncreated soul, the creator of all other souls. Parameshvara has many other names and titles, including those denoting the five divine actions—Sadasiva, the revealer; Maheshvara, the obscurer; Brahma, the creator; Vishnu the preserver; and Rudra the destroyer.

parampara (paramparā): परंपरा "Uninterrupted succession." A lineage.

Parasiva (Paraśiva): परशिव "Transcendent Siva." The Self God, Siva's first perfection, Absolute Reality. Parasiva is *That* which is beyond the grasp of consciousness, transcends time, form and space and defies description. To merge with the Absolute in mystic union is the ultimate goal of all incarnated souls, the reason for their living on this planet, and the deepest meaning of their experiences. Attainment of this is called Self Realization or nirvikalpa samadhi.

parivrajaka (*parivrājaka*): परिव्राजक "Spiritual wanderer." An itinerent Hindu monk.

Parvati (Pārvatī): पार्वती "Mountain's daughter." One of many names for the Universal Mother. Prayers are offered to Her for strength, health and eradication of impurities. Mythologically, Parvati is wedded to Siva. See: *Goddess, Shakti.*

Patanjali (Patañjali): पतञ्जलि A Saivite Natha siddha (ca 200 bce) who codified the ancient Yoga Darshana (philosophy) which outlines the path to enlightenment through purification, control and transcendence of the mind.

pathashala (*pāṭhaśāla*): पाठशाल "Place of lessons." A school for training temple priests.

Pati: पति "Master; lord; owner." A name for God Siva indicating His commanding relationship with souls as caring ruler and helpful guide. See: *Pati-pashu-pasha.*

Pati-pashu-pasha (Pati-paśu-pāśa): पति पशु पाश Literally, "Master, cow and tether." These are the three primary elements *(padartha,* or *tattvatrayi)* of Saiva Siddhanta philosophy: God, soul and world—Divinity, man and cosmos—seen as a mystically and intricately interrelated unity. Pati is God, envisioned as a cowherd. *Pashu* is the soul, envisioned as a cow. *Pasha* is the all-important force or fetter by which God brings souls along the path to Truth. The various schools of Hinduism define the rapport among the three in varying ways. For pluralistic Saiva Siddhantins they are three beginningless verities, self-existent, eternal entities. For monistic Saiva Siddhantins, *pashu* and *pasha* are the temporary, emanational creation of Pati, God Siva, destined to be reabsorbed into Him like waves into the ocean; He alone is eternal reality. See: *Saiva Siddhanta, soul.*

penance: *Prayashchitta.* Atonement, expiation. An act of devotion (bhakti), austerity *(tapas)* or discipline *(sukritya)* undertaken to soften or nullify the anticipated reaction to a past action.

pilgrimage: *Tirthayatra.* Journeying to a holy temple, near or far, performed by all Hindus at least once each year.

Pillaiyar: பிள்ளையார் Ganesha in the form of the Noble Child.

pingala (piṅgalā): पिंगला "Tawny channel." The masculine psychic current flowing along the spine. See: *nadi.*

pitham (pīṭha): पीठ "Seat; pedestal; foundation." 1) The base or pedestal of the Sivalinga, or of any Deity idol. 2) A religious seat, such as the throne of the abbot of a monastery. 3) An *aadheenam,* ashrama or matha established around such a seat of spiritual authority.

Pongal festival: *See:* Tai Pongal.

pottu: பொட்டு "A drop, small particle, dot." Small dot worn on the forehead between the eyebrows, or in the middle of the forehead, made of red powder *(kunkuma),* sandalpaste, clay, cosmetics or other substance. The pottu is known as *bindu* in Sanskrit, and *bindi* in Hindi.

prana (prāṇa): प्राण Vital energy or life principle. Literally, "vital air," from the root *pran,* "to breathe." Prana in the human body moves in the *pranamaya* kosha as five primary life currents known as vayus, "vital airs or winds." Prana sometimes denotes the power or animating force of the cosmos, the sum total of all energy and forces.

pranam(a) (praṇāma): प्रणाम "Obeisance; bowing down." Reverent salutation in which the head or body is bowed. There are two types of prostration, as follows. 1) ashtanga *pranama* ("Eight-limbed obeisance"): the full prostration for men, in which the hands, chest, forehead, knees and feet touch the ground (it is the same as *shashtanga* pranama); and 2) *panchanga* pranama ("Five-limbed obeisance"): the woman's form of prostration, in which the hands, head and knees touch the ground (with the ankles crossed, right over the left). A more exacting term for prostration is *pranipata,* "falling down in obeisance."

pranayama (prāṇāyāma): प्राणायाम "Breath control." Science of controlling prana through breathing techniques in which the lengths of inhalation, retention and exhalation are modulated. Pranayama prepares the mind for meditation. See: *ashtanga yoga.*

pranic (prāṇic): Of or related to prana. See: *prana.*

pranic body (prāṇic body): The subtle, life-giving sheath called *pranamaya* kosha. See: *kosha.*

prapatti: प्रपत्ति "Throwing oneself down." Bhakti—total, unconditional submission to God, often coupled with the attitude of personal helplessness, self-effacement and resignation. A term especially used in Vaishnavism to name a concept extremely central to virtually all Hindu schools. See: *grace.*

prarabdha karma (prārabdha karma): प्रारब्धकर्म "Action that has been unleashed or aroused." See: *karma.*

prasada(m) (prasāda): प्रसाद "Clarity, brightness; grace." 1) The virtue of serenity and graciousness. 2) Food offered to the Deity or the guru, or the blessed remnants of such food. 3) Any propitiatory offering.

pratyahara (pratyāhāra): प्रत्याहार "Withdrawal." The drawing in of forces. In yoga, the withdrawal from external consciousness. (Also a synonym for *pralaya.*) See: *ashtanga yoga.*

prayashchitta (prāyaścitta): प्रायश्चित्त "Predominant thought or aim." Penance. Acts of atonement. An act of devotion (bhakti), austerity *(tapas)* or discipline *(sukritya)* undertaken to soften or nullify the anticipated reaction to a past action. Penance is uncomfortable karma inflicted upon oneself to mitigate one's karmic burden caused by wrongful actions *(kukarma).* It includes such acts as prostrating 108 times, fasting, self-denial, or carrying *kavadi* (public penance), as well as more extreme austerities, or *tapas.* Penance is often suggested by spiritual leaders and elders.

prayopavesha (prāyopaveśa): प्रायोपवेश "Resolving to die through fasting." Self-willed death by fasting.

Pretaloka: प्रेतलोक "World of the departed." The realm of the earth-bound souls. This lower region of Bhuvarloka is an astral duplicate of the physical world. Bhuvarloka is one of the seven upper worlds: Bhuloka, Bhuvarloka, Svarloka, Maharloka, Janaloka, Tapoloka and Satyaloka. See: *loka.*

Primal Soul: The uncreated, original, perfect soul—Siva Parameshvara—who emanates from Himself the inner and outer universes and an infinite plurality of individual souls whose essence is identical with His essence. God in His personal aspect as Lord and Creator, depicted in many forms: Nataraja by Saivites, Vishnu by Vaishnavites, Devi by Shaktas.

puja (pūjā): पूजा "Worship, adoration." An Agamic rite of worship performed in the home, temple or shrine, to the murti, shri *paduka,* or other consecrated object, or to a person, such as the satguru. Its inner purpose is to purify the atmosphere around the object worshiped, establish a connection with the inner worlds and invoke the presence of God, Gods or one's guru. *Atmartha* puja is done for oneself and immediate family, usually at home in a private shrine. *Parartha* puja is public puja, performed by authorized or ordained priests in a public shrine or temple.

pujari (pujāri): पूजारी "Worshiper." A general term for Hindu temple priests, as well as anyone performing puja.

pandit (paṇḍita): पण्डित "Learned one." A Hindu religious scholar or theologian, well versed in philosophy, liturgy, religious law and sacred science.

pundit: See *pandit.*

punya (puṇya): पुण्य "Holy; virtuous; auspicious." 1) Good or righteous. 2) Meritorious action. 3) Merit earned through right thought, word and action. Punya includes all forms of doing good, from the simplest helpful deed to a lifetime of conscientious beneficence. Punya produces inner contentment, deep joy, the feeling of security and fearlessness. See also: *papa.*

Purana (Purāṇa): पुराण "Ancient (lore)." Hindu folk narratives containing ethical and cosmological teachings relative to Gods, man and the world. They revolve around five subjects: primary creation, secondary creation, genealogy, cycles of time and history. There are 18 major *Puranas* which are designated as either Saivite, Vaishnavite or Shakta.

Puranic (Purāṇic): Of or related to the *Puranas.*

purushartha (purushārtha): पुरुषार्थ "Human wealth or purpose." The four pursuits in which humans may legitimately engage, a basic principle of Hindu ethics. They are: dharma, artha, kama and moksha. 1) dharma ("Righteous living"): The fulfillment of virtue, good works, duties and responsibilities, restraints and observances—performing one's part in the service and upliftment of society. This includes pursuit of truth under a guru of a particular parampara and sampradaya. See: *dharma.* 2) artha ("Wealth"): Material welfare and abundance, money, property, possessions. Artha is the pursuit of wealth, guided by dharma. It includes the basic needs—food, money, clothing and shelter—and extends to the wealth required to maintain a comfortable home, raise a family, fulfill a successful career and perform religious duties. See: *yajna.* 3) kama ("Pleasure, love; enjoyment"): Earthly love, aesthetic and cultural fulfillment, pleasures of the world (including sexual), the joys of family, intellectual satisfaction. Enjoyment of happiness, security, creativity, usefulness and inspiration. 4) moksha ("Liberation"): Freedom from rebirth through the ultimate attainment, realization of the Self God, Parasiva. The spiritual attainments and superconscious joys attending renunciation and yoga leading to Self Realization. Moksha comes through the fulfillment of dharma, artha and kama in the current or past lives, so that one is no longer attached to worldly joys or sorrows. See: *liberation.*

Rajagopura(m) (rājagopura): राजगोपुर "Royal gateway." *Gopura* names a temple entry tower in the South Indian style of architecture. Large temples may have several gopuras. The main tower is the *rajagopura.*

rajas: रजस् "Passion; activity." See: *guna.*

rasatala chakra (rasātala chakra): रसातलचक्र "Subterranean region." The fifth chakra below the *muladhara,* centered in the ankles. Region of selfishness, self-centeredness and possessiveness. *Rasa* means "earth, soil; moisture." See: *chakra, Narakaloka.*

reincarnation: "Re-entering the flesh." *Punarjanma;* metempsychosis. The process wherein souls take on a physical body through the birth process.

renunciation: See: *sannyasa.*

restraints: See: *yama-niyama.*

revealing grace: See: *anugraha shakti, grace.*

rishi (ṛishi): ऋषि "Seer." A term for an enlightened being, emphasizing psychic perception and visionary wisdom.

Rudra: रुद्र "Controller of terrific powers;" or "red, shining one." The name of Siva as the God of dissolution, the universal force of reabsorption. Rudra is revered both as the "terrifying one" and the "Lord of tears," for He wields and controls the terrific powers which may cause lamentation among humans. See: *Nataraja, Siva.*

rudraksha (rudrākṣa): रुद्राक्ष "Eye of Rudra; or red-eyed." Refers to the third eye, or *ajna* chakra. Marble-sized, multi-faced, reddish-brown seeds from the *Eleocarpus ganitrus*, or blue marble tree, which are sacred to Siva and a symbol of His compassion for humanity.

Sacrament: 1) Holy rite, especially one solemnized in a formal, consecrated manner which is a bonding between the recipient and God, Gods or guru. This includes rites of passage (samskara), ceremonies sanctifying crucial events or stages of life. 2) Prasada. Sacred substances, grace-filled gifts, blessed in sacred ceremony or by a holy person.

sadhaka (sādhaka): साधक "Accomplished one; a devotee who performs sadhana." A serious aspirant who has undertaken spiritual disciplines, is usually celibate and is under the guidance of a guru. He wears white and may be under vows, but is not a sannyasin.

sadhana (sādhana): साधन "Effective means of attainment." Religious or spiritual disciplines, such as puja, yoga, meditation, japa, fasting and austerity.

sadhu (sādhu): साधु "Virtuous one; straight, unerring." A holy man dedicated to the search for God. A sadhu may or may not be a yogi or a sannyasin, or be connected in any way with a guru or established lineage. Sadhus usually have no fixed abode and travel unattached from place to place, often living on alms.

sahaja: सहज "Spontaneous, natural," a term used by Satguru Yogaswami to name the state of the knower of Truth. Ananda Coomaraswamy described it as "a recognition of the identity of spirit and matter, subject and object."

sahasrara chakra (sahasrāra chakra): सहस्रारचक्र "Thousand-spoked wheel." The cranial psychic force center. See: *chakra.*

Saiva (Śaiva): शैव Of or relating to Saivism or its adherents, of whom there are about 400 million in the world today. Same as *Saivite.* See: *Saivism.*

Saiva Agamas (Śaiva Āgamas): शैव आगम The sectarian revealed scriptures of the Saivas. Strongly theistic, they identify Siva as the Supreme Lord, immanent and transcendent. They are in two main divisions: the 64 *Kashmir Saiva Agamas* and the 28 *Saiva Siddhanta Agamas.* The latter group are the fundamental sectarian scriptures of Saiva Siddhanta.

Saiva Atmartha Puja (Śaiva Ātmārtha Pūjā): शैव आत्मार्थपूजा "Saivite personal worship rite." Home puja, Sanskrit liturgy performed in the home shrine. See: *puja.*

Saiva Parartha Puja (Śaiva Parārtha Pūjā): शैव परार्थपूजा "Saivite public worship rite." Formal temple puja in the Agamic tradition. See: *puja.*

Saiva Samayam: சைவசமயம் "Saiva religion." See: *Saivism.*

Saiva Siddhanta (Śaiva Siddhānta): शैवसिद्धान्त "Final conclusions of Saivism." The most widespread and influential Saivite school today, predominant especially among the Tamil people of Sri Lanka and South India. It is the formalized theology of the divine revelations contained in the twenty-eight *Saiva Agamas.* For Saiva Siddhantins, Siva is the totality of all, understood in three perfections: Parameshvara (the Personal Creator Lord), Parashakti (the substratum of form) and Parasiva (Absolute Reality which transcends all). Souls and world are identical in essence with Siva, yet also differ in that they are evolving. A pluralistic stream arose in the Middle Ages from the teachings of Aghorasiva and Meykandar. See: *Saivism.*

Saivism (Śaivism, Śaiva): शैव The religion followed by those who worship Siva as Supreme God.

Oldest of the four sects of Hinduism. The earliest historical evidence of Saivism is from the 8,000-year-old Indus Valley civilization in the form of the famous seal of Siva as Lord Pashupati, seated in a yogic pose. There are many schools of Saivism, six of which are Saiva Siddhanta, Pashupata Saivism, Kashmir Saivism, Vira Saivism, Siddha Siddhanta and Siva Advaita. They are based firmly on the *Vedas* and *Saiva Agamas,* and thus have much in common, including the following principal doctrines: 1) the five powers of Siva—creation, preservation, destruction, revealing and concealing grace; 2) the three categories: Pati, *pashu* and *pasha* ("God, souls and bonds"); 3) the three bonds: *anava,* karma and maya; 4) the threefold power of Siva: *iccha* shakti ("desire; will"), kriya shakti ("action power") and jnana shakti ("power of wisdom"); 5) the thirty-six tattvas, or categories of existence; 6) the need for initiation from a satguru; 7) the power of mantra; 8) the four *padas* (stages of spiritual progress): charya (selfless service), kriya (devotion), yoga (meditation), and jnana (illumination); 9) the belief in the Panchakshara as the foremost mantra, and in rudraksha and *vibhuti* as sacred aids to faith; 10) the beliefs in satguru (preceptor), Sivalinga (object of worship) and *sangama* (company of holy persons).

Saivite (Śaivite, Śaiva): शैव Of or relating to Saivism or its adherents, of whom there are about 400 million in the world today. See: *Saivism.*

Saivite Shastras (Śaivite Śāstras): शैव शास्त्र The inner-plane prophecy that has guided Saiva Siddhanta Church since Sivaya Subramuniyaswami read it from the akasha in 1973. *The Saivite Shastras* were written for the Saiva Siddhanta Yoga Order by a group of devas in the Second World, in English. Their purpose is to bring forward the applicable patterns of the Lemurian and Dravidian monasteries, molding the monastics into the culture and ideals expressed therein, including relationships with the guru, attitudes and guidelines for monastic life.

samadhi (samādhi): समाधि "Enstasy," "standing within one's Self." "Sameness; contemplation; union, wholeness; completion, accomplishment." Samadhi is the state of true yoga, in which the meditator and the object of meditation are one. Samadhi is of two levels. The first is savikalpa samadhi ("enstasy with form" or "seed"), identification or oneness with the essence of an object. Its highest form is the realization of the primal substratum or pure consciousness, Satchidananda. The second is nirvikalpa samadhi ("enstasy without form" or "seed"), identification with the Self, in which all modes of consciousness are transcended and Absolute Reality, Parasiva, beyond time, form and space, is experienced.

samayam: சமயம் "Religion."

sampradaya (sampradāya): संप्रदाय "Tradition," "transmission;" a philosophical or religious doctrine or lineage. A living stream of tradition or theology within Hinduism, passed on by oral training and initiation. Typically, a sampradaya is represented by many paramparas.

samsara (saṁsāra): संसार "Flow." The phenomenal world. The cycle of birth, death and rebirth; the total pattern of successive earthly lives experienced by a soul.

samskara (saṁskāra): संस्कार "Impression, activator; sanctification, preparation." 1) The imprints left on the subconscious mind by experience (from this or previous lives), which then color all of life, one's nature, responses, states of mind, etc. 2) A sacrament or rite done to mark a significant transition of life.

Sanatana Dharma (Sanātana Dharma): सनातनधर्म "Eternal religion" or "Everlasting path." It is a traditional designation for the Hindu religion. See: *Hinduism.*

sanga(m) (saṅga): सङ्ग "Association," "fellowship." Coming together in a group, especially for religious purposes.

Sankara, Adi: See: *Shankara.*

San Marga (San Mārga): सन्मार्ग "True path." The straight, spiritual path leading to the ultimate goal, Self Realization, without detouring into unnecessary psychic exploration or pointless development of siddhis. *San Marga* also names the jnana *pada.*

San Marga Sanctuary: A meditation *tirtha* at the foot of the extinct volcano, Mount Waialeale, on Hawaii's Garden Island, Kauai. Founded in 1970, it is among the many public services of Saiva Siddhanta Church, one of America's senior Hindu religious institutions.

sannidhana(m) (sannidhāna): सन्निधान "Nearness; proximity; provost; taking charge of." A title of heads of monasteries: Guru Mahasannidhana. See: *sannidhya.*

sannidhya (sānnidhya): सान्निध्य "(Divine) presence; nearness, indwelling." The radiance and blessed presence of shakti within and around a temple or a holy person.

sannyasa (sannyāsa): संन्यास "Renunciation." "Throwing down or abandoning." Sannyasa is the repudiation of the dharma, including the obligations and duties, of the householder and the acceptance of the even more demanding dharma of the renunciate.

sannyasin (sannyāsin): संन्यासिन् "Renouncer." One who has taken sannyasa *diksha*. A Hindu monk, swami, and one of a world brotherhood (or holy order) of sannyasins. Some are wanderers and others live in monasteries.

Sanskrit (Saṁskṛita): संस्कृत "Well-made," "refined," "perfected." The classical sacerdotal language of ancient India, considered a pure vehicle for communication with the celestial worlds. It is the primary language in which Hindu scriptures are written, including the *Vedas* and *Agamas*. Employed today as a liturgical, literary and scholarly language, but no longer as a spoken vernacular.

santosha: संतोष "Contentment." See: *yama-niyama.*

***sapta* rishi (*sapta ṛishis*):** सप्तऋषि Seven inner-plane masters who help guide the karmas of mankind.

sari (sārī): (Hindi, साड़ी) The traditional garment of a Hindu woman.

Satchidananda (Sacchidānanda): सच्चिदानन्द "Existence-consciousness-bliss." Lord Siva's Divine Mind and simultaneously the pure superconscious mind of each individual soul. It is perfect love and omniscient, omnipotent consciousness, the fountainhead of all existence, yet containing and permeating all existence. It is also called pure consciousness, pure form, substratum of existence. A synonym for *Parashakti.* See: *Siva.*

satguru (sadguru): सद्गुरु "True weighty one." A spiritual preceptor of the highest attainment and authority—one who has realized the ultimate Truth, Parasiva, through nirvikalpa samadhi—a *jivanmukta* able to lead others securely along the spiritual path. He is always a sannyasin, an unmarried renunciate. He is recognized and revered as the embodiment of God, Sadasiva, the source of grace and liberation.

satsanga (satsaṅga): सत्सङ्ग "Association with the good." Gathering in the company of good souls.

sattva guna (sattva guṇa): सत्त्वगुण "Perfection of Being." The quality of goodness or purity. See: *guna.*

satya: सत्य "Truthfulness." See: *yama-niyama.*

Sat Yuga: सत्युग (Also Satya) "Age of Truth," also called Krita, "accomplished, good, cultivated, kind action; the winning die of four dots." The first in the repetitive cycle of yugas, lasting 1,728,000 years, representing the brightest time, when the full light of the Central Sun permeates Earth. See: *Central Sun, cosmic cycle, yuga.*

sayuja (sāyujya): सायुज्य "Intimate union." Perpetual God Consciousness. Often *sayujya samadhi.*

Self (Self God): God Siva's perfection of Absolute Reality, Parasiva—That which abides at the core of every soul. See: *Parasiva.*

Self Realization: Direct knowing of the Self God, Parasiva. Self Realization is known in Sanskrit as nirvikalpa samadhi; "enstasy without form or seed;" the ultimate spiritual attainment (also called *asamprajnata* samadhi). See: *God Realization.*

seva (sevā): सेवा "Service," karma yoga, an integral part of the spiritual path, doing selfless, useful work for others, such as volunteer work at a temple, without preference or thought of reward or personal gain. *Seva,* or Sivathondu in Tamil, is the central practice of the charya *pada.*

shakahara (śākāhāra): शाकाहार "Vegetarian diet." From *shaka,* "vegetable;" and *ahara,* "eating; taking food." See: *yama-niyama.*

Shakta (Śākta): शाक्त Of or relating to Shaktism. See: *Shaktism.*

Shakti (Śakti): शक्ति "Power, energy." The active power or manifest energy of Siva that pervades all of existence. Its most refined aspect is Parashakti, or Satchidananda, the pure consciousness and primal substratum of all form. This pristine, divine energy unfolds as *iccha* shakti (the power of desire, will, love), kriya shakti (the power of action) and jnana shakti (the power of wisdom, knowing), represented as the three prongs of Siva's *trishula,* or trident. From these arise the five powers of revealment, concealment, dissolution, preservation and creation. In Saiva Siddhanta, Siva is All, and His divine energy, Shakti, is inseparable from Him. This unity is symbolized in the image of Ardhanarishvara, "half-female God." In popular, village Hinduism, the unity of Siva and Shakti is replaced with the concept of Siva and Shakti as separate entities. Shakti is represented as female, and Siva as male. In Hindu temples, art and mythology, they are everywhere seen as the divine couple. Within the Shakta religion, the worship of the Goddess is paramount, in Her many fierce and benign forms. Shakti is most easily experienced by devotees as the sublime, bliss-inspiring energy that emanates from a holy person or sanctified Hindu temple. See: *Shaktism*.

shaktinipata (*śaktinipāta*): शक्तिनिपात "Descent of grace," occurring during the advanced stage of the soul's evolution called *arul,* at the end of the *sakala avasthai*. *Shaktinipata* is two–fold: the internal descent is recognized as a tremendous yearning for Siva; the outer descent of grace is the appearance of a satguru. At this stage, the devotee increasingly wants to devote himself to all that is spiritual and holy. Same as *shaktipata*.

shaktipata (*śaktipāta*): शक्तिपात Same as *shaktinipata*. See: *shaktinipata*.

Shaktism (*Śāktism, Śākta*): शाक्त "Doctrine of power." The religion followed by those who worship the Supreme as the Divine Mother—Shakti or Devi—in Her many forms, both gentle and fierce. Shaktism is one of the four primary sects of Hinduism. Shaktism's first historical signs are thousands of female statuettes dated ca 5500 bce, recovered at the Mehrgarh village in India. In philosophy and practice, Shaktism greatly resembles Saivism, both faiths promulgating, for example, the same ultimate goals of advaitic union with Siva and moksha. But Shaktas worship Shakti as the Supreme Being exclusively, as the dynamic aspect of Divinity, while Siva is considered solely transcendent and is not worshiped. See: *Shakti*.

Shankara (*Śaṅkara*): शङ्कर "Conferring happiness;" "propitious." A name of Siva. Also one of Hinduism's most extraordinary monks, Adi Shankara (788-820), preeminent guru of the Smarta Sampradaya, noted for his monistic philosophy (Advaita Vedanta), his many scriptural commentaries, and his formalizing of ten orders of sannyasins with pontifical headquarters at strategic points across India. He lived only 32 years, but traveled throughout India and transformed the Hindu world of that time.

Sharavanabhava (*Śaravaṇabhava*): शरवणभव "Thicket of reeds." The mantra which calls upon Lord Karttikeya, son of God Siva and guardian of the spiritual quest, who arose from Sharavana, the sacred lake of primal consciousness. Its mirror-like surface symbolizes a quieted, peaceful mind. This mantra is prescribed for Saivites not yet initiated by a satguru into the mantra Namah Sivaya.

shastra (*śāstra*): शास्त्र "Sacred text; teaching." Any religious or philosophical treatise, or body of writings. Also a department of knowledge, a science; e.g., the *Artha Shastras* on politics.

shastri (*śāstrī*): शास्त्री One who is knowledgeable in shastra (scriptures or books of law).

shaucha (*śauca*): शौच "Purity." See: *yama-niyama*.

shishya (*śiṣya*): शिष्य "A pupil or disciple," especially one who has proven himself and been accepted by a guru.

shloka (*śloka*): श्लोक A verse, phrase, proverb or hymn of praise, usually composed in a specified meter. Especially a verse of two lines, each of sixteen syllables.

Shri Rudram (*Śrī Rudram*): श्रीरुद्रम् "Hymn to the wielder of terrific powers." Preeminent Vedic hymn to Lord Siva as the God of dissolution, chanted daily in Siva temples throughout India. It is in this long prayer, located in the *Yajur Veda, Taittiriya Samhita,* in the middle of the first three *Vedas,* that the Saivite mantra Namah Sivaya first appears.

Shum (Shūm): ᴖ The Natha mystical language of meditation revealed in Switzerland in 1968 by Sivaya Subramuniyaswami. Its primary alphabet looks like this:

shumif (shūmif): ᴖ One of four basic perspectives designated in the Shum language and philosophy, the meditative viewpoint of being awareness flowing from one area of the inner mind to another, the mind itself being stationary. Also simply the Shum perspective. In Saiva Siddhanta it includes the deeper meditative practices. It is an advaitic, or monistic, viewpoint.

shumsimnisi (shūmsimnīsī): ᴖ The warm thoughts that lead to passion.

siddha: सिद्ध A "perfected one" or accomplished yogi, a person of great spiritual attainment or powers. See: *siddhi*.

siddhanta (*siddhānta*): सिद्धान्त "Final attainments;" "final conclusions." Ultimate understanding in any field.

siddhanta shravana (*siddhānta śravaṇa*): सिद्धान्तश्रवण "Scriptural listening." See: *yama-niyama*.

siddhi: सिद्धि "Power, accomplishment; perfection." Extraordinary powers of the soul, developed through consistent meditation and deliberate, grueling, often uncomfortable *tapas,* or awakened naturally through spiritual maturity and yogic sadhana. Through the repeated experience of Self Realization, siddhis naturally unfold according to the needs of the individual. Before Self Realization, the use or development of siddhis is among the greatest obstacles on the path because it cultivates ahamkara, I-ness, and militates against the attainment of *prapatti,* complete submission to the will of God, Gods and guru.

simshumbisi (simshūmbīsī»): ੨ੳ ੦ਯ The actinic energy within the spine; the pure life force, yellow in color, flowing through the spine and out into the nerve system. *Simshumbisi* is the area of fourteen strong psychic nerve currents of the subsuperconscious state. These fourteen currents, or *nadis,* include the *vumtyeudi* and *karehana* currents, termed *pingala* and *ida* in Sanskrit, as well as the central *nadi,* called *sushumna.* When a yogi lives in *simshumbisi,* his consciousness is that of a being, neither man (aggressive) nor woman (passive).

Siva (Śiva): शिव The "Auspicious," "Gracious," or "Kindly one." Supreme Being of the Saivite religion. God Siva is All and in all, simultaneously the creator and the creation, both immanent and transcendent. As personal Deity, He is Creator, Preserver and Destroyer. He is a one Being, perhaps best understood in three perfections: Parameshvara (Primal Soul), Parashakti (Pure Consciousness) and Parasiva (Absolute Reality). See: *Parameshvara.*

Sivadhyana (Śivadhyāna): शिवध्यान "Meditation on Siva." See: *ashtanga yoga.*

Sivalinga(m) (Śivaliṅga): शिवलिङ्ग "Mark (or sign) of Siva." The most prevalent icon of Siva, found in virtually all Siva temples. A rounded, elliptical, aniconic image, usually set on a circular base, or *pitha.* The Sivalinga is the simplest and most ancient symbol of Siva, especially of Parasiva, God beyond all forms and qualities. The *pitha* represents Parashakti, the manifesting power of God. Lingas are usually of stone (either carved or naturally existing, *svayambhu,* such as shaped by a swift-flowing river), but may also be of metal, precious gemstone, crystal, wood, earth or transitory materials such as ice. See: *murti, Saivism.*

Sivaloka (Śivaloka): शिवलोक "Realm of Siva." See: *loka.*

Siva Purana(m) (Śiva Purāṇa): शिवपुराण "Ancient [lore] of Siva." A collection of six major scriptures sacred to Saivites. Also the name of the oldest of these six texts, though some consider it a version of the *Vayu Purana.* See: *Hinduism, Puranas.*

Sivaratri (Śivarātri): शिवरात्रि "Night of Siva." See: *Mahasivaratri.*

Sivathondu: சிவதொண்டு "Service to Siva." Akin to the concept of karma yoga.

Skanda: स्कन्द "Quicksilver;" "leaping one." One of Lord Karttikeya's oldest names, and His form as scarlet-hued warrior God.

Skanda Shashthi (Skanda Shashṭhī): स्कन्दषष्ठी A six-day festival in October-November celebrating Lord Karttikeya's, or Skanda's, victory over the forces of darkness.

Smarta (Smārta): स्मार्त "Of or related to smriti," the secondary Hindu scriptures. See: *Smartism.*

Smartism (Smārtism): स्मार्त Sect based on the secondary scriptures (smriti). The most liberal of the four major Hindu denominations, an ancient Vedic brahminical tradition (ca 700 bce) which from the 9th century onward was guided and deeply influenced by the Advaita Vedanta teachings of the reformist Adi Shankara.

soul: The real being of man, as distinguished from body, mind and emotions. The soul, known as atman or purusha, has two aspects, its essence and its form, or body. The essence or nucleus of the soul is man's innermost and unchanging being, eternally identical with God Siva's first two perfections, Parasiva (Absolute Reality) and Parashakti (Satchidananda, Pure Consciousness). The body of the soul, *anandamaya* kosha ("sheath of bliss"), is also called the soul body, causal body *(karana sharira),* innermost sheath, actinic body and body of light. These terms refer to the soul's manifest nature as an individual being—an effulgent, human-like form composed of light (quantums). See: *evolution of the soul.*

sphatika (sphaṭika): स्फटिक "Quartz crystal." From *sphat,* "to expand; blossom; to burst open or into view." See: *sphatika Sivalinga.*

sphatika Sivalinga(m) (sphaṭika Śivaliṅga): स्फटिकशिवलिङ्ग "Crystal mark of God." A quartz-crystal Sivalinga. See: *San Marga Sanctuary, Sivalinga, Svayambhu Linga.*

spiritual unfoldment: The unfoldment of the spirit, the inherent, divine soul of man. The gradual expansion of consciousness as kundalini shakti slowly rises through the *sushumna nadi.* The term *spiritual unfoldment* indicates this slow, imperceptible process of uncovering soul qualities that are already there, likened to a lotus flower's emerging from bud to effulgent beauty.

subconscious mind: Samskara *chitta.* The storehouse of past impressions, reactions and desires and the seat of involuntary physiological processes. See: *mind.*

Subramaniam: சுப்பிரமணியம் (Sanskrit—Subrahmaṇya: सुब्रह्मण्य) "Very pious; dear to holy men." A name of Lord Karttikeya.

Subramuniyaswami: சுப்பிரமுனியசுவாமி The 162nd satguru (1927–2001) of the Nandinatha Sampradaya's Kailasa Parampara. He was recognized worldwide as one of the foremost Hindu ministers of our times, contributing to the revival of Hinduism in immeasurable abundance. He was simultaneously a staunch defender of traditions, as the tried and proven ways of the past, and a fearless innovator, setting new patterns of life for contemporary humanity.

sub-subconscious mind: Vasana *chitta.* See: *mind (five states).*

subsuperconscious mind: *Anukarana chitta.* The superconscious mind working through the conscious and subconscious states, which brings forth intuition, clarity and insight.

subtle body: *Sukshma sharira,* the nonphysical, astral body or vehicle in which the soul encases itself to function in the Antarloka, or subtle world. The subtle body includes the *vijnanamaya* kosha (mental, cognitive-intuitive sheath), *manomaya* kosha (instinctive-intellectual sheath) and, while the soul is physically embodied, the *pranamaya* kosha (life-energy sheath). After death, the pranamaya kosha disintegrates and the subtle body consists of only *manomaya* and *vijnanamaya.* Just before rebirth, or when higher evolutionary planes are entered, manomaya kosha is dropped off as well; at that point, the subtle body consists of only *vijnanamaya* kosha. Also part of the subtle body are the *antahkarana* (mental faculty: intellect, instinct and ego—buddhi, manas and ahamkara) and, during physical embodiment, the five *jnanendriyas* (agents of perception: hearing, touch, sight, taste and smell); and the five *karmendriyas* (agents of action: speech, grasping, movement, excretion and generation). Its composition spans the 6th to the 36th tattva.

summa: சும்மா "Stillness."

superconscious mind: *Karana chitta.* See: *mind (five states), mind (three phases).*

sutra (sūtra): सूत्र "Thread." An aphoristic verse; the literary style consisting of such maxims. From 500 bce, this style was widely adopted by Indian philosophical systems and eventually employed in works on law, grammar, medicine, poetry, crafts, etc.

svadharma: स्वधर्म "One's own way." See: *dharma.*

svarnasharira vishvagrasa (svarṇaśarīra viśvagrāsa): स्वर्णशरीरविश्वग्रास The final merging with Siva where there exists no individual soul, only Siva. See: *vishvagrasa.*

svayambhu Linga(m) (svayambhū Liṅga): स्वयम्भूलिङ्ग *Svayambhu* Sivalinga. See: *svayambhu Sivalinga.*

svayambhu Sivalinga(m) (svayambhū Śivaliṅga): स्वयम्भूशिवलिङ्ग "Self-existent mark or sign of God." Names a Sivalinga discovered in nature and not carved or crafted by human hands; often a smooth cylindrical stone, called *banalinga,* such as found in India's Narmada River. See: *Sivalinga.*

swami (svāmī): स्वामी "Lord; owner; self-possessed." He who knows or is master of himself. A respectful title for a Hindu monk, usually a sannyasin, an initiated, orange-robed renunciate, dedicated wholly to religious life. As a sign of respect, the term *swami* is sometimes applied more broadly to include non-monastics dedicated to spiritual work.

Tai Pongal: தைப்பொங்கல் A four-day home festival held in the Tamil month of Tai (January-February), celebrating the season's first harvest. Surya, the Sun God, is honored at this time as the giver of all good fortune and as the visible Divine One. Newly harvested rice is ceremoniously cooked outdoors over an open fire in a giant pot (hence *pongal,* from *pongu,* "to cook"). The direction of the overflow of boiling milk is an augury for the coming year.

Tai Pusam: தைப்பூசம் A festival held on the Pushya *nakshatra* near the full-moon day of January-February to worship Lord Siva or Karttikeya, depending on the locality. It is an important holiday, especially dear to the Tamil people, celebrated with great pomp, fervor and intensity in India, Sri Lanka, Malaysia, Fiji, South Africa and Réunion, often marked by the carrying of *kavadi*. In Mauritius and Singapore it is a national holiday.

tali: தாலி Wedding pendant. A gold ornament worn by the Hindu wife around the neck representing her vows of matrimony. Known as *mangala* sutra in Sanskrit. She reveres it as an image of her husband and ritually worships it during her morning devotions.

tamas(ic): तमस् "Force of inertia." See: *guna*.

tambura (taṁbūrā): तंबूरा (Hindi) A long-necked, four-stringed fretless lute that provides a drone accompaniment for a singer or instrumentalist.

Tamil: தமிழ் The ancient Dravidian language of the Tamils, a Caucasoid people of South India and Northern Sri Lanka, who have now migrated throughout the world. The official language of the state of Tamil Nadu, India, spoken by 60 million people.

tandava (tāṇḍava): தாண்டவ "Violent dance." Any vigorous dance sequence performed by a male dancer. There are many forms of *tandava*. Its prototype is Siva's dance of bliss, ananda *tandava,* in which there are 108 traditional poses. The much softer feminine dance is called *lasya,* from *lasa,* "lively." Dance in general is *nartana.* See: *Nataraja.*

tantra: तन्त्र "Loom, methodology." 1) Most generally, a synonym for shastra, "scripture." 2) A synonym for the Agamic texts, especially those of the Shakta faith, a class of Hindu scripture providing detailed instruction on all aspects of religion, mystic knowledge and science. The *Tantras* are also associated with the Saiva tradition. 3) A specific method, technique or spiritual practice within the Saiva and Shakta traditions. 4) In Shaktism, tantra includes disciplines and techniques with a strong emphasis on worship of the feminine force, often involving sexual encounters, with the purported goal of transformation and union with the Divine.

tapas: तपस् "Heat, fire; ardor." Purificatory spiritual disciplines, severe austerity, penance and sacrifice. The endurance of pain, suffering, through the performance of extreme penance, religious austerity and mortification.

tapasvin: तपस्विन् One who performs *tapas* or is in the state of *tapas.* See: *tapas.*

tattva: तत्त्व "That-ness" or "essential nature." Tattvas are the primary principles, elements, states or categories of existence, the building blocks of the universe. Lord Siva constantly creates, sustains the form of and absorbs back into Himself His creations. Rishis describe this emanational process as the unfoldment of tattvas, stages or evolutes of manifestation, descending from subtle to gross. At *mahapralaya,* cosmic dissolution, they enfold into their respective sources, with only the first two tattvas surviving the great dissolution. The first and subtlest form—the pure consciousness and source of all other evolutes of manifestation—is called Siva tattva, or Parashakti-nada. But beyond Siva tattva lies Parasiva—the utterly transcendent, Absolute Reality, called *attava.* That is Siva's first perfection. The Sankhya system discusses 25 tattvas. Saivism recognizes these same 25 plus 11 beyond them, making 36 tattvas in all.

tavil: தவில் A large drum, native to South India, energetically played at Hindu pujas and processions in accompaniment to the nagasvara, a long, shrill woodwind.

Tayumanavar: தாயுமானவர் A Tamil Saiva yogi, devotional mystic and poet saint (ca 17th century) whose writings are a harmonious blend of philosophy and devotion. In his poem "Chinmayananda Guru," Tayumanavar places himself in the lineage of Rishi Tirumular. See: *Tirumular.*

teradi: தேரடி "Chariot shed." Tamil term for the "garage" shelter that houses the temple cart or chariot *(ter)* in which the parade Deity, *utsava* murti, is taken in procession on festival days.

That: When capitalized, this simple demonstrative refers uniquely to the Ultimate, Indescribable or Nameless Absolute: The Self God, Parasiva.

theism: Belief that God exists as a real, conscious, personal Supreme Being, creator and ruler of the universe. May also include belief in the great Mahadevas (Gods) created by the Supreme Being.

Third World: Sivaloka, "realm of Siva," or Karanaloka. The spiritual realm or causal plane of existence wherein Mahadevas and highly evolved souls live in their own self-effulgent forms. See: *loka, three worlds.*

three worlds: The three worlds of existence, *triloka,* are the primary hierarchical divisions of the cosmos. 1) Bhuloka: "Earth world," the physical plane. 2) Antarloka: "Inner or in-between world," the subtle or astral plane. 3) Sivaloka: "World of Siva," and of the Gods and highly evolved souls; the causal plane, also called Karanaloka.

tirtha (*tīrtha*): तीर्थ "Passageway; ford." A bathing ghat or place of pilgrimage, especially on the banks of sacred waters. Also refers to water offered in puja.

tirthayatra (*tīrthayātrā*): तीर्थयात्रा "Journey to a holy place." Pilgrimage.

Tirukural: திருக்குறள் "Holy couplets." A treasury of Hindu ethical insight and a literary masterpiece of the Tamil language, written by Saiva Saint Tiruvalluvar (ca 200 bce) near present-day Chennai. One of the world's earliest ethical texts, the *Tirukural* could well be considered a bible on virtue for the human race.

Tirumantiram: திருமந்திரம் "Holy incantation." The Nandinatha Sampradaya's oldest Tamil scripture; written ca 200 BCE by Rishi Tirumular. It is the earliest of the *Tirumurai* texts, and a vast storehouse of esoteric yogic and tantric knowledge. It contains the mystical essence of raja yoga and siddha yoga, and the fundamental doctrines of the 28 *Saiva Siddhanta Agamas*, which are the heritage of the ancient prehistoric traditions of Saivism. As the *Agamas* themselves are now partially lost, the 3,000-verse *Tirumantiram* is a rare source of the complete *Agamanta* (collection of Agamic lore).

Tirumular: திருமூலர் An illustrious siddha yogi and rishi of the Nandinatha Sampradaya's Kailasa Parampara who came from the Himalayas (ca 200 bce) to Tamil Nadu to compose the *Tirumantiram*. In this scripture he recorded the tenets of Saivism in concise and precise verse form, based upon his own realizations and the supreme authority of the *Saiva Agamas* and the *Vedas*. Tirumular was a disciple of Maharishi Nandinatha.

Tirumurai: திருமுறை "Holy book." A twelve-book collection of hymns and writings of South Indian Saivite saints, compiled by Saint Nambiyandar Nambi (ca 1000). The first seven books are known as *Devarams*.

tiruvadi: திருவடி The feet of the satguru or his holy sandals, known in Sanskrit as shri *paduka*, worshiped as the source of grace. The guru's feet are especially sacred, being the point of contact of the divine and physical spheres.

tiruvadi puja: திருவடி பூஜை Ritual worship of the feet of a guru or his holy sandals. See: *puja*.

Tiruvalluvar: திருவள்ளுவர் "Holy weaver." Tamil weaver and householder saint (ca 200 bce) who wrote the classic Saivite ethical scripture *Tirukural*. He lived with his wife Vasuki, famed for her remarkable loyalty and virtues, near modern-day Chennai.

Tiruvasagam: திருவாசகம் "Holy Utterances." The lyrical Tamil scripture by Saint Manikkavasagar (ca 850). Considered one of the most profound and beautiful devotional works in the Tamil language, it discusses every phase of the spiritual path—from doubt and anguish to perfect faith in God Siva, from earthly experience to the guru-disciple relationship and freedom from rebirth.

tithe (tithing): The spiritual discipline, often a *vrata*, of giving one tenth of one's gainful and gifted income to a religious organization of one's choice, thus sustaining spiritual education and upliftment on earth. The Sanskrit equivalent is *dashamamsha*, called *makimai* in the Tamil tradition.

trishula (*triśūla*): त्रिशूल A three-pronged spear or trident wielded by Lord Siva and certain Saivite ascetics. Symbolizes God's three fundamental shaktis, or powers—*iccha* (desire, will, love), kriya (action) and jnana (wisdom).

Unfoldment: See: *spiritual unfoldment*.

upadesha (*upadeśa*): उपदेश "Advice; religious instruction." Often given in question-and-answer form from guru to disciple. The satguru's spiritual discourses.

upadeshi (*upadeśī*): उपदेशी A liberated soul who chooses to teach, actively helping others to the goal of liberation. Contrasted with *nirvani*. See: *nirvani and upadeshi*.

Upanishad: उपनिषद् "Sitting near devotedly." The fourth and final portion of the *Vedas*, expounding the secret, philosophical meaning of the Vedic hymns. The *Upanishads* are a collection of profound texts which are the source of Vedanta and have dominated Indian thought for thousands of years. They are philosophical chronicles of rishis expounding the nature of God, soul and cosmos, exquisite renderings of the deepest Hindu thought.

Vaishnava (**Vaishṇava**): वैष्णव Of or relating to Vishnu; same as Vaishnavite. A follower of Lord Vishnu or His incarnations. See: *Vaishnavism, Vishnu.*

Vaishnavism (Vaishṇava): वैष्णव One of the four major religions, or denominations, of Hinduism, representing roughly half of the world's one billion Hindus. It gravitates around the worship of Lord Vishnu as Personal God, His incarnations and their consorts. Vaishnavism stresses the personal aspect of God over the impersonal, and bhakti (devotion) as the true path to liberation.

Vaishnavite: Of or relating to Vishnu; same as Vaishnava. A follower of Vishnu or His incarnations. See: *Vaishnavism, Vishnu.*

vasana (vāsanā): वासना "Abode." Subconscious inclinations. From *vas,* "dwelling, residue, remainder." The subliminal inclinations and habit patterns which, as driving forces, color and motivate one's attitudes and future actions.

vasana *daha* tantra (vāsanā *daha* tantra): वासनादहतन्त्र "Purification of the subconscious by fire." *Daha* means burning, tantra is a method, and vasanas are deep-seated subconscious traits or tendencies that shape one's attitudes and motivations. Vasanas can be either positive or negative. One of the best methods for resolving difficulties in life, of dissolving troublesome vasanas, the vasana *daha* tantra is the practice of burning confessions, or even long letters to loved ones or acquaintances, describing pains, expressing confusions and registering grievances and long-felt hurts. Also called spiritual journaling, writing down problems and burning them in any ordinary fire brings them from the subconscious into the external mind, releasing the suppressed emotion as the fire consumes the paper. This is a magical healing process. A special form of this discipline is maha vasana daha tantra. It is the sadhana of looking back over and writing about the various aspects of one's life in order to clear all accumulated subconscious burdens, burning the papers as done in the periodic vasana *daha* tantra. Ten pages are to be written about each year. Other aspects of this tantra include writing about people one has known and all sexual experiences.

Veda: वेद "Wisdom." Sagely revelations which comprise Hinduism's most authoritative scripture. They, along with the *Agamas,* are shruti, that which is "heard." The *Vedas* are a body of dozens of holy texts known collectively as the *Veda,* or as the four *Vedas: Rig, Yajur, Sama* and *Atharva.* In all they include over 100,000 verses, as well as additional prose. The knowledge imparted by the *Vedas* ranges from earthy devotion to high philosophy.

Vedanta (Vedānta): वेदान्त "Ultimate wisdom" or "final conclusions of the *Vedas.*" Vedanta is the system of thought embodied in the *Upanishads* (ca 1500-600 bce), which give forth the ultimate conclusions of the *Vedas.* Through history there developed numerous Vedanta schools, ranging from pure dualism to absolute monism.

Vedic-Agamic (Vedic-Āgamic): Simultaneously drawing from and complying with both of Hinduism's revealed scriptures (shruti), *Vedas* and *Agamas,* which represent two complementary, intertwining streams of history and tradition.

vel: வேல் "Spear, lance." The symbol of Lord Karttikeya's divine authority as Lord of yoga and commander of the devas. (Known as *shula* in Sanskrit.)

veshti: வேஷ்டி A long, unstitched cloth, like a sarong, wound about the waist and reaching below the ankles. Traditional Hindu apparel for men. It can be wrapped in many different styles. A Tamil word derived from the Sanskrit *veshtana,* "encircling." Also called *vetti* (Tamil) or *dhoti* (Hindi).

vibhuti (vibhūti): विभूति "Resplendent, powerful." Holy ash, prepared by burning cow dung along with other precious substances (milk, ghee, honey, etc). It symbolizes purity and is one of the main sacraments given at puja in all Saivite temples and shrines.

Vishnu (Vishṇu): विष्णु "All-pervasive." Supreme Deity of the Vaishnavite religion. God as personal Lord and Creator, the All-Loving Divine Personality, who periodically incarnates and lives a fully human life to reestablish dharma whenever necessary. In Saivism, Vishnu is Siva's aspect as Preserver.

***vishuddha* chakra (*viśuddha* chakra):** विशुद्धचक्र "Wheel of purity." The fifth chakra. Center of divine love. See: *chakra.*

vishvagrasa (viśvagrāsa): विश्वग्रास "Total absorption." The final merger of the soul in Siva at the fulfillment of its evolution. It is the ultimate union of the individual soul body with the body of Siva—Parameshvara—within the Sivaloka, from whence the soul was first emanated.

vitala chakra: वितलचक्र "Region of negation." The second chakra below the *muladhara,* centered in the thighs. Region of raging anger and viciousness. See: *chakra, Narakaloka.*

vrata: व्रत "Vow, religious oath." Often a vow to perform certain disciplines, such as penance, fasting, specific mantra repetitions, worship or meditation.

vritti (vṛitti): वृत्ति "Whirlpool, vortex." In yoga psychology, the fluctuations of consciousness, the waves of mental activity *(chitta vritti)* of thought and perception. A statement from Patanjali's *Yoga Sutras* (1.2) reads, "Yoga is the restraint *(nirodha)* of mental activity *(chitta vritti)*." In general use, *vritti* means: 1) course of action, mode of life; conduct, behavior; way in which something is done; 2) mode of being, nature, kind, character.

vumtyeudi (vūmtyēūdī): ⌐க⌐ The current, blue in color, that flows upward, ending on the right side of the body. Called *pingala* in Sanskrit, this current, masculine-aggressive in nature, is the intellectual-mental energy within the being, the intellectual energy which causes one to think and to become aware of the intellectual mind. *Vumtyeudi* is one of the currents of *simshumbisi.*

Yagam: யாகம் "Worship; sacrifice." Colloquially, a public feeding. See: *yajna.*

yajna (yajña): यज्ञ "Worship; sacrifice." One of the most central Hindu concepts—sacrifice and surrender through acts of worship, inner and outer. 1) Primarily, yajna is a form of ritual worship especially prevalent in Vedic times, in which oblations—ghee, grains, spices and exotic woods—are offered into a fire according to scriptural injunctions while special mantras are chanted. The element fire, Agni, is revered as the divine messenger who carries offerings and prayers to the Gods. Yajna requires four components, none of which may be omitted: *dravya,* sacrificial substances; *tyaga,* the spirit of sacrificing all to God; devata, the celestial beings who receive the sacrifice; and mantra, the empowering word or chant. 2) *Manushya* yajna or often simply yajna, "homage to men," is feeding guests and the poor, the homeless and the student. *Manushya* yajna includes all acts of philanthropy, such as tithing and charity. In Sri Lanka, yajna (Tamil, *yagam*) also refers to large, ceremonious mass feedings.

yagasala: யாகசாலை (Sanskrit—*yajñaśālā:* यज्ञशाला) "Place of worship." A temporary structure under which Hindu rituals are conducted, such as for elaborate *homas* or the reconsecration of a temple.

yama-niyama: यम नियम The first two of the eight limbs of raja yoga, the yamas and niyamas are Hinduism's fundamental ethical codes, the essential foundation for all spiritual progress. Here are the ten traditional yamas and ten niyamas. The yamas: 1) ahimsa: "Noninjury." Not harming others by thought, word, or deed. 2) *satya:* "Truthfulness." Refraining from lying and betraying promises. 3) *asteya:* "Nonstealing." Neither stealing nor coveting, nor entering into debt. 4) brahmacharya: "Divine conduct." Controlling lust by remaining celibate when single, leading to faithfulness in marriage. 5) *kshamā:* "Patience." Restraining intolerance with people and impatience with circumstances. 6) *dhriti:* "Steadfastness." Overcoming nonperseverance, fear, indecision and changeableness. 7) *daya:* "Compassion." Conquering callous, cruel and insensitive feelings toward all beings. 8) *arjava:* "Honesty, straightforwardness." Renouncing deception and wrongdoing. 9) *mitahara:* "Moderate appetite." Neither eating too much nor consuming meat, fish, fowl or eggs. 10) *shaucha:* "Purity." Avoiding impurity in body, mind and speech. The niyamas: 1) *hrī:* "Remorse." Being modest and showing shame for misdeeds. 2) *santosha:* "Contentment." Seeking joy and serenity in life. 3) *dana:* "Giving." Tithing and giving generously without thought of reward. 4) *astikya:* "Faith." Believing firmly in God, Gods, guru and the path to enlightenment. 5) Ishvarapujana: "Worship of the Lord." The cultivation of devotion through daily worship and meditation. 6) *siddhanta shravana:* "Scriptural listening." Studying the teachings and listening to the wise of one's lineage. 7) *mati:* "Cognition." Developing a spiritual will and intellect with the guru's guidance. 8) *vrata:* "Sacred vows." Fulfilling religious vows, rules and observances faithfully. 9) japa: "Recitation." Chanting mantras daily. 10) *tapas:* "Austerity." Performing sadhana, penance, *tapas* and sacrifice. Patanjali lists the yamas as: ahimsa, *satya, asteya,* brahmacharya and *aparigraha* (noncovetousness); and the niyamas as: *shaucha, santosha, tapas, svadhyaya* (self-reflection, private scriptural study) and Ishvarapranidhana (worship). See: *ashtanga yoga.*

Yama(n) (Yama): यम "The restrainer." Hindu God of death; oversees the processes of death transition, guiding the soul out of its present physical body.

yatra (**yātrā**): यात्रा "Journey." Pilgrimage. Usually *tirthayatra,* "journey to a holy place."

yoga: योग "Union." From *yuj,* "to yoke, harness, unite." The philosophy, process, disciplines and practices whose purpose is the yoking of individual consciousness with transcendent or divine consciousness.

yoga pada (**yoga pāda**): योगपाद The third of the successive stages in spiritual unfoldment in Saiva Siddhanta, wherein the goal is Self Realization. See: *pada.*

Yogaswami (**Yogaswāmī**): யோகசுவாமி "Master of yoga." Sri Lanka's most renowned contemporary spiritual master (1872–1964), a Sivajnani and Natha siddhar revered by both Hindus and Buddhists. He was trained by Satguru Chellappaswami, from whom he received guru *diksha.* Siva Yogaswami was the satguru of Sivaya Subramuniyaswami. Yogaswami conveyed his teachings in songs, published in a book called *Natchintanai,* "Good Thoughts." See: *Kailasa Parampara.*

yogi (**yogī**): योगी One who practices yoga.

yogini (**yoginī**): योगिनी Feminine counterpart of *yogi.*

yuga: युग "Eon," "age." One of four ages which chart the duration of the world according to Hindu thought: Satya (also Sat or Krita), Treta, Dvapara and Kali. In the first period, dharma reigns supreme, but as the ages revolve, virtue diminishes and ignorance and injustice increase. At the end of the Kali Yuga, in which we are now, the cycle begins again with a new Satya Yuga.

of *Tirumurai*, 44; reciting with Yogaswami, 314

Devotees: ensuring Yogaswami's visits, 340; three types, 272; vs. curiosity-seekers, 120-122; Yogaswami's, 270-272, 275. See also *Shishyas*

Devotion (kriya, bhakti): catching a satguru, 196; Chellappaswami's teachings, 156-157, 159; foundation for yoga, 526; in *Tirumantiram,* 524; temple worship, 403, 405. See also *Love*

Dharma (duty, rectitude): becoming steadfast, 336; feeding the hungry, 322; harnessing computer technology, 592; importance, 140; in child rearing, 542, 610; sannyasins', 464, 508, 534; Yogaswami's emphasis, 299. See also *Svadharma*

Dharmapura Aadheenam: monism-pluralism debate, 563

Dharmarajah C.S.: on Yogaswami, 295, 316

Diabetes: Yogaswami, 314

Diamond ring: Kadaitswami and, 99

Diet: Gurudeva's recommendations, 574; qualities associated with meat-eating, 662; *Tirukural* verse, 532; vow of vegetarianism, 576. See also *Food; Vegetarianism*

Diksha. See *Initiation*

Dimensions of the mind: Gurudeva describes fourth dimension, 678

Dipavali festival: new clothes, 273

Disciples. See *Guru-disciple relationship; Shishyas*

Discipline: civilized methods, 378, 668; four vows for all shishyas, 576. See also *Corporal punishment; Sadhana*

Disharmony: zero-tolerance policy, 635

Divali. See *Dipavali*

Divine Life Society: sending Swami Satchidananda to Ceylon, 280

Divine Mother. See *Amman; Goddess; Shakti; Thaiyalnayaki*

Doctors: appropriate care for Hindu patients, 594; diagnosing Gurudeva's cancer, 700; Gurudeva refuses tests, 673

Door of Brahman: Gurudeva's experience, 481

Dowry: Yogaswami's help, 270, 272

Dravidians: ancient race, 34-35

Dream(s): Saravanamuthu's, 190; shared, 394; Yogaswami's teachings, 224. See also *Visions*

Drought. See *Rain*

Drugs, psychedelic. See *Psychedelic drugs*

Duality, dualism, pluralism (dvaita): a matter of perspective, 418; perspective expressed in *Mahabharata,* 249. See also *Monism-pluralism debate; Siddhanta*

Duraiswamy V., Sir: Chellachi Ammaiyar and, 229, 235; healed by Yogaswami, 289; Yogaswami and, 213, 302

Dutch: in Sri Lanka, 83, 117, 132-133

Duty. See *Dharma*

Dvaita. See *Duality*

Dvaita Saiva Siddhanta: philosophical rather than experiential, 528

Earth: vulnerability, 602; Yogaswami's reverence, 323-325. See also *Ecology; Nature*

Ecology: Eastern perspective, 610. See also *Earth; Global Forums for Human Survival*

Editing: Gurudeva's collaborative methods, 641-643, *741*

Edmonton Maha Ganapathy Temple: Gurudeva prostrates at future site, 651; Gurudeva's guidance, 629

Education: British Christians' control, 100; vs. daily dharma, 320. See also *Pedantry; Schools*

Eelathu Thiruneri Thamil Mandram: Gunanayagam A., 587

Ego/egoism: abyss, 220; cured by Sivathondu (service), 342; empowerment of, 232

Eknath Ranade: inspiring modern Hindu renaissance, 538

Elangovan M.: on Gurudeva's picture, 621

Elayathamby M.S.: association with Yogaswami, 194, 203, 213

Elders: interrogating Hansen, 404

Elements: subtle and gross, 29

Elephant Pass: bomb, 616; Robert Hansen, 409

Embezzler: Yogaswami and, 305

Encounter groups: Enter-Ins, 473

Endowment(s): for Iraivan Temple, 691; power of, 638; Yogaswami's emphasis, 277. See also *Hindu Heritage Endowment; Self-sufficiency*

Energy: Hansen's study, 386; transmuting for higher purpose, 638. See also *Transmutation*

Engine: temporarily inoperable, 2, 230

English: inadequate for inner states, 474-475

Enright, Cora. See *Mother Christney*

Enter-In: monastics' encounter group, 473

Environment. See *Earth; Global Forums for Human Survival*

Epics: Gurudeva's rejection, 522

Episcopalians (Christian sect): open to Eastern thought, 445

Erlalai: room and meals for pilgrims, 85

Esala Perahera: Murugan festival, 184

Vaidyeshwara Vidyalayam: Yogaswami and, 251

Vairamuthu Chettiar (later Chinnaswami): devotee of Kadaitswami, 83; renouncing the world, 84, 92

Vairamuthu M. (later Chinnaswami): Yogaswami and, 252. See also *Chinnaswami*

Vaishnavism: preserving a great tradition, 539

Vaithialingam: confronting Chellappaswami, 192; on Yoganathan's tapas, 177; Yoganathan's cousin, 154

Vallipuram: Chellappaswami's father, 111; quoting Yogaswami about his pilgrimage, 183-184; Yogaswami and, 195

Vannarpannai: Vaidyeshwara Vidyalayam, 251

Vannarpannai Nilayam. See *Sivathondan Nilayam*

Vannarpannai Vaitheesvaran-Thaiyalnayaki Sivan Temple: environs, 340; Kadaitswami, 103-104; opened to harijans, 252; Yogaswami and, 211-212, 331

Varanasi. See *Kashi*

Vasana daha tantra: purification of subconscious by fire, 666

Vasanas: from unresolved disharmony, 636

Vedanta: harmony with Siddhanta, 419, 524-526; in Tirumular's time, 526; simplistic modern form, 550; united with Siddhanta, 41. See also *Nonduality; Upanishads*

Vedanta Society: Hansen's study, 388

Vedas: Hinduism's revealed scriptures, 522; quoted in the Kremlin, 604

Vedda tribesmen: Yogaswami and, 183

Veeragathiyar, Puvanesam: a mother's love, 621

Veerasingham: on guru protocol, 280

Vegetarianism (shakahara): Alaveddy, 413; Saivism, 90, 93; vow for all shishyas, 576. See also *Diet*

Vel (Lord Skanda's): Gurudeva echoes *Sukshma Agama,* 667

Velikhov, Yevgeny, Dr.: on threats to human survival, 602

Vellupillai, Mr.: hosting Yogaswami, 341; Yogaswami and, 289-290

Velvindron, Retnon: calling Gurudeva to Mauritius, 571

Venice: Gurudeva's opera-singer life, 468; instructions from Mahadeva, 476

Vettivelu S.A., Dr.: attending Yogaswami in hospital, 346; Yogaswami's mahasamadhi, 358-359

Veylan, Aran: Gurudeva's guidance of Edmonton temple, 629

Veylanswami. See *Bodhinatha Veylanswami*

Vibhuti (holy ash): connecting devotee to temple, 501; in Natha initiation ceremony, 26; visible to devas, 586

Vinacinthamby S.: on Yogaswami, 248-249

Vinayagamoorthy Amma: indicating where Hansen stayed, *725*

Vinayagamoorthy Chettiar: and family, with Gurudeva, *723*; and Gurudeva's Alaveddy ashram, 268, 424; and Yogaswami, 268; on Gurudeva's ordination, 422; taking Hansen to Yogaswami, 415-416

Vipulananda Swami: Vaidyeshwara Vidyalayam, 251. See also *Mylvaganam T., Pundit*

Virginia City: Mountain Desert Monastery, 450

Vishvagrasa: ultimate merger, 430

Vishvanatha Temple: devotees personally bathe Sivalingam, 34

Vision(s): clairvoyance, 647; crystal Sivalingam, 597; Durga, Lakshmi and Saraswati, 654; flame at top of head, 409; inner-plane library, 495-496; of Chellachi Ammaiyar, 230; of Ganesha, 572; of Kadaitswami, 98; of Murugan, 53, 190, 493; of Siva, 511; of soul body, 368; of Yogaswami, 365, 419; peacock tail, 400; Siva as Cosmic Dancer, 409; Siva dancing on head, 436. See also *Clairvoyance*

Vision Kauai 2020: island leaders envisioning Kauai's future, 674

Vithanayar: Yoganathan/Yogaswami and, 144, 303-304, 309

Vivekananda, Swami: bringing Vedanta to West, 526; Hansen's study, 388; modern Hindu renaissance, 538; Yogaswami and, 142, 213, 331

Voice loss: healed, 294

Vows (vratas): for potential monastics, 826; Gurudeva's requirements, 576; karmic effects, 577; obedience to, 683-684

V.S.S.K. Vegetarian Cafe: frequented by Yogaswami, 340

Vyaghrapada, Sage: Chidambaram Sivalinga, 38; disciple of Nandinatha, 19

Waialeale, Mount: healing energies, 489

Waitering: Silent Ministry, 483

Waitress: gift of boots, 613

Waloopillai N., Dr.: attending Yogaswami in hospital, 346

War in Sri Lanka: foreseen by Gurudeva, 558; long-standing conflict, 345

Bibliography

Chellappa Swami of Nallur, by Dr. Mrs. Vimala Krishnapillai; an English translation of *Yalpana Nallur Terati Cellappa Cuvamikal,* by K.C. Kularatnam (Jaffna, Sri Lanka, 1984, Tamil)

Guruvum Seedarum ("Guru & Disciple"), by K.C. Kularatnam (Jaffna, Sri Lanka, 2005, Tamil)

Homage to Yogaswami, by Susunaga Weeraperuma (Poets' and Painters' Press, London, 1972, English)

Nandikeshvara Kashika (manuscript), translation by Dr. S.P. Sabharathnam Sivachariyar (Himalayan Academy, Kapaa, Hawaii, USA, 2011, English)

Natchintanai, Songs and Sayings of Yogaswami (Sivathondan Society Ltd., Jaffna, Sri Lanka, 1974, English)

Eelathu Sitharkkal (Siddhars of Eelam), by N. Muthaiya, a.k.a. Athmajothy, editor of *Atmajothy* magazine (Jaffna, Sri Lanka, 1980 & 1994, Tamil)

Saint Yogaswami and the Testament of Truth, by Ratna Ma Chelliah Navaratnam (Sivathondan Society, Jaffna, Sri Lanka, 1972, English)

Tamil Sages and Seers of Ceylon, by V. Muttucumaraswamy (Jaffna, Sri Lanka, 1972, English)

The Sivathondan magazine (Sivathondan Society Ltd., Jaffna, Sri Lanka, Tamil)

The Tirumandiram, T. N. Ganapathy, gen. ed. (Saint-Étienne-de-Bolton, Québec, Canada: Babaji's Kriya Yoga and Publications, copublished with Varthamanan Publications, Theyagaraya Nagar, Chennai, India, 2010, English)

Varalarum Sathanaihallum, by M. Arunasalam (Jaffna, Sri Lanka, 1985, Tamil)

Words of Our Master, by Markanduswami, A. Chellathurai, Sandaswami and M. Srikhantha (The Jaffna Cooperative Tamil Books, Publication and Sale Society Ltd., Jaffna, Sri Lanka, 1972, English)

Yogaswamigal, S. Ampikaipaakan (Siva Yoga Swamikal Endowment Trust, Colombo, Sri Lanka, Second Edition 1972, Tamil)

Yogaswami, Life and Teachings (manuscript), by Mrs. Inthumathy Navaratnarajah, (The Sivathondan Centre, Chenkaladi, Sri Lanka); an English translation of *Yogaswamihal: Vaalkaiyum Vallikattalum,* by Chellathurai Swami (Sivathondan Society Ltd., Jaffna, Sri Lanka, Tamil), with additional biographical material and stories from devotees

Colophon

This book was designed by the acharyas and swamis of the Saiva Siddhanta Yoga Order at Kauai Aadheenam, Kauai's Hindu Monastery on Hawaii's Garden Island. It was produced on Apple MacBook Pro and Mac Pro computers using Adobe's Creative Suite, including InDesign, Photoshop and Illustrator. The text is set in the Relato family of fonts created by Spanish designer Eduardo Manso. The main body type is set in 11.5-point regular on 14.25-point linespacing and 8.25 on 11 for the glossary and index. Sanskrit and Tamil fonts are by Ecological Linguistics and Srikrishna Patil. The cover art and the book's primary story illustrations are taken from fifty-six watercolors that were the last major work of Tiru S. Rajam (1919–2009) of Chennai, with supplemental illustrations taken from his broader portfolio. The map illustrations of the Indian subcontinent, Sri Lanka and the Jaffna peninsula were created by Michael Gibbons of Midvale, Utah. Embellishments to a few stories of the ancient gurus were contributed by Darshak Jeyanandarajan of San Luis Obispo, California. John Loudon, a book publishing consultant from San Anselmo, California, helped shape the book with his critique. Special thanks go to T. Sivayogapathy of Toronto, who knew Yogaswami as a boy, and whose family were close devotees, for providing a living connection to the many stories and assuring the accuracy of facts, names and history from his own memory, that of associates and from various Tamil biographies. The book's index was created by Chamundi Sabanathan of Kapaa, Hawaii, using Adobe InDesign. Sheela Venkatakrishnan of Chennai, India, advised on Tamil language and cultural matters. We know that Gurudeva is smiling down upon this book from the inner planes, pleased with its production, happy that his original vision, begun in 1972, has been fulfilled, lending his blessings to all those who read these words and strive to apply the wisdom and living example of the Kailasa Parampara to their daily life. Aum.

Like the great masters in this book, there are a few unusual young men who have had enough of the materialistic world and choose to live and serve as Hindu monks.

These rare souls follow the path of the traditional Hindu monastic, vowed to poverty, humility, obedience and purity. They pursue the disciplines of charya, kriya, yoga and jnana that lead to realization of the Self. It is this ancient faith that most fully carries forward the traditions spoken of in this book. There are over one billion Hindus on the planet today, and by conservative estimate, three million swamis, sadhus and satgurus in India alone. The BAPS Swaminarayan order has over 800; Ramakrishna Mission over 700 worldwide. The Bharat Sevashram Sangha has over 500. The head of the Juna Akhara has been known to give initiation to 25,000 on a single day. Other organized Hindu orders number into the thousands. Temples to the Gods of Sanatana Dharma are estimated at 500,000—with 1,000 in the USA. The priests serving in these temples outnumber those in several of the great religions. We invite you, if you feel a calling and are under the age of 25, to consider joining our order, the Saiva Siddhanta Yoga Order. Knowing God Siva and serving others is our only goal in life. We live in monasteries apart from the world to worship, meditate, serve and realize the Truth of the *Vedas* and *Agamas*, uplifting the world by our example, fulfilling the ultimate human purpose by realizing the Self at the core of a perfectly stilled mind. Guided by our satguru, Bodhinatha Veylanswami, and headquartered at Kauai Aadheenam in Hawaii, our order ranks among Hinduism's foremost traditional monastic orders, accepting candidates from every nation on Earth. Young men considering life's renunciate path who believe they have found their spiritual master in Bodhinatha are encouraged to write to him—he is available—sharing their personal history, spiritual aspirations, thoughts and experiences, and to visit his monastery and meet others who are following this highest path on Earth. Entrance is slow. The first step is to come to Kauai island on a taskforce program for six months, then return home and think over the experience. After that, vows for six months at a time are given for the first year or two. Renewable two-year vows are given until final lifetime vows, holy orders of sannyasa, may be given after ten to twelve years of training. More about our order can be found at: www.himalayanacademy.com/monks/

Kauai's Hindu Monastery
107 Kaholalele Road, Kapaa, Hawaii 96746-9304 USA
E-mail: bodhi@hindu.org

The Hindu Heritage Endowment

The spiritual centers of South India, the *aadheenams,* tradition-ally support Hindu organizations such as temples, orphanages and priest training schools. In ancient times, farm land or shops owned by these monastic-run institutions supplied the revenue for regular charitable assistance for local religious and social activities. In today's world, *aadheenam* endowments include stocks and bonds. The charitable activities of Kauai's Hindu Monastery are more global than local, and are significant enough to be responsibly overseen by a separate organiza-tion, called Hindu Heritage Endowment (HHE), which Gurudeva founded in 1994. Through HHE, a wide variety of activities are funded, includ-ing temples, festivals and feedings, orphanages, children's retreat camps, youth education, ashrams and mathas, religious publications, pilgrim-age sites, priest training centers, support for pandits, shelters for sadhus, elderly homes, scriptural or philosophical research centers, support of ayurveda and jyotisha, the missions of various swamis and institutes for music, art, drama, dance and yoga. An organization can easily create an HHE fund to sustain its mission. Individuals can donate to existing funds or create new funds for their favorite Hindu charities or causes. Once contributions are put into HHE, they cannot be removed or used for anything other than the fund's stated purpose. Grants, generated by investment gains, are regularly distributed to the beneficiaries to use in furthering their plans and goals. Contributions are tax-deductible in the US. As of 2011, there are over 80 individual funds within HHE, which together exceed $10 million. These assets are professionally overseen by Halbert Hargrove LLC of Long Beach, California, an investment counsel-or respected for their utilization of multi-manager institutional mutual funds. Contributions to an HHE fund can be made in several ways, in-cluding outright gifts of cash, securities or real estate, a bequest through a will or living trust, life insurance or a gift through a life income plan, such as a charitable remainder trust, gift annuity or pooled income fund.

HINDU HERITAGE ENDOWMENT
Kauai's Hindu Monastery
107 Kaholalele Road
Kapaa, Hawaii, 96746-9304 USA
Phone: (800) 890–1008, Ext. 244
Outside US: (808) 822–3152, Ext. 244
Fax: (808) 822-4351
www.hheonline.org
E-mail: hhe@hindu.org

Our Wide Range of Hindu Resources

Himalayan Academy provides savvy, well-designed resources for Hindus and those teaching Hinduism. Whether it is for your own pursuit of dharma or for sharing with others in classes and seminars, you will find our materials articulate, contemporary and grounded in tradition. Links below will guide you to our books, pamphlets, children's courses and more.

Explore the Basics of Hinduism

www.himalayanacademy.com/basics/
www.himalayanacademy.com/teaching/
www.himalayanacademy.com/basics/nineb/

Listen to Inspired Talks & Study the Hindu Path

www.himalayanacademy.com/audio/
www.himalayanacademy.com/study/mc/
www.himalayanacademy.com/innersearch/

Discover Our Books And Global Magazine

www.himalayanacademy.com/books/
www.hinduismtoday.com
www.minimela.com

Learn About Kauai's Hindu Monastery and Monks' Life

www.himalayanacademy.com
www.himalayanacademy.com/monks/
www.himalayanacademy.com/visitors/

Kauai's Hindu Monastery

A 363-acre sanctuary in Hawaii, dedicated to strengthening Hinduism worldwide through its publications, Hindu Heritage Endowment funds and Saiva Siddhanta Church fellowship